BURT FRANKLIN: BIBLIOGRAPHY AND REFERENCE SERIES #211

American Classics in History & Social Science #41

THE

ISSUES OF THE PRESS

IN

PENNSYLVANIA

1685—1784

VOL. II.
1764—1784

A CENTURY OF PRINTING

THE

ISSUES OF THE PRESS

IN

PENNSYLVANIA

1685—1784

BY

CHARLES R. HILDEBURN

VOL. II.
1764—1784

BURT FRANKLIN: BIBLIOGRAPHY AND REFERENCE SERIES #211

American Classics in History & Social Science #41

BURT FRANKLIN
NEW YORK

Published By
BURT FRANKLIN
235 East 44th St.
New York, N.Y. 10017

ORIGINALLY PUBLISHED
PHILADELPHIA: 1836
Reprinted 1968

Printed in U.S.A.

THE ISSUES OF THE PRESS

IN PENNSYLVANIA.

1764.

AN ACCOUNT of the Births and Burials in St. Peter's | and Christ-Church Parish, in Philadelphia, from De- | cember 25, 1763, to December 25, 1764. By Caleb | Cash, Clerk, and James Weyley, Sexton. | [*Philadelphia:* 1764.] Folio, 1 leaf. 1936

AN | ACCOUNT | of | Two | Terrible | Fires. | Which hap- pened in the City of | Brotherly-Love, | On Friday the 26th of October. | . . . | . . . . | [*Philadelphia:*] *Printed* [*by Anthony Armbruster*] *in the Year* MDCCXLIV. [1764.] | Sm. 8vo. pp. 7, (1). L. C. P. 1937

[Cut.] THE ADDITION to the Epitaph, without the Copper- Plate. | [*Philadelphia: Anthony Armbruster.* 1764.] Folio, 1 leaf.

A burlesque in the form of a prayer, by David James Dove?

AN ADDRESS | Lately presented to | J[oseph] G[alloway] Esq. | [*Philadelphia: Printed by William Bradford.* 1764.] 4to. 1 leaf. L. C. P. 1939

AN | ADDRESS | Of Thanks to the Wardens of Christ Church and St. Peters, and the Reverend | W[illiam] S[mit]h, D.D. Pro- vost of the College and Tool to the P[roprieto]r, and J[aco]b | D[uch]é, A.M. and MV.D. from F[rancis] A[liso]n D.D. and J[oh]n E[win]g in their | own Name and in the Name of all the Presbyterian Ministers in Pennsylvania. | [*Philadelphia: Anthony Armbruster.* 1764.] Folio, 1 leaf. L. C. P. 1940

THE | ADDRESS | of the | People call'd Quakers, | In the Province of Pennsylvania, | To John Penn, Esquire, | Lieutenant-Governor of the said | Province, &c. | *Philadelphia :* | *Printed by Andrew Steuart, at the Bible-in-* | *Heart in Second-street, a little below the* | *Friend's Meeting-House.* 1764. | Sm. 8vo. pp. 11.   1941

In defence of their conduct towards the Indians and the settlers. They were charged with being " profuse to Savages, and carefully avoiding to contribute to the Relief and Support of the distressed Families on the Frontiers."

AN | ADDRESS | to the | Freeholders | and | Inhabitants | of the | Province | of | Pennsylvania. | In Answer to a Paper called | The Plain Dealer. | *Philadelphia :* | *Printed and sold by Anthony Armbruster, at the* | *German and English Printing-Office ; in* | *Moravian-Alley.* 1764. | 8vo. pp. 12.   L. C. P. 1942

ADVERTISEMENT, and not a Joke. | A Speech there is, which no Man spoke : | [*Philadelphia : William Bradford.*] 4to. 1 leaf.   L. C. P. 1943

AGUECHEEK. (A.) The Universal American Almanac for 1765. By Andrew Aguecheek. *Philadelphia : Andrew Steuart.* 1764.   1944

DJE | ALLMÄCHTJGE Errettungs= | Hand Gottes | Aus den wilden | Meeres=Wellen; | Wunderbar erwiesen an einer | Anno 1735 den 10den October | von Altona nach London schif= | fenden Frauens= Person. | *Germantown :* | *Gedruckt bey Chr. Saur,* 1764. | 16mo. pp. 14.   H. S. P. 1945

AN | Die Freyhalter | und Einwohner | Der | Stadt und County Philadelphia, deutscher Nation. | [*Philadelphia :*] *Gedruckt* [*bey Anton Armbruester,*] *im Jahre* 1764. | 4to. pp. 4.   L. C. P. 1946

EJNE ANDERE ANREDE an die deutschen Freyhalter der Stadt und County Philadelphia von etlichen von ihren Landsleuten. [n. p. 1764.]   1947

Title from Seidensticker's Bibliography.

𝕬𝕹𝕸𝕰𝕽𝕶𝖀𝕹𝕲𝕰𝕹 | über | (Ein noch nie erhört und gesehen Wunder | Thier in Pennsylvanien, | genannt | Streit= und Strauß= | Vogel, | Heraus gegeben von einer | Teutschen Gesellschaft freyer Bürger und | getreuer Unterthanen Seiner Groß= | Brittanischen Majestät. | [*German-town :*] *Gedruckt* [*bey Christoph Saur*] *in diesem Jahr.* [*1764.*] | 8vo. pp. 16.   H. S. P.   1948

ANNO Quarto | Georgii III. Regis. | An Act for preventing Tumults and riotous | Assemblies, and for the more speedy and ef- | fectual punishing the Rioters. | [*Philadelphia : B. Franklin.*] Folio, pp. 4.   1949

ANNO Regni | Georgii III. | Regis, | Magnæ Britanniæ, Franciæ & Hiberniæ, | Quarto. | At a General Assembly of the Province of Penn- | sylvania, begun and holden at Philadelphia, | the Fourteenth Day of October, Anno Domini 1763, in | the Third Year of the Reign of our Sovereign Lord | George III. by the Grace of God, of Great- | Britain, France and Ireland, King, Defender of the | Faith, &c. | And from thence continued by Adjournments to the | Twenty-fourth Day of March, 1764. | [*Penn Arms.*] | *Philadelphia :* | *Printed and Sold by B. Franklin, at the New-* | *Printing-Office, near the Market.* MDCCLXIV. | Folio, Title, 1 leaf; pp. 315–330. + And from thence continued . . . to the | Thirtieth Day of May, 1764. | *Ibid.*] Title, 1 leaf; pp. 333–358. + And from thence continued . . . to the | Twenty-second Day of September, 1764. | [*Ibid.*] Title, 1 leaf; pp. 361–369.   H. S. P.   1950

𝕰𝕵𝕹𝕰 | 𝕬𝕹𝕽𝕰𝕯𝕰 an die Deutschen | Freyhalter | der | Stadt und County | Philadelphia. | *Philadelphia, gedruckt* [*bey Anton Armbruester*] *in der Arch-Strasse* | 1764 | 8vo. pp. 8.   H. S. P.   1951

AN | ANSWER | to | Mr. Franklin's | Remarks | on a late | Protest. | *Philadelphia :* | *Printed and Sold by William Bradford at his Book-* | *Store, in Market-street, adjoining the London Coffee-house.* | M.DCC.LXIV. | 8vo., pp. 22.   H. S. P.   1952

AN | ANSWER, | to the | Pamphlet | Entituled the Conduct of the Paxton Men, | impartially represented : Wherein the un- |

generous Spirit of the Author is Mani- | fested, &c. And the spotted Garment | pluckt off. | . . . | . . . | . . . | . . . | . . . | . . . | . . . | . . . | . . . | . . . | . . . | . . . . | *Philadelphia : Printed by Anthony Armbruster, | in Moravian Alley, 1764.* | Sm. 8vo. pp. 28. H. S. P. 1953

AN | ANSWER | to the | Plot. | [*Philadelphia : Anthony Armbruster. 1764.*] Narrow folio, 1 leaf. L. C. P. 1954

Ten verses not very complimentary to Franklin.

AUTENRIETH. (F. W.) Merkwürdige Nachricht von F. W. Autenrieths Ehrlichen Abkunft, gottlosen Leben, und gerichtlichen Tode, als eines verlornen und wieder gefundenen Sohns. *Philadelphia : Anthon Armbruester.* 1764. 1955

THE | AUTHOR | of | Quaker Unmask'd, | strip'd | Start Naked, | Or The | Delineated | Presbyterian | Play'd | Hob With. | *Philadelphia.* | *Printed [by Anthony Armbruster] in the Year* M,DCC,LXIV. | Sm. 8vo. pp. 12. H. S. P. 1956

Charges Franklin with the authorship of the Quaker Unmasked.

[BARTON. (Thomas).] The | Conduct | of the | Paxton-Men, | impartially represented : | With some | Remarks | on the | Narrative. | *Philadelphia :* | *Printed by Andrew Steuart.* MDCCLXIV. | *Second title :* The Conduct of | The Paxton-Men, | Impartially represented ; | The Distresses of the Frontiers, and the | Complaints and Sufferings of the People fully | stated ; and the Methods recommended by the wisest | Nations, in such Cases, seriously consider'd. | With some | Remarks upon the Narrative, | Of the Indian-Massacre, lately publish'd. | Interspers'd with several interesting Anecdotes, relating to the | Military Genius, and Warlike Principles of the | People call'd Quakers : Together with proper Reflec- | tions and Advice upon the whole. | In a Letter from a Gentleman in one of the | Back-Counties, to a Friend in Philadelphia. | . . . | . . . . | . . . | . . . | . . . . | . . . | . . . | . . . | . . . | . . . | . . . | . . . | . . . . | *Philadelphia :* | *Printed by A. Steuart, and sold by John Creaig, Shop- | keeper in Lancaster.* 1764. | Sm. 8vo. pp. (2), 24. H. S. P. 1957

A | BATTLE! A Battle! | A Battle of Squirt, | Where no man is kill'd, | and no man is hurt! | To the Tune of three blue Beans, | in a blue Bladder; | Rattle Bladder Rattle. | To which is added, | The Quaker's Address, | And the | School-Boy's Answer | To an insolent Fellow | Who accus'd him of Stealing his Cherries. | . . . | . . . | . . . | . . . | . . . | . . . | . . . . | *Sold by Edward Merefield, at the Corner of | Arch-Street, and opposite the Church-Burying- | Ground, in Philadelphia.* 1764. | 8vo. pp. 20.

The following title appears on page 17 :
King Wampum. | Or | Harm Watch, | Harm Catch. | And the Lord departed from Is . . . l, | and behold He went a Whore- | ing after his own Invention un- | til his abominable Iniquity was | found out. | [*Printed by Anthony Armbruster.*] *Sold by Edward Merefield, at the Corner | of Arch-Street, and opposite the Church- | Burying-Ground, in Philadelphia.* 1764. |

A BATTLE! a Battle! a Battle a Squirt; | Where no Man is kill'd, and no Man is hurt! | To the Tune of | Three new blue Beans, in a new blue blown Bladder ; | rattle Bladder rattle Bladder! | To which is added, | The | Quaker's Address, versify'd; | and | King Wampum, on Harm watch Harm | catch. | . . . | . . . | . . . | . . . . | [*Philadelphia :*] *Printed [by Andrew Steuart] and sold at the Blue-Nose, near | Brazen-Nose-College, Germantown.* [1764.] | Sm. 12mo. pp. 11, (1), 1 Plate. H. S. P. 1959

The plate is an etching—probably by Jas. Claypoole—divided in two compartments, that to the left illustrative of "King Wumpum," and the other of "A battle, a battle," &c. The Paxton Boys are seen approaching from the country, and the Philadelphians, under the command of a Quaker, are drawn up to defend the Barracks, supported by a piece of artillery manned by Jos. Fox and another Quaker. Franklin stands on the right, exclaiming, "Fight Dog! fight Bear! you're both my Friends, By you I shall attain my Edns : For I can never be content till I have got the Government."

BOSTWICK. (D.) A Fair and Rational Vindication, of the Right of Infants to the Ordinance of Baptism. By David Bostwick, A.M. *Philadelphia : William Bradford.* 1764. 1960

THE BRITISH Plutarch; or Biographical Entertainer. Being a Select Collection of the Lives at large of the most Eminent Men, Natives of Great Britain and Ireland ; from the Reign of Henry VIII. to George II. Adorned with Copper Plates. In Six Volumes. *Philadelphia : William Bradford.* 1764. 1961

A CATECHISM for the use of the Baptist Churches. *Philadelphia: Andrew Steuart.* 1764.   1962

C. (G.)   A | Little Looking-Glass | For the Times; | Or, | A brief Remembrancer | for | Pennsylvania. | Containing | Some serious Hints, affectionately addressed to People of | every Rank and Station in the Province : | With an Appendix, by Way of Supplication to | Almighty God. | By G. C. | . . . | . . . | . . . | . . . | . . . | . . . | . . . | . . . . | *Wilmington,* | *Printed and Sold by James Adams,* 1764. | Sm. 8vo. pp. 24.   H. S. P.   1963

THE | CHARTER, | Laws, | and | Catalogue of Books, | of the | Library Company | of | Philadelphia. | . . . . | *Philadelphia :* | *Printed by B. Franklin and D. Hall.* | M,DCC,LXIV. | 8vo, pp. 1–26, 1–150.   H. S. P.   1964

THE | CHEAT Unmask'd : | Being | A Refutation | Of that Illegitimate | Letter, | Said to be wrote by | A Clergyman in Town : | In a true Copy of | A Letter | from that | Clergyman to his Friend. | [*Philadelphia :*] *Printed* [*by Henry Miller*] *in the Year* M,DCC,LXIV. | Sm. 8vo pp. 8.   L. C. P.   1965

THE CLOVEN Foot Discovered. *Ephrata.* 1764. + *Philadelphia: Andrew Steuart.* 1764.   1966

A CONFERENCE between the D[evi]l and Doctor D[ov]e. | Together with the Doctor's Epitaph on himself. | [*Philadelphia : Andrew Steuart.* 1764.] Folio, 1 leaf.   L. C. P.   1967

Headed by a copper plate.

A CONFESSION of Faith.   Adopted by the Philadelphia Baptist Association. 1742. *Philadelphia: Andrew Steuart.* 1764.

A | DECLARATION | and | Remonstrance | Of the distressed and bleeding Frontier Inhabitants | Of the Province of Pennsylvania, | Presented by them to the Honourable the Governor and | Assembly of the Province, | Shewing the | Causes | Of their late Discontent and Uneasiness and the | Grievances | Under which they have laboured, and which they humbly pray to | have redress'd. | [*Philadelphia:*] *Printed* [*by William Bradford*] *in the Year* M,DCC,LXIV. | 8vo. pp. 18.   H. S. P.   1969

DELAWARE. Anno Quarto | Georgii III. Regis. | At a General Assembly begun at | New-castle, in the Government of the Counties | of New-castle, Kent and Sussex, upon Dela- | ware, the Twentieth Day of October, in the | Third Year of the Reign of our Sovereign Lord | George the Third, King of Great-Britain, | &c. Annoque Domini 1763, and continued by | Adjournments till the Thirty-first Day of March | follow- ing, The following Acts were passed by | the Honourable John Penn, Esq., Governor; | [*Wilmington: James Adams*, 1764.] Folio, pp. 83–97. + Anno Quinto | Georgii III. Regis. | At a General Assembly begun | at New-castle, . . . | . . . | . . . in the | Fourth Year of the Reign of our Sovereign | Lord George the Third, . . . | . . . 1764, The | following Act was passed . . . | . . . . | [*Ibid.*] pp. 99–106.   L.   1970

ＥＪＮＥ | ＤＥＭ Hochedlen Herrn Guvernör | und der Landesver- sammlung | der Provinz Pennsylvanien | übergebene | Erklärung | und | Vorstellung | von den | bedrängten und in Todesgefahr stehenden | Einwohnern an den Grenzen dieser Provinz: | Worin | die Ursachen | ihrer letztheringen | Unzufriedenheit und Kummers | angezeigt werden: | Samt den | Beschwerungen, | die sie ausgestanden haben, und um deren | Abschaffung | sie unterthänig bitten. | Aus dem Englischen übersetzt. | [*Philadelphia:*] *Gedruckt* [*bey Henrich Miller*] *im Jahr* 1764. | 8vo. pp. 16.   H. S. P.   1971

A translation of No. 1969, *supra*.

A | DIALOGUE, | Between | Andrew Trueman, | And | Thomas Zealot; | About the killing the Indians | At | Can- nestogoe | And | Lancaster. | *Printed at Ephesus.* | [*Philadelphia: Anthony Armbruster.* 1764.] Sm. 8vo. pp, 7.   H. S. P.   1972

A | DIALOGUE, | Between | Andrew Trueman, | and | Thomas Zealot; | About the killing the Indians | At Cannestogoe | And | Lancaster. | [*Philadelphia: Anthony Armbruster.* 1764] | Sm. 8vo. pp. 8.   N. Y. H. S.   1973

The copy in the New York Historical Society shows traces of an imprint, which has had the ink wiped from the type before printing.

A | DIALOGUE, | Containing some Reflections on the late | Declaration and Remonstrance, | Of the Back-Inhabitants of the | Province of Pennsylvania. | With a serious and short Address, to those | Presbyterians, who (to their dishonor) have | too much abetted, and conniv'd at the late | Insurrection. | By a Member of that Community. | . . . | . . . | . . . | . . . . | *Philadelphia,* *printed:* | *[by Andrew Steuart] And sold by all the Pamphlet-sellers.* M,DCC,LXIV. | 16mo. pp. 16.　　　　　　　　　　H. S. P.　**1974**

DICKINSON. (J.) "Last Tuesday morning Mr. Galloway carried a writing containing some reflections on me, to a printer in this city, ... [*Philadelphia: Printed by W. Bradford.* 1764.] 8vo. pp. 4.　　　　　　　　　　　　　　　L. C. P.　**1975**

A reply to the broadside published by Galloway, signed John Dickinson, and dated September 29.

DICKINSON. Eine | Rede, | gehalten | in dem Haufe der Affembly der Provinz | Pennfylvanien, am 24ten May, 1764. | Von | Herrn John Dickinfon, | einem der Mitglieder des Haufes für | Philadelphia Caunty. | Bey Gelegenheit einer Vittfchrift, die auf Befehl des | Haufes aufgefetzt, und damals in Ueberlegung genom= | men war, worin Seine Königliche Majeftät um eine | Veränderung des Guvernements diefer Provinz er= | fucht wird. | Mit einer Vorrede | . . . | . . . | . . . | . . . | . . . | . . . | . . . | . . . | . . . . | Aus dem Englifchen über= fetzt, nach der zweyten Auflage. | *Philadelphia, Gedruckt und zu finden bey Henrich* | *Miller, in der Zweyten-Strasse.* [1764.] | 8vo. pp. xvi, 35.

DICKINSON. A | Reply | To a Piece called | the | Speech | Of Joseph Galloway, Esquire. | By | John Dickinson. | . . . | . . . | . . . | . . . | . . . | . . . . | *Philadelphia:* | *Printed and Sold by* *William Bradford,* | *At his Book-Store, in Market-street, adjoining the* | *London Coffee-House,* M,DCC,LXIV. | 8vo. pp. iv, 45, xiii.

DICKINSON. A | Speech, | Delivered in the House of Assembly of the Province of | Pennsylvania, May 24th, 1764. | By John Dickinson, Esq; | One of the Members for the County of Philadelphia. | On Occasion of a Petition, drawn up by Order, and then | under Consideration, of the House; praying His Majesty for a | Change of the Government of this Province.

| With a Preface. | . . . | . . . | . . . | . . . | . . . | . . . | . . . . |
| *Philadelphia:* | *Printed and Sold by William Bradford, at his* |
Book-Store adjoining the London Coffee-House. | M,DCC,LXIV. |
8vo. pp. xii, 30. + The Second Edition. [*Ibid.*] 8vo. pp. xv,
30. 	 H. S. P. 	1978

DOCK. (C.) Sdul=Drbnung. Bon Chriftoph Dod. *German-*
town: Christoph Saur. 1764. 8vo ? pp. 54. 	1979

Title from Haven's List. See No. 2522, *infra*, which according to Mr. S. W.
Pennypacker, is the earliest edition of Dock's Rules.

[DODSLEY. (Robert)] Fragments of the Chronicles of Nathan
Ben Saddi. Constantinople, 5707. *Philadelphia:* 1764. 	1980

Title from Haven's List.

[DOVE. (David James)] The | Quaker unmask'd; | or | Plain
Truth: | Humbly address'd to the Consideration of all the |
Freemen of Pennsylvania. | . . . | . . . . | . . . | . . . . | *Phila-*
delphia: | *Printed [by Andrew Steuart] in the Year of our Lord,*
M,DCC,LXIV. | Sm. 8vo. pp. 15. 	 H. S. P. 	1981

Attributed to Franklin. See No. 1956, *supra*. The real author's name has been
ascertained from contemporaneous memorandum on the title page of a copy in the
"Moravian Archives" at Bethlehem.

[DOVE.] The | Quaker unmask'd; | or, | Plain Truth: |
Humbly address'd to the Consideration of all the | Freemen of
Pennsylvania. | . . . | . . . . | . . . | . . . . | The Second Edition.
| *Philadelphia: Printed by Andrew Steuart, in* | *Second-Street.* 1764.
| 16mo. pp. 16. 	 L. C. P. 	1982

The last page contains a list of fifteen pamphlets relating to the Paxton Boys to
be sold by the printer.

THE ELECTION a Medley, Humbly Inscribed to Squire
Lilliput Professor of Scurrility. | *Philadelphia:* 1764. Folio, 1
leaf. 	 L. C. P. 	1983

Engraved on copper, with a view of the election at the top.

AN ESSAY on the Trade of the Northern Colonies of Great Britain in North America. *Philadelphia:* 1764.   1984

See Sabin's Dictionary, No. 22970.

[ESTEN. (Cornelius)] To the Public. [*Philadelphia:* 1764.] 8vo. pp. 4.   L. C. P. 1985

Against bribery. Contains two pages of doggerel verse.

𝕰𝖙𝖑𝖏𝖈𝖍𝖊 merkwürdige Punkten, betreffende die Verwechſelung des *Governments*, gerichtet an die deutſchen Einwohner der Provinz Pen= ſylvanien. *Philadelphia: Gedruckt bey Anton Armbrüster in der Aert-Strasse.* 1764.   1986

Title from Seidenstreker's Bibliography.

EXPLANATORY Remarks on the Assembly's | Resolves, published in the Pennsylvania Gazette, No. 1840. | [*Philadelphia: B. Franklin, and D. Hall.* 1764.] Folio, pp. 2. H. S. P. 1987

In support of the Assembly's resolution asking for the substitution of a Royal for the Proprietary Government of the Province.

FINLEY. (S.) The successful Minister of Christ dis- | tinguished in Glory. | A | Sermon, | Occasioned by the Death of the Reverend | Mr. Gilbert Tennent, | Pastor of the Second Presbyterian Congre- | gation, in Philadelphia. | Preached on the 2d Day of September, 1764. | By Samuel Finley, D.D. | President of the College of New-Jersey. | . . . | . . . . | *Phila-delphia.* | *Printed and Sold by William Brad-* | *ford, at his Book-Store in Market-Street,* | *adjoining the London Coffee-House.* | M,DCC,LXIV. | 8vo. pp. 28, xv, xvi.   c. 1988

Dr. Finley's Sermon is followed by " A | Funeral | Eulogy, | Sacred to the Memory of the late Reverend | Gilbert Tennent, A.M. | Pastor of the Second Pres-byterian Church in | Philadelphia." | pp. xvi. " Wrote by a young Gentleman of Philadelphia."

FOX. (T.) The Wilmington Almanac for 1765. By Thomas Fox. *Wilmington; James Adams.* 1764.   1989

[FRANKLIN. (Benjamin)] Cool Thoughts | on the | Present Situation | of our | Public Affairs. | In a Letter to a Friend in the

Country. | *Philadelphia:* | *Printed by W. Dunlap.* M,DCC,LXIV. | 8vo. pp. 22.   H. S. P.   1990

First published as a Supplement to the Pennsylvania Journal, No. 1116, Ap'l 26, 1764.

[FRANKLIN.] Cool Thoughts | on the present | Situation | of our | Public Affairs. | In a Letter to a Friend in the Country. [Cut.] | *Philadelphia:* | *Printed by A. Steuart at the Bible-in-* | *Heart.* M,DCC,LXIV. | Sm. 8vo. pp. 20.   N. Y. H. S.   1991

[FRANKLIN.] A | Narrative | of the late | Massacres, | in | Lancaster County, | of a | Number of Indians, | Friends of this Province, | By Persons Unknown. | With some Observations on the same. | [*Philadelphia:*] *Printed* [*by Anthony Armbruster*] *in the Year* M,DCC,LXIV. | 8vo. pp. 31.   H. S. P.   1992

FRANKLIN. Proteſtation | gegen die Beſtellung | Herrn Benjamin Franklins zu einem Agenten für | dieſe Provinz. | [Followed by] An= merkungen | über eine neuliche | Proteſtation | gegen die Beſtellung | Herrn Benjamin Franklins zu einem Agenten für | dieſe Provinz. | [*Germantown: Christoph Saur.* 1764.] Folio, pp. (4).

The Protest occupies the first page, the other three being filled with Franklin's Remarks upon it.

[FRANKLIN.] Remarks | on a late | Protest | Against the Appointment of | Mr. Franklin an Agent | for this Province. | [*Philadelphia: Printed by B. Franklin and D. Hall.* 1764.] 8vo. pp. 7.   H. S. P.   1994

GALLOWAY. (J.) Die | Rede, | Herrn Joseph Galloways, | eines der Mitglieder des Hauſes für | Philadelphia Caunty, | Zur Beant= wortung | Der Rede welche Hr. John Dickinſon | gehalten | im Hauſe der Aſſembly der Provinz | Pennſylvanien, am 24ten May, 1764. | Bey Gelegenheit einer Bittſchrift, welche auf Befehl | des Hauſes aufgeſetzt, und damals in Ueberlegung ge= | nommen war, worin Seine König= liche Majeſtät um | ein Königliches anſtatt des jetzigen Proprietors Gu= | vernements erſucht wird. | Mit einer Vorrede. | . . . | . . . | . . . . | Aus dem Engliſchen überſetzt. | *Philadelphia, Gedruckt und zu finden*

bey Henrich | Miller, in der Zweyten-strasse. [1764.] | 8vo. pp. xliv, (4), 46.
1995

GALLOWAY. The | Speech | Of | Joseph Galloway, Esq; | One of the Members for Philadelphia County: | In Answer | To the Speech of John Dickinson, Esq; | Delivered in the House of Assembly, of the | Province of Pennsylvania, May 24, 1764. | On Occasion of a Petition drawn up by Order, and | then under the Consideration of the House; | praying his Majesty for a Royal, in lieu of | a Proprietary Government. | . . . . | *Philadelphia: | Printed and sold by W. Dunlap, in Market-street. | MDCCLXIV.* | 8vo. pp. xxxv, (3), 45.   + The Second Edition.

GALLOWAY. To the | Public. | Philadelphia, September 29, 1764. | [*Philadelphia:* 1764.] Folio, 1 leaf.   L. C. P.   1997

Galloway's answer to Dickinson's charge that his Speech of May 24 was never spoken.

𝔈𝔍𝔑 | 𝔊𝔈𝔍𝔖𝔗𝔏𝔍𝔆𝔥𝔈𝔖 | Magazien, | Oder: | Aus den Schätzen der Schrifftgelehr= | ten zum Himelreich gelehrt, dargereichtes | Altes und Neues. | *Germantown: | Gedruckt bey Christoph Saur,* 1764. | 8vo.   H. S. P.   1998

Collation. Title 1 l. Preface, pp. (4) Magazein pp. 406. (Numbers I–50.) Register pp. (4) Herlichkeit Gottes in der Natur, aus Pf. 104. pp. (4). The first religious periodical printed in America. It ceased to appear in 1770.

𝔊𝔈𝔗𝔑𝔈𝔘𝔈 | Warnung | gegen die | Lockvögel, | Samt einer Ant= wort auf die andere Anrede | an die deutsche Freyhalter der Stadt und | County von Philadelphia, | durch Germanicus | . . . . | *Philadelphia, gedruckt im Jahr* 1764. | 8vo. pp. 15.   H. S. P.   1999

HABERMANN. (J.) Christliche | Morgen= und | Abend Gebäter, | Auf alle Tage in der Wochen, | Durch | D. Joh. Habermann. | Samt andern schönen | Gebätern, | Wie auch | D. Neumanns | Kern aller Gebät und | schönen | Morgen= Abend= u. andern | Liedern. | *Germanton: | Gedruckt und zu finden bey | Christoph Saur.* 1764. | 24mo. 62, 55.
2000

HAYES. (R.) The Negociator's Magazine: Or the Most Authentic Account yet published of the Monies, Weights and

Measures, of the Principal Places of Trade in the known World. By Richard Hayes. *Philadelphia: William Bradford.* 1764.   2001

AN | HISTORICAL | Account, | of the late | Disturbance, | between the Inhabitants; | Of the Back | Settlements; | Of Pennsylvania, | and the Philadelphians, &c. | Impartially related by a well Wisher. | *Printed at Rome, by A. S.* | [*Philadelphia: Anthony Armbruster.* 1764.] Sm. 8vo. pp. 8.   L. C. P.   2002

> This was the second edition. I have not met with the first.

AN | HISTORICAL | Account, | of the late | Disturbance, | between the Inhabitants | Of the Back | Settlements; | Of Pennsylvania, | and the Philadelphians, &c. | Impartially related by a well Wisher. | ☞ The Second Edition, may be called a Pira- | cy. I said Printed at Rome; I meant | nothing but ✚ Printed in Second - Street, by | Andrew Steuars - Stockfish. | [*Philadelphia:*] *Printed by Anthony Armbruster, in* | *Moravian-Alley.* [1764.] | Sm. 8vo. pp. 8.   H. S. P.   2003

𝕰𝕴𝕹𝕰 𝕳𝕴𝕾𝕿𝕺𝕽𝕴𝕾𝕮𝕳𝕰 Beschreibung von den Letzthin geschehenen Unruhen zwischen den Hintern Einwohnern d. Proving Pennsylvanien u. denen zu Philadelphia. . . . aus dem Englischen ins Hochteutsche ueberseßet. *Philadelphia, gedruckt bey Anton Armbruester.* 1764. Sm. 8vo. pp. 8.   2004

𝕳𝕴𝕾𝕿𝕺𝕽𝕴𝕾𝕮𝕳𝕰 | Nachricht | von dem | neulich in Lancaster Caunty durch unbekante | Personen ausgeführten | Blutbade | über eine | Anzahl Indianer, | welche Freunde dieser Proving waren. | Mit einigen hinzu gefügten | Anmerkungen. | Aus dem Englischen übersetzt. | [*Ephrata?*] *Gedruckt im Jahr* 1764. | 8vo. pp. 31.   H. S. P.   2005

𝕯𝕰𝕽 | 𝕳𝕺𝕮𝕳=𝕯𝕰𝕌𝕿𝕾𝕮𝕳𝕰 | Americanische | Calender, | Auf das Jahr | . . . | . . . | 1765. | (Welches ein gemein Jahr von 365 Tagen ist.) | . . . | . . . | . . . | . . . | . . . | . . . | . . . | . . . | . . . | . . . . | Zum sieben und zwanßigsten mal heraus gegeben. | *Germantown: Gedruckt und zu finden bey Christoph Saur.* | . . . | . . . . [1764.] 4to. pp. (48).   H. S. P.   2006

[HUNT. (Isaac)] A | Letter | From a Gentleman | in | Transilvania | To his Friend in America giving some Account | of the late disturbances that have happen'd in that | Government; with some Remarks upon the | political revolutions in the Magistracy, and the | Debates that happened about the change. | Humbly inscribed to Counsellor Quondam | By his Friend | Isaac Bickerstaff, of the Middle Temple. | . . . | . . . | . . . | . . . | . . . | . . . | . . . | . . . | *New-York,* [*Philadelphia:*] *Printed* [*by Anthony Armbruster*] *in the Year* 1764. | Sm. 8vo. pp. 12. 2007

JOHNSON. (J.) The | Advantages and Disadvantages | of the | Marriage-State, | As entered into with | Religious or Irreligious Persons: | Represented under the Similitude of a | Dream. | By the Reverend Mr. John Johnson. | The Seventh Edition. | *Philadelphia:* | *Printed by Andrew Steuart, at the Bible-in-Heart, in* | *Second-street:* M,DCC,LXIV. | . . . | . . . . | Sm. 8vo. pp. 24. F. 2008

KINNERSLY. (E.) A | Course | of | Experiments, | In that curious and entertaining Branch of | Natural Philosophy, called | Electricity; | Accompanied with explanatory Lectures: | In which Electricity and Lightning, will | be proved to be the same Thing. | By Ebenezer Kinnersley, M.A. | Professor of English and Oratory, | in the College and Academy of | Philadelphia. | [*Philadelphia:*] *Printed by A. Armbruster,* MDCCLXIV. | Sm. 8vo. pp. 8. L. C. P. 2009

LEBENS-REGUL | Wie sie zu Rom aus Päbstlichem Befehl an der Pabstlichen Cantzley-Thür angeschrieben stehet. | [*Ephrata:* 1764?] Folio, 1 leaf. H. S. P. 2010

A | LETTER | From a Clergyman in Town; | Vindicating himself against the | Malevolent Aspersions | Of a late Pamphelteer Letter-Writer. | [*Philadelphia:*] *Printed* [*by Andrew Steuart*] *in the Year* M,DCC,LXIV. | Sm. 8vo. pp. 8. L. C. P. 2011

Relates to the Rev. Wm. McClanachan, and in part to the Paxton Boys.

A | LETTER | from | A Gentleman | at | Elizabeth-Town, | to his Friend in | New-York. | *Philadelphia:* | *Printed by Andrew Steuart,* MDCCLXIV. | Sm. 8vo. pp. 8. H. S. P. 2012

A reply to Charles Read's Letter to John Ladd, in defence of the Paxton Men. Signed W. P., which, from its tone, might stand for " Wrathy Presbyterian."

A | LETTER, | from | Batista Angeloni, | Who resided many Years in London, | To his Friend | Manzoni. | Wherein the Quakers are politically and religiously | considered. | To which is added, | The Cloven-Foot discovered. | . . . . | *Printed at Carolina :* | [*Philadelphia : ?*] *And sold by Edward Merefield, at the Corner of* | *Arch-street, and opposite the Church Burying-Ground,* | *in Philadelphia.* [1764 ?] | 8vo. pp. 8.   L. C. P.   2013

A | LETTER, | from | Batista Angeloni, | Who resided many Years in London, | To his Friend | Manzoni. | Wherein the Quakers are politically and religiously | considered. | To which is added, | The Cloven - Foot discovered. | . . . . | *Ephrata :* | *Re-printed, and sold by several Store-Keepers in the* | *County of Lancaster.* [1764.] | 8vo. pp. 8.   L. C. P.   2014

LOCKE. (J.)   A | Letter | Concerning | Toleration. | By John Locke, Gent. | The Fourth Edition. | *Wilmington,* | *Printed and Sold by James Adams, in Market-* | *street.* 1764. | 16mo. pp. 77.   F.   2015

𝕯𝕰𝕽 𝕷𝕺𝕮𝕶𝕭𝕺̈𝕲𝕰𝕷 | Warnungsgefang | Vor den | Stoſsvögeln : | Oder | Nöthige Beantwortung | der ſogenannten | Getreuen Warnung gegen die Lockvögel, ꝛc | *Gedruckt* [*bey Henrich Miller*] *am* 29ten *September, im Jahr* 1764. | Sq. 8vo. pp. 8.   2016

(Numb. I.)   A | LOOKING-GLASS | for | Presbyterians. | Or | A brief Examination of their Loyalty, Merit, | and other Qualifications for Government. | With some Animadversions on the Quaker | unmask'd. | Humbly Address'd to the Consideration | of the Loyal Freemen of | Pennsylvania. | . . . | . . . | . . . | . . . | . . . | . . . . | *Philadelphia :* | *Printed* [*by Anthony Armbruster*] *in the Year* M,DCC,LXIV. | 8vo. pp. 18.   H. S. P.   2017

A | LOOKING - GLASS, | for | Presbyterians. | . . . | . . . | . . . | . . . | . . . | . . . | . . . | . . . | . . . . | [Cut.] [*Philadelphia :*] *Printed* [*by Anthony Armbruster.*] *in the Year* MDCCXLIV. [1764] | 8vo. pp. 43.   H. S. P.   2018

Title 1 leaf. Dedication 1 leaf. A Looking-Glass, &c., Numb. I. pp. 5 to 12. Numb. II. pp. 13 to 23. Appendix. The Substance of a Council ... at Lancaster, August the 28th 1764 by ... Presbyterian Ministers, ... pp. [27] to 34. A Dialogue between a Churchman and a Presbyterian pp. 35–38; Letter from a Gentleman in Transylvania: pp. 38–43. Perhaps by Isaac Hunt.

MARKHAM, (J.) and G. JEFFERIES. The | Citizen and Countryman's | experienced | Farrier. | Containing, | I. The most best approved Method of Ordering, Dieting, Ex- | ercising, Purging, Scouring, and Cleansing of Horses; Al- | so choice Restoratives to chear the Heart, procure an Appe- | tite, and to clear the Lungs and Pipes, so as to strengthen | Wind, and give large Breath to the Running or Race-Horse. | II. A certain sure Method to know the true State of any | Horse's Body, as to Sickness or Health. | III. The true Shape of a Horse explained: With choice Di- | rections for buying. | IV. An experienced and approved Method for Raising of Horses, | as to Ordering, Keeping, &c. Also Mares, Colts and Stali- | ons. | V. A Sure and certain Rule to know the Age of any Horse, from | one Year to ten, with good Observations as he further ad- | vances in Years. | VI. The best and experienced Way of keeping the common | Hackney, or Hunting Horse, so as to keep him lively, chear- | ful, free from Colds, Strains, Windgalls, and gross Hu- | mours. | VII. An approved Method of Purging, Bleeding and Feeding | Cattle; with choice approved Receipts for the Diseases they | are incident to; with Signs to know the Disease, and Direc- | tions for the Use of Medicines. | To all which is added, | A valuable and fine Collection of the surest and best Receipts | in the known World for the Cure of all Maladies and Distem- | pers that are incident to Horses of what Kind soever, with Di- | rections to know what is the Ailment, or Disease. | By J. Markham, G. Jefferies, and | Discreet Indians. | *London, Printed; and,* | *Wilmington, Re-printed, and Sold by James* | *Adams, at his Printing-Office,* 1764. | 16mo. pp. 364. H. S. P. 2019

THE | MAY Be | Or Some | Observations | Occasion'd by reading a Speech deliver'd in | the House of Assembly, the 24th of May | last, by a certain eminent Patriot. | . . . | . . . . | . . . | . . . | . . . | . . . | . . . | . . . | . . . | . . . | . . . | . . . . |

Philadelphia: | *Printed by Anthony Armbruster, in Arch - street.*
[1764.] | Sm. 8vo. pp. 7.   H. S. P.   2020

𝕹𝕰𝖀 = 𝕰𝕴𝕹𝕲𝕰𝕽𝕴𝕮𝕳𝕿𝕰𝕿𝕰𝕽 Americaniſher Calender, auf das
Jahr 1765. *Philadelphia: Anton Armbruester.* 1764.   2021

𝕰𝕴𝕹𝕰 𝕹𝕰𝖀𝕰 | Anrede | an die | Deutſchen | in | Philadelphia
County, ꝛc. | . . . . *[Philadelphia:]* *Gedruckt [bey H. Miller] zur*
Zeit und in dem Jahr, | *Da einer wider'n andern war.* [1764.] |
4to. pp. (4).   H. S. P.   2022

𝕯𝕰𝕽 𝕹𝕰𝖀𝕰𝕾𝕿𝕰, Verbeſſerte= und Zuverläßige Americaniſche
Calender Auf das 1765ſte Jahr Chriſti. *Philadelphia: Henrich*
Miller. 1764.   2023

THE | NEW-YEAR | Verses, | Of the Printers Lads, who
carry about the Penn- | sylvania Gazette to the Customers. | Jan-
uary 1, 1764. | *[Philadelphia: B. Franklin, and D. Hall.* 1764.]
Folio, 1 leaf.   L. C. P.   2024

NEW-YEAR Verses of the Carriers of the Pennsylvania
Journal. *Philadelphia: William Bradford.* 1764.   2025

NORCOTT. (J.) Baptism | discovered, | Plainly and Faith-
fully, according to | the Word of God. | Agreeable to the Glorious
Pattern given by our | Blessed Saviour Jesus Christ. | To the Ex-
amples of Thousands baptized | after they believed. | Recorded in
Sacred Scripture. | By John Norcott, | A Servant of Jesus Christ,
and of His Church. | The Fifth Edition, with Amendments. |
Philadelphia: Printed by Andrew Steuart, at the Bible-in- | *Heart, in*
Second-Street. 1764. | Sm. 8vo. pp. 47, (1).   2026

OBSERVATIONS | On a late | Epitaph, | In a Letter from
a Gentleman in the | Country, | To his Friend in Philadelphia : |
. . . . | *Philadelphia:* | *Printed by Anthony Armbruster, in Arch-*
street, | *by whom all Manner of Printing-work is* | *done, both in Eng-*
lish and German, with | *the greatest Accuracy and Expedition.* [1764.]
| Sm. 8vo. pp. 8.   L. C. P.   2027

THE ORIGINAL States of Thirty One Baptist Churches
whose Messengers An- | nually meet in Association at Phila-
delphia. | *[Philadelphia:* 1764.] Folio, 1 leaf.   2028

THE | PAXTON BOYS, | a | Farce. | Translated from the Original French, | By a Native of Donegall. | [*Philadelphia:*] *Printed* [*by Anthony Armbruster*] *in the Year*, MDCCLXIV. | 16mo. pp. 16.   H. S. P.   2029

THE | PAXTON Boys, | A | Farce. | Translated from the Original | French, | By a Native of Donegall. | The Second Edition. | *Philadelphia:* | *Printed and sold by Anthony Armbruster,* | *at the German and English Printing-* | *Office; in Moravian-Alley.* 1764. | 16mo. pp. 16.   L. C. P.   2030

THE | PAXTON Boys, | a | Farce. | Translated from the Original French, | By a Native of Donegall. | [n. p. 1764?]   8vo. pp. 8.   C.   2031

This reprint of the preceding is without a title page, and may not be from any press in Pennsylvania. The only copy I have seen is in the Library of Congress.

THE PAXTON Expedition. Inscribed to the Author of the Farce, by H. D. | [*Philadelphia:* 1764.]   L. C. P.   2032

A copper plate, representing the citizens of Philadelphia at the Court House in arms to repel the Paxton Boys. With six doggerel verses.

THE | PAXTONIADE. | A | Poem. | By Christopher Gymnast, Esq; | With the Prolegomenà and Exercitations of | Scriblerus. | [*Philadelphia:*] *Printed* [*by Anthony Armbruster,*] *in the Year*, 1764. | Sm. 4to. pp. 8.   H. S. P.   2033

THE | PAXTONIADE. | A | Poem. | By Christopher Gymnast, Esq; | With the Prolegomana and Exercitations of | Scriblerus. | The Second Edition. | Printed word for word, from the first Grand Edition. | *Philadelphia: Printed and sold by* | *John Morris, opposite the three Reapers in Third-street.* [1764.] | Sm. 8vo. pp. 8.   L. C. P.   2034

THE PENNSYLVANIA Gazette.   2035

Numbers 1828 (Jan. 5, 1764) to 1879 (Dec. 27, 1764), four pages each, with extra sheets of four pages to Numbers 1842, and 1843. Title and Imprint as in No. 1232, *supra.*

THE PENNSYLVANIA Journal.   H. S. P.   2036

Numbers 1100 (Jan. 5, 1764) to 1151 (Dec. 27, 1764), four pages each, with extra half sheets of two pages each to Numbers 1100, 1101, 1108–1110, 1112–1115, 1118–1123, 1126–1130, 1138, 1140–1145, 1150 and 1151, and a "Supplement" of two pages to No. 1116. Title and imprint as in No. 1693, *supra*.

THE PENNSYLVANIA Pocket Almanac for 1765. *Philadelphia: William Bradford.* 1764.   2037

A PETITION to the King. *Philadelphia: B. Franklin, and D. Hall.* 1764.   2038

Hall says 300 copies were printed by the firm. No doubt a petition for revocation of the Proprietary Charter.

PIKE. (S.) and S. HAYWARD. Important Cases of Conscience Answered at the Casuistical Lecture, in Little St. Helen's Bishopgate Street. By Samuel Pike and Samuel Hayward. In Two Volumes. *Philadelphia: William Bradford.* 1764.   2039

THE | PLOT. | By way of a | Burlesk, | To turn F[rankli]n out of the Assembly; between | H [ockley]. and P [ugh]; Proprietary Officers, being two | of the Wiser [Conrad Weiser] Sort. | [*Philadelphia: Printed [by Anthony Armbruster] in the Year* 1764. | Narrow folio, 1 leaf.   2040

POWELL. (T.) The Writing Master's Assistant. By Thomas Powell. *Philadelphia?* 1764.   2041

A PRIMER; *Philadelphia: B. Franklin, and D. Hall.* 1764.

In a statement of account rendered Franklin by Hall, it is said that between 1749 and 1765, thirty-five thousand one hundred Primers were printed.

PROCLAMATION. [*Royal Arms.*] By the Honourable | John Penn, Esq; | Lieutenant - Governor and Commander in Chief of the Province of Pennsylvania, | and Counties of New-Castle, Kent and Sussex, on Delaware, | A Proclamation. | *Philadelphia: Printed by B. Franklin, and D. Hall.* [1764.] | Folio, 1 leaf.   2043

A proclamation against the "Paxton Boys," dated January 2, 1764.

PROCLAMATION. [*Royal Arms.*]   By the Honourable |
John Penn, Esq; | Lieutenant Governor and Commander in Chief
of the Province of Pennsylvania, | and Counties of New-Castle,
Kent and Sussex, on Delaware, | A Proclamation. | *Philadelphia:*
Printed by B. Franklin, and D. Hall.   [1764.] | Folio, 1 leaf.   2044

Proclamation offering rewards for Indian scalps, &c., dated July 7, 1764. " For
every Male Indian Enemy above Ten years old, who shall be taken prisoner 150
Spanish Dollars.   For every Female Indian Enemy, and every Male under Ten
years 130 Pieces of Eight.   And for the Scalp of every Male Indian Enemy above
the age of Ten years, produced as Evidence of their being killed 134 Pieces of Eight,
and for the Scalp of every Female Indian Enemy above the age of Ten years, 50
Pieces of Eight."

PSALTERSPIEL.   Das kleine. | Davidische | Pſalterſpiel | Der |
Kinder Zions, | Von | Alten und Neuen auserleſenen | Geiſtes-Geſängen
Allen wahren | Heyls-begieri= | gen Sanglingen der Weisheit, | In-
ſonderheit aber | Denen Gemeinden des Herrn, zum | Dienſt und Gebrauch
mit Fleiß zuſammen | getragen, | Und in gegenwätig-beliebiger Form | und
Ordnung, | Nebſt einem doppelten, darzu nützlichen und der | Materien
halben nötligen, | Regiſter, | Zum dritten mal ans Licht gegeben. | *Ger-*
mantown, gedruckt bey Christoph Sauer, 1764.   12mo. pp. (6), 570,
(24), 4.   H. S. P.   2045

THE | QUAKER Vindicated; | or, | Observations | on | A
late Pamphlet, | entituled, | The Quaker Unmask'd, | or, | Plain
Truth. | . . . | . . . . | . . . | . . . | . . . | . . . | . . . | . . .
| [*Philadelphia:*]   *Printed* [*by Andrew Steuart*]   *in the Year*
MDCCLXIV. | 8vo. pp. 16.   H. S. P.   2046

THE | QUAKERS Assisting | To preserve the Lives of the
Indians in the | Barracks, | Vindicated | And proved to be con-
sistant with Reason, agreeable | to our Law, hath an inseperable
Connection | with the Law of God, and exactly agreeable with |
the Principles of the People call'd Quakers. | . . . | . . . | . . . .
| . . . | . . | . . | . . . | . . | . . | . . . | . . . | . . . | . . .
| . . . | . . . . | *Philadelphia: Printed by Anthony Armbruster,* | *in*
Moravian Alley, 1764. | 16mo. pp. 16.   H. S. P.   2047

THE | QUAKERS | Assisting, | To preserve the Lives of the
Indians, in the | Barracks, vindicated : Shewing | wherein, the

Author of the Quaker Un- | mask'd, hath turned King's Evidence; im- | peached himself, and cleared the Quakers | from all the heavy Charges he hath Publish- | ed against them. | . . . | . . . | . . . . | . . . | . . . | . . . | . . . . | Number II. | *Philadelphia:* | *Printed [by Anthony Armbruster] in the Year* MDCCLXIV. | Sm. 8vo. pp. 12.   L. C. P.   2048

RANDALL. ([John]) The Semi - Virgilian Husbandry, deduced from various experiments: Or, an Essay towards a new Course of National Farming. By Mr. Randall. *Philadelphia: William Bradford.* 1764.   2049

READ. (C.) Copy of a | Letter | From Charles Read, Esq; | To | The Hon: John Ladd, Esq; | And his Associates, Justices of the Peace for the | County of Gloucester. | [Cut.] | *Philadelphia: Printed and sold by Andrew | Steuart, at the Bible-in-Heart, in Second-street,* | *(Price 3 old Pennies.)* 1764. | 8vo. pp. 8.+The Second Edition.   H. S. P.   2050

READ. Copy of a | Letter | From Charles Read, Esq; | To | The Hon: John Ladd, Esq; | And his Associates, Justices of the Peace for | the County of Gloucester. | The Third Edition. | [Cut] | *Philadelphia:* | *Printed by Andrew Steuart, at the Bible-in- | Heart, in Second-street.* M,DCC,LXIV. | *Of whom may be had, all the Pamphlets that | have been publish'd on the same Subjects.* | Sm. 8vo. pp. 8.   N. Y. H. S.   2051

DIE REGELN der Teutschen Gesellschaft in Philadelphia. *Germantown. Gedruckt bey Christoph Saur.* 1764. 8vo. pp. 8.   2052

REMARKS | on the | Quaker Unmask'd; | Or Plain Truth found to be Plain Falshood: | Humbly address'd to the Candid. | . . . | . . . | . . . | . . . | . . . . | *Philadelphia:* | *Printed and sold by John Morris, oppo- | site the Three Reapers, in Third-Street.* [1764.] | Sm. 8vo. pp. 8.   H. S. P.   2053

REMARKS | Upon The | Delineated Presbyterian | Play'd Hob With; | or | Clothes | For a | Stark Naked | Author. | . . . . | *Philadelphia:* | *Printed and sold by Anthony Armbruster,* | *at*

the German and English Printing- | *Office; in Moravian - Alley.*
1764. | Sm. 8vo. pp. 8. H. S. P. 2054

ROUSSEAU, (J. J.) Emilius and Sophia: Or, A New System
of Education. Translated from the French of Mr. J. J. Rousseau, Citizen of Geneva. By the Translator of Eloisa. In Four
Volumes. *Philadelphia: William Bradford.* 1764. 2055

SAUNDERS. (R.) A Pocket | Almanack | For the Year
1765. | Fitted to Use of Penn- | sylvania, and the neighbour- |
ing Provinces. | With several useful Additions. | By R. Saunders,
Phil. | *Philadelphia:* | *Printed and sold by B. Franklin,* | *and D.*
Hall. [1764.] | 24mo. pp. (24). c. 2056

Hall says the number of Pocket Almanacs printed for the years 1752 to 1765,
inclusive, was 25,735.

SAUNDERS. Poor Richard improved: | Being an | Al-
manack | . . . | . . . | . . . | . . . | . . . | . . . | . . . | . . . | . .
| . . . | For the | Year of our Lord 1765: | Being the First after
Leap - Year. | . . . | . . . | . . | . . | . . . | . . . | . . . | . . . |
. . . . | By Richard Saunders, Philom. | *Philadelphia: Printed*
and Sold by B. Franklin, and D. Hall. [1764.] | Sm. 8vo. pp. (36).

According to Hall statement of the partnership account, 141,257 Poor Richard's
Almanacs were printed for the years 1752 to 1765, inclusive.

[SAUR. (Christopher)] 𝔈𝔍𝔑𝔈 | Zu dieser Zeit höchstnöthige
Warnung und Erinnerung an die freye Einwohner der Provinz | Pen=
sylvanien von Einem, dem die Wohlfahrt des Landes angelegen und
darauf bedacht ist. | [*Germantown: Christoph Saur.* 1764.] Folio,
pp. (2). H. S. P. 2058

A | SCENE | in the first Act | of the new | Farce. | Published
as a Specimen. | . . . . | [*Philadelphia:*] *Printed:* | [*by Anthony Arm-*
bruster] *In the first Year of the New Hegira* | *Secundus, the Paxtonian*
Expedition. [1764.] | Sm. 8vo. pp. 8. L. C. P. 2059

THE | SCRIBLER | Being a | Letter | From a Gentleman in
Town | To his | Friend in the Country, | concerning the present
State of Public | Affairs; | with a | Lapidary Character. | . . . .

| [*Philadelphia :*] *Printed* [*by Anthony Armbruster*] *in the Year* MDCC,LXIV. | Sm. 8vo. pp. 24. H. S. P. 2060

This is a reply to the epitaph on Franklin, and concludes with an imitation of it in a "Lapidary Character" of Dr. Wm. Smith.

𝕾𝕰𝕴𝕹𝕰𝕽 Königlichen Erhabensten Majestät | im Hohen Rath, | nahe sich | Diese demüthigste Vorstellung und Bitte | von | Seiner Majestät gehorsamst-getreuen Unterthanen, den freyen | Einwohnern der Provinz Pennsylvanien. | [*Philadelphia : Anton Armbruester.* 1764.] Folio, pp. (2). H. S. P. 2061

A | SERIOUS | Address, | To | Such of the Inhabitants of | Pennsylvania, | As have cannived at, or do approve of, the | late Massacre of the Indians at Lancaster; | or the Design of killing those who are | now in the Barracks at Philadelphia. | *Philadelphia :* | *Printed* [*by Anthony Armbruster*] *for the Author,* 1764. | 16mo. pp. 12.+The Second Edition. H. S. P. 2062

A SERIOUS | Address, | To such of the Inhabitants of | Pennsylvania, | As have connived at, or do approve of, the | late Massacre of the Indians at Lancaster, | or the Design of killing those who are now | in the Barracks at Philadelphia. | Re-printed from the First Edition (printed by Mr. | Armbruster) and diligently compared and revised with | the same. | *Philadelphia :* | *Printed by Andrew Steuart, at the* | *Bible-in-Heart, in Second-street,* 1764. | Sm. 8vo. pp. 8. L. C. P. 2063

A SERIOUS | Address, | To such of the | Inhabitants of Pennsylvania, | As have connived at, or do approve of, the late | Massacre of the Indians at Lancaster; or the | Design of killing those who are now in the Bar- | racks at Philadelphia. | The Demand for this Piece has been so great, that this Fourth | Edition is call'd for in a few Days! | To which is now added, | A Dialogue between | Andrew Trueman and Thomas Zealot, | About the killing the Indians at Connestogoe and Lancaster. | (An Excellent Piece!) | *Philadelphia : Printed by Andrew Steuart, in* | *Second-street.* M,DCC,LXIV. | Sm. 8vo. pp. 8. L. C. P. 2064

THE | SQUABBLE, | a | Pastoral Eclogue. | By Agricola. |

The Second Edition. | [*Philadelphia:*] *Printed* [*by Anthony Armbruster*] *in the Year* MDCCLXIV. | 4to. pp. 8.   H. S. P.   2065

THE | SQUABBLE; | A | Pastoral Eclogue. | By Agricola. | With a curious and well-design'd Frontispiece. | *Printed* (*from The First Edition.*) | *By Andrew Steuart, in Second-street, Philadelphia.* [1764.] | Sm. 8vo. pp. 8.   L. C. P.   2066

The Frontispiece, which, by the way, is on page 4, is a rude metal cut representing "Thyrsis, with a Pr*sb*t*rian Nose," and "Corin, with a Q**k*ronian Nose."

STEUART. (A.) The Gentleman and Citizen's Pocket Almanac for 1765. By Andrew Steuart. *Philadelphia: Andrew Steuart.* 1764.   2067

THE | SUBSTANCE, | of a | Council | Held at Lancaster August the 28th 1764. By | a Committee of Presbyterian Ministers | and Elders deputed from all Parts of Penn- | sylvania, in order to settle the ensuing E- | lection of Members for the Assembly. | Published, | At the Request of their respective | Congregations. | . . . | . . . | . . . | . . . | . . . . | [*Philadelphia:*] *Printed* [*by Anthony Armbruster*] *in the Year* MDCC,LXIV. | Sm. 8vo. pp. 19.   L. C. P.   2068

THE SYNOD of New York and Philadelphia vindicated. In a Reply to Mr. Samuel Harker's Appeal to the Christian World. By a Member of the Synod. *Philadelphia: William Dunlap,* 1764.   2069

DIE TÄGLICHEN Loosungen der Brüder Gemeine für das Jahr 1765.   2070

Henry Miller printed 400 copies of an index, of about twelve pages, to the edition printed in Germany.

[TERSTEEGEN. (Gerhard)] Das | Anhangen | an Gott, | ein | Unterricht | des | Albertus Magnus, | gewesenen Bischoffs | zu | Regensburg. | *Germantown gedruckt bey* | *Christoph Saur,* 1764. | Sm. 16mo. pp. (7), 56.   H. S. P.   2071

[*Penn Arms.*] TO the | Commissioners | and | Assessors, |

of | Chester County, | for the Year 1764. | [*Philadelphia: B. Franklin, and D. Hall.* 1764.] Folio, 1 leaf. ᴌ. ᴄ. ᴘ. 2072

A return of the tax paper in doggerel verse, in double columns.

TO the | Freeholders | and | Electors | Of the City and County of Philadelphia. | [*Philadelphia: William Bradford.* 1764.] Folio, pp. 2. ᴌ. ᴄ. ᴘ. 2073

An Anti-Franklin election address.

TO the Freeholders and other Electors for the City | and County of Philadelphia, and Counties of Chester and | Bucks. | [*Philadelphia: B. Franklin, and D. Hall.* 1764.] Folio, pp. (2).

An Anti-Proprietory election address.

TO the | Freemen | of | Pennsylvania. | [*Philadelphia: William Bradford.* 1764.] Folio, 1 leaf. ᴌ. ᴄ. ᴘ. 2075

An attack upon the new "Militia Law," dated Sept. 28, 1764.

TOBLER. (J.) The Pennsylvania Town and Countryman's Almanac for 1765. By John Tobler. *Wilmington: James Adams.* 1764. 2076

TRUE Copy of a | Letter, | from a | Member of St. P[au]l's, | to an | Intimate Friend : | Shewing the real Source from which | the present Wranglings in that Congre- | gation have sprung. | [*Philadelphia:*] *Printed* [*by Andrew Steuart*] *in the Year* M,DCC,LXIV. | Sm. 8vo. pp. 8. ᴌ. ᴄ. ᴘ. 2077

THE | TRUE QUAKER, | Reproving the | False One. | Or | Them that would be counted | Quakers, and are not : | So set forth | By John Buffin, former Bookseller | in the Jerseys, and Pennsylvania. | Being his Third Impresion. | . . . | . . . | . . . | . . . . | *Philadelphia, printed* [*by Anthony Armbruster*] *for the Author* accord- | *ing to Copy.* 1764. | Sm. 8vo. pp. 17. ᴌ. ᴄ. ᴘ. 2078

TUNES | in | Three Parts, | For the several metres in Dr. Watts's | version of the Psalms; some of which tunes | are new. This Collection of tunes is | made from the works of eminent

mas- | ters; consisting of six tunes for short me- | tre; eight
for common metre; seven for | long metre; and a tune for
each special | metre. | To which are added the gamut, with |
directions to learners of music. | The second adition, Price 1s.
6d. stitched. | *Philadelphia:* | *Printed by Anthony Armbruster, in
Arch-Street,* 1764. | 12mo. pp. viii, 43, (1).   H. S. P. 2079

THE | UNIVERSAL | Peace-Maker, | or | Modern Author's |
Instructor. | By Philanthropos. | *Philadelphia: Printed by Anthony
Armbruster | in Moravian Alley,* 1764. | Sm. 8vo. pp. 15.   2080

Von der | Historia | Des | Apostolischen Kampffs, | Zehen Bücher,
| Wie sie der Abdias anfänglich in der Hebräischer | Sprache be-
schrieben, Eutropius aber ins Griechische | und Julius Africanus ins
Lateinische übersetzte haben, | Welchen dann Wolfgangus Lazius aus
alten Scri | = | benten auch beygefüget hat | Das Leben des Apostels
Matthaei | und des heiligen Marci, Clementis, Cipriani und | Apol-
linaris; | Nunmehro für einige unpaffionirte Liebhaber Wahrheit ins
Deutsche | übersetzet; Nebst etlichen | Merckwürdigen Reden Jesu, die
man | zwar nicht in den Evangelien, aber bey andern bewährten |
Scribenten findet: | Auch der Marter = Geschichte der heiligen und hoch-
berühmten ersten Märtyrin und | Apostolischen Jungfrau Theclä. |
*Vormals in Amsterdam; nun aber in Ephrata ge- | druckt durch die
Brüderschafft auf Kosten der | Brüder in Canegotshiken, im Jahr*
1764. | 16mo. 388, 52.   2081

Appended to this work, with separate paging (1–52), but continuous signatures, is
the Gospel of Nicodemus, which has the following title:

Des | Jüngers Nicodemi | Evangelium | von unsers Meisters und | Heylands Jesu
Christi Ley- | den und Auferstehung. | *Ephrata:* | *Gedruckt im Jahr* MDCCLXIV.
| 16mo. pp. 52.

VOTES | and | Proceedings | of the | House of Representatives
| of the | Province of Pennsylvania, | Met at Philadelphia, on
the Fourteenth of October, Anno | Domini 1763, and continued
by Adjournments. | [*Penn Arms.*] | *Philadelphia:* | *Printed and
Sold by B. Franklin, and D. Hall, at the | New Printing-Office near
the Market.* MDCCLXIV. | Folio, pp. 113.   H. S. P. 2082

WEATHERWISE. (A.) Father Abraham's Almanac for

1765.   By Abraham Weatherwise.   *Philadelphia: William Dunlap.*
1764.   2083

WHEREAS the Number of poor in and around this City, is at | present great, and every Year increasing; and as for want of Employment, many | of them, especially in Winter, are reduced to great Straits, and rendered | burthensome to their Neighbours; therefore, in order to alleviate their Wants, by finding | them Employment, it is proposed to erect a Linen Manufactory, in or near this City; | and for that End the following Articles are agreed on, viz. | [*Philadelphia:* 1764.] Folio, pp. 2.   L. C. P.   2084

WIDDER. (P.)   Er. Ehrw. Hrn. Philip Widders, ehmaligen Chur=Pfälzischen Reformirten Kirchenraths und Pfarrherrn in Mannheim, Sechs und zwanzig Paßions=Predigten.   *Philadelphia: Henrich Miller.* 1764.

[WILLIAMSON. (Hugh)]   The | Plain Dealer: | Or, | A few Remarks upon | Quaker-Politicks, | And their Attempts to | Change the Government | Of Pennsylvania. | With | Some Observations on the false and | abusive Papers which they have | lately publish'd. | Numb. I. | To be continued. | *Philadelphia:* | *Printed,* [*by Andrew Steuart*] *Anno* MDCCLXIV. | 16mo. pp. 19.

THE | PLAIN Dealer: | Numb. II. | Being a | Tickler, | For the leisure Hour's Amusement of the Author of | Cool Thoughts. | Wherein the Force of his several Arguments in Favour | of a Change of Government is stated in a clear | Light and accommodated to the Comprehension of Readers | of every capacity. | By X. Y. Z. Gentleman. | To be continued. | *Philadelphia:* | *Printed* [*by Andrew Steuart*] *in Second-street, where Numb. I. may be had.* 1764. | Sm. 8vo. pp. 16.

THE | PLAIN Dealer: | or | Remarks on Quaker Politics | In Pennsylvania. | Numb. III. To be continued. | By W. D. Author of No. I. | *Philadelphia:* | *Printed,* [*by William Dunlap*] *Anno* MDCCLXIV. | 8vo. pp. 24.

[WILLIAMSON.]   The | Plain Dealer; | Numb. I. | Or, | A Few Remarks upon | Quaker-Politicks, | and their attempts to | Change the Government of Pennsylvania. | With some Observations on the false and abusive | Papers which they have lately publish'd. | To be Continued. | *Philadelphia:* | *Printed by Andrew Steuart, at the Bible-in-Heart, in Second- | street; of whom all the succeeding Numbers may be had; and | all other political Pamphlets*

that have been publish'd since the Commencement of the present Disputes.
[1764.] | 8vo. pp. 16.   N. Y. H. S.   2087

[WILLIAMSON.]   What is Sauce for a Goose is also Sauce
for a | Gander. | Being | A small Touch in the Lapidary Way.
| Or | Tit for Tat, in your own Way. | An Epitaph | On a
certain great Man. | Written by a departed Spirit and now |
Most humbly inscrib'd to all his dutiful Sons and | Children,
Who may hereafter chose to dis- | tinguish him by the Name of
| A Patriot. | . . . | . . . | . . . | . . . | . . . | . . . . | *Phila-*
delphia, printed [by A. Armbruster] in Arch-Street 1764. | Sm. 8vo.
pp. 8.   H. S. P.   2088

WILSON. (S.)   The Ordinance of Baptism, set in a clear light,
by the late learned and pious Mr. Samuel Wilson, of London.
The Third Edition. *Philadelphia: Anthony Armbruster.* 1764.   2089

WISTER. (J.)   Bekanntmachung! [Von Johannes Wister, Apotheker
zu Germantown! | *Germantown: Christoph Saur, 1764.*]   12mo.
pp. (4).   H. S. P.   2090

[WITHERSPOON. (John)]   A Letter from a Blacksmith,
to the Ministers and Elders of the Church of Scotland; in
which the manner of public Worship in that Church is considered; its Inconveniences and Defects pointed out and
methods for removing them humbly proposed. *Philadelphia:*
William Dunlap. 1764.   2091

[YOUNG. (Edward)]   Resignation. | In Two Parts, | and | A
Postscript. | To Mrs. B[oudinot.] . . . | . . . . | *London, Printed:*
| *Philadelphia, Re-printed: By W. Bradford, at* | *the Corner of Market*
and Front-Streets. | M.DCC.LXIV. | 8vo. Half title 1 l. pp. 74.   2092

The Postscript was written by Miss Eliz. Græme, afterwards Mrs. Ferguson.

ZWEY wahrhafte neue Zeitungen von gantz besondern | Himmels=
Zeichen, | Welches erstere | sich bey der Haupt= und Seestadt Riga in
Lifland zugetragen, allwo | sehr viele Menschen, am Himmel einen Sarg,
feurige Ruthen, 3 Todtenköpfe, eine | Schlange und Pyramide gesehen.
Daß zweyte ist gesehen worden zu Kirschberg, 4 | Meilen von der Stadt

und Feſtung Elbing, und zehn Meilen von der Kauf= und | Handel=
ſtadt Dantzig gelegen, allwo nemlich vom 6 zum 7 May 1763 dieſes |
Himmels = Zeichen, 48. Stunden lang mit einem ſtarcken Blitz und
Donner= | ſchlag geſtanden. | Welches aus nachfolgenden mit mehrerm
zuerſehen iſt. | [Cut.] | *Philadelphia gedruckt bey Anton Armbruester in
Moraevien Alley, 1764.* | Sm. 4to. pp. 4.   H. S. P.   2093

ZWÖLFF Sibyllen. | Weiſſagungen, | Viel wunderbarer Zukunft,
von An= | fang bis zum Ende der Welt | beſagend, | Auch der Königin
von Saba, dem König | Salomon gethane Prophezeyung. | Wie auch |
Merklicher künftiger Dinge, von St. Bri= | gitten, Cyrillo, Methodio,
Joachimo, Bruder Rein= | hard, Johanne Lichtenberger, und Bruder
Jacob aus | Hiſpanie, beſchrieben. | [Cut of St. Brigitta.] | *Phila-
delphia, gedruckt und zu haben bey A. Arm-* | *bruester und N. Hassel-
bach, in Moraevien* | *Ally naechst der Bruder Kirche* . . . . [1764?]
| 8vo.   2094

1765.

AN ACCOUNT | Of a surprising | Phœnomenon, | Which
appeared in the Sky at the City of Phi- | ladelphia and different
Parts of Pennsylva- | nia, on Saturday the 2d. of February 1765.
| . . . | . . . . | [Cut] | *Philadelphia, printed by Anthony Armbruster
in Arch-Street* 1765. | *This may be depended upon for Truth.* | 4to.
pp. 4.   L. C. P.   2095

AN ACCOUNT of the Births and Bu- | rials in Christ-Church
and St. Peter's Parish, | in Philadelphia, from December 25,
1764, to De- | cember 25, 1765. By Caleb Cash, Clerk, and |
James Weyley, Sexton. | [*Philadelphia:* 1765.] Folio, 1 leaf. 2096

ACT of Parliament commonly called The Billeting Act.
Philadelphia: William Dunlap. 1765.   2097

AN | ADDRESS | to the | Rev. Dr. Alison, the Rev. Mr.
Ewing, and | others, Trustees of the Corporation for the Relief
| of Presbyterian Ministers, their Widows and Children: |
Being | A Vindication | of the | Quakers | From the Aspersions
of the said Trustees | in their Letter published in the London
Chronicle, | No. 1223. | To which is prefixed, the said Letter.

| By a Lover of Truth. | . . . . | [*Philadelphia :*] *Printed* [*by William Dunlap*] *in the Year* 1765. | 16mo. Half-title, 1 leaf; Title, 1 leaf; Letter, pp. i–iii ; text, pp. 1–47. H. S. P. 2098

AGUECHEEK. (A.) The Universal American | Almanack, | or yearly | Magazine. | . . . | . . . | . . . . | For the Year of our Lord 1766. | . . . | . . . | . . . | . . . . | Being the 2d after Bissextile, or Leap-Year. | [20 lines.] | By Andrew Aguecheek, Philom. | *Philadelphia: Printed by Andrew Steuart, at the | Bible-in-Heart, in Second-street.* [1765.] | Sm. 8vo. pp. (40). L. C. P. 2099

𝔄𝔫 die | Deutſchen, | vornemlich die zum Wahlen berechtigen, | in Philadelphia= Bucks= und Berks County. | *Philadelphia, Gedruckt bey Henrich Miller, in der Zweyten-strasse.* | Folio, pp. (2). L. C. P. 2100

ANNO REGNI | Georgii III. | Regis | Magnæ Brittaniæ, Franciæ, & Hiberniæ, | Quinto. | At the Parliament begun and hold- | en at Westminster, the Nine- | teenth Day of May, Anno. | Dom. 1761, in the First Year | of the Reign of our Sovereign | Lord George the Third, | by the Grace of God, of Great- | Britain, France, and Ireland, | King, Defender of the Faith, &c. | And from thence continued by several Prorogations to | the Tenth Day of January 1765, being the Fourth | Session of the Twelfth Parliament of Great-Britain. | *London : Printed by Mark Basket, Printer to the King's Most | Excellent Majesty : And, re-printed by William | Dunlap, at the Newest-Printing-Office, in Market- | Street, Philadelphia.* [1765.] | 8vo. pp. 40. L. C. P. 2101

The title of the Act on page 3, is, "An Act for granting and applying certain Stamp Duties, and other Duties, in the British Colonies and Plantations in America, towards further defraying the Expences of defending, protecting, and securing the same ;" &c. This is the celebrated "Stamp Act ;" there were probably several editions printed in Philadelphia.

ANNO Regni | Georgii III. | Regis, | Magnæ Britanniæ, Franciæ & Hiberniæ, | Quinto. | At a General Assembly of the Province of Penn- | sylvania, begun and holden at Philadelphia, | the Fourteenth Day of October, Anno Domini 1764, in | the Fourth Year of the Reign of our Sovereign Lord | George III. by the Grace of God, of Great- | Britain, France and Ireland, King,

Defender of the | Faith, &c. | And from thence continued by Adjournments to the | Fifteenth Day of February, 1765. | [*Penn Arms.*] | *Philadelphia:* | *Printed and Sold by B. Franklin, at the New-* | *Printing-Office, near the Market.* MDCCLXV. | Folio, Title, 1 leaf; pp. 373–410.+And from thence continued . . . to the | Eighteenth Day of May, 1765. | [*Ibid.*] Title, 1 leaf; pp. 413–428.+And from thence continued . . . to the | Twenty-first Day of September, 1765. | [*Ibid.*] Title,·1 leaf; pp. 431–448.   2102

ANTWORT | auf | Hrn. Fränklins | Anmerckungen | über ein ohn= längst herausgekommenes | Protestations= | Schreiben, | Uebersetzt aus dem Englischen. | [*Germantown:*] *Gedruckt* [*bey Christoph Saur*] *im Jahr 1765.* | 16mo. pp. 27.   2103

ARNDT. (J.) Des | Gottseligen und Hocherleuchteten | Lehrers, | Hrn. Johann Arnds | Weiland | General = Superintendentens des | Fürstenthums Lüneburg, | Paradieß= | Gärtlein, | zur Uebung des wahren Christenthums | Durch | Geistreiche Gebäter, | in die Seele zu pflantzen, | Nebst einem wahrhafftigen Bericht, | was sich mit diesem Büchlein denk= | würdiges zugetragen, | Mit der Vorrede des Hrn. | Authoris selbsten. | *Germantown;* | *Gedruckt bey Christoph Saur,* 1765. | 24mo. pp. (34), 531, (11).   H. S. P.   2104

AT a general Meeting of the Merchants and Traders . . . . [*Philadelphia:* 1765.] 4to. 1 leaf.   L. C. P.   2105

Dated, "Philadelphia, November 7, 1765." A form of a non-importation agreement circulated for signatures.

BACHMAIR. (J. J.) A Complete German Grammar. By John James Bachmair. *Philadelphia:* 1765.   2106

Title from Haven's List. See No. 2745, *infra.*

BEVERIDGE. (J.) Epistolæ Familiares | et | Alia quædam Miscellanea. | Familiar Epistles, | and | Other Miscellaneous Pieces, | Wrote originally in Latin Verse, | By John Beveridge, A.M. | Professor of Languages in the College and Academy | of Philadelphia. | To which are added several Translations into English | Verse, by different Hands, &c. | . . . . | *Philadelphia.*

| *Printed for the Author by William Bradford, at the London Coffee-* | *House, at the Corner of Market and Front-Streets.* | M,DCC,LXV. | 8vo. pp. xi, 88.   H. S. P.   **2107**

A | CATALOGUE | of | Books, | Belonging to the | Association Library Company | of | Philadelphia : | Alphabetically digested. | To which is Prefixed, | the | Articles | of the said Company, &c. | *Philadelphia :* | *Printed by William Bradford, at the Corner of Mar-* | *ket and Front-Streets.* M.DCC.LXV. | 8vo. pp. 68.   H. S. P.   **2108**

A | CATALOGUE | of | Books, | belonging to the | Union Library Company | of | Philadelphia. | *Philadelphia :* | *Printed by Henry Miller, in Second-street.* MDCCLXV. | 8vo. pp. xxiv, 40.   H. S. P.   **2109**

A CATECHISM. *Philadelphia : B. Franklin, and D. Hall.* 1765.

Four thousand copies, according to Hall's account rendered to Franklin, were printed about 1765.

𝕯𝕰𝕽 𝕶𝕷𝕰𝕵𝕹𝕰 𝕮𝕬𝕿𝕰𝕮𝕳𝕵𝕾𝕸𝖀𝕾 Lutheri, mit der Ordnung des Heils, und dem Würtembergischen Kurzen Kinder-Examen, ꝛc. wie auch Der Ungeänderten Augspurgischen Confeſſion, ꝛc. Zum Gebrauch der Jugend und Alten. *Philadelphia : Henrich Miller.* 1765.   **2111**

THE | CHRISTIAN Letter | To | Presbyterian, Church & Quaker. | . . . | . . . | . . . | . . . | . . . | . . . . | *Philadelphia,* *printed by Anthony Armbruster,* | *in Arch-Street,* 1765. | Sm. 8vo. pp. 12.   H. S. P.   **2112**

COLLECTION of Hymns, By Watts, Willison and Gillis. *Wilmington : James Adams.* 1765.   **2113**

Saturday, September 21, 1765. Num. 1 | THE CONSTITUTIONAL Courant. | Containing Matters interesting to Liberty, and no wise repugnant to Loyalty. | [*Philadelphia : Andrew Steuart.* 1765.] Folio, 1 leaf.   L. C. P.   **2114**

A reprint from the original issued at New York.

THE COUNTER Medley: Being a proper answer to all the dunces of the Medley, and their abettors. *Philadelphia: Anthony Armbruster.* 1765. 2115

CRISP. (S.) A Short History of a Long Travel from Babylon to Bethel. By Stephen Crisp. *Philadelphia: Anthony Armbruster.* 1765. 2116

[DICKINSON. (John)] Friends and Countrymen. | [*Philadelphia. William Bradford.* 1765.] Folio, pp. (2). H. S. P. 2117

An Address by John Dickinson urging opposition to the Stamp Act, published Dec. 5, 1765.

[DICKINSON.] The | Late Regulations | Respecting the | British Colonies | on the Continent of | America | considered, | In a Letter from a Gentleman in Philadelphia | to his Friend in London. | . . . | . . . . | *Philadelphia:* | *Printed and Sold by William Bradford, at the Corner of* | *Market and Front-Streets.* M.DCC.LXV. | 8vo. pp. 38. H. S. P. 2118

[DULANEY. (Daniel)] Considerations on the propriety of imposing taxes in the British colonies. *Philadelphia: ? B. Franklin, and D. Hall.* 1765. 2119

The existence of a Philadelphia edition is doubtful.

THE ELECTION. Humbly Inscribed to the Saturday-Nights Club in Lodge Alley. Folio, 1 leaf. L. C. P. 2120

About 150 lines of blank verse engraved on copper, with a picture of the election at the top.

ELLWOOD. (T). Davideis. By Thomas Ellwood. *Wilmington: James Adams.* 1765. 2121

DJE ERSTE Frucht | der | Teutschen Gesellschaft. | Ein Lands=Gesetz | Worin noch fernere Verordnungen hinzu | gethan werden zu demjenigen Landes=Gesetz | welches den Titul führet „Ein Landes=Ge= | „setz worin verboten wird daß von den | „Teutschen so wohl als andern Passagie= | „ren nicht zu viele mit einander in ein | „Schiff gepackt und hieher übergebracht | „werden mögen," nebst einem Auszug aus | demselben Lands=Gesetz. | Auf Verordnung der Teutschen Ge=sellschaft | Aus dem Englischen übersetzt. | *Germantown:* | *Gedruckt bey Christoph Saur.* 1765. | 8vo. pp. 15.   H. S. P.   2122

EVANGELISCHER | Auterricht, | Wie die | Confirmation, | Das ist: | Die Taufs=Bunds= | Erneurung | Mit benenjenigen Kindern, welche das er= | ste mal zum Heiligen Abendmahl geben | wollen, | In den | gesamten Evangelisch Würtembergischen | Kirchen | Zur Besserung der Gemeinde Gottes an= | zustellen. | Mit Hoch Fürstl. gnädigstem | Privilegio. | *Gedruckt in Stuttgard und Tuebingen, in Phila-* | *delphia nachgedrukt bey Anton Armbruester in der* | *Raess-Strasse, im Jahr* 1765. | 24mo. pp. 1–51?; 1–57.   H. S. P.   2123

FOX. (T.) The Wilmington Almanac for 1766. By Thomas Fox. *Wilmington: James Adams,* 1765.   2124

FRANKLIN. (W.) The Answer of his Excellency William Franklin, Esq; Governor . . . | . . . of New Jersey, to the invidious Charges of the Proprietary Party, con- | tained in a Libel, read by Mr. James Biddle, Clerk of the Common Pleas for the County of | Philadelphia, on Saturday last, and afterwards published and industriously dispersed through the | Province. | [*Philadelphia: B. Franklin and D. Hall.* 1765.] Folio, 1 leaf.   2125

Printed also in the Pennsylvania Gazette, Oct 3, 1765.

A | FULL and True | Relation, | of | Count Martini, in Silesia, | Who was transformed into a Dog, all but the Head, which you will see | in the Cut, hereunto annexed. | Was occa-sioned by way of striving for Worldly Pelf, ruining his | Sub-jects, and Blaspheming his Lord and Creator. | . . . | . . . | . . . . | [Cut.] . . . | . . . . | *Philadelphia, Printed by Anthony Armbruster,* 1765. | Sm. 4to. pp. 4.   L. C. P.   2126

[GALLOWAY. (Joseph)] Advertisement. | Philadelphia, December 20, 1765. | To the Publick. | [*Philadelphia: B. Frank-lin, and D. Hall.* 1765.] Folio, 1 leaf.   L. C. P.   2127

Galloway's denial of the charge that he opposed the transaction of Judicial busi-ness except on "Stampt Paper."

𝔇𝔍𝔈 𝔊𝔈𝔥𝔈𝔍𝔏𝔍𝔊𝔗𝔈𝔑 Wiſſenſchaften | unter dem Kreuße. | Ein Traum. | Aus dem IIIten Stück der Gelehrten Dresdniſchen | Anzeigen auf das Jahr 1762. | *Philadelphia, Nachdruckt bey Henrich Miller.* 1765. | 8vo. pp. 8.   H. S. P.   2128

GODFREY. (J.)   Juvenile Poems | on | Various Subjects. | With the | Prince of Parthia, | A | Tragedy. | By the late | Mr. Thomas Godfrey, Junr. | of Philadelphia. | To which is pre-fixed | Some Account of the Author and his Writings. | . . . . | *Philadelphia:* | *Printed by Henry Miller, in Second - Street.* | MDCCLXV. | 4to. pp. xxvi, (2), 223.   H. S. P.   2129

HALBERT. (H.)   The | Last Speech and Confession, | of | Henry Halbert, | Who was executed at Philadelphia, October | 19, 1765, for the inhuman Murder of the | Son of Jacob Wool-man. | To which is added, | A Letter from the Criminal to the Father of the | murdered Son. | . . . | . . . | . . . | . . . | . . . | . . . . | *Philadelphia: Printed by Anthony Arm-* | *bruster, in Race-Street.* [1765.] | Sm. 8vo. pp. 8.   L. C. P.   2130

THE HEIDELBURG Catechism, in English.   Translated from the German, for the use of the Reformed and other schools. *Philadelphia: Anthony Armbruster.* 1765.   2131

𝔇𝔈𝔑 | 𝔥𝔒𝔆𝔥=𝔇𝔈𝔘𝔗𝔖𝔆𝔥𝔈 | Americaniſche | Calender, | Auf das Jahr | . . . | . . . | 1766. | . . . | . . . | . . . | . . . | . . . | . . . | . . . | . . . | . . . | . . . | . . . . | Zum acht und zwanßigſten mal heraus gegeben. | *Germantown: Gedruckt und zu finden bey Christoph Saur.* | . . . | . . . . [1765.] | 4to. pp. (48).   H. S. P.   2132

HONEYCOMB. (W.) *Pseud.*   No. I. | The | Bee. | By | Wil-liam Honeycomb. | Tuesday February 12th. 1765. | . . . | . . . . | [*Philadelphia:*] *Printed* [*by Anthony Armbruster*] *in the Year* M,D,CC,LXV. | (This Paper will be published weekly.) | Sm. 8vo. pp. 8.+Number II. pp. 9–16.+Number III. pp. 17–22, Advertise-ment, 1 leaf.   H. S. P.   2133

[HUNT. (Isaac)]   A | Humble Attempt | at | Scurrility. | In Imitation of | Those Great Masters of the Art | the Rev. Dr.

S——th; the Rev. Dr. Al[iso]n; the Rev. | Mr. Ew[i]n[g]; the Irreverent D. J. D[o]ve, and the Heroic | J[oh]n D[ickinso]n, Esq; | Being a | Full Answer | to the | Observations | on | Mr. H[ughe]s's | Advertisement. | By Jack Retort, Student in Scurrility. | *Quilsylvania: Printed*, 1765. [*Philadelphia: Anthony Armbruster*.] | 8vo. pp. 42, Errata, 1 leaf.   H. S. P.   2134

Attributed to William T. Franklin (who was born about 1760!) in the catalogue of the Library of the American Philosophical Society, and elsewhere, when the absurdity of the statement had been noticed, to Governor William Franklin. It was, however, one of the several scurrilous productions of the pen of Leigh Hunt's father. Hunt was graduated at the College and Academy of Philadelphia in 1763, and in 1765 applied to the Trustees to be admitted to the degree of Master of Arts, but was refused on technical grounds. In 1766 he renewed his request, which was refused on the grounds of his being the "author and publisher of several scurrilous and scandalous pieces," among which were "A Letter from a Gentleman in Transylvania" (see No. 2002, *supra*) and the "Exercises for Scurrility Hall," &c.

[HUNT.] The | Substance | of an | Exercise, | Had this Morning in | Scurrility-Hall. | [*Philadelphia:*] *Printed* [*by Andrew Steuart*] *in the Year*, M,DCC,LXV. | Sm. 8vo. pp. 6.   H. S. P.   2135

No. II. | A Continuation | Of the | Exercises, | in | Scurrility Hall. | . . . | . . . | . . . . | [*Philadelphia:*] *Printed* [*by Anthony Armbruster*] *in the Year* MDCC,LXV. | Sm. 8vo. pp. 7.

No. III. | A Continuation | Of the | Exercises, | in | Scurrility Hall. | With a Dialogue between the Professor [D. J. Dove] and | Sir John Brute. | [Sir J. St. Clair, Bart.] . . . | . . . . | [*Philadelphia:*] *Printed* [*by Anthony Armbruster*] *in the Year* MD,CC,LXV. | Sm. 8vo. pp. 7, (1).

No. IV. | A Continuation | Of the | Exercises, | in | Scurrility Hall. | . . . | . . . | . . . . | [*Philadelphia:*] *Printed* [*by Anthony Armbruster*] *in the Year* MD,CC,LXV. | Sm. 8vo. pp. 8.

No. V. | A Continuation | Of the | Exercises, | in | Scurrility Hall. | . . . | . . . . | [*Philadelphia:*] *Printed* [*by Anthony Armbruster*] *in the Year* MD,CC,LXV. | Sm. 8vo. pp. 7.

No. VI. | A Continuation | Of the | Exercises, | in | Scurrility Hall. | With the Reasons of their Publication. | . . . | . . . . | [*Philadelphia:*] *Printed* [*by Anthony Armbruster*] *in the Year* MD,CC,LXV. | Sm. 8vo. pp. 7.

No. VII. | A Continuation | Of the | Exercises, | in | Scurrility Hall. | [*Philadelphia:*] *Printed* [*by Anthony Armbruster*] *in the Year* MD,CC,LXV. | Sm. 8vo pp. 8.

No. VIII. | A | Dialogue, | between the Giant | Polypheme | and his Son | Jack Nothing: | On Occasion of his Eye being put out by a | Stranger: with a Dedication to Sir John Brute. | . . . | . . . . | . . . | . . . | . . . | . . . | . . . . | *Printed at*

Constantinople, [*Philadelphia: Anthony Armbruster*] *in the Year* 1696. [1765.] | Sm. 8vo. pp. 8.

O! JUSTITIA. | [Cut.] | A | Complete Trial. | God gives, and takes away, | Well, | Justice Shall Take Place. | [*Philadelphia: Anthony Armbruster,* 1765.] Sm. 8vo. pp. 16. L. C. P. 2136

THE | LAMENTATION, | of | Pennsylvania, | On Account of the Stamp-Act, together with the Prayer of J[oh]n | H-ws. [Hughes.] | [*Philadelphia: Anthony Armbruster.* 1765.] Folio, 1 leaf. L. C. P. 2137

A LAMENTATION over Zion, on the Declension of the Church. *Wilmington: James Adams.* 1765. 2138

A LAMPOON on Modern Scribblers. | [*Philadelphia: Anthony Armbruster.* 1765?] Narrow Folio, 1 leaf. L. C. P. 2139

LAND-OFFICE, 17th of June, 1765. | [*Philadelphia:* 1765.] Folio, 1 leaf. H. S. P. 2140

Notice, signed William Peters, Secretary, of certain changes in the mode of taking up large quantities of land in Pennsylvania.

LATELY imported, and to be sold by | David Hall, | At the New-Printing-Office, in Market-street, Philadelphia, the following Books, ... | [*Philadelphia: B. Franklin, and D. Hall.* 1765.] Folio, 1 leaf. L. C. P. 2141

[LEE. (Arthur)] An Essay in Vindication of the Continental Colonies of America from a Censure of Mr. Adam Smith, in his Theory of Moral Sentiments. With some Reflections on Slavery in General. By An American. *Philadelphia: William Bradford.* 1765. 2142

LUCIFER'S Decree, | After a Fray. | Or, | A Friendly Warning to all Persons | Of | Whatsoever Station, Nation, or Qualification, | In the City of Deceit, | And Province of Transylvania. | . . . | . . . | . . . | . . . . | The Mysterious Truth. | [*Philadelphia:*] *Printed in the Year,* 1765. | Sm. 8vo. pp. 7, (1). L. C. P. 2143

MAGNA Britania her Colonies Reduc'd. | [*Philadelphia :* 1765.]
Folio, 1 leaf.   L. C. P.   2144

A copper plate, engraved in line, of the well-known Female figure with her limbs
cut off. With 34 lines (also engraved) of "Explanation" and a Moral. "Engraved in
Philadelphia," says Du Simitiere. The original part, an etching 2½ by 4¼ inches,
designed by Franklin, was engraved and printed on the back of Message Cards used
by him.

[MILLER. (Peter)] A | Dissertation on | Mans Fall, | Trans-
lated from the High-German Original. | [Cut.] | *Printed : Ephrata,
Anno* MDCCLXV. | *Sold at Philadelphia by Messieurs Christoph |
Marshal and William Dunlap.* | 8vo. Title, 1 leaf; pp. 37.   2145

THE MERCHANTS and Traders of the City of Philadelphia,
taking into their Consideration the melancholy State | of the
North American Commerce . . . | . . . do unanimously agree. |
[*Philadelphia :* 1765.]   Folio, 1 leaf.   L. C. P.   2146

The Non-importation agreement.

MORGAN. (J.)   A | Discourse | Upon the Institution of |
Medical Schools | In America; | Delivered at a Public Anni-
versary Commence- | ment, held in the College of Philadelphia |
May 30 and 31, 1765. | With a | Preface | Containing, amongst
other things, | The Author's | Apology | For attempting to in-
troduce the regular mode of | practicing Physic in Philadelphia;
| By John Morgan M.D.: | Fellow of the Royal Society at
London; Corre- | spondent of the Royal Academy of Surgery
at | Paris; Member of the Arcadian Belles Lettres So- | ciety
at Rome; Licentiate of the Royal Colleges of | Physicians in
London and in Edinburgh; and | Professor of the Theory and
Practice of Medicine | in the College of Philadelphia. | *Philadel-
phia : | Printed and sold by William Bradford, at the | Corner of
Market and Front-Streets,* M,DCC,LXV. | 8vo. pp. vii, i–xxvi,
(2), 1–63.   H. S. P.   2147

𝔑𝔢𝔲=𝔈𝔦𝔫𝔤𝔢𝔯𝔦𝔠𝔥𝔱𝔢𝔱𝔢𝔯 Amerikanischer Calender, auf das Jahr
1766. *Philadelphia : Anton Armbruester.* 1765.   2148

DER NEUESTE, Verbeffert= und zuverläßige Americanifche Ca=
lender Auf das 1766fte Jahr Chrifti. *Philadelphia: Henrich Miller.*
1765.   2149

A | NEW | Song. | To the Tune of "Hearts of Oak, &c." |
[*Philadelphia:* 1765 ?] Folio, 1 leaf.   L. C. P.   2150

> " Then join Hand in Hand brave Americans all,
> By *uniting* We stand, by *dividing* We fall ;
> In so Righteous a Cause let us hope to succeed,
> For Heaven approves of each generous Deed."

A NEW Song Suitable to the Season. [*Philadelphia:* 1765.]
4to. 1 leaf.   L. C. P.   2151

Three verses and chorus, headed by a picture of three persons at a table, &c. Engraved on copper.

THE | NEW-YEAR | Verses, | Of the Printers Lads, who
carry about the Penn- | sylvania Gazette to the Customers. |
January 1, 1765. | [*Philadelphia: B. Franklin, and D. Hall,* 1765.]
Folio, 1 leaf.   L. C. P.   2152

NEW-YEAR Verses of the Carriers of the Pennsylvania
Journal. *Philadelphia: William Bradford.* 1765.   2153

A NUMBER of the Inhabitants of this City, desirous of
encouraging the Poor . . . | . . . did . . . form themselves
into a Company . . . | . . . to manufacture . . . | . . . coarse
Linen. | [*Philadelphia:* 1765.] Folio, pp. (2).   L. C. P.   2154

Articles of Agreement proposed to be signed for the purpose.

OPPRESSION. A Poem. By an American. With Notes by
a North-Briton. *Philadelphia? William Bradford.* 1765.   2155

First published in London, and reprinted in Boston and New York. The title
here given may be from an advertisement of one of these editions.

THE PENNSYLVANIA Gazette.   2156

Numbers 1880 (Jan. 3, 1765) to 1931 (Dec. 26, 1765), four pages each, with an
extra sheet of four pages to Numbers 1911 and 1923. The latter appeared in mourn-

ing, and in place of 1924, a half sheet (1 leaf) headed "No Stamped Paper to be had," was issued. The next issue (No. 1925) is called "Remarkable Occurances" and contains four pages. With number 1926 the regular heading was resumed. Title and imprint as in No. 1693, *supra*, until No. 1924, the substitutes for which and for 1925, and the remaining numbers printed during the year were issued without an imprint. This was done to avoid responsibility for violating the Stamp Act.

THE PENNSYLVANIA Journal. H. S. P. 2157

Numbers 1152 to 1203, four pages each, with an extra half sheet of two pages to No. 1193; Title and imprint as in No. 1693, *supra*.

THE | PENNSYLVANIA | Pocket Almanack | For the Year 1766. | Calculated for the Use of the Province | of Pennsylvania, and the neighbour- | ing Provinces. | *Philadelphia:* | *Printed and Sold by W. Bradford,* | *at the London Coffee-House.* [1765.] | 24mo. pp. (36). H. S. P. 2158

The last twelve pages contain "The Substance of the Act of Parliament, entitled 'An Act for granting certain Stamp Duties in the British Colonies and Plantations in America.'" It was issued in July to escape the tax.

[PETERS. [Richard)] Dialogue, &c. | For the Commencement in the College of | Philadelphia, | May 30th, 1765. | [*Philadelphia:* *W. Dunlap.* 1765.] 8vo. pp. 4. H. S. P. 2159

The original manuscript in the author's handwriting is in the possession of D. McN. Stauffer, Esq., of New York City.

THE PLAN | Of a Performance of | Solemn Musick; | To be in the Hall of the College of | Philadelphia, | On Wednesday Evening, April 10th, 1765, | For the Benefit of the Charity-Schools. | [*Philadelphia: W. Dunlap.* 1765.] 8vo. pp. 4. L. C. P. 2160

CITY OF PHILADELPHIA. | By the Mayor, Recorder, and Aldermen, and the | Commissioners for paving and cleansing the Streets, &c. | [*Philadelphia: B. Franklin, and D. Hall.* 1765.] Folio, 1 leaf. L. C. P. 2161

Notice that a scavenger had been appointed, and extracts from the Act of Assembly.

A PRIMER. *Philadelphia: B. Franklin, and D. Hall.* 1765. 2162

Between March, 1765, and Feb. 1, 1766, Two thousand Primers were printed by Hall for the firm's account.

THE | QUAKERS Grace, Prayer, | and | Thanksgiving, | On Sunday Sixth, Tenth Month, 1765, for their late Victory over the Rebels, | in their Province of Quylsylvania, in electing Law-Makers for the same. | [*Philadelphia : Anthony Armbruster.* 1765.] Folio, 1 leaf.   L. C. P.   2163

RHYMES Relating to the present Times, &c. *Philadelphia : Printed for the Author and sold by W. Dunlap.* 1765.   2164

SAUNDERS. (R.) A Pocket | Almanack | For the Year 1766. | Fitted to the Use of Penn- | sylvania, and the neighbour- | ing Provinces. | With several useful Additions. | By R. Saunders, Phil. | *Philadelphia :* | *Printed by B. Franklin,* | *and D. Hall.* [1765.] | 24mo. pp. (24).   c.   2165

SAUNDERS. Poor Richard improved : | Being an | Al-manack | . . . | . . . | . . . | . . . | . . . | . . . | . . . | . . . | . . . | . . . . | For the Year of our Lord 1766 : | Being the Second after Leap - Year. | . . . | . . . | . . . | . . . | . . . | . . . | . . . | . . . | . . . . | By Richard Saunders, Philom. | *-Philadelphia :* | *Printed and Sold by B. Franklin, and D. Hall.* [1765.] | Sm. 8vo. pp. (36).

The edition consisted of Nine thousand seven hundred and seventy-one copies.

[SAUR. (Christopher)] Werthefte Landes=Leute, | Sonderlich in Philadelphia Bucks und Bercks = Caunty ! | [*Germantown : Christoph Saur.* 1765.] Folio, pp. (2).   H. S. P.   2167

SHORT. (T.) Medicina Britannica. By Thomas Short. *Philadelphia : B. Franklin, and D. Hall.* 1765.   2168

[SMITH. (William)] An | Historical Account | of the | Expedition | Against the | Ohio Indians, in the Year 1764. | Under the Command of | Henry Bouquet, Esq ; | Colonel of Foot, and now Brigadier General in America. | Including | His Transactions with the Indians, relative to the delivery of their prisoners, | and the preliminaries of Peace. | With an | Introductory Account | Of the Preceeding Campaign, and Battle at Bushy-

Run. | To which are annexed | Military Papers, | Containing | Reflections on the war with the Savages; a method of forming frontier settle- | ments; some account of the Indian country, with a list of nations, fight- | ing men, towns, distances and different routs. | The whole illustrated with a Map and Copper-plates. | Published from authentic Documents, by a Lover of his Country. | *Philadelphia:* | *Printed and sold by William Bradford, at the London* | *Coffee-House, at the corner of Market and Front-streets.* M.DCC.LXV. | 4to. pp. (2), xiii, 71, 2 maps, 1 plate.   H. S. P.   2169

THE STAMP Act. *Philadelphia: William Bradford.* 1765. 2170

Advertised in the Pa. Journal, June 20, 1765. There were probably several other editions published in Philadelphia, for one of which see No. 2101, *supra.*

STEUART. (A.) The Gentleman and Citizen's Pocket Almanac for 1766. By Andrew Steuart. *Philadelphia: Andrew Steuart.* 1765.   2171

TENNANT. (G.) The Blessedness of Peace-Makers repre- | sented; and the Danger of Persecution | considered; | In two | Sermons, | On Mat. v. 9. | Preach'd at Philadelphia, the 3d Wednesday | in May, 1759, before the Reverend the Synod, of | New-York and Philadelphia, | By | Gilbert Tennant, A.M. | · · · | · · · · | · · · | · · · | · · · | · · · | · · · | · · · | · · · | · · · | · · · | · · · · | *Philadelphia:* | *Printed and Sold by William Bradford,* | *at the London Coffee-House, the corner of Mar-* | *ket and Front-streets.* M,DCC,LXV. | 8vo. pp. 50.   L. C. P.   2172

TO the | Freeholders and Electors | Of the Province of Pennsylvania. | [*Philadelphia: William Bradford.* 1765.] Folio, 1 leaf.   L. C. P.   2173

An anti-Franklin election address. "You have seen how the same faction have gratified an ambitious man in frequent embassies to England, under pretence of extinguishing a flame designedly kindled by himself! And . . . how this man, altho' he originally crept into confidence under the character of a commonwealth's man 'with the cry of our constitution and charter rights in his mouth' returned from England an arrant courtier and state tool; . . . determined to maintain himself and his associates here in power by a total change of our government and surrender of our charter." It is signed "James Biddle," and was perhaps written by him.

William Franklin, in his reply, says the principal Officers of the Government employed "the Clerk of the Court [James Biddle] to read it aloud to the Public."

TO the | Freeholders | And other Electors of Assembly-Men, for | Pennsylvania. | [*Philadelphia : Anthony Armbruster.* 1765.] Folio, pp. (2).   L. C. P.   2174

    A Franklin election circular.

TOBLER. (J.) The Pennsylvania Town and Countryman's Almanac for 1766. *Wilmington : James Adams.* 1765.   2175

THE | TRUE State | of the | Case | between | John Fenwick, Esq; | and | John Edridge & Edmund Warner, | concerning | Mr. Fenwick's Ten Parts of his | Land in West-New-Jersey, | in America. | *London, Printed in the Year* 1677. *And* | *Philadelphia, Re-printed by Andrew Steuart, for* | *John Hart,* MDCCLXV. | Sm. 8vo. pp. 8.   H. S. P.   2176

VOTES and Proceedings of the Assembly. *Philadelphia : B. Franklin.* 1765.   2177

WATKINSON. (E.) An | Essay | upon | Oeconomy. | The Fourth Edition. | By | Edward Watkinson, M.D. | Rector of Little Chart in Kent. | . . . . | *London, Printed :* | *Re-printed and Sold at the Newest Printing - Office , near the Market,* | *Philadelphia :* | M.DCC.LXV. | 8vo. pp. 35.   2178

WEATHERWISE. (A.) Father Abraham's | Almanack, | (On an entire New Plan.) | For the Year of our Lord, | 1766. | Being the Second after Leap Year. | [24 lines.] | By Abraham Weatherwise, Gent. | *Philadelphia : Printed by W. Dunlap,* | *at the Newest-Printing-Office, in Market-Street.* [1765.] | Sm. 8vo. pp. (40).   L. C. P.   2179

WESLEY. (J.) Primitive Physic, or An easy and natural Method of curing most Diseases. By John Wesley. The 12th Edition. *Philadelphia : Andrew Steuart.* 1765.   2180

WHITEFIELD. (G.) A Collection of Hymns for Social Worship, More particularly designed for the use of the Tabernacle Congregation in London. By George Whitefield, late of Pembroke College, Oxford, &c. *Philadelphia: William Bradford.* 1765.

WHITEFIELD. The Two First Parts of his Life with his Journals, revised, corrected, and abridged. By George White-field. *Philadelphia: William Bradford.* 1765. **2182**

THE WHITEOAK Anthum, taken from the | Pilgrims Progress. Newly translated from | the Original Dutch, By Mr. Sagasity. | [*Philadelphia: Anthony Armbruster.* 1765.] Narrow Folio, 1 leaf. L. C. P. **2183**

WILLISON. (J.) Young Communicant's Catechism. By J. Willison. *Wilmington: James Adams.* 1765. **2184**

[WITHERSPOON. (John)] A | Letter | from a | Blacksmith, | to the | Ministers and Elders | of the | Church of Scotland. | In which the Manner of Public Worship in that Church | is considered; its Inconveniences and Defects pointed out; | and Methods for removing them humbly proposed. | . . . | . . . | . . . . . . | . . . . | The Fourth Edition. | *London Printed:* | *Philadel-phia Reprinted, and Sold by Andrew* | *Steuart, in Second-street,* 1765. | Sm. 8vo. pp. 51, (1). C. **2185**

YOUR attendance at the Court House. . . . | [*Philadelphia:* 1765.] 4to. 1 leaf. L. C. P. **2186**

Call for a public meeting in regard to non-importation, dated " Philadelphia, November 6, 1765."

1766.

AN ACCOUNT of the Births and Bu- | rials in Christ-Church Parish, in Philadelphia, | from December 25, 1765, to December 25, 1766. | By Caleb Cash, Clerk, and James | Weyley, Sexton. | [*Philadelphia:* 1766.] Folio, 1 leaf. L. C. P. **2187**

AN ACT for the better Employment, Relief | and Support of the Poor, within the City of Philadel- | phia, the District of South-wark, the Townships of Moya- | mensing and Passyunk, and the

Northern Liberties. | [*Philadelphia : B. Franklin, and D. Hall.* 1766.] Folio, pp. 4.   L. C. P.   2188

ADVERTISEMENT. | . . . | . . . | . . . | . . . | . . . . | Pro-posals, | For Printing by Subscription, | A General History of the Lives | Raised and propogated by the Pr—y Faction, since the Year 1753; | with Remarks; in Four Volumes, in Folio. | [*Phila-delphia :* 1766.] Folio, 1 leaf.   L. C. P.   2189

A Franklin election squib. Probably by Isaac Hunt.

AGUECHEEK. (A.) The Universal American | Almanack, | or yearly | Magazine. | . . . | . . . | . . . | . . . . | For the Year of our Lord 1767 ; | . . . | . . . | . . . | . . . . | Being the 3d after Bissextile, or Leap-Year. | [19 lines.] | By Andrew Aguecheek, Philom. | *Philadelphia : Printed by Andrew Steuart, at the* | *Bible-in-Heart, in Second-street, between Market and Arch* | *streets, near Coombe's Alley.* [1766.] | Sm. 8vo. pp. (40).   H. S. P.   2190

THE AMERICAN Calendar for 1767.   *Philadelphia : William Bradford.*   1766.   2191

ANNO Regni | Georgii III. | Regis, | Magnæ Britanniæ, Franciæ & Hiberniæ, | Sexto. | At a General Assembly of the Province of Penn- | sylvania, begun and holden at Philadelphia, | the Fourteenth Day of October, Anno Domini 1765, in | the Fifth Year of the Reign of our Sovereign Lord | George III. by the Grace of God, of Great- | Britain, France and Ireland, King, Defender of the | Faith, &c. | And from thence continued by Ad-journments to the | Eighth Day of February, 1766. | [*Penn Arms.*] | *Philadelphia :* | *Printed and Sold by David Hall, at the New-* | *Printing-Office, near the Market.* MDCCLXVI. | Folio, Title, 1 leaf; pp. 451–485.+And from thence continued . . . to the | Twentieth Day of September, 1766. | [*Penn Arms.*] | *Philadelphia :* | *Printed and Sold by D. Hall, and W. Sellers, at the* | *New Printing-Office, near the Market.* MDCCLXVI. | Title, 1 leaf; pp. 489–498.   2192

THE ASSOCIATION Letter. | [*Philadelphia.* 1766.] Folio, pp. (2).   2193.

Letter from, and Minutes of, the Baptist Association of Churches in Pennsylvania, New Jersey, &c.

BENEZET. (A.)   A | Caution | and | Warning | to | Great Britain | and | Her Colonies, | in | A Short Representation | of the | Calamitous State | of the | Enslaved Negroes | in the British Dominions. | Collected from various Authors, and submit- | ted to the Serious Consideration | of all, and more especially of Those in | Power. | By Ant. Benezet. | *Philadelphia: Printed by Henry Miller,* | *in Second-street.* MDCCLXVI. | 8vo. pp. 35.   H. S. P.   2194

THE | BIRTH, Parentage, and Education, | of | Praise-God Barebone. | To which is added, | An Election Ballad, | or | the Lamentation of Miss * * * * * * *. | A true but doleful Ditty. | [*Philadelphia:*] *Printed* [*by Andrew Steuart*] *for Jack Northwester, at the* | *Sign of the White-Oak in Heart of Oak* | *Street,* MDCCLXVI. | 8vo. pp. 16. + [*Ibid.*] 8vo. pp. 17.   L. C. P.   2195

The ballad refers to Dickinson's defeat as a candidate for the Assembly, and the whole of this Hudibrastic performance was probably aimed at Dickinson by Isaac Hunt.

BLAIR. (J.) Animadversions on a Pamphlet entitled "Thoughts on the Examination and Trials of Candidates for the sacred Ministry," in a Letter to the unknown Author.   By Rev. John Blair, M.A. *Philadelphia:* 1766. 12mo. pp. 44.   2196

Title from Sabin's Dictionary.

BUCHANAN. (G.) De Juri Regni: Or The due right of Government, by way of a dialogue betwixt George Buchanan and Thomas Maitland; by the said George Buchanan, and translated out of the original Latin into English, by Philalethes. *Philadelphia: Andrew Steuart.* 1766.   2197

BUELL. (S.)   A Faithful Narrative of the Remarkable Revival of Religion in East-Hampton on Long-Island. In the Year of our Lord 1764. With Some Reflections. By Samuel Buell, A.M. Minister of the Gospel there. *Philadelphia: William Bradford.* 1766.   2198

CHALONER. (R.) The Morality of the Bible : Extracted from all the Canonical books both of the Old and New Testament. By R. Chaloner. *Philadelphia : Andrew Steuart.* 1766. 2199

THE | CHARTER, | Laws, | Catalogue of Books, | List of | Philosophical Instruments, &c. | of the | Juliana Library-Company, | in | Lancaster. | To which are prefixed, | Some Reflections on the Advantages of Knowledge; the | Origin of Books and Libraries, shewing how they | have been encouraged and patronized by the Wise and Virtuous | of every Age. | With | A Short Account of its Institution, Friends and Benefactors. | . . . | . . . | . . . | . . . | . . . | . . . | . . . . | Published by Order of the Directors. | *Philadelphia :* | *Printed by D. Hall, and W. Sellers.* MDCCLXVI. | Sq. 8vo. Title, 1 leaf; Dedication, 1 leaf; pp. 1–56. H. S. P. 2200

THE CHILD'S Best Instructor in Spelling and Reading. *Philadelphia : William Bradford.* 1766. 2201

CHILDS. (I.) The | Vision | of | Isaac Childs, | Which he saw in the Year 1757, | concerning | Pennsylvania, | The Land of his Nativity. | (Never published before this Year 1766.) | To which is annexed, | The Explanation. | [*Philadelphia :* 1766.] 12mo. pp. 12. L. C. P. 2202

CHRISTIAN Piety, | freed | From the many Delusions | of | Modern Enthusiasts | Of all Denominations. | By Philalethes. | The Third Edition. | With | The Life of Armelle Nicholas. | *London : Printed.* | *Philadelphia :* | *Reprinted by Henry Miller, in Second-Street.* | MDCCLXVI. | 16mo. pp. 22. H. S. P. 2203

A COLLECTION of Hymns, for Social Worship. Extracted from various Authors, and published by the Revd. Mr. Madan, and the Revd. Mr. Whitefield. *Philadelphia : W. and T. Bradford.* 1766. 2204

A | CONGRATULATORY, | Letter, | To | Mr. G[arne]r. | In | Philadelphia. | . . . | . . . | . . . | . . . | . . . . | [*Philadelphia :*] *Printed by [Anthony Armbruster] in the Year* 1766. | Sm. 8vo. pp. 8. L. C. P. 2205

CONSIDERATIONS upon the Rights of the Colonists to the Privileges of British Subjects, Introduced by a brief Review of the Rise and Progress of English Liberty, And concluded with some Remarks upon our present Alarming Situation. *Philadelphia: William Bradford.* 1766.   2206

DELAWARE. Anno Regni Sexto | Georgii III. Regis. | At a General Assembly begun at | New-castle, in the Government of the Coun- | ties of New-castle, Kent and Sussex, upon | Dela- ware, the Twentieth Day of October, | in the Sixth Year of the Reign of our Sove- | reign Lord George the Third, King of | Great-Britain, &c. Annoque Domini 1766, | The following Acts were passed by the Ho- | nourable John Penn, Esq; Governor; | [*Wilmington: James Adams.* 1766.] Folio, pp. 107–123. L. 2207

A | DEMONSTRATION | of the | Uninterrupted Succession | and | Holy Consecration | of the first | English Bishops. | Being | An Extract from Mr. Ward's Second | Canto of his England's Reformation. | With an Introduction, Notes, and an Appendix, con- | taining the solemn Funeral Song of the Native Irish. | Very useful for all Christians. | [*Philadelphia:*] *Printed* [*by Andrew Steuart*] *in the Year* M,DCC,LXVI. | Sm. 8vo. pp. 47.   L. C. P. 2208

[DICKINSON. (John)] An | Address | to | The Committee of Correspondence | in | Barbadoes. | Occasioned by a late letter from them | to | Their Agent in London. | By a North American. . . . | . . . . | *Philadelphia:* | *Printed and Sold by William Bradford, at* | *his Book-Store in Market-Street, adjoining the* | *London Coffee- House.* M,DCC,LXVI. | 8vo. Title, 1 leaf; pp. vi, 18.   2209

DILWORTH. (T.) A New Guide to the English Tongue. By Thomas Dilworth. *Philadelphia: D. Hall.* 1766.   2210

The edition, two thousand copies, was more than half printed at the dissolution of the partnership between Franklin and Hall.

EVANS. (N.) The Love of the World incompatible with the Love of God: A Discourse. Preached upon I John II. 15,

16, 17. By the Rev. Nathaniel Evans. *Philadelphia: Henry Miller.* 1766. 8vo. pp. 22. 2211

[FENELON. (F. Salignac de la Mothe)] The Uncertainty of a | Death-Bed | Repentance, | Illustrated under the Character of Penitens, | [*Germantown: Christopher Sower.* 1766.] Sm. 8vo. pp. 16. F. 2212

FOUR | DISSERTATIONS, | on the | Reciprocal Advantages | of a | Perpetual Union | between | Great-Britain | and her | American Colonies. | Written | For Mr. Sargent's Prize-Medal. | To which (by Desire) is prefixed, | An Eulogium, | Spoken on the Delivery of the Medal | at the Public Commencement in the College of | Philadelphia, May 20th, 1766. | *Philadelphia: | Printed by William and Thomas Bradford, at the | London Coffee-House.* M,DCC,LXVI. | Sm. 8vo. H. S. P. 2213

Collation: Title, 1 leaf; List of subscribers, pp. iii.–x.; Preface, pp. i.–viii.; Eulogium by William Smith, D.D., pp. 1–12; Dissertation, by John Morgan, M.D.; Title and Dedication, pp. (2), text, pp. 1–45; Essay, by Stephen Watts, pp. 47–77; Dissertation III., by Joseph Reed, pp. 79–104; Dissertation IV., by Francis Hopkinson, pp. 105–112.

FOX. (T.) The Wilmington | Almanack, | or | Ephemeries, | for | The Year of our Lord, 1767: | (On an exceeding good Old Plan.) | Containing | The Motions of the Sun and Moon; the true Places | and Aspects of the Planets; the rising and setting | of the Sun; and the rising setting and southing of the Moon.—Also, | The Lunations, Conjunctions, Eclipses, Judgment of | the Weather, rising and setting of the Planets, | | Length of Days and Nights, Fairs, Courts, Roads, | Quakers General Meetings, &c. Together with | useful Tables, chronological Observations, and en- | tertaining Remarks, in Prose and Verse. Likewise, | The Continuation of Mr. Hervey's Thoughts on the | Starry Heavens.—An Hymn to God.—A Piece on | Liberty;—on Justice;—on Health; on Sincerity; | —Virtuous Love and Lust; A Vision.—A Revd. | D——r's Lamentation for the Loss of his Hearing. | Valuable Receipts, &c. &c. &c. | . Fitted to the Latitude of Forty Degrees, and a Meridian of | near five Hours West from London; but may, without | sensible

Error, serve all the Northern Colonies. | By Thomas Fox, Philom. | *Wilmington, Printed and Sold by James Adams.* [1766.] | Sm. 8 pp. (40).   **2214**

FRANKLIN. (B.)   Die | Verhörung | Doctor Benjamin Franklins | von der | Hohen Versammlung | des | Hauses der Gemeinen | von Großbrittanien, | die Stämpel-Act, zc. betreffend. | Aus dem Englischen übersetzt. | *Philadelphia, Gedruckt und zu finden bey H. Miller,* | *in der Zweyten-Strasse.* 1766. | 8vo. pp. 43.   H. S. P.   **2215**

[FRANKLIN.] The Examination of Doctor | Benjamin Franklin, before an | August Assembly, relating to the Repeal of | the Stamp-Act, &c. | [*Philadelphia: Hall and Sellers.* 1766.] 8vo. pp. 16.   H. S. P.   **2216**

FRIENDS, Brethren, and Countrymen, | If the memory of your ancestors, your own honour, and that of your Posterity, pos- | sess . . . a just affection in your bosoms, . . . | . . . | . . . Consider the irrevocable disgrace. . . . | . . . of Pennsylvania, . . . should | her . . . Sons call into her Assembly, the author of Americanus, the | . . . Advocate for American Slavery . . . . | [*Philadelphia:* 1766.] 4to. 1 leaf.   L. C. P.   **2217**

An anti-Franklin election address, issued Sept. 30, 1766.

FROM the | Merchants and Traders | Of Philadelphia, in the Province of Pennsylvania; | to the | Merchants and Manufacturers | Of Great Britain. | [*Philadelphia:* 1766?] Folio, pp. (3).   **2218**

[GARRIGUES. (Samuel)] Philadelphia, May 19, 1766. | To the Printers of the Pennsylvania Gazette. | [*Philadelphia: Hall and Sellers.* 1766.] 4to. 1 leaf.   H. S. P.   **2219**

Samuel Garrigues' reply to John Macpherson's vindication.

[GODDARD. (William)]. Philadelphia, December 23, 1766. | Proposals, | For Printing by Subscription, | In Four Pages, large Folio, on a beautiful Letter, and good Paper, | The Pennsylvania Chronicle, | and | Universal Advertiser. | [*Philadelphia : William Goddard.* 1766.] Folio, pp. (2).   N. Y. H. S.   **2220**

The " Proposals" occupy one page, the other contains specimens of Goddard's various types.

A GRAND | Chorus, | To be sung on the Fourth of June, being His | Majesty's Birth Day ; at an Enter- | tainment on the Banks of Schuylkill, by | a large Company of the Inhabitants of the | City of Philadelphia | [*Philadelphia :* 1766.] Folio, 1 leaf.

HAYES. (A.)　A | Legacy, | or | Widow's Mite ; | Left by | Alice Hayes, | To | Her Children and others. | Being a Brief | Relation of her Life ; | With an | Account | of some | Of her Dying Sayings. | The Second Edition. | . . . | . . . . | *London*, *printed : And* | *Philadelphia, Re-printed by Andrew Steuart, at* | *the Bible-in-Heart, in Second-street,* MDCCLXVI. | Sm. 8vo. pp. 48.

HAYES. (A.)　A | Legacy, | or | Widow's Mite ; | Left by | Alice Hayes, | To | Her Children and others. | Being a Brief | Relation of her Life ; | With an | Account | of some | Of her Dying Sayings. | The Third Edition. | . . . | . . . . | *London, printed : And* | *Philadelphia, Re-printed by Andrew Steuart, at* | *the Bible-in-Heart, in Second-street,* MDCCLXVI. | Sm. 8vo. pp. 44. +.

𝕯𝕰𝕾 | 𝕳𝕰𝕽𝖀𝕸𝕿𝕽𝕬𝕲𝕰𝕽𝕾 des Staatsboten | Neujahrs-Verse, | bey seinen resp. | Geehrten Kundleuten | abgelegt | den 6ten Jenner, 1766. | [*Philadelphia : Henrich Miller.* 1766.] Sm. Folio, 1 leaf.　2224

𝕯𝕰𝕽 | 𝕳𝕺𝕮𝕳-𝕯𝕰𝖀𝕿𝕾𝕮𝕳𝕰 | Americanische | Calender, | Auf das Jahr | . . . | . . . | 1767. | . . . | . . . | . . . | . . . | . . . . | . . . | . . . | . . . | . . . | . . . | . . . | . . . . Zum neun und zwanzigsten mal heraus gegeben. | [*Germantown : Gedruckt und zu finden bey Christoph Saur.* | . . . | . . . . [1766.] 4to. pp. (48).　' H. S. P.　2225

[HOPKINSON. (Francis)]　A Psalm of | Thanksgiving, | Adapted to the Solemnity of | Easter : | To be performed on Sunday, the 30th of March, | 1766, at Christ-Church, Philadelphia. | [*Philadelphia :* 1766.] Folio, 1 leaf.　　L. C. P.　2226

[HOPKINSON. (Thomas)]　An | Exercise, | containing | a | Dialogue and two Odes | Performed at the public Commencement in the College of | Philadelphia, May 20th, 1766. | *Philadel-*

phia : | *Printed by* **W. Dunlap,** *in Market-Street,* M,DCC,LXVI. | Sm.
4to. pp. 8.   H. S. P.   2227

> The Pa. Journal, June 5, 1766, says it was written chiefly by Thos. Hopkinson.

[HUME. (Sophia)]   Extracts | from | Divers antient Testi-
monies of | Friends and others, corresponding with | the Doctrines
of Christianity, recommended to | the Consideration, First, Of
Ministers. | Secondly, Elders.   Thirdly, To every | Member of the
Church, who makes a plain | outward Appearance ; as a Touch-
stone from the Spirit of Christ, through his Servants, to | try our
Practice by ; First, In the Education | of our Children, and In-
struction of our Fami- | lies in Religion.   Secondly, In getting and
Spend- | ing Riches ; in Buildings, and furnishing them | and our
Tables.   Thirdly, In Marriages, and | costly Entertainments at the
same.   Fourthly, | In paying Tithes. | Fifthly, In Trades or Occu-
| pations, and Merchandize. | [*Wilmington : James Adams.* 1766?]
16mo. pp. 85, (1).   H. S. P.   2228

JOYFUL News | to | America, | a | Poem. | Expressive of Our
more than ordinary | Joy, on the Repeal of the | Stamp-Act. |
Together-with the | Praise of Liberty, | And | Two Acrosticks.
| [*Philadelphia :*] *Printed* [*by Andrew Steuart*] *in the Year* 1766. |
Sm. 8vo. pp. 8.   F.   2229

𝕯𝕰𝕽 𝕶𝕷𝕰𝕴𝕹𝕰 𝕮𝕬𝕿𝕰𝕮𝕳𝕵𝕾𝕸𝖀𝕾 des seligen D. Martin Luthers.
*Philadelphia.   Gedruckt und zu haben bey Anton Armbruester in der
Raesz-strasse, ohnweit dem grünen Baum.* 1766.   2230

> Title from Seidensticker's Bibliography.

LAW. (W.)   An | Extract | from a | Treatise | By William
Law, M.A. | Called, | The Spirit of Prayer ; | or, | the Soul rising
out of the Vanity of | Time, into the Riches of Eternity. | With |
Some Thoughts | on the Nature of War, | and its Repugnancy |
to the Christian life, &c. &c. | *Philadelphia : Printed by Henry Mil-
ler,* | *in Second-Street.* MDCCLXVI. | Sm. 8vo. pp. 48.   2231

L[ETCHWORTH]. (T[homas])   A | Morning and Evening's |
Meditation, | or, a | Descant | on the | Times. | A | Poem. | By T.

L. | . . . | . . . | . . . | . . . | . . . | . . . | . . . | . . . . | *London,*
Printed. | *Philadelphia, Re-printed and Sold by B.* | *Franklin, and D.*
Hall. 1766. | 8vo. pp. 58.   F.   2232

> The edition consisted of five hundred copies.

MACPHERSON (J.) Mount-Pleasant, May 5, 1766. | Mr.
David Hall. | That Duty incumbent on every honest Man, to vin-
dicate his Character. . . . | [*Philadelphia: Hall and Sellers.* 1766.]
Folio, 1 leaf.   L. C. P.   2233

> John Macpherson's defence against a charge of retaining a stray horse.

METHOD of Hearing Sermons to Advantage. *Philadelphia:*
1766.   2234

> Title from Haven's List.

MUHLENBERG. (H[enrich]) Ein Zeugniß von der Güte und
Ernst (sic) Gottes gegen sein Bundesvolk in alten und neuen Zeiten
und des Volkes Undankbarkeit, gelegentlich des Dankfestes wegen Auf-
hebung der Stempel-Acte 1. August 1766. Von Hochw. H. Mühlenberg.
Philadelphia: Henrich Miller. 1766.   2235

NEU-EINGERICHTETER Americanischer Calender, auf das Jahr
1767. *Philadelphia: Anton Armbrüster.* 1766.   2236

DER NEUESTE, Verbessert- und Zuverläßige | Americanische |
Calender | Auf das 1767ste Jahr Christi, | Welches ein gemein Jahr
von 365 Tagen ist. | . . . | . . . | . . . | . . . | . . . | . . . | . . . .
| Wie auch | Eine kurze Beschreibung aller Europäischen Länder und
Staaten, 2c. 2c. | . . . | . . . . | Zum Fünftenmal herausgegeben. |
Zweyte Auflage. | *Philadelphia, Gedruckt und zu finden bey Henrich*
Miller, in der Zweyten-strasse. | . . . | . . . | . . . . [1766.] | 4to.
pp. (40).   H. S. P.   2237

> The first page contains a rude copy of Heap's View of Philadelphia, and also a half
> title "Philadelphischer Calender," &c. The first edition has not been met with. A
> third edition was announced in Miller's paper of Jan. 26, 1767.

A | NEW Song, | On the Repeal of the Stamp-Act, Tune, | A

late worthy Qld Lyon. | [*Philadelphia:* 1766.]   Narrow Folio, 1 leaf.

L. C. P.   2238

THE | NEW-YEAR | VERSES, | Of the Printers Lads, who carry about the | Pennsylvania Gazette to the Customers. | January 1, 1766. | [*Philadelphia: B. Franklin and D. Hall.* 1766.] Folio, 1 leaf.

2239

THE NEW-YEAR Verses of the Carriers of the Pennsylvania Journal.   *Philadelphia: William Bradford.* 1766.

2240

NOW in the Press, and will be speedily published, | The Life and Adventures | of a certain | Quaker Presbyterian Indian | Colonel. | To which will be added, | The Qualifications necessary to entitle a Man to the dignified Name | of a modern moderate Quaker. | By Tim Trimmer. | [*Philadelphia:* 1766.]   Folio, 1 leaf.

An election squib aimed at John Dickinson.

𝕻𝖆𝖗𝖆𝖉𝖏𝖘𝖏𝖘𝖈𝖍𝖊𝖘 | Wunder=Spiel, | Welches sich | In diesen letzten Zeiten und Tagen in denen Abend= | ländischen Welt=Theilen, als ein Vorspiel | der neuen Welt hervorgethan. | Bestehend in einer neuen Sammlung andächticher und zum Lob | des grosen Gottes eingerich= teter geistlicher, und ehedessen | zum Theil publicirter Lieder. | [Cut.] | *Ephratæ: Typis & Consensu Societatis A : D :* MDCCLXVI. | 4to. pp. 9, (1), 472, (6).

H. S. P.   2242

For the first edition, see Addenda.

THE PENNSYLVANIA Gazette.

H. S. P.   2243

Numbers 1932 (Jan. 2, 1766) to 1983 (Dec. 25, 1766), four pages each, with an extra half sheet of two pages to No. 1948, and "Supplements," of 1 leaf to No. 1951, of two pages to Numbers 1954 and 1975, and of four pages to 1968 and 1977.   Title as in No. 1692, *supra.*   No imprint on Numbers 1932 to 1936.   The imprint of No. 1937 is: *Philadelphia: Printed by David Hall, at the New Printing-Office, | near the Market.* | This was continued till No. 1950, when it was changed to the form given in No. 2308, *infra.*

THE PENNSYLVANIA Journal.

H. S. P.   2244

Numbers 1204 to 1255, four pages each, with extra half sheets of two pages each to Numbers 1237, 1246, and 1248, and "Supplements" of two pages to Numbers 1204,

1207, 1209, 1212, 1218, 1221, 1225, 1239, 1241, and 1242. Title and imprint as in No. 1693, *supra*, until the latter was changed, in No. 1239, to the form given under No. 2317, *infra*.

THE PENNSYLVANIA Pocket Almanac for 1767. *Philadelphia: W. and T. Bradford.* 1766.   2245

[Cut.] . . . 𝔓𝔥𝔦𝔩𝔞𝔡𝔢𝔩𝔭𝔥𝔦𝔞 den 19ten May 1766. | [*Philadelphia: Anthony Armbruster.* 1766.] Folio, 1 leaf. H. S. P.   2246

An account of the arrival of the news of the repeal of the Stamp Act, in German, headed by an allegorical cut, under which are twenty-six lines of verse disposed in two columns.

POLITICAL | Debates. | . . . | . . . | . . . | . . . . | *A Paris,* | *Chez J. W. Imprimeur, Rue du Colombier* | *Fauxbourg St. Germain,* à *l' Hotel de Saxe.* | MDCCLXVI. | " [*Prix 30 Sous.*]" | *Avec Approbation & Privilege.* | 8vo. Half title, 1 leaf; Title, 1 leaf; pp. 18.

Printed either in Philadelphia or New York, I think by W. Dunlap.

PROCLAMATION. [*Royal Arms.*] | By the Honourable | John Penn, Esquire, | Lieutenant-Governor, and Commander in Chief of the Province of Penn- | sylvania, and Counties of New-Castle, Kent and Sussex, on Delaware, | A Proclamation. | *Philadelphia: Printed by D. Hall, and W. Sellers, at the New Printing- | Office, near the Market.* [1766.] | Folio, 1 leaf.   H. S. P.   2248

Against settlers upon Indian Lands, dated Sept. 23, 1766.

RAY. (N.) The Importance of the Colonies of North America, and the Interest of Great Britain with regard to them considered; together with Remarks on the Stamp Duty. By Nicholas Ray. *Philadelphia: ? David Hall.* 1766.   2249

A | RECEIPT | To make a | Speech. | By J[oseph] G[alloway], Esquire. | [*Philadelphia: William Bradford.* 1766.] 4to. 1 leaf.

DIE | REGELN | der | Teutschen Gesellschaft | in | Philadelphia. | *Germantown* | *Gedruckt bey Christoph Saur,* 1766. | 8vo. pp. 8.   2251

ROBERTS. (D.) Some | Memoirs | Of the Life of | John Roberts. | Written by his Son | Daniel Roberts. | The Fifth Edition. |

. . . | . . . | . . . . | *London and Bristol: Printed.* | *Philadelphia:* *Reprinted* | *by Henry Miller.* | *And Sold by James Der Kinderen,* | *in* *Strawberry-Alley.* 1766. | Sm. 8vo. pp. 67. H. S. P. 2252

ROMAINE. (W.) Twelve Sermons upon the Law & the Gospel. By William Romaine. *Philadelphia: Andrew Steuart.* 1766. 2253

RUSSEL (R.) Seven | Sermons; | viz. | I. Of the Unpardon- able | Sin against the Holy- | Ghost; or, The Sin | unto Death. | II. The Saint's Duty and | Exercise: In two Parts. | Being an Ex- hortation | to, and Directions for | Prayer. | III. The Accepted Time | and Day of Salvation. | IV. The End of Time, | and Be- ginning of E- | ternity. | V. Joshua's Resolution | to serve the Lord. | VI. The Way to Heaven | made Plain. | VII. The Future State of | Man; or, A Treatise of | the Resurrection. | A Funeral Sermon. | By Robert Russel, | At Wardhurst in Sussex. | The Fifty-Second Edition. | *Philadelphia:* | *Printed and Sold by W. Dun- lap, at the* | *Newest-Printing-Office, the South Side of the* | *Jersey Market,* MDCCLXVI. | 12mo. pp. 172. H. S. P. 2254

SAUNDERS. (R.) A Pocket | Almanack | For the Year 1767. | Fitted to the Use of Penn- | sylvania, and the neighbour- | ing Provinces. | With several useful Additions. | By R. Saunders, Phil. | *Philadelphia:* | *Printed and Sold by D. Hall, and* | *W. Sellers.* [1766.] | 24mo. pp. (24). H. S. P. 2255

SAUNDERS. Poor Richard improved: | Being an | Alma- nack | . . . | . . . | . . | . . | . . | . . | . . | . . | . . . | . . . | For the | Year of our Lord 1767: | Being the Third after Leap-Year. | . . . | . . . | . . | . . | . . . | . . . | . . . | . . . | . . . . | By Richard Saunders, Philom. | *Philadelphia:* | *Printed and Sold by D. Hall, and W. Sellers.* [1766.] | Sm. 8vo. pp. (36). 2256

[SCOUGAL. (Henry)] The | Life of God | in the | Soul of Man: | or, the | Nature and Excellency | of the | Christian Re- ligion. | Also | An Account of the Beginnings and Advan- | ces of a Spiritual Life, | With | A Recommendatory Preface by | Gilbert Burnet, Late Lord Bi- | shop of Sarum. | *Philadelphia:* |

Printed and Sold by W. Dunlap, | *in Market-Street,* M.DCC.LXVI. |
Sm. 12mo. pp. xxiv, 196.   2257

SIX Arguments | Against Chusing | Joseph Galloway | An As-
semblyman at the ensuing Election; | Addressed to himself by one
heretofore his Friend. | [*Philadelphia: W. and T. Bradford.* 1766?]
Folio, 1 leaf.   L. C. P. 2258

STEUART. (A.) The Gentleman and Citizen's Pocket Almanac for 1767. By Andrew Steuart. *Philadelphia: Andrew Steuart.*
1766.   2259

𝔇𝔍𝔈 𝔗𝔄𝔊𝔏𝔍𝔆𝔈𝔑 Loofungen der Brüder-Gemeine für das Jahr
1766. *Philadelphia: Henrich Miller.* 1766.   2260

Henry Miller, in January, printed 400 copies of an index, and in February the
same number of copies of changes to the " Watch Words" for 1766.

TOBLER. (J.) The Pennsylvania Town and Countryman's Almanac for 1767. *Wilmington: James Adams.* 1766.   2261

A TRUE State of the Establishment of the Church of England
in the Province, by the Royal Charter . . . to the . . . Pro-
prietor of Pennsylvania, &c. By a Layman and member of the
Church of England. *Philadelphia:* 1766.   2262

TUCKER. (J.) Interest of Great Britain considered, with
regard to her Colonies. By Josiah Tucker, Dean of Gloucester.
Philadelphia: 1766?   2263

Title from Haven's List. No doubt intended for Tucker's True Interest of Great
Britain, first printed at Gloucester in 1774, and reprinted in Philadelphia in 1776.

𝔙𝔈𝔕𝔅𝔈𝔖𝔖𝔈𝔑𝔗𝔈 𝔄-𝔅-𝔆- oder Namenbücher, nach der richtigen
Buchstabier-Art. *Philadelphia: Henrich Miller.* 1766.   2264

VOTES and Proceedings of the House of Representatives.
Philadelphia: D. Hall and W. Sellers. 1766.   2265

𝔚𝔄𝔥𝔯𝔈 und wahrscheinliche Begebenheiten auf ungestempelten
Papier, weil kein gestempeltes zu haben ist. [n. p. dated March 5,
1766.]   2266

Title from Seidensticker's Bibliography.

WEATHERWISE. (A.) Father Abraham's Almanac for 1767.
Philadelphia : William Dunlap.   1766.   2267

1767.

AN ACCOUNT of the Births and Bu- | rials in the United
Churches of Christ-Church | and St. Peter's, in Philadelphia,
from December | 25, 1766, to December 25, 1767. By Caleb |
Cash, Clerk, and James Weyley, | Sexton. | [*Philadelphia :* 1767.]
Folio, 1 leaf.   L. C. P.   2268

AN ACCOUNT of the Burials and Baptized | in the Baptist
Church, in Philadelphia, from December 25, 1766, | to December
25, 1767.   By Samuel Burkloe, Sexton. | [*Philadelphia :* 1767.]
Folio, 1 leaf.   L. C. P.   2269

AN ACCOUNT of the Burials in the Second | Presbyterian
Church, in Philadelphia, from December 25, 1766, | to December
25, 1767. By Adam Hope, Sexton. | [*Philadelphia :* 1767.] Folio,
1 leaf.   L. C. P.   2270

AGUECHEEK. (A.) The Universal American Almanac for
1768. By Andrew Aguecheek.   *Philadelphia : Andrew Steuart.*
1767.   2271

THE AMERICAN Calendar for 1768.   *Philadelphia : W. and
T. Bradford.*   1767.   2272

THE AMERICAN Pocket Almanac for 1768.   *Philadelphia :
W. and T. Bradford.*   1767.   2273

ANNO Regni | Georgii III. Regis, | Magnæ Britanniæ,
Franciæ & Hiberniæ, | Septimo. | At a General Assembly of
the Province of Penn- | sylvania, begun and holden at Phila-
delphia, | the Fourteenth Day of October, Anno Domini 1766,
in | the Sixth Year of the Reign of our Sovereign Lord | George
III. by the Grace of God, of Great- | Britain, France and Ireland,
King, Defender of the | Faith, &c. | And from thence continued by

Adjournments to the | Twenty-first Day of February, 1767. | [*Penn Arms.*] | *Philadelphia:* | *Printed and Sold by D. Hall, and W. Sellers, at the* | *New Printing-Office, near the Market.* MDCCLXVII. | Folio, Title, 1 leaf; pp. 501–538.+And from thence continued . . . to the | Twentieth Day of May, 1767. | [*Royal Arms.*] | *Philadelphia:* | *Printed and sold by William Goddard, at the New* | *Printing-Office, in Market-Street.* | MDCCLXVII. | Title, 1 leaf; pp. 541–583, (1).+And from thence continued . . . to the | Twenty-sixth Day of September, 1767. | Title, 1 leaf; pp. 587–593.   2274

𝔄𝔘𝔖𝔅𝔘𝔑𝔇, | Das ift: | Etliche schöne | Chriftliche | Lieder, | Wie fie in dem Gefäng= | nüß zu Baffau in dem Schloß | von den Schweißer=Brüdern, und | von anderen rechtglaubigen Chriften | hin und her gedichtet worden. | Allen und jeden Chriften wel= | cher Religion fie feßen, unpar= | theßifch faft nußlich. | Nebft einem Anhang von fünff Lie= | dern. | Zum dritten mal aufgelegt in Pennfylvanien. | *German-town:* | *Gedruckt, und zu finden bey Christoph Saur,* 1767. | 16mo. pp. (10), 812, (6), 96.   H. S. P. 2275

AUTHENTIC Account of the Proceedings of the Congress held at New York in 1765, on the Subject of the American Stamp Act. *Philadelphia:* 1767. 8vo. pp. 37.   2276

Title from Haven's List.

BENEZET. (A.) A | Caution | and | Warning | to | Great-Britain, | and | Her Colonies, | in | A Short Representation | of the | Calamitous State | of the | Enslaved Negroes | in the British Dominions. | Collected from various Authors, and submitted to the | Serious Consideration of all, more | especially of Those in Power. | To which is added, | An Extract of a Sermon, preached by the Bishop of | Gloucester, before the Society for the Propagation | of the Gospel. | By Anthony Benezet. | *Phila-delphia: Printed by D. Hall, and W. Sel-* | *lers, at the New Printing-Office, in Market-street.* | MDCCLXVII. | 16mo. Half title, 1 leaf; Title, 1 leaf; pp. 52.   H. S. P. 2277

𝔅𝔈𝔑𝔍𝔈ℭ𝔖𝔗 von den Brüdern im Schweizerland in dem Züricher

Gebiet wegen der Trübfalen, welche über fie ergangen find. *German-town: Christoph Saur*. 1767. 2278

Title from Seidensticker's Bibliography. This was not, I think, a separate publication, but only a part of the matter appended to the "Ausbund," No. 2275, *supra*.

A | BILL | in the | Chancery of New-Jersey, | At the Suit of | John Hunt, | against | William Earl of Stirling, | And Others, | Proprietors of the Eastern Division of the Province | of New-Jersey. | [*Royal Arms.*] | *Philadelphia:* | *Printed by William Goddard, at the New Printing-Office,* | *in Market-Street.* | M.DCC.LXVII. | Folio, pp. 21. H. S. P. 2279

BLAIR. (J.) The | New Creature | Delineated. | In a | Sermon, | Delivered in Philadelphia, | February 26, 1767, | By John Blair, A.M. Minister of the | Gospel at Fag's Manor. | Published at the Request of a Number of the | Hearers. | ... | ... | .... | *Philadelphia:* | *Printed by William and Thomas Bradford, at* | *the London Coffee-House.* | M,DCC,LXVII. | 8vo. pp. 32. C. 2280

BOSTON. (T.) Sermons and Discourses on Several important Subjects in Divinity. By the late Reverend and Learned Mr. Thomas Boston, Minister of the Gospel at Ettrick. *Philadelphia: W. and T. Bradford*. 1767. 2281

[BROOKS. (Seth)] A | Plowman's Complaint | against a | Clergyman: | Being a | Letter | to the | Baptist Association | at | Philadelphia. | Written by an alient Baptist Dissenter. | ... | ... | .... | *Philadelphia:* | *Printed [by W. and T. Bradford] for the Author.* | M.DCC.LXVII. | 8vo. pp. vii, 27. L. C. P. 2282

BY Authority. | By the American Company, | at the New Theatre in Southwark; on Tuesday | The Seventh of April, will be presented, by Particular Desire, | A Tragedy called | Romeo and Juliet, | Romeo by Mr. Hallam, | Mercutio by Mr. Douglass, | Capulet by Mr. Morris, | Fryar Lawrance by Mr. Allyn, | Mountague by Mr. Tomlinson. | [42 lines.] | [*Philadelphia:* 1767.] Folio, 1 leaf. 2283

CATECHISM. The Assembly's Shorter Catechism explained,

by Way of Question and Answer. In two parts. By some Ministers of the Gospel. *Philadelphia: W. and T. Bradford.* 1767.

𝕯𝕰𝕽 𝕶𝕷𝕰𝕵𝕹𝕰 𝕮𝕬𝕿𝕰𝕮𝕳𝕵𝕾𝕸𝕌𝕾 Lutheri, mit der Ordnung
des Heils, und dem Würtembergischen Kurzen Kinder-Examen, oder
Confirmations-Büchlein, ꝛc., wie auch der Ungeänderten Augspurgischen
Confeßion, und einer Zugabe der 7 Buß-Psalmen. *Philadelphia:
Henrich Miller*, 1767. 2285

CHANDLER. (T. B.) An Appeal to the Public, in behalf of the
Church of England in America. By Thomas Bradbury Chandler,
D.D. *Philadelphia: William Goddard.* 1767. 2286

THE | CHARACTER | of | Eusebius : | Containing | Remarks
| on a late | Pamphlet, | intitled, | True Pleasure, Chearfulness,
and | Happiness, the immediate Conse- | quence of Religion, fully
and | concisely proved. | In a Letter from Atticus to his Friend. |
. . . | . . . | . . . | . . . | . . . . | *Philadelphia:* | *Printed and Sold
by William & Thomas* | *Bradford, at the London Coffee-House.* |
M.DCC.LXVII. | 8vo. pp. 19. H. S. P. 2287

A | COLLECTION | of some | Writings | Of the most noted of
the | People called Quakers, in their Times. | Collected together, in
order that such who profess that Way | now may compare their
Sentiments with those of their | Forefathers, as they term them, or
such as were deem- | ed worthy Ancients, whose writings have
been approv- | ed of by the Society in general. | *Philadelphia,* |
Printed [by W. and T. Bradford] for the Compiler, 1767. | 8vo. pp.
34. H. S. P. 2288

DAILY Conversation with God, | Exemplified in the | Holy Life
| of | Armelle Nicholas, | A poor ignorant Country Maid in |
France, commonly known by the Name of | The Good Armelle, |
Deceas'd in Bretaigne in the Year 1671. | Done out of French. |
. . . | . . . | . . . | . . . | . . . | . . . | . . . | . . . | . . . | . . . |
. . . . | *London: Printed.* | *Philadelphia:* | *Reprinted by Henry
Miller, in Second-Street.* | MDCCLXVII. | 12mo. pp. 16. 2289

[DE FOE. (Daniel)] The | Dreadful Visitation: | In a | Short
Account | of the | Progress and Effects | of the | Plague, | The last

Time it spread in the City | of London, in the Year 1665 ; | Extracted | From the Memoirs of a Person who | resided there during the whole Time of | that Infection : | With | Some Thoughts on the Advantage which would | result to Christianity, if a Spirit of Impartiality | and true Charity was suffered to preside amongst | the several religious denominations, &c. | . . . | . . . | . . . . | *Philadelphia :* | *Printed by Henry. Miller, in Second-Street,* | MDCCLXVII. | 16mo. pp. 16.   H. S. P.   2290

DELAWARE.   Anno Regni Septimo | Georgii III. Regis. | At a General Assembly begun at | New-castle, in the Government of the Coun- | ties of New-castle, Kent and Sussex, upon | Delaware, the Twentieth Day of October, | in the Seventh Year of the Reign of our So- | vereign Lord George the Third, King of | Great-Britain, &c. Annoque Domini 1767, | The following Acts were passed by the Ho- | nourable John Penn, Esq; Governor; | [*Wilmington : James Adams.* 1767.] Folio, pp. 125–131.   2291

THE | EMPTINESS and Vanity | of | A Life | Spent in the Pursuit of Worldly Profit, | Ease or Pleasure, | compared with | A Life | Wholly employed in endeavouring to glo- | rify God, and do good to Mankind : | Illustrated in | An Extract | of the | Life and Death | Of the pious Lady | Elizabeth Hastings. | With | Some Remarks on the Universality | of the Love of God to Mankind. | *Philadelphia :* | *Printed by Henry Miller, in Second-Street,* | MDCCLXVII. | 16mo. pp. 16.   H. S. P.   2292

ERSKINE. (E.)   Sermons and Discourses upon the Most Important and Interesting Subjects.   By the late Reverend Mr. Ebenezer Erskine, Minister of the Gospel at Sterling.   In Four Volumes.   *Philadelphia : W. and T. Bradford.* 1767.   2293

AN | EXERCISE, | containing | a | Dialogue and two Odes, | Performed at the Public Commencement in the College | of Philadelphia, November 17, 1767. | [*Royal Arms.*] | *Philadelphia :* | *Printed by William Goddard, in Market-Street.* [1767.] | Sm. 4to. pp. 8.   H. S. P.   2294

The Dialogue was written by Thomas Coombe.   Pa. Chronicle, Nov. 23, 1767.

EXTRACT | From an Address | in the | Virginia Gazette, | of March 19, 1767. | [*Philadelphia: Henry Miller.* 1767.] Sm. 8vo. pp. 4.   H. S. P.   2295

EXTRACT of a Letter, | Wrote by a pious Person, describing the Progress of the | Soul in her Spiritual Warfare, as typically pointed | out in the Travels of the Children of Israel | from Egypt to Canaan, particularly treating of | the barren and fruitful Wilderness State, &c. | [*Philadelphia:* 1767?] Sm. 8vo. pp. 8.   2296

THE FAMILY | Prayer Book | containing | Morning and Evening | Prayers, | for Families and private Persons, | To which are annexed Directions for a de- | vout and decent behaviour in the publick Wor- | ship of God; more particularly in the Use | of Common Prayer appointed by the | Church of England: | Together with the Church Catechism. | Collected and published chiefly for the Use of the | Episcopal Congregations of | Lancaster, Pequea, and Caerracoon (?). | . . . . | *Ephrata: Printed for William Barton.* MDCCLXVII. | 2297

I am indebted to the Rev. Joseph Henry Dubbs, D.D., of Lancaster, for the above title. He supposes the copy of the Prayer-Book from which it was taken now to be in the Lenox Library, in New York City.

FOX. (T.) The Wilmington Almanac for 1768. By Thomas Fox. *Wilmington: James Adams.* 1767.   2298

[FOTHERGILL. (Samuel)] Two | Discourses | and | A Prayer, | publickly delivered | On Sunday the 17th and Tuesday | the 19th Days of May, 1767. | At the Quakers Yearly Meeting, | At the Fryers, in Bristol. | The whole taken down in Characters, | By a Member of the Church of England. | To which is added, a Preface. | *Bristol Printed; And* | *Philadelphia Re-printed, and sold by Andrew* | *Steuart, at the Bible-in-Heart, in Second-street.* [1767?] | Sm. 8vo. pp. 30.   H. S. P.   2299

THE GENUINE Letter from the Baptist Association met in Philadelphia. *Philadelphia: Henry Miller.* 1767.   2300

GOODLET. (J.) A | Vindication | of the | Associate Synod,

| upon the | Head of their Principles | about the | Present Civil Government: | Against | The gross Misrepresentations and Reproaches by which | they are abused in the Supplement to a Performance, | intituled, Act, Declaration and Testimony, &c. by | the Reformed Presbytery. | In which | It is proven, contrary to the shameless Pretences of the pre- | tended Reformed Presbytery, That an owning of the | present Civil Government is agreeable to the Principles | and Practice of our Reformers; and of our Martyrs, in | the bloody Reigns of Charles II. and James II. | By Mr. John Goodlet, Minister of the | Gospel in the Associate Congregation at Sanquhar. | *Edinburgh, Printed:* | *Philadelphia, Reprinted by D. Hall, and* | *W. Sellers, at the New Printing-Office, near* | *the Market,* MDCCLXVII. | 8vo. pp. 115, (3).

THE GOSPEL Explained According to the iii Chapter of St. John, and 3d Verse, &c. Delivered in five Propositions. *Philadelphia : Anthony Armbruster.* 1767. 2302

HARTLEY. (T.) Auszug aus einer Rede | Thomas Hartleys, | eines Lehrers der Englischen Kirche, | über | die Mißbegriffe, | die Religion, ꝛc. | betreffend. | Aus dem Englischen übersetzt. | *Philadelphia, Gedruckt bey Henrich Miller,* | *in der Zweyten-strasse.* 1767. | 8vo. pp. 8. H. S. P. 2303

THE HEIDELBERG Catechism; Translated from the German into English, by the New York Synod. *Philadelphia: Anthony Armbruster.* 1767. 2304

DER | HOCH = DEUTSCHE | Americanische | Calender, | Auf das Jahr | . . . | . . . | 1768. | (Welches ein Schalt = Jahr von 366 Tagen ist.) | . . . | . . . | . . . | . . . | . . . | . . . | . . . | . . . | . . . | . . . . | Zum dreyßigsten mal heraus gegeben. | *Germantown: Gedruckt und zu finden bey Christoph Saur.* | . . . | . . . . [1767.] | 4to. pp. (48). H. S. P. 2305

LYON. (J.) Urania: Or, A choice collection of Psalm Tunes, Anthems and Hymns, from the most approved Authors: With some entirely new. In two, three and four parts. By James Lyon, A.M. *Philadelphia : 1767.* 2306

" A new and neat Edition" was advertised in the Pa. Journal, Nov. 19, 1767. See No. 1743, *supra*.

McEWEN. (W.) Grace and Truth; or, The Glory and Fulness of the Redeemer displayed. In an attempt to explain, illustrate, and enforce the most remarkable Types, Figures, and Allegories of the Old Testament. To which is added, Thoughts on Various Subjects. By the late Reverend Mr. William McEwen, Minister of the Gospel at Dundee. *Philadelphia: W. and T. Bradford.* 1767.   2307

HENRICH MILLER, | Buchdrucker in der Zweyten-straſſe, | zwiſchen der Rees- und Wein-ſtraſſe, | gegenüber Herrn John Lukens, dem General - Landmeſſer, | Hat folgende Bücher zu verkaufen: | [*Philadelphia: Henrich Miller.* 1767.] 4to. 1 leaf. H. S. P. 2308

THE | MINISTERS, Elders, and Messengers, | from the several Churches Baptized on | Profession of Faith, in Pennsylvania, and | Provinces adjacent, Met in Annual | Association in Philadelphia, the | 13th, 14th, and 15th Days of October, | Anno Domini 1767. | To the several Churches, we relate unto, do send our | loving Salutation. | [Colophon.] *Philadelphia, Printed by Henry Miller, in Second-Street.* [1767.] | Folio, pp. (3).   2309

NEU - EJNGERJCHTETER | Americaniſche | Stadt und Land | Calender, | Auf das Jahr | ... | ... | 1768. | (Welches ein Schalt-Jahr von 366. Tagen iſt.) | ... | ... | ... | ... | ... | ... | ... | ... | ... | ... | .... | Zum Fünfzehenden mahl ans Licht gegeben. | *Philadelphia gedruckt und zu haben bey Anton Armbruester in der Raesz-Strasse,* | *ohnweit dem gruenen Baum-Wirth; auch sind solche zu haben bey Andreas Geyer, Buch-* | *binder in der Second-strasse, bey Ludwig Lauman in Lancaster, bey Bern-* | *hard Holzinger* | *in Yorktaun, bey Kraft Huener in Rieding, bey Wil-* | *helm Baesz und Henrich Landes in An-* | *weil, bey Michael Hofman und Jacob Huth in Neu-yorck, und bey Mr. Laschy in Ger-* | *manton,* | *bey Mr. Hochstrasser, Kraemer in Albanien, bey Henrich Miller,* | *Kraemer in Neu-* | *Germanton in Neu-Jersey, und andern auswaertigen* | *Kraemern.* [1767.] | 4to. pp. (40). H. S. P. 2310

DER NEUESTE, Verbeſſert- und zuverläßige | Americaniſche |

Calender | Auf das 1768ſte Jahr Chriſti, | Welches ein Schalt=Jahr von 366 Tagen iſt. | . . . | . . . | . . . | . . . | . . . | . . . | . . . | . . . . | Wie auch | Eine kurze Hiſtoriſche Nachricht von der Staatsklugheit und dem Einfluß | Frankreichs, ſeitdem das Haus Bourbon ſelbige Krone beſitzt, ꝛc. ꝛc. | . . . | . . . . | Zum Sechſtenmal herausgegeben. | *Philadelphia, Gedruckt und zu finden bey Henrich Miller, in der Zweyten-strasse.* | . . . | . . . | . . . . [1767.] | 4to. pp. (40).   H. S. P.   2311

THE | NEW-YEAR | Verses, | Of the Printers Lads, who carry the Pennsylva- | nia Gazette to the Customers. | January 1, 1767. | [*Philadelphia: Hall and Sellers.* 1767.]   Folio, 1 leaf.   2312

NEW-YEAR Verses of the Carriers of the Pennsylvania Journal. *Philadelphia: W. and T. Bradford.* 1767.   2313

PENNINGTON. (Edward) A Description of Pennsbury Manor, which, as attorney for Ann Penn, he offers to sell. [*Philadelphia.* 1767.] Folio, 1 leaf.   H. S. P.   2314

It sets forth Ann Penn's title to the estate and gives some descriptive and historical details concerning it.

(January, M.DCC.LXVII.) (Numb. 1.) | THE | PENNSYLVA-NIA : Chronicle, | And Universal : Advertiser. | Containing the freshest Advices, : both Foreign and Domestic ; | with a Variety of other Matter, : useful, instructive and entertaining. | . . . . | Monday, January 26, 1767. (Vol. I.) | [Colophon.] *Philadelphia: Printed by William Goddard, at the New-Printing-Office, in Market-Street, near | the Post-Office, and opposite Mr. John Wister's, where Subscriptions, Advertisements, Articles and Letters | of Intelligence are gratefully received for this Paper, and where all Manner of Printing Work is performed with Care, | Fidelity and Expedition.* | Folio, pp. 4.   H. S. P.   2315

Numbers 1 (Jan. 26, 1767) to 54 (Jan. 18 to 25, 1768) of four pages each, except Number 46, which is only two pages, pp. 1–214. There are unpaged " Postscripts" of two pages each to Numbers 5, 10, 16, 18, 19, 20, 21, 24, 25, 37, 38, 42, and 45, and "Postscripts Extraordinary," of two pages each, dated Oct. 28, and Nov. 11, 1767. In the centre of the heading is a large cut of the Royal Arms. The dotted lines indicate the division of the wording which its insertion caused. Additions were made to the imprint in Numbers 5 and 42.

THE PENNSYLVANIA Gazette. *Philadelphia: Printed by David Hall, and William Sellers, | at the New Printing-Office, near the Market. |* H. S. P. 2316

Numbers 1984 (Jan. 1, 1767) to 2036 (Dec. 31, 1767) four pages each, with "Supplements" of two pages each to Numbers 1989, 1991, 1993, 1997, 2008, 2009, 2012, 2013, and 2016. Title as in No. 1692, *supra.* Imprint as above until No. 2002, when it was changed to the form given in No. 2381, *infra.*

THE PENNSYLVANIA Journal. *Philadelphia: Printed and Sold by William and Thomas Bradford, at the Corner of Front and Market-Streets, where | Persons may be supplied with this Paper at Ten Shillings a Year. And where Advertisements are taken in. |* Folio.

Numbers 1256 (Jan. 1, 1767) to 1308 (Dec. 31, 1767) four pages each, with extra half sheets of two pages each to Numbers 1256, 1258 to 1262, 1264 to 1271, 1273 to 1277, 1279 to 1284, 1286 to 1289, 1292 to 1297, 1299 to 1301, and 1304 to 1308; extra sheets of four pages each to Numbers 1302 and 1303; and "Supplements" of four pages each to Numbers 1278 and 1285. Title as in No. 1693, *supra.*

THE PENNSYLVANIA Pocket Almanac for 1768. *Philadelphia: W. and T. Bradford.* 1767. 2318

𝕯𝕰𝕽 𝕲𝕬𝕹𝕿𝕵𝕰 | Pfalter | Königs und Propheten | Davids, | Verdeutscht | Von | D. Martin Luthern: | Mit | Jedes Pfalms kurtzen | Summarien, | und | Nöthigsten Parallelen. | *Philadelphia, Gedruckt bey Anton | Armbruster, in der Raesz-Strasse,* | 1767. | Sm. 12mo. pp. 350, (10). H. S. P. 2319

[ROWE. (Elizabeth)] The | History | of | Joseph; | A | Poem. | In Ten Books. | By a Female Hand. | To which is added, | The Hermit; A Poem: | And | An Essay on the Creation. | *Philadelphia: | Printed and Sold by David Hall, and | William Sellers.* 1767. | 16mo. Title, 1 leaf; pp. 1–66. 2320

RUSTON. (T.) An Essay on Inoculation for the Small Pox. Wherein the Nature of the Disease is explained, the various Methods of Preparation that have been practised in America are critically examined, and that which the Author has found, from his own experience, to be most successful, is clearly laid down. With an Appendix, containing a Chymical Examination of Mr. Sutton's

Medicines. By Thomas Ruston, M.D. *Philadelphia: W. and T. Bradford.* 1767.   2321

SAUNDERS. (R.) A Pocket | Almanack | For the Year 1768. | Fitted to the use of Penn- | sylvania and the neighbour- | ing Provinces. | By R. Saunders, Phil. | *Philadelphia:* | *Printed and Sold by D. Hall, and W. Sellers.* [1767.] | 24mo. pp. (24).   2322

SAUNDERS. Poor Richard improved : | Being an | Almanack | . . . | . . . | . . . | . . . | . . . | . . . | . . . | . . . | . . . | . . . | For the | Year of our Lord 1768 : | Being Bissextile, or Leap-Year. | . . . | . . . | . . . | . . . | . . . | . . . | . . . | . . . | . . . | By Richard Saunders, Philom. | *Philadelphia:* | *Printed and Sold by D. Hall, and W. Sellers.* [1767.] | Sm. 8vo. pp. (36).   2323

SMITH. (R.) The Principles of Sin and Holiness, And the Conflict Between these in the Heart of Believers. In Two Sermons, Preached by Robert Smith, A.M. Minister of the Gospel at Pequea. *Philadelphia: W. and T. Bradford.* 1767.   2324

STATEMENT of the Case respecting the Controversy between New York and Massachusetts respecting the Boundaries of these States. *Philadelphia:* 1767.   2325

Title from Haven's List.

STEUART. (A.) The | Gentleman and Citizen's | Pocket Almanack, | By Andrew Steuart, Bookseller. | For the Year 1764. | . . . | . . . | . . . | . . . | . . . | . . . | . . . | . . . | . . . . | *Philadelphia:* | *Printed by Andrew Steuart, at the* | *Bible-in-Heart, in Second-street.* [1767.] | 24mo. pp. (24), 1 leaf folded.   2326

DIE | TÆGLICHEN | Loosungen | der | Brüder-Gemeine | Für das Jahr | 1767. | *Gedruckt bey Bethlehem in der Fork Dellawar. Bey Johann Brandmiller.* MDCCLXVII. 8vo. Title, 1 leaf; pp. (60).   H. S. P. 2327

THOUGHTS | on the | Nature of War, | and its | Repugnancy | to the | Christian Life. | Extracted from a Sermon, | on the 29th November, 1759; | Being the Day of Public Thanksgiving | for the Successes obtained in the late War. | With | Some Extracts |

from the Writings of Will. Law | and Th. Hartley, both Clergy-men | of the Church of England, on the Neces- | sity of Self-Denial, and bear- | ing the Daily Cross, in order to be true | Fol-lowers of Christ. | . . . | . . . | . . . | . . . | . . . | . . . . | *Philadelphia :* *Printed by Henry Miller,* | *in Second-Street.* MDCCLXVI. | Sm. 8vo. pp. 30.   H. S. P.   2328

This title was accidentally misplaced. It should have appeared in 1766.

TOBLER. (J.) The | Pennsylvania | Town and Country-man's | Almanack, | For the Year of our Lord, 1768 : | Being Bissex-tile or Leap-Year. | [20 lines.] | By John Tobler, Esq ; | *Wilming-ton,* | *Printed and Sold by James Adams, and to be had in* | *Philadelphia* *of Jonathan Zane and William Wilson,* | *both in Second-street, between* *Chesnut- and Arch-street.* [1767.] | Sm. 8vo. pp. (40).   2329

A TRANSLATION of a Passage from the Letters of Julius, an antient Italian Missionary, residing in China, of the Manner there of draining and flooding their Rice and Grass Lands along the Sides of Tide Rivers. *Philadelphia : William Goddard.* **1767.**

TRUE | Pleasure, Chearfulness, | aad | Happiness, | The im-mediate Consequence of | Religion | Fully and concisely proved. | With some Remarks on the | Theatre. | Addressed to a Young Lady in | Pennsylvania. | . . . | . . . | . . . | . . . | . . . | . . . . | *Philadelphia :* | *Printed by William and Thomas Bradford,* | *at the Lon-don Coffee-House.* M.DCC.LXVII. | 8vo. pp. 22.   H. S. P.   2331

ΚURTZE | UNTERWEJSUNG | Vor | Keine | Kinder, | Woburch man felbige, | Durch Gottes Gnade, | Frühzeitig | Weifen und anleiten | möge | Zu Jefu Chrifto ; | Auf daß er fie umfahe, hertze | und fegne, | In Zeit und Ewigkeit; | Aus Liebe, zum Lob Gottes, | Aus dem Munde der Unmündigen dargeftellet. | *Germantown :* | *Gedruckt bey* *Christoph Saur,* 1767. | 24mo. pp. 48.   H. S. P.   2332

VERBESSERTE A = B = C = oder Namenbücher, nach der richtig=ften Buchftabier = Art. *Philadelphia : Henrich Miller.* **1767.**   2333

VOTES and Proceedings of the Assembly. *Philadelphia : D.* *Hall and W. Sellers.* **1767.**   2334

WATTS. (I[saac]) Hymns | and | Spiritual Songs. | In Three Books. | I. Collected from the Scriptures. | II. Composed on Divine Subjects. | III. Prepared for the Lord's Supper. | By I. Watts, D.D. | The Twentieth Edition. | . . . | . . . | . . . | . . . | . . . . | *Philadelphia : | Printed and Sold by D. Hall, and | W. Sellers, at the New-Printing- | Office, | in Market-street.* MDCCLXVII. | 24mo. pp. xiii, 1–281, (4).   H. S. P.   2335

WEATHERWISE. (A.) Father Abraham's | Almanack, | . . . | For the Year of our Lord, 1768. | Being Bissextile, or Leap-Year. | [26 lines.] | By Abraham Weatherwise, Gent. | *Philadelphia : | Printed and Sold by W. Dunlap, at the | Newest-Printing-Office, in Market-Street.* [1767.] | Sm. 8vo. pp. (40).   L. C. P.   2336

WITHERSPOON. (J.) Ecclesiastical | Characteristics: | Or the | Arcana of Church-Policy. | Being an | Humble Attempt, | to open the | Mystery of Moderation. | Wherein is shewn, | A plain and easy Way of attaining to the Character of | a Moderate Man, as at present in Repute in the | Church of Scotland. | The Seventh Edition. | By John Witherspoon, D.D. | *London : Printed, | Philadelphia : | Re-Printed, by William and Thomas Bradford, | at the London Coffee-House.* | M,DCCLXVII. | 8vo. pp. 60.   H. S. P.   2337

1768.

AN ACCOUNT of the Births and Bu- | rials in the United Churches of Christ-Church | and St. Peter's, in Philadelphia, from December | 25, 1767, to December 25, 1768. By Caleb | Cash, and William Young, Clerks, and James | Weyley, and George Stokes, Sextons. | [*Philadelphia :* 1768.] Folio, 1 leaf.   2338

AN ACCOUNT of the Burials of the Second | Presbyterian Church, in Philadelphia, from December 25, 1767, | to December 25, 1768. By Adam Hope, Sexton. | [*Philadelphia :* 1768.] Folio, 1 leaf.   L. C. P.   2339

AN ADDRESS to the Merchants, Freehold- | ers, and all other the Inhabitants of the Pro- | vince of Pennsylvania in particular, and the | Southern Colonies in General. | [*Philadelphia: William Goddard?* 1768.] Folio, pp. (2). H. S. P. 2340

An Anti-Non-Importation address, signed " An Englishman," who says, " The establishment of a Bishop or Bishops, would, amongst other things, have this very excellent effect, that it would draw the attention, and awaken the jealousy of the [New England] Puritans, who would give their spleen some vent, in discharging it upon the ceremonies, forms, &c., of the church, . . . and this will answer as good an end as stuffing a skin to amuse a puppy, to prevent his worrying the sheep."

THE FOLLOWING | ADDRESS | Was read at a Meeting of the Merchants, at the Lodge, in Philadelphia, on Monday, | the 25th of April, 1768. | [*Philadelphia: W. and T. Bradford.* 1768.] Folio, 1 leaf. H. S. P. 2341

Recommending a renewal of the Non-Importation agreement.

AGUECHEEK. (A.) The Universal American Almanac for 1769. By Andrew Aguecheek. *Philadelphia: Andrew Steuart.* 1768. 2342

ALLEN (B.) An Address to the Vestrymen, Church-Wardens, and Parishioners of All-Saints, in Frederick County, Maryland. In which the Author's Conduct is explained, and his Character vindicated from the Aspersions thrown upon it in the Maryland Gazette. By Bennet Allen, Chaplain and Agent to the Right Honourable the Proprietary, in Maryland. *Philadelphia: William Goddard.* 1768. 2343

THE AMERICAN Calendar for 1769. *Philadelphia: W. and T. Bradford.* 1768. 2344

THE AMERICAN Pocket Almanac for 1769. *Philadelphia: W. and T. Bradford.* 1768. 2345

ANNO Regni | Georgii III. Regis, | Magnæ Britanniæ, Franciæ & Hiberniæ, | Octavo. | At a General Assembly of the Province of Penn- | sylvania, begun and holden at Philadelphia, | the Fourteenth Day of October; Anno Domini 1767, in | the Seventh Year of the Reign of our Sovereign Lord | George III. by the Grace of God, of Great- | Britain, France and Ireland, King, Defender of the | Faith, &c. | And from thence continued by

Adjournments to the | Twentieth Day of February, 1768. | [*Penn Arms.*] | *Philadelphia:* | *Printed and Sold by D. Hall, and W. Sellers, at the* | *New Printing-Office, near the Market.* MDCCLXVIII. | Folio, Title, 1 leaf; pp. 597–636. + [*Royal Arms.*] | *Philadelphia:* | *Printed and sold by William Goddard, at the New* | *Printing-Office, in Market-Street.* | MDCCLXVIII. | Folio, pp. 44, 1 leaf.   2346

THE | BAPTIST Association, | held | In Philadelphia, | the 11th, 12th and 13th Days of October, Anno Domini 1768; | To the Churches thereunto belonging. | [Colophon.] *Philadelphia, Printed by Henry Miller, in Second-street.* [1768.] | Folio, pp. (3).

CATALOGUE of Books to be sold at Auction, May 4, 1768, by Robert Bell. *Philadelphia: William Goddard.* 1768.   2348

CHAUNCY. (C.) The Appeal to the Public Answered, In Behalf of the Non-Episcopal Churches in America; containing Remarks on what Dr. Thomas Bradbury Chandler has advanced, on the four following Points, The Original and Nature of the Episcopal Office. Reasons for sending Bishops to America. The Plan on which it is proposed to send them. And the Objections against sending them obviated and refuted. Wherein the Reasons for an American Episcopate are shown to be insufficient, and the Objections against it in full force. By Charles Chauncy, D.D. and Pastor of the first Church of Christ in Boston. *Philadelphia: W. and T. Bradford.* 1768.   2349

CHAUNCY. A Letter to a Friend, Containing Remarks on certain Passages in a Sermon Preached by the Right Reverend Father in God, John, Lord Bishop of Landaff, before the incorporated Society for the Propagation of the Gospel in Foreign Parts, at their Anniversary-Meeting in the Parish Church of St. Mary Le-Bow, February 20, 1767. In which the highest Reproach is undeservedly cast upon the American Colonies. By Charles Chauncy, D.D. Pastor of the first Church of Christ in Boston. *Philadelphia: W. and T. Bradford.* 1768.   2350

CHESAPEAK. | [*Philadelphia:* 1768.] Sm. 8vo. pp. 18 +.

In favor of a canal between the Chesapeake and Delaware Bays.

A COPY of a Letter from a Gentleman in Virginia, | To a Merchant in Philadelphia. | [*Philadelphia :* 1768.] Folio, pp. (2).

In regard to violations of the Non-Importation agreement by Philadelphia merchants.

CROSSWELL. (A.)　Observations on Bishop Warburton's Sermon before the Society for the Propagation of the Gospel, Feb. 21, 1766. By Andrew Crosswell. *Philadelphia :* 1768. 8vo.　2353

Title from Haven's List.

[DICKINSON. (John)] Letters | from a | Farmer | in | Pennsylvania, | to the | Inhabitants | of the | British Colonies. | *Philadelphia :* | *Printed by David Hall, and William Sellers.* | MDCCLXVIII. | 8vo. pp. 71. + The Second Edition. | [*Ibid.*] 8vo. pp. 71.　2354

The first edition was published in March and the second in June following. The publication of these letters produced a greater sensation throughout the colonies than anything ever before printed. They appeared simultaneously in the Pennsylvania Chronicle and Gazette, in twelve issues, beginning on Dec. 3, 1767 ; towards the close of the series the Chronicle was a few days ahead of the Gazette and Journal, which joined the others with numbers one and two, on the 10th of Dec. They were promptly reprinted in nearly all the twenty-five papers then published on the continent, Miller's and Sower's German papers and the Boston Evening Post being among the exceptions. The latter paper published a series of letters in reply, and Goddard (Partnership, p. 16) hints that Galloway also wrote a series of letters in answer to the Farmer, which were not, however, published. The publication of the letters in the Chronicle led to a breach between the partners,—Galloway, Wharton, and Goddard, which resulted finally in the latter's overthrow.

The Town Meeting held in Boston, March 17, 1768, voted that " The Thanks of the Town be given to the Author." " This," says the Pa. Gazette, " is the first Honour of the kind ever given by a City to any person in America." Other towns in New England followed the example of Boston ; in New York, the " Author of the Farmer's Letters" was a toast at public dinners ; in Pennsylvania, when Dickinson appeared in Court, proceedings were delayed by the presentation of complimentary addresses from the Grand Juries. From Maryland and the southern colonies came addresses from Grand Juries and other public bodies. The French edition says thirty editions were printed in America within six months. This statement may have included the newspaper reprints, as only eight in pamphlet form are now known to have been printed in America. Two editions were also published in London and one in Dublin. A long notice in the Monthly Review, vol. xxxix., concludes, " If reason is to decide between us and our colonies, in the affairs here controverted, our Author, whose name the advertisements inform us is Dickinson, will not perhaps easily meet with a satisfactory refutation."

[EDWARDS. (Morgan)] The | Customs of primitive churches; | or | A set of propositions relative to name, matterials, constitution, power, | officers, ordinances, rites, business, worship, discipline, government, &c. | of a church; to which are added their proofs from scripture; and his- | torical narratives of the manner in which most of them have been re- | duced to practice. | . . . | . . . | . . . | . . . | . . . . | [*Philadelphia: Andrew Steuart.* 1768.] 4to. pp. 110.   2355

The reverse of the title-page contains a list of errata. The only copy I have seen contains what appears to be a cancelled title-page: " Customs of the churches; | Or | A set of propositions relative to the name, matterials, constitutions, pow- | ers, officers, ordinances, rites, business, worship, discipline, govern- | ment, &c., of a church; to which are added their proofs from | scripture; and historical narratives of the manner in which some have | been reduced to practice." | . . . | . . . | . . . | . . . | . . . | . . . . | [n. p. n. d.]. On the reverse is an " Advertisement" of 16 lines.

This attempt to formulate the ritual of the Baptist Church was written by Rev. Morgan Edwards, who had a few copies printed for private distribution among the Ministers and Elders of that sect, " with an earnest request that each of them will consider the plan; mend it; or propose a better." It does not seem to have met with a favorable reception, and the Philadelphia Association, in their Letter for 1774, express their disapproval.

EXTRACTS | From the Proceedings | of the | Court of Vice-Admiralty | in | Charles-Town, South-Carolina; | In the Cause, | George Roupell, Esq; v. the Ship Ann and Goods: | With a few | Explanatory Remarks. | To which is subjoined, some | General Observations | on | American Custom-House Officers, | and | Courts of Vice-Admiralty. | . . . | . . . | . . . | . . . | . . . | . . . . . . | . . . . | *America:* | [*Philadelphia: W. and T. Bradford.*] *Printed, Anno Domini,* M,DCC,LXVIII. | 4to. pp. iv, 20.   2356

[FOTHERGILL. (Samuel)] The | Prayer of Agur, | illustrated in | A Funeral Discourse: | And the | Advantages Resulting | from an | Early and Stedfast Piety. | Preached extempore, | By the Author of Two Discourses, and a | Prayer. | Publickly delivered at the Quakers Yearly | Meeting, in Bristol. | The whole taken down in Characters, | By a Member of the Church of England. | *Bristol, Printed:* | *Philadelphia, Re-printed, and sold by D. Hall,* | *and W. Sellers, at the New Printing-Office,* | *opposite the Jersey Market.* MDCCLXVIII. | 8vo. pp. 43.   H. S. P.   2357

FOX. (T.)   The Wilmington Almanac for 1769.   By Thomas Fox. *Wilmington : James Adams.*   1768.   2358

THE FREEMEN . . . of Philadelphia are desired | to attend at the State-House . . . | . . . to consider of proper Instructions to . . . | our Representatives on the present and alarming critical situation | of these Colonies. | [*Philadelphia :* 1768.]   4to. 1 leaf.

Dated " Philadelphia, Saturday, July 30, 1768."

FROM our | Yearly Meeting, | Held in London, by Adjournments, from | the 23d Day of the Fifth Month, 1768, to | the 28th of the same, inclusive, | To the ensuing Yearly-Meeting of Friends, for | Pennsylvania and New Jersey. | [Colophon.] *Philadelphia : Printed by D. Hall, and W. Sellers, | in Market-street.* [1768.] | Folio, pp. 2.   M. S.   2360

THE GENUINE Letter from the Baptist Association met in Philadelphia. *Philadelphia : Henry Miller.* 1768.   2361

GOLDSMITH. (O.)   The | Traveller : | or, a | Prospect of Society. | A Poem. | Containing | A Sketch of the Manners | of | Italy, | Switzerland, | France, | Holland, | and | Britain. | To which is added, | True Beauty : A Matrimonial Tale. | Likewise, | The Adventures of Tom Dreadnaught. | Who served as a Soldier, and also as a Sailor, | in the Late War. | By Oliver Goldsmith, M.B. | Author of the Vicar of Wakefield, &c. | *America :* [*Philadelphia : Robert Bell.*] *Printed for every Purchaser,* | MDCCLXVIII. | 8vo. pp. 24.   N. Y. H. S.   2362

GRIFFITH. (J.)   Some | Brief Remarks | upon sundry | Important Subjects, | Necessary to be understood and attended to by all | professing the Christian Religion. | Principally addressed to | The People called Quakers. | By John Griffith. | *London, Printed : | And Wilmington, Re-printed, by James Adams,* | M.DCC.LXVIII. | 8vo. pp. (8), 89.   H. S. P.   2363

THE | GROUND and Nature | of | Christian Redemption. | *Philadelphia : | Printed and Sold by John Dunlap, at the Newest | Printing-Office, on the South Side of the Jersey Market, | the third Door below Second-street,* 1768. | 12mo. pp. 28.   L. C. P.   2364

𝕯𝕰𝕽 𝕳𝕰𝖄𝕯𝕰𝕷𝕭𝕰𝕽𝕲𝕵𝕾𝕮𝕳𝕰 Catechismus, Samt der Haus=
Tafel. *Philadelphia: Henrich Miller.* 1768.   2365

𝕯𝕰𝕽 | 𝕳𝕺𝕮𝕳=𝕯𝕰𝖀𝕿𝕾𝕮𝕳𝕰 | Americanische | Calender, | Auf das
Jahr | Nach der Gnadenreichen Geburth unsers | Herrn und Heylandes
Jesu Christi | 1769. | (Welches ein gemein Jahr von 365 Tagen ist.) |
In sich haltende; Die Wochen=Tage; den Tag des Monaths; Tage
welche | bemerckt werden; Des Monds Auf= und Untergang; Des
Monds Zeichen und Grad; | Des Monds Virtel: Aspecten der
Planeten samt der Witterung; des 7 Gestirns | Aufgang, Süd=Platz
und Untergang; Der Sonnen Auf= und Untergang; Der | Venus, |
des Morgen= oder Abend=sterns | Auf= und Untergang. Nebst ver= |
schiedenen andern Berichten; Erklärung der Zeichen, Aderlaß=Täfflein,
An= | zeigung der Finsternüsse, Courten, Fären, 2c. 2c. | Eingerichtet vor
40 Grad Norder= Breite, sonderlich vor Pennsylvanien; | Jedoch an
denen angrentzenden Länden ohne mercklichen Unterschied zu gebrauchen.
| Zum ein und dreyßigsten mal heraus gegeben. | *Germantown: Ge-
druckt und zu finden bey Christoph Saur.* | . . . | . . . . [1768.] |
4to. pp. (48).   H. S. P.   2366

JANEWAY. (J.) Heaven upon Earth or the Best Friend
in the Worst Times. By Rev. James Janeway. *Philadelphia:
Benjamin Mecom.* 1768.   2367

[JOHNSON. (Samuel)] The | History | of | Rasselas, | Prince
of Abissinia. | An Asiatic Tale. | The Two Volumes complete in
One. | Volume the First. | . . . | . . . | . . . | . . . | . . . . |
America: | *Printed for every Purchaser.* | MDCCLXVIII. | 12mo.
pp. 192, 1 plate.   H. S. P.   2368

> The " Frontispiece " is an etching called " A Perspective View of Grand Cairo."
> It is a very crude performance by some local workman, Dawkins or perhaps Clay-
> poole. The first volume ends on page 94, and is followed by the title to the second
> volume, of which the reverse is blank. Rasselas ends on page 188, and is followed
> by The | Voyage | of | Life. | By Samuel Johnson, L.L.D. | Author of the Rambler,
> Rasselas, &c. | pp. 189–192.

𝕯𝕵𝕰 𝕷𝕰𝕳𝕽 = 𝕿𝕰𝕏𝕿 | der | Brüder=Gemeine, | und insonderheit |
der Kinder, | für das Jahr | 1769. | . . . | . . . | . . . . | *Phila-
delphia: Gedruckt [bey Henrich Miller] im Jahr,* 1768. | Sm. 8vo.
pp. (39).   2369

A | LETTER, | concerning | an | American Bishop, &c. | to | Dr. Bradbury Chandler, | Ruler of St. John's Church, in | Elizabeth - Town. | In Answer to the | Appendix | Of His | Appeal to the Public, &c. | [*Philadelphia :*] *Printed,* [*by W. and T. Bradford*] *A.D.* 1768. | 8vo. pp. 19.   H. S. P.   2370

LIBERTY. | A | Poem. | By Rusticus. | . . . . | *Philadelphia :* | *Printed by John Dunlap, in Market-Street.* | MDCCLXVIII. | 4to. pp. 27.   H. S. P.   2371

𝕰𝕴𝕹 𝕾𝕮𝕳Ö𝕹 𝕷𝕴𝕰𝕯 | von dem | Schweizerischen Erz = Freyheits= sohn | Wilhelm Thellen, | dem Urheber der Löbl. Eydgenoßenschaft. | Samt einem andern Liede | von dem | Ursprung und Herkommen der Schweizer. | [Cut.] | *Philadelphia,* | *Nach einem Schweizerischen Exemplar treulich nachge-* | *druckt, und zu finden bey Henrich Miller,* *in* | *der Zweyten-strasse.* 1768. | 16mo. pp. (16).   H. S. P.   2372

LIVINGSTON. (W.) A Letter To the Right Reverend Father in God John, Lord Bishop of Landaff; Occasioned by some Passages in his Lordship's Sermon, on the 20th of February, 1767, in which the American Colonies are loaded with great and undeserved Reproach. By William Livingston. *Philadelphia : W. and T. Bradford.* 1768.   2373

𝕰𝕴𝕹 𝕸𝕰𝕽𝕶𝕨Ü𝕽𝕯𝕴𝕲𝕰𝕽 Traum, | der im Jahr 1757 von einer gewißen Person, betreffend Philadelphia, | Zum erstenmal, und dann eilf Jahren nachher wiederum von | der nemlichen Person, geträumet worden. | [*Germantown : Christopher Saur.* 1768.] 4to. pp. (2).   H. S. P.   2374

MONTAGUE. (M. W.) Additional Volume to the Letters of the Right Honourable Lady Mary Wortley Montague. *Philadelphia : Robert Bell.* 1768.   2375

𝕯𝕰𝕽 𝕹𝕰𝖀𝕰𝕾𝕿𝕰, Verbeßert= und Zuverläßige Americanische Calender Auf das 1769ste Jahr Christi. *Philadelphia : Henrich Miller.* 1768.   2376

NEW JERSEY. [*Royal Arms.*] | By his Excellency | William Franklin, Esquire, | . . . | . . . | . . . . | A Proclamation.

| *Philadelphia: Printed by   William   Goddard,   in   Market-Street.*
[1768.] | Folio, 1 leaf.   L. C. P.   2377

The house of the Treasurer of East Jersey having been broken into, the Governor offered £50 reward for the apprehension of the Robbers.

NEW-YEAR Verses of the Carriers of the Pennsylvania Chronicle. *Philadelphia: William Goddard.* 1768.   2378

NEW-YEAR Verses of the Carriers of the Pennsylvania Journal. *Philadelphia: W. and T. Bradford.* 1768.   2379

OLD | Mr. Dod's | Sayings. | *Philadelphia:* | *Printed by John Dunlap, in Market-Street.* | MDCCLXVIII. | 12mo. pp. 11.   F.   2380

THE | PENNSYLVANIA Chronicle, | and | Universal Advertiser. | From February 1, 1768, to January 23, 1769. | . . . . | Volume II. | [*Royal Arms.*] | *Philadelphia:* | *Printed by William Goddard, in Market-Street.* | 4to.   H. S. P.   2381

Collation: Title, 1 leaf; text, in numbers of eight pages each, pp. 1–452; with unpaged "Postscripts" of two pages each, to Numbers 55, 57, 78, 98, and 106; of four pages each to Numbers 58, 62, 63, 66, 67, 68, 73, 74, 75, and 97; of eight pages each to Numbers 60, 61, 69, 70, and 71; and "Postscripts Extraordinary" of two pages each to Numbers 93 and 96. These "Postscripts" vary in size from *octavo* to *folio*. "Postscripts" to many numbers are regularly paged. The paper was modelled after the London Chronicle, to which, however, it was much superior in appearance and contents.

THE PENNSYLVANIA Gazette. *Philadelphia: Printed by David Hall, and William Sellers, at the | New Printing-Office, near the Market.* | H. S. P.   2382

Numbers 2037 (Jan. 7, 1768) to 2088 (Dec. 29, 1768), four pages each, with "Supplements" of two pages to Numbers 2038 to 2050 inclusive, 2052, 2053, 2056 to 2067 inclusive, 2069, 2070, 2072 to 2076 inclusive, 2079, 2080, 2082, and 2084; of four pages to Numbers 2051, 2054, and 2055; "Supplement Extraordinary" to No. 2066; and "Postscripts" of 1 leaf to Numbers 2067 and 2068, and of two pages to 2071, and 2073 to 2079 inclusive. Title as in No. 1693, *supra*.

THE PENNSYLVANIA Journal.   H. S. P.   2383

Numbers 1309 (Jan. 7, 1768) to 1360 (Dec. 29, 1768), four pages each, with extra half sheets of two pages each to Numbers 1309–13, 1315–17, 1319, 1325–28, 1338,

1341–42, 1344, 1347, and 1353–60 ; "Supplements" of two pages each to 1314, 1316, 1322, 1332–34, 1336–37, 1339, 1345–46, and 1349–51 ; "Supplements" of four pages each to 1318, 1320–25, 1329–31, 1335, and 1352 ; "Postscripts" of one leaf to 1318 and 1338 ; "Postscripts" of two pages to 1347 and 1348.   Title and imprint as in No. 2317, *supra*.

THE | PENNSYLVANIA | Pocket Almanack | For the Year 1769. | Being the First after Bissextile | or Leap Year. | Calculated for the Use of the Province | of Pennsylvania, and the neighbour- | ing Provinces. | *Philadelphia:* | *Printed and Sold by W. and T.* | *Bradford at the London Coffee-House.* [1768.] | 24mo. pp. (26).   H. S. P.   2384

THE | POWER and Grandeur | of | Great-Britain, | founded on | The Liberty | of the | Colonies, | and | The Mischiefs attending the Taxing them by Act | of Parliament | Demonstrated. | . . . | . . . . | *Philadelphia:* | *Printed and Sold by William Goddard,* *at the New Printing-* | *Office, in Market-Street.* | M,DCC,LXVIII. | 8vo. pp. 22.   H. S. P.   2385

PROCLAMATION.   [*Royal Arms.*]   By the Honourable | John Penn, Esquire, | Lieutenant-Governor, and Commander-in-Chief of the Province of Pennsylvania, and | Counties of New-Castle, Kent, and Sussex, on Delaware. | A Proclamation. | *Philadelphia: Printed by D. Hall, and W. Sellers.* 1768. | Folio, 1 leaf.   H. S. P.   2386

Dated March 16, 1768.   Offering a reward for the apprehension of Frederick Stump and John Ironcutter, who had been rescued from jail at Carlisle, where they were confined upon a charge of having murdered ten Indians.

PROCLAMATION.   [*Royal Arms.*]   By the Honourable | John Penn, Esquire, | Lieutenant-Governor, and Commander in Chief | of the Province of Pennsylvania, and Counties | of New-Castle, Kent, and Sussex, on Delaware, | A Proclamation. | *Philadelphia: Printed by D. Hall, and W. Sellers.* [1768.] | Folio, 1 leaf.   H. S. P.   2387

Proclamation of a Robbery of the Treasurer of New Jersey, dated Aug. 6, 1768. See No. 2376, *supra.*

PROCLAMATION.   [*Royal Arms.*] | By the Honourable |

John Penn, Esquire, | Lieutenant-Governor, and Commander in Chief of the Province of Pennsylvania, and | Counties of New-Castle, Kent, and Sussex, on Delaware, | A Proclamation. | *Philadelphia: Printed by D. Hall, and W. Sellers.* [1768.] | Folio, 1 leaf.   H. S. P.   2388

Proclamation of an Act imposing the penalty of death on any person then settled, or who should thereafter settle on land not purchased from the Indians, who shall fail to remove therefrom within thirty days after notice being given to him.

DER | PSALTER | Des | Königs und Propheten | Davids, | verteutschet von | D. Martin Luther. | Mit kurtzen Summarien, oder | Inhalt jedes Psalmen. | Mit | vielen parallelen oder gleichen | Schrifft = Stellen. | *Germantown zum fünfften mal ge-* | *druckt bey Christoph Saur, 1768.* | 24mo. pp. 252.   H. S. P.   2389

DER | PSALTER | des | Königs und Propheten | Davids, | Verteutschet von | D. Martin Luther. | Mit | Kurtzen Summarien, oder In= | halt jedes Psalmen; | wie auch | Vielen Parallelen, oder gleichlau= | tenden Schriftstellen. | *Philadelphia,* | *Gedruckt und zu finden bey Henrich Miller, in der Zweyten-strasse.* 1768. | 24mo. pp. 252.   2390

JOSEPH REED, Defendant, vs. John Reed. Argument for the Defendant in Error. *Philadelphia:* 1768 ? 4to. pp. 28.   2391

Title from Haven's List.

SAUNDERS. (R.) A Pocket Almanac for 1769. By Richard Saunders, Phil. *Philadelphia: Hall and Sellers,* 1768.   2392

SAUNDERS. Poor Richard improved: | Being an | Al-manack | . . . | . . . | . . | . . | . . | . . | . . | . . | . . . | . . . | For the | Year of our Lord 1769: | Being the First after Leap - Year. | . . . | . . . | . . . | . . . | . . . | . . . | . . . | . . . | . . . . | By Richard Saunders, Philom. | *Philadelphia:* | *Printed and Sold by D. Hall, and W. Sellers.* [1768.] | Sm. 8vo. pp. (36).

SCHABALIE (J. P.) Die | Wandlende Seel, | Das ist: | Gespräch | der | Wandlenden Seelen mit Adam, | Noah und Simon Cleophas; | verfasset die | Geschichten von Erschaffung der | Welt an, biß zu und nach der | Verwüstung Jerusalems. | Daraus ordentlich zu erſehen, wie eine | Monarchie und Königreich auf die andere gefolget, | wie dieſe angefangen, jene aber vergangen, | und auch der ausführ= liche Verlauff der | Zerſtöhrung Jeruſalem. | Durch | Johann Philip Schabalie | in Niederländiſcher Sprach beſchrieben; | Anjetzo aber in die Hochdeutſche Sprach überſetzt | von | B. B. B. | *Germantown:* | *Gedruckt und zu finden, bey Christoph Saur, 1768.* | 16mo. pp. (8), 463, (25).   H. S. P.   2394

SERMONS, | or, | Declarations, | Made | by some of the | Ancient Preachers | amongst the | People called Quakers, | viz. | Stephen Crisp. | William Dewsbury. | William Penn. &c. | Taken in Short Hand, as they were delivered | by them. | *Philadelphia:* | *Printed and sold by John Dunlap, on the* | *south side of Market-Street, the third* | *Door below Second-Street.* MDCCLXVIII. | 12mo. pp. 71.   2395

A SHORT and True | Account | Of a | Young Youth; | Born in Philadelphia of honest and true | Christian Parents; who was taken a- | way by an Angel the 31st of January | 1768. up to the Cœlestical Parts, | where the Lord of Host show'd her | great Wonders and supernatural Things. | . . . | . . . | . . . | . . . | . . . . | Translated from the German. | *Philadelphia printed by Anthony Arm-* | *bruster in Third-street,* 1768. | 8vo. pp. 8.   L. C. P.   2396

SIEGVOLCK (G. P.) Das von | Jeſu Chriſto | Dem Richter der Lebendigen und der Todten, | Aller Creatur zu predigen befohlene | Ewige Evangelium, | Von der durch Ihn erfundenen | Ewigen Er= löſung, | Wodurch alles, was da heiſſet Teufel, Sünde, | Hölle und Tod endlich gantz und gar vernichtiget, und | alſo alle Geſchöpfe, die von Gott ſehr gut erſchaffen wor= | den, nach gnugſam geoffenbahrter Gött= lichen Straff= | Gerechtigkeit, wiederum in ihre uranfängliche Rei= | nigkeit und Seligkeit gebracht werden ſollen; | Allen Menchen unter allen Nationen, und Religi= | ons = Partheyen, welche deſſen Schall hören, inſonderheit | aber denen, welche es zu Hertzen nehmen, und ſich zu ei= | ner heiligen Gegen=Liebe gegen den ſo liebreichen | Gott erwecken laſſen wollen. | Anjetzo | Vor denen nächſt=inſtehenden, ja bey denen bereits angegan= | genen erſchrecklichen Gerichten über dieſe gegen= wärtige | Wider=Chriſtiſche Welt, | Entweder zu ihrer Bekehrung und

Stärckung in dem Guten, | oder Zufalls-Weise zu ihrer Verstockung und Reiffmachung zum | Gerichte; aus erbarmender Liebe verkündiget; an unzeh= | lich vielen Orten durch diesen Druck verbessert, und | nebst Hinzufügung eines | Neuen Capitels über Hebr. II. v. 16. | vom | Samen Abrahä | handlend, vermehret, | von | Georg Paul Siegvolck, | einem einfältigen Schüler der Himmlischen Weisheit. | *Germantown:* | *Gedruckt und zu finden bey Christoph Saur, 1768.* | 16mo. pp. (9), 175.   H. S. P.   2397

SOME Brief Remarks upon sundry important Subjects, principally addressed to the People called Quakers. *Wilmington: James Adams.* 1768.   2398

SOME | Observations | of | Consequence, | In Three Parts. | Occasioned by the | Stamp-Tax, | Lately imposed on the | British Colonies. | [*Philadelphia:*] *Printed [by Hall and Sellers?] for the Author,* MDCCLXVIII. | 8vo. pp. 80.   L. C. P.   2399

STEUART. (A.) The | Gentleman and Citizen's | Pocket Almanack, | By Andrew Steuart, Bookseller. | For the Year 1769. | Fitted to the Use of Pennsylvania and | the neighbouring Provinces. | Containing | Many useful Lists and Tables, | not in any other Almanack printed | on the Continent. | This Almanack contains more than | double the Quantity of any other Pocket- | Almanack printed in this Place. | *Philadelphia:* | *Printed by Andrew Steuart, at the* | *Bible-in-Heart, in Second-street.* [1768.] | 24mo. pp. (48).   H. S. P.   2400

DIE TÄGLICHEN Loosungen der Brüder-Gemeine für das Jahr 1768. *Philadelphia: Henrich Miller.* 1768.   2401

In February, Miller printed 500 copies of this work for the Moravians.

DIE | TÄGLICHEN | Loosungen | der | Brüder-Gemeine | für das Jahr | 1769. | *Philadelphia, Gedruckt [bey Henrich Miller] im Jahr* 1768. | Sm. 8vo. pp. (46).   H. S. P.   2402

TO the Public. | *Philadelphia: Printed by William Goddard.* [1768.] | 4to. 1 leaf.   H. S. P.   2403

Signed "Pacificus," and dated "July 25, 1768." An answer to a "Letter from a Gentleman in Virginia."

TO the | Public. | [*Philadelphia :. William Goddard.* 1768.] Sm. 8vo. pp. 8.　　　　　　　　　　　　　　H. S. P.　2404

Signed "Pacificus," and dated "Philadelphia, July 16, 1768." Relates to the renewal of the "Non-Importation Agreement."

TOBLER. (J.)　The | Pennsylvania | Town and Country-Man's | Almanack, | for | The Year of our Lord, 1769, | Being the First after Leap-year. | [21 lines] | By John Tobler, Esq ; | *Wilmington,* | *Printed and Sold by James Adams.*　[1768.] | Sm. 8vo. pp. (40).

THE Trial of Frederick Calvert, Esq ; Baron of Baltimore, in the Kingdom of Ireland, for a Rape on the Body of Sarah Wood-cock.　*Philadelphia : W. and T. Bradford.*　1768.　　　2406

VERSES, | Of the Printers Lads, who carry the Pennsylva- | nia Gazette to the Customers. | Ode on the New Year. | January 1, 1768. | [*Philadelphia : Hall and Sellers.* 1768.]　Folio, 1 leaf.

VOTES | and | Proceedings | of the | House of Representatives | of the | Province of Pennsylvania, | Met at Philadelphia, on the Fourteenth of October, Anno | Domini, 1767, and continued by Adjournments. | [*Royal Arms.*] | *Philadelphia :* | *Printed and Sold by William Goddard, at the New Printing-* | *Office, in Market-Street.* | MDCCLXVIII. | Folio, pp. 137.　　　　　　　　　　2408

THE WHOLE Duty of Woman, by a Lady.　Written at the Desire of a Noble Lord.　The Fourth Edition, corrected.　*Phila-delphia : Hall and Sellers.*　1768.　　　　　　　　　2409

WOOLMAN. (J.)　Considerations | on | Pure Wisdom, | and | Human Policy; | on | Labour; | on | Schools; | And on the right use of the | Lord's outward Gifts. | By John Woolman. | . . . | . . . | . . . | . . . . | *Philadelphia :* | *Printed by D. Hall, and* | *W. Sellers, at the* | *New Printing-Office, opposite the Jersey Market.* 1768. | 16mo. pp. 28.　　　　　　　　　N. Y. H. S.　2410

1769.

AN ACCOUNT of the Births and Bu- | rials in the United Churches of Christ-Church | and St. Peter's, in Philadelphia, from December | 25, 1768, to December 25, 1769. By Caleb | Cash, and William Young, Clerks, and James | Weyley, and George Stokes, Sextons. | [*Philadelphia:* 1769.] Folio, 1 leaf.   L. C. P.   2411

AN ACCOUNT of the Burials and Baptisms in the Baptist Church, Dec. 25, 1768, to Dec. 29, 1769. *Philadelphia:* 1769.   2412

AN ACCOUNT of the Burials in the Second Presbyterian Church, Dec. 25, 1768, to Dec. 25, 1769. *Philadelphia:* 1769.

AGUECHEEK. (A.)   The Universal American Almanac for 1770. By Andrew Aguecheek. *Philadelphia: Thomas Magee?* 1769.   2414

THE AMERICAN Calendar for 1770. *Philadelphia: W. and T. Bradford.* 1769.   2415

THE AMERICAN Magazine. *Philadelphia: W. and T. Bradford.* 1769. 8vo. Preface, pp. ii; text, pp. 1–328; 1 plate. 2416

This magazine, edited by Lewis Nichola, was begun in January, and continued until September. Sixteen pages of the Proceedings of the American Philosophical Society were appended, separately paged, to each number except the first. See No. 2491, *infra.* Page 38 is followed by 44, and page 67 by 69. The plate which should face page 80 represents "The Manner of Fowling in Norway." It is probable that no title-page was printed. The title of the cover of the first number is: Number I. of | The | American | Magazine, | or | General Repository, | For January, 1769. | . . . . | *Philadelphia:* | *Printed by William and Thomas Bradford, at the* | *London Coffee House.*

THE AMERICAN Pocket Almanac for 1770. *Philadelphia: W. and T. Bradford,* 1769.   2417

ANNO Regni | Georgii III. Regis, | Magnæ Britanniæ, Franciæ & Hiberniæ, | Nono. | At a General Assembly of the Province of Penn- | sylvania, begun and holden at Philadelphia, | the Fourteenth Day of October, Anno Domini 1768, in | the Eighth Year of the Reign of our Sovereign Lord | George III. by the Grace of God, of Great- | Britain, France and Ireland, King, De- fender of the | Faith, &c. | And from thence continued by Adjourn- ments to the | Eighteenth Day of February, 1769. | [*Penn Arms.*] | *Philadelphia:* | *Printed and Sold by D. Hall and W. Sellers, at the* | *New Printing-Office, near the Market.* MDCCLXIX. | Folio, Title, 1 leaf; pp. 639–737, (1). + And from thence continued . . . to the | Twenty-seventh Day of May, 1769. | [*Ibid.*] Title, 1 leaf; pp. 741–744. + And from thence continued . . . to the | Thirtieth Day of September, 1769. | [*Ibid.*] Title, 1 leaf; pp. 749–754.

ANNO REGNI | Georgii III. Regis, | Magnæ Britanniæ, Franciæ & Hiberniæ, | Nono. | At a General Assembly of the Province of Penn- | sylvania, begun and holden at Philadelphia, | the Fourteenth Day of October, Anno Domini 1768, in | the Eighth Year of the Reign of our Sovereign Lord | George III. by the Grace of God, of Great- | Britain, France and Ireland, King, De- fender of the | Faith, &c. | And from thence continued by Adjourn- ments to the | Eighteenth Day of February, 1769. | [*Royal Arms.*] | *Philadelphia:* | *Printed and Sold by Henry Miller, in Second-Street.* | MDCCLXIX. | Folio, pp. 101. + And from thence continued by Adjournments to the | Twenty-seventh Day of May, 1769. | [*Ibid.*] Title, 1 leaf; pp. 105–108, (1).   H. S. P.   2419

𝔄ℜ𝔒ℒ𝔒𝔊𝔍𝔈 des Ordens der Freimaurer. *Philadelphia:* [*Dieterich in Goettingen.*] 1769.   2420

From the French by J. A. Stark. Title from Weller's *Die falschen Druckorte.*

BEATTY (C.)   The Journal of a Two Months Tour; With a view of Promoting Religion, among the frontier inhabitants of Pennsylvania, and of introducing Christianity among the Indians to the Westward of the Alegh-geny Mountains.   To which are added, Remarks on the Language and Customs of some particular tribes among the Indians, with a brief account of the various at- tempts that have been made to civilize and convert them, from the first settlement of New-England to this day.   By Charles Beatty, A.M. *Philadelphia?* 1769.   2421

Advertised in the Pa. Journal, Aug. 31, 1769.

[BENEZET. (Anthony)] Some | Serious and Awful | Considerations, | Recommended to All, particularly the Youth, | In | A Representation of the Uncertainty of a | Death-Bed Repentance. | Also some | Christian Instructions, | Agreeable to the Precepts of our blessed Saviour | Jesus Christ; | Under the Character of a devout Parent | advising his Children. | Extracted from a late pious Author. | . . . | . . . | . . . | . . . | . . . | . . . . | *Philadelphia : | Printed by Joseph Crukshank, in Second-street, two | Doors below the Corner of Chestnut-street.* [1769.] | 12mo. pp. 48.   H. S. P.   2422

[BUSHE. (Gervase Parker)] .The | Case | of | Great-Britain | and | America, | addressed to the King, | and both | Houses of Parliament. | . . . | . . . | . . . | . . . | . . . . | *London : Printed, | Philadelphia, Re-Printed by William and Thomas | Bradford, at the London Coffee-House.* MDCCLXIX. | 8vo. Title, 1 leaf; pp. 16.

CATALOGUE of a Circulating Library, kept by Thomas Bradford. *Philadelphia : W. and T. Bradford.* 1769.   2424

CATALOGUE of Books to be sold at Auction by Robert Aitken. *Philadelphia : John Dunlap.* 1769.   2425

CATALOGUE of Books, | to be sold, by | Public Auction, | at the | City Vendue-Store, | In Front-Street : | Notice of the Time of Sale will be given in the Public Papers. | [*Philadelphia : W. and T. Bradford.* 1769.] Folio, 1 leaf.   H. S. P.   2426

CATALOGUE of the Library of the late David James Dove. To be sold at Auction by Robert Bell, May 8, 1769. *Philadelphia : William Goddard.* 1769.   2427

CATALOGUS | von | mehr als 700 meist Deutschen | Büchern, | Welche entweder zusammen oder einzeln | zu Verkaufen sind. | ☞ Wo selbige zu sehen sind, solches kan man | erfahren bey Henrich Miller, Buchdrucker | in der Rees-strasse, gegenüber Morävien= | Alley, zu Philadelphia; bey welchem dieser | Catalogus zu haben ist, wie auch bey Herrn | Christoph Saur, in Germantaun. | [*Philadelphia : Henrich Miller.* 1769?] 16mo. pp. (32).   H. S. P.   2428

CHANDLER. (T. B.) The Appeal Defended; Or the proposed American Episcopate Vindicated, In Answer to the objections and misrepresentations of Dr. Chauncey, and others. By Thomas Bradbury Chandler. *Philadelphia: William Goddard.* 1769. 2429

CHURCHILL. (C.) Charles Churchill's Works. In two Volumes. *Philadelphia: W. and T. Bradford.* 1769. 2430

Advertised in the Pa. Journal, Jan. 19, 1769, as "This day is published and ready for the Subscribers."

DELAUNE. (T.) A Plea for the Non-Conformists. In three Parts. By Thomas Delaune. *Philadelphia: W. and T. Bradford.* 1769. 2431

DELAWARE. Anno Regni Octavo | Georgii III. Regis. | At a General Assembly begun at | New-castle, in the Government of the Coun- | ties of New-castle, Kent and Sussex, upon | Delaware, the Twentieth Day of October, | in the Eighth Year of the Reign of our So- | vereign Lord George the Third, King of | Great-Britain, &c. Annoque Domini 1768, | the following Acts were passed by the Ho- | nourable John Penn, Esquire, Governor; [June 16, 1769.] | [*Wilmington: James Adams.* 1769.] Folio, pp. 133–153. L. 2432

[DICKINSON. (John)] Letters | from a | Farmer | in | Pennsylvania, | to the | Inhabitants | of the | British Colonies. | The Third Edition. | *Philadelphia:* | *Printed by William and Thomas Bradford, at the* | *London Coffee-House.* M,DCC,LXIX. | 8vo. Title, 1 leaf; pp. 104. H. S. P. 2433

A | DISCOURSE | publickly delivered | By a Female Friend, | From Old England, | In the Friends Meeting-House, in Pine-Street, | Philadelphia, | On the Third Day of the 5th Month, 1769: | Also, | A Prayer, | By Another Friend: | The Whole taken down in Characters | (at the Time | they were spoken) | By William Darragh: | To which is added, | A Short Preface, | By the Editor. | *Philadelphia:* | *Printed in the Year* M,DCC,LXIX. | 8vo. pp. 24. · L. C. P. 2434

DISCOURSES on Several Subjects. *Philadelphia: John Dunlap.* 1769.   2435

Title from Haven's List.

EDWARDS. (J.) A Treatise concerning Religious Affections, in three Parts. By Jonathan Edwards. *Philadelphia: John Dunlap.* 1769.   2436

EIGHT Dollars Reward. | Run - Away | Last Sunday Night, Two Servant Boys, from the Subscribers, living in Philadelphia; | [*Philadelphia:* 1769.] 4to. 1 leaf.   H. S. P.   2437

Dated "Philadelphia, July 24, 1769." And signed "Peter Sutter and David Cuming."

EVERY Man his own Lawyer. *Philadelphia: John Dunlap.* 1769.   2438

AN | EXTRACT | of | Miss Mary Gilbert's | Journal. | With | Some Account of the Lady | Elizabeth Hastings, &c. | . . . | . . . | . . . | . . . | . . . . | *London, Printed:* | *Philadelphia, Reprinted and Sold by David* | *Hall, and William Sellers.* | MDCCLXIX. | 16mo. pp. viii, 66.   2439

FATHER Abraham's Pocket Almanac for 1770. *Philadelphia: John Dunlap.* 1769.   2440

FOX. (T.) The Wilmington | Almanack, | or | Ephemeris, | for | The Year of our Lord, 1770, | Being the Second after Leap-Year. | [22 lines.] | By Thomas Fox, Philom. | *Wilmington,* | *Printed and Sold by James Adams.* [1769.] | Sm. 8vo. pp. (40). 2441

FROM the | Meeting for Sufferings, | In London the 10th Day of the Third | Month, 1769, | To Friends . . . in North America. | [Followed by] From our Meeting for Sufferings, | held at Philadelphia, | For Pennsylvania and New-Jersey, the 1st | Day of the Ninth Month, 1769, | To our Friends and Brethren in these and the adjacent | Provinces. | [*Philadelphia:* 1769.] Folio, pp. 2.

Two letters against Non-Importation agreements.

THE GENTLEMAN and Citizen's Pocket Almanac for 1770. *Philadelphia: William Evitt.* 1769. + The Second Edition. 2443

𝕯𝕴𝕰 | 𝕲𝕰𝕾𝕮𝕳𝕴𝕮𝕳𝕿𝕰 | der | Tage | des | Menschen = Sohnes | von | der Marter-Woche an | bis | zu Seiner Himmelfahrt. | *Philadelphia, Gedruckt im Jahr* 1769. | *Bey Henrich Miller zu haben mit oder ohne* | *Wilcocks Honig-* | *Tropfen.* | 16mo. pp. 88. H. S. P. 2444

Thomas Wilcocks' Honig-Tropfen, which was appended, was printed at "Leipzig und Ebersdorf," in 1757.

[GREEN ? (Jacob)] The Controversy Between Great-Britain and her Colonies Reviewed; The several Pleas of the Colonies in support of their Right to all the Liberties and Privileges of British Subjects, and to Exemption from the Legislative Authority of Parliament stated and considered; And the Nature of their Connection with, and Dependence on Great-Britain, shewn upon the Evidence of Historical Facts and Authenticated Records. *Philadelphia: W. and T. Bradford.* 1769. 2445

"My own father wrote a pamphlet entitled, as well as I can recollect, Observations on the Present Controversy between Great Britain and her American Colonies." Life of Ashbel Green, p. 46.

GUALDO. (J.) Philadelphia, November 21, 1769. | To the Philharmonical | Merchants, and others. [*Philadelphia:* 1769.] Folio, 1 leaf. L. C. P. 2446

Mr. Gualdo's announcement of his Concerts on Thursday during the winter.

THE HERMIT of New-Jersey; a Collection of Poetical Essays; an Ode to Liberty, and a Dialogue between Lorenzo and the Hermit, on Human Happiness. *Philadelphia: William Goddard.* 1769.

THE HISTORY of Hypolitus, Earl of Douglas. Interspersed with Historical Anecdotes. Translated from the French. *Philadelphia: W. and T. Bradford.* 1769. 2448

H. (G.) I saw the other day, in the Pennsylvania Chronicle, a short state of the Connecticut people's claim to the lands at

Wioming, ... [*Philadelphia: W. and T. Bradford.* 1769.]
Folio, pp. (2).   H. S. P. 2449

Signed G. H., and dated May 1, 1769. An argument against the Connecticut
claim to the Wyoming region.

DAVID HALL, | At the New Printing-Office, in Market-street,
Philadelphia, has to dis- | pose of, Wholesale and Retail, the fol-
lowing Books, &c. | [*Philadelphia: D. Hall, and W. Sellers.* 1769.]
| Folio, pp. (2).   L. C. P. 2450

𝔇𝔈ℜ | 𝔥𝔒𝔠𝔥-𝔇𝔈𝔘𝔗𝔖𝔠𝔥𝔈 | Americaniſche | Calender, | Auf das
Jahr | . . . | . . . | 1770. | . . . | . . . | . . . | . . . | . . . |
. . . | . . . | . . . | . . . | . . . | . . . | Zum zwey und dreyßigſten mal her-
aus gegeben. | [*Germantown: Gedruckt und zu finden bey Christoph
Saur.* | . . . | . . . . [1769.] | 4to. pp. (48).   H. S. P. 2451

IMPORTED in the Last Vessels from London, and to be Sold
by | William and Thomas Bradford, | Printers, Booksellers, and
Stationers, | At their Book-Store in Market-Street, adjoining the
London Coffee-House; | or by | Thomas Bradford, | At his House
in Second-Street, one Door from Arch-Street, . . . | . . . | A large
and neat Assortment of | Books and Stationary. | [*Philadelphia:
W. and T. Bradford.* 1769.] Folio, pp. (2).   H. S. P. 2452

Contains the titles of over 400 works in every department of literature.

𝔇𝔍𝔈 𝔏𝔈𝔥ℜ - 𝔗𝔈𝔛𝔗 der Brüder - Gemeine, und inſonderheit der
Kinder, für das Jahr 1770. *Philadelphia: Henrich Miller.* 1769. 2453

LIBERTY, | a | Poem, | lately found in a bundle of papers, |
said to be written by | A Hermit in New-Jersey. | . . . | . . . |
. . . . | *Philadelphia:* | *Printed by William Goddard, in Market-
Street.* | MDCCLXIX. | Sm. 4to. pp. 12.   L. C. P. 2454

LIFE truly painted in the History of Tommy and Harry. *Philadelphia: Robert Bell.* 1769.   2455

[MACGOWAN. (John)] Priestcraft Defended. | A | Sermon
| occasioned by the | Expulsion | of | Six Young Gentlemen |
from the | University of Oxford. | For | Praying, Reading and

Expounding the Scriptures. | Humbly Dedicated to | Mr. V[ice] C[hancello]r and the H[ea]ds of H[ouse]s. | By Their Humble Servant, | The Shaver. | The Sixth Edition. | *London, Printed.* | *Philadelphia,* | *Re-printed, and Sold, by William and Thomas Brad-* ford | *At the London Coffee-House.* | M.DCC.LXIX. | 8vo. pp. v, 25.

MARTIN. (A.) America. | A | Poem. | By Alexander Martin, Esq; | . . . | . . . | . . . | . . . | . . . . | To which is added, | Liberty. | A | Poem. | By Rusticus. | . . . . | The Second Edition longe emendatior priore: | Likewise from Mr. Addison, in Praise of Li- | berty with Something suitable to the Times. | [*Philadelphia: Andrew Steuart.* 1769?] 12mo. pp. 28.   2457

THE MERCHANTS of this City are earnestly requested to meet at | the Coffee-House, on Monday. . . . | [*Philadelphia:* 1769. | 4to. 1 leaf.   L. C. P.   2458

<small>Call for a Non-Importation meeting, dated Feb. 4, 1769.</small>

MINUTES | of | Conferences, | held at | Fort-Pitt, | In April and May, 1768, | under the direction of | George Crogan, Esquire, | Deputy Agent for Indian Affairs, | with the | Chiefs and Warriors | of the | Ohio and other Western Indians. | [*Royal Arms.*] | *Philadelphia:* | *Printed and Sold by William Goddard, at the New Printing-* | *Office, in Market-Street.* | M,DCC,LXIX. | Folio, pp. 22.   H. S. P.   2459

MINUTES | Of the | Philadelphian | Association | in MDCCLXIX. | *Germantown:* | *Printed by Christopher Sower,* 1769. | Sm. 4to. pp. 7.   2460

MONTAGUE. (M. W.) Poetical Works of Lady Mary Wortley Montague. *Philadelphia: Robert Bell.* 1769.   2461

[MOSS.] (C.) A | Sermon | Preached before | The House of Lords, | in the | Abbey Church | of | Westminster, | On Monday, January 30, 1769. | Being the Day appointed to be observed as the Day | of the Martrydom of King Charles I. | By the Right Reverend Father in God | Charles Lord Bishop of St. David's | *London Printed:* | *Philadelphia: Re-printed, and sold by Joseph* |

Crukshank, in Second-street, two Doors below | the Corner of Chestnut-street. 1769. | 8vo. pp. 20.   H. S. P.   2462

[MURREY. (James)] Sermons | to | Asses. | The Third Edition. | *Philadelphia:* | *Re-printed by John Dunlap, at the Newest-* | *Printing-Office in Market-street,* MDCCLXIX. | 12mo. pp. 114.

" These curious Sermons have been so well received by the Publick, that an Edition of One Thousand Copies has been sold within two months." Pennsylvania Chronicle, Dec. 25, 1769. In the earlier advertisements it is said of these Sermons that they were " supposed to be written by the ingenious Dr. F[ranklin]."

[MURREY.] Sermons | to | Asses. | The Fourth Edition. | *Philadelphia:* | *Re-printed by John Dunlap, at the Newest Print-* | *ing-Office in Market-street,* MDCCLXIX. | 12mo. pp. 63, (1).   2464

𝕯𝖆𝖘 | 𝕹𝖊𝖚𝖊 | Teſtament. | Unſers | Herrn und Heylandes | Jeſu Chriſti, | Verteutſchet | Von | D. Martin Luther. | Mit | Jedes Capitels kurtzen | Summarien, | Auch beygefügten vielen richtigen | Parallelen. | Sechſte Auflage. | *Germantown:* | *Gedruckt und zu finden bey Christoph Saur,* 1769. | 12mo. Title, 1 leaf; pp. 1–529, (3). 2465

𝕯𝖊𝖗 𝕹𝖊𝖚𝖊𝖘𝖙𝖊, Verbeſſert= und Zuverlaßige Americaniſche Cal= ender Auf das 1770ſte Jahr Chriſti. *Philadelphia: Henrich Miller.* 1769.   2466

NEW-YEAR Verses of the Carriers of the Pennsylvania Chronicle. *Philadelphia: William Goddard.* 1769.   2467

THE | NEW-YEAR | VERSES, | Of the Printers Lads, who carry about the Penn- | sylvania Gazette to the Customers. | [*Philadelphia: Hall and Sellers.* 1769.] Folio, 1 leaf.   L. C. P.   2468

NEW-YEAR Verses of the Carriers of the Pennsylvania Journal. *Philadelphia: W. and T. Bradford.* 1769.   2469

A | NORTH Briton | Extraordinary: | Containing | A Concise and Comprehensive Review of | English and Scottish History, concerning im- | portant Events relative to the Union of the two | Kingdoms — Commerce — National Independency— | and the Grand Cause of Liberty: By which | it is clearly demonstrated that the Scots Nation (both | in Words and Actions) hath always been strenuous | and warm Assertors of the Liberties of the People : | Likewise some Observations on Property—Revenue | Officers— Pensioners—and rapacious Courtiers. | Written by | A Young Scotsman, | Formerly a Volunteer in the Corsican Service. | . . . | . . . | . . . . | Third Edition, with Additions. | *London, Printed :* | *Philadelphia : Re-printed by John Dunlap,* | *at the Newest Printing-Office, in Market-street.* | M,DCC,LXIX. | 12mo. pp. 50. L. C. P. 2470

OBSERVATIONS | on the | Angina Maligna : | Or, the | Putrid and Ulcerous Sore Throat. | With a | Method | Of Treating it. | By A Lover of Pennsylvania. | *Philadelphia :* | *Printed by William and Thomas Bradford, at the* | *London Coffee-House.* M.DCC.LXIX. | 8vo. pp. 7.   2471

By Dr. Rush ? " The description of the disease, which would now be called diphtheria," says Dr. W. F. Atlee, " is admirable. The treatment advised is very remarkable, inasmuch as it denounces bleeding in all cases of the disease, and is the one generally adopted nowadays." It was published in Nichola's American Magazine for 1769, and the only known copy, now in the Library of the College of Physicians, Philadelphia, is from the same type, the paging having been altered and a title-page added.

THE | PENNSYLVANIA Chronicle, | and | Universal Advertiser. | From January 23, 1769, to January 22, 1770. | . . . . | Volume III. | [*Royal Arms.*] *Philadelphia :* | *Printed by William Goddard, and Company, in Market-Street.* | 4to. Title, 1 leaf; text, pp. 1–428.   H. S. P. 2472

THE PENNSYLVANIA Gazette.   H. S. P. 2473

Numbers 2089 (Jan. 5, 1769) to 2140 (Dec. 28, 1769), four pages each, with " Supplements" of two pages to Numbers 2090, 2091, 2093, 2095, 2096, 2101, 2105, 2121, 2132, and 2134, of four pages to Numbers 2106, 2107, 2108, and 2110; " Postscripts" of 1 leaf to Numbers 2089 and 2124, and of two pages to No. 2138. Title and imprint as in No. 2382, *supra.*

THE PENNSYLVANIA Journal.   H. S. P. 2474

Numbers 1361 (Jan. 5, 1769) to 1412 (Dec. 28, 1769), four pages each, with extra half-sheets of two pages each to Numbers 1362, 1364 to 72, 1374 to 76, and 1380 to 1410; " Supplement Extra" of one leaf, to 1361; " Supplements" of two pages each to 1373–74, 1377, 1393, 1409–10; " Supplements" of four pages to 1378–79; " Postscript" of one leaf to 1403; and " Postscripts" of. two pages to 1365 and 1398. Title and imprint as in No. 2317, *supra.*

THE | PENNSYLVANIA | Pocket Almanack | For the Year
1770. | (Being the Second after Bissextile | or Leap-Year.)   Cal-
culated for the Use of the Province | of Pennsylvania, and the
neighbour- | ing Provinces. | *Philadelphia :* | *Printed and Sold, by
W. and T.* | *Bradford, at the London Coffee-House.*   [1769.] | 24mo.
pp. (28).   H. S. P.   2475

THE | PENNY Post, | Containing Fresh News, Advertise-
ments, Useful Hints, &c. | No. I. Monday, January 9, 1769. | [*Phil-
adelphia :*] *Printed and Sold by Benjamin Mecom, opposite the Pres-
byterian Meeting, in Arch-street.* | 8vo. pp. (4).   L. C. P.   2476

   Numbers 1 to 9 (Jan. 27, 1769), four pages each except the last two, which contain only two pages. It was published three times a week.

PETERS. (R.)   A | Sermon, | preached | In the New Lutheran
| Church of Zion, | in the | City of Philadelphia, | At the In-
stance of the Ministers, Wardens, | and Vestry-Men, of the incor-
porated Congre- | gation of St. Michael's, | On the 26th Day of
June, 1769. | By the Revd. Mr. Richard Peters, | Rector of Christ-
Church and St. Peter's, in | the said City. | *Philadelphia :* | *Printed
by John Dunlap, at the Newest Printing-Office,* | *in Market-street, the
Third Door below Second-street.* | M.DCC.LXIX. | 8vo. pp. 37.   2477

POOR WILL'S Almanac for 1770.   *Philadelphia : Joseph Crukshank.*   1769.   2478

PROCLAMATION.   [*Royal Arms.*]   By the Honourable |
John Penn, Esquire, | Lieutenant-Governor, and Commander in
Chief of the Province of Pennsylvania, | and Counties of New-
Castle, Kent and Sussex, upon Delaware, | A Proclamation. | *Phil-
adelphia : Printed by D. Hall, and W. Sellers.*   1769. | Folio, 1 leaf.

   Against the Connecticut settlers at Wyoming, dated May 16, 1769.

[ROOSEN. (Gerhard)] Chriſtliches | Gemüths=Geſpräch | Von dem
| Geiſtlichen und ſeligmachenden | Glauben, | Und | Erkäntnüß der
| Warheit, ſo zu | der Gottſeligkeit führet in der Hoffnung | des ewigen
Lebens, | Tit. iv. 1. | In | Frag und Antwort für die ankommende Ju-
| gend, wodurch dieſelbe zu einer heilſamen | Lebens=Uebung möchte
gereizt | und gebracht werden. | . . . . | . . . | . . . . | . . . . | . . . . |
Ephratæ Typis Societatis Anno MDCCLXIX. | 8vo. pp. 168.   2480

SAUNDERS. (R.) A Pocket Almanac for 1770. By Richard Saunders, Phil. *Philadelphia: D. Hall, and W. Sellers.* 1769.

SAUNDERS. Poor Richard improved: | Being an | Almanack | ... | ... | ... | ... | ... | ... | ... | ... | ... | ... | For the | Year of our Lord 1770 : | Being the Second after Leap-Year. | ... | ... | ... | ... | ... | ... | ... | ... | ... | By Richard Saunders, Philom. | *Philadelphia :* | *Printed and Sold by D. Hall, and W. Sellers.* [1769.] | Sm. 8vo. pp. (36).   2482

THE | SENTIMENTS | and | Plan | Of the Warren | Association. | *Germantown :* | *Printed by Christopher Sower,* 1769. | 4to. pp. 4.

An Association of Baptists, formed Sept. 8, 1767, at Warren, in Rhode Island.

SIEGVOLK. (G. P.) Das von | Jesu Christo | Dem Richter der Lebendigen und der Todten, | Aller Creatur zu predigen befohlene | Ewige Evangelium, | Von der durch Ihn erfundenen | Ewigen Erlösung, | Wodurch alles, was da heisset, Teufel, Sünde, | Hölle und Tod endlich gantz und gar vernichtiget, und | also alle Geschöpfe, die von Gott sehr gut erschaffen wor= | den, nach gnugsam geoffenbahrter Gött= lichen Straff= | Gerechtigkeit, wiederum in ihre uranfängliche Rei= | nigkeit und Seligkeit gebracht werden sollen; | Allen Menshen unter allen Nationen, und Religi= | ons=Partheyen, welche dessen Schall hören, insonderheit | aber denen, welche es zu Hertzen nehmen, und sich zu ei= | ner heiligen Gegen=Liebe gegen den so liebreichen | Gott erwecken lassen wollen. | Anjetzo | Vor denen nächst=instehenden, ja bey denen bereits angegan= | genen erschrecklichen Gerichten über diese gegenwärtige Wider=Christische Welt, | Entweder zu ihrer Bekehrung und Stärckung in dem Guten, | oder Zufalls=Weise zu ihrer Verstockung und Reissmachung | zum Gerichte; aus erbarmender Liebe verkündiget; an unzeh= | lich vielen Orten durch diesen Druck verbessert, | und nebst Hinzufügung eines | Neuen Capitels über Hebr. II. v. 16. | vom | Samen Abrahä | handlich, vermehret, | von | Georg Paul Siegvolck, | einem einfältigen Schüler der Himmlischen Weisheit. | *Germantown :* | *Gedruckt und zu finden bey Christoph Saur,* 1769. | 16mo. pp. (9), 1–175.   H. S. P.   2484

SMITH. (W.) Some | Account | of the | Charitable Corporation, | lately erected | For the Relief of the Widows and Chil- | dren of Clergymen, in the Communion of the | Church of England in America; with a Copy of | their Charters, and fundamental Rules. | And also a | Sermon, | Preached in Christ-Church, Philadelphia, Octo- | ber 10, 1769, before the said Corporation, | on Occasion of their First Meeting. | By William Smith, D.D. Provost of the | College and Academy of Philadelphia. | Published by Order, for the Benefit of the Charity. | *Philadelphia :* | *Printed by D. Hall, and W. Sellers, op-* | *posite the Jersey Market.* MDCCLXIX. | Sq. 8vo. pp. 48.   H. S. P.   2485

STANLY. (J. W.) John Wright Stanly's | Reply | to | A Few Observations, | lately Published | By Jonathan Cowpland. | *Philadelphia : Printed [by Henry Miller] in the Month of June,* 1769. | 12mo. pp. 22, (1).   N. Y. H. S.   2486

[STANLY.] Remarks | on | Scurrility and Oppression. | *Philadelphia :* | *Printed in the Year* MDCCLXIX. | 8vo. pp. 8.   2487

𝄐𝅘𝅥 𝕿𝕬𝕲𝕷𝕴𝕮𝕳𝕰𝕹 Loosungen der Brüder-Gemeine für das Jahr 1770. *Philadelphia : Henrich Miller.* 1769.   2488

[TERSTEEGEN. (Gerhard)] Geistliches | Blumen - Gärtlein | Inniger Seelen; | Oder kurtze | Schluß-Reimen | Betrachtungen und Lieder | Uber allerhand Wahrheiten des | Innwendigen Christenthums; | Zur Erweckung, Stärckung | und Erquickung | in dem | Verborgenen Leben | Mit Christo in Gott; Fünffte und vermehrte Edition. | Nebst der | Frommen Lotterie. | *Germantown,* | *Gedruckt und zu finden bey Christoph Saur.* | 1769. | 24mo. pp. (12), 517, (29).   2489

TOBLER. (J.) The Pennsylvania Town and Countryman's Almanac for 1770. By John Tobler. *Wilmington : James Adams.* 1769.   2490

THE | TRANSACTIONS | of the | American Philosophical Society, &c. | [*Philadelphia : W. and T. Bradford.* 1769.] 8vo. pp. 118, 2 plates.   L. C. P.   2491

Published in monthly parts as a supplement to the American Magazine, see No. 2416, *supra.*

VOTES | and | Proceedings | of the | House of Representatives | of the | Province of Pennsylvania, | Met at Philadelphia, on the Fourteenth of October, Anno | Domini 1768, and continued by Adjournments. | [*Royal Arms.*] | *Philadelphia:* | *Printed and Sold by William Goddard, at the New Printing-* | *Office, in Market-Street.* | MDCCLXIX. | Folio, pp. 109.   H. S. P.   2492

WEATHERWISE. (A.) Father Abraham's | Almanack, | For the Year of our Lord, | 1770 ; | Being the Second after Leap-Year. | [24 lines.] | By Abraham Weatherwise, Gent. | *Philadelphia:* | *Printed by John Dunlap, at the Newest-Print-* | *ing-Office, the South Side of the Jersey Market, and three* | *Doors below Second-street.* [1769.] | Sm. 8vo. pp. (36).   L. C. P.   2493

WHITEFIELD. (G.) Letter to his Excellency Governor Wright; giving an account of the Steps taken relative to Converting the Georgia Orphan House into a College; with the Correspondence between the Archbishop of Canterbury and Mr. Whitefield. By the Rev. George Whitefield. *Philadelphia:* 1769.   2494

WOOLMAN. (J.) First Book for Children. By John Woolman. The Third Edition. *Philadelphia:* 1769.   2495

This Title and the preceding are from Haven's List. See No. 3138, *infra.*

1770.

AN ACCOUNT of the Births and Bu- | rials in the United Churches of Christ-Church | and St. Peter's, in Philadelphia, from December 25, 1769, to December 25, 1770. By Caleb | Cash, and William Young, Clerks, and James | Weyley, and George Stokes, Sextons. | [*Philadelphia:* 1770.] Folio, 1 leaf.

AN ACCOUNT of the Burials and Baptisms in the Baptist Church, from Dec. 25, 1769, to Dec. 25, 1770. *Philadelphia:* 1770.   2497

AN ACCOUNT of the Burials in the Second Presbyterian Church, to Dec. 25, 1770. *Philadelphia:* 1770.   2498

THE ADVENTURES of a Black Coat, containing a series of remarkable occurrences and entertaining incidents; as related by itself. *Philadelphia: Robert Bell.* 1770.   2499

AGUECHEEK. (A.) The Universal American Almanac for 1771. By Andrew Aguecheek. *Philadelphia: William Evitt.* 1770.

THE ALPHABET. | Roman Letters. | A B C D E F G H I J K L M N O | P Q R S T U V W X Y Z. | a b c d e f g h i j k l m n o p q r s | t u v w x y z. | Italian Letters. | *A B C D E F G H I J K L M N | O P Q R S T U V W X Y Z. | a b c d e f g h i j k l m n o p q r s t | u v w x y z.* | English Letters. | 𝕬𝕭𝕮𝕯𝕰𝕱𝕲𝕳𝕴𝕵𝕶𝕷𝕸 𝕺 | 𝕻𝕼𝕽𝕾𝕿𝖀𝖁𝖂𝖃𝖄𝖅. | 𝔞𝔟𝔠𝔡𝔢𝔣𝔤𝔥𝔦𝔧𝔨𝔩𝔪𝔫𝔬𝔭𝔮𝔯𝔰𝔱 𝔲𝔳𝔴𝔵𝔶𝔷. | Double Letters. | ct ff ffi ffl fi fl sb sh si sk sl ss ssi st & &c. | Vowels. | a e i o u y. | Dipthongs. | ai au aw ay, ea ee ei eo ew ey, ie, oa oi oo | ou ow oy, ua ue ui uo uy. | [*Philadelphia: Henry Miller.* 1770.] 24mo. pp. 47.   H. S. P. 2501

This school-book was printed by Miller for the Moravians according to an entry in their Bethlehem Ledger dated Oct. 18, 1770.

THE | AMERICAN Calendar; | or, an | Almanack, | For the Year of our Lord, | 1771. | (Being the Third after Bissextile or Leap-Year.) | Fitted to the Latitude of 40 Degrees North, and near | Five Hours West from London ; but may, with- | out sensible Error, serve all the Northern Pro- | vinces. | Containing, | The Motions of the Sun and Moon; the true Places | and Aspects of the Planets ; the Rising and Setting | of the Sun ; the Rising, Set- ting, and Southing of | the Moon ; the Lunations, Conjunctions, Eclipses, | Rising, Setting, and Southing of the Planets ; Judg- | ment of the Weather ; Festivals, and other Re- | markable Days ; Quakers Yearly Meetings ; Fairs ; | Courts ; Table of Interest ; Roads, &c. &c. | Also, | An Essay in Praise of Husbandry ; On the Raising and | Dressing of Hemp ; To a Friend after a Debauch, An | Epigram ; Receipts for the Cure of Disorders in Sheep ; | Anecdote of the famous Mr. Sydney ; Love and Wine, | an Epi- gram ; A Lady ridiculed for Gaming ; A humour- | ous Account of one Day's Expedition ; New Methods of | killing Bugs and Fleas ; A New and approved Method of | Planting Potatoes ; Char- acter of a Miser, a Story founded | on Fact ; December, an Ode ; Genealogical List of the | Royal Family of Great-Britain ; Births and Marriages of | the Sovereign Princes of Europe ; A List of the Civil and | Military Establishment in America ; Ode on Time, &c.

| By Philo Copernicus. | *Philadelphia:* | *Printed and Sold by Wil-liam & Thomas Bradford,* | *at the London Coffee-House.* [1770.] | Sm. 8vo. pp. (48).   L. C. P. 2502

ANNO Regni | Georgii III. Regis, | Magnæ Britanniæ, Franciæ & Hiberniæ, | Decimo. | At a General Assembly of the Province of Penn- | sylvania, begun and holden at Phila-delphia, | the Fourteenth Day of October, Anno Domini 1769, in | the Ninth Year of the Reign of our Sovereign Lord | George III. by the Grace of God, of Great- | Britain, France and Ireland, King, Defender of the | Faith, &c. | And from thence continued by Adjournments to the | Twenty-fourth Day of February, 1770. | [*Penn Arms.*] | *Philadelphia:* | *Printed and Sold by D. Hall, and W. Sellers, at the | New Printing-Office, near the Market.* MDCCLXX. | Folio, pp. 34. + And from thence continued . . . to the | Six-teenth Day of May, 1770. | [*Ibid.*] Title, 1 leaf; pp. 37–38. + And from thence continued . . . to the | Twenty-ninth Day of September, 1770. | [*Ibid.*] Title, 1 leaf; pp. 41–50.   2503

BARCLAY. (R.) The | Anarchy | of the | Ranters, | And other Libertines; | The | Hierarchy | of the | Romanists, | and other | Pretended Churches, equally refused and re- | futed, in a two-fold Apology for the Church | and People of God, called in Derision, Quakers. | Wherein | They are vindicated from those that accuse them of Disorder and Confu- | sion on the one Hand, and from such as calumniate them with Tyranny | and Imposition on the other; shewing, that as the true and pure Prin- | ciples of the Gos-pel are restored by their Testimony; so is also the an- | tient Apos-tolick Order of the Church of Christ re-established among | them, and settled upon its right Basis and Foundation. | By Robert Bar-clay. | . . . | . . . | . . . | . . . . | *Philadelphia:* | *Re-printed by Joseph Crukshank,* | MDCCLXX. | 8vo.   H. S. P. 2504

Collation: Title, 1 leaf; Preface, pp. iii.–vii.; Contents, 1 page; text, pp. 1–111. See Numbers 2573 and 2578, *infra.*

CATALOGUE of Second-hand Greek and Latin Classics for sale by Robert Bell. *Philadelphia: Robert Bell.* 1770.   2505

CATALOGUE of Books to be sold at Auction, October 25, 1770. *Philadelphia: Robert Bell.* 1770. 2506

CATALOGUE of old Physical and Surgical Authors to be sold at the prices marked therein. *Philadelphia: Robert Bell.* 1770.

CATALOGUS Eorum qui in Collegio Novæ Cæsarea Laurea . . . donati sunt, 1748–1770. *Philadelphia: W. and T. Bradford.* 1770. Folio, 1 leaf. 2508

THE SHORTER CATECHISM of the Assembly of Divines at Westminster. *Philadelphia: Robert Aitkin.* 1770. 2509

From entries in Robert Aitkin's " Waste Book" it would seem that he printed the above, as well as The Longer Catechism; Mother's Catechism; Father's Catechism; Church of England Catechism; and the Proofs of the Catechism, before 1771.

DER KLEJNE | CATECHJSMUS | Des sel | D. Martin Luthers, | Nebst | Den Gewöhnlichen Morgen- Tisch- und | Aben Ge-bethern. | Welchem | Die Ordnung des Heils, | in einem Liede, in kurzen Sängen, in Frag | und Antwort, und in einer Tabelle; | Wie auch | Das Würtembergische | Kurze Kinder Examen, | Die Confirmation, Beicht, Communion- | Gebether, Lieder, ꝛc. | beygefüget; | Und | Die Ungeänderte | Augspurgische Confession, | Jngleichen das Güldene A-B-C der Kinder | angehänget ist. | Zum Gebrauch der Jugend und Alten. | Siebente Auflage. | *Philadelphia: Gedruckt und zu finden bey* | *Henrich Miller, in der Zweyten-Strasse.* 1770. | Sm. 12mo. pp. (4), 144. 2510

THE | CHARTER, | Laws, | and | Catalogue | of | Books, | of the | Library Company | of | Philadelphia. | With a Short Ac-count of the Library prefixed. | . . . . | *Philadelphia:* | *Printed by Joseph Crukshank, in Second-street.* | M,DCC,LXX. | 8vo. pp. 38, (316). H. S. P. 2511

CHRIST'S Temptations real Facts, or a defence of the Evan-gelical History. *Philadelphia: Peter Barker ?* 1770. 2512

[CLUNY. (Alexander)] The | American Traveller: | con-taining | Observations | on the | Present State, Culture and Commerce | of the | British Colonies in America, | And the further Improvements of which | they are capable; | with | An Account of the Exports, Imports and Returns | of each Colony respectively,—and of the Numbers | of British Ships and Seamen, Merchants, Traders | and Manufacturers employed by all collectively: | Together with | The Amount of the Revenue arising to Great-Britain | therefrom. | In | A Series of Letters, | Written originally to the | Right Honourable the Earl of * * * * * * * * | By an Old and Experienced Trader. | [*Philadelphia :*] *Printed* [*by Crukshank and Collins*] *in the Year* MDCCLXX. 16mo. pp. 89, (1).   H. S. P. 2513

[CRISP. (Stephen)] A | Short History | of a | Long Travel | from | Babylon | to | Bethel. | The Eighth Edition. | *Philadelphia :* | *Printed, and Sold by Joseph Crukshank, in* | *Second-street, and by Benjamin Ferriss,* | *Stationer and Book-binder in Wilmington.* [1770?] | 12mo. pp. 24.   H. S. P. 2514

DAVID. (E.) Offers of Christ | No Gospel Preaching. | To which is added, | A Word of Advice | to | A young Gospel Minister. | Written in Verse, | By Enoch David. | *Philadelphia :* | *Printed for the Author ;* | *By Henry Miller, in Second-street.* 1770. | Sm. 8vo. pp. 20.   H. S. P. 2515

DAVIES. (R.) An | Account | of the | Convincement, Exercises, | Services and Travels, | of that | Ancient Servant of the Lord, | Richard Davies. | With | Some Relation of Ancient Friends, | and the Spreading of Truth in | North-Wales, &c. | The Third Edition. | *London Printed ; And,* | *Philadelphia Reprinted by Joseph* | *Crukshank, and Isaac Collins,* | *in Third-street,* | *opposite the Work-house.* | M,DCC,LXX. | 24mo. pp. (24), 257, 6, (1).

DEIGENDESCH. (J.) Nachrichters: | Oder | Nützliches und aufrichtiges | Roß-Artzney- | Büchlein. | In welchem die meisten innerliche | Kranckheiten und äusserliche Zustände | der Roß aufs deutliche beschrieben und | erkläret werden : | Samt Beyfügung der darzu gehörigen | und nöthigsten Artzney-Mittel und approbirte | Recepte was ein jeder Zustand wird nöthig | haben, und mit deutlicher Anwei- | sung versehen. | Auch wird gelehret einige Composita | selbsten zu machen, insonderheit das sympateti- | sche Pulver und dessen Applicirung, wie | auch der Freyſchnitt mit dem | Kletten=Stock; | Welchem annoch beygefüget ein | Anhang von Rind=Viehs Artzneyen, | ſamt einem dienlichen Re= giſter. | Alles mit Fleiß zuſammen getragen, und in den | Druck verfertiget | von | Einem Scharffrichter | Johannes Deigenbeſch. | *Germantown:* | *Gedruckt bey Christoph Saur.* 1770. | 24mo. pp. 209, (7). 2517

DELAWARE. Anno Regni Nono | Georgii III. Regis. | At a General Assembly | begun at New-castle, in the Govern- | ment of the Counties of New-castle, | Kent and Sussex, upon Delaware, the | Twentieth Day of October, (and continued by Adjournment to the Twen- | ty-fourth of March following,) in the | Ninth Year of the Reign of our So- | vereign Lord George the Third, | King of Great-Britain, &c. Annoque Domini 1769, the following Acts | were passed by the Honourable John | Penn, Esquire; Governor; . . . . | [*Wilmington: James Adams.* 1770.] Folio, pp. 155–222. L. 2518

DELAWARE. Anno Regni Decimo | Georgii III. Regis. | At a General Assembly | . . . | . . . | . . . | Twentieth Day of Octo- ber, in the | Tenth Year of the Reign of our Sove- | reign Lord George the Third, | . . . 1770 . . . and continued by Ad- | journ- ment to the Third of Novem- | ber following, the following Act was passed by the Honourable John | Penn, Esquire, Governor; . . . . | [*Wilmington: James Adams.* 1770.] Folio, pp. 223–227.

DILWORTH. (T.) A New Guide to the English Tongue. By Thomas Dilworth. *Philadelphia: T. and W. Bradford.* 1770? 12mo. + *Philadelphia: Robert Aitken.* 1770. 2520

A DISCOURSE upon Perfection and Universal Redemption: To which is added, Discourses on the following Subjects, viz. 1. On Original Sin; shewing wherein Original Sin is. 2. On Election and Reprobation; shewing wherein they each stand. 3. On Baptism; occasioned by the Reading of Two Sermons on Matth. xxviii. 19, shewing the Weakness of the Author, and his Misapplication of Water Baptism, which never was more than a Type of Christ's Baptism. And A further Discourse on the same Text of Scripture; wherein it is shewed, that Christ could not mean elementary Water; neither can the Text of Scripture be taken literally, as it stands recorded. By the Author of a former Discourse on Perfection and Universal Redemption. *Philadelphia: John Dunlap.* 1770.   2521

DOCK. (C.) Eine | Einfältige und gründlich abgefaßte | Schul-Ordnung, | Darinnen deutlich vorgestelt wird, auf welche | Weiße die Kinder nicht nur in denen in Schu= | len gewöhnlichen Lehren bestens angebracht, | sondern auch in der Lehre der Gottseligkeit | wohl unterrichtet werden mögen. | Aus Liebe zu dem menschlichen Geschlecht aufgesetzt durch den | wohlerfahrnen und lang geübten Schulmeister, | Christoph Dock. | Und durch einige Freunde des gemeinen Bestens | dem Druck übergeben. | *Germantown:* | *Gedruckt und zu finden bey Christoph Saur,* 1770. | 8vo. pp. (8), 54. + The Second Edition. H. S. P. 2522

EDWARDS. (M.) A | New-Year's-Gift. | Being a sermon delivered at Phila- | delphia, on January 1, 1770 ; | and published for rectifying some | wrong reports, and preventing | others of the like sort; but chiefly | for the sake of giving it another | chance of doing good to them | who heard it. | By Morgan Edwards, A M. Fel- | low of Rhode Island college, and | minister of the Baptist church in | Philadelphia. | *Philadelphia:* | *Printed by Joseph Crukshank, in Second-* | *Street, two Doors below Chestnut-Street.* [1770.] | 8vo. pp. 14.   L. C. P. 2523

EDWARDS. Materials | towards | A History of the American Baptists, | in xii volumes. | By Morgan Edwards, A.M. | Fellow of Rhodeisland college, and Overseer | of the Baptist church in Philadelphia. | . . . | . . . . | *Philadelphia:* | *Printed by Joseph Crukshank, and* | *Isaac Collins,* MDCCLXX. | 16mo. 2524

Collation : Title, 1 leaf ; 1 plate, Title and Advertisement to Vol. I. pp. (2) ; Advertisement [Preface], pp. i.-iv. ; text, pp. 5-132 ; Errata, pp. 133-134. The title to Vol. I. is as follows : Materials | towards a history of the | Baptists in Pennsylvania both Bri- | tish and German, distinguished into | Firstday Baptists | Kerthian Baptists | Seventhday Baptists | Tuncker Baptists | Mennonist Baptists. | Vol. I. | . . . | . . . . | *Philadelphia:* | *Printed by Joseph Crukshank, and* | *Isaac Collins,* MDCCLXX. | The first historical work written and printed in Pennsylvania, and one of the most valuable contributions to our local history extant. It is not only an epitome of Baptist history, but is replete with biographical and genealogical data relating to the early settlers of the Province who were connected with that sect. It was probably not a financial success, and the second volume was not issued till 1792.—Materials | towards a history of the | Baptists in Jersey ; | distinguished into

| Firstday Baptists, | Seventhday Baptists, | Tuncker Baptists, | Rogerene Baptists. | Vol. II. | By Morgan Edwards, A.M. | And Quondam Fellow of R. I. College. | . . . | . . . . | *Philadelphia :* | *Printed by Thomas Dobson, at the Stone-* | *House, in Second-Steet.* | MDCCXCII. | 12mo. pp. 155, (1). H. S. P. The History of the Baptists in Rhode Island was printed in the sixth volume of the Collections of the Rhode Island Historical Society, and of the Delaware Baptists in the Pennsylvania Magazine of History and Biography, Vol. IX. A small edition of the latter was struck off separately. Mr. Horatio Gates Jones has in manuscript the volumes relating to Virginia, North and South Carolina, and Georgia.

EXTRACT | From an Address | in the | Virginia Gazette, | of March 19, 1767. | [*Philadelphia : Joseph Crukshank.* 1770 ?] 16mo. pp. 4. 2525

An Anti-slavery address to the Virginia Assembly.

DJE | ERNSTHAFFTE | Chriſten ﹦ Pflicht, | Darinnen | Schöne Geiſtreiche | Gebäter, | Darmit | Sich fromme Chriſten ﹦ Hertzen zu | allen Zeiten und in allen Nö﹦ | then tröſten können. | *Ephrata,* | *Drucks u. Verlags der Bruederschaft.* | *Anno* MDCCLXX. | 12mo. pp. 99, (1). H. S. P. 2526

FATHER Abraham's Pocket Almanac for 1771. *Philadelphia : John Dunlap.* 1770. 2527

FISHER, (G.) The | American Instructor : | Or, | Young Man's Best Companion. | Containing | Spelling, Reading, Writing and Arithmetic, in an | easier Way than any yet published ; and how to qualify any Person | for Business, without the Help of a Master. | Instructions to write Variety of Hands, with Copies both in Prose | and Verse. How to write Letters on Business or Friendship. | Forms of Indentures, Bonds, Bills of Sale, Receipts, Wills, | Leases, Releases, &c. | Also Merchants Accompts, and a short and easy Method of Shop and | Book-keeping ; with a Description of the several American | Colonies. | Together with the Carpenter's plain and exact Rule ; Shewing how | to measure Carpenters, Joiners, Sawyers, Bricklayers, Plaisterers, | Plumbers, Masons, Glasiers and Painters Work. How to un- | dertake each Work, and at what Price ; the Rates of each Com- | modity, and the common Wages of Journeymen ; with Gunter's | Line and Coggeshal's Description of the Sliding-Rule. | Likewise the Practical

Gauger made Easy; the Art of Dialing, and | how to erect and fix any Dial; with Instructions for Dying | and Colouring, and making Colours. | To which is added, | The Poor Planters Physician. | With Instructions for Marking on Linnen; how to Pickle and Pre- | serve; to make divers Sorts of Wine; and many excellent Plaisters | and Medicines, necessary in all Families. | And also | Prudent Advice to young Trademen and Dealers. | The whole better adapted to these American Colonies, than | any other Book of the like Kind. | By George Fisher, Accomptant. | The Fifteenth Edition Revised, and Corrected. | *Philadelphia:* | *Printed and sold by John Dunlap, at the Newest* | *Printing-Office, in Market-Street,* M,DCC,LXX. | 24mo. pp. v, 390, 1 plate.   H. S. P.   2528

THE | FOLLY and Vanity | of | A Life spent in the Pursuit of | Worldly Profit, Ease or Pleasure, | compared with | A Life wholly employed in | endeavouring to glorify God, and do | Good to Mankind; | illustrated in | Some Account | Of the pious Lady | Elizabeth Hastings, | and of | Armelle Nicolas, | A poor ignorant Country Maid in France, | Commonly known by the name of | The Good Armelle. | . . . | . . . | . . . | . . . | . . . | . . . | . . . . | *Philadelphia:* | *Printed by John Dunlap, at the Newest* | *Printing-Office, in Market-Street.* | M.DCC.LXX. | 12mo. pp. 24.   2529

FOR the Benefit of Miss Storer. | By Authority. | Never Acted There. | By the American Company, | At the Theatre in Southwark, On Friday | Next, the Thirtieth of March, will be presented A Comedy, written by | Sir Richard Steele, called, | The Tender Husband, | [17 lines.] | To which will be added a Farce, (Not perform'd this Season) called, | Miss In Her Teens. | [*Philadelphia:* 1770.]   Folio, 1 leaf.   H. S. P.   2530

FOX. (T.) The Wilmington | Almanack, | or | Ephemeris, | for | The Year of our Lord, 1771, | Being the Third after Leap-Year. | Containing | . . . | . . . | . . . | . . . | . . . | . . . | . . . | . . . | . . . | . . . . | The continuation of Mr. Harvey's Thoughts on the | Starry Heavens.—A Comparative View of | the Faculties of the Mind and Body, in order to il- | lustrate the Spirituality of the Soul.—Thoughts | Political and Moral, viz. On Subversion of Go- | vernment;—Infringment of Liberty;—Freedom; | —Conduct of Superiors; — A Country's Greatness; | — Duty of a King;—Effects of Oppression ;—Ef- | fects of two great Inequality among the Members | of a Community ;—True Oecon- omy;—Education; | —Duty to the Public ;—True Courage, &c. &c. &c. | . . . | . . . | . . . . | By Thomas Fox, Philom. | *Wilmington,* | *Printed and Sold by James Adams.* [1770.] | Sm. 8vo. pp. (40).

[FRANCKE. (August Hermann)] Der | heilige und sichere | Glaubensweg | eines | Evangelischen Christen. | . . . | . . . | . . . | . . . . | Die Zweyte Auflage. | *Philadelphia,* | *Gedruckt und zu finden bey Henrich Miller,* | *in der Zweyten-strasse.* 1770. | The | Holy and Sure | Way of Faith | of an | Evangelical Christian. | . . . | . . . | . . . | . . . . | The Second Edition. | *Philadelphia :* | *Printed and Sold by Henry Miller, in* | *Second-Street.* MDCCLXX. | 16mo. pp. 16.　　　　　　　　　　　　　　　　　　　　H. S. P.　2532

German and English on alternate pages. See No. 1804, *supra.*

FRANCKE. (M.) Einfältige | Lehr = Betrachtungen, | und kurtz- gefaßtes | Glaubens= | bekäntniß | des gottseligen Lehrers | Michael Frantzen; | Weyland gewesenen Vorstehers | der Täuffer=Gemeine in Canastogoe. | Nun zum gemeinen Besten dem Druck übergeben. | *Ger- mantown : Gedruckt bey* | *Christoph Saur,* 1770. | 16mo. pp. 47, (1).

FRANKLIN, (Benjamin) and John NEUFFVILLE. Letters, | To the Merchants Committee of Philadelphia, | Submitted to the Consideration of | The Public. | [*Philadelphia :* 1770.] Folio, 1 leaf.　　　　　　　　　　　　　　　　　　　　　　　L. C. P.　2534

THE FRIENDLY Instructor ; or, a Companion for Young La- dies and Young Gentlemen : In which their Duty to God, and their Parents, their Carriage to Superiors and Inferiors, and several other very useful and instructive Lessons, are recommended. In plain and familiar Dialogues. With a recommendatory Preface, by the Reverend Dr. Doddridge. The Seventh Edition. *Phila- delphia : Hall and Sellers.* 1770.　　　　　　　　　　　　2535

FROM the | Merchants and Traders | Of Philadelphia, in the Province of Pennsylvania, | To the | Merchants and Manufacturers | Of Great Britain. | [*Philadelphia : W. and T. Bradford.* 1770.] Folio, pp. (3).   L. C. P. 2536

" A brief view of the restrictions and burthens on our Trade," signed by 204 merchants, &c.

THE GENTLEMAN and Citizen's Pocket Almanac for 1771. *Philadelphia : William Evitt.* 1770.   2537

A GERMAN Freeholder, to his Countrymen. | [*Philadelphia : William Goddard.* 1770.] 4to. 1 leaf.   L. C. P. 2538

An Anti-Galloway election circular.

GESSNER. ([Solomon]) The | Death | of | Abel. | In | Five Books. | Attempted from the | German of Mr. Gessner. | *Lon-don, Printed ; | Philadelphia, Re-printed and Sold by Joseph | Cruk-shank, and Isaac Collins, in Third-street, | opposite the Work-house,* M,DCC,LXX. | 12mo. pp. 106.   F. 2539

GODDARD. (W.) Advertisement. | [*Philadelphia : William Goddard.* 1770.] 4to. 1 leaf.   2540

Dated Philadelphia, August 1, 1770, and signed by Wm. Goddard, in answer to Towne's To the Public, and announcing the forthcoming of " The Partnership," &c.

GODDARD. The | Partnership : | or the | History | of the | Rise and Progress | of the | Pennsylvania Chronicle, &c. | wherein the Conduct of Joseph Gallo-way, Esq; Speaker of the Honourable House | of Representatives of the Province of Penn- | sylvania, Mr. Thomas Wharton, sen. | and their Man Benjamin Towne, my late | Partners, with my own, is properly delineated, | and their calumnies against me fully refuted. | By William God-dard. | . . . | No. I. | *Philadelphia : | Printed by William Goddard, in Arch-street, between | Front and Second Streets.* | M,DCC,LXX. | 8vo. pp. 24. + No. II. pp. 25–64. + Postscript to Numb. II. pp. 65–72. + The Second Edition. + The Third Edition.   2541

DAVID HALL, | At the New Printing-Office, in Market-street, Philadelphia, has to dis- | pose of, Wholesale and Retail, the fol-lowing Books, &c. | [*Philadelphia : D. Hall, and W. Sellers.* 1770.] Folio, pp. (2).   L. C. P. 2542

HAMMOND. (W.)   Advice | to | Youth : | Being the Instruc-
tions of a Father to a Son, | On several interesting Occasions, | a
| Poem. | By William Hammond. | . . . | . . . . | *Philadelphia :* |
Printed and Sold by William Evitt, at his Printing-Office, at the | *Sign
of the Bible-in-Heart, in Strawberry-Alley.*   MDCCLXX. | 4to. pp.
13, (1).   2543

𝔇𝔈𝔖 𝔥𝔈ℜ𝔘𝔐𝔗ℜ𝔄𝔊𝔈ℜ𝔖 ber ℙennſylvaniſche Staat𝔰bote | 𝔈m=
pfehlung | an ſeine reſp. 𝔊eehrten Kunbleute, | beÿm 𝔈intritt in ba𝔰
Jahr 1770. | [*Philadelphia : Henrich Miller.* 1770.]   Folio, 1 leaf.

𝔇𝔈ℜ | 𝔥𝔒𝔆𝔥 = 𝔇𝔈𝔘𝔗𝔖𝔆𝔥𝔈 | 𝔄mericaniſche | 𝔆alenber, | 𝔄uf ba𝔰
Jahr | . . . | . . . | 1771. | . . . | . . . | . . . | . . . | . . . | . . .
. . . | . . . | . . . | . . . . | 3um breÿ unb breÿ𝔰zigſten mal herau𝔰
gegeben. | *Germantown : Gedruckt und zu finden bey Christoph Saur.*
| . . . | . . . . [1770.] | Sq. 8vo. pp. (48).   H. S. P.   2545

THE INHABITANTS of the City of New York, having broke
their | Non-Importation Agreement, . . . | . . . the Inhabitants
of this City and County, | are . . . requested to meet at the State
House, on | Saturday next, ... | [*Philadelphia :* 1770.] 4to. 1 leaf.

Dated Philadelphia, July 12, 1770.

JACKY and Maggy's Courtship.   *Philadelphia : Robert Aitken.*
1770.   2547

𝔇𝔈ℜ 𝔎𝔩𝔈𝔍ℜ𝔈 𝔎𝔄𝔗𝔈𝔆𝔥𝔍𝔈𝔐𝔘𝔖. Siebente 𝔄uflage.   *Philadelphia : Henrich Miller.* 1770.   2548

Title from Seidensticker's Bibliography.

KEARSLEY. (J.)   A | Narrative, | of many | Facts, relating
to the late disputed Will of | Samuel Flower, Esq ; | published
with a view to defend an | Injured Reputation, | and to remove |
Ill-Grounded Prejudices. | By Dr. John Kearsley, Junr. | . . . |
. . . . | *Philadelphia :* | *Printed by J. Crukshank, and I. Collins, in
Second-street, two Doors below Chestnut-street.* | M,DCC,LXX. | 4to.
pp. 16.   L. C. P.   2549

KENNEDY. (R.) To the worthy Tradesmen, Artificers, Mechanics, &c. Electors of the City and | County of Philadelphia. | [*Philadelphia:* 1770.] 4to. 1 leaf. L. C. P. 2550

Robert Kennedy soliciting the office of Sheriff, dated Oct. 1, 1770.

DIE | LEHR = TEXTE | der | Brüder = Gemeine, | für das Jahr | 1771. | enthaltend | lauter Worte | unfers | lieben Herrn und Heilandes. | . . . | . . . . | *Philadelphia,* | *Gedruckt bey Henrich Miller, im Jahr* 1770. | 8vo. Title, 1 leaf; pp. (64). H. S. P. 2551

A LETTER | From a Gentleman travelling through | Bucks County, to his Friend in | Town. | [*Philadelphia:* 1770.] Folio, pp. (4). L. C. P. 2552

Against the removal from Newtown to Bristol of the County-seat of Bucks Co.

LIBERTY. A Poem. In Imitation of Churchill. *Philadelphia: W. and T. Bradford.* 1770. 2553

THE | LIFE | and | Confession | of | Herman Rosencrantz; | Executed in the City of Philadelphia, on the 5th Day | of May, 1770, for Counterfeiting and Uttering the | Bills of Credit of the Province of Pennsylvania. | In which is an Account who were his | Confederates. | Taken from his own Mouth, in one of the Cells of the | Gaol, a short Time before he was Executed; and, by | his Request Published, as a Warning to all others. | . . . | . . . . | *Philadelphia: Printed [by Joseph Crukshank] for James Chattin, and Sold by him | at Mr. Graham's in Second-street, the second Door from | Market-street Corner, and next Door to Mr. Miles, Jeweller.* [1770.] | 8vo. pp. 10, (1). N. Y. H. S. 2554

"The sale of 2000 of this Piece makes it necessary that a new impression be struck off." Pa. Journal, June 7, 1770.

LITURGISCHE | Gesänge | der | Brüder=Gemeinen | aufs neue | revidirt. | . . . | . . . | . . . | . . . . | *Philadelphia,* | *Gedruckt bey Henrich Miller, im Jahr* 1770. | 16mo. pp. 48. 2555

[LIVINGSTON. (William)] A Review of the Military Operations in North-America; From the Commencement of the French

Hostilities on the Frontiers of Virginia, in 1753, to the surrender of Oswego, on the 14th of August, 1756. *Philadelphia: W. and T. Bradford.* 1770.   2556

[MACPHERSON (John)] Letter to John Dickinson, Esq; | [*Philadelphia: Robert Bell.* 1770.] 8vo. pp. 4.   L. C. P. 2557

Dated Philadelphia, November 13, 1770.

[MACPHERSON. (John)] Macpherson's | Letters, &c. | *Phila-delphia: | Printed for the Author, [by Wm. Evitt] in the Year* 1770. | 8vo. Half title, 1 leaf; pp. vii, 105, 1 leaf of Errata. H. S. P. 2558

MANY respectable Freeholders . . . of this City . . . justly alarmed at the Resolutions . . . of the Dry Goods Importers, ... [*Philadelphia:* 1770.] 4to. 1 leaf.   H. S. P. 2559

Call for a public meeting, dated " Thursday, September 27, 1770."

MANY respectable Freeholders, &c. [*Philadelphia:* 1770.] 4to. 1 leaf.   L. C. P. 2560

A reprint of the preceding, with proceedings and resolves of the meeting. Dated " Philadelphia, Thursday, September 27, 1770."

𝔙𝔒𝔏𝔏𝔖𝔗Ä𝔑𝔇𝔍𝔊𝔈𝔖 | 𝔐𝔄𝔕𝔅𝔘𝔕𝔊𝔈𝔕 | Gefang= | Buch | Zur | Uebung der Gottseligkeit | in 649 Christlichen und Trostreichen | Psalmen und Gesängen | Hrn. D. Martin Luthers. | und andrer | Gottseliger Lehrer, | Ordentlich in XII. Theile verfasset, | Und mit nöthigen Re= gistern auch einer Verzeichniß versehen, | unter welche Titul die im Anhang befindlichen Lieder gehörig: | Auch zur beförderung | des so Kirchen= als Privat=Gottesdienstes, | Mit erbaulichen | Morgen= Abend= Buß= Beicht= und | Communion=Gebätlein vermehret. | *Germantown: | Gedruckt und zu finden bey Christoph Saur,* 1770. | 12mo. pp. (12), 490, (15), 13, 82, (1).   H. S. P. 2561

MARMONTEL. ([Jean François]) The | History | of | Beli-sarius, | the heroick and humane | Roman General. | A Man who possessed the most immoveable Fidelity, and practised | the most disinterested Patriotism, in the Court of a weak Empe- | ror, sur-rounded by a Junto of as corrupt and abandoned Mini- | sters, as ever enslaved and disgraced Humanity; whose Malice | and Envy remained unsatiated, till by misrepresentation and per- | jury they accomplished the Downfal of this greatest and most ex- | cellent of all human Beings, in whose amiable and exalted | Character every Virtue exists that is admirable or desirable, | in the | Sage Lawgiver, | Brave Hero, | Noble Patriot, | Profound Politician, | Exploring Philosopher, | Sober Citizen, | Judicious Farmer, | Honest Lawyer, | Or in the most humble, | And most perfect Divine. | A New Translation from the French of M. Marmontel, | Member of the Royal Academy. | *Philadelphia : Printed and sold by Joseph Crukshank, in Third-street.* | MDCCLXX. | 12mo. pp. viii, 135.   2562

[MECOM. (Benjamin)] Philadelphia, Sept. 11, 1770. | [*Philadelphia : Benjamin Mecom.* 1770.] Sm. 4to. pp. (2). H. S. P.   2563

A printed letter from a nephew of Benjamin Franklin, to the Mayor, Recorder, and Aldermen : "Sir, Be pleased to permit me to inform you, that I have been in this City, a few Months more than two Years, during which Time I have endeavoured to get constant Employment at my own Business, but being disappointed, my Wife (the Bearer hereof) has been frequently advised to apply to your Worship for a Recommendation to his Honour the Governor, to grant us a Licence to sell spirituous Liquors by small Measure, at a House we have now liv'd in almost a Quarter, where such Sale has been continued. We are not fond of the Prospect it affords, farther than as it may contribute to support a Number of young growing Children, whose Welfare we would earnestly and honestly endeavour to secure. If you, Sir, after Inquiry, should judge we are improper Persons to recommend, in this Case, I have only to desire that you will excuse the Application from Your respectful humble Servant, *Benjamin Mecom*, Printer."

MILTON. (J.) An old | Looking-Glass | for the | Laity and Clergy | of all denominations, | Who either give or receive Money under Pretence | of the Gospel : | Being | Considerations | touching | The likeliest Means to remove Hirelings out of the | Church of Christ. | Wherein are also discoursed of | Tythes, | Church-Fees, Church-Revenues, | Christenings, | Marriages, | Burials, | and | Whether any Maintenance of Gospel-Servants | ought to be settled by Law. | By John Milton, Author of Paradise Lost. | With the Life of Milton : | Also large Extracts from his Works, concerning Bishops. | . . . | . . . | . . . | . . . | . . . | . . . | . . . | . . . | . . . . . . | . . . | . . . | . . . | . . . | . . . | . . . . | *Philadelphia :* | *Printed for Robert Bell, and sold by J. Crukshank, and | I. Collins, Printers in Third-street.* M,DCC,LXX. | 12mo. pp. i–x, 1–74. H. S. P.   2564

MINUTES | of the | Philadelphian Association | In MDCCLXX. | [*Philadelphia: Henry Miller*. 1770.] Sm. 4to. pp. 8.

[MURREY. (James)] Sermons to Asses. The Fifth Edition. *Philadelphia: John Dunlap*. 1770.   2566

DER NEUESTE, Verbeffert= und Zuverläßige | Americanifche | Calender | Auf das 1771fte Jahr Chrifti, | Welches ein gemein Jahr von 365 Tagen ift. | . . . | . . . | . . . | . . . | . . . | . . . | . . . . | Wie auch | Eine kurzgefaßte Hiftorifche Nachricht von America; nebft verfchiedenen | wißigen Stücken, 2c. 2c. | . . . | . . . . | Zum Achtenmal herausgegeben. | *Philadelphia, Gedruckt und zu finden bey Henrich Miller, in der Zweyten-strasse.* | . . . | . . . | . . . . [1770.] | 4to. pp. (40).   H. S. P. 2567

THE NEW ENGLAND Primer improved. *Philadelphia: Robert Aitken*. 1770.   2568

NEW-YEAR Verses of the Carriers of the Pennsylvania Chronicle. *Philadelphia: William Goddard*. 1770.   2569

THE | NEW-YEAR | Verses, | Of the Printers Lads, who carry about the Penn- | sylvania Gazette to the Customers. | [*Philadelphia: Hall and Sellers*. 1770.] Folio, 1 leaf.   L. C. P. 2570

NEW-YEAR Verses of the Carriers of the Pennsylvania Journal. *Philadelphia: W. and T. Bradford*. 1770.   2571

DIE | PARADIESISCHE Aloe | der Jungfräulichen Keufchheit | welche Gott giebet allen, die da | find aus dem Glauben an den | Herren Jefum; | Wobey gelehret wird, wie | diefes | Himlifche Gewächs | mit Chrifti Dornen=Cron, | Als | Einem Leb=Hag umzäunet werden müffe, | damit es nicht von der höchft=fchädlichen, | gifftigen Fleifches=Luft verder= | bet werde. | Gefammlet und ausgepreffet | von | Gratiano Chriftophilo. | . . . | . . . . | *Germantown: | Gedruckt bey Christoph Saur*, 1770. | 16mo. pp. 303, (1).   H. S. P. 2572

PENN. (W.) A Brief | Account | of the | Rise and Progress | Of the People called | Quakers, | in which | Their Fundamental Principle, Doctrines, Worship, | Ministry and Discipline, are plainly declared. | With a Summary Relation | Of the Former Dispensations of God in the | World by Way of Intro-duction. | . . . . | The Sixth Edition. | By William Penn. | *Phila-delphia* : | *Re-printed by Joseph Crukshank.* | MDCCLXX. | 8vo.

Collation : Title, 1 leaf; Epistle, pp. (2) ; Contents, pp. (2) ; text, pp. 1–88. The first of " Three Treatises," No. 2598, *infra.* It is, however, sometimes found sepa-rately.

THE PENNSYLVANIA Chronicle. Folio, pp. 1–210. 2574

Numbers 159 (Jan. 29, 1770) to 210 (Jan. 21, 1771), four pages each. Title as in No. 2315, *supra,* but in smaller type and with a smaller cut of the Royal Arms. The imprint varies frequently. Until No. 183, it was printed by Goddard and Towne, but from that Number Towne's name was withdrawn. The paper was printed in three columns on a smaller folio sheet than during the first year.

THE PENNSYLVANIA Gazette. 2575

Numbers 2141 (Jan. 4, 1770) to 2192 (Dec. 27, 1770), four pages each, with " Sup-plements" of two pages to Numbers 2141, 2146 to 2152, 2158 to 2172, 2174 and 2175, and " Postscripts" of one leaf to Numbers 2152, 2157, 2158, 2160, and 2161, and of two pages to No. 2159. Title and imprint as in No. 2382, *supra.*

THE PENNSYLVANIA Journal. 2576

Numbers 1413 (Jan. 4, 1770) to 1464 (Dec. 27, 1770), four pages each, with extra half sheets of two pages to Numbers 1416, 1437, 1439, 1440, 1442, 1446, 1448, 1450, 1451, 1452, 1454, 1456, 1458, 1460, and 1461 ; " Supplements" of two pages to Num-bers 1413, 1419 (misnumbered 1491), 1420, 1422 to 1426, 1429, 1433, 1435, 1445, and 1449, of four pages to Numbers 1430 and 1444 ; " Postscripts" of two pages to Num-bers 1424 and 1430. Title and imprint as in No. 2317, *supra.*

THE PENNSYLVANIA Pocket Almanac for 1771. *Phila-delphia : W. and T. Bradford.* 1770. 2577

PIKE. (J.) An | Epistle | to the | National Meeting | of | Friends, | in | Dublin, | Concerning good Order and Discipline in | the Church. | Written by Joseph Pike. | *Philadelphia :* | *Re-printed by Joseph Crukshank,* 1770. | 8vo. pp. 24. H. S. P. 2578

See Numbers 2598 and 2573, *infra.*

POOR Robin's Almanac for 1771. *Philadelphia : William Evitt.* 1770. 2579

POOR Will's Almanac for 1771. *Philadelphia: Joseph Cruk-shank.* 1770. 2580

POOR Will's | Pocket Almanack, | For the Year 1771; | Fitted to the Use of Pennsylvania, | and the neighbouring Prov-inces. | Containing, | A great Variety of useful Lists | and Tables. | *Philadelphia:* | *Printed and Sold by Joseph Cruk-* | *shank, in Third-street, near the Harp-* | *and-Crown Tavern, and opposite the* | *Work-House.* [1770.] | 24mo. pp. (36). H. S. P. 2581

. . . A RIDDLE. | [*Philadelphia:* 1770.] 4to. 1 leaf. 2582

An election squib signed " A White Oak." Du Simitiere's copy is dated in ink " 7ber, 1770."

ROBERTSON. (W.) The | History | of the | Reign | of | Charles the Fifth, | Emperor of Germany; | And of all the King-doms and States in Europe, | during his Age. | To which is pre-fixed, a View of the | Progress of Society | In Europe, | From the Subversion of the Roman Empire, to the | Beginning of the Six-teenth Century. | Confirmed by | Historical Proofs and Illustra-tions. | In Three Volumes. | By William Robertson, D.D. | . . . | . . . | . . . . | Volume the First. | *America:* [*Philadelphia:*] *Printed for the Subscribers,* [*by Robert Bell.*] | M,DCC,LXX. | 8vo. 2583

Collation : Advertisement, 1 leaf; Dedication to the English Edition, pp. (2); Dedication of the American Edition, pp. (2); Contents, pp. (10); Preface, pp. v.–viii.; Title to the " Progress of Society," 1 leaf; text, pp. 360.+Volume the Second. [*Ibid.*] 8vo. Title, 1 leaf; Contents, pp. (14); text, pp. 374.+Volume the Third. [*Ibid.*] 8vo. Advertisement, 1 leaf; Title, 1 leaf; List of Subscribers, pp. (19); Address from the Publisher, pp. (6); Contents, pp. (14); text, pp. 351; Adver-tisement, 1 page; Index to Progress of Society, pp. (14); Index to Charles V. pp., (45).

[ROOSEN. (Gerhard)] Chriſtliches | Gemüths = Geſpräch | Von dem | Geiſtlichen und ſeligmachenden | Glauben, | Und | Erkäntnuſz der Warheit, | ſo zu der Gottſeligkeit führet in | der Hoffnung des ewigen | Lebens, Tit. I, i. | Ans Licht gegeben | In Frag und Antwort für die ankommende Ju= | gend, wodurch dieſelbe zu einer heilſamen Le= | bens=Uebung möchte geretſzt und gebracht | werden, | Der Warheit zum Beſten. | *Ephrata: Typis Societatis* | *Anno* MDCCLXX. | 12mo. pp. 248. 　　　　　　　　　　　　　　H. S. P.　2584

Printed with " Der Ernsthaffte Christen-Pflicht." The paging is begun anew, but the signatures are continuous.

SAUNDERS. (R.) A Pocket Almanac for 1771. By Richard Saunders, Phil. *Philadelphia: Hall and Sellers.* 1770.　2585

SAUNDERS. Poor Richard improved: | Being an | Almanack | . . . | . . . | . . . | . . . | . . . | . . . | . . . | . . . | . . . | . . . | . . . | For the | Year of our Lord 1771 : | Being the Third after Leap-Year. | . . . | . . . | . . . | . . . | . . . | . . . | . . . | . . . | . . . | . . . . | By Richard Saunders, Philom. | *Philadelphia:* | *Printed and Sold by D. Hall, and W. Sellers.* [1770.] | Sm. 8vo. pp. (36).　　2586

SAUVAGES, (François Bossier de) and (—) PULLIEN. Directions | for the | Breeding and Management | of | Silk-Worms. | Extracted from the Treatises of | The Abbé Boissier de Sauvages, and Pullien. | With a | Preface, | giving some | Account | Of the Rise and Progress | of the | Scheme | For encouraging the | Culture of Silk, | In Pennsylvania, and the adjacent Colonies. | *Philadelphia:* | *Printed by Joseph Crukshank, and Isaac Collins.* | M,DCC,LXX. | 8vo. pp. xv, (1), 32.　　　　　　H. S. P.　2587

[SEARSON. (John)] Two | Discourses | Delivered in the Prison of | Philadelphia, | On the two following Texts ; | Matthew xv. 25. | . . . | Isaiah xlv. 15 | . . . | . . . . | By a Lay-Man of the Church of England. | . . . | . . . . | *Philadelphia:* | *Printed and sold by William Evitt, at the Sign of the* | *Bible-in-Heart, in Strawberry-Alley, for the Benefit of* | *the Prisoners of the said Prison.* [1770.] | 8vo. pp. 17.　　　　　　　　　　　　　　N. Y. H. S.　2588

SECCOMBE. (J.) Eine zu Halifax den 3ten July 1770 gehaltene Predigt an der Hochdeutſch = Reformirte Gemeine zu Lüneburg in Nova Scotia, bey der Ordination des Ehrw. Herrn Bruin Romcas Comingoe. Durch Mag. John Seccombe; nebſt einem Anhange. Aus dem Engliſchen überſetzt. *Philadelphia: Henrich Miller.* 1770.　　2589

Advertised in Der Pennsylvanische Staatsbote, Feb. 5, 1770.

SEVEN Hints | For all who will take them. | By | A Church of England-Man. | [*Philadelphia :* 1770.]   L. C. P.   2590

Anti-Non-Importation circular signed " J. S."   M. Hillegas says published July 17, 1770.

A SHORT but serious Address to the Inhabitants of Pennsylvania, by a Well wisher to his King and Country. *Philadelphia : William Goddard.* 1770.   2591

A SHORT Narrative of the Massacre in Boston, perpetrated by a party of Soldiers under the command of Captain Preston of the 29th Regiment. *Philadelphia : Robert Bell.* 1770.   2592

SMITH. (W.) An | Account | of the | Charitable Corporation, | lately erected | For the Relief of the Widows and Chil- | dren of Clergymen, in the Communion of | the Church of England in America; with a | Copy of their Charters, and Funda- | mental Rules. | And also a | Sermon, | Preached in Christ-Church, Philadelphia, | October 10, 1769, before the said Corpora- | tion, on Occasion of their First Meeting. | By William Smith, D.D. Provost of | the College and Academy of Philadelphia. | Published, by Order, for the Benefit of the Charity. | The Second Edition. | *Philadelphia :* | *Printed by D. Hall, and W. Sellers,* | *opposite the Jersey Market.* MDCCLXX. | 8vo. pp. 56.   L. C. P.   2593

A | SOLILOQUY. | . . . | . . . | . . . | . . . | . . . . | [*Philadelphia :*] *Printed* [*by John Dunlap*] *in the Year* 1770. | 4to. Title, 1 leaf; pp. 15.   L. C. P.   2594

SPERBER. (J.) Kabalisticae precationes, d. i. auserlefene ſchöne Gebete, denen auch beigefüget Iſagoge, d. i. Einleitung zur wahren Erkenntniſs des dreieinigen Gottes und der Natur, ꝛc. *Philadelphia :* 1770.   2595

Title from Weller's *Die falschen Druckorte.*

STEVENSON. (R.) Military Instructions for Officers. By Roger Stevenson. *Philadelphia :* 1770. 12mo.   2596

Title from Haven's List.   Probably misdated 1770 for 1776.

𝔇𝔍𝔈 | 𝔗𝔄𝔊𝔏𝔍𝔈𝔥𝔈𝔑 | Loofungen | der | Brüder=Gemeine | für das Jahr | 1771. | *Philadelphia,* | *Gedruckt bey Henrich Miller, im Jahr* 1770. 8vo. pp. (58). 　　　　H. S. P.　2597

THREE | Treatises, | in which | The Fundamental Principle, | Doctrines, Worship, Ministry | and Discipline of the People called | Quakers, | are plainly declared. | The first, | By William Penn, in England; | The second, | By Robert Barclay in Scotland; | The third | By Joseph Pike, in Ireland. | *Philadelphia:* | *Re-printed by Joseph Crukshank,* | MDCCLXX. | 8vo. 1 leaf.　　H. S. P.　2598

The three tracts are sometimes met with separately, and will be found under their respective authors. When found together, some copies contain a list of books, &c., "To be Sold by Benjamin Ferris . . . in Wilmington," pp. (4).

TO the Free and Patriotic Inhabitants of the City of | Philad. & Province of Pennsylvania; | [*Philadelphia:* 1770.] Folio, 1 leaf.

Dated "May 31st, 1770," and signed "A Lover of Liberty and a Mechanic's Friend."

TO the Freeholders, Merchants, Tradesmen and Farmers, of the City and County of Philad. | [*Philadelphia:* 1770.] 4to. 1 leaf.

"A Freeholder," against indiscriminate Non-Importation, dated "Sept. 26, 1770." In answer to "A Tradesman"'s address of the 24th of Sept.

TO the Inhabitants of the City and County of | Philadelphia. | [*Philadelphia:* 1770.] Folio, 1 leaf.　　　　L. C. P.　2601

"A Pennsylvanian" in favor of Non-Importation. "The New Yorkers have betrayed a Meanness and Cowardice in deserting us in the present important Juncture, which wants a name."

TO the Merchants, and Traders, of | the City of Philadelphia. | [*Philadelphia:* 1770.] Folio, 1 leaf.　　　　L. C. P.　2602

Address in favor of a Non-Importation agreement.

TO the Merchants Committee, the Dry Goods Merchants, &c. | [*Philadelphia:* 1770.] 4to. 1 leaf.　　　　L. C. P.　2603

In favor of home manufactures. Signed "An American," and dated "Philadelphia, May 12, 1770."

TO the Public. | [*Philadelphia*: 1770.]   Folio, 1 leaf.   2604

Philadelphus against Non-Importation agreements.

TO the Public. | [*Philadelphia*: 1770.]   Folio, 1 leaf.   2605

Messrs. Semple, Bartram, Steuart, and Wilson's acknowledgment of having
violated the Non-Importation agreement, dated "June 30 and July 4, 1770."

TO the | Tradesmen, Farmers, and other Inhabitants of the
City and County | of Philadelphia. | [*Philadelphia*: 1770.]   4to.
1 leaf.   L. C. P.   2606

"A Tradesman" in favor of Non-Importation, dated "Northern Liberties, September 24, 1770."

TOBLER (J.)   The | Pennsylvania | Town and Country-
man's | Almanack, | for | The Year of our Lord, 1771, | Being
the Third after Leap-Year. | [21 lines.] | By John Tobler, Esq;
| *Wilmington,* | *Printed and Sold by James Adams.* [1770.] | Sm.
8vo. pp. (40).   2607

TOWNE. (Benjamin)   To the Public, and particularly the
kind Customers | of the Pennsylvania Chronicle, &c. | [*Phila-
delphia*: 1770.]   Folio, pp. (2).   2608

THE TRADESMEN, Artificers and other Inhabitants | . . .
are ear- | nestly requested to attend at the State House on |
Wednesday . . . . | [*Philadelphia*: 1770.] 4to. 1 leaf. L. C. P.   2609

Dated "Philadelphia, May 22, 1770."   A call for a public meeting.

THE TRIAL of His R. H. the D[uke] of C[umberland]
for Criminal Conversation with Lady Harriet G[rosverno]r.   To
which is Prefixed, an Introductory Discourse upon the ancient
and modern Punishments of Adultery, and the uncommon Progress of that Crime.   Including all the Letters which have
passed between his Royal Highness and her Ladyship, and were
read in Court.   *Philadelphia: John Dunlap.* 1770.   2610

TWO Letters from Brutus to the Duke of Cumberland.
Philadelphia: William Evitt. 1770.   2611

UNIVERSAL Restitution, a Scripture doctrine. Proved in several letters wrote on the nature and extent of Christ's Kingdom. *Philadelphia: Peter Barker?* 1770.   2612

VOTES | and | Proceedings | of the | House of Representatives | of the | Province of Pennsylvania, | Met at Philadelphia, on the Fourteenth of October, Anno | Domini 1769, and continued by Adjournments. | [*Royal Arms.*] | *Philadelphia:* | *Printed and Sold by Henry Miller, in Second-Street,* | MDCCLXX. | Folio, Title, 1 leaf; pp. 113–201.   H. S. P.   2613

WE, the Shopkeepers of Philadelphia, and Places adjacent, | whose Names are hereunto subscribed, labouring under many and great | Difficulties in the present languishing Condition of Trade in this City, | partly owing to the unrestrained Liberties of Vendues, have found it necessary | and expedient to come into an Agreement not to purchase any Goods so exposed to | publick Sale, ... | [18 lines.] | *Philadelphia, Printed by Henry Miller, in Second-street.* [1770.] | 4to. 1 leaf. + The same in German. [*Ibid.*] 4to. 1 leaf.   2614

WEATHERWISE. (A.)   Father Abraham's | Almanack, | For the Year of our Lord, | 1771; | Being the Third after Leap-Year. | [25 lines.] | By Abraham Weatherwise, Gent. | *Philadelphia:* | *Printed and Sold by John Dunlap, at the* | *Newest-Printing-Office, the South Side of the Jersey* | *Market, and Three Doors below Second-street.* [1770.] | Sm. 8vo. pp. (36).   H. S. P.   2615

WESLEY. (J.) Primitive Physic, or an easy and natural Method of curing most Diseases. The Fourteenth Edition. By John Wesley. *Philadelphia: Joseph Crukshank.* 1770. 12mo. pp. xviii, 83.   2616

WHEATLEY. (P.) An Elegiac Poem, on the Death of that celebrated Divine and eminent servant of Jesus Christ the Rev. Geo. Whitefield. By Phillis Wheatley. *Philadelphia: William Goddard.* 1770.   2617

WITHERSPOON. (J.) Practical Discourses on the Leading Truths of the Gospel. By John Witherspoon, D.D. *Philadelphia: W. and T. Bradford.* 1770.   2618

WOOLMAN. (J.) Considerations | on the | True Harmony | of | Mankind; | And how it is to be maintained. | By John Woolman. | . . . | . . . | . . . | . . . . | *Philadelphia : Printed by Joseph Crukshank,* | *in Third-Street,* MDCCLXX. | 12mo. pp. 33.   2619

WOOLMAN. An | Extract | from | John Woolman's | Journal in Manuscript, | concerning the | Ministry. [*Philadelphia :* 1770 ?] 8vo. pp. 7.   F.   2620

ZIGUERER. (C.) Theologisches | Bedenken | zur | Beantwortung der Frage : | Woher das jetzige Verderben der Chri= | stenheit in Lehr und Leben komme ? | von | Christian Ziguerer, | Prediger zu Grüsch, in Grau-bündten | *Berlin, Gedruckt bey L. Winter,* 1769. | *Philadelphia, Nach-gedruckt und zu finden bey* | *Henrich Miller, in der Zweyten-strasse.* 1770. | Sm. 8vo. pp. 46.   2621

1771.

AN ACCOUNT of the Burials and Baptisms in the Baptist Church. *Philadelphia :* 1771.   2622

AN ACCOUNT of the Burials in the Second Presbyterian Church. *Philadelphia :* 1771.   2623

AN | ACT | for the | Relief | of the | Poor. | [*Penn Arms.*] | *Philadelphia :* | *Printed and Sold by D. Hall, and W. Sel-* | *lers, at the New-Printing-Office, near the* | *Jersey-Market.* | MDCCLXXI. | 8vo. Title, 1 leaf; pp. 30.   H. S. P.   2624

AGUECHEEK. (A.) The Universal American | Almanack, | or yearly | Magazine. | . . . | . . . | . . . . | For the Year of our Lord 1772, | Being Bissextile or Leap - Year. | [22 lines.] | By Andrew Aguecheek, Esq; Philom. | *Philadelphia : Printed by William* | *Evitt, at the Bible-in-Heart, in Strawberry-Alley,* | *opposite the Bull's-Head Tavern.* [1771.] | Sm. 8vo. pp. (40). H. S. P. 2625

THE AMERICAN Calendar for 1772. *Philadelphia : W. and T. Bradford.* 1771.   2626

DER | AMERICANISCHE | Calender | Auf das 1772ste Jahr Christi, | Welches ein Schalt=Jahr von 366 Tagen ist. | Enthaltend |

Die Wochen= Monaths= Namen= und Feyer=Tage, | Der Sonnen und
des Monden Auf= und Untergang, die Monds= | Viertel und Zeichen,
das Hohe Wasser in Philadelphia, | und andere gewöhnliche Calender=
Arbeit; | Wie auch | Einige Politische und andere Moralische Stücke. |
Nach der Pennsylvanischen Himmels = Gegend berechnet. | *Ephrata, mit
Bewilligung der Bruederschaft gedruckt von Albert Conrad Reben.*
[1771.] | Sm. 4to. pp. (40).   2627

ANDERSON. (W.)   The History of France, during the
Reigns of Francis II. and Charles IX. By Walter Anderson,
D.D. In Two Volumes. *Philadelphia?* 1771.   2628

Advertised by W. and T. Bradford for more than eighteen months, but probably
referring to an English edition.

ANNO Regni | Georgii III. Regis, | Magnæ Britanniæ, Franciæ
& Hiberniæ, | Undecimo. | At a General Assembly of the Province
of Penn- | sylvania, begun and holden at Philadelphia, | the
Fourteenth Day of October, Anno Domini 1770, in | the Tenth
Year of the Reign of our Sovereign Lord | George III. by the
Grace of God, of Great- | Britain, France and Ireland, King,
Defender of the | Faith, &c. | And from thence continued by
Adjournments to the | Ninth Day of March, 1771. | [*Penn Arms.*]
| *Philadelphia:* | *Printed and Sold by D. Hall, and W. Sellers
at the* | *New Printing-Office, near the Market.* MDCCLXXI. | Folio,
Title, 1 leaf; pp. 53–153, (1). + And from thence continued . . .
to the | Twenty-fifth Day of September, 1771. | [*Ibid.*] Title, 1
leaf; pp. 157–165.   H. S. P.   2629

BATES. (W.) The | Harmony | of the | Divine Attributes,
| in the | Contrivance and Accomplishment | of | Man's Re-
demption | by the | Lord Jesus Christ: | or, | Discourses |
Wherein is shewn | How the Wisdom, Mercy, Justice, Holiness,
Pow- | er, and Truth of God are glorified in that | great and
blessed Work. | By William Bates, D.D. | . . . . | *London, Printed:*
| *Wilmington, Reprinted, and Sold by* | *James Adams, in Market-
street,* 1771. | 16mo. pp. iv, 501, (11).   H. S. P.   2630

BELL. (Robert) Proposals for reprinting Ferguson's Essay
on the History of Civil Society. *Philadelphia: Robert Bell.* 1771.

BELL. Proposals for reprinting Hume's History of England, in eight volumes. *Philadelphia: Robert Bell.* 1771.   2632

BENEZET. (A.) Some | Historical Account | of | Guinea, | Its Situation, Produce and the general Dis- | position of its Inhab- itants. | With | An inquiry into the Rise and Progress of the | Slave-Trade, its Nature and lament- | able Effects. | Also | A Re- publication of the Sentiments of seve- | ral Authors of Note, on this interesting | Subject; particularly an Extract of a | Treatise, by Granville Sharp. | By Anthony Benezet. | . . . | . . . | . . . | . . . | . . . | . . . | . . . | . . . | . . . | . . . | . . . | . . . | . . . | *Philadelphia : Printed by Joseph Cruk- | shank, in Third-street, opposite the Work-house.* | M,DCC,LXXI. | 12mo.   H. S. P.   2633

Collation: Title, 1 leaf; Contents, pp. (3); Introduction, pp. i.–iv.; text, pp. 1–144; Extract, &c., pp. 1–53; Index, pp. (6). The "Extract" has the following title: Extract | from a | Representation | of the | Injustice | and | Dangerous Tendency | of tolerating | Slavery, | or | Admitting the least Claim of private Pro- | perty in the Persons of Men in England. | By Granville Sharp. | *London: Printed* MDCCLXIX. | *Philadelphia : Re-printed by Joseph Cruk- | shank, in Third-street, opposite the Work-house.* | MDCCLXXI. |

[BLACKBURNE. (Francis)] A Critical | Commentary | on | Archbishop Secker's Letter | to the | Right Honourable Horatio Walpole, | concerning | Bishops in America. | . . . | . . . | . . . . | *Philadelphia : | Printed and Sold by John Dunlap, at the | Newest Printing-Office, in Market-Street.* | M,DCC,LXXI. | 8vo. pp. 72.

BLACKSTONE. (W.) Commentaries | on the | Laws | of | England. | In Four Books. | By | Sir William Blackstone, Knt. | One of his Majesty's Judges of the Court of Common Pleas. | Re- Printed from the British Copy, | Page for Page with the Last Edi- tion. | *America: | Printed for the Subscribers, | By Robert Bell, at the late Union Library, in Third-street, | Philadelphia.* MDCCLXXI. | 8vo. pp. (12), 485. + Book the Second. | [*Ibid.*] MDCCLXXI. pp. (8), 520, xix.   H. S. P.   2635

For the third and fourth volumes, see 1772.

CADOGAN. (W.) A | Dissertation | on the | Gout, | and all | Chronic Diseases, | jointly considered, | As proceeding from the same Causes; | What those Causes are; | And | A rational and natural Method of Cure | proposed. | Addressed to all Invalids. | By William Cadogan, | Fellow of the College of Physicians. | . . . . | *London, Printed :* | *Philadelphia : Re-printed and Sold by* | *William and Thomas Bradford.* | M.DCC.LXXI. | 8vo. pp. v, 51.

CATALOGUE of Books to be sold at Auction, October 7, 1771. *Philadelphia : Robert Bell.* 1771. 2637

CATALOGUE of Books to be sold at Auction, December 2, 1771. *Philadelphia : Robert Bell.* 1771. 2638

CATALOGUE | of | Drugs, | Chymical and Galenical | Preparations, | Shop Furniture, | Patent Medicines, | and | Surgeons Instruments, | sold by | John Day, and Co. | Druggists and Chymists, | in | Second-Street, | Philadelphia. | *Philadelphia :* | *Printed by John Dunlap, in Market-Street.* | M.DCC.LXXI. | 8vo. pp. 33. 2639

DEIGENDESCH. (J.) Nachrichters, oder Roß-Arßney = Büchlein. Von Johannes Deigendesch. Zweite Auflage. *Germantown : Christoph Saur.* 1771. 2640

Title from Seidensticker's Bibliography.

DIMSDALE. (T.) The | Present Method | of | Inoculating | for the | Small-Pox. | To which are added, | Some Experiments, | instituted with a | View to discover the Effects of a similar | Treatment in the Natural Small-Pox. | By Thomas Dimsdale, M.D. | *Philadelphia :* | *Printed by John Dunlap, for John Sparhawk,* | MDCCLXXI. | 8vo. pp. 82. 2641

DUCHÉ. (J.) Human Life a Pilgrimage : | Or | The Christian a Stranger and | Sojourner upon Earth : | A | Sermon, | Occasioned by the Death of the | Hon. Richard Penn, Esq ; | One of the Proprietaries of the Province | of Pennsylvania : | Preached before the united Congregations of | Christ-Church and St. Peter's, in the City | of Philadelphia, on Sunday, April xxi. 1771. | By the Reverend | Jacob Duché, A.M. | *Philadelphia :* | *Printed by D. Hall and W. Sel-* | *lers.* MDCCLXXI. | 8vo. pp. iv, 19. L. C. P. 2642

ELMER. (J.) Dissertatio Medica, | Inauguralis, | de | Sitis in Febribus Causis | et Remediis. | Quam, | Sub Moderamine Viri admodum Reverendi | Gulielmi Smith, S. T. P. | Collegii et Academiae Philadelphiensis | Praefecti, | Ex per illustrium Curatorum Auctoritate, | nec non | Amplissimae Collegii et Academiae Facultatis decreto, | Deo ter Optimo Maximo Annuente, | Pro Gradu Doctoratus, | summisque in Medicina honoribus et privilegiis | rite ac legitime consequendis, | Eruditorum examini subjectam sustinuit | Jonathan Elmer, M.B. | Novo-Caesariensis | Ad diem 28 Junii, hora locoque solitis. | . . . | . . . . | *Philadelphiae,* | *Apud Henricum Miller.* | MDCCLXXI. | Title, 1 leaf; Dedication, 1 leaf; text, pp. 1–23.   A. P. S.   2643

FATHER Abraham's Pocket Almanac for 1772. *Philadelphia: John Dunlap.* 1771.   2644

MR. FAULKS, | The Noted Performer in Horsemanship. | [*Philadelphia:* 1771.] 4to. 1 leaf.   L. C. P.   2645

Advertisement of Faulks's performances, dated " Philadelphia, Sept. 23, 1771."

FOX. (T.) The Wilmington | Almanack, | or | Ephemeris, | for | The Year of our Lord 1772. | Being Bissextile or Leap-Year. | Containing | . . . | . . . | . . . | . . . | . . . | . . . | . . . | . . . | . . . | . . . . | Philosophical Enquiries concerning the Vir- | tues of Tar Water, &c. By Dr. George | Berkley, Lord Bishop of Cloyne, in Ireland.— | Thoughts on Various Subjects.—On the Dissec- | tion of a Body.—Ode to Gratitude.—The Spring, | &c. &c. &c. | . . . | . . . | . . . . | By Thomas Fox, Philom. | *Wilmington,* | *Printed and Sold by James Adams.* [1771.] | Sm. 8vo. pp. (40).   H. S. P.   2646

[FOTHERGILL. (Samuel)] The Grace of our Lord Jesus Christ, the Love of God, and a Divine Communion recommended and enforced, in a Sermon publicly delivered at a meeting of the People called Quakers, held in Leeds, the 26th of the Sixth Month, commonly called June, 1769. *Philadelphia: Joseph Crukshank.* 1771.   2647

FURMAN. (Moore) An das Publicum. | [*Philadelphia: Henry Miller*, 1771.] Folio, pp. (4).   H. S. P.   2648

FURMAN. To the Public. | [*Philadelphia:* 1771.] Folio, pp. (2).   H. S. P.   2649

In answer to " Wikoff's Appeal," specifically charging Wikoff with selling adulterated rum.

THE GENTLE Shepherd. *Philadelphia: Robert Aitken.* 1771.

THE GENTLEMAN and Citizen's Pocket Almanac for 1772. *Philadelphia: William Evitt.* 1771.   2651

GOLDSMITH. ([Oliver]) The | Deserted Village, | a | Poem. | By | Doctor Goldsmith. | *London: Printed.* | *Philadelphia: Re-printed,* | *By William and Thomas Bradford, at the* | *London Coffee-house.* | M.DCC.LXXI. | 8vo. Half title, 1 leaf; pp. iv, 22.   2652

GRAVINES. (— de) The Ladies' Friend. By M. de Gravines. *Philadelphia: John Dunlap.* 1771. 8vo. pp. 80 +.   2653

GURNALL. (W.) The | Christian | in | Compleat Armour : | Or, a | Treatise | of the | Saints War against the Devil. | Wherein | A Discovery is made of that Great Enemy of God | and his People, in his Policies, Power, Seat of his Empire, | Wicked-ness, and chief Design he hath against the Saints. | A | Magazine Opened, | From whence the Christian is furnished with Spi- | ritual Arms for the Battle, helped on with his Armour, and | taught the Use of his Weapon, together with the happy Issue | of the whole War. | By William Gurnall, M.A. | formerly Pastor of the Church of Christ at Lavenham, in Suffolk. | The Seventh Edition, carefully corrected. | *Philadelphia:* | *Printed by Joseph Cruk-shank, for John McGibbons.* [1771.] | 8vo. pp. 8 +.   H. S. P.   2654

[HARMER. (Thomas)] Observations on Divers Passages of Scripture, Placing many of them in a light altogether new, ascer-taining the meaning of several not determinable by the methods commonly made use of by the learned, and proposing probable conjectures on others, different from what have been hitherto recommended to the attention of the curious; grounded on circumstances incidentally mentioned in books of Voyages and Travels into the East. *Philadelphia: W. and T. Bradford.* 1771.

A HISTORY and Defence of Magna Charta. Containing a Copy of the Original Charter at large, with an English Translation; The Manner of its being obtained from King John. With its Preservation and Final Establishment in the Succeeding Reigns; with an Introductory Discourse, Containing a short Account of the Rise and Progress of National Freedom, from the Invasion of Cæsar to the present Times. Also the Liberties which are confirmed by the Bill of Rights, &c. To which is added, An Essay on Parliaments, Describing their Origin in England, &c. *Philadelphia: W. and T. Bradford.* 1771.   2656

𝕯𝕰𝕽 | 𝕳𝕺𝕮𝕳 = 𝕯𝕰𝖀𝕿𝕾𝕮𝕳𝕰 | Americanische | Calender | Auf das Jahr | . . . | . . . | 1772. | (Welches ein Schalt=Jahr von 366 Tagen ist.) | . . . | . . . | . . . | . . . | . . . | . . . | . . . | . . . | . . . . | Zum vier und dreyßigsten mal heraus gegeben. | *Germantown: Gedruckt und zu finden bey Christoph Saur.* | . . . | . . . [1771.] | Sq. 8vo. pp. (48).   H. S. P.   2657

HOSKINS. (J.) The | Life | and | Spiritual Sufferings | of | That Faithful Servant of Christ | Jane Hoskins, | A Public Preacher among the People called | Quakers. | Never before printed. | *Philadelphia: | Printed and Sold by William Evitt, at his Printing- | Office, the Sign of the Bible-in-Heart, in Strawberry- | Alley, opposite the Bull's Head Tavern.* | M,DCC,LXXI. | Sm. 8vo. pp. 31, (1).   F.   2658

HUSSEY. (J.) The | Glory of Christ | Vindicated, | in the | Excellency of his Person, Righteousness, | Love and Power. | Being | An Explication of the Mystery which was kept Secret | since the World began. | Wherein the Doctrine of the Holy Trinity is ma- | nifest in the Glory-Man, the Lord Jesus, and that bearing | the Filth of Sin, in his sufferings, was Part of the Atonement | he made to God for the Elect. | It is likewise demonstrated, | That an Interest in Christ is founded alone, upon | the free, absolute Love of the Father, Son, and Spirit. | Proving | That their free Grace-Union, according to God's An- | cient Settlements of their Supreme Relation to Christ, was | never destroyed by their natural Relation and Fall in Adam. | To which is added, | The spiritual Operations of the Holy Ghost, as | the immediate Spring, Life and Source of all practical Reli- | gion. | The Whole containing, | A concise, and comprehensive Answer, to a Book en- | titled, The Saint's Treasury; or Christ the | most Excellent. | Wrote Originally by Joseph Hussey, Minister of the· Gospel of | Christ, at Cambridge, and now faithfully abridged. | *Philadelphia:* | *Printed by Joseph Crukshank, for John McGibbons.* [1771.] | 8vo. pp. 8 +.

IRWIN. (Thomas) To the Public. | [*Philadelphia:* 1771.] Folio, pp. (2). L. C. P. 2660

In reply to Wikoff's "Appeal," charging Wikoff with selling adulterated rum.

KEYSER. (J. G.) Travels through Germany, Bohemia, Hungary, Switzerland, Italy and Lorraine. By John George Keyser. In Four Volumes. *Philadelphia:?* 1771. 2661

Advertised in the Pa. Journal, March 7, 1771, as "just published and to be sold by W. and T. Bradford." This I think, however, refers to an imported edition.

K[ING]'S | Answer | to | Junius. | Taken from an English Paper. | *Philadelphia:* | *Re-printed and sold by William Goddard, in* | *Arch-Street, between Front and Second* | *Streets.* | MDCCLXXI. | 8vo. pp. 8. L. C. P. 2662

THE Lancaster Almanac for **1772**. *Lancaster: Francis Bailey.* 1771. 2663

𝔇𝔌𝔈 𝔏𝔈𝔥𝔯 ═ 𝔗𝔈𝔵𝔱 ber 𝔅rüber ═ 𝔊emeine, unb infonberheit ber 𝔨inber, für baß 𝔍ahr 1772. *Philadelphia: Henrich Miller.* 1771.

𝔇𝔄𝔖 𝔏𝔒𝔗𝔗𝔒 bi 𝔊enua in feiner wahren 𝔊röſſe. *Philadelphia:* [*Donatus in Luebeck.*] **1771.** 2665

Title from Weller's *Die falschen Druckorte.*

LOTTERY. December 6, 1771. | Christiana-Bridge Land & Cash | Lottery, | [*Philadelphia:* 1771.] Folio, 1 leaf. 2666

Scheme of a lottery for disposing of **48 Plantations** in the Province of Penna.

LOTTERY. Dover Land and Cash | Lottery, | To be Drawn in Dover, in the County of Kent, on Delaware, For Disposing of certain Valuable and Improved Farms, and Tracts of Land, with Stock, Mills, &c. | situate on the River Saint Croix, in the Township of Newport, and Province of Nova Scotia. | [*Philadelphia:* 1771.] Folio, 1 leaf.   L. C. P. 2667

LOTTERY. Christiana Bridge, March 23, 1771. | The Adventurers in the Second Class of the New-Ark Land and | Cash Lottery, are desired to call upon the managers who | signed their respective Tickets, . . . | . . . that they may get them renewed in the Third Class; . . . . | [*Philadelphia:* 1771.] 4to. 1 leaf. 2668

LOTTERY. New-Ark Land and Cash | Lottery, | In New Castle County on Delaware, | [*Philadelphia:* 1771.] Folio, 1 leaf.

Scheme of a lottery to dispose of certain property in Lancaster Co.

LOTTERY. Christiana Bridge, July 13, 1771. | Newcastle Lottery, | Instituted by the Friends of the | American China Manufactory, | [*Philadelphia:* 1771.] Folio, 1 leaf. L. C. P. 2670

LOTTERY. Pettie's Island | Land and Cash | Lottery, | . . . | . . . The Drawing will begin as soon as the Tickets are | disposed of, . . . | [signed] W. M. [*Philadelphia:* 1771.] Folio 1 leaf. + . . . The Drawing will begin on the First Day of | July, 1771, . . . | [signed] William Masters. | [*Philadelphia:* 1771.] Folio 1 leaf. + . . . The Drawing shall begin on Monday, the | Twenty-first Day of October, 1771, under the Inspection of William Heysham, | John Chevalier, Abraham Beeckley, and Thomas Bond, Jun. . . . | [signed] William Masters. | [*Philadelphia:* 1771.] Folio, 1 leaf.   L. C. P. 2671

LOTTERY. Advertisement. | For the Satisfaction of the Adventurers | in Pettie's Island Land and Cash | Lottery, . . . | . . . | . . . the Drawing will . . . begin on | Monday, the 9th Day of September next, ... | [*Philadelphia:* 1771.] 4to. 1 leaf. 2672

LOTTERY. New-Castle, June 15, 1771. | A | Scheme | of a | Lottery, | For raising . . . Three Hundred and Seventy-five Pounds

. . . | to discharge a Debt upon the Methodist Preaching-House, | in Philadelphia; and towards the Building a Preaching-House in | New-Castle County. | [*Philadelphia :* 1771.] Folio, 1 leaf.

[MACPHERSON. (John)] A | Pennsylvania Sailor's | Letters, | alias the | Farmer's Fall : | With Extracts from a Tragic Comedy, called | Hodge Podge improved : | Or, | The Race Fairly Run. | The Author's Sympathy for an innocent Woman, pre- | vents his publishing the Whole of that Dramatic Piece. | . . . | . . . . | Number I. | *Philadelphia :* | *Printed for the Author,* [*by Robert Bell.*] 1771. | 8vo. pp. 64.   L. C. P.   2674

[MACPHERSON.] To be Published and Sold, by | William Woodhouse, | . . . | . . . | Every Saturday, until a Pamphlet is complete, | A | Pennsylvania Sailor's Letters ; | alias the | Farmer's Fall. | [*Philadelphia : Robert Bell.* 1771.] 4to. 1 leaf.

MANY members of the Library Company of Philadelphia, ... | [*Philadelphia :* 1771.] Folio, 1 leaf.   L. C. P.   2676

Call for a meeting of the Stockholders to consider the question of a new building.

MARY Somerville. A Tale. *Philadelphia : Robert Aitken.* 1771.   2677

MINUTES | Of the | Philadelphian Association | in MDCCLXXI. | [*Philadelphia : Henry Miller.* 1771.] Sm. 4to. pp. 8.   2678

NELSON. (John) The | Case | of | John Nelson. | Written by Himself. | . . . | . . . | . . . . | The Third Edition. | *Wilmington,* | *Printed by James Adams, in Market-street,* 1771. | 16mo. pp. 32.

DER NEUESTE, Verbessert= und Zuverläßige | Americanische | Calender | Auf das 1772ste Jahr Christi, | Welches ein Schalt=Jahr von 366 Tagen ist. | [12 lines.] | Zum Zehntenmal herausgegeben. | *Philadelphia, Gedruckt und zu finden bey Henrich Miller, in der Rees-strasse.* | . . . | . . . | . . . | . . . | . . . . [1771.] | 4to. pp. (56).

THE | NEW-ENGLAND | Primer | Enlarged. | For the more easy attaining the true | Reading of English. | To which is added,

| The Assembly's Catechism. | *Philadelphia :* | *Printed and Sold by D. Hall, and W. Sellers, in Market-street,* 1771. | Sm. 16mo. pp. (80).

On the reverse of the first leaf is a portrait ? of Geo. III. Mr. J. P. Wickersham, in his History of Education in Pa., p. 195, says an edition of The New England Primer was printed at Germantown, in 1771, by Christopher Sower.

A NEW Song, in high Vogue in Northampton | County, in the Province of Pennsylvania. | *Printed for the Author, Anno Domini* 1771. | Folio, 1 leaf. L. C. P. 2682

NEW-YEAR Verses of the Carriers of the Pennsylvania Chronicle. *Philadelphia: William Goddard.* 1771. 2683

THE | NEW-YEAR | Verses, | Of the Printers Lads, who carry about the Penn- | sylvania Gazette to the Customers. | [*Philadelphia: Hall and Sellers,* 1771.] Folio, 1 leaf. L. C. P. 2684

NEW-YEAR Verses of the Carriers of the Pennsylvania Journal. *Philadelphia: W. and T. Bradford.* 1771. 2685

NOW in the Press and speedily will be Published | by | John Dunlap, | . . . | . . . | . . . | . . . | All the | Poetical Writing, and some other Pieces, | Of the Rev. Nathaniel Evans, A.M. | [*Philadelphia: John Dunlap.* 1771.] Folio, pp. (2). H. S. P. 2686

NOW in the Press. | . . . | . . . | The true art of mixing every kind of Wine and Spirits, | [*Philadelphia:* 1771.] 4to. 1 leaf.

See Wikoff, to whom it relates, Furman, and Irwin.

OBSERVATIONS on the late Law for re- | gulating the Nightly Watch, fixing Lamps, and taking care of the Pumps, | in the City of Philadelphia—humbly offered to the Consideration of | the Inhabitants of the said City. | [*Philadelphia:* 1771.] Folio, 1 leaf.

OTTOLENGHE. (J.) Directions | for breeding | Silk-Worms, | Extracted from a Letter of | Joseph Ottolenghe, Esq ; | Late Superintendent | of the | Public Filature | in | Georgia. | *Philadelphia:* | *Printed by Joseph Crukshank, in Third-Street.* | M,DCC,LXXI. | 8vo. pp. 8. H. S. P. 2689

PEMBERTON. (E.) A Sermon on the Death of the Rev. George Whitefield. By Ebenezer Pemberton, D.D. *Philadelphia: W. and T. Bradford.* **1771.** 2690

(January, M.DCC.LXXI.) (Number 211.) | THE | PENNSYL-VANIA Chronicle, | and | Universal Advertiser. | Monday, January 28, 1771. (No. I, of Vol. V.) | *Philadelphia: Printed by William Goddard, at the New Printing-Office, in Arch-Street, between Front and Second Streets, where Subscriptions,* | *(at Ten Shillings per Annum) Advertisements, Articles and Letters of Intelligence are gratefully received for this Paper, and where all manner of Print-* | *ing Work is performed with Care, Fidelity and Expedition—Blanks and Hand-Bills, in particular are done on the shortest Notice, in a neat and correct Manner.* | Folio, pp. 1–204.   H. S. P. 2691

Numbers 211 (Jan. 28, 1771) to 261 (Jan. 13, 1772), four pages each, with unpaged " Postscripts" of two pages each to Numbers 226, 250 to 253, and 255. The cut of the Royal Arms was withdrawn from the title.

THE PENNSYLVANIA Gazette.   2692

Numbers 2193 (Jan. 3, 1771) to 2244 (Dec. 26, 1771), four pages each, with "Supplements" of two pages to Numbers 2207, 2208, 2209, 2213, 2217, 2226, and 2236; " Postscripts" of 1 leaf to Numbers 2211 and 2212, and " List of Prizes," one leaf to No. 2205. Title and imprint as in No. 2382, *supra.*

THE PENNSYLVANIA Journal.   2693

Numbers 1465 (Jan. 3, 1771) to 1516 (Dec. 26, 1771), four pages each, with extra half-sheets of two pages to Numbers 1468 to 1472, 1476, 1477, 1479 to 1483, 1486 to 1490, 1492 to 1497, 1500, 1501, 1503, 1504, 1505, and 1509 to 1516; " Supplements" of one leaf to No. 1484, two pages to Numbers 1467, 1478, 1485, and 1502, of four pages to Numbers 1491 and 1507; " Postscripts" of one leaf to Numbers 1479, 1485, and 1507, of two pages to Numbers 1483 and 1508. Title and imprints as in No. 2317, *supra.*

October, 1771. Numb. 1. | THE | PENNSYLVANIA : Packet; | and : the | General : Advertiser. | Monday, : October 28th, 1771. | *Philadelphia: Printed by John Dunlap, at the Newest Printing-Office, in Market-Street, where* | *Subscriptions at Ten Shillings per Annum, Advertisements, &c. are thankfully received for this Paper.* | Folio.   H. S. P. 2694

Numbers 1 (Oct. 28, 1771) to 10 (Dec. 30, 1771), four pages each, with " Supplements" of two pages each to every number. The title is divided by a cut of a ship, as indicated by the dotted lines.

THE PENNSYLVANIA Pocket Almanac for 1772. *Philadelphia: W. and T. Bradford.* 1771.   2695

PHIPPS. (J[oseph]) Brief | Remarks | on the | Common Arguments | Now used in Support of divers | Ecclesiastical Impositions | In this Nation, | Especially as they relate to | Dissenters. | By J. Phipps. | . . . | . . . . | *Norwich Printed: And | Philadelphia: | Re-printed by Joseph Crukshank, in | Market-Street,* MDCCLXXI. | 12mo. pp. 27.   H. S. P.   2696

See Two Treatises containing Reasons why Quakers do not pay Tythes, &c., of which this is the second. Although separately paged the signatures are continuous.

POTTS. (J.) Dissertatio Medica | inauguralis | de | Febribus | Intermittentibus, | Potentissimum Tertianis; | quam, | sub moderamine viri admodum reverendi, | Gulielmi Smith, S. S. T. P. | Collegii et Academiæ Pennsylvaniensis Præfecti; | Ex Curatorum Perillustrium auctoritate, | nec non | Amplissimae Collegii et Academiæ Facultatis decreto; | Deo Maximo Annuente, | Pro Gradu Doctoratus, | summisque in medicina honoribus et privilegiis | rite et legitime consequendis; | eruditorum examini subjectam sustinuit | Jonathan Potts, M.B. | Pennsylvaniensis. | Ad Diem 28 Junii, hora locoque solitis. | . . . | . . . . | *Philadelphiæ: | Typis Johannis Dunlap.* | M.DCC.LXXI. | 8vo. pp. vii, 37.

POOR Robin's Almanack for 1772. *Philadelphia: William Evitt.* 1771.   2698

POOR Will's Almanac for 1772. *Philadelphia: Joseph Crukshank.* 1771.   2699

POOR Will's Pocket Almanac for 1772. *Philadelphia: Joseph Crukshank.* 1771.   2700

PROCLAMATION. [*Royal Arms.*] By the Honourable | John Penn, Esquire, | Lieutenant-Governor, and Commander in Chief of the Province of Pennsylvania, and | Counties of New-Castle, Kent, and Sussex, on Delaware. | A Proclamation. | *Philadelphia: Printed by D. Hall, and W. Sellers.* 1771. | Folio, 1 leaf.   2701

Offering a reward for the apprehension of Lazarus Stewart, and others of Lancaster County, for the murder of Nathan Ogden, dated " Feb. 9, 1771."

REASONS | why | The People called | Quakers | do not pay | Tythes. | *London Printed: And, | Philadelphia: | Re-printed by Joseph Crukshank, in | Third-Street*, MDCCLXXI. | 12mo. pp. 10.

THE | ROYAL Spiritual | Magazine; | or | The Christian's | Grand Treasure. | By several Divines. | Vol. I. | *Philadelphia: | Printed by Joseph Crukshank for John | M'Gibbons.* [1771.] | 8vo. pp. vi, 24 +.   H. S. P.   2703

SAUNDERS. (R.) A Pocket Almanac for 1772. By Richard Saunders, Phil. *Philadelphia: Hall and Sellers.* 1771.   2704

SAUNDERS. Poor Richard improved: Being an Almanack for the Year of our Lord 1772. By Richard Saunders, Philom. *Philadelphia: Printed and Sold by D. Hall, and W. Sellers.* 1771.

SCHABALIE (J. P.) Die | Wandlende Seel, | Das ift: | Gespräch | der | Wandlenden Seelen mit Adam, | Noah und Simon Cleophas; | verfaffet die | Geschichten von Erschaffung der | Welt an, biß zu und nach der | Verwüftung Jerufalems. | Daraus ordentlich zu erfehen, wie eine | Monarchie und Königreich auf die andere gefolget, | wie diefe angefangen, jene aber vergangen, | und auch der ausführ= liche Verlauff der | Zerftöhrung Jerufalem. | Durch | Johann Philip Schabalie | in Niederländifcher Sprach befchrieben; | Anjetzo aber in die Hochteutfche Sprach überfetzt | von | B. B. B. | Die Zweyte Auflage. | *Germantown: | Gedruckt und zu finden, bey Christoph Saur,* 1771. | 16mo. pp. (8), 463, (23).   2706

SHARP. (G.) Extract | from a | Representation | of the | Injustice | and | Dangerous Tendency | of tolerating | Slavery, | or, | Admitting the least Claim of private Pro- | perty in the Persons of Men in England. | By Granville Sharp. | *London: Printed* MDCCLXIX. | *Philadelphia: Re-printed by Joseph Cruk- | shank, in Third-street, opposite the Work-house.* | MDCCLXXI. | Sm. 8vo. pp. 53.   L. C. P.   2707

SPROUTT. (J.) A | Discourse, | occasioned | By the Death of the Reverend | George Whitefield, A.M. | Late Chaplain to the Right Honourable the | Countess of Huntingdon; | delivered October 14, 1770, | In the Second Presbyterian Church, in | the

City of Philadelphia, | By | James Sproutt, A.M. | Pastor of the said Church. | *Philadelphia :* | *Printed and Sold by W. and T. Brad-* *ford, at the* | *London Coffee-House.* | M.DCC.LXXI. | 8vo. Half-title, 1 leaf; pp. 25.   H. S. P.   2708

STACKHOUSE. (T.) A New History of the Bible. By Thomas Stackhouse. *Philadelphia : ?* 1771.   2709

> Advertised in the Pa. Journal, March 7, 1771, *et seq.*, as "Just published and to be sold by W. and T. Bradford." Referring, I think, to an imported edition.

STERNE. ([Laurence]) Yorick's Sentimental Journal through France and Italy. By the late celebrated Dr. Sterne, of double entendre memory. Two volumes in one. *Philadelphia : Robert Bell.* 1771.   2710

STEUART. (J.) An Inquiry into the Principles of Political Œconomy: Being an Essay on the Science of Domestic Policy in Free Nations. In which are particularly considered Population, Agriculture, Trade, Industry, Money, Coin, Interest, Circulation, Banks, Exchange, Public Credit, and Taxes. By Sir James Steuart, Bart. In Three Volumes. *Philadelphia : W. and T. Bradford.* 1771.   2711

𝕯𝕴𝕰 𝕿𝖀𝕲𝕷𝕴𝕮𝕳𝕰𝕹 Loofungen der Brüder=Gemeine für das Jahr 1772. *Philadelphia : Henrich Miller.* 1771.   2712

THOUGHTS on Government; applicable to the present State of America. *Philadelphia :* 1771.   2713

> Title from Haven's List. This tract was not printed till 1776. See No. 3477, *infra.*

TILTON. (J.) Dissertatio Medica, | inauguralis | Quam | Sub Moderamine Viri admodum reverendi | Gulielmi Smith, S. T. P. | Collegii et Academiæ Philadelphiensis Praefecti, | Ex Cura-torum Auctoritate perillustrium | Nec non | Amplissimæ Col-legii et Academiæ Facultatis decreto. | Deo optimo maximo annuente, | Pro Gradu Doctoris, | Summisque in Medicina Honoribus et Privi- | legiis rite et legitime consequendis, | Eru-ditorum Examini Subjectam sustinuit | Jacobus Tilton, M.B. | Doveriensis apud Delaware, | Ad Diem 28 Junii hora locoque solitis. | . . . . | *Philadelphiæ:* | *Typis Gulielmi & Thomæ Bradford,* | M.DCC.LXXI. | 8vo. Title, 1 leaf; Dedication, 1 leaf; pp 23.

TISSOT. ([Simon André]) Advice | to the | People in General, | with | Regard to their Health: | But particularly cal- culated for those, who are the | most unlikely to be provided in Time with the best | Assistance, in acute Diseases, or upon any sudden | inward or outward Accident. | With | A Table of the most cheap, yet effectual Remedies, | and the plainest Directions for preparing them | readily. | Translated from the French Edi- tion of | Dr. Tissot's Avis au Peuple, &c. | Printed at Lyons; with all the Notes in the former | English Editions, and a few additional ones. | By J. Kirkpatrick, M.D. | . . . | . . . | . . . . | The Fourth Edition revised and corrected. | With some further additional Notes and Prescrip- | tions. | *Philadelphia:* | *Printed [by John Dunlap] for John Sparhawk.* | M,DCC,LXXI. | 8vo. pp. xviii, (4), 1–307.   H. S. P. **2715**

TO the Citizens of Philadelphia. | [*Philadelphia: W. and T. Bradford.* 1771.] Folio, 1 leaf.   H. S. P. **2716**

In reply to " A Piece . . ." addressed " To the Inhabitants of Philadelphia," in answer to " Observations on the late Law for Regulating the Nightly Watch, &c." The Author of which labors to prove that " The Servants of the Public are wrong- fully, maliciously and falsely charged with misapplying the Public Money."

TO the Inhabitants of | Philadelphia. | [*Philadelphia: W. and T. Bradford.* 1771.] Folio, 1 leaf.   H. S. P. **2717**

In regard to the cost of maintaining the public pumps and the nightly watch.

TO the Merchants and other Inhabitants of | Pennsylvania. | [*Philadelphia:* 1771.] Folio, 1 leaf.   L. C. P. **2718**

" A Friend to Trade" recommending canals between the Susquehanna and the Schuylkill, and the Chesapeake and the Delaware, dated " Dec. 13, 1771."

TOBLER. (J.) The Pennsylvania Town and Countryman's Almanac for 1772. By John Tobler. *Wilmington: James Adams.* 1771.   **2719**

TRANSACTIONS, | of the | American | Philosophical Society, | held at | Philadelphia, | for promoting | Useful Knowledge. |

Volume I. | From January 1st, 1769, To January 1st, 1771. | *Philadelphia:* | *Printed by William and Thomas Bradford, at the* | *London Coffee-House.* | M.DCC.LXXI. | Sq. 8vo. pp. i–xxviii, i–xix, 1–116, 1–340, 5 plates.   H. S. P.   2720

A TRUE and Faithful | Narrative | of the | Modes and Measures pursued | at the Anniversary Election, for Representa- | tives, of the Freemen of the Province of | Pennsylvania, held at New- town, in and for | the County of Bucks, on Monday the first Day | of October, Anno Domini 1770. | By a Bucks County Man. | | . . . | . . . . | [Cut.] | *Philadelphia:* | *Printed by William God- dard, in Arch-street,* | *between Front and Second streets.* 1771. | 8vo. pp. 7.   H. S. P.   2721

TWO | Treatises, | containing | Reasons | why | The People called Quakers | do not pay | Tythes | and other | Ecclesiastical Impositions. | *Philadelphia:* | *Re-printed by Joseph Crukshank, in* | *Market-Street,* MDCCLXXI. | 12mo.   H. S. P.   2722

Collation: Title 1 leaf; Reasons why the Quakers do not pay Tythes, pp. 10; Phipps' Brief Remarks, &c., pp. 27.

USEFUL Tables, whereby the Money of England is reduced into Money of Portugal; and the Money of Portugal reduced into English Money.   Also the Coins, Weights and Measures of both Kingdoms, compared. *Philadelphia: Hall and Sellers.* 1771.   2723

VOTES and Proceedings of the House of Representatives of the Province of Pennsylvania.   Met at Philadelphia, on the Fourteenth of October, Anno Domini 1770, and continued by Adjournments. [*Royal Arms.*] *Philadelphia: Printed and Sold by Henry Miller.* MDCCLXXI.   Folio, Title, 1 leaf; pp. 205–300.   2724

WATT'S Complete Spelling Book.   The Tenth Edition. *Phil- adelphia?* 1771.   2725

Advertised in the Pa. Journal, March 7, 1771, as "just published and to be sold by W. and T. Bradford."

WAY. (N.) Dissertatio Medica, | inauguralis, | de | Variolarum Insitione. | Quam, | Sub Moderamine Reverendi admodum Viri |

Gulielmi Smith, S. S. T. P. | Collegii et Academiae Philadelphiensis | Praefecti, | Ex perillustrium Curatorum Auctoritate, | nec non | Amplissimae Collegii et Academiae Facultatis decreto, | Deo ter optimo maximo annuente, | Pro Gradu Doctoratus, | Summisque in medicina honoribus et privilegiis | rite ac legitime consequendis, | Eruditorum examini subjectam sustinuit | Nicolaus Way, M.B. | Wilmingtoniensis apud Delaware. | Ad diem 28 Junii, hora locoque solitis. | *Philadelphiae,* | *Apud Henricum Miller.* | MDCCLXXI. | 8vo.   Title, 1 leaf; Dedication, pp. (2); pp. 19.   L. C. P.   2726

WEATHERWISE. (A.)   Father Abraham's | Almanack, | For the Year of our Lord | 1772; | Being Leap-Year. | [27 lines.] | By Abraham Weatherwise, Gent. | *Philadelphia:* | *Printed and Sold by John Dunlap, at the* | *Newest-Printing-Office, in Market-Street.* [1771.] | Sm. 8vo. pp. 36.   L. C. P.   2727

𝕯𝕰𝕽 𝖂𝕰𝕲 der Gottſeligkeit oder Empfindungen und Erfahrungen im Chriſtenthum auf dem Wege zum Himmel.   *Germantown: Christoph Saur.*   1771.   2728

Title from Seidensticker's Bibliography.

WIKOFF. (Isaac)   An Address to my Fellow Citizens. | [*Philadelphia:* 1771.]   Folio, 1 leaf.   L. C. P.   2729

WIKOFF.   To the Public. | [*Philadelphia:* 1771.]   Folio, pp. (4).   L. C. P.   2730

Isaac Wikoff's reply to Moore Furman's charge of selling poor rum.

𝖂𝕺𝕳𝕷= | 𝕰𝕴𝕹𝕲𝕰𝕽𝕴𝕮𝕳𝕿𝕰𝕿𝕰𝕾 | Vieh = Arzney = Buch, | worin enthalten | die Wartung und Pflege, | ſowol als | die Krankheiten und Heilungsmittel | I. Der Pferde, | II. Des Rindviehes, | III. Der Schaafe, | IV. Der Schweine; und | V. Der Gänſe und Hiner. | Aus den Schriften bewährteſten Vieh=Aerzte, | und derer welche die Vieh= zucht getrieben und | beſchrieben haben, mit Fleiß zuſammen getragen; | Und | zum Allgemeinen Nutzen, beſonders aber zum Gebrauch | des Landmanns heraus gegeben. | *Philadelphia,* | *Gedruckt und zu finden bey Henrich Miller, in der Zweyten-strasse.* 1771. | Sm. 8vo. pp. (10), 184.   H. S. P.   2731

THE YOUNG Clerk's Vade Mecum, or complete English Law Tutor.   The Seventh Edition.   *Philadelphia: ?* 1771.   2732

Advertised "To be sold by W. and T. Bradford," in the Pa. Journal, Feb. 14, 1771.   The edition printed in New York by Hugh Gaine is no doubt there referred to.

1772.

AN ACCOUNT of the Births and Burials in the | United Churches of Christ-Church and St. Peter's in | Philadelphia, from New-Year's Day, 1771, to New-Year's Day, | 1772.   By Caleb Cash, and William Young, Clerks, | and James Weyley, and George Stokes, Sextons. [*Philadelphia :* 1772.] Folio, 1 leaf.

AN ACCOUNT of the Births and Burials in the | United Churches of Christ-Church and St. Peter's in | Philadelphia, from December 25, 1771, to December 25, | 1772.   By Caleb Cash, and William Young, Clerks, | and Jacob Digle, and George Stokes, Sextons. | [*Philadelphia:* 1772.] Folio, 1 leaf.   L. C. P.   2734

AN ACCOUNT of the Births and Burials | in St. Paul's Church, in Philadelphia, from | December 25, 1771, to December 25, 1772. | By Alexander Hall, Clerk, | James Harris, Sexton. | [*Philadelphia :* 1772.]   Folio, 1 leaf.   L. C. P.   2735

AN ACCOUNT of the Burials in the Second Presbyterian Church.   *Philadelphia:* 1772.   2736

By Charles Wilson, | Sexton of the Baptist Church in Philadelphia. | AN ACCOUNT of the Births and Burials in the | United Churches of Christ Church and St. Peter's, in Phila- | delphia, from New-Year's Day, 1771, to New-Year's Day, 1772. | [*Philadelphia:*] *Printed by William Evitt, at the Bible-in-Heart in Strawberry-Alley.* [1772.] | Folio, 1 leaf.   L. C. P.   2737

AN ACT for raising a Fund to pay the Damages, done by Dogs within the City and County of Philadelphia, and the County of Bucks.   *Philadelphia: D. Hall, and W. Sellers.* 1772.   2738

AN ADDRESS from the Clergy of New-York and New-Jersey, to the Episcopalians in Virginia; Occasioned by some late Transactions in that Colony, relative to an American Episcopate. *Philadelphia: John Dunlap.* 1772.   2739

AITKEN'S | General American | Register, | and the | Gentleman's and Tradesman's | complete | Annual Account Book, | and | Calendar, | For the Pocket or Desk; | For the Year of our Lord, | 1773. | *Philadelphia :* | *Printed by Joseph Crukshank,* | *For R. Aitken, bookseller, opposite the | London-coffee-house, Front-street.* [1772.] | Sm. 8vo. pp. (110); Second title, 1 leaf; pp. 1–64.   2740

> The second title is as follows: Aitken's | General American | Register, | for the | Year of our Lord | 1773. | *Philadelphia:* | *Printed* | *by Joseph Crukshank,* | . . . | . . . . |

THE | AMERICAN Calendar; | or, an | Almanack, | For the Year of our Lord, | 1773. | (Being the First after Bissextile or Leap-Year.) | [25 lines.] | By Philo Copernicus. | *Philadelphia:* | *Printed and Sold by William & Thomas Bradford,* | *at the London Coffee-House.* [1772.] | Sm. 8vo. pp. (36 ?).   L. C. P.   2741

ANNO Regni | Georgii III. Regis, | Magnæ Britanniæ, Franciæ & Hiberniæ, | Duodecimo. | At a General Assembly of the Province of Penn- | sylvania, begun and holden at Philadelphia, | the Fourteenth Day of October, Anno Domini 1771, in | the Eleventh Year of the Reign of our Sovereign Lord | George III. by the Grace of God, of Great- | Britain, France and Ireland, King, Defender of the | Faith, &c. | And from thence continued by Adjournments to the | Twenty-first Day of March, 1772. | [*Penn Arms.*] | *Philadelphia:* | *Printed and Sold by D. Hall, and W. Sellers, at the | New Printing-Office, near the Market.* MDCCLXXII. | Folio, Title, 1 leaf; pp. 169–286, 2. + And from thence continued . . . to the | Nineteenth Day of September, 1772. | [*Ibid.*] Title, 1 leaf; pp. 289–290.   H. S. P.   2742

ARMSTRONG. (J.) The Oeconomy of Love; A Poetical Essay. By John Armstrong. *Philadelphia: William Mentz.* 1772. + The Second Edition. [*Ibid.*]   2743

𝕯𝕴𝕰 𝕬𝕽𝕿𝕴𝕵𝕽𝕰𝕷 | der | Patriotiſchen Geſellſchaft | der | Stadt und Caunty Philadelphia. | *Philadelphia, Gedruckt bey Henrich Miller, in der Rees-strasse.* [1772.] | Folio, 1 leaf.   L. C. P.   2744

BACHMAIR. (J. J.)   A Complete | German Grammar, | in | Two Parts. | The First Part | containing | The Theory of the Language | through all the Parts of Speech; | The Second Part | is | The Practice in as ample a Manner | as can be desired. | The Third Edition, | Greatly Altered and Improved. | By John James Bachmair, M.A. | To which is added | An Appendix, | containing | I. An Index of German Words similar in Sound but of | different Orthography and Signification.   II. Names of the | most common Occupations and Trades, as also the Names | of the Materials and Implements, &c. thereto belonging. | III. Explication of a German Proverb. | *London, Printed: | Philadelphia, Reprinted, and Sold by | Henry Miller, in Race-Street.*   MDCCLXXII. | 8vo.   Title, 1 leaf; Preface, pp. (2); text, pp. 1–313; Index, pp. (2).   H. S. P.   2745

BELL. (Robert)   To the Encouragers of Literature : The Third Volume of Blackstone's Commentaries is now Published, and the fourth Volume being now in the Press, will be Published with great expedition; and as many of the Subscribers to this book have expressed an earnest desire for an American edition of An Interesting Appendix to Sir William Blackstone's Commentaries, . . . The Editor always attentive to the Desire of the Public and ever willing to gratify the growing Taste for the Advancement of Literature in America, Proposeth to publish by subscription the above . . . . [*Philadelphia : Robert Bell.* 1772.] 8vo. 1 leaf.

[BENEZET. (Anthony)]   A | Mite cast into the Treasury: | Or, | Observations | on | Slave-Keeping. | . . . | . . . . | *Philadelphia, Printed* 1772. | *To be had at most of the Booksellers in Town.* | 12mo. pp. 24.   L. C. P.   2747

[BENEZET.]   A | Mite | cast into the | Treasury : | Or, Observations | on | Slave-Keeping. | . . . | . . . . | *Philadelphia : | Printed by Joseph Crukshank, in Market-street, | between Second and Third-Streets.*   [1772.] | 12mo. pp. 24.   F.   2748

BLACKSTONE. (W.)   Commentaries | on the | Laws | of | England. | Book the Third. | By | Sir William Blackstone, Knt. | One of his Majesty's Judges of the Court of Common Pleas. | Reprinted from the British Copy, | Page for Page with the Last

Edition. | *America :* | *Printed for the Subscribers,* | *by Robert Bell, at the late Union Library, in Third-street,* | *Philadelphia.* MDCCLXXII. | 8vo. Title, 1 leaf; Contents, pp. (5); text, pp. 1–455, (1); Appendix, pp. i–xxvii. + Book the Fourth. | [*Ibid.*] 8vo. List of Subscribers, pp. (22); Title, 1 leaf; Contents, pp. (5); text, pp. 1–436; Appendix, pp. i–vii; Index, pp. (39).   H. S. P.   2749

BLACKSTONE.   An interesting | Appendix | to | Sir William Blackstone's Commentaries | on the | Laws of England. | Containing, | I. Priestley's Remarks on some | Paragraphs in the Fourth Volume | of Blackstone's Commentaries, | relating to the Dissenters. | II. Blackstone's Reply to | Priestley's Remarks. | III. Priestley's Answer to | Blackstone's Reply. | IV. The Case of the late Election | of the County of Middlesex consi- | dered on the Principles of the Con- | stitution and the Authorities of | Law. | V. Furneaux's Letters to the | Hon. Mr. Justice Blackstone | concerning his Exposition of the | Act of Toleration, and some Posi- | tions relative to Religious Liberty, | in his celebrated Commentaries on | the Laws of England. | VI. Authentic Copies of the Ar- | gument of the late Hon. Mr. Jus- | tice Foster in the Court of Jud- | ges Delegates, and of the Speech | of the Right Hon. Lord Mans- | field in the House of Lords, in | the Cause between the City of | London and the Dissenters. | *America:* | *Printed for the Sub- | scribers,* | *By Robert Bell, at the late Union-Library, in Third-street,* | *Philadelphia.* MDCCLXXII. | 8vo.   H. S. P.   2750

Collation : General Title, 1 leaf; Priestley's Remarks, Title, 1 leaf; Contents, pp. i.–iv. ; text, pp. 5–34; Blackstone's Reply, Title, 1 leaf; text, pp. 37–47 ; Priestley's Answer, Title, 1 leaf; text, pp. 51–56; Case of the Middlesex Election, Title, 1 leaf; text, pp. 59–119; Furneaux's Letters, Title, 1 leaf; Preface to 2d edition, pp. iii.–v. ; Preface to 1st edition, pp. vii.–xii. ; text, pp. 1–119; Appendix, Half-title, p. 121 ; Advertisement, pp. 122–126 ; Dodson's Letter, p. 127 ; Foster's Argument, pp. 128–135; Appendix 2, Half-title, 1 leaf; Mansfield's Speech, pp. 139–155 ; Advertisement, 1 page.   There are copies on large paper.   The several title-pages are as follows :

PRIESTLEY. (J.)   Remarks | on | Some Paragraphs | In the Fourth Volume of | Dr. Blackstone's Commentaries on the | Laws of England, | relating to | The Dissenters. | By Joseph Priestley, LL.D. F.R.S. | . . . | . . . . | [Imprint as in the general title.]

[BLACKSTONE. (William)]   A | Reply | to | Dr. Priestley's | Remarks | on the | Fourth Volume | of the | Commentaries | on the | Laws of England. | By the | Author of the Commentaries. | [Imprint as in the general title.]

PRIESTLEY. An | Answer | to | Dr. Blackstone's | Reply | to | Remarks | on the | Fourth Volume | of the | Commentaries | on the | Laws of England. | By Joseph Priestley, LL.D. F.R.S. | [Imprint as in the general title.]

[BLACKSTONE.] The | Case | of the | Late Election | for the | County of Middlesex, | considered | On the Principles of the Constitution, | and the | Authorities of Law. | [Imprint as in the general title.]

For the title to Furneaux's Letters, see *infra*, No. 2881. See also No. 2859, *infra*, and No. 3072, *infra*.

BLACKSTONE.   The | Law | of | Crimes and Misdemeanors. | With the means of their | Prevention and Punishment. | Exhibiting, | The Pleas of the State against the Offenders of Society, | Under the following heads : | I. The general nature of Crimes and Punishments. | II. The Persons capable of committing Crimes. | III. Their several degrees of Guilt, as Principals or Accessories. | IV. The several species of Crimes, with the punishment annexed to each | by the Law. | V. The means of preventing the perpetration of Crimes. | VI. The method of inflicting those Punishments, which the Law has | annexed to each several Crime and Misdemeanor. | Containing a Valuable Code of Criminal Law; Being | the Complete Book, of the Celebrated Judge | Blackstone's Commentaries on Public Wrongs. | *Philadelphia :* | *Printed and Sold by Robert Bell, in Third-street.* | MDCCLXXII. | 8vo. 1 leaf.   L. C. P.   2751

The fourth volume of Blackstone, with an additional title-page, as above given. Collation as in No. 2750, *supra*, excepting the list of subscribers, which is omitted.

BUCHAN. (W.) Domestic Medicine; | or, the | Family Physician : | Being an attempt | To render the Medical Art more generally | useful, by shewing people what is in their own | power both with respect to the Prevention | and Cure of Diseases. | Chiefly | Calculated to recommend a proper attention to | Regimen and Simple Medicines. | By | William Buchan, M.D. | . . . | . . . | . . . | . . . | . . . . | To which is added, | Dr. Cadogan's Dissertation on the Gout. | *Philadelphia :* | *Printed by John Dunlap, for R. Aitken, at his* | *Book-Store, nearly opposite the London Coffee-House,* | *in Front-Street.* | M.DCC.LXXII. | 8vo.   H. S. P.   2752

Collation : Title, 1 leaf; Advertisement, pp. iii.–vii., 1 p. blank; Contents, pp. (3), 1 p. blank; text, pp. 1–368; Cadogan on the Gout, pp. iv., 39 (1). For title of Cadogan's tract, see No. 2753, *infra*.

CADOGAN. (W.) A | Dissertation | on the | Gout, | and all | Chronic Diseases, | jointly considered, | As proceeding from the same Causes; | What those Causes are; | and | A rational and natural Method of Cure | proposed. | Addressed to all Invalids. | By William Cadogan, | Fellow of the College of Physicians. | . . . . | *Philadelphia:* | *Printed [by John Dunlap] for and Sold by R. Aitken, at his Book-Store, | nearly `opposite the London-Coffee-house, in Front-street.* [1772.] | 8vo. pp. i–iv, 1–39, (1).   H. S. P.   2753

CANDID Remarks | on | Dr. Witherspoon's Address | To the Inhabitants of | Jamaica, | And the other West-India Islands, &c. | In a Letter to those Gentlemen. | . . . | . . . | . . . . | *Philadelphia:* | *Printed [by Wm. Goddard] in the Year* MDCCLXXII. | 8vo. Title, 1 leaf; pp. 59; Errata, 1 page.   2754

CATALOGUE of New and Old Books for Sale by William Woodhouse. *Philadelphia: Robert Bell.* 1772.   2755

𝔇𝔈𝔕 𝔆𝔥𝔯𝔦𝔰𝔱𝔩𝔦𝔠𝔥𝔢 𝔥ülender. *Ephrata.* 1772.   2756

[Cut.] WILLIAM COATES, | Takes this method of acquainting the Public . . . | . . . that he has for Sale, . . . | *Philadelphia: Printed by John Dunlap, at the Newest | Printing-Office, in Market-street.* [1772.] | 4to. 1 leaf.   L. C. P.   2757

COCKINGS. (G.) The | Conquest of Canada, or the Siege of Quebec: An Historical Tragedy of Five Acts. By George Cockings. *Philadelphia: William Magill.* 1772.   2758

Some by old Words to fame have made pretence, | . . . | . . . . . . | THE CONSTABLES of the City beg leave to present their respectful | compliments to Mr. Isaac Gray, ... | [*Philadelphia:* 1772.]   4to. 1 leaf.   L. C. P.   2759

Mr. Gray having paid his fine to escape service as constable, was included in the published list of Acting Constables. He published a card in the Gazette, No. 2274. This handbill, dated " Philadelphia, July 25, 1772," ridicules the card, particularly the " Latin sentence" by which it is preceded.

CUMBERLAND. (R.) The Fashionable Lover. By Richard Cumberland. *Philadelphia: William Laplain.* 1772.   2760

Advertised in the Pa. Packet, Sept. 14, 1772, as " now in the press," and by Robert Macgill in the Pa. Gazette, Feb. 10, 1773.

CUMBERLAND. (R.)   The West Indian, a Comedy.   By Richard Cumberland.   *Philadelphia : John Dunlap.*   **1772.**   **2761**

Also advertised in the Pa. Gazette, Feb. 10, 1773, by Robert Macgill, possibly referring to another edition.

CUMBERLAND.   The | West Indian: | a | Comedy. | As it is performed at | the Theatre Royal, in Drury Lane. | By Richard Cumberland.   *Philadelphia : Robert Bell.*   **1772.**   **2762**

DELAWARE.   Anno Regni Undecimo | Georgii III. Regis. | At a General Assembly | begun at New-Castle, in the Govern- | ment of the Counties of New-Castle, | Kent and Sussex, upon Delaware, the | Twentieth Day of October, in the | Eleventh Year of the Reign of our Sove- | reign Lord George the Third, | King of Great-Britain, &c. Annoque | Domini 1771, and contin- ued by Ad- | journment to the Thirteenth of June | following, the following Acts were | passed by the Honourable Richard Penn, Esq, Governor . . . . | [*Wilmington : James Adams.*   **1772.**] Folio, pp. 229–278.   **L.   2763**

THE DEVIL upon Crutches in England; or Night Scenes in London; a satyrical work, Written upon the plan of the celebrated Diable Boiteux of Monsieur Le Sage.   In two parts.   By a Gentleman of Oxford.   *Philadelphia : William Evitt.*   **1772.**   **2764**

DILWORTH. (T.)   A Spelling Book.   By Thomas Dilworth. *Philadelphia : John Dunlap.*   **1772.**   **2765**

This edition consisted of 10,000 copies.

[DODSLEY (Robert)]   The Oeconomy of Human Life.   *Philadelphia : Joseph Crukshank.*   **1772?**   **2766**

EDWARDS. (J.)   The Great Christian Doctrine of Original Sin defended; evidences of its Truth produced: And arguments to the contrary answered.   By the Reverend Jonathan Edwards. *Wilmington : James Adams.*   **1772.**   **2767**

ELMER. (J.) A | Funeral Eulogium; | Sacred to the Memory | Of the late Reverend | William Ramsay, A.M. | . . . | . . . | . . . | . . . | . . . | . . . | . . . . | By Jonathan Elmer, M.D. | *Philadelphia: | Printed by D. Hall, and W. Sellers, | in Market-street,* MDCCLXXII. | 8vo. pp. 18.   N. Y. H. S.   2768

ERSKINE. (R.) Gospel Sonnets. By Ralph Erskine. *Philadelphia: Robert Aitken.* 1772.   2769

EVANS. (N.) Poems | on | Several Occasions, | with | Some other Compositions. | By Nathaniel Evans, A.M. | Late Missionary (appointed by the Society for Pro- | pagating the Gospel) for Gloucester County, | in New-Jersey; and Chaplain to the Lord Vis- | count Kilmory, of the Kingdom of Ireland. | *Philadelphia: | Printed by John Dunlap, in Market-Street.* | M.DCC.LXXII. | 8vo. pp. xxviii, 160, 24, 1 leaf.   H. S. P.   2770

FALK. (N. D.) The Ready Observator; Or an Infallible Method for determining the Latitude at Sea : By Altitudes of the Sun, At any Time of the Day, either Fore-noon or After-noon, Independent of a Meridional Observation. By N. D. Falk. *Philadelphia: W. and T. Bradford.* 1772.   2771

FATHER Abraham's Pocket Almanac for 1773. *Philadelphia: John Dunlap.* 1772.   2772

FELLOW Citizens, | and | Countrymen. | [*Philadelphia :* 1772.] Folio, 1 leaf.   H. S. P.   2773

An Election circular, dated Oct. 1, 1772, and headed by a ticket composed of John Dickinson, Michael Hillegas,° Joseph Parker,° Israel Jacobs,° John Cox, junr., Jonathan Roberts,° Charles Thomson, and George Gray,° for the Assembly, and Samuel Shoemaker° and Thomas Mifflin,° for Burgesses. " Most of the above named . . . have declined accepting . . . on this Occasion . . .. if when chosen they should refuse to serve, let them be forever considered as pusillanimous Men, who either neglect or dare not stand forth to save their oppressed Country. As no Tickets are wrote to be delivered at the State-House, it is requested, that every Gentleman, who approves of the above List will please to write a few spare Tickets to furnish his Friends with." The seven candidates marked ° were elected.

A | FEW Reasons | in favour of | Vendues. | [*Philadelphia : Henry Miller.* 1772.] Folio, 1 leaf.   L. C. P.   2774

FOX. (T.)   The Wilmington | Almanack, | or | Ephemeris, | for | The Year of our Lord 1773, | Being the First after Leap-Year. | Containing | . . . | . . . | . . . | . . . | . . . | . . . | . . . | . . . | . . . | . . . . | Extracts, from a late Publication, intituled, | The Family Physician; shewing People what is in | their own Power both with respect to the Prevention | and Cure of Diseases.—Also approved Re- | ceipts for the Glanders and many other Disorders in | Horses, &c. | . . . | . . . | . . . . | By Thomas Fox, Philom. | *Wilmington,* | *Printed and Sold by James Adams.* [1772.] | Sm. 8vo. pp. (40).   H. S. P.   2775

[FRENEAU. (Philip)]   A | Poem, | on the | Rising Glory | of | America ; | being an | Exercise | Delivered at the Public Com- mencement at | Nassau-Hall, September 25, 1771. | . . . | . . . | . . . | . . . | . . . | . . . | . . . | . . . . | *Philadelphia : | Printed by Joseph Crukshank, for R. Aitken, | Bookseller, opposite the London-Coffee- | House, in Front-street.* | M,DCC,LXXII. | Sm. 8vo. pp. 27, (1).

Attributed to Judge H. H. Brackenridge, and also to Brackenridge and Freneau jointly.   In the edition of Freneau's Poems, printed on his own press and under his supervision at Monmouth in 1809, this poem is given a prominent place without any reference being made to Brackenridge's share in its composition.   On the title- page of Brackenridge's Poem on Divine Revelation, that piece is said to be " By the same person who on a similar occasion . . . *delivered* a small poem on the rising glory of America."   This may have been the ground on which the last-named poem was attributed to Brackenridge.   But as it admits of the construction that he only read or recited the earlier poem, of which Freneau claims the sole authorship, I have placed it under the latter's name.

THE FRIENDS of Liberty and Justice think it necessary, at this Juncture, to re- | publish the following Piece, which made its Appearance some Time ago in the | New-York Journal, and which was written by a Gentleman of dis- | tinguished Merit in the City of New-York. | [*Philadelphia : W. Goddard,* 1772.]   Folio, 1 leaf.

An anti-Galloway election circular, very laudatory of William Goddard.

GESANG = BUCH.   Neu = vermehrt = und vollständiges | Gesang= Buch, | Worinnen sowohl die | Psalmen Davids, | Nach | D. Ambrosii Lobwassers, | Uebersetzung hin und wieder verbessert, | Als auch | 730. auserlesener alter und neuer | Geistreichen Liedern | begriffen sind, | Welche anjetzo sämtlich | in denen Reformirten Kirchen | der Hessisch=

Hanauiſch=Pfältziſch=Pennſilvaniſchen | und mehreren andern angräntzen=
den Landen zu finden ge= | bräuchlich, in nützlicher Ordnung eingetheilt,
| Auch | Mit den Heydelbergiſchen Catechiſmo und | erbaulichen Gebätern
verſehen. | Dritte Auflage. | *Germantown: | Gedruckt und zu finden
bey Christoph Saur,* | 1772. | 16mo. 1 plate; pp. (2), 404, (8), 18,
58 +. H. S. P. 2778

GUTHRIE. (W.) A New Geographical, Historical and Com-
mercial Grammar. By William Guthrie. *Philadelphia: ?* 1772.

Advertised by Robert Aitken in the Pa. Journal, Feb. 6, 1772, as just published,
but probably referring to an English edition.

[GOLDSMITH. (Oliver)] The | Vicar | of | Wakefield: | A
Tale. | Supposed to be written by Himself. | . . . . | Vol. I. |
*Philadelphia: | Printed for William Mentz, and sold by | most of the
Booksellers in America.* | M,DCC,LXXII. | 12mo. pp. 92. + Vol. II.
| [*Ibid.*] | 12mo. Title, 1 leaf; pp. 95–180. H. S. P. 2780

GREEN. (E.) Slothfulness reproved, | and | Example of the
Saints proposed | for Imitation: | A | Sermon, | Occasioned by the
Death of the Reverend | Mr. William Ramsay, M.A. | Who de-
parted this Life November 5, 1771. | In the 39th Year of his Age.
| Delivered at | Fairfield, in Cohansie, | December 9, 1771. | By
Enoch Green, A.M. | *Philadelphia: | Printed by D. Hall, and W. Sel-
lers, | in Market-street,* MDCCLXXII. | 8vo. pp. 32. N. Y. H. S. 2781

HAWLES. (J.) The Englishman's Right: A Dialogue between a Barrister at Law, and a Juryman; setting forth the An-
tiquity, Use, Office, and just Privileges of Juries, by the Law of
England. By Sir John Hawles, Kt. *Philadelphia: ?* 1772. 2782

The advertisement in the Pa. Chronicle, March 9, 1772, may refer to the New
York edition.

DER | HOCH=DEUTSCH= | Americaniſche | Calender, | Auf das
Jahr | . . . | . . . | 1773. | (Welches ein gemein Jahr von 365
Tagen iſt.) | . . . | . . . | . . | . . . | . . | . . . | . . . | . . . |
. . . | . . . | . . . . | Zum fünf und dreyßigſten mal heraus gegeben. |
Germantown: Gedruckt und zu finden bey Christoph Saur. | . . . |
. . . [1772.] | Sq. 8vo. pp. (48). H. S. P. 2783

INVITATION | Serieuse | aux | Habitants | des | Illinois. | [*Philadelphia: W. and T. Bradford. 1772.*] 8vo. pp. 15.   2784

" A Philadelphié MDCCLXXII," says Du Simitiere.   It is signed " Un Habitant des Kaskaskia."

JONES. (S.) Resignation, a Funeral Sermon, occasioned by the Death of Rev. Isaac Eaton, A.M. late Minister of the Baptist Church, at Hopewell, in New-Jersey; preached at Hopewell, by Samuel Jones, A.M. *Philadelphia: James Humphreys, junior.* 1772.   2785

THE LANCASTER Almanac for 1773. *Lancaster: Francis Bailey.* 1772.   2786

𝕯𝕴𝕰 | 𝕷𝕰𝕳𝕽 = 𝕿𝕰𝕏𝕿𝕰 | ber | Brüber = Gemeine | für baß Jahr | 1773. | . . . | . . . . | *Philadelphia,* | *Gedruckt bey Henrich Miller, im Jahr* 1772. | 8vo. pp. (72).   H. S. P.   2787

𝕷𝕴𝕯𝕰𝕽 für Freimaurer. *Philadelphia:* [*Kanter in Koenigsberg.*] 1772.   2788

Title from Weller's *Die falschen Druckorte.*

LOTTERY. Pettie's Island | Cash | Lottery, | [*Philadelphia: J. Dunlap.* 1772.] Folio, 1 leaf.   L. C. P.   2789

Scheme of a lottery to assist in finishing a Presbyterian Church, in Norrington Township, a German Lutheran Church, in Whitpain Township, the Newark Academy, and for the benefit of three School-masters in Philadelphia.

LOTTERY. Pettie's - Island | Land and Cash | Lottery, | [*Philadelphia:* 1772.] Folio, 1 leaf.   L. C. P.   2790

Scheme of a lottery for disposing of several Houses and Lots in Lancaster, Penna.

LOTTERY. Pettie's - Island | Lottery, | For disposing of a great Variety of curious Pictures, Jewellery, &c. &c. | [*Philadelphia:* 1772.] Folio, 1 leaf.   L. C. P.   2791

LOTTERY. New-Castle, February 6, 1772. | Scheme | of a | Lottery, | For . . . | the Building | A Methodist Preaching House | In New-Castle County; and to discharge a Debt upon

the | Preaching - House | In Philadelphia. | [*Philadelphia:* 1772.]
Folio, 1 leaf. L. C. P. 2792

MADEN. (M[artin]). A Scriptural Comment upon the Thirty-
Nine Articles of the Church of England. By Rev. M. Maden.
Philadelphia: Robert Aitken. 1772. 2793

THE MIRACULOUS Power of Clothes; Or, the Dignity
of the Taylors. Being an Essay on the words Clothes Make
Men. *Philadelphia: William Mentz.* 1772. 2794

𝕯𝕰𝕽 𝕹𝕰𝖀𝕰𝕾𝕿𝕰, Verbeſſert= und Zuverlaßige Americaniſche Cal=
ender auf das 1773ſte Jahr Chriſti. *Philadelphia: Henrich Miller.*
1772. 2795

𝕰𝕵𝕹𝕰 | 𝕹𝖀𝕰𝕿𝖅𝕷𝕵𝕮𝕳𝕰 | Anweiſung | oder | Beyhülffe vor
Deutſche | um Engliſch zu lernen: | Wie es vor Neu=Ankommende und
an= | dere im Land gebohrne Land= und Handwerksleute, | welchen in
der Engliſchen Sprache erfahrene und geübte | Schulmeiſter und Pre-
ceptores ermangelen, | vor das be= | quemſte erachtet worden; mit
ihrer gewöhnlichen Ar= | beit und Werckzeug erläutert. | Nebſt einer
| Grammatic, | Vor diejenigen, welche in andern Sprachen und |
deren Fundamenten erfahren ſind. | Dritte Auflage. | *Germanton:* |
Gedruckt und zu bekommen bey Christoph Saur 1772. | 16mo. Title,
1 leaf; Vorrede, pp. (2); text, pp. 1–262; A | Short Appendix |
to a | German Grammar, | pp. (4). H. S. P. 2796

NEW-YEAR Verses of the Carriers of the Pennsylvania
Chronicle. *Philadelphia: William Goddard.* 1772. 2797

THE | NEW-YEAR | Verses, | Of the Printers Lads, who carry
about the Pennsyl- | vania Gazette to the Customers. | January,
1772. | [*Philadelphia: Hall and Sellers.* 1772.] Folio, 1 leaf. 2798

NEW-YEAR Verses of the Carriers of the Pennsylvania Journal. *Philadelphia: W. and T. Bradford.* 1772. 2799

NEW-YEAR Verses of the Carriers of the Pennsylvania
Packet. *Philadelphia: John Dunlap.* 1772. 2800

OTTO. (Johann Henrich.) Ein geiftlich Lied | auf Paul Springs
Helbftmord | mit | einer Piftole, | So fich im Jahr 1772, im Monat
September in | Lancäfter Caunty, Cocallico Taunfchip, zutrug. | [n. p.
1772.] Folio, 1 leaf.   H. S. P.   2801

THE PENNSYLVANIA Chronicle. Folio, pp. 1–212.   2802

Numbers 263 (Jan. 27, 1772) to 314 (Jan. 16, 1773), four pages each, with unpaged
" Postscripts" of two pages each to Numbers 277, 279, and 300. Title as in No.
2691, *supra*.

THE PENNSYLVANIA Gazette.   2803

Numbers 2245 (Jan. 2, 1772) to 2297 (Dec. 30, 1772), four pages each, with " Supplements" of two pages to Numbers 2245, 2246, 2248, 2249, 2251, 2252, 2254, 2255,
2257 to 2264, 2268 to 2272, 2274, 2276, 2277, 2279, 2283, 2285 to 2293, 2295, and 2296 ;
" Postscripts" of one leaf to Numbers 2259 and 2283, and of two pages to No. 2287.
Title and imprint as in No. 2382, *supra*, except last number.

THE PENNSYLVANIA Journal.   2804

Numbers 1517 (Jan. 2, 1772) to 1569 (Dec. 30, 1772), four pages each, with extra
half-sheets of two pages all but Numbers 1517, 1530, 1531, 1548, 1551, 1558, 1559, and
1568 ; " Supplements" of two pages to Numbers 1517, 1530, 1531, 1548, 1551, 1558,
and 1559 ; " Postscripts" of one leaf to Numbers 1531, 1532, and 1534. Title and
imprint as in No. 2317, *supra*.

THE PENNSYLVANIA Packet.   2805

Numbers 11 (Jan. 6, 1772) to 62 (Dec. 28, 1772), four pages each, with " Supplements" of four pages to Numbers 26 and 51, and of two pages to all the other numbers ; and a " Postscript" of one leaf to No. 53. Title and imprint as in No. 2694,
supra, until No. 53, when " Vol. II." was inserted in the first line of the title between
the date and number.

THE PENNSYLVANIA Pocket Almanac for 1773. *Philadelphia: W. and T. Bradford.* 1772.   2806

THE | PLAIN Path | to | Christian Perfection, | shewing |
That we are to seek for Reconciliation and | Union with God,
solely by renouncing our- | selves, denying the World, and follow-
ing our | Blessed Saviour, in the Regeneration. | Translated from
the French. | . . . | . . . | . . . | . . | . . . | . . . | . . . | . . . |
. . . . | *Philadelphia:* | *Printed by Joseph Crukshank, in Third-street,*

| *opposite the Work-House.* | MDCCLXXII. | Sm. 8vo. pp. i–xi, 1–124, 1–16.   H. S. P. 2807

Translated, compiled, and with a preface by Anthony Benezet. The last sixteen pages begin with, "To the foregoing testimonies of the happiness of a life spent in the service of God, may be added that of a faithful servant of Christ from amongst ourselves, to wit, David Brainard," &c. This is entered in my "List" as printed in 1774, ends on page 10, and is followed by "The following experience of some men of note," &c., pp. 11–14; and an "Extract from a letter wrote by the Earl of Essex," &c., pp. 15–16.

POOR WILL'S Almanac for 1773. *Philadelphia: Joseph Crukshank.* 1772.   2808

POOR Will's | Pocket Almanack, | for the Year 1773; | . . . | . . . | . . . | . . . | . . . . | *Philadelphia :* | *Printed and Sold by J. Crukshank,* | *at his Printing-Office, in Third-street,* | *opposite the Work-House.* [1772.] | 24mo. pp. (36).   H. S. P. 2809

PRIESTLEY, (J.) Experimental Philosophy; containing the History and Present State of Discoveries relating to Vision, Light and Colours. The Second Volume. By Joseph Priestley. *Philadelphia :* 1772.   2810

Title from Haven's List.

PROJET d'une représentation sur les ordonnances somptuaires. Par un Patriote. *A Philadelphie : [Genève.]* 1772.   2811

Title from Weller's *Die falschen Druckorte.*

JOHN RHEA | Desires to return his Thanks to all . . . who have . . . | . . . countenanced his proposed Plan of a Pott and Pearl Ash | Works ; . . . . | [*Philadelphia :* 1772.] Folio, 1 leaf.

In reply to the protest of the Soap-Boilers.

RULES | and | Constitutions | of the | Society | Of the Sons of | St. George. | *Philadelphia :* | *Printed by James Humphreys, Junior,* | *in Front-street, at the lower Corner of* | *Black-horse Alley.* M,DCC,LXXII. | 8vo. pp. 28.   L. C. P. 2813

[RUSH. (Benjamin)] Sermons | to | Gentlemen | upon | Temperance | and | Exercise. | . . . | . . . | . . . | . . . | . . . | . . . |

. . . | . . . . | *Philadelphia:* | *Printed by John Dunlap, in Market-Street.* | M.DCC.LXXII. | 8vo. pp. 44.   L. C. P.   2814

In Aitken's Ledger, Feb. 4, 1772, Dunlap is charged for stitching 102 Rush's Sermons.

SAUNDERS. (R.) A Pocket Almanac for 1773. By Richard Saunders, Phil. *Philadelphia: Hall and Sellers.* 1772.   2815

SAUNDERS. Poor Richard improved; | Being an | Alma-nack | . . . | . . . | . . . | . . . | . . . | . . . | . . . | . . . | . . . | . . . | For the | Year of our Lord 1773 : | Being the First after Leap-Year. | . . . | . . . | . . . | . . . | . . . | . . . | . . . | . . . | . . . . | By Richard Saunders, Philom. | *Philadelphia:* | *Printed and Sold by D. Hall, and W. Sellers.* [1772.] | Sm. 8vo. pp. (36). 2816

SELLERS. (R.) An | Account | of the | Sufferings | of | Rich-ard Sellers, | Of Keinsey, a Fisherman, | Who was pressed in Scarborough-Piers, in the | Time of the two last Engagements be-tween the | Dutch and English, in the Year 1665. | *Philadelphia:* | *Printed and Sold by Joseph Crukshank, in Third-Street,* | *opposite the Work-House,* MDCCLXXII. | 12mo. pp. 26.   F.   2817

A SERMON on the present Situation of Affairs of America and Great Britain. Written by a Black; and printed at the request of several persons of distinguished characters. *Philadelphia:* 1772. 8vo. pp. 11.   2818

Title from Haven's List.

STANTON. (D.) A | Journal | of the | Life, Travels, and Gospel Labours, | of a | Faithful Minister | of | Jesus Christ, | Daniel Stanton, | Late of Philadelphia, in the Province of | Pennsylvania. | With the Testimony of the Monthly-Meeting of | Friends in that City concerning him. | . . . | . . . | . . . | . . . . | *Philadelphia:* | *Printed and sold by Joseph Crukshank, in Third-* | *street, opposite the Work-House.* | MDCCLXXII. | 8vo. pp. xvii, 184, 4, 1 leaf.   H. S. P.   2819

STEPHENS. (G. A.) Lecture upon Heads. By George Alexander Stephens. *Philadelphia: Samuel Dellap.* 1772.   2820

THE SENATORS, A Poem: Or, A Candid Examination into the Merits of the Principal Performers of St. Stephen's Chapel. *Philadelphia: William Goddard.* 1772.   2821

𝖣𝖨𝖤 | 𝖳𝖠𝖦𝖫𝖨𝖢𝖧𝖤𝖭 | Loosungen | der | Brüder-Gemeine | für das Jahr | 1773. | *Philadelphia,* | *Gedruckt bey Henrich Miller, im Jahr* 1772. | 8vo. pp. (55).   H. S. P. 2822

[TERSTEEGEN (Gerhard)] Die Kraft | der | Liebe Christi, | Angepriesen und angewiesen | in einer | Erweckungs = Rede, | Ueber die Worte Pauli | 2 Corinth. 5, 14. | Die Liebe Christi bringet uns also. | Gehalten | den 18ten October, 1751. | zu Mühlheim an der Ruhr; | Und | auf Verlangen verschiedener Freunde | aufgeschrieben, | Und dem Druck übergeben, | G. T. St. | Zweyte Auflage. | *Essen,* *Gedruckt von J. C. Straube, 1752.* | *Philadelphia, Gedruckt und zu finden bey Henrich Miller, in der Rees-strasse,* 1772. | Sm. 8vo. pp. 64.

TO All | Farmers and Tradesmen, | Who want good Settlements for themselves and Families, especially | those lately arrived, or that may yet come, from Scotland or Ireland. | *Philadelphia: Printed by John Dunlap, at the Newest Printing-Office | in Market-Street.* 1772. | 4to. 1 leaf.   L. C. P. 2824

Recommending Central New York.

TO the | Freemen | Of Pennsylvania. | [*Philadelphia : 1772.*] Folio, 1 leaf.   H. S. P. 2825

" A. P." on the Excise Law, dated in manuscript by Du Simitiere, Feb. 18, 1772. Michael Hillegas noted on his copy " said to be by Thomas Mifflin."

TO the | Freemen | of | Pennsylvania. | [*Philadelphia: 1772.*] Folio, 1 leaf.   L. C. P. 2826

" Civis" on the Excise Law, dated in manuscript by Du Simitiere, Feb. 21, 1772.

TO the Inhabitants of the City of | Philadelphia, and Parts adjacent. | [*Philadelphia: 1772.*] 4to. 1 leaf.   L. C. P. 2827

Protest of the Soap-Boilers against John Rhea's methods of procuring ashes, dated " 15th February, 1772."

TO the printur of the Penselvaney Kronical. | [*Philadelphia :*
1772.]   4to. 1 leaf.   L. C. P.   2828

An anti-excise, &c., election squib, signed "Terence sweep," and dated by Du
Simitiere, Oct. 1, 1772.

TO the Public. | [*Philadelphia :* 1772.]   4to. 1 leaf.   2829

Address in favor of canals between the Susquehanna and Schuylkill, and Delaware and Chesapeake, dated "Philadelphia, January 15, 1772."

TOBLER. (J.) The | Pennsylvania | Town and Country-man's
| Almanack, | for | The Year of our Lord 1773, | Being the
First after Leap-Year. | [22 lines.] | By John Tobler, Esq; |
Wilmington, | *Printed and Sold by James Adams.* [1772.] | Sm.
8vo. pp. (36).   H. S. P.   2830

A TRADESMAN'S Address to his Countrymen. | [*Phila-
delphia :* 1772.]   4to. 1 leaf.   L. C. P.   2831

"A Tradesman" on the Excise Law, dated "March 2, 1772."

TURFORD. (H.) The | Grounds | of a | Holy Life : | Or |
The Way by which many who | were Heathens, came to be
Renowned | Christians ; and such as | are now Sinners, may
come to be | numbered with Saints ; by little | Preaching. | To
which is added, | Paul's Speech | to the | Bishop of Cretia. |
As also, | A True Touch-stone or Trial | of Christianity. | By
Hugh Turford. | The Tenth Edition. | *Philadelphia.* | *Printed and
Sold by Joseph Crukshank, in* | *Third-street, opposite the Work-House,*
1772. | Sm. 12mo. pp. viii, 123.   F.   2832

THE UNIVERSAL Almanac for the Year of our Lord, 1773 ;
Philadelphia : James Humphreys, jun.   [1772.]   2833

A second edition was advertised in the Pa. Packet, Feb. 15, 1773.

[VANSANT. (John)]   To the Public. | [*Philadelphia :* 1772.]
Folio, pp. (2).   L. C. P.   2834

A statement of his business troubles which led to his imprisonment, dated "Philadelphia Gaol, the 12th of the 10th Month, 1772."

VOTES | and | Proceedings | of the | House of Representatives | of the | Province of Pennsylvania, | Met at Philadelphia, on the Fourteenth of October, Anno | Domini 1771, and continued by Adjournments. | [*Royal Arms.*] | *Philadelphia:* | *Printed and Sold by Henry Miller, in Race-Street.* | MDCCLXXII. | Folio, Title, 1 leaf; pp. 303–412.   H. S. P.   2835

The votes were also issued weekly by Miller.

WALKER. (R.)   Sermons on Practical Subjects.   By the Rev. Robert Walker.   *Philadelphia|: Robert Aitken.*   1772.   2836

Printed by Crukshank for Aitken.   Some copies were printed on extra fine paper.

WEATHERWISE. (A.)   Father Abraham's Almanac for 1773.   By Abraham Weatherwise.   *Philadelphia: John Dunlap.* 1772.   2837

WILLISON. (J.)   Songs for Children.   By the Rev. John Willison.   *Philadelphia: Robert Aitken.*   1772.   2838

[WITHERSPOON. (John)]   Address | to the | Inhabitants | of | Jamaica, | and other | West-India Islands, | In Behalf of the | College of New-Jersey. | *Philadelphia:* | *Printed by William and Thomas Bradford, at* | *the London Coffee-House.* | M.DCC.LXXII. | 8vo. pp. 27.   H. S. P.   2839

[WOOLMAN. (John)]   An | Epistle | to the | Quarterly and Monthly | Meetings of Friends. | [*Philadelphia: ? 1772.*]   8vo. pp. 16.   H. S. P.   2840

1773.

AN | ABSTRACT | of the | Proceedings | of the | Corporation | For the Relief of the | Widows and Children | of | Clergymen, | In the Communion of the Church of England | In America. | *Philadelphia, Printed:* | *By James Humphreys junior,* | *in Front-street,* M,DCC,LXXIII. | 8vo. pp. 52.   H. S. P.   2841

AN ACCOUNT of the Births and Burials in the | United Churches of Christ-Church and St. Peter's, in | Philadelphia, from December 25, 1772, to December 25, 1773. | By Matthew White-

head, and William Young, | Clerks, and Jacob Digle, and George
Stokes, Sextons. | [*Philadelphia:* 1773.] Folio, 1 leaf. L. C. P. 2842

AN ACCOUNT of the Births and Burials in St. Paul's Church.
Philadelphia: 1773.   2843

AN ACCOUNT of the Baptisms and Burials in the Baptist
Church. *Philadelphia:* 1773.   2844

AN ACCOUNT of Burials in the Second Presbyterian Church.
Philadelphia: 1773.   2845

THE ADVENTURES of Bampfylde Moore Carew, King of the
Beggars, containing an account of the great number of characters
and shapes he has appeared in, both before and after his preferment
to that high office. *Philadelphia: Robert Bell.* 1773.   2846

ADVERTISEMENT. [Signed S. Bogle.] *Philadelphia:* 1773.

AITKEN. ([Robert]) Aitken's | General American | Register,
| and | Calendar, | For the Year | 1774. | *Philadelphia:* | *Printed
for R. Aitken, Bookseller,* | *Stationer, and Bookbinder, op-* | *posite the
London-Coffee-* | *House, Front-Street.* [1773.] | 12mo. pp. 200, (4).

THE AMERICAN Calendar for 1774. *Philadelphia: W. and
T. Bradford.* 1773.   2849

𝔄𝔫 bie guten Einwohner in Pennſylvanien. | [*Philadelphia: Henrich
Miller.* 1773.] Folio, pp. (2).   H. S. P. 2850

Dated " Jan. 5, 1773," and signed " Publicus." For the English edition, see No.
2939, *infra.*

THE | ANCIENT Testimony | of the | People called Quakers,
| reviv'd. | By the Order and Approbation of the Yearly | Meet-
ing, held for the Provinces of Penn- | sylvania and New-Jersey,
1722. | *Philadelphia:* | *Printed by Joseph Crukshank, in* | *Market-
street.* MDCCLXXIII. | 12mo. pp. 64, (3).   H. S. P. 2851

Printed with Barclay's Catechism. See No. 2853, *infra.*

ANNO Regni | Georgii III. Regis, | Magnæ Britanniæ,
Franciæ & Hiberniæ, | Decimo Tertio. | At a General Assembly

of the Province of Penn- | sylvania, begun and holden at Phila- | delphia, | the Fourteenth Day of October, Anno Domini 1772, in | the Twelfth Year of the Reign of our Sovereign Lord | George III. by the Grace of God, of Great- | Britain, France and Ireland, King, Defender of the | Faith, &c. | And from thence continued by Adjournments to the | Twenty-sixth Day of February, 1773. | [*Penn Arms.*] | *Philadelphia :* | *Printed and Sold by Hall and Sellers,* | *at the* | *New Printing-Office, near the Market.* MDCCLXXIII. | Folio, Title, 1 leaf; pp. 293–355, (1). + And from thence continued . . . to the | Twenty-eighth Day of September, 1773. | [*Ibid.*] Title, 1 leaf; pp. 359–364. H. S. P. 2852

[BARCLAY. (David)] A | Catechism | and | Confession of Faith, | Which containeth a true and Faithful Account | of the Principles and Doctrines of the Peo- | ple called Quakers. | To which is added, | the | Ancient Testimony | Of the said People reviv'd, | With some of the Rules of the Discipline Established | among them. | Extracted from the Minutes of their Yearly Meet- | ings. | *Philadelphia :* | *Printed by Joseph Crukshank, in Market-* | *street, between Second and Third street.* | MDCCLXXIII. | 8vo. 2853

Collation : General Title, 1 leaf; Barclay's Catechism, Title, 1 leaf; Preface, pp. (6) ; Text, pp. 1–147; Contents, pp. (3) ; Ancient Testimony, Title, 1 leaf; text, pp. 3–64; List of Books, pp. (3). The title to Barclay's Catechism is as follows : A | Catechism | and | Confession of Faith, | Approved of and Agreed unto, by the Gen- | eral Assembly | of the Patriarchs, Prophets and Apostles, | Christ himself Chief Speaker in and among them. | Which containeth a true and faithful Account of the | Principles and Doctrines, which are most surely believed by the | Churches of Christ in Great Britain and Ireland, who are reproachfully | called by the Name of Quakers ; yet are found in the one | Faith with the Primitive Church and Saints, as is most clearly de- | monstrated by some plain Scripture Testimonies, (without Con- | sequences or Commentaries) which are here collected, and in- | serted by way of Answer to a few weighty, yet easy and familiar | Questions, fitted as well for the wisest and largest, as for the weakest | and lowest Capacities. | To which is added, | An Expostulation with, and Appeal to, all other | Professors. | By Robert Barclay. | The Tenth Edition. | . . . | . . . | . . . . | *Philadelphia :* | *Printed by Joseph Cruk-* | *shank, in* | *Market-street.* MDCCLXXIII. | For the title to the Ancient Testimony, see No. 2851, *supra.* The edition consisted of 1000 copies.

[BELL. (Robert)] Observations relative to the Manufactures of Paper | and Printed Books in the Province of Pennsylvania. | [*Philadelphia : Robert Bell.* 1773.] Folio, 1 leaf. L. C. P. 2854

BELL. Proposals for printing by Subscription John Leland's History of Ireland, in four volumes. *Philadelphia: Robert Bell.* 1773.   2855

ROBERT BELL'S Sale Catalogue of a Collection of New and Old Books, for the Fall of the Year 1773. Containing above Fifteen Hundred Volumes. *Philadelphia: Robert Bell.* 1773.

BELL. To the Sons of Science in America Robert Bell, Bookseller of Philadelphia, notifieth, that in the fall of this present year 1773, he will Publish by Subscription Ferguson's Essay on the History of Civil Society. . . . . [*Philadelphia: Robert Bell.* 1773.] 8vo. 1 leaf.   2857

BENEZET? (A.) Brief Considerations upon Slavery, and the Expediency of its Abolition. By Anthony Benezet. *Philadelphia:* 1773. 8vo.? pp. 16.   2858

Title from Haven's List, in which it is said of this tract, "The same. Burlington." I have not met with a Philadelphia edition, if there be one. The tract printed at Burlington with the above title is anonymous, and was certainly *not* written by Benezet.

BLACKSTONE. (W.) An interesting | Appendix | to | Sir William Blackstone's Commentaries | on the | Laws of England. | . . . . | [28 lines in two columns.] | *America:* | *Printed for the Subscribers,* | *by Robert Bell,* . . . | *Philadelphia,* MDCCLXXIII. | 8vo.   H. S. P. 2859

General title and collation as in No. 2750, *supra.* The special titles are also exactly the same except Priestley's Remarks, which has an additional quotation of two lines, and the Case of the Late Election, to which is added " By the Author of | Commentaries on the Laws of England." | See No. 2881, *infra,* and No. 3072, *infra.*

BLAIR, (R.) and ([Thomas]) GRAY. The | Grave. | A | Poem. | By Robert Blair. | To which is added | An | Elegy | Written in a Country | Church-Yard. | By Mr. Gray. | *Philadelphia:* | *Printed and sold by R. Aitken, Book-seller* | *and Stationer, Opposite the London Coffee-house,* | *in Front-Street.* M,DCC,LXXIII. | 8vo. pp. 31, (1).

BY the Medium of the Curious Numerical Machine, invented by the ingenious Mr. Cox, are to be disposed of, | the following Two Hundred and Fifty Lots of ornamented rich Plated Goods, ... | [*Philadelphia: Henry Miller.* 1773.] Folio, 1 leaf.

Dated "Philadelphia, Dec. 9, 1773."

CADOGAN. (W.) An | Essay | upon | Nursing, | and the | Management of Children, | From their Birth to Three Years of Age. | By William Cadogan of Bristol, M.D. | In a Letter to one of the Governors of | the Foundling Hospital. | Published by Order of the General Committee for | transacting the Affairs of the said Hospital. | The Fifth Edition, with Additions. | *London, Printed: | Philadelphia: Re-printed and Sold by | William and Thomas Bradford, at the London | Coffee-House.* | MDCCLXXIII. | 8vo. pp. 36.   H. S. P.   2862

A CARD. | [*Philadelphia:* 1773.] Sm. 4to. 1 leaf.   2863

"The Public present their Compliments to Messieurs James and Drinker." Calling on them to renounce in writing to be left at the Coffee House their Commissions under Tea tax Act.

THE CHRISTIAN Œconomy. Translated from the original Greek of an old manuscript, found in the island of Patmos, where St. John wrote his book of Revelation. *Philadelphia: James Humphreys, jun.* 1773.   2864

COLLES. (C.) Syllabus | Of a Course of Lectures in | Natural Experimental Philosophy. | By Christopher Colles. | *Philadelphia: Printed by John Dunlap.* [1773.] | Folio, 1 leaf.   L. C. P.   2865

A | CONFESSION | of | Faith | put forth by the | Elders and Brethren | of many | Congregations | of | Christians, | (Baptized upon Profession of their Faith) | In London and the Country. | Adopted by the Baptist Association met at | Philadelphia, Sept. 25, 1742. | The Seventh Edition | To which are added, | Two Articles viz. Of Imposition of Hands, and | Singing of Psalms in public Worship. | Also | A short Treatise of Church Discipline, | . . . | . . . | . . . . | *Philadelphia: | Printed by John Dunlap, at the Newest | Printing-Office, in Market-street.* | M,DCC,LXXIII. | 12mo. pp. vii, 56, (2), 31.   H. S. P.   2866

CRISP. (S.) Sermons | or | Declarations, | made by | Stephen Crisp, | one of the | Antient Preachers | amongst the | People called Quakers. | Taken in Short Hand, as they were delivered by him. | *Philadelphia:* | *Printed by Joseph Crukshank, in Third-* | *street, opposite the Work-House.* | MDCCLXXIII. | Sm. 8vo. pp. 60. 2867

CUMBERLAND. (R.) The Fashionable Lover; A Comedy. By Richard Cumberland. *Philadelphia: John Dunlap.* 1773. + *Philadelphia: Robert Macgill.* 1773. 2868

A DISSERTATION on the Laws of Excise, In which the arguments urged in their favour by Publicus will be considered, and the dangerous consequences, resulting from them to Liberty and Commerce will be pointed out. By Causidicus Mercatorius. *Philadelphia: John Dunlap.* 1773. 2869

Advertised in the Pa. Packet, Feb. 8, 1773, as "shortly to be published."

DELAWARE. Anno Regni Duodecimo | Georgii III. Regis. | At a General Assembly | begun at New-Castle, . . . | . . . | . . . | Twentieth Day of October, (and con- | tinued by Ad- journment to the Twelfth | of April following) in the Twelfth | Year of the Reign of our Sovereign | Lord George the Third, King of | Great-Britain, &c. Annoque Domini | 1772, the fol- lowing Acts were | passed by the Honorable Richard | Penn, Esquire, Governor; . . . . | [*Wilmington: James Adams.* 1773.] Folio, pp. 279–286. L. 2870

DELAWARE. Anno Regni Decimo Tertio | Georgii III. Regis. | At a General Assembly | begun . . . | . . . | . . . | Twentieth Day of October, in the | Thirteenth Year of the Reign of our | Sovereign Lord George the Third, | . . . | . . . 1773, the following Acts | were passed by the Honorable John | Penn, Governor; . . . . | [*Wilmington: James Adams.* 1773.] Folio, pp. 287–299. L. 2871

DELICIÆ Ephratenses, | Pars I. | Oder des ehrwürdigen Vat= ters | Friedsam Gottrecht, | Wehland Stiffters und Führers des Christ= lichen Ordens | der Einsamen in Ephrata in Pennsylvania, | Geistliche

Reben. | . . . | . . . | . . . | . . . . | *Ephratæ : Typis Societatis, Anno* MDCCLXXIII. | Sq. 8vo. pp. 8, 340.   H. S. P.   **2872**

THE DEVIL upon Crutches, or Night Scenes in London. *Philadelphia: Robert Bell?* 1773.   **2873**

A | DIALOGUE, | spoken at opening the Public | Grammar-School | At Wilmington, on Tuesday, October 26. 1773. | [*Wilmington : James Adams.* 1773.] Folio, 1 leaf.   L. C. P.   **2874**

DILWORTH. (T.) The | Schoolmasters Assistant: | Being a | Compendium of Arithmetic, | both | Practical and Theoretical, | In Five Parts. | Containing | I. Arithmetic in Whole Numbers, | wherein all the common Rules, | having each of them a sufficient | Number of Questions, with their | Answers, are methodically and | briefly handled. | II. Vulgar Fractions, wherein se- | veral Things, not commonly met | with are there distinctly treated | of, and laid down in the most | plain and easy Manner. | III. Decimals, in which among other | Things, are considered the Extrac- | tion of Roots, Interest, both Sim- | ple and Compound; Annuities, Re- | bate, and Equation of Payments. | IV. A large Collection of Questions, | with their Answers, serving to | exercise the foregoing Rules; | together with a few others, both | pleasant and diverting. | V. Duodecimals, commonly called | Cross Multiplication; wherein | that Sort of Arithmetic is tho- | roughly considered, and rendered | very plain and easy; together | with the Method of proving all | the foregoing Operations at once | by Division of several Denomi- | nations, without reducing them | to the lowest Term mentioned. | The Whole being delivered in the most familiar Way of Question and An- | swer, is recommended by several eminent Mathematicians, Accomptants, | and Schoolmasters, as necessary to be used in Schools by all Teachers, who | would have their Scholars thoroughly understand, and make a quick | Progress in Arithmetic. | To which is prefixt, An Essay on the Education of Youth; humbly | offer'd to the Consideration of Parents. | The Seventeenth Edition. | By Thomas Dilworth, | Author of the New Guide to the English Tongue; Young Book- | keeper's

Assistant; &c. &c. and Schoolmaster in Wapping. | . . . | . . . |
. . . | . . . | . . . | . . . | . . . . | *Philadelphia:* | *Printed and Sold
by Joseph Crukshank, in* | *Third-street, opposite the Work-house,*
MDCCLXXIII. | 12mo. Portrait, 1 leaf; pp. i–xiv, (10), 1–192,
1 folded leaf.   H. S. P.   2875

A FAITHFUL Narrative of the Conversion and Death of
Count Struensee, late Prime Minister of Denmark; together
with Letters from his Parents to him, and also a Letter of his
own; wherein he relates how he came to alter his Sentiments of
Religion. Published by D. Munter, an eminent Divine, who was
ordered by the King to prepare him for Death. To which is
added, the History of Count Enevold Brandt, from the Time of
his Imprisonment to his Death. Together with two Anonymous
Letters, found in his Pocket-book, wherein he was forewarned of
what happened to him four Months after; and likewise an Exact
Copy of his Sentence. The Whole translated from the original
German. Embellished with Heads and Coats of Arms of both
the unhappy Counts. *Philadelphia: Robert Bell?* 1773.   2876

FATHER Abraham's Pocket Almanac for 1774. *Philadelphia:
John Dunlap.* 1773.   2877

FERGUSON. (A.) An Essay on the History of Civil Society.
By Adam Ferguson. *Philadelphia: Robert Bell.* 1773.   2878

FOX. (T.) The Wilmington Almanac for 1774. By Thomas
Fox. *Wilmington: James Adams.* 1773.   2879

FRÜHAUF. (D.) Beschreibung | der bevorstehenden | Partial
Monds=Finsterniß, | so aus dem | Meridian zu Philadelphia und America
| sichtbar seyn wird, | den 7ten April, im Jahr 1773. | Von Daniel
Frühauf. | *Philadelphia,* | *Gedruckt und zu finden bey Henrich Miller,
in der Rees-strasse,* 1773. | Sq. 8vo. pp. 16.   L. C. P.   2880

FURNEAUX. (P.) Letters | To the Honourable | Mr. Justice
Blackstone, | concerning | His Exposition of the Act of Tolera-
tion, | and | Some Positions relative to Religious Liberty, | in his
celebrated | Commentaries on the Laws of England. | By Philip

Furneaux, D.D. | The Second Edition with Additions, | and | An Appendix, containing Authentic Copies of the Argument | of the late Honourable Mr. Justice Foster in the Court of Judges De- | legates, and of the Speech of the Right Honourable Lord Mansfield | in the House of Lords, in the Cause between the City of London | and the Dissenters. | *America:* | *Printed for the Subscribers,* | *By Robert Bell, at the late Union Library, in Third-street,* | *Philadelphia.* MDCCLXXIII. | 8vo. pp. xii, 155, (1). 2881

Issued as part of "An interesting Appendix to Blackstone's Commentaries," No. 2750, *supra.* See also No. 2859, *supra,* and No. 3072, *infra.* There are copies on large paper.

GARRICK. (D.) The Irish Widow. By David Garrick. As it is performed at the Theatre Royal, in Drury Lane. *Philadelphia: John Dunlap.* 1773. + *Philadelphia: James Humphreys, junior·* 1773. + *Philadelphia: Robert Macgill.* 1773. 2882

ANDREAS GEYER, | Buchbinder in der Zweyten-straffe, nahe | bey der Arch-straffe, | Hat mit den allerletzten Schiffen aus Deutsch- land folgende Bücher bekommen, | Welche er für billige Preife verkaufen wird, näml. | [*Philadelphia: Henrich Miller,* 1773.] 4to. 1 leaf. 2883

GOLDSMITH. ([Oliver)] She Stoops to Conquer. | Or the | Mistakes of a Night. | A | Comedy. | As it is Acted at the | Theatre Royal | In Covent Garden. | Written by | Doctor Goldsmith. | *Philadelphia.* | *Re-printed and sold by John Dunlap,* | *in Market-street.* | MDCCLXXIII. | 12mo. Title, 1 leaf; Dedication, 1 page; Prologue, Epilogue, &c., pp. (3); text, pp. 1–75. 2884

GOLDSMITH. The Vicar of Wakefield. By the celebrated Dr. Goldsmith. *Philadelphia: James Humphreys, jun.* 1773. 2885

"Printed on fine Pennsylvania made paper."

GOOD Public Roads, are of the greatest Utility . . . . | [*Philadelphia:* 1773.] 4to. 1 leaf. L. C. P. 2886

A new road to the westward having been laid out by order of the Governor, and there being no Public money to defray the expense, the citizens of Philadelphia are requested to contribute towards its completion.

A GREAT Variety of Ornamental, Rich Pla- | ted Goods, Just Imported by Samuel Bogle, | [*Philadelphia : Henry Miller.* 1773.] Folio, 1 leaf.   2887

Dated " Philadelphia, November 27, 1773."

GREGORY. (J.) A Father's Legacy to his Daughters. By John Gregory. *Philadelphia :* 1773. 12mo.   2888

Title from Haven's List. Perhaps intended for No. 3217, *infra.*

FRANCIS HASENCLEVER, | Jn dem Haufe worin Leonhard Melchior ehedem gewohnt hat, in | der Zweyten-ftraffe, Halbwegs zwifchen der Rees- und Arch- | ftraffe, zu Philadelphia, | Hat neulich folgende fchöne Sammlung von Büchern | aus Deutfchland erhalten, | Welche er um billigften Preife verkaufen will, näml. | [*Philadelphia : Henrich Miller.* 1773.] Folio, pp. (2).   H. S. P.   2889

DER | HOCH = DEUTSCH= | Americanifche | Calender, | Auf das Jahr | . . . | . . . | 1774. | . . . | . . . | . . . | . . . | . . . | . . . | . . . | . . . | . . . | . . . | . . . | . . . | . . . . | Zum fechs und dreyffigften mal heraus gegeben. | *Germantown : Gedruckt und zu finden bey Chris-* *toph Saur.* | . . . | . . . . [1773.] | Sq. 8vo. pp. (48).   H. S. P.   2890

INHABITANTS of Pennsylvania. | [*Philadelphia :* 1773.] 4to. 1 leaf.   L. C. P.   2891

Call for a Public Meeting to take measures to prevent the landing of Tea, dated " October 13, 1773."

JOSEPHUS. (F.) The | Works | of | Flavius Josephus : | Translated into English, by | Sir Roger L'Estrange, Kt. | Viz. | I. The Life of Josephus. Writ- | ten by himself. | II. The Antiquities of the Jews. | In Twenty Books. | III. His Book against Aprion, in | Defense of the said Antiquities | of the Jews. In Two Parts. | IV. Their Wars with the Ro- | mans. In Seven Books. | V. The Martyr bow of the Mac- | cabees. As also | All carefully revised and compared with the original Greek. | To which are prefixed, | Two Discourses, and several Remarks and Observa- | tions upon Josephus. | The Seventh Edition. | Vol. I. | *London, Printed,* | *Philadelphia :* | *Re-printed, by W. and T. Bradford, for John Mc-* *Gibbons.* | MDCCLXXIII. | 8vo. Title, 1 leaf; pp. 1–520.   2892

The second volume was not issued till October, 1774, and the third and fourth did not appear till October, 1775. I have met with the first volume only. The last two volumes may have been printed by James Humphreys, jun.

KEMPIS. (T. á) Der kleine | Kempis, | oder | kurze Sprüche | und | Gebätlein, | aus denen meistens unbekann= | ten Werklein | des | Thomae á Kempis | zusammen getragen | zur Erbauung der Kleinen. | Fünfte und vermehrte Auflage. | *Germantown,* | *gedruckt u. zu finden bey Christoph Saur,* 1773. | 16mo. pp. (10), 155, 1 plate. H. S. P. 2893

THE LANCASTER Almanac for 1774. *Lancaster. Francis Bailey.* 1773. 2894

[*Royal Arms.*] LANCASTER County, to wit: | To the | Electors | Of the Borough and | County of Lancaster. | *Lancaster: Printed by Francis Bailey, in King's-Street.* [1773.] | Folio, 1 leaf.

Proclamation by F. Stone, Sheriff, of an election to fill a vacancy in the Assembly.

DIE | LEHRTEXTE | der | Brüder=Gemeine | für das Jahr | 1774. | . . . | . . . . | *Philadelphia:* | *Gedruckt bey Henrich Miller, im Jahr* 1773. | 8vo. pp. (71). H. S. P. 2896

A LETTER from the Country, | To a Gentleman in Philadelphia. | [*Philadelphia:* 1773.] Folio, 1 leaf. L. C. P. 2897

"Rusticus" on the Tea tax, dated "Fairview, Nov. 27, 1773." Probably by John Dickinson.

LOTTERY. Philadelphia, September 23, 1773. | Pettie's-Island | Cash Lottery, | [*Philadelphia:* 1773.] Folio, 1 leaf. 2898

Scheme of a lottery to raise £1100.12.6 for the purpose of securing and improving a Public Vineyard.

LOTTERY. Pettie's Island | Cash Lottery, | In Three Classes. | *Philadelphia:* 1773.] Folio, 1 leaf. L. C. P. 2899

Scheme of a lottery to raise £2000 for the American Glass Manufactory at Manheim.

LOTTERY. The German Charitable Society's | Lottery, | On Petty's Island, in Two Classes. | [*Philadelphia:* 1773.] Folio, 1 leaf.

MARVEL. (Andrew) *Pseud.* No. I. | Philadelphia, June 10th, 1773. | To my Fellow Citizens, | Friends to Liberty, | and | Enemies to Despotism. | [*Philadelphia:* 1773.] Folio, 1 leaf. 2901

> In answer to " A Philadelphian" 's address, dated " May 29, 1773." It is in opposition to the proposed Market-Houses in Market Street. The next following tract is on the same subject.

MARVELL. Andrew Marvell's | Second | Address | to the | Inhabitants of Ppiladelphia. [*sic.*] . . . | . . . | . . . | . . . | . . . . | *Philadelphia: Printed Anno* 1773. | 8vo. pp. 16.   2902

MINUTES | of the | Philadelphian Association | In MDCCLXXIII. | [*Philadelphia: Printed by Henry Miller.* 1773.] Sm. 4to. pp. 8.   2903

MORE. (H.) Search | after | Happiness: | A | Pastoral Drama. | By | Miss Hannah More. | Performed by some young Ladies of Bristol, in | England. | . . . | . . . | . . . | . . . | . . . . | *London, Printed:* | *Philadelphia: Re-printed,* | *and Sold by all the Printers and Book-Sellers,* [1773.] | Sm. 4to. pp. (4), 29, (3). 2904

[MURREY. (James)] Sermons | to | Doctors in Divinity; | being the | Second Volume | of | Sermons to Asses. | *Philadelphia:* | *Re-printed, and sold by John Dunlap,* | *in Market-Street.* | MDCCLXXIII. | Sm. 8vo. pp. viii, 144.   L. C. P. 2905

𝖉𝖊𝖗 𝕹𝕰𝖀𝕰𝕾𝕿𝕰, Verbeffert= und Zuverläßige | Americanifche | Calender | Auf das 1774fte Jahr Chrifti, | Welches ein gemein Jahr von 365 Tagen ift. | [12 lines.] | Zum Zwölftenmal herausgegeben. | *Philadelphia, Gedruckt und zu finden bey Henrich Miller,* . . . | . . . | . . . | . . . | . . . . [1773.] | 4to. pp. (48 ?). H. S. P. 2906

THE NEW-YEAR Verses of the Carriers of the Pennsylvania Chronicle. *Philadelphia: William Goddard.* 1773.   2907

THE NEW-YEAR Verses of the Carriers of the Pennsylvania Journal. *Philadelphia: W. and T. Bradford.* 1773.   2908

THE NEW-YEAR Verses of the Carriers of the Pennsylvania Packet. *Philadelphia: John Dunlap.* 1773.   2909

THE | NEW-YEAR | Verses, | Of the Printers Lads, who carry about the Penn- | sylvania Gazette to the Customers. | January 1773. | [*Philadelphia: Hall and Sellers.* 1773.] Folio, 1 leaf. 2910

OETINGER. (F. C.) Prebigt von ber weinenben Seele Jefu. Von F. C. Oetinger. *Philadelphia:* 1773.   2911

Title from Weller's *Die falschen Druckorte.*

THE PENNSYLVANIA Chronicle. *Philadelphia: William Goddard.* Folio, pp. 1–208.   H. S. P.   2912

THE PENNSYLVANIA Gazette. *Philadelphia: Printed by Hall and Sellers, at the New Printing-* | *Office, near the Market.* | 2913

Numbers 2298 (Jan. 6, 1773) to 2349 (Dec. 29, 1773), four pages each, with "Supplements" of four pages to Numbers 2309, 2313, 2314, 2316, 2328, 2333, 2334, 2335, and 2338, and of two pages to all the others except Numbers 2318, 2324, 2344, and 2347; and "Postscripts" of one leaf to Numbers 2346 and 2348, and of two pages to No. 2324. Title as in No. 1693, *supra.*

THE PENNSYLVANIA Journal.   2914

Numbers 1570 (Jan. 6, 1773) to 1621 (Dec. 29, 1773), four pages each, with extra half-sheets of two pages to Numbers 1577 to 1580 (misnumbered 1560), 1587, 1594, 1596, 1604, 1605, 1613, and 1620; "Supplements" of two pages to Numbers 1576, 1580, 1582, 1592, 1597, 1598, and 1602; "Postscripts" of one leaf to Numbers 1575, 1584, 1618, and 1620, of four pages to No. 1611; and "Christmas Box" of one leaf to No. 1620. Title and imprint as in No. 2317, *supra.*

THE PENNSYLVANIA Packet.   2915

Numbers 63 (Jan. 4, 1773) to 114 (Dec. 27, 1773), four pages each, with "Supplements" of four pages to Numbers 78 and 81, and of two pages to all the other numbers from 63 to 104 inclusive; and a "Postscript" of one leaf to No. 113, and one of two pages to No. 112. Title and imprint as in No. 2694, *supra,* until No. 105, when they were changed to the form given in No. 3076, *infra,* and the paper was enlarged and a fourth column added.

THE PENNSYLVANIA Pocket Almanac for 1774. *Philadelphia: W. and T. Bradford.* 1773.   2916

PERSONAL Slavery | Established, | By the Suffrages | of | Custom and Right Reason. | Being a full | Answer | To the gloomy and visionary Reveries, of all | the fanatical and enthusi-

astical Writers on | that subject. | . . . | . . . | . . . | . . . | . . . |
. . . | . . . | . . . | . . . | . . . . | *Philadelphia : | Printed by John Dunlap, in Market-Street.* | M,DCC,LXXIII. | 8vo. pp. 26.   2917

POOR WILL'S | Almanack, | for the | Year of our Lord, 1774; | Being the second after Leap-Year, and the 14th Year of | the King's Reign, till October 26. | Fitted to the Latitude of Forty Degrees, and a Meridian of near five | Hours West from London. | Containing, | The Motions of the Sun and Moon; the true Places | and Aspects of the Planets; the Rising and Setting of | the Sun; the Rising, Setting, and Southing of the | Moon; the Lunations, Conjunctions, Eclipses, Rising, | Setting, and Southing of the Planets; Length of Days, | Judgment of the Weather; Festivals, and other Re- | markable Days; Table of Tide; Tables of Interest, | Table of the Value and Weight of Coins; Quakers | Yearly Meetings; Fairs, Courts, Roads, &c. | Also, | A liquid Remedy for decayed Teeth, Sir Hans | Sloane's Eye-salve; On Drunkenness; Contentment | and Avarice; and a Variety of other useful and en- | tertaining Matter. | *Philadelphia : | Printed and sold by Joseph Crukshank, in Market-street, | between Second and Third Streets, and opposite the Presbyterian | Meeting-House.* [1773.] | Sm. 8vo. pp. (36).   H. S. P.   2918

POOR Will's Pocket Almanac for 1774. *Philadelphia : Joseph Crukshank.* 1773.   2919

PORTEUS. (B.) Death : | A | Poetical Essay. | By Beilby Porteus, M.A. | Fellow of Christ College. | The Fourth Edition. | *Philadelphia : | Printed by Robert Bell, in Third-street, | And Sold by | William Woodhouse, in Front-street.* | MDCCLXXIII. | 8vo. pp. 20.   L. C. P.   2920

PROCLAMATION. [*Royal Arms.*] | By the Honourable | John Penn, Esquire, | Governor, and Commander in Chief of the Province of Pennsylvania, and Counties of New-Castle, | Kent and Sussex, on Delaware, | A Proclamation. | *Philadelphia : Printed by Hall and Sellers.* 1773. | Folio, 1 leaf.   H. S. P.   2921

Against settlers on land not yet purchased from the Indians, dated "Sept. 20, 1773."

GEORG CHRISTOPH REINHOLDT, | Buchbinder in der Marft = ſtraſſe, neben dem Wirthshauſe zum Schwarzen | Bären, zu Philadelphia, hat folgende Bücher zu Verkaufen: | [*Philadelphia: Henrich Miller.* 1773.] Folio, 1 leaf.   L. C. P.   2922

ROBERTS. (D.) Some | Memoirs | Of the Life of | John Roberts. | Written by his Son | Daniel Roberts. | The Sixth Edition. | ... | ... | .... | *Philadelphia:* | *Printed by Joseph Crukshank, in* | *Market-Street, between Second and Third* | *Streets.* MDCCLXXIII. | 12mo. pp. 57, (2).   2923

[RUSH. (Benjamin)] An | Address | to | The Inhabitants | of the | British Settlements, | on the | Slavery of the Negroes | in | America. | The Second Edition. | To which is added, A | Vindication of the Address, | in Answer to a Pamphlet entitled, " Slavery | not forbidden in Scripture ; or, a Defence of the | West India Planters." | By a Pennsylvanian. | ... | ... | ... | ... | ... | ... | ... | ... | ... | ... | ... | ... | ... | ... | ... | .... | *Philadelphia:* | *Printed and Sold by John Dunlap.* | M,DCC,LXXIII. | 8vo. Title, 1 leaf; pp. 28, 1 leaf.   F.   2924

[RUSH.] An | Address | to | The Inhabitants | of the | British Settlements | in | America, | upon | Slave-Keeping. | The Second Edition. | To which are added, | Observations on a Pamphlet, entitled, | " Slavery not forbidden by Scripture ; or, A | Defence of the West-India Planters." | By a Pennsylvanian. | ... | ... | ... | ... | ... | ... | ... | ... | ... | ... | ... | ... | ... | .... | *Philadelphia:* | *Printed and Sold by John Dunlap.* | M.DCC.LXXIII. | 8vo. Title, 1 leaf; pp. 28, 1 leaf.

RUSH. Experiments | and | Observations | on the | Mineral Waters | of | Philadelphia, Abington, | and Bristol, | In the Province of Pennsylvania. | Read June 18, 1773, before the American Philo- | sophical Society, held at Philadelphia. | By Benjamin Rush, M.D. | Professor of Chemistry in the College of | Philadelphia. | ... | ... | ... | .... | *Philadelphia:* | *Printed by James Humphreys, junior,* | *In Front-street.* | MDCCLXXIII. | 8vo. pp. 30.   H. S. P.   2926

The waters of Abington, and Bath, near Bristol, were much resorted to till near the middle of the present century. The fame of the *supposed* " Philadelphia Mineral Water," on the disagreeable taste and fetid smell of which Dr. Rush has much to say, was short-lived. The true cause of these qualities being soon discovered to arise not from mineral sources, but from one which put an immediate stop to the use of the water, and made its advocates and their disciples a subject of ridicule.

[RUSH.]   A | Vindication | of the | Address, | To the Inhabitants of the British | Settlements, on the Slavery of | the Negroes in America, in An- | swer to a Pamphlet entitled, | " Slavery not Forbidden | by | Scripture; | Or a Defence of the West-India | Planters from the Aspersions | thrown out against them by the Author | of the Address." | . . . | . . . | . . . | . . . | . . . | . . . | . . . | . . . | . . . . | By a Pennsylvanian. | *Philadelphia:* | *Printed by John Dunlap, in Market-Street.* | M,DCC,LXXIII. | 8vo. pp. 54.   F. 2927

This was appended to the second edition of Rush's Address to the Inhabitants of the British Settlements.

SAUNDERS. (R.)   A Pocket | Almanack | for the Year 1774. | . . . | . . . | . . . | . . . . | By R. Saunders, Phil. | *Philadelphia:* | *Printed and Sold by Hall, and | Sellers.* [1773.] | 24mo. pp. 24.

SAUNDERS.   Poor Richard improved: | Being an | Almanack | . . . | . . . | . . . | . . | . . | . . | . . | . . | . . | . . | . . | . . . | For the | Year of our Lord 1774: | . . . | . . . | . . . | . . . | . . . | . . . | . . . | . . . | . . . . | By Richard Saunders, Philom. | *Philadelphia:* | *Printed and Sold by Hall and Sellers.* [1773.] | Sm. 8vo. pp. (36).   H. S. P. 2929

SHIPLEY. (J.)   A | Sermon | Preached before the | Incorporated Society | for the | Propagation of the Gospel in Foreign Parts; | at their | Anniversary Meeting | in the | Parish Church of St. Mary-le-Bow, | On Friday, February 19, 1773. | By the Right Reverend | Jonathan Lord Bishop of St. Asaph, | *Philadelphia:* | *Printed by Robert Bell, in Third-street,* | *And Sold by* | *William Woodhouse, in Front-street.* | MDCCLXXIII. | 8vo. Halftitle, &c. pp. (2); Title, 1 leaf; pp. 3–20. L. C. P. + *Philadelphia:* *Robert Aitken.* 1773.   2930

SLAVERY | not forbidden by | Scripture. | Or a defence | of the | West-India Planters, | From the Aspersions thrown out against | them, by the author of a pamphlet, entitled, | " An Address to the inhabitants of | the British settlements in America, upon | Slave - Keeping. | By a West-Indian. | . . . | . . . | . . . | . . . | . . . . | *Philadelphia.* | *Printed* [*by John Sparhawk*] M,DCC,LXXIII. | 8vo. Title, 1 leaf; pp. iii, 30.   L. C. P.   2931

SMITH. (W.) An | Oration, | Delivered, January 22 1773, | before | The Patron, Vice-Presidents | and Members | of the | American | Philosophical Society, | held at | Philadelphia, | for promoting | Useful Knowledge. | By William Smith, D.D. | One of the Secretaries of the said Society, and Provost of the | College of Philadelphia. | *Philadelphia :* | *Printed by John Dunlap, in Market-Street.* | M,DCC,LXXIII. | 4to. pp. 15.   H. S. P.   2932

SOMMERS. ([John, Baron]) The Judgment of | Whole Kingdoms and Nations, | Concerning the | Rights, Power and Prerogative | of | Kings, | and the | Rights, Priviledges, and Properties | of the | People : | Shewing | The Nature of Government in general, both from | God and Man. An Account of the British Go- | vernment ; and the Rights and Priviledges of | the People in the Time of the Saxons, and since the Con- | quest. The Government which God ordain'd over the Children | of Israel; and that all Magistrates and Governors proceed from | the People, by many Examples in Scripture and History; and the | Duty of Magistrates from Scripture and Reason. An Account | of Eleven Emperors, and above Fifty Kings depriv'd for their | evil Government. The Right of the People and Parliament of | Britain, to Resist and Deprive their Kings for | evil Government, by King Henry's Charter; and likewise in Scotland, | by many Examples. | The Prophets and ancient Jews were Strangers to absolute Pas- | sive-Obedience. Resisting of Arbitrary Government | is allow'd by many Examples in Scriptures; by most Nations; and | by undeniable Reason. | A large Account of the Revolution; with several | Speeches, Declarations, and Addresses; and the Names and | Proceedings of Ten Bishops, and above Sixty Peers, concern'd | in the Revolution before King James went out of England. | Several Declarations in Queen Elizabeth's Time of the Clergy | in Convocation, and the Parliament | who assisted, and justified the Scotch, French, and Dutch, in Re- | sisting of their Evil and Destructive Princes. | By Lord Sommers. | The Eleventh Edition Corrected. | *Phila-* *delphia:* | *Re-printed, and sold by John Dunlap,* | *in Market-Street.* | MDCCLXXIII. | 8vo. pp. 156, (1).   H. S. P.   2933

[STERNE. (Laurence)]   Letters | from | Yorick to Eliza. | *London, Printed:* | *Philadelphia, Re-printed, by John Dunlap,* | *in Market-street,* | M,DCC,LXXIII. | 12mo. pp. 71.   L. C. P.   2934

𝕯𝕴𝕰 | 𝕿𝕬𝕲𝕷𝕴𝕮𝕳𝕰𝕹 | Loosungen | der | Brüder=Gemeine | für das Jahr | 1774. | *Philadelphia,* | *Gedruckt bey Henrich Miller, im Jahr* 1773. | 8vo. pp. (48).   H. S. P.   2935

THE TEA-SHIP being arrived, every Inhabitant, . . . | . . . is desired to meet at the | State-House . . . . | [*Philadelphia:* 1773.] 4to. 1 leaf.   L. C. P.   2936

Dated "Monday Morning, December 27, 1773."

[TERSTEEGEN. (Gerhard)]   Geistliches | Blumen = Gärtlein | Inniger Seelen; | Oder kurze | Schluß=Reimen, | Betrachtungen und Lieder | Ueber allerhand Wahrheiten des | Inwendigen Christenthums ; | Zur | Erweckung, Stärkung und Erquickung | in dem | verborgenen Leben mit Christo | in Gott; | Nebst der | Frommen Lotterie. | Sechste und vermehrte Auflage. | *Germantown,* | *gedruckt und zu finden bey* *Christoph Saur,* | 1773. | 24mo. pp. (12), 547.   H. S. P.   2937

TO the | Advocates | for | Ministerial Oppression. | [*Philadel-* *phia:* 1773.] Folio, 1 leaf.   L. C. P.   2938

"Clodius" on the Tea tax.

TO the | Commissioners | Appointed by the East-India Company, | for the Sale of | Tea, in America. | [*Philadelphia:* 1773.] Folio, 1 leaf.   L. C. P.   2939

"Scævola" warning the Commissioners not to act.

TO the | Delaware Pilots. | [*Philadelphia:* 1773.]   4to. 1 leaf.

The Committee for Tarring and Feathering's warning to Pilots not to bring up the Tea Ship Polly, Capt. Ayres.

TO the | Delaware Pilots. | [And] To | Capt. Ayres. | [*Philadelphia:* 1773.] Folio, 1 leaf.   L. C. P.   2941

The Committee on Tarring and Feathering's renewal of the warning to the Pilots, and threatening Capt. Ayres with "Ten Gallons of liquid Tar, and the Feathers of a dozen wild Geese," dated "Nov. 27, 1773."

TO the | Delaware | Pilots. | [*Philadelphia:* 1773.] Folio, 1 leaf.   L. C. P.   2942

The Committee for Tarring and Feathering warning pilots not to bring up the Tea Ship Polly, Capt. Ayres, dated "Dec. 7, 1773."

TO the Freemen of America. | [*Philadelphia:* 1773.] Folio, 1 leaf.   L. C. P.   2943

"Mucius" on the Tea tax.

TO the Freemen, Citizens of Philadelphia. | [*Philadelphia:* 1773.] Folio, 1 leaf.   L. C. P.   2944

"A Philadelphian" in support of the project to erect market sheds in Market Street, dated "May 29, 1773."

To the Freemen, Citizens of Philadelphia. | [*Philadelphia:* 1773.] Folio, 1 leaf.   L. C. P.   2945

"A Philadelphian" against the action of the Corporation in occupying the river ends of the streets with wharfs, and renting them, dated "June 16, 1773."

TO the | Freemen | of | Pennsylvania. | [*Philadelphia:* 1773.] Folio, 1 leaf.   L. C. P.   2946

"Regulus" on the Tea tax.

TO the Freeholders and Freemen, | In Pennsylvania. | [*Philadelphia:* 1773.] Folio, 1 leaf.   L. C. P.   2947

"A Countryman" against the Tea tax, dated "Chester County, October 14, 1773."

TO the Good People of Pennsylvania. | [*Philadelphia :* 1773.]
Folio, pp. (3).　　　　　　　　　　　　　　　　L. C. P.　2948

" Publicus" in defence of the Excise Law, dated " January 5, 1773."

TO the | Tradesmen, Mechanics, &c. | Of the Province of |
Pennsylvania. | [*Philadelphia :* 1773.] Folio, 1 leaf.　H. S. P.　2949

" A Mechanic" on the Tea tax, dated " December 4, 1773."

TOBLER. (J.) The Pennsylvania Town and Countryman's
Almanac for 1774. By John Tobler. *Wilmington : James Adams.*
1773.　　　　　　　　　　　　　　　　　　　　　　2950

TOPLADY. (A. [Montague]) The Doctrine of Absolute Pre-
destination Stated and Asserted : With a Preliminary Discourse
on the Divine Attributes. Translated in great measure from the
Latin of Jerom Zanchius. By Augustus Toplady. *Philadelphia :*
Robert Aitken. 1773.　　　　　　　　　　　　　　2951

THE | UNIVERSAL | Almanack, | For the Year of our Lord,
| 1774 ; | Being the Second after Bissextile or Leap- | Year.
(The Fourteenth Year of the Reign of | King George III.) | Con-
taining ; | The Motions of the Sun and Moon ; | The true Places
and Aspects of the Planets ; | The Rising and Setting of the Sun—
And, | The Rising, Setting and Southing of the Moon. | Also, The
Lunations, Conjunctions, Eclipses, Judg- | ment of the Weather,
Rising and Setting of the | Planets, Length, Increase and Decrease
of Days | and Nights, Equation of Time, Fairs, Courts, | Roads,
&c. Together with useful Tables, chrono- | logical Observations,
and entertaining Remarks. | Fitted to the Latitude of Forty De-
grees North, and | near Five Hours West from London ; but may,
with- | out material Error, serve all the Northern Colonies. | *Phil-*
adelphia : | *Printed & Sold by James Humphreys, jun.* | *in Front-street,*
at the Corner of Black-horse Alley. [1773.] | Sm. 8vo. pp. (36).

VOTES | and | Proceedings | of the | House of Representatives
| of the | Province of Pennsylvania, | Met at Philadelphia, on the
Fourteenth of October, Anno | Domini 1772, and continued by
Adjournments. | [*Royal Arms.*] | *Philadelphia :* | *Printed and Sold by*

Henry Miller, in Race-Street. | MDCCLXXIII. | Folio, Title, 1 leaf; pp. 415–498.   H. S. P.   2953

VOTES | of the | House of Representatives. | [Colophon.] *Philadelphia: Printed by Henry Miller, in Race-Street.* [1773.] Folio, pp. 41 +.   H. S. P.   2954

Issued weekly, in parts of from two to eight pages each. The first imprint is on page 25. With the third part the date was regularly inserted thus : " From Monday, January 18 to Saturday, January 23, 1773," &c.

VOTES | of the | House of Representatives, | From Thursday, October 14, to Saturday, October 16, 1773. | [*Philadelphia: Henry Miller.* 1773.] Folio, pp. 4.   H. S. P.   2955

Continued weekly to December 24, 1773, pp. 17.

WATTS. (I.) Divine Songs, attempted in easy Language for the use of Children. By Isaac Watts. *Philadelphia: Printed by Joseph Crukshank for Robert Aitken.* 1773.   2956

WEATHERWISE. (A.) Father Abraham's Almanac for 1774. By Abraham Weatherwise. *Philadelphia: John Dunlap.* 1773.

WESLEY. (J.) Primitive Physic, or an easy and natural Method of Curing most Diseases. By John Wesley. *Philadelphia: Joseph Crukshank.* 1773.   2958

WHITTENHALL. ([Edward]) A | Short Introduction | to | Grammar, | For the Use of the | College and Academy | in | Philadelphia: | Being a New Edition of | Whittenhall's Latin Grammar, | With many Alterations, Additions and Amend- | ments, from antient and late Grammarians. | The Second Edition. | . . . | . . . | . . . . | *Philadelphia, Printed; | By James Humphreys, junior, | For the College and Academy of Philadelphia, | and Sold by him at his Printing-office, at the | lower Corner of Black-horse Alley, in Front- | street.* MDCCLXXIII. | Sm. 8vo. pp. i–v, 1–145.   2959

The author's name is variously spelled on different editions of his works.

THE WITS of Westminster, A New Select Collection of Jests, Bon Mots, Humorous Tales, Brilliant Repartees, Epigrams, and other sallies of Wit and Humour. Chiefly New and Original. By a Member of the Calcannon Club. *Philadelphia: John Dunlap.* 1773.   2960

YOU are earnestly requested to meet a Number of the Free- | holders of this City, at John Little's, . . . | . . . to consider of the | best Method, to prevent the Mayor and Commonalty from car- | rying their present Intentions, of erecting Shambles in High- | Street, into Execution. | [*Philadelphia:* 1773.] 4to. 1 leaf.

Dated " Philadelphia, June — 1773."

1774.

AN ACCOUNT of the Births and Burials in St. | Paul's Church, in Philadelphia, from Decem- | ber 25, 1773, to December 25, 1774. By Alex. | Hale, Clerk, and James Harris, Sexton. | [*Philadelphia :* 1774.] Folio, 1 leaf.   L. C. P.   2962

AN ACCOUNT of the Births and Burials in the | United Congregations of Christ-Church and St. Peter's, in | Philadelphia, from December 25, 1773, to December 25, 1774. | By Matthew Whitehead, and William Young, Clerks, | and Jacob Diegel, and George Stokes, Sextons. | [*Philadelphia:* 1774.] Folio, 1 leaf.

AN ACCOUNT of the Burials and Baptisms in the Baptist Church. *Philadelphia:* 1774.   2964

AN ACCOUNT of the Burials in the Second Presbyterian Church. *Philadelphia:* 1774.   2965

ACT of the Associate Presbytery in Pennsylvania, for a Public Fast. At Philadelphia, the seventh Day of November, one thousand seven hundred and seventy-four Years. *Philadelphia: Robert Aitken.* 1774.   2966

Reprinted at Glasgow in 1775. By an entry in Aitken's Ledger, July 29, 1777, it would seem that he had not been paid for printing this tract up to that time.

ADVERTISEMENT. *Philadelphia: Robert Aitken.* 1774.   2967

Aitken's Ledger during 1774 contains the following charges :

April 24. Wilday and Montgomery for printing 100 copies of Abraham Ritchie's Advertisement.

May 11. Ezekiel Letts, tailor, for printing 200 folio Advertisements.

June 21. George Bartram, for printing 500 large folio Advertisements.

ADVERTISEMENT. Millstones to be sold by Clarkson and Bonsall. *Philadelphia : Robert Aitken.* 1774.   2968

THE AMERICAN Calendar for 1775. *Philadelphia : W. and T. Bradford.* 1774.   2969

AMERICAN CHRONICLES. The first Book of the Ame- | rican Chronicles of the | Times. | [Colophon.] *Philadelphia : Printed and Sold by B. Towne.* [1774.] | 8vo. pp. 70.   L. C. P.   2970

Chapters I. to VI., of twelve pages each, except II., which contains only ten, and III. only eleven pages. The imprint appears at the end of each chapter. The first was issued in October, the second in November, the third and fourth in December, 1774, and the fifth and sixth in February, 1775. A third edition of the first chapter was announced.

AMERICANUS | examined, | and his | Principles | Compared with those of the | Approved Advocates | for | America, | By a Pennsylvanian. | *Philadelphia : | Printed in the year,* MDCCLXXIV. | 8vo. pp. 24.   L. C. P.   2971

An die Einwohner | der Stadt und County Philadelphia. | [*Philadelphia : Henrich Miller.* 1774.] 4to. 1 leaf.   H. S. P.   2972

On the Boston Port-Bill.

ANNO Regni | Georgii III. Regis, | Magnæ Britanniæ Franciæ & Hiberniæ, | Decimo Quarto. | At a General Assembly of the Province of Penn-' | sylvania, begun and holden at Phila- delphia, | the Fourteenth Day of October, Anno Domini 1773, in | the Thirteenth Year of the Reign of our Sovereign Lord | George III. by the Grace of God, of Great- | Britain, France and Ireland, King, Defender of the | Faith, &c. | And from thence continued by Adjournments to the | Twenty-second Day of January, 1774. | [*Penn Arms.*] | *Philadelphia : | Printed and Sold by Hall and Sellers, at the | New Printing-Office, near the Market.* MDCCLXXIV. | Folio, Title, 1 leaf; pp. 367–407, (1). + [Continued to July 23,

1774.] pp. 409–411. + And from thence continued . . . to the | Twenty-ninth Day of September, 1774. | [*Ibid.*] Title, 1 leaf; pp. 413–436.   H. S. P.   2973

AUSZÜGE | aus den | Stimmungen | und | Verhandlungen | des | Americanischen | Congresses | vom Besten Lande, | Gehalten zu Phila= delphia, den 5ten Sept. 1774. | Enthaltend | Die Bill der Rechten, eine Liste von Be= | schwerden, gelegentliche Schlüsse, eine | Addresse an des Volk von Großbrit= | tannien, und ein Memorial an die Ein= | wohner der Brittisch=Americanischen | Colonien. | Herausgegeben auf Befehl des Congresses; | und aus dem Englischen übersetzt. | *Philadelphia,* | *Gedruckt und zu haben bey Henrich Miller,* | 1774. | 16mo. pp. 76.   H. S. P.   2974

BACHMAIR. (J. J.)   The German Grammar.   By John James Bachmair.   *Philadelphia: Henry Miller.*   1774.   2975

BARKER. (P.)   Vindiciæ Veritates : Or, A Further Testimony to Theses Theologiæ, being an illustration of the fifth and sixth theological propositions, which are defended by Robert Barclay, in his Apology, for the true church divinity, as the same is held forth and preached, by the people called Quakers. By Peter Barker, M.S. Professor of truth and the plain language in the most unholy courts of Star-Chamber and Inquisition of the Quaker Church in North America.   *Philadelphia : Peter Barker.*   1774.   2976

[BELL.] (Robert)   Philadelphia, January 17th, 1774. | Memorandum. | The more Books are sold, the more will be sold, is an established | Truth, well known to every liberal Reader, and to every Bookseller of Experience ; | [*Philadelphia : Robert Bell.* 1774.]   Folio, 2 leaves.   L. C. P.   2977

In support of a petition to the Assembly to authorize Book auctions in Philadelphia.

BELL. (R.)   Proposals by Robert Bell for Printing by Subscription Lectures on Materia Medica, by William Cullen, M.D. *Philadelphia: Robert Bell.*   1774.   2978

BELL. (R.)   Proposals | For Printing by Subscription, | the | Catholic Christian | Instructed. | In the | Sacraments, Sacrifice,

Ceremonies, and Observances of the | Church. | By way of | Question and Answer. | By R[ichard] C[halloner.] | *Philadelphia:* | *Printed by Robert Bell, in Third-street.* | MDCCLXXIV. | 12mo. pp. (4).   2979

[BENEZET. (Anthony)] The | Mighty Destroyer | Displayed, | In some Account of the | Dreadful Havoc made by the mistaken Use as | well as Abuse of | Distilled Spirituous Liquors. | By a Lover of Mankind. | . . . | . . . | . . . | *Philadelphia:* | *Printed by Joseph Crukshank, between Second* | *and Third Streets, in Market-Street.* | M.DCC.LXXIV. | Sm. 8vo. pp. 48.   H. S. P.   2980

[BENEZET.] The | Potent Enemies | of | America | Laid Open: | Being | Some account of the baneful effects attending the use of | Distilled Spirituous Liquors, | and the | Slavery | of the | Negroes. | *Philadelphia:* | *Printed by Joseph Crukshank in Market-* | *Street, between Second and Third Streets.* [1774.] | 16mo. pp. (2). •

This is only a general title-page to two pamphlets separately printed for Benezet. See Wesley, No. 3134, *infra*, and the preceding.

B[ERNARD] (F[rancis]) The | Causes | of the | Present Distractions | in | America | explained: | In | Two Letters | to a | Merchant | In London. | By F—. B—. | [*Philadelphia:*] *Printed* [*by W. and T. Bradford*] *in the Year* 1774. | 8vo. pp. 16.   L. C. P.   2982

BOSTWICK. (D.) A Fair and Rational Vindication of the right of Infants to the ordinance of Baptism. By David Bostwick, A.M. *Wilmington: James Adams.* 1774.   2983

[BRACKENRIDGE. (Hugh Montgomery)] A | Poem | on | Divine Revelation; | being an | Exercise | Delivered | At the Public Commencement | at | Nassau-Hall, | September 28. 1774. | By the same Person, who on a similar occasion, Sept. 25. 1771. | delivered a small Poem on the rising Glory of America. | *Philadelphia:* | *Printed and sold by R. Aitken, Bookseller,* | *opposite the London-coffee-house,* | *Front-street.* | M.DCC.LXXIV. | 8vo. pp. (6), 22.   L. C. P.   2984

In Aitken's Ledger, sales of this pamphlet are always entered as Brackenridge's Poem on Divine Revelation. In later life the author was well known as Judge Hugh *Henry* Brackenridge. In his first acknowledged work, No. 3678, *infra*, his name appears as Hugh Montgomery Brackenridge, and in his second, No. 3856, *infra*, as Hugh M. Brackenridge. His son, in reprinting the latter as by H. H. Brackenridge, alludes to the former as also by his father. Judge B. also called himself Hugh Montgomery B. in the advertisement of his School at Frederick Town, Md., which appeared in the Pa. Gazette, May 2, 1778.

BROOKE. ([Henry]) Juliet Grenville: | Or, the | History | of the | Human Heart. | Three volumes in two. | By Mr. Brooke. | Vol. I. | *London, Printed:* | *Philadelphia:* | *Re-printed, for John Sparhawk,* | *and John Dunlap.* | MDCCLXXIV. | 12mo. pp. 293. + Vol. II. | [*Ibid.*] | 12mo. pp. 276.   L. C. P.   2985

BUCHAN. (W.) Domestic Medicine; | Or, the | Family Physician: | Being an Attempt | To render the Medical Art more generally useful, by | shewing people what is in their own power both with re- | spect to the Prevention and Cure of Diseases. | Chiefly | Calculated to recommend a proper attention to | Regimen and Simple Medicines. | By William Buchan, M.D. | Of the Royal College of Physicians, Edinburgh. | . . . | . . . | . . . | . . . . | The Second American Edition, | with considerable Additions, by the Author. | *Philadelphia:* | *Printed by Joseph Crukshank,* | *For R. Aitken, at his Book-Store, opposite the* | *London Coffee-House, in Front-Street.* | M.DCC.LXXIV. | 8vo. pp. xxiv, 461.   H. S. P.   2986

[CARTWRIGHT. (Edmund)] Armine | and | Elvira. | A | Legendary Tale. | In Two Parts. | *Philadelphia, Re-printed* | *By James Humphreys, junior, in Front-street.* | MDCCLXXIV. | 8vo. pp. 30, 1 leaf.   H. S. P.   2987

Printed with More's Search after Happiness (see No. 3061, *infra*), but the pagination and signatures are begun anew, and it is sometimes found separately.

CATALOGUE of New and Old Books, to be sold by Auction, by Robert Bell, Bookseller, and Professor of Book-Auctioneering, on Monday the Seventh of February, 1774. *Philadelphia: Robert Bell.* 1774.   2988

CATALOGUE of Books to be Sold at Auction March 14, 1774. *Philadelphia: Robert Bell.* 1774.   2989

CATALOGUE of Books to be Sold at Auction on May 19th, 1774. *Philadelphia: Robert Bell.* 1774.   2990

CATALOGUE of Books to be Sold at Auction on December 16th, 1774. *Philadelphia : Robert Bell.* 1774.   2991

THE CHILD of Nature, a Philosophical Novel. In Two Volumes. *Philadelphia : James Humphreys, junior.* 1774.   2992

COLMAN. (G.) The Man of Business. A Comedy. By George Colman. *Philadelphia : John Dunlap.* 1774.   2993

COLMAN, and D. GARRICK. The Clandestine Marriage. By George Colman and David Garrick. *Philadelphia : Robert Bell.* 1774.   2994

COMMITTEE Chamber, December 6, 1774. | [*Philadelphia :* 1774.] 4to. 1 leaf.   L. C. P.   2995

Resolves of the Committee of Philadelphia in regard to the 10th Article of the Association of the General Congress, requiring the opening of all packages of goods imported after Dec. 1st.

A | COMPENDIOUS | History | of the | World, | from | The Creation to the Dissolution | of the Roman Republic. | Compiled for the use of Young Gentlemen | and Ladies. | Embellished with Variety of Copperplates. | Vol. II. | *Philadelphia : | Printed and sold by R. Aitken, | bookseller, opposite the London | Coffee-house, Front-Street.* | M.DCC.LXXIV. | 16mo. pp. 176, 7 plates.   2996

COOKE'S Voyage round the World. In Two Volumes. *Philadelphia : James Humphreys, junior.* 1774. 8vo.   2997

COOMBE. (T[homas]) The Harmony between the Old and New | Testaments respecting the Messiah : | Being the Substance of | Two Sermons | Preached before the United Congre- | gations of Christ-Church and | St. Peter's, Philadelphia, | On Christmas-Day, 1773 ; | And | On the Sunday when a Collection was | made for the relief of the Poor of those | Congregations. | By T. Coombe, M.A. | Chaplain to the Most Noble the Marquis of | Rockingham, and one of the Assistant Ministers | of Christ-Church and St. Peter's. | . . . | . . . | . . . . | *Philadelphia : | Printed by John Dunlap, in Market-Street.* | M,DCC,LXXIV. | 12mo. pp. 59.   N. Y. H. S.   2998

THE COUNTRY-MAN'S Almanac for 1775. *Lancaster:*
Stewart Herbert, junior. 1774. 2999

THE COUNTING-HOUSE Almanac for 1775. *Philadelphia:*
Robert Aitken. 1774. 3000

[DE FOE. (Daniel)] The | Dreadful Visitation, | in a | Short
Account of the Progress and Effects | of the | Plague, | The last
time it spread in the city of London, in | the year 1665, extracted
from the memoirs | of a person who resided there during the |
whole time of that infection. | . . . | . . . . | *Philadelphia :* | *Printed*
by Joseph Crukshank on the North side | *of Market-Street, between*
Second and Third Streets. | MDCCLXXIV. | 16mo. pp. 16. 3001

A | DIALOGUE, | between | A Southern Delegate, | and | His
Spouse, | on his return from | The Grand Continental Congress.
| A Fragment, | inscribed | To the Married Ladies of America, |
By their most sincere, | And affectionate Friend, | And Servant,
| Mary V. V. | *Printed in the Year* M,DCC,LXXIV. | 8vo. pp. 14.

Said to have been printed in Philadelphia, but I think it came from the Press of
James Rivington in New York.

[DICKINSON. (John)] An | Essay | on the Constitutional
Power of | Great-Britain | over the Colonies in | America ; | with
the | Resolves | of the | Committee | for the Province of | Penn-
sylvania, | and their | Instructions | To their Representatives | in
Assembly. | *Philadelphia:* | *Printed and Sold, by William and Thomas*
| *Bradford, at the London Coffee-House.* | M.DCC.LXXIV. | 8vo.
pp. vii, 127, (1). H. S. P. 3003

[DICKINSON.] Letters from a Farmer in Pennsylvania, To
the Inhabitants of the British Colonies. *Philadelphia :* 1774. 3004

Title from Sabin's Dictionary and Haven's List. The former says there are copies
in the libraries of Harvard College and Congress, but these proved to be copies of a
London edition with the following imprint : *Philadelphia printed, and London re-*
printed, MDCCLXXIV. From this I think it has been assumed that there was an
edition printed during 1774 in Philadelphia, and as I have been unable to find a trace
of it, I do not believe that there ever was such an edition.

DILWORTH. (T.) A New Guide to the English Tongue. By
Thomas Dilworth. *Philadelphia : Robert Aitken.* 1774. 3005

DIRECTIONS | for the | Gulph and River | of | St. Lawrence, | with | some occasional | Remarks, | *Philadelphia:* | *Printed by William and Thomas Bradford,* | *at the London Coffee-House.* | M,DCC,LXXIV. | 8vo. Title, 1 leaf; pp. 36.   H. S. P.   3006

[DRINKER. (John)] Observations | on the late | Popular Measures, | Offered to the serious Consideration of the sober | Inhabitants of Pennsylvania, | By a Tradesman of | Philadelphia. | *Philadelphia:* | *Printed for a Tradesman.* | MDCCLXXIV. | 8vo. pp. 24.   H. S. P.   3007

[DUCHÉ. (Jacob)] Observations | on a | Variety of Subjects, | Literary, Moral and Religious; | In a Series of | Original Letters, | Written by a Gentleman of Foreign | Extraction, who resided some Time in | Philadelphia. | Revised by a Friend, to whose Hands the | Manuscript was committed for Publication. | *Philadelphia:* | *Printed by John Dunlap.* | M,DCC,LXXIV. | 12mo. pp. x, 241, (1).

EIGHT Propositions respecting the closing of the Port of Boston. [*Philadelphia?* 1774.] 4to.   3009

AN | EPISTLE | from our | Yearly-Meeting, | Held at Philadelphia, for Pennsylvania and | New-Jersey, by Adjournments, from the 24th | Day of the 9th Month, to the 1st of the 10th | Month, inclusive, 1774 : | To our Friends and Brethren in these and the | neighbouring Provinces. | [*Philadelphia: Joseph Crukshank.* 1774.] Folio, pp. 4.   F.   3010

EPITAPH, &c. | [*Philadelphia:* 1774.] 8vo. pp. 4.   L. C. P.   3011

Two mock epitaphs, the first on Alexander Wedderburne, and the second on Gov. Thomas Hutchinson.

ERZEHLUNG | derer durch | Samuel Brand | verübten gantz un= menfchi= | chen Thaten, | und | feiner derauf erfolgten Hinrichtung. | . . . | . . . | . . . | . . . . | Andere Auflage. | Welcher ein erbaulicher und denen mei= | ften unbefanter gefang beygefügt worden. | *Lancaester:* *Gedruckt und zu fin-* | *den bey Francis Bailey.* 1774. | Sm. 8vo. pp. 34 +.   L. C. P.   3012

AN EXAMINATION into the Conduct of the Delegates at
their Grand Convention, held in Philadelphia, September, 1774.
Philadelphia: 1774.   3013

Title from Haven's List, and the Catalogue of the Library Company of Philadelphia. Upon examination of the volume referred to by the latter, it proves to be :
The | Congress | Canvassed : | Or, | An Examination | into | The Conduct of the
Delegates, | at their | Grand Convention, | Held in Philadelphia, Sept. 1, 1774. |
Addressed | To the Merchants of New-York. | By A. W. Farmer. | Author of
Free Thoughts, &c. | [six lines.] | Printed in the Year M,DCC,LXXIV. |

It was not printed in Philadelphia, but, like other tracts by Isaac Wilkins (A
Westchester Farmer), by James Rivington in New York.

THE EXAMINATION of Baron Messeres and Mr. Hey, at
the Bar of Parliament, on the same account and at the same time
with Dr. Marriot. *Philadelphia: James Humphreys.* 1774. 3014

EXTRACTS | From the | Votes and Proceedings | Of the
American Continental | Congress, | Held at Philadelphia on the
| 5th of September, 1774. | Containing | The Bill of Rights,
a List of Griev- | ances, Occasional Resolves, the | Association, an
Address to the People | of Great Britain, and a Memorial | to
the Inhabitants of the British | American Colonies. | Published
by order of the Congress. | *Philadelphia:* | *Printed by William and
Thomas Bradford,* | *October 27th,* M,DCC,LXXIV. | 8vo. Title, 1
leaf; pp. 1–23, 1–50.   H. S. P. 3015

FATHER Abraham's Pocket Almanac for 1775. *Philadelphia:
John Dunlap.* 1774.   3016

FENNING. (D.) Der | Geſchwinde Rechner. | Oder: des | Händ=
lers nützlicher Gehülfe ; | in | Kauffung und Verkauffung allerley Sa= |
chen ſowohl im Groſſen als Kleinen. | da auf einmal gezeigt wird |
Der Werth von allerley Waaren oder Sachen, | von einem Viertel
Pens bis auf 19 Schilling | und 9 Pens; und von einem Pfund,
Jard, | Galle, Buſchel, ꝛc. bis auf 10,000. | Und ſolches auf eine ſo
leichte Weiſe, das ſich eine | Perſon, die ſonſt nichts von der Rechen=
kunſt ge= | lernt hat, doch darnach richten kan, und dem der | rechnen
kan, iſt es eine geſchwinde anzeige, wo= | durch er Mühe und Zeit
erſpahrt. | In der engliſchen Sprache zum 7ten mal herausgegeben |

burd Daniel Fenning. | unb nun verbeffert, Deutfd ans Licht gebradt. | *Germantown:* | *gedruckt und zu finden bey Christ. Saur,* 1774. | Sm. 8vo. pp. (280). H. S. P. 3017

FENNING. The | Ready Reckoner; | Or | Trader's most useful Assistant, | In | Buying and Selling all Sorts of Commodities | either Wholesale or Retail. | Shewing at one View | The Amount or Value of any Number or Quantity | of Goods or Merchandise from one Farthing to Twen- | ty Shillings, either by the long or short Hundred, | half Hundred or Quarter, Pound or Ounce, Ell or | Yard, &c. &c. | In so plain and easy a Manner, that Persons quite unac- | quainted with Arithmetic may hereby ascertain the | Value of any Number of Hundreds, Pounds, Ounces, | Ells or Yards, &c. at any Price whatever: And to | the most ready in Figures, it will be equally useful | by saving much Time in casting up what is here cor- | rectly done to their Hand. | The Seventh Edition, | With Additions on Bord and Timber Measure, | Brick Work, and Gauging by the Pen and Slip-Rule. | By Daniel Fenning, | *London Printed: Germantown Reprinted by* | *Christopher Sower.* 1774. | Sm. 8vo. pp. (280). 3018

FOX. (T.) The Wilmington Almanac for 1775. By Thomas Fox. *Wilmington: James Adams.* 1774. 3019

THE FREEHOLDERS | and other | Electors, | In the City of Philadelphia, in the Northern Liberties, and District | of Southwark, | Are requested to attend at Ten o'clock to-morrow morning at the | State-House, . . . | . . . | . . . . | [*Philadelphia:* 1775.] 4to. 1 leaf. L. C. P. 3020

A call for a meeting to "chuse a Committee, agreeable to the Resolves of Congress," dated "Nov. 11, 1774."

FRIENDS, Countrymen, | and Fellow-Electors. | [*Philadelphia:* 1774.] Folio, 1 leaf. L. C. P. 3021

An Election circular, dated by Du Simitiere Oct. 1, 1774.

THE | GARDEN of the Soul: | Or, a | Manual | of | Spiritual Exercises | and | Instructions | for | Christians who (living in the | World) aspire to Devotion. | The Seventh Edition, Correction. |

London : Printed. | *Philadelphia : Re-printed,* | *by Joseph Crukshank,* | *in Market-* | *Street, between Second and Third Streets.* [1774?] | 36mo. pp. 364.   3022

The first Roman Catholic prayer-book printed in English in America. Dr. J. Gilmary Shea, to whom I am indebted for an opportunity of examining a copy, writes, " My grandmother gave me her father's Garden of the Soul, telling me that it was printed a couple of years before her birth (*i.e.* 1776)." The imprint indicates that it could not have been printed before the middle of the year 1772, as Crukshank's office was not in Market street until about June of that year.

GESANG = BUCH. Neu = vermehrt = und vollständiges | Gesang= Buch, | Worinnen sowohl die | Psalmen Davids, | Nach | D. Ambrosii Lobwassers, | Uebersetzung hin und wieder verbessert, | Als auch | 730. auserlesener alter und neuer | Geistreichen Liedern | begriffen sind, | Welche anjetzo sämtlich | in denen Reformirten Kirchen | der Hessisch= Hanauisch=Pfältzisch=Pensylvanischen | und mehreren andern angräntzen= den Landen zu singen | gebräuchlich, in nützlicher Ordnung eingetheilt, | Auch | Mit dem Heydelbergischen Catechismo und | erbaulichen Gebätern versehen. | Vierte Auflage. | *Philadelphia :* | *zu finden bey Ernst Ludwig Baisch, in der zweyten-* | *Strasse, nahe bey der Rees-Strasse.* 1774. | 24mo. pp. 1–192, (2), 1–480, (11), 1–72.   H. S. P.   3023

This book was printed in Germany. For the American editions, see Numbers 1301, 1896, and 2778, *supra.*

GESCHICHTE von der Pfaltz = Gräfin Genovesa. *Lancaster :* *F. Bailey.* 1774.   3024

[GILLIES. (John)] The Memoirs of the Life of the Reverend George Whitefield, M.A. *Philadelphia : Printed for the Subscribers.* 1774.   3025

GRUBER. (E. L.) Eberhard Ludwig Grubers | Grundforschende | Fragen, | welche denen | neuen Täufern | im Witgensteinschen, in= sonder= | heit zu beantworten vorgelegt waren, | sammt : | beygefügten kurzen und einfältigen Ant= | worten auf dieselben, vormals schriftlich | heraus gegeben von einem | Aufrichtigen Mitglied | der Gemeinde zu Witgenstein, | zum öffentlichen Druck befördert. | Zweyte Auflage. | *Germantown,* | *gedruckt und zu finden bey Christoph Saur,* 1774. | 24mo. pp. 58.   H. S. P.   3026

WILLIAM HALL, | At the New Printing-Office, in Market-street, Philadelphia, has to dispose of, | Wholesale and Retail, the following | Books, &c. | [*Philadelphia: Hall and Sellers.* 1774.] Folio, pp. (2).   H. S. P.   3027

HAPPINESS, A Characteristic Poem. Written by a Gentleman of Newcastle upon Tyne in Old England. *Philadelphia: Robert Bell?* 1774.   3028

[HITCHCOCK. (Robert)] The Macaroni. A Play. *Philadelphia: William Woodhouse.* 1774.   3029

𝔇𝔈ℜ | 𝔥𝔬𝔠𝔥 = 𝔇𝔈𝔘𝔗𝔖𝔠𝔥 = | Americanische | Calender, | Auf das Jahr | . . . | . . . | 1775. | . . . | . . . | . . . | . . . | . . . | . . . | . . . | . . . | . . . | . . . | . . . | . . . | . . . . | Zum sieben und dreyßigsten mal heraus gegeben. | *Germantown: Gedruckt und zu finden bey Christoph Saur.* | . . . | . . . . [1774.] | Sq. 8vo. pp. (48).   H. S. P.   3030

[HOPKINSON. (Francis)] A | Pretty Story | written in the | Year of our Lord 2774, | By | Peter Grievous, Esq; | A. B. C. D. E. | . . . . | *Philadelphia:* | *Printed and Sold by John Dunlap.* | M,DCC,LXXIV. | Sm. 8vo. pp. 29 + The Second Edition. [*Ibid.*] Sm. 8vo. pp. 32.   H. S. P.   3031

IN Committee, December 14, 1774. | [*Philadelphia:* 1774.] 4to. 1 leaf.   3032

Notice from the Committee of Philadelphia, "to discourage the Killing and Sale of Ewe Mutton and Lamb."

Philadelphia. | IN Congress, Thursday, September 22, 1774. | Resolved, | That the Congress request the Merchants . . . | . . . not to send to | Great Britain any Orders for Goods, ... | [*Philadelphia:*] *Printed by W. and T. Bradford.* [1774.] | 4to. 1 leaf.   L. C. P.   3033

[JEFFERSON. (Thomas)] A | Summary View | of the | Rights | of | British America. | Set forth in some | Resolutions | Intended for the | Inspection | Of the present | Delegates | Of the | People of Virginia, | Now in | Convention. | By a Native, and Member of the | House of Burgesses. | *Williamsburg: Printed:* | *Philadelphia: Re-Printed by John Dunlap.* | M,DCC,LXXIV. | 8vo. pp. 23.

JINGLE. (Bob) The | Association, &c. | of the | Delegates of the Colonies, | at the | Grand Congress, | Held at Philadelphia, Sept. 1, 1774, | Versified, and adapted to Music, | Calculated | For Grave and Gay Dispositions; | with a short | Introduction. | By Bob Jingle; | Poet Laureat to the Colonies. | . . . | . . . . | *Printed in the Year* M,DCC,LXXIV. | 8vo. pp. 22.   L. C. P.   3035

Printed in Philadelphia, according to Sabin and the J. Carter Brown Catalogue. In my opinion it was printed at New York, by James Rivington.

JOURNAL | of the | Proceedings | of the | Congress, | Held at Philadelphia, | September 5, 1774. | [Cut.] | *Philadelphia:* | *Printed by William and Thomas Bradford,* | *at the London Coffee-House.* | M,DCC,LXXIV. | 8vo. Half-title, 1 leaf; Title, 1 leaf; pp. 1–144.   H. S. P.   3036

THE LADIES Memorandum-Book, or Daily Pocket-Journal, for the Year 1775. *Philadelphia: Robert Aitken.* 1774.   3037

THE LANCASTER Almanac for 1775. *Lancaster: Francis Bailey.* 1774.   3038

THE LAST solemn Confession and Declaration of John Hurrin, and Alexander Buchan, who were executed at Easton, Northampton County, in the Province of Pennsylvania, on the first of January, 1774. The first for Murder committed in the Year 1768, and the last for a late Burglary committed at Easton. Containing a Particular Account of the many Thefts, &c. they have been guilty of from their Childhood, and by which they have been unhappily led, as it were step by step, to this ignominious and untimely End. *Philadelphia: James Humphreys, junior.* 1774.   3039

[LEE. (Arthur)] A | True State | of the | Proceedings | In the Parliament of Great Britain, | and | In the Province of Massachusetts Bay, | relative to | The Giving and Granting the Money of the People of that Pro- | vince, and of all America, in the House of Commons, in | which they are not represented. | [*Philadelphia: Hall and Sellers.* 1774.] Folio, pp. 24.   3040

See R. H. Lee's Life of Arthur Lee, Vol. I. pp. 262. Attributed to Franklin when first published. See Pa. Gazette, Sept. 21, 1774.

[LEE.] A | True State | of the | Proceedings | in the | Parliament of Great Britain | and in the | Province of Massachusetts Bay, | relative to | The Giving and Granting the Money of the | People of that Province, and of all America, | in the House of Commons, in which they are not | represented. | *London, Printed :* | *Philadelphia :* | *Re-printed by Joseph Crukshank, in Market-Street, between* | *Second and Third Streets.* | MDCCLXXIV. | 8vo. pp. 39. L. C. P. 3041

[LEE. (Charles)] Strictures | on a | Pamphlet, | entitled | a | "Friendly Address | to | All Reasonable Americans, | on the | Subject of our Political Confusion." | Addressed to the | People of America. | . . . | . . . . | *Philadelphia :* | *Printed and Sold by William and Thomas Bradford,* | *at the London Coffee-House.* | M.DCC.LXXIV. | 8vo. pp. 15. L. C. P. 3042

𝕯𝕴𝕰 | 𝕷𝕰𝕳𝕽𝕿𝕰𝕿𝕰 | der | Brüder = Gemeine | für das Jahr | 1775. | Enthaltend | lauter Worte unsers lieben Herrn | und Heilandes. | . . . . | *Philadelphia,* | *Gedruckt bey Henrich Miller, im Jahr* 1774. | 8vo. pp. (60). H. S. P. 3043

LELAND. (T.) The | History | of | Ireland | from the | Invasion of Henry II. | With a | Preliminary Discourse | on the | Antient State of that Kingdom. | By Thomas Leland, D.D. | Senior Fellow of Trinity College, and Prebendary of St. Patrick's, Dublin. | Vol. I. | *Philadelphia and New York :* | *Printed by Hugh Gaine, Robert Bell,* | *and John Dunlap.* | MDCCLXXIV. | 8vo. pp. (4), xliv, 456. + Vol. II. [*Ibid.*] 8vo. Title, 1 leaf; pp. 601. + Vol. III. [*Ibid.*] 8vo. Title, 1 leaf; pp. 359. + Vol. IV. [*Ibid.*] 8vo. Title, 1 leaf; pp. 372, (50). H. S. P. 3044

LETTER | From a Virginian, | to the | Members of the Congress | to be held | At Philadelphia, | on | The first of September, 1774. | [*Philadelphia : H. Miller*] *Printed in the Year* 1774. | 8vo. Half title, 1 leaf; pp. 1–29. N. Y. H. S. 3045

A | LETTER | to the | Inhabitants | of the | Province | of | Quebec. | Extract from the Minutes of the Congress. | *Philadelphia :*

| *Printed by William and Thomas Bradford*, | October, 1774. | 8vo. Title, 1 leaf; pp. 37–50. H. S. P. 3046

Published as part of No. 3015, *supra*.

LETTER to the People of Great Britain from the Delegates of the American Congress. [*Philadelphia:* 1774.] 8vo. pp. 16. 3047

Title from Sabin's Dictionary, No. 40,508.

LETTRE | adressée | Aux Habitans | de la Province | de | Quebec, | Ci-devant le Canada. | De la part du Congrés Général de ∙ l'Amé- | rique Septentrionale, tenu à Philadelphie. | Imprimé & publié par Ordre du Congrès. | *A Philadelphie*, | *De l'Imprimerie de Fleury Mesplet*. | M.DCC.LXXIV. | 8vo. Half title, 1 leaf; pp. 18.

[LILLO. (George)] The London Merchant, or the History of George Barnwell. *Philadelphia: John Douglas M'Dougall.* 1774.

THE LIVES of the Apostles. *Philadelphia: Robert Aitken.* 1774. 3050

LOTTERY. Wind Mill Island | Cash Lottery. | [*Philadelphia:* 1774.] Folio, 1 leaf. L. C. P. 3051

Scheme of a lottery to raise £5250, for the purchase and improvement of public landings on the Delaware front of Philadelphia.

LOTTERY. January 17, 1774. | Supplement | to the | American Flint Glass Manufactory Pettie's Island | Cash Lottery. | [*Philadelphia:* 1774.] Folio, 1 leaf. L. C. P. 3052

LOTTERY. Philadelphia, March ·24, 1774. | The Managers | of the Delaware | Lottery, | for the | College of | New-Jersey, &c. | Have . . . resolved to begin the drawing of | said Lottery at New-Castle, on Monday the 23d of May next. | [*Philadelphia:* 1774.] 4to. 1 leaf. L. C. P. 3053

LOTTERY. List of the Prizes drawn in the Delaware Lottery. *Philadelphia:* 1774. 3054

MACK. (A.) Kurße und einfältige Vorſtellung | der äuſſern, aber doch heiligen | Rechten | und | Ordnungen | des | Hauſes Gottes, | Wie es der wahre Haus=Vater | Jesus Christus | beofhlen, und in sei= | nem Testament schriftlich hinterlassen. | vorgestellt in einem Gespräch= | unter Vater und Sohn, | durch | Frag und Antwort, | von | Alexander Mack, | einem Mitberuffenen, zu dem grossen | Abendmahl. | Zweyte Auflage. | *Germantown,* | *gedruckt u. zu finden bey Christoph Saur,* 1774. | 24mo. pp. (22), 133, (1).   H. S. P.   3055

A | MANUAL | of | Catholic Prayers. | . . . | . . . | . . . . | *Philadelphia :* | *Printed for the Subscribers,* | *By Robert Bell, Bookseller, in Third-street.* | MDCCLXXIV. | 12mo. pp. 272 +, 1 plate.

MARSHALL. (W.) The Propriety of Singing the Psalms of David, in New Testament Worship. A Sermon Preached at Middle-Octorara, April 13th, 1774, at the opening of the Associate Presbytery of Pennsylvania. By William Marshall. *Philadelphia : Robert Aitken.* 1774.   3057

[MASON. (William)] Methodism displayed, and Enthusiasm detected ; intended as an Antidote against, and a Preservative from the delusive Principles and unscriptural Doctrines of a Modern Sett of seducing Preachers : And as a Defence of our regular and orthodox Clergy, from their unjust Reflections. Addressed to the Rev. Mr. Romaine, the Rev. Mr. Jones, &c. *Philadelphia : William Woodhouse.* 1774.   3058

A MELANCHOLY Narrative of the unhappy Samuel Brand, who was executed at Lancaster, in the Province of Pennsylvania, on the 18th Day of December, 1773, for the barbarous and inhuman Murder of his only Brother ; containing a succinct Account of his Person, Parentage, Principles and temper, interspersed with some interesting Reflections, moral and religious. *Lancaster : Francis Bailey.* 1774.   3059

MINUTES | of the | Baptist Association | held in Philadelphia, | October the 12th, 13th, 14th, 1774. | [*Philadelphia : Henry Miller.* 1714.] Sq. 8vo. pp. 11.   L. C. P.   3060

[MORE. (Hannah)] Search | after | Happiness : | A | Pastoral Drama. | And | Armine and Elvira : | A | Legendary Tale ;

| In Two Parts. | *Bristol: Printed.* | *Philadelphia, Re-printed.* | *By James Humphreys, junr. in Front-Street.* | MDCCLXXIV. | 8vo.

Collation: Title, 1 leaf; Search after Happiness, pp. 1–62; Cartwright's Armine and Elvira, pp. 1–30; 1 plate. The title to More's Drama is as follows: Search | after | Happiness: | A | Pastoral Drama. | As it was performed by some young Ladies | of Bristol, in England. | . . . | . . . | . . . | . . . | . . . . | The Fourth Edition. | *Philadelphia:* | *Printed, by James Humphreys, junior,* | *in Front-street.* MDCCLXXIV. | Some copies are called "The Fifth Edition." But these differ in no other respect from the one described. Cartwright's poem was issued separately. For title, &c., see No. 2987, *supra.*

[MURRAY. (James)] New | Sermons | to | Asses. | By the Author of Sermons to Asses. | . . . | . . . . | *Philadelphia: John Sparhawk.* 1774. 8vo. pp. 94. 3062

𝕯𝕰𝕽 𝕹𝕰𝖀𝕰𝕾𝕿𝕰, Verbeſſert= und Zuverläßige | Americaniſche | Calender | Auf das 1774ſte Jahr Chriſti, | [13 lines.] | Zum Drey= zehntenmal herausgegeben. | *Philadelphia, Gedruckt und zu finden bey Henrich Miller,* . . . | . . . | . . . | . . . | . . . . [1774.] | 4to. pp. (48). H. S. P. 3063

A NEW Journal of a voyage round the World. Performed in the years 1768, 1769, 1770, and 1771, in his Majesty's ship Endeavor, Captain James Cook. Undertaken in pursuit of Natural Knowledge, at the desire of the Royal Society: Containing all the Occurrences of the Voyage, with Descriptions of several new discovered Countries, in the Southern Hemisphere, with account of their soil and productions, and of many singularities in the structure, apparel, customs, manners, policy, manufactures, &c. of the inhabitants. To which is added, a Vocabulary of the language of the Otahitee. *Philadelphia: John Douglas M'Dougall.* 1774.

NEW-YEAR Verses of the Carriers of the Pennsylvania Chronicle. *Philadelphia: William Goddard.* 1774. 3065

NEW-YEAR Verses of the Carriers of the Pennsylvania Gazette. *Philadelphia: Hall and Sellers.* 1774. 3066

THE NEW-YEAR'S | Verses | Of Those who carry the | Pennsylvania Journal | To the Customers. | Philadelphia, January 1, 1774. | [*Philadelphia: W. and T. Bradford.* 1774.] Folio, 1 leaf.

THE | NEW-YEAR | Verses, | Of the Printer's Lads, who carry the | Pennsylvania Packet | To the Customers. | January 1st, 1774. | [*Philadelphia : John Dunlap.* 1774.] 4to. 1 leaf. 3068

OGILVIE. (J.) Providence. An Allegorical Poem. By John Ogilvie, A.M. *Philadelphia : Robert Bell.* 1774.   3069

OPIFERQUE per Orbem Dicor. *Philadelphia : Robert Aitken.* 1774.   3070

An Advertisement, by Benjamin Duffield, of some kind of " quack medicine." Aitken charged £2.5.0 for printing 100 copies.

[ORTON. (Job)] Memoirs of the Life, Character and Writings of the late Rev. Philip Doddridge, of Northampton. *Philadelphia : Robert Bell.* 1774.   3071

THE | PALLADIUM of Conscience ; | or, the | Foundation of Religious Liberty displayed, asserted, and established, | agreeable to its true and genuine Principles, above the reach of all petty Tyrants, | who attempt to Lord it over the Human Mind. | Containing, | Furneaux's Letters to Blackstone. | Priestley's Remarks on Blackstone. | Blackstone's Reply to Priestley. | And | Blackstone's Case of the Middlesex Election ; | With some other curious Tracts, worthy of high Rank in every | Gentleman's Literary Repository. | Being a necessary Companion for every Lover of Religious Liberty. | And an | Interesting Appendix | to | Blackstone's Commentaries | on the | Laws of England. | *America :* | *Printed for the Subscribers,* | *By Robert Bell, at the late Union Library,* | *in Third-street,* | *Philadelphia,* MDCCLXXIV. | 8vo. Advertisement, 1 leaf ; Title, 1 leaf.   3072

The Third edition of An interesting Appendix to Blackstone's Commentaries, with a new general title. For a collation, see No. 2750, *supra.* The special titles, except to Furneaux's Letters, are dated 1773, and are precisely the same as in the second edition, No. 2859, *supra.* The title to Furneaux's Letters is also dated 1773, but the spacing is somewhat different. Pages 97–119 of the Case of the Late Election, &c., the title-page, Prefaces, and pp. 1–4 of Furneaux's Letters (Signatures N to R), were reprinted for this edition, which is in other respects the same as the second edition.

THE PENNSYLVANIA Chronicle.   H. S. P.   3073

Numbers 367 (Feb. 1, 1774) and 368 (Feb. 8, 1774), four pages each. Title as in No. 2691, *supra*. The imprint is as in No. 2912, *supra*, except the difference in spacing made necessary by the use of a larger type. No. 368 contains Goddard's valedictory.

THE PENNSYLVANIA Gazette.   3074

Numbers 2350 (Jan. 5, 1774) to 2401 (Dec. 28, 1774), four pages each, with "Supplements" of four pages to Numbers 2361, 2367, 2368, 2374, and 2392, and of two pages to all the others except Numbers 2352, 2365, 2375, 2377, and 2379 to 2384; "Postscripts" of one leaf to Numbers 2365, 2369, and 2373, and of two pages to Numbers 2375, 2377, 2378, 2379, 2383, 2386, 2393, and 2394, and an extra sheet of four pages to No. 2390. Title and imprint as in No. 2913, *supra*.

THE PENNSYLVANIA Journal.   3075

Numbers 1622 (Jan. 5, 1774) to 1673 (Dec. 28, 1774), four pages each, with extra sheets of four pages to Numbers 1649 and 1663, extra half-sheets of two pages to Numbers 1658 to 1662, 1666, and 1668 to 1673; "Supplements" of two pages to Numbers 1640, 1646 to 1648, 1650, 1651, and 1654, and of four pages to No. 1638; "Postscripts" of one leaf to Numbers 1641, 1643, 1645 (Quarto), 1647, 1648, and 1654, of two pages to Numbers 1632, 1637, 1645, 1646, 1650, 1651, 1658, and 1659, and "Postscript Extraordinary" of two pages to No. 1650. Title as in No. 2317, *supra*, until 1651, when a cut of a divided snake, with the motto "Unite or die," was substituted for the old cut in the heading. Imprint as in No. 2317, *supra*.

Vol. III. Numb. 115. | DUNLAP'S | PENNSYLVANIA: Packet. | Or,: the | General : Advertiser. | Monday, : January 3d, 1774. | 3076

Numbers 115 to 166 (Dec. 26, 1774), four pages each, large folio, printed in four columns. There are "Postscripts" of two pages to Numbers 118, 124, 129, 130, 131, 133, 135, 136, 138 to 143, 145, 146, 147, 149, 152, 153, 154, 156 to 160, 162, 164, and 165, of four pages to No. 144, of one leaf to No. 162, and two "Postscripts" of two pages to No. 150. "Postscripts Extraordinary" of two pages to Numbers 144, 147, and 152. A new cut of a ship appears in the title. Imprint as in No. 2694, *supra*.

THE PENNSYLVANIA Pocket Almanac for 1775. *Philadelphia: W. and T. Bradford.* 1774.   3077

THE PHILADELPHIA Newest Almanac for 1775. *Philadelphia: Robert Aitken.* 1774.   3078

PHILADELPHIA, September 1st, 1774. | [*Philadelphia:* 1774.] Folio, 1 leaf.   L. C. P.   3079

"A Tradesman," against Non-Importation, beginning with five lines from Milton's translation of Euripides.

POMP. (N[icholas]) Kurzgefaßte | Prüfungen | der Lehre | des | Ewigen Evangeliums: | Womit | deutlich gezeiget wird, | Daß man die Wiederbringung | aller Dringe in der heiligen Schrift, | vergeblich suchet. | Auf Begehren vieler Freunde zum Druck | befördert | von | N. Pomp, V.D.M. | *Philadelphia: | Gedruckt bey Henrich Miller,* | 1774. | 16mo. pp. xvi, 200.   H. S. P.   3080

POOR Will's Almanac for 1775. *Philadelphia: Joseph Cruk-shank.* 1774.   3081

POOR Will's Pocket Almanack for 1775. *Philadelphia: Joseph Crukshank.* 1774.   3082

A | PRESENT | for an | Apprentice: | Or, a | Sure Guide | To gain both | Esteem and Estate. | With Rules for his Conduct to his | Master, and in the World. | More especially, while an Apprentice, his Behavi- | our after he is free, Care in setting up, Com- | pany with the Ladies, Choice of a Wife, Be- | haviour in Courtship, and Wedding-Day, | Complaisance after Marriage, Education of | Children, &c. | By a late Lord-Mayor of London. | *London, Printed; | Philadelphia: Re-printed by J. | Crukshank, for James Williamson, | Bookbinder in Wilmington.* | MDCCLXXIV. | Sm. 12mo. pp. 83.   H. S. P.   3083

[PRIESTLEY. (Joseph)] An Address to Protestant Dissenters of all Denominations, on the approaching election of Members of Parliament, with respect to the state of Public Liberty in general, and American Affairs in particular. *Wilmington: James Adams.* 1774.   3084

[PRIESTLEY.] An | Address | to | Protestant Dissenters | of all Denominations, | On the Approaching Election of | Members of Parliament, | With Respect to the State of | Public Liberty in General, | and of | American Affairs in Particular. | *London, Printed. | Philadelphia, Re-printed: | And Sold by James Humphreys, junr. | In Front-street.* MDCCLXXIV. | 8vo. pp. 24.   H. S. P.   3085

PROCLAMATION. [*Royal Arms.*] By the Honourable | John Penn, Esquire, | Governor and Commander in Chief of the Province of Pennsylvania, and Counties of New- | Castle, Kent and Sussex, on Delaware, | A Proclamation. | *Philadelphia : Printed by Hall and Sellers.* 1774. | Folio, 1 leaf.   H. S. P.   3086

Against the Connecticut settlers, dated "Feb. 28, 1774."

PROCLAMATION. [*Royal Arms.*] By the Honourable | John Penn, Esquire, | . . . | . . . | A Proclamation. | *Philadelphia : Printed by Hall and Sellers.* [1774.] | Folio, 1 leaf.   H. S. P.   3087

Dated "July 14, 1774." Reward for the apprehension of the murderers of an Indian.

PROCLAMATION. [*Royal Arms.*] By the Honourable | John Penn, Esquire, | . . . | . . . | A Proclamation. | *Philadelphia : Printed by Hall and Sellers.* 1774. | Folio, 1 leaf.   3088

Dated "Sept. 15, 1774." Extending the authority of Pennsylvania to the Maryland boundary.

PROCLAMATION. [*Royal Arms.*] By the Honourable | John Penn, Esquire, | . . . | . . . | A Proclamation. | *Philadelphia : Printed by Hall and Sellers.* 1774. | Folio, 1 leaf.   H. S. P.   3089

Dated "Oct. 12, 1774." Against the encroachments of Lord Dunmore on the western lands of Pennsylvania.

PROCLAMATION. [*Royal Arms.*] By the Honourable | John Penn, Esquire, | . . . | . . . | A Proclamation. | *Philadelphia : Printed by Hall and Sellers.* 1774. | Folio, 1 leaf.   H. S. P.   3090

Dated "Nov. 2, 1774." Revoking the Proclamation of Sept. 15th.

QUINCY (J.) Observations | on the | Act of Parliament | commonly called the | Boston Port-Bill; | with | Thoughts | on | Civil Society | and | Standing Armies. | By Josiah Quincy, junior. | . . . | . . . | . . . | . . . | . . . | . . . | . . . | . . . | . . . | . . . | . . . | . . . | . . . | . . . . | *Philadelphia.* | *Printed for John Sparhawk.* | MDCCLXXIV. | 8vo. pp. 60.   H. S. P.   3091

THE RATES of Porterage and Carriage, &c. to any Parts of the City and Suburbs, proper to be stuck up in Taverns, Stores, Shops, &c. &c. *Philadelphia : James Humphreys, junior.* 1774.

REED. (J.)   An | Explanation | of the | Map of the City and Liberties | of | Philadelphia. | By John Reed. | *Philadelphia:* | *Printed for the Author, and Sold by Mr. Nicholas Brooks, in Se-* | *cond-Street, between Market and Chesnut Streets.* | M.DCC.LXXIV. | 4to. pp. 24, (8), 23, (9).   H. S. P.   3093

[ROBINSON, (Matthew—Baron Rokeby.)]   Considerations | on the | Measures Carrying On | with respect to the | British Colonies | in | North America. | . . . | . . . | . . . | . . . | . . . | . . . | . . . . | *Philadelphia:* | *Re-printed and Sold by Benjamin Towne,* | *near the Coffee House.*   MDCCLXXIV. | 8vo. pp. 60.

RULES | and | Constitutions | of the | Society of Englishmen, | and | Sons of Englishmen, | Established at Philadelphia, for the Ad- | vice and Assistance of Englishmen in | Distress. | [Cut.] | *Philadelphia:* | *Printed by Benjamin Towne.* | MDCCLXXIV. | Sm. 8vo. pp. 24.   N. Y. H. S.   3095

RUSH. (B.)   An | Oration, | Delivered February 4, 1774, | before the | American Philosophical | Society, | held at | Philadelphia. | Containing, | An Enquiry into the Natural History of Medicine | among the Indians in North-America, | and | A comparative View of their Diseases and Reme- | dies, with those of civilized Nations. | Together with an Appendix, containing | Proofs and Illustrations. | By Benjamin Rush, M.D. | Professor of Chemistry in the College of Philadelphia. |. . . . | . . . | . . . | . . . . | *Philadelphia:* | *Printed by Joseph Crukshank, in Market-* | *Street, between Second and Third Streets.*   [1774.] | 8vo. pp. 118.

SAUNDERS. (R.)   A Pocket Almanac for 1775.   By Richard Saunders, Phil.   *Philadelphia: Hall and Sellers.*   1774.   3097

SAUNDERS.   Poor Richard improved; | Being an | Almanack | . . . | . . . | . . . | . . . | . . . | . . . | . . . | . . . | . . . | . . . | For the | Year of our Lord 1775: | Being the Third after Leap-Year. | . . . | . . . | . . . | . . . | . . . | . . . | . . . | . . . . | By Richard Saunders, Philom. | *Philadelphia:* | *Printed and Sold by Hall and Sellers.*   [1774.] | Sm. 8vo. pp. (36).   H. S. P.   3098

SAY, (T.) and I. WATTS. The | Visions | of a certain |
Thomas Say, | Of the City of Philadelphia, | which he saw in a
| Trance : | To which is added, another | Vision. | By the late
Reverend | Isaac Watts, D.D. | *Philadelphia :* | *Printed, and Sold by,*
William Mentz, | *near the Great Lutheran Church.* | MDCCLXXIV.
| 12mo. pp. 23.   L. C. P.   3099

" Whereas a certain William Mentz has printed and published for sale without
my knowledge or consent, ' The Vision of Thomas Say,' which is but an incorrect and
imperfect part of what I propose to make public. And as I never intended what I had
wrote on that head to be published during my life, all persons are desired not to encourage the said Mentz in such wrong proceeding. Thomas Say." Pa. Journal,
March 2, 1774. Watts' Vision begins on page 11 with a separate title, as follows :
A | Near Prospect | of | Heaven, | seen in a | Vision. | By the late Reverend | Isaac
Watts, D.D. | [Imprint as in general title.]

THE SCHOOL for Husbands, a Sentimental Novel.   In Two
Volumes.   *Philadelphia : James Humphreys, junior.* 1774.   3100

𝔈𝔍𝔑 | 𝔖𝔠𝔥𝔯𝔢𝔍𝔅𝔢𝔑 | An die | Einwohner | der | Provinz |
Quebec. | Auszug aus dem Protocoll des Congresses. | *Philadelphia,* |
Gedruckt und zu haben bey Henrich Miller, | 1774. | 8vo. pp. (2), 63–76.

[SCOTT. (Sarah)]   The Man of Real Sensibility; or the History of Sir George Ellison.   *Philadelphia : James Humphreys,* ˎ
junior. 1774.   3102

SCOTT. (W.) O Tempora! O Mores! | or | The best New
Year's Gift | for a | Prime Minister, | Being the Substance of two
Sermons preached at a | few small Churches only, and published at
the | repeated Request of the Congregations, | By the Rev. Wil-
liam Scott, M.A. | Late Scholar of Eton, | Dedicated to Lord
North. | The Pulpit was refused at eight of the most capital
Churches | in London. | *Philadelphia :* | *Reprinted and sold by Ben-*
jamin Towne. | MDCCLXXIV. | 8vo. pp. xii, 20.   L. C. P.   3103

A | SERMON | on | Tea. | . . . | . . . | [Cut.] | . . . | . . .
| . . . | . . . . | *Lancaster :* | *Printed by Francis Bailey.* [1774 ?] |
8vo. pp. 8.   c.   3104

SETHONIA, a Tragedy.   *Philadelphia : John Sparhawk.* 1774.

SHARP. (G.) A | Declaration | of the | People's Natural Right | to a | Share in the Legislature, | which is the | Fundamental Principle | of the | British Constitution of State. | By Granville Sharp. | . . . | . . . . | *London, Printed:* | *Philadelphia, Reprinted* | *And sold by Benjamin Towne, in Front-street, near* | *the Coffee-House.* 1774. | 8vo. pp. 21. + *London, Printed:* | *Philadelphia, Reprinted* | *And sold by John Dunlap, at the Newest Printing-Office,* | *in Market-Street.* 1774. | 8vo. pp. 21.   L. C. P.   3106

[SHIPLEY. (Jonathan)] A | Speech | Intended to have been spoken | on the | Bill | for | Altering the Charters | of the | Colony of Massachusett's Bay. | The Third Edition. | *London, Printed:* | *Philadelphia:* | *Re-printed and Sold, by William and Thomas* | *Bradford, at the London Coffee-House.* | M.DCC.LXXIV. | 8vo. pp. vi, 29.   H. S. P.   3107

[SHIPLEY.] A | Speech | intended to have been spoken | By the Bishop of St. Asaph, | on the | Bill | for | Altering the Charters | of the | Colony of Massachusetts Bay. | *London, Printed:* | *Philadelphia, Reprinted and Sold by* | *Benjamin Towne, in Front-Street, near the* | *Coffee-House.* [1774.] | 8vo. pp. 18.   H. S. P.   3108

SHIPLEY. A | Speech, | intended to have been spoken | on the | Bill | for altering the Charters | of the Colony of | Massachusetts Bay. | By the Rev. Dr. Jonathan Shipley, | Lord Bishop of St. Asaph. | Though it is not above three weeks since this piece | appeared first in America, this is the Fifth | Edition; besides several in England, where | it sold at One Shilling Sterling. | *Lancaster:* | *Printed and Sold by Francis Bailey.* | MDCCLXXIV. | Sm. 8vo. pp. 24.   L. C. P.   3109

THE | SINGULAR and Diverting Behaviour | of | Doctor Marriot, | His Majesty's | Advocate General: | Who was Examined concerning the Religion and Laws of | Quebec: | And found means from his incomparable | Wit and Subtilty, | To defeat the Purposes for which he was brought to the | Bar of Parliament, | on the 3d of June, 1774. | *Philadelphia:* | *Printed and Sold by James Humphreys junr. in Front-* | *street.* 1774. *Price Fourpence.* | 16mo. pp. 16.   L. C. P.   3110

SIR, | You are desired to attend a Special Meeting of | the
Committee this — at — | o'Clock, precisely, at the Carpenter's
Hall. | To — | [*Philadelphia:* 1774.]   4to. 1 leaf.   **3111**

SIR, | You are desired to attend a Special Meeting of the |
Committee at the Philosophical Hall, ... | [*Philadelphia:* 1774.]
4to. 1 leaf.   L. C. P.   **3112**

Call for a meeting of the Committee of Philadelphia "to consider of the Subscriptions for Boston."

[SMITH. (William)]   An | Examination | of the | Connecticut
Claim | to | Lands in Pennsylvania. | With | An Appendix,
containing Extracts and Copies | taken from Original Papers. |
Philadelphia: | *Printed by Joseph Crukshank, in Market Street.* |
MDCCLXXIV. | 8vo.   Title, 1 leaf; pp. 1–93, 1–32, 1 map.

STERNE. (L.)   The | Works | of | Laurence Sterne, A.M. |
Prebendary of York, | and | Vicar of Sutton on the Forest,
| and of | Stillington, near York. | With the | Life of the
Author. | In Five Volumes. | Vol. I. | *London printed.* | *Phila-
delphia, re-printed;* | *By James Humphreys, junior,* | *in Front-street.*
MDCCLXXIV. | 12mo. pp. xiv, 370, 1 plate. + Vol. II. [*Ibid.*]
12mo. pp. 348. + Vol. III. [*Ibid.*] 12mo. pp. 270; List of Books,
pp. (2). + Vol. IV. [*Ibid.*] 12mo. pp. 257. + Vol. V. [*Ibid.*]
12mo. pp. 250; Advertisement and List of Subscribers, pp. (5).

[STERNE.]   The | Sermons | of | Mr. Yorick. | In Two Vol-
umes. | Volume I. | *Philadelphia:* | *Printed by James Humphreys,*
junr. | [1774.] 12mo. pp. 270. + Volume II. | *Ibid.*] 12mo. pp. 257.

THE STORY of Æneas and Dido burlesqued: By a Gentleman of South Carolina.   *Philadelphia: James Humphreys, junior.*
1774.   **3116**

DIE | TÄGLICHEN | Loosungen | der | Brüder=Gemeine | für das
Jahr | 1775. | *Philadelphia,* | *Gedruckt bey Henrich Miller, im Jahr*
1774. | 8vo. pp. (55).   H. S. P.   **3117**

TENNENT. (W.)   An | Address, | occasioned by the | Late
Invasion of the | Liberties | of the | American Colonies | by the |

British Parliament, | Delivered in Charlestown, South Carolina. | By William Tennent, A.M. | *Philadelphia :* | *Printed and Sold by William and Thomas* | *Bradford, at the London Coffee-House.* | MDCCLXXIV. | 8vo. pp. 20.   H. S. P. 3118

THOMAS. ([Antoine Léonard]) Essay | on the | Character, | Manners, and Genius | of | Women | in different Ages. | Enlarged from the French of Mr. Thomas. | By Mr. Russell. | In Two Volumes. | Vol. I. | *Philadelphia :* | *Printed and sold by R. Aitken, Book-* | *seller, opposite the London-Coffee-* | *House, Front-Street.* | M,DCC,LXXIV. | 12mo. pp. v, (2), 124. + Vol. II. [*Ibid.*] 12mo. Title, 1 leaf; Contents, 1 leaf; pp. 129, (2).   L. C. P. 3119

TO the | Electors | and | Freeholders | of the | City of Philadelphia. | [*Philadelphia :* 1774.] Folio, 1 leaf.   L. C. P. 3120

Election circular concerning the choice of four additional members of the Assembly from Philadelphia on May 1st.

TO the Inhabitants of the Township of | | *Philadelphia,* *Printed by James Humphreys, junior, in Front-street.* [1774.] | Folio, 1 leaf.   L. C. P. 3121

A circular to the people of Chester County, calling upon them to meet at Chester and choose a Committee, with certain " Propositions" agreed upon at a meeting held at that place June 18, 1774.

TO | The Manufacturers and Mechanics of | Philadelphia, the Northern Liberties, | and District of Southwark. | [*Philadelphia :* 1774.] 4to. 1 leaf.   L. C. P. 3122

Call for a public meeting to aid the people of Boston, dated " June 8, 1774."

TO the Philadelphians, on the Abandonment of the non-importation Resolution, in New York. *Philadelphia :* July 14, 1774.

Signed a " Pennsylvanian." Title from Haven's List, which follows, I suppose, the Catalogue of the Library Company of Philadelphia. The broadside described in the latter is dated " 1770," and will be found No. 2601, *supra.*

TO the | Representatives | of the | Freemen | Of the Counties of Chester, Bucks, and Philadelphia, | Now met at the State-House. | [*Philadelphia :* 1774.] 4to. 1 leaf.   L. C. P. 3124

"A great Number of your Constituents," in regard to Indian affairs, dated "Chester County, May 9, 1774."

TOBLER. (J.) The Pennsylvania Town and Countryman's Almanac for 1775. By John Tobler. *Wilmington: James Adams.* 1774.   3125

[TOWGOOD. (Micaiah)] A Calm and plain Answer to the Enquiry, " Why are you a Dissenter from the Church of England ?" Containing some remarks on its doctrine, spirit, constitution, and some of its offices and forms of devotion. By the author of the Dissenting Gentleman's Letters to White. *Philadelphia: James Humphreys, junior.* 1774.   3126

THE | UNIVERSAL | Almanack, | For the Year of our Lord, | 1775; | . . . | . . . | . . . | . . . | . . . | . . . | . . . | . . . | . . . | . . . | . . . | . . . | . . . | . . . . | ☞ The ingenious D. Rittenhouse, A.M. has a- | gain favour'd us with the Calculations for this Al- | manack. | . . . | . . . . | *Philadelphia: | Printed & Sold by James Humphreys, jun. | in Front-street, at the Corner of Black-horse Alley.* [1774.] | Sm. 8vo. pp. (36).   H. S. P. 3127

VIAUD, (P.) and W. FALCONER. The | Surprizing | yet real and true | Voyages | and | Adventures | of | Monsieur Pierre Viaud. | A French Sea-Captain. | To which is added, | The Shipwreck. | A Sentimental and Descriptive Poem, | In Three Cantos. | By William Falconer, an English Sailor. | . . . | . . . . | *Philadelphia: | Printed by Robert Bell in Third-street. |* MDCCLXXIV. | 12mo.   H. S. P. 3128

Collation : Advertisement, 1 leaf; 1 plate; General Title, 1 leaf; Title to Viaud, 1 leaf; French Editor's Preface, pp. vii.–viii. ; Griffith's Preface, pp. ix.–x. ; Certificate, pp. xi.–xii. ; text, pp. 1–144; Title to " The Shipwreck," 1 leaf; Argument, &c., pp. (2) ; text, pp. 1–108. The title to Viaud is as follows: The | Surprizing | yet real and true | Voyages | and | Adventures | of | Monsieur Pierre Viaud, | A Native of Bordeaux, and Captain of a Ship. | Translated from the French | By Mrs. Griffith. | Author of Henry and Frances. | . . . | . . . . | *Philadelphia: | Printed by Robert Bell, in Third-street. |* MDCCLXXIV. | The title to " The Shipwreck" is as follows: The | Shipwreck. | A Sentimental and Descriptive Poem. | In Three Cantos. | By | William Falconer. | An English Sailor. | . . . | . . . | . . . | . . . . | *Philadelphia: | Printed by Robert Bell, in Third-street. |* MDCCLXXIV. |

VOTES and Proceedings of the House of Representatives of the Province of Pennsylvania. Met at Philadelphia, the Four-teenth of October, Anno Domini, 1773. [*Royal Arms.*] *Phil-adelphia: Printed and Sold by Henry Miller, in Race-Street.* MDCCLXXIV. Folio, Title, 1 leaf; pp. 501–578.   H. S. P.   3129

VOTES | and | Proceedings | of the | House of Representatives | of the | Province of Pennsylvania. | Beginning the Fifteenth Day of October, 1744. | Volume The Fourth. | [*Penn Arms.*] *Philadelphia: | Printed and Sold by Henry Miller, in Race-Street. |* MDCCLXXIV. | Folio, Title, 1 leaf; pp. 856.   H. S. P.   3130

VOTES | of the | House of Representatives, | From Wednes-day, December 29, 1773, to Saturday, January 8, 1774. | [*Philadel-phia: Henry Miller.* 1774.] Folio, pp. 19–23.   H. S. P.   3131

Continued weekly to January 22, and from July 18 to July 23, and from Sept. 19 to —, pp. 51 or 52. Votes of the new Assembly from Oct. 14 to Dec. 24, 1774, pp. 53–74.

WEATHERWISE. (A.) Father Abraham's | Almanack, | For the Year of our Lord | 1775; | Being the Third after Leap-Year. | (The Fifteenth Year of the Reign of King George III.) | Con-taining, | The Motions of the Sun and Moon; | the true | Places and Aspects of the Planets; | the | Rising and Setting of the Sun; | And the Rising, Setting and Southing of the Moon; | Also, | The Lunations, Conjunctions, Eclipses, Judgment of the | Weather, Rising and Setting of the Planets, Length | of Days and Nights, &c. &c. | Fitted to the Latitude of Forty Degrees, and a Meridian | of near five Hours West from London. | By Abraham Weather-wise, Gent. | *₊* Our kind customers are requested to observe, that the | ingenious David Rittenhouse, A.M. of this city, has | favoured us with the astronomical calculations of our Al- | manack for this year, therefore they may be most firmly | relied on. | *Philadelphia: | Printed and Sold by John Dunlap, at the | Newest-Printing-Office, in Market-Street.* [1774] | Sm. 8vo. pp. 36.   H. S. P.   3132

[WELLS. (Richard)] A few | Political Reflections | sub-mitted | To the Consideration | of the | British Colonies, | by | A Citizen of Philadelphia. | *Philadelphia: | Printed and Sold by John Dunlap.* | M,DCC,LXXIV. | Sm. 8vo. pp. 86.   A. P. S.   3133

WESLEY. (J.) Thoughts | upon | Slavery. | By John Wesley, A.M. | . . . | . . . | . . . . | *London, Printed: | Re-printed in Philadelphia, with notes, | and sold by Joseph Crukshank.* | MD,CC,LXXIV. | 12mo. pp. 83.   H. S. P.   3134

This was printed as the second tract of Benezet's Potent Enemies of America laid open, but is found sometimes separately.

WHEATLEY. (P.) Poems on Various Subjects, Religious and Moral. By Phillis Wheatley. *Philadelphia : ? W. and T. Bradford.* 1774.   3135

Advertised in the Pa. Journal, June 15, 1774. Probably referring to the London edition.

WILCOCKS. (T.) Thoma Wilcocks köstlicher Honig = Tropfen aus dem Felsen Christo: Oder, Ein kurzes Wort der Ermahnung an alle Heilige und Sünder. Welchem angehänget ist, des weiland vortrefflichen Deutschen Gottesgelehrten Herrn August Herman Frankens heiliger und sicherer Glaubens-Weg eines Evangelischen Christen. In Englisch und Deutscher Sprache gedruckt. *Philadelphia : Henrich Miller,* 1774.   3136

[WILSON. (James)] Considerations | on the | Nature | and the | Extent | of the | Legislative Authority | of the | British | Parliament. | *Philadelphia : | Printed and Sold by William and Thomas Bradford, | at the London Coffee-House.* | M.DCC.LXXIV. | 8vo. pp. iv, 35.   H. S. P.   3137

WOOLMAN. (J.) A First Book for Children, A. B. C. D. &c. Much useful reading being sullied and torn by Children in Schools before they can read, this Book is intended to save unnecessary expense. By John Woolman, The Third Edition, enlarged. *Philadelphia : Printed and sold by Joseph Crukshank, in Second-street; and by Benjamin Ferriss, Stationer and Bookbinder, in Wilmington.* [1774 ?] 48mo. ? pp. 16 ?   3138

Title from Smith's Catalogue of Friends' Books. The year assigned is undoubtedly wrong, as Crukshank removed from Second Street in 1770. See No. 2495, *supra.*

WOOLMAN. The | Works | of | John Woolman. | In Two Parts. | *Philadelphia : | Printed by Joseph Crukshank, in Market- | Street, between Second and Third Streets.* | M.DCC.LXXIV. | 16mo.

Collation: Title, 1 leaf; Testimony of Friends in Yorkshire, pp. iii–xiv; Title to Journal, 1 leaf; text, pp. 1–250; Title to Part II., 1 leaf; text, pp. 253–436. The special titles are as follows: A | Journal | of the | Life, Gospel Labours, | and | Christian Experiences | of that | Faithful Minister | of | Jesus Christ, | John Woolman, | Late of Mount-Holly, in the Province of | New-Jersey. | ... | ... | ... | .... | *Philadelphia :* | *Printed by Joseph Crukshank, in Market Street,* | *between* | *Second and Third Streets.* | M.DCC.LXXIV. | —The | Works | of | John Woolman. | Part the Second. | Containing his Last Epistle and his | other Writings. | *Philadelphia :* | *Printed by Joseph Crukshank, in Market-* | *Street, between Second and Third Streets.* | M.DCC.LXXIV. |

THE | YOUNG Clerk's | Magazine : | Or, | English Law-Repository : | Containing, | A Variety of the most useful Pre- | cedents | of Articles of Agreement, Bonds, Bills, Re- | cog- nizances, Releases, Letters and Warrants | of Attorney, Awards, Bills of Sale, Gifts, | Grants, Leases, Assignments, Mortgages, Sur- | renders, Jointures, Covenants, Copartner- | ships, Charter- parties, Letters of Licence, Com- | positions, Conveyances, Parti- tions, Wills, and | all other Instruments that relate to Publick | Business. | With | Necessary Directions for making Distresses for Rent, | &c. as the Law between Landlord and Tenant | now stands. | To which is added, | The Doctrine of Fines and Recoveries, and their | Forms. | Together with | Those of Com- mon Writs, Affidavits, Memorials for | registering Deeds, &c. in Middlesex; as also a | choice Collection of Declarations in the King's | Bench and Common Pleas. | The Fifth Edition, revised and corrected. | *London Printed :* | *Philadelphia :* | *Re- printed by John Dunlap and Joseph Crukshank,* | *in Market-street.* | M.DCC.LXXIV. | 8vo. Title, 1 leaf; Preface, pp. (2); pp. 303.

1775.

AN ACCOUNT of the Bap- | tisms and Burials in all the | Churches and Meetings in | Philadelphia. From Dec. 25, 1774, | to December 25, 1775. | By their respective Clerks and Sextons. | [*Philadelphia :* 1775.] 4to. 1 leaf.   L. C. P.   3141

AN ACCOUNT of the Births and Burials in the | United Churches of Christ-Church and St. Peter's, in Phi- | ladelphia, from December 25, 1774, to December 25, 1775. By | Matthew

Whitehead, and William Young, Clerks, and | Jacob Diegel, and George Stokes, Sextons. | [*Philadelphia:* 1775.] Folio, 1 leaf.

AN ACCOUNT of the Births and Burials in the St. Paul's Church. *Philadelphia:* 1775.   3143

AN ACCOUNT of the Burials and Baptisms in the Baptist Church. *Philadelphia:* 1775.   3144

AN ACCOUNT of the Burials in the Second Presbyterian Church. *Philadelphia:* 1775.   3145

ACCOUNT of the Commencement | in the | College of Philadelphia, | May 17, 1775. | [*Philadelphia:* 1775.]   8vo. pp. 15.

THE | ACTS of Assembly | of the | Province | of | Pennsylvania, | Carefully compared with the Originals. | And an | Appendix, | Containing such Acts, and Parts of Acts, relating to | Property, as are expired, altered or repealed. | Together with | The Royal, Proprietary, City and Borough Charters; | and the Original Concessions of the Honourable | William Penn to the First Settlers of the Province. | Published by Order of Assembly. | [*Penn Arms.*] | *Philadelphia:* | *Printed and Sold by Hall and Sellers, in Market-street, between* | *Front and Second-streets.* MDCCLXXV. | Folio, pp. xxi, 536, 22, (12), 3.   H. S. P.   3147

Edited by Joseph Galloway. The Appendix has the following title: An | Appendix: | Containing a | Summary | of such | Acts of Assembly | As have been formerly in Force within this Province, | For Regulating of Descents, | And Transferring the Property of Lands, &c. | But since expired, altered or repealed. | With Notes upon Divers of them, by the late Learned in the | Law, Chief Justice Kinsey. | [*Penn Arms.*] | *Philadelphia:* | *Printed by Hall and Sellers, in Market-street.* MDCCLXXV. |

AN | ADDRESS | of the | Presbyterian Ministers, | of the | City of Philadelphia, | to the | Ministers | and | Presbyterian Congregations, | in the County of | | In | North Carolina. | *Philadelphia: Printed* MDCCLXXV. | 8vo. pp. 8.   N. Y. H. S.   3148

THE ADDRESS of | Liberty, | To the Buckskins of Pennsylvania, on hearing of the | intended Provincial Congress. | [*Phila-delphia:* 1775.] 4to. 1 leaf. L. C. P. 3149

An anti-Revolutionary address in doggerel verses, dated "Jan. 7, 1775."

THE ADDRESS of the Lords and Commons to | his Majesty, on the present State of America, &c. | [*Philadelphia:*] *Printed by John Dunlap.* [1775.] | 4to. 1 leaf. H. S. P. 3150

AN | ADDRESS | of the | Twelve United Colonies | of | North-America, | By their | Representatives | in | Congress, | To the People of | Ireland. | *Philadelphia :* | *Printed by W. and T. Bradford,* 1775. | 8vo. Title, 1 leaf; pp. 1–10. L. C. P. 3151

ADVERTISEMENT. *Philadelphia: Robert Aitken.* 1775. 3152

The following entries appear in Aitken's Ledger during 1775 :

April 29. Matthew Clarkson for printing 100 Advertisements for Anthony Duché.
June 27. Somerville and Noble for printing 200 quarto Advertisements, and 4000 Price Currents.
August 3. Peter Wright for printing 400 Advertisements.
September 4. Estate of John Inglis for reprinting 200 quarto Advertisements.
September 9. John Willis for printing 100 Advertisements.

ALEXANDER. (W.) History of Women. By William Alexander. *Philadelphia:* 1775. 12mo. 3153

Title from Haven's List.

[ALLEN. (—)] An | Oration, | Upon the Beauties of Liberty; | Or the Essential Right of the Americans. | Delivered | At the Second Baptist-Church in Boston. | Upon the last Annual Thanksgiving. | Humbly dedicated to the Right-Honourable the | Earl of Dartmouth. | Published at the Request of many. | Micha VII. 3. | ... | ... | .... | *Wilmington,* | *Printed and Sold by James Adams, in High-Street,* | M,DCC,LXXV. | 8vo. pp. 21. 3154

"Boston, Thursday, December 10, 1775. Last Thanksgiving, P.M. Mr. Allen, a British Bostonian, preached a Sermon at the Rev. Mr. Davis's Baptist Meeting House from Micah VII. 3." Essex Gazette, Dec. 15, 1775. Perhaps Jolley Allen, who is noticed in Sabine's Loyalists.

THE AMERICAN Calendar for 1776. *Philadelphia: W. and T. Bradford.* 1775. 3155

Aπ die | Einwohner von Irland, | von | Den Abgeordneten der Ver= einigten Colonien | Newhampschire, Massachusetts=Bay, Rhode= | Eyland und Providenz, Connecticut, Neu= | york, New=Jersey, Pennsylvanien, der | Niedern Grafschaften an der Delaware, | Maryland, Virginien, Nord= und Sud= | Carolina, im General=Congreß zu Phila= | phia, [*sic*] den 16ten May, 1775. | Nebst der | Meinung des General=Con= gresses, | betreffend | Einem Entschluß des Hauses der Ge= | meinen von Großbrittannien, | von 20sten February, 1775. | *Philadelphia,* | *Gedruckt und zu bekommen bey Henrich Miller, in* | *der Rees-strasse,* 1775. | 16mo. pp. 16.   H. S. P.   3156

AN | ANECDOTE | Recommended to the Friends. | [*Phila- delphia:* 1775.]   Folio, 1 leaf.   L. C. P.   3157

The Presbyterians in New Jersey, by raising a religious question, succeeded in de- feating a Quaker " of known Abilities and good Reputation," for a seat in the Assembly.

ANNO Regni | Georgii III. Regis, | Magnæ Britanniæ, Fran- ciæ & Hiberniæ, | Decimo Quinto. | At a General Assembly of the Province of Penn- | sylvania, begun and holden at Philadel- phia, | the Fourteenth Day of October, Anno Domini 1774, in | the Fourteenth Year of the Reign of our Sovereign Lord | George III. by the Grace of God, of Great- | Britain, France and Ireland, King, Defender of the | Faith, &c. | And from thence continued by Adjournments to the | Eighteenth Day of March, 1775. | [*Penn Arms.*] | *Philadelphia:* | *Printed and Sold by Hall and Sellers, at the* | *New Printing-Office, near the Market.* MDCCLXXV. | Folio, Title, 1 leaf; pp. 439–464. + And from thence . . . to the | Twenty-Ninth Day of 'June, 1775. | [*Ibid.*] + And from thence . . . to the | Thirtieth Day of September, 1775. | [*Ibid.*]

I have not been able to ascertain whether any of the acts passed by the last Colo- nial Assembly, which met Oct. 14, 1775, and was continued by several adjournments to Sept. 26, 1776, were ever separately printed.

ARTICLES of Association in Pennsylvania. | [*Philadelphia:* *Henry Miller.* 1775.]   Folio, pp. (2).   H. S. P. + [The same in German. *Ibid.*]   3159

ARTICLES | of | Capitulation, | Made and entered into between Richard | Montgomery, Esquire, Brigadier Ge- | neral of the Continental Army, and the Citi- | zens and Inhabitants of Montreal . . . . | [*Philadelphia :*] *Printed by John Dunlap.* [1775.] | Folio, 1 leaf.   L. C. P. 3160

AT a Meeting of the | Committee | Of Inspection and Observation of the County | of Lancaster, . . . on the 29th Day of May, 1775. | *Lancaster: Printed by Francis Bailey, in King's Street.* [1775.] | Folio, 1 leaf.   H. S. P. 3161

Against violence to persons whose " religious tenets forbid their forming military associations." Printed also in German.

BARCLAY. (R.) An Apology for the true Christian Divinity; being an Explanation and Vindication of the Principles and Doctrines of the People called Quakers. By Robert Barclay. The Ninth Edition. *Philadelphia: Printed and Sold by Joseph Crukshank, in Market-Street, between Second and Third-Streets.* 1775. 8vo. pp. 574.   3162

BARTLET. (J.) The | Gentleman Farrier's Repository, | of | Elegant and approved Remedies | for the | Diseases of Horses; | In Two Books. Containing, | I. The Surgical; II. The Medical Part of | Practical Farriery; | Also, | Directions for the proper Treatment of Post | Chaise and other Horses, after violent Exercise. | With suitable Remarks on the Whole. | To. which are now added; | Observations on broken-winded Horses, endea- | vouring to prove the Seat of that Malady not | to be in the Lungs. | . . . | . . . | . . . | . . . . | The Third Edition. | By J. Bartlet, Surgeon. | *Philadelphia :* | *Printed and sold by Joseph Crukshank,* | *in Market-street, between Second and Third* | *Streets.* M,DCC,LXXV. | 12mo. pp. xii, 293; Advertisement, pp. (3).   L. C. P. 3163

BATWELL. (D.) A | Sermon, | Preached at York-Town, | Before Captain Morgan's and Captain | Price's Companies of Rifle-Men, | On Thursday, July 20, 1775. | Being the Day recommended by the | Honorable Continental Congress | for | A General Fast | throughout the | Twelve United Colonies | Of North-America. | By Daniel Batwell, M.'A. | Published by Request.

| *Philadelphia:* | *Printed by John Dunlap, in Market-Street.* | M,DCC,LXXV. | 8vo. Title, 1 leaf; pp. 20.   L. C. P.   3164

[BENEZET. (Anthony)] Remarks on the Nature and bad Effects | of Spirituous Liquors. | [*Philadelphia:* 1775 ?] 12mo. pp. 12.   F.   3165

[BENEZET.] Serious Reflections affectionately recom- | mended to the Well-disposed of every | Religious Denomination, particularly | those who mourn and lament on ac- | count of the Calamities which attend | us; and the insensibility that so gene- | rally prevails. | [*Philadelphia:* 1775 ?] Sm. 8vo. pp. 3.   F.   3166

[BELL. (Robert)] Proposals for Printing by Subscription, Lectures on the Duties and Qualifications of a Physician, with the Elements of the Practice of Physic. By John Gregory, M.D. *Philadelphia: Robert Bell.* 1775.   3167

BIBLIA, | Das ist: | Die ganze | Heilige Schrift | Alten uub Neuen Testaments, | Nach der teutschen Uebersetzung | D. Martin Luthers, | Mit vorgesetztem kurzen | Inhalt eines jeden Capitels, | wie auch mit richtigen | Summarien und vielen Schriftstellen | auf das allersorgfäl= tigste versehen, | Nach denen bewahrtesten und neusten Aufgaben | mit grossem Fleisse ausgefertiget. | Sammt einer Vorrede | von | Herrn D. Johann Gottlieb Faber, | Herzogl. Wurtemb. Oberhofprediger, Con= sistorials | Rath, General = Superintendenten und Abbten | des Klosters Adelberg. *Philadelphia,* | *zu finden bey Ernst Ludwig Baisch,* | *in der zweyten Strasse nahe bey der Rees-Strasse.* 1775. | 8vo. pp. (32), 909, 265, (4).   3168

    Title from O'Callaghan's American Bibles, which see for collation.

[BURGH. (James)] The | Art | of | Speaking. | Containing, | I. An Essay; in which are given Rules for expres- | sing properly the principal Passions and Humours, | which occur in Reading, or public Speaking; | and | II. Lessons taken from the Ancients and Moderns, | (with Additions and Alterations, where thought use- | ful) exhibiting a Variety of Matter for Practice; the | emphatical Words printed in Italics; with Notes of | Direction referring to the Essay. | To which are added, | A Table of the

Lessons; | and | An Index of the various Passions and Humours | in the Essay and Lessons. | . . . | . . . | . . . | . . . . | The Fourth Edition. | *Philadelphia:* | *Printed and sold by R Aitken Bookseller,* | *opposite the London - coffee - house,* | *Front - street.* | M,DCC,LXXV. | . . . . | 12mo. 299, (11).   L. C. P.   3169

BURGH.   Political | Disquisitions; | or, | An Enquiry into public Errors, Defects, | and Abuses.   Illustrated by, and established upon | Facts and Remarks, extracted from a Variety | of Authors, Ancient and Modern. | Calculated | To draw the timely Attention of Government | and People, to a due Consideration of the | Necessity, and the Means, of Reform- | ing those Errors, Defects, and | Abuses; of Restoring the | Constitution, and Sav- | ing the State. | By J. Burgh, Gentleman; Author of the Dignity of | Human Nature, and other Works. | Volume the First. | *Philadelphia:* | *Printed and Sold by Robert Bell, in Third-Street; and* | *William Woodhouse, in Front-Street.* | M.DCC.LXXV. | 8vo. pp. xxiii, (8), 486, (2). + Volume the Second. [*Ibid.*] pp. vii, (7), 477, (3). + Volume the Third and Last.   [*Ibid.*] pp. (16), 460, (54).

BURKE.   (E[dmund]) Speech | of | E. Burke, Esq; | on | American Taxation, | April 19, 1774. | The Third Edition. | *London, printed:* | *Philadelphia, reprinted and sold by Benjamin* | *Towne, in Front-street, near the Coffee-House.* | MDCCLXXV. | 8vo. pp. iv, 76.   L. C. P.   3171

BURKE.   The Speech of Edmund Burke, Esq; on moving his Resolutions for Conciliation with the Colonies, March 22, 1775.   *Philadelphia: Benjamin Towne.*   1775.   3172

From the advertisement in the Pa. Gazette, Sept. 20, 1775, it is probable that James Humphreys, jr., also reprinted both these speeches.

BY an Express arrived at Philadelphia on Saturday evening, | last we have the following account of the battle at Charlestown, on Saturday the 18th of | June, Instant. | June 26th, 1775. *Lancaster: Printed by Francis Bailey.* | Folio, 1 leaf.   H. S. P.   3173

BY an Express just arrived, we have the following. | [*Philadelphia:*] *Printed by John Dunlap.* [1775.] | 8vo. 1 leaf.   L. C. P.   3174

Dated " Philadelphia, April 26, 1775. Wednesday, 12 o'clock." Additional particulars of the battle of Lexington, &c.

BY the Lord Hyde Packet, Captain Jefferies, arrived at New- | York in six weeks from Falmouth, we have | His Majesty's most gracious | Speech, | To both Houses of Parliament. | On Wednesday, November 30, 1774. | [*Philadelphia:*] *Printed by John Dunlap.* [1775.] | Folio, 1 leaf.　　　　　　　　　　　　H. S. P.　3175

Dated " Philadelphia, February 3, 1775."

BYRNES. (Daniel)　A Short Address to the English Colonies in North America, on a Fast Day.　*Wilmington:* 1775.　Folio, pp. 2.　　　　　　　　　　　　　　　　　　　　　　　3176

Title from Haven's List.

CARMICHAEL. (J.)　A Self-defensive War lawful, proved in a Sermon, preached at Lancaster, before Captain Ross's Company of Militia, June 4, 1774, by the Rev. John Carmichael.　*Lancaster:* 1775.　　　　　　　　　　　　　　　　　　　3177

CARMICHAEL.　A | Self-defensive War | Lawful, | proved in | A Sermon, | Preached at Lancaster, before Captain Ross's | Company of Militia, in the Presbyterian | Church, on Sabbath Morning, June 4, 1775. | By the Rev. John Carmichael, A.M. | Now published at the Request of the Author, and corrected by | himself from the Copy printed at Lancaster; | Humbly offered to the Perusal of the Military Asso- | ciators of the City, Liberties and County of Phi- | ladelphia. | . . . |, . . | . . . | . . . | . . . . | *Philadelphia:* | *Printed* [*by Henry Miller*] *for and Sold by John Dean, Bookbinder,* | *in Lœtitia-Court.* 1775. | 8vo. pp. 34.　　　3178

CATALOGUE.　The | Second Part | of the | Catalogue | of | Books, | of the | Library Company | of | Philadelphia. | . . . . | *Philadelphia:* | *Printed by R. Aitken, Bookseller, opposite* | *the London Coffee-House, Front-Street.* | M,DCC,LXXV. | 8vo. pp. 67.　　3179

CATALOGUE of Books to be sold at Auction by Robert Bell, January 18, 1775.　*Philadelphia: Robert Bell.* 1775.　　　3180

Bell advertised another sale to take place on Nov. 23, 1775.

[CHANDLER. (Thomas Bradbury)] The Strictures on the Friendly Address examined, and a refutation of its principles attempted. Addressed to the People of America. *Philadelphia:* 1775. 8vo. pp. 14. Two editions.   3181

Title from Haven's List, where the same tract is also attributed to Lieut. Henry Barry. Haven has probably followed a very slovenly piece of work in Sabin's Dictionary. Under T. B. Chandler, Sabin has given a *title* as above, but with the following *imprints,* &c.: " Printed in the Year 1775, 8vo, pp. 14. + [Another edition.] Philadelphia. 1775. 8vo.," and adds P, meaning that these pamphlets are in the Philadelphia Library. That Library possesses four or five copies of a tract (probably by Lieut. Henry Barry) with the following title : The | General, | attacked | By a Subaltern: | Or THE | STRICTURES | ON | THE FRIENDLY ADDRESS | EXAMINED, | AND | A REFUTATION OF ITS PRINCIPLES | ATTEMPTED. | ADDRESSED TO THE PEOPLE OF AMERICA. | . . . . | *Boston, Printed :* | *New-York, re-printed by James Rivington.* [n. d.] | 8vo. pp. 11. From this it is apparent where Sabin's *title* came from. The Philadelphia Library also contains four or five copies of an edition of Lee's reply to Chandler, with the following title and *imprint:* Strictures | on a | Pamphlet, | entitled | a | " Friendly Address | to | All Reasonable Americans, | on the | Subject of our Political Confusions." | Addressed to the | People of America. | . . . | . . . . | PRINTED IN THE YEAR 1775. | 8vo. Title, 1 leaf, pp. 15–25. Paging and signatures in continuation of Barry's tract, the title and first two pages forming the last four pages of sheet B. This shows the source of Sabin's first *imprint.* Whoever made up the title for him had a pamphlet containing two tracts on opposite sides of a question (each of which has a title-page), and took part of the title of the first tract and the imprint of the second to make up his description. This style of cataloguing recalls a criticism on Macaulay's way of handling the evidence against Sir Elijah Impey, which the critic said was very much the same as if we added to a verse in the New Testament which says, " And Judas went and hanged himself," Christ's command on another occasion, " Go thou and do likewise."

CHEW. (S.) The | Speech | of | Samuel Chew, Esq. | Chief Judge of the Counties of Newcastle, Kent and | Sussex, on Delaware. | On the | Lawfulness of Defence against an | armed Enemy. | Delivered from the Bench to the Grand | Jury of the County of Newcastle, | Nov. 21, 1741. | First Published at the request of said Grand Jury; and now re-pub- | lished by desire of several Gentlemen. | *Philadelphia :* | *Printed and Sold by R. Aitken, Front-Street.* | M.DCC.LXXV. | 8vo. pp. 8.   L. C. P.   3182

COOMBE. ([Thomas]) Edwin : | Or the | Emigrant. | An Eclogue. | To which are added | Three Other Poetical Sketches. | By the Rev. Mr. Coombe. | . . . . | *Philadelphia :* | *Printed by John Dunlap, in Market-street.* | M,DCC,LXXV. | 4to. pp. 24.   3183

COOMBE. A | Sermon | Preached before the Congregations of | Christ Church and St. Peter's, | Philadelphia, | On Thursday, July 20, 1775. | Being the Day recommended by the | Honorable Continental Congress | for | A General Fast | throughout the | Twelve United Colonies | Of North-America. | By Thomas Coombe, M.A. | Chaplain to the Most Noble the Marquis | of Rockingham. | Published by Request. | *Philadelphia:* | *Printed by John Dunlap, in Market-street.* | M,DCC,LXXV. | 8vo. Title, 1 leaf; Dedication, 1 leaf; text, pp. 1–29.   H. S. P.   3184

There was a second edition, which differs only from the first in the substitution on the title-page of "The Second Edition," for "Printed by Request." It was reprinted at Newport, Rhode Island. For a notice of the author, see Appendix to *Inscriptions in St. Peter's Church-Yard*, Philadelphia, 1879.

THE | CRISIS. | Number I. | [*Philadelphia: B. Towne.* 1775.] 8vo. pp. 8. + Number XIV. | Saturday, April 22, 1775. | [*Ibid.*] pp. 113–119. + Number XV.   L. C. P.   3185

This is a reprint of an English publication very strongly in favor of the Americans, of which Towne reprinted the fifteen numbers of eight pages each. I have seen only fourteen. The fifteenth was advertised in the Pa. Evening Post, Nov. 25, 1775. A second edition of the following title was advertised by Towne, Nov. 23, 1775.

A | CRISIS | Extraordinary. | Wednesday, August 9, 1775. | [*Philadelphia: B. Towne.* 1775.] 8vo. pp. 16.   L. C. P.   3186

CROWLEY. (A.) Some Expressions of Ann Crowley, daughter of Thomas and Mary Crowley, of London, during her last illness. With an introductory Testimony concerning her, from the family. *Philadelphia? Joseph Crukshank?* 1775.   3187

Advertised in the Pa. Packet, Feb. 6, 1775, as "just published by Joseph Crukshank, and may be had of Isaac Collins, in Burlington." I have seen a "Third Edition" of this tract, "Burlington: Printed by Isaac Collins. 1775." The first and second editions were published in London in 1774, and it is not unlikely that Crukshank's advertisement refers to Collins's edition.

CULLEN. (W.) Lectures | on the | Materia Medica, | as delivered | By William Cullen, M.D. | Professor of Medicine in the University of Edinburgh. | Now Published by Permission of the Author, | And with many Corrections from the Collation of different | Manuscripts by the Editors. | *America:* | *Printed for the Subscribers, by Robert Bell,* | *next Door to St. Paul's Church, Third-Street, Philadelphia.* | MDCCLXXV. | 4to. pp. i–viii, 1–512.   3188

A | DECLARATION | by the | Representatives | of the | United Colonies | of | North-America, | now met in | General Congress | at | Philadelphia, | Seting [*sic*] forth the Causes and Necessity of their | taking up | Arms. | *Philadelphia:* | *Printed by William and Thomas Bradford,* 1775. | 8vo. pp. (2), 13.   H. S. P. 3189

DELAWARE. Anno Regni Decimo Quarto | Georgii III. Regis. | At a General Assembly | begun at New-Castle, in the Govern- | ment of the Counties of New-Castle, | Kent and Sussex, upon Delaware, the | Twentieth Day of October, in the | Four-teenth Year of the Reign of our | Sovereign Lord George the | Third, King of Great-Britain, &c. | Annoque Domini 1774, (and continu- | ed by Adjournments to the Twenty- | first of August following) the follow- | ing Acts were passed by the Ho- | norable John Penn, Esq; Gover- | nor. | [*Wilmington: James Adams.* 1775.] Folio, pp. 301–351.   c. 3190

DELAWARE. Anno Regni Decimo Quinto | Georgii III. Regis. | At a General Assembly be- | gun at New-Castle, in the Government | of the Counties of New-Castle, Kent and | Sussex, upon Delaware, the Twentieth | Day of October, in the Fifteenth Year | of the Reign of our Sovereign Lord | George the Third, King of Great- | Britain, &c. Annoque Domini 1775, the | following Act was passed by the Ho- | norable John Penn, Esq; Governor. | [*Wilmington: James Adams.* 1775.] Folio, pp. 353–355, 336–337 [for 356–357].   c. 3191

The last Law passed in the Three Lower Counties, under the Provincial Govern-ment. The error in the paging is continued in the Laws of the next Assembly, which sat from Oct. 28, 1776, to Feb. 22, 1777.

A DESCANT on the Command, Matt. xxviii. 19, 20. Written in a Letter to a Friend. By a Wellwisher to Truth. Wherein the Ministerial Office is considered in a just Light. *Philadelphia: Robert Bell?* 1775.   3192

DILWORTH. (T.)   A New Guide to the English Tongue.   By Thomas Dilworth.   *Philadelphia: Robert Aitken.*   1775.   3193

Aitken's Ledger shows sales of 3000 copies in January and February, 1775.

DIRECTIONS | For Manouvres, to be Performed by the Brigade composed | of the Three City Battalions, on Tuesday, the Fourteenth | of November, 1775. | [*Philadelphia:* 1775.] Folio, 1 leaf.   H. S. P.   3194

[DODSLEY. (Robert)]   The Chronicle of the Kings of England from the Reign of William the Conqueror (first King of England) down to his present Majesty George the Third.   By Nathan Ben-Saddi.   *Lancaster: Stewart Herbert, jun.* 1775. + *Philadelphia: Robert Bell and Benjamin Towne.* 1775.   3195

DUCHÉ. (J.) The | American Vine, | A | Sermon, | Preached in Christ-Church, Philadelphia, | before the honourable | Continental Congress, | July 20th, 1775. | Being the day recommended by them | For a General Fast | throughout the | United English Colonies | of America. | By the Reverend | Jacob Duché, M.A. | *Philadelphia.* | *Printed by James Humphreys, junior.* | M,DCC,LXXV. | 8vo. pp. 34.   H. S. P.   3196

DUCHÉ.   The Duty of Standing Fast in our | Spiritual and Temporal | Liberties, | A | Sermon, | Preached in Christ-Church, | July 7th, 1775. | Before the First Battalion of the City | and Liberties of Philadelphia; | And now published at their Request. | By the Reverend | Jacob Duché, M.A. | *Philadelphia.* | *Printed and Sold by* | *James Humphreys, junior,* | *The Corner of Black-horse Alley, Front-street.* | M,DCC,LXXV. | 8vo. pp. (4), iv, 25.   3197

AN | EARNEST Address | to such of | The People called Quakers | As are Sincerely Desirous of | Supporting and Maintaining | the | Christian Testimony | of their | Ancestors. | Occasioned by a Piece, intituled, | "The Testimony of the People Called Quakers, given | forth by a Meeting of the Representatives | of said People, in Pennsylvania and New-Jersey, | held at Philadelphia the Twenty-fourth Day of | the First Month, 1775." | . . . | . . . | . . . | . . . | . . . | . . . | . . . | . . . | . . . | . . . | . . . . |

Philadelphia, | *Printed for John Douglas M'Dougal,* 1775. | Sm. 8vo. pp. 56.　　　　　　　　　　　　　H. S. P.　3198

ELLWOOD. (T.)　The | History | of the | Life | of | Thomas Ellwood: | Or, | An Account of his Birth, Education, &c. | with divers Observations on his Life and Manners when a | Youth: And how he came to be convinced of the Truth; | with his many Sufferings and Services for the same. | Also, | Several other remarkable Passages and Occurrences. | Written by his own Hand. | To which is added, | A Supplement | by J[oseph] W[yeth.] | . . . . | The Fourth Edition. | *Philadelphia:* | *Printed by Joseph Crukshank in Market-* | *Street, between Second and Third Streets.* | M,DCC,LXXV. | 16mo. pp. 24, 360.　　　　　　3199

ENSLIN. (G. E.)　$\mathfrak{H}$armonie | ber | Evangelien unb Epiſteln. | Ober: | Lehrreiche Verbinbung | ber | evangeliſch= unb epiſtoliſchen Texte | auf alle | Feſte, Sonn= unb Feyertäge, | nebſt einigen | Paßions= Prebigten, | entworfen von | M. Georg Ernſt Enslin, | Prebiger zu Wolfenhauſen ohnweit Tübingen. | Mit einer Vorrebe von | D. Chriſtoph Friberich Sartorius, | orbentlichen öfentlichen Lehrer ber Gottesgelahrt= heit, auch Superattenbenten | bes Herzogl. Stifts in Tübingen. | Mit gnäb. Genehmigung bes Herzogl. Würtembergiſchen Conſiſtorii. | *Phila-delphia:* | *Bey Ernſt Ludwig Baiſch, in der zweyten Strasse nahe der Rees-Strasse.* | MDCCLXXV. | Sq. 8vo. pp. (16), 708, 142, 1 leaf.

Printed in Germany, as were the Bible and Hymn-Book sold by Baisch.

AN | EPISTLE | from the | Meeting for Sufferings, | Held in Philadelphia for Pennsylvania and | New-Jersey, the 5th Day of the First Month | 1775 ; | To our Friends and Brethren in these and the | adjacent Provinces. | [*Philadelphia:* 1775.]　Folio, pp. 3.

THE | EPISTLE | from the | Meeting for Sufferings in London. | To Friends and Brethren in New-England. | [Followed by] The Epistle from the Yearly-Meeting held in London by Ad- | journments, from the 5th of the 6th Month, 1775, to the 10th | of the same, inclusive. | [*Philadelphia:* 1775.]　Folio, pp. (2).　F.　3202

THE | EPISTLE | from the | Yearly-Meeting, | Held in London, by Adjournments, from | the 5th of the Sixth Month, 1775, to the | 10th of the same, inclusive. | To the Quarterly and Monthly-Meetings of Friends | in Great-Britain, Ireland, and elsewhere. | [*Philadelphia:* 1775.] Folio, pp. (4).   F. 3203

AN | ESSAY | upon | Government, | adopted by | The Americans. | Wherein, | The lawfulness of revolutions, are De- | monstrated in a Chain of consequences | from the Fundamental Principles of society. | *Philadelphia:* | *Printed and sold by the Booksellers.* | MDCCLXXV. | 12mo. pp. 125.   H. S. P. 3204

AN | EXERCISE; | Containing, | a | Dialogue and Two Odes | Set to Music, | for the | Public Commencement, | in the | College of Philadelphia, | May 17th, 1775. | *Philadelphia:* | *Printed by Joseph Crukshank, in Market-* | *Street, between Second and Third Streets.* | MDCCLXXV. | 8vo. pp. 8.   L. C. P. 3205

AN EXPRESS arrived at Five O'clock this Evening, by which we have the | following Advices; | Watertown, Wednesday Morning, near ten of the clock. | To all Friends of American Liberty, ... | *Lancaster: Printed by Francis Bailey.* [1775.] | Folio, 1 leaf.   3206

Dated "Philadelphia, April 25th, 1775." This account of the Battle of Lexington was issued at Lancaster on April 26th.

EXTRACT of a letter wrote by the Earl of Essex, to his | particular friend the Earl of Southampton, some- | time before his death. | [*Philadelphia:* 1775?] 12mo. pp. 12.   F. 3207

One of Benezet's numerous tracts, published without date. It contains besides extracts from letters by John Locke, Count Oxenstiern, David Brainerd, and others, Locke's Universal Prayer and The Hermit, a Poem.

EXTRACTS | from the | Votes and Proceedings | Of the American Continental | Congress, | Held at Philadelphia, Septem- .ber 5, 1774. | Containing | The Bill of Rights, a List of Grievances, | Occasional Resolves, the Association, an | Address to the People of Great-Britain, | A Memorial to the Inhabitants of the | British American Colonies, and a Petition | to the King. | To which is added, | The Proceedings of the | Provincial Convention, | Held at Philadelphia, January 23, 1775. | Published by order of the Provincial Convention. | *Philadelphia :* | *Printed by William and Thomas Bradford,* | *at the London Coffee-House.* | M,DCC,LXXV. | 8vo. pp. 80. H. S. P. 3208

FATHER Abraham's | Pocket Almanack, | For the Year 1776 ; | Fitted to the Use of Pennsylvania, | and the neighbouring Provinces. | Containing, | A great Variety of useful Lists | and Tables. | *Philadelphia :* | *Printed and Sold by J. Dunlap, at* | *the Newest Printing-Office, in* | *Market-street.* [1775.] | 24mo. pp. (48).

LA FERME | de | Pensylvanie. | Les Avantages | De la Vertu. | Plan | D' Instruction | Pour le Peuple ; | Avec quelques Observations sur la Liberté | du Commerce des Grains. | . . . . | *A Philadelphie,* | *Et à Paris,* | *Chez Ribou, Libraire, Cloître Saint-* | *Germain l'Auxerrois, attenant l'Eglise* | *à la Nouveauté.* | M.DCC.LXXV. | 24mo. pp. xii, 96. H. S. P. 3210

FOX. (T.) The Wilmington Almanac for 1776. By Thomas Fox. *Wilmington : James Adams.* 1775. 3211

[FRENEAU. (Philip)] A | Voyage | to | Boston. | A | Poem. | . . . | . . . | . . . | . . . | . . . | . . . . | By the Author of American Liberty, a Poem : General | Gage's Soliloquy, &c. | *Philadelphia :* | [*Printed by Benjamin Towne.*] *Sold by William Wood-house,* | *in Front-street.* | M,DCC,LXXV. | 8vo. pp. 24. 3212

FRESH Intelligence. | Monday, November 6, 1775. | *Philadelphia : Printed by John Dunlap.* [1775.] | Folio, 1 leaf. H. S. P. 3213

Probably issued as a Postscript to the Pa. Packet. An account of Lord Dunmore's proceedings in Virginia.

[GALLOWAY. (Joseph)] A Plan of a proposed Union between Great Britain and the Colonies. *Philadelphia ?* 1775. 3214

Title from Haven's List, where, however, it is erroneously attributed to Samuel Galloway. This mistake is probably copied from the title of the London edition of Chandler's " What think ye of the Congress now ?" This plan was laid before Congress Sept. 28, 1774. It was reprinted in " Observation," &c., No. 3427, as " First printed at New York."

LES GOUT Anecdotes. *A Philadelphie : Fleury Mesplet.* 1775.

GREGORY. ([John]) A | Father's Legacy | to his | Daughters. | By the late | Dr. Gregory, | Of Edinburgh. | *London, Printed:* | *Philadelphia:* | *Re-printed by John Dunlap,* | *In Market-Street.* | M,DCC,LXXV. | Sm. 8vo. pp. i–viii, 1 leaf, 1–132.   H. S. P.   3216

HANCOCK. (J.)   An | Oration: | Delivered March 5, 1774 | at the | Request of the Inhabitants | of the | Town of Boston: | To Commemorate the Bloody | Tragedy of the Fifth of | March, 1770. | By the Honorable John | Hancock, Esquire. | *Philadelphia: J. Douglas M'Dougall,* 1775.   8vo. pp. 24.   3217

HANSON. (T.)   The | Prussian Evolutions | in | Actual Engagements; | both in | Platoons, Sub, and Grand-Divisions; | Explaining, | All the different Evolutions, and Manœuvres, in Firing, | Standing, Advancing, and Retreating, which | were exhibitted before his present Majesty, | May 8, 1769; and before John Duke of | Argyle, on the Links of Leith, near | Edenburgh, in 1771. | With some Additions, since that Time, | explained with Thirty Folio Copper-Plates. | To which is added, | The Prussian Manual Exercise: | Also | The Theory and some Practices of Gunnery. | By Thomas Hanson, Adjutant to the 2d Battalion. | And Teacher of part of the American Militia. | *Philadelphia: Printed for the Author, by J. Doug-* | *lass M'Dougall, Printer, Book-biner and Stationer, at* | *his Shop in Chestnut-Street, three Doors below Second-* | *Street.*   [1775.] | Sq. 8vo.   H. S. P.   3218

Collation: Title, 1 leaf; Dedication, 1 page; List of Subscribers, pp. (5); Preface, pp. i.–iv.; text, pp. 1–64; Second title, 1 leaf; text, pp. 1–56; 30 folded plates. The second title reads: Book | The Second, | containing | The Theory and Practice | of | Gunnery. | With some Methods | of the | English Larbartary. | *Philadelphia:* | *Printed for Thomas Hanson, by J. Douglas* | *M'Dougall, Printer, Book-binder and Stationer* | *at his Shop in Chestnut-Street, three Doors below* | *Second-Street.* |

HAUSAM, (A.) S. CULBERTSON and J. SMITH. [*Philadelphia:* 1775.]   4to. 1 leaf.   L. C. P.   3219

Three depositions, dated "May 26, 1775," subscribed by Anthony Hausam, Samuel Culbertson, and Jacob Smith, before Isaac Davis, "one of his Majesty's Justices for" Chester County, setting forth that "William Moore, of Moore Hall, had said that some of the Congress had taken into their Heads to send an Army against the King's Troops, for which they were Fools and damned Rascals; and that Moore said the People of Boston were a vile set of Rebels, that he wondered the Magistrates of

Philadelphia did not commit every man to Prison who associated or mustered, that he was determined to commit to Prison every person who would associate near him, if they should be sixty," &c.

HILL. (J[ohn]) The | Old Man's Guide | To | Health and Longer Life : | With Rules for | Diet, Exercise, and Physic ; | for | Preserving a Good Constitution | and | Preventing Disorders in a Bad One. | By J. Hill, M.D. | Member of the Imperial Academy. | *London, Printed ; | Philadelphia : Re-Printed by John Dunlap, | In Market-Street.* | M,DCC,LXXV. | Sm. 8vo. pp. 48.   L. C. P.   3220

DER | HOCH=Deutsch= | Americanische | Calender, | Auf das Jahr | . . . | . . . | 1776. | (Welches ein Schalt=Jahr von 366 Tagen ist.) | . . . | . . . | . . . | . . . | . . . | . . . | . . . | . . . | | . . . | . . . . | Zum acht und dreyßigsten mal heraus gegeben. | *Germantown : Gedruckt und zu finden bey Christoph Saur.* | . . . | . . . . [1775.] | Sq. 8vo. pp. (48).   H. S. P.   3221

HUGHES. (J.) Letters | of | Abelard | and | Heloise. | To which is prefix'd a particular Account of their | Lives, Amours, and Misfortunes. | By the late John Hughes, Esq. | To which is now first added, | The Poem of Eloisa to Abelard. | By Mr. Pope. | *Philadelphia : | Printed for Samuel Delap.* | M.DCC.LXXV. | 12mo. pp. 124, 1 plate.   3222

HUNT. (I.) The | Political Family : | Or a | Discourse | pointing out the | Reciprocal Advantages, | Which flow from an uninterrupted Union between | Great-Britain and her American Colonies. | By Isaac Hunt, Esquire. | Numb. I. | [Cut.] | *Philadelphia : | Printed, By James Humphreys, junior.* | MDCCLXXV. | 8vo. pp. 32.   L. C. P.   3223

The cut on the title is an engraving of two pitchers at sea, with the motto, " If we strike we break."

IN Congress, | Monday, June 12, 1775. | *Philadelphia : Printed by William & Thomas Bradford.* [1775.] | Folio, 1 leaf.   3224

Recommending the observance of Thursday, July 20th, as a day of " Humiliation, Fasting, and Prayer."

IN Congress, June 12, 1775. | [*Philadelphia :*] *Printed by John Dunlap.* [1775.] | Folio, 1 leaf.   3225

Recommendation by Congress that July 20th be observed as a Fast-Day, and an address " To the oppressed Inhabitants of Canada." Dated " Philadelphia, June 15."

IN Congress. | December 6, 1775. | [*Philadelphia :*] *Printed by J. Dunlap.* [1775.] | Folio, 1 leaf.   H. S. P.   3226

In answer to a " Proclamation issued from the Court of St. James's on the Twenty-Third day of August last."

JNWENDJGE | Glaubens= | und | Liebes = Uebung | einer Seelen gegen Gott | und dessen Gegenwart. | Kurz und einfältig entworffen und | angewiesen | Von und vor eine Seele, so nach Got= | tes Gegenwart und Vereinigung | durch seine Gnade ist begierig | worden. | *Partheno-polis :* [*Ephrata :*] *Gedruckt Anno* 1775, | *vor Jacob Kimmel.* | 16mo. pp. 80.   H. S. P.   3227

JONES. (D.) Defensive War in a just Cause | Sinless. | A Sermon, | Preached | On the Day of the Continental Fast, | at | Tredyffryn, in Chester County, | by | The Rev.ᵈ | David Jones, A.M. Published by Request. | . . . | . . . . | *Philadelphia :* | *Printed by Henry Miller.* 1775. | 8vo. pp. 27.   H. S. P.   3228

JOURNAL | of the | Proceedings | of the | Congress, | held at | Philadelphia, | May 10, 1775. | [Cut.] | *Philadelphia :* | *Printed and Sold, by William and Thomas | Bradford, at the London Coffee-House.* | M.DCC.LXXV. | 8vo. Half title, 1 leaf; Title, 1 leaf; List of Delegates, pp. iv; text, pp. 1–239.   H. S. P.   3229

EJNE KURZGEFASZTE | Historische Nachricht | von den | Kämpfen der Schweizer | für die | Freyheit. | NB. Diese Schrif tist erstlich als ein Anhang zu einer | Predigt gedruckt worden, betitelt, Das Gesetz der Freyheit, welche bey dem Drucker in Englisch | zu haben ist. | *Philadelphia,* | *Gedruckt und zu haben bey Henrich Miller.* 1775. | 8vo. pp. 16.   H. S. P.   3230

LEE. (Charles) Letters of Major-General Lee to Earl Percy and General Burgoyne ; with their Answers. *Philadelphia ? James Humphreys, junr.* 1775.   3231

Advertised with the Speeches of Edmund Burke (see Numbers 3171 and 3172, *supra*) in the Pa. Ledger, Oct. 21, 1775. As the latter probably refer to pamphlets printed by Towne, the above perhaps has reference to Rivington's edition of these Letters.

DIE | LEHRTEXTE | der | Brüder = Gemeine | für das Jahr | 1776. | Enthaltend | lauter Worte unsers lieben Herrn | und Heilandes | . . . . | *Philadelphia,* | *Gedruckt bey Henrich Miller, im Jahr* 1775. | 8vo. pp. (68).   H. S. P.   3232

LETTRE | Addressée | Aux Habitans | Opprimés de la Province | de | Quebec. | De la port du Congrés Général de l'Amérique Sep- | tentrionale, tenu à Philadelphie. | [*Philadelphia: Fleury Mesplet.* 1775.] 8vo. pp. 7.   L. C. P.   3233

THE | LIFE | of the late | Earl of Chesterfield : | Or, the | Man of the World. | Including | His Lordship's principal Speeches in Parlia- | ment ; his most admired Essays in the Paper | called The World ; his Poems ; and the | Substance of the System of Education | Delivered in a | Series of Letters to his Son. | *London, Printed :* | *Philadelphia, Re-printed for John Sparhawk.* | MDCCLXXV. | 8vo. pp. iv, 388.   H. S. P.   3234

LOWTH. (R.) A | Short | Introduction | to | English | Grammar. | With | Critical Notes. | By the Right Reverend | Robert Lowth, D.D. | Lord Bishop of Oxford. | . . . | . . . | . . . | . . . | . . . | . . . . | *Philadelphia :* | *Printed by R. Aitken Bookseller, opposite the London | Coffee-House, Front-Street.* | M.DCC.LXXV. | 12mo. pp. xii, 132.   H. S. P.   3235

MAGAW. (S.) A | Discourse | Preached in Christ-Church, | Philadelphia, | On Sunday, October 8th, 1775. | By the Rev. Samuel Magaw, M.A. | of Kent County, on Delaware. | *Philadelphia :* | *Printed and Sold by Story and Humphreys,* | *in Norris's Alley, near Front-Street.* | M,DCC,LXXV. | 8vo. pp. 14.   H. S. P.   3236

THE | MANUAL Exercise, | As Ordered by His | Majesty, | In 1764. | Together with | Plans and Explanations, | of the Method generally practis'd | at | Reviews and Field-Days, &c. | *Wilmington,* | *Printed by James Adams, at his Printing-Office | in High-street,* M,DCC,LXXV. | 8vo. pp. 37, (2 ?).   H. S. P.   3237

THE | MANUAL | Exercise, | As Ordered by His | Majesty, | In 1764. | *Philadelphia: | Printed and Sold, by William and Thomas Bradford, at the London Coffee-House.* | MDCCLXXV. | 8vo. pp. 8 +.   N. Y. H. S.   3238

THE MANUAL Exercise as ordered by his Majesty in 1764. *Philadelphia: Robert Aitken.* 1775.   3239

THE | MANUAL Exercise, | As Ordered by His | Majesty, | In 1764. | Together with | Plans and Explanations, | of the Method generally practised | at | Reviews and Field-Days, &c. | *Lancaster: | Printed by Francis Bailey, in King's-Street.* | M,DCC,LXXV. | 8vo. pp. 40.   H. S. P.   3240

THE | MIDDLE Line: | Or, | An Attempt | to | Furnish Some Hints | For ending the | Differences | subsisting | Between Great-Britain and the Colonies. | *Philadelphia: | Printed and Sold by Joseph Crukshank, | in Market-Street.* M.DCC.LXXV. | 12mo. pp. 48.   L. C. P.   3241

MINUTES | of the | Philadelphian Association | In MDCCLXXV. | [Colophon.] *Philadelphia: Printed by Henry Miller.* [1775.] | Sq. 8vo. pp. 11.   3242

MONTGOMERY. (J.) A | Sermon, | preached at | Christiana Bridge and Newcastle, | The 20th of July, 1775. | Being the day appointed by the | Continental Congress, | As a Day of Fasting, Humiliation, | and Prayer. | Published by Request. | By Joseph Montgomery, A.M. | . . . | . . . | . . . . | *Philadelphia: | Printed by James Humphreys, junr. | The Corner of Black-Horse Alley, Front-street.* | MDCCLXXV. | 8vo. pp. 30.   H. S. P.   3243

MORE, (Hannah) and [Edmund] CARTWRIGHT. The Search after Happiness, A Pastoral Drama. By Miss Hannah More. With Armine and Elvira, A Legendary Tale, in Two Parts. By Mr. Cartwright. The Second Edition. *Philadelphia: James Humphreys, jun.* 1775.   3244

DAS NEUE | Teſtament | unſers | Herrn und Heylandes | Jeſu Chriſti, | Nach der Deutſchen Ueberſetzung | D. Martin Luthers, | mit kurzem | Inhalt eines jeden Capitels, | und vollstandiger | Anweisung gleicher Schrift-Stellen. | Wie auch | aller Sonn= und Fest-tägigen | Evangelien und Episteln. | Siebente Auflage. | *Germantown,* | *Gedruckt und zu finden bey Christoph Saur,* 1775. | 16mo. pp. 529, (3).   3245

     According to O'Callaghan, some copies of this edition are incorrectly called "Sechte Auflage."

DER NEUESTE, Verbessert= und Zuverläßige | Americänische | Calender | Auf das 1776ste Jahr Christi, | Welches ein Schalt-Jahr von 366 Tagen ist. | [12 lines.] | Zum Vierzehntenmal herausgegeben. | *Philadelphia, Gedruckt und zu finden bey Henrich Miller,* . . . | . . . | . . . | . . . | . . . . [1775.] | 4to. pp. (48).   H. S. P.   3246

NEW-YEAR Verses of the Carriers of the Pennsylvania Gazette. *Philadelphia: Hall and Sellers.* 1775.   3247

NEW-YEAR Verses of the Carriers of the Pennsylvania Journal. *Philadelphia: W. and T. Bradford.* 1775.   3248

THE NEW-YEAR | Verses, | Of Those who Carry the | Pennsylvania Packet | To the Customers. | Philadelphia, January, 1775. | [*Philadelphia: John Dunlap.* 1775.] Folio, 1 leaf.   3249

DIE | OFFENBAHRUNG | von dem | Wunder=Wesen | Gottes | vor, in und nach der Schöpfung, | zum | Schauen, Glauben und Ver= trauen | an den | wahren einigen Gott. | In Versen vorgestellet, | und auf | Begehren und Kosten guter Freunde zum | Druck befördert. | *Anno* 1775. | 12mo. pp. 48.   H. S. P.   3250

     This title is included in Seidensticker's Bibliography. In my opinion it was printed in Germany.

PENN. (W.) Argumentum ad Hominem: | Being an | Extract | From a Piece intitled, | England's present Interest considered, | with | Honour to the Prince, | and | Safety to the People. | In Answer to this one Question: | What is most Fit, Easy and Safe at this Juncture of Affairs to | be done, for quieting of Differences, allaying the Heat of | contrary Interests, and making them subservient to the | Interest of the Government, and consistent with the Pros- | perity of the Kingdom? | By

William Penn, | Founder of the Province of Pennsylvania. | To which are added, | Some Extracts from the Writings | of divers Authors, more particularly re- | commended to the Notice of the People | called Quakers. | *Philadelphia :* | *Printed [by John Dunlap ?] in the Year* M,DCC,LXXV. | 8vo. pp. 28.   H. S. P.   3251

THE | PENNSYLVANIA | Evening Post. | MDCCLXXV. | Volume I. | *Philadelphia :* | *Printed by Benjamin Towne, in Front-Street.* [1775.] | 4to. pp. (2), 604.   3252

Published on Tuesdays, Thursdays, and Saturdays.

THE PENNSYLVANIA Gazette.   3253

Numbers 2402 (Jan. 4, 1775) to 2453 (Dec. 27, 1775), four pages each, with " Supplements" of four pages to Numbers 2409, 2413, and 2416, and of two pages to all the others except 2407, 2448, 2450, 2452, and 2453 ; " Postscripts" of one leaf to Numbers 2418, 2429, and 2445, and of two pages to Numbers 2406, 2411, 2416, and 2418. Title and imprint as in No. 2913, *supra.*

THE PENNSYLVANIA Journal.   3254

Numbers 1674 (Jan. 4, 1775) to 1725 (Dec. 27, 1775), four pages each, with extra half-sheets of two pages to Numbers 1674, 1675, 1676, 1677, 1679, 1680, 1681, 1684, 1685, 1687, 1691, 1692, 1693, 1694, 1697, 1698, 1701, 1703, 1705, 1710, and 1712 ; "Supplements" of two pages to Numbers 1678, 1682, 1683, 1686, 1689, 1690, and 1700 ; " Postscripts" of one leaf to Numbers 1678, 1679, and 1690 ; and of two pages to Numbers 1683 (March 8), 1683 (March 9), and 1688. No. 1709 is misnumbered 1708. Title with the cut of the divided snake until 1715, when the old cut was reintroduced. Imprint as in No. 2317, *supra.*

January 28, 1775. Numb. I. | THE | PENNSYLVANIA : Ledger : | Or the Virginia, Maryland, : Pennsylvania, & New-Jersey | Weekly : Advertiser. | Saturday, : January 28, 1775. | *Philadelphia : Printed by James Humphreys, junr. in Front-street, at the Corner of Black- | horse Alley :— Where Essays, Articles of News, Advertisements, &c. are gratefully received and impartially inserted.* | Folio.   3255

Number I. (Jan. 28, 1775) to XLIX. (Dec. 30, 1775), four pages each, with " Supplements" of one leaf to Numbers 5 and 6, and of two pages to Numbers 3, 8, 12, and 25. A cut of the royal arms divides the title, as indicated by the dotted lines. In No. 2 the words, " And | where Subscriptions are taken in for this Paper, at Ten Shillings per Year," were added to imprint.

THE | PENNSYLVANIA | Magazine : | Or, | American | Monthly Museum. | MDCCLXXV. | Volume I. [Vignette.] | *Philadelphia : | Printed and sold by R. Aitken, printer and bookseller, | opposite the London Coffee-house, Front-street.* [1775.] | 8vo. pp. 625 ; Index, pp. (5) ; 15 plates.   H. S. P.   3256

THE PENNSYLVANIA Mercury. *Philadelphia : Printed by Storey and Humphreys.* Folio.   3257

This paper was begun in April, 1775, and was discontinued in December, the publishers having been burnt out. See Thomas's History of Printing.

THE PENNSYLVANIA Packet.   3258

Numbers 167 (Jan. 2, 1775) to 208 (Dec. 25, 1775), four pages each, with "Post-scripts" of one leaf to Numbers 171, 202, 207, and 216 ; of two pages to Numbers 173, 175, 176, 177, 179 to 183, 186, 187 (two Postscripts, one dated "May 24"), 188, 191, 193, 194, 195, 198 to 201, 204, and 211 ; and one of four pages to No. 182. Title and imprint as in No. 3076, *supra.*

THE PENNSYLVANIA Pocket Almanac for 1776. *Philadelphia : W. and T. Bradford.* 1775.   3259

THE | PETITION | of the | Continental Congress | to the | King. | And | General Gage's Letter | to the Honorable | Peyton Randolph, Esq ; | In Answer to one wrote by the Congress. | *Philadelphia : | Printed by William and Thomas Bradford, | at the London Coffee-House.* | MDCCLXXV. | 8vo. Title, 1 leaf ; pp. 133–144.   3260

An Appendix to the Journals of the Congress of 1774.

THE PHILADELPHIA Newest Almanac for 1776. *Philadelphia : Robert Aitken.* 1775.   3261

[PHIPPS. (Joseph)] To the Youth | of | Norwich Meeting. | [*Lancaster : Francis Bailey.* 1775.] Sm. 12mo. pp. 12.   F.   3262

The first page contains a preface dated "Lancaster | Quarterly-Meeting. | First Month, 1775."

PITT, (William — Earl of Chatham.) The | Speech, | Of the Right Honourable | The Earl of Chatham, | in the | House of

Lords, | January 20th, 1775. | On a Motion for an Address to His | Majesty, to give immediate orders for remov- | ing his Troops from Boston forthwith, in order | to quiet the minds and take away the apprehensions of | His good Subjects in America. | *Philadelphia :* | *Printed by John Dunlap, in Market-Street.* | M,DCC,LXXV. | 8vo. pp. 16.   H. S. P.   3263

PITT. Des Hoch=Edlen | Grafen von Chatham | Rede, | gehalten | im Hause der Lords, | den 20ften Jenner, 1775, | Bey Gelegenheit eines Vorschlags, | zu einer | Abdresse an Seine Majestät den König, | Daß derselbe unverzüglich Befehle ertheilen möge | seine Truppen von Boston sogleich wegzuzie= | hen, um die Gemüther seiner guten Unter= thanen | in America zu beruhigen, und ihre Besorgnisse | aus dem Wege zu schaffen. | *Philadelphia,* | *Gedruckt und zu haben bey Henrich Miller,* *in der* | *Rees-strasse.* 1775. | 3264

POOR Will's Almanac for 1776. *Philadelphia : Joseph Cruk-shank.* 1775.   3265

POOR Will's Pocket Almanac for 1776. *Philadelphia : Joseph Crukshank.* 1775.   3266

PORTEUS. (B.) A Review of the Life and Character of Arch-bishop Secker. By Beilby Porteus, D.D. *Philadelphia :?* 1775.

From some entries in Robert Aitken's Ledger it seems possible that an edition was printed in Philadelphia, but they may have referred to that printed in New York in 1773, or to a London edition.

THE | PRESENT Situation | of | Affairs in North-America. | A Poem. | [*Philadelphia : B. Towne.* 1775.] 8vo. pp. 8.   3268

PROCEEDINGS | of the | Convention, | for the | Province | of | Pennsylvania, | held at | Philadelphia, | January 23, 1775, and continued | by Adjournments, to the 28th. | *Philadelphia :* | *Printed by William and Thomas Bradford,* | *at the London Coffee-House.* | M.DCC.LXXV. | 8vo. Title, 1 leaf; pp. 10.   L. C. P.   3269

PROCLAMATION. G. [*Royal Arms.*] R. | By the Honoura-ble | John Penn, Esquire, | . . . | . . . | A Proclamation. | *Phila-*

delphia: Printed by Hall and Sellers, in Market-street.   [1775.] |
Folio, 1 leaf.   H. S. P.   3270

Dated "April 8, 1775." Revoking the Proclamation of Nov. 2, 1774, and re-
proclaiming the extension of authority to the Maryland Lines.

[RAYNAL. (William Thomas Francis)] The | Sentiments | of
a | Foreigner, | on the | Disputes | of | Great-Britain with
America. | Translated from the French | . . . . | *Philadelphia:*
| *Printed by James Humphreys, junior;* | *in Front-Street.* |
M,DCC,LXXV. | 8vo. pp. 27, (1).   H. S. P.   3271

RESOLUTIONS directing the Mode of Levying Taxes on Non-
Associators in Pennsylvania. *Philadelphia: Henry Miller.* 1775.

Printed in English and German by order of the Assembly. Minutes Nov. 25,
1775.

RITTENHOUSE. (D.) An | Oration, | Delivered February 24,
1775, | before the | American | Philosophical Society, | held at |
Philadelphia, | for promoting | Useful Knowledge. | By David Rit-
tenhouse, M.A. | Member of the said Society. | *Philadelphia:* |
Printed by John Dunlap, in Market-Street. | M,DCC,LXXV. | 4to.
pp. 27.   H. S. P.   3273

[ROBINSON, (Matthew — Baron Rokeby.)] Appendix | to
the | Considerations | on the | Measures Carrying On | with re-
spect to the | British Colonies | in | North America. | *Philadelphia.*
| *Reprinted and Sold by Benjamin Towne,* | *near the Coffee-House.*
M,DCC,LXXV. | 8vo. pp. 19.   L. C. P.   3274

ROMANS. (B.) It is Proposed to Print, | A | . . . | Map, |
From Boston to Worcester, Pro- | vidence and Salem. | Shewing
the Seat of the present unhappy Civil War in | North-America. |
Author, Bernard Romans. | [*Philadelphia: Robert Aitken.* 1775.]
8vo. 1 leaf.   L. C. P.   3275

Dated "Philadelphia, July 12, 1775."

RULES | and | Articles, | for the better | Government | of the
| Troops | Raised, or to be raised, and kept in pay by and at |

the joint Expence of the | Twelve united English Colonies | of | North-America. | *Philadelphia :* | *Printed by William and Thomas Bradford,* 1775. | 8vo. pp. 16.   H. S. P. 3276

RULES | For establishing Rank of | Precedence amongst the | Pennsylvania Associators. | [*Philadelphia : Henry Miller.* 1775.] Sm. 8vo. pp. 12.   H. S. P. 3277

Also printed in German, as were Numbers 3159 and 3272, *supra.*

SAUNDERS. (R.) A Pocket Almanac for 1776. By Richard Saunders, Phil. *Philadelphia : Hall and Sellers.* 1775.   3278

SAUNDERS. Poor Richard improved : | Being an | Almanack | . . . | . . . | . . . | . . . | . . . | . . . | . . . | . . . | . . . | . . . | ... | For the | Year of our Lord 1776 : | Being Bissextile or Leap-Year. | . . . | . . . | . . . | . . . | . . . | . . . | . . . | . . . | . . . . | By Richard Saunders, Philom. | *Philadelphia :* | *Printed and Sold by Hall and Sellers.* [1775.] | Sm. 8vo. pp. (36). H. S. P. 3279

[SAYRE. (John)] From the | New-York Journal. | [*Philadelphia :* 1775.] Sm. 8vo. pp. 6.   F. 3280

The Rev. John Sayre's letter to the Committee of Fairfield, Conn., giving his reasons for refusing to sign the " Continental Association." Probably reprinted for Anthony Benezet.

SCHREIBEN | des | Evangelisch = Lutherisch und Reformirten | Kirchen=Raths, | wie auch | der Beamten der Teutschen Gesellschaft | in der Stadt Philadelphia, | an die | Teutschen Einwohner | der Provinzen | von Newyork und Nord=Carolina. | *Philadelphia,* | *Gedruckt bey Henrich Miller, in der Rees-strasse,* | 1775. | 16mo. pp. 40.   3281

THE SEVERAL Assemblies of New Jersey, | Pennsylvania and Virginia, having re- | ferred to the Congress a resolution of the House of | Commons of Great Britain, which resolution | is in these words : | [*Philadelphia : W. and T. Bradford.* 1775.] 8vo. pp. 8.   L. C. P. 3282

The resolution (which expressed the sentiments of the House of Commons in regard to the taxes imposed by Colonial Assemblies being approved by the King) is followed by the opinion of Congress, signed John Hancock, and dated " July 31, 1775."

SEVERAL Methods | of making | Salt-Petre; | recommended to the | Inhabitants | of the | United Colonies, | by their | Representatives | In Congress. | *Philadelphia: | Printed by W. and T. Bradford.* 1775. | 8vo. pp. 12. L. C. P. 3283

In Haven's List the authorship of this tract is attributed to W. Shewell.

SHARP. (A.) Der Gantz Neue Verbefferte Nord = Americanifche Calender, auf das 1776ste Jahr Chrifti. Zum Erftenmal herausgegeben und verfertiget von Anthony Sharp, Philom. *Lancaster: Francis Bailey.* 1775. 3284

SHARP. The Lancaster Almanac for 1776. By Anthony Sharp, Philom. *Lancaster: Francis Bailey.* 1775. 3285

[SHIPLEY. (Jonathan)] A Speech Intended to have been spoken on the Bill for Altering the Charter of Massachusetts-Bay. By the Bishop of St. Asaph. *Philadelphia: W. and T. Bradford.* 1775. 3286

A SHORT and sincere Declaration, | To our Honorable Assembly, and all others in high or low Station of Admi- | nistration, and to all Friends and Inhabitants of this Country, to whose | Sight this may come, be they English or Germans. | [n. p. 1775.] Folio, 1 leaf. L. C. P. 3287

A Mennonite protest against military service, presented to the Assembly Nov. 7, 1775.

SMITH. (W.) A | Sermon | On the Present Situation of | American Affairs. | Preached in Christ-Church, | June 23, 1775. | At the Request of the Officers of the | Third Battallion of the City of | Philadelphia, and District of Southwark. | By William Smith, D.D. | Provost of the College in that City. | *Philadelphia. | Printed and Sold by | James Humphreys, junior, | The Corner of Black-horse Alley, Front-street.* | M,DCC,LXXV. | 8vo. pp. (4), iv, 32. H. S. P. + *Wilmington, | Printed and Sold by James Adams, in High-street,* | M,DCC,LXXV. | 8vo. pp. 17. H. S. P. 3288

STANHOPE, (Philip Dormer — Earl of Chesterfield.) Letters, Written by the late Earl of Chesterfield to his son Philip Stanhope. In Four Volumes. *Philadelphia? James Humphreys, jun.* 1775. 3289

Advertised in the Pa. Ledger Sept. 2d, and by Dunlap in the Packet about the same time. Perhaps both refer to an English edition.

STEVENSON. (R.) Military | Instructions | for | Officers | Detached in the Field : | Containing, | A Scheme | for forming | A Corps of a Partisan. | Illustrated | With Plans of the Manoeuvres | necessary in carrying on the | Petite Guerre. | . . . . | By Roger Stevenson, Esq; | *Philadelphia :* | *Printed and sold by R. Aitken, Printer and* | *Bookseller, opposite the London Coffee-* | *House, Front-Street.* | M.DCC.LXXV. | . . . . | 12mo. L. C. P. 3290

Collation : Title, 1 leaf ; Dedication to Gen. Washington, by the Editor, pp. (4) ; Contents, pp. (2) ; Preface, pp. i.–vii. ; 1 blank page ; text, pp. 1–232 ; Index, pp. (4) ; Plates, i. to xii. The editor was Hugh Henry Ferguson, who was then residing at Græme Park, the property of his wife, the well-known Mrs. Ferguson.

SWAN. (A.) A | Collection | of | Designs | in | Architecture, | containing | New Plans and Elevations of Houses, | for general use. | With | A great Variety of Sections of Rooms; from a | common Room, to the most grand and magnificent. | Their | Decorations, viz. Bases, Surbases, Architraves, Freezes, | and Cornices, properly inriched with Foliages, Frets and Flowers, | in a New and Grand Taste. | With | Margins and Mouldings for the Panelling. All large enough for Practice. | To which are added, | Curious Designs of Stone and Timber Bridges, | Extending from Twenty Feet to Two Hundred and Twenty, in One Arch. | Likewise some Screens and Pavilions. | In Two Volumes. | Each containing Sixty Plates, curiously engraved on Copper. | Designed by Abraham Swan, Architect : | And Engraved, by John Norman. | Vol. I. | *Philadelphia :* | *Printed by R. Bell, Bookseller, next Door to St. Paul's Church, in Third-Street.* | M,DCC,LXXV. | Folio. 3291

I have only met with a fragment of the first volume, consisting of the title-page, dedication, preface, and two pages of the text, in all ten pages, with the first ten plates. The dedication by Bell and Norman to John Hancock and the members of the Continental Congress, is headed with a copper-plate.

𝔇𝔍𝔈 | 𝔗𝔄𝔊𝔏𝔍𝔈𝔥𝔈𝔑 | Lofungen | der | Brüder=Gemeine | für das Jahr | 1776. | *Philadelphia,* | *Gedruckt bey Henrich Miller, im Jahr* 1775. | 8vo. pp. (60).   H. S. P.   3292

THE TESTIMONY of the People | called Quakers, given forth by a Meeting of the | Representatives of said People, in Pennsylvania | and New-Jersey, held at Philadelphia the twenty- | fourth Day of the first Month, 1775. | [*Philadelphia:* 1775.] Folio, 1 leaf.   H. S. P.   3293

"We . . . publicly declare against every usurpation of power and authority, in opposition to the laws and government, and against all combinations, insurrections, conspiracies, and illegal assemblies, and as we are restrained from them by the conscientious discharge of our duty to almighty God, 'by whom kings reign, and princes decree justice,' we hope . . . to maintain our testimony against any requisitions . . . inconsistent with our religious principles, and *the fidelity we owe to the king in his government.*"

THIS Day is Published, and to be Sold by | John Dunlap, | In Market-street, Philadelphia, | A Father's Legacy | to his | Daughters. | By the late | Dr. Gregory, of Edinburgh. | [*Philadelphia: John Dunlap.* 1775.] Folio, 1 leaf.   H. S. P.   3294

TO the | Associators | of the | City of Philadelphia. | [*Philadelphia:* 1775.] 4to. 1 leaf.   L. C. P.   3295

Dated by Du Simitiere, May 18, 1775. Advocating the adoption of a "Hunting Shirt" as part of the Associators' uniform.

TO the | King's most Excellent Majesty | In Council, | The Humble | Petition | and | Memorial | Of The | Assembly of Jamaica | (Voted in Assembly, on the 28th of | December, 1774.) | *Philadelphia:* | *Printed by William and Thomas Bradford, at* | *the London Coffee-House.* | M.DCC.LXXV. | 8vo. pp. 8.   H. S. P.   3296

TO the Non-Commissioned Officers and Privates, of the | several Companies of Associators, belonging to the | City and Liberties of Philadelphia. | [*Philadelphia:* 1775.] Folio, pp. (2). 3297

Urging the Associators to sign the Articles of Agreement given out by the Assembly.

TO the | Representatives of the Freemen of the Province of

| Pennsylvania, in General Assembly met. | The Address of the People called Quakers. | [*Philadelphia:* 1775.] Folio, pp. (2). 3298

An anti-Revolutionary address dated "10th mo. 26th, 1775."

. . . | . . . . | TO the Three Generals, | with Scotch Orders, on their | Voyage to North-America. | . . . . | Critical and faithful Extracts from Colonel | Cavallier's Memoirs of the Wars | of the Cevennes, or Lower Lan- | guedoc, in his own handwriting, and | in the French language. | [*Philadelphia: John Dunlap.* 1775.] Folio, 1 leaf. H. S. P. 3299

From the London Evening Post, 29th of April, 1775.

TOBLER. (J.) The Pennsylvania Town and Countryman's Almanac for 1776. By John Tobler. *Wilmington: James Adams.* 1775. 3300

[TRUMBULL. (John)] M'Fingal: | A Modern | Epic Poem. | Canto First, | or | The Town-Meeting. | *Philadelphia:* | *Printed and Sold by William and Thomas Brad-* | *ford, at the London Coffee-House,* 1775. | Sm. 8vo. Title, 1 leaf; pp. 40. H. S. P. 3301

All published at this time. See J. H. Trumbull's Origin of McFingal.

THE | TWELVE United Colonies, | By their Delegates in | Congress, | To the Inhabitants of | Great Britain. | [*Philadelphia: W. and T. Bradford.* 1775.] 8vo. pp. 8. L. C. P. 3302

No title-page, signed by John Hancock, President, and attested by Charles Thomson, Secretary, Philadelphia, July 8, 1775.

THE | UNIVERSAL | Almanack, | For the Year of our Lord | 1776; | [16 lines.] | *Philadelphia:* | *Printed & Sold by James Humphreys, jun.* | *in Front-street, at the Corner of Black-horse Alley.* [1775.] | Sm. 8vo. pp. (36). H. S. P. 3303

VOTES | of the | House of Representatives, | From Monday, February 20, to Saturday, February 25, 1775. | [Colophon.] *Philadelphia: Printed and Sold by Henry Miller, in Race-street.* [1775.] | Folio, pp. 75–80. H. S. P. 3304

Continued weekly to March 18, and from May 1 to May 13, and from June 19 to

June 30, and from Sept. 18 to Sept. 30, pp. 75–123.   Votes of the new Assembly, from Oct. 14 to Nov. 25, pp. 124–172.

VOTES | and | Proceedings | of the | House of Representatives | of the | Province of Pennsylvania, | Beginning the Fourteenth Day of October, 1758. | Volume The Fifth. | [*Penn Arms.*] | *Philadelphia :* | *Printed and Sold by Henry Miller, in Race-Street.* | MDCCLXXV. | Folio, Title, 1 leaf; pp. 560.   H. S. P.   3305

VOTES | and | Proceedings | of the | House of Representatives | of the | Province of Pennsylvania, | Met at Philadelphia, on the Fourteenth of October, | Anno Domini 1774, and continued by Adjournments. | [*Royal Arms.*] | *Philadelphia :* | *Printed and Sold by Henry Miller, in Race-Street.* | MDCCLXXV. | Folio, Title, 1 leaf; pp. 581–682.   H. S. P.   3306

[WARREN. (Mercy)]   The | Group, | a | Farce : | As lately Acted, and to be Re-acted, to the Wonder | of all superior Intelligences ; | Nigh Head Quarters, at | Amboyne. | In Two Acts. | *Jamaica, Printed ;* | *Philadelphia, Re-printed ;* | *By James Humphreys, junior, in Front-street.* | M,DCC,LXXV. | 16mo. pp. 16.   3307

WEATHERWISE. (A.) Father Abraham's | Almanack, | For the Year of our Lord | 1776 ; | Being Bissextile or Leap-Year. | (The Sixteenth Year of the Reign of King George III.) | . . . | . . . | . . . | . . . | . . . | . . . | . . . | . . . | . . . | . . . | . . . | . . . | . . . . | By Abraham Weatherwise, Gent. | . . . | . . . | . . . | . . . | . . . . | *Philadelphia :* | *Printed and Sold by John Dunlap, at the | Newest-Printing-Office, in Market-Street.* [1775.] | Sm. 8vo. pp. 36.   H. S. P.   3308

Prof. Seidensticker refers to Miller's newspaper as authority for saying that an edition of this almanac was presented by Dunlap in German. The advertisement in the Pennsylvanischer Staatsbote of Oct. 27, 1775, frequently inserted before and after that date, is always the same, and is not, in my opinion, sufficient to warrant such an assertion.

WOOLMAN. (J.)   The | Works | of | John Woolman. | In Two Parts. | The Second Edition. | *Philadelphia :* | *Printed by Joseph Crukshank, in Market-* | *Street, between Second and Third Streets.* | M.DCC.LXXV. | 8vo.   H. S. P.   3309

Collation : Title, 1 leaf; Testimony of Friends in Yorkshire, pp. iii.–xvi. ; Title to Journal, 1 leaf; text, pp. 1–250; Title to Part II., 1 leaf; text, pp. 253–432. The title to the Journal is, except the date, the same as in the first edition, No. 3139, *supra.* The title to Part II. is also the same, except the date and the spacing of the sixth and seventh lines.

[ZUBLY. (Johann Joachim)] Great Britain's | Right to tax her | Colonies. | Placed in the clearest Light, | By a Swiss. | . . . . | [*Philadelphia ?* 1775.] 8vo. pp. 55.   3310

Printed in Philadelphia, according to the Catalogue of the Library Company of Philadelphia and Haven's List. Upon examining the four copies of the tract referred to by the former, I found one bearing a London imprint and that the other three were of the same edition, but all lacked the title-page. The author's name is given in Miller's Pennsylvanischer Staatsbote, Oct. 20, 1775.

ZUBLY. The Law of Liberty. | A Sermon | on | American Affairs, | preached | At the Opening of the Provincial | Congress of Georgia. | Addressed | To the Right Honourable | The Earl of Dartmouth. | With an Appendix, | Giving a concise Account of the Struggles of | Swisserland to recover their Liberty. | By John J. Zubly, D.D. | . . . | . . . . | *Philadelphia :* | *Printed and Sold by Henry Miller,* 1775. | *Also to be had of Messieurs Bradford, in Phila-* | *delphia; Noel and Hazard, at New York; William Scott, on the Bay, in Charles-Town,* | *South-Carolina; and at Mr. Bard's Store, at Sa-* | *vannah, Georgia.* | 8vo. pp. xx, 41, List of Book (1).   3311

1776.

AN ACT, | Directing the Mode and Time of electing Justices of the | Peace for the City of Philadelphia, and the several and | respective Counties in this Common-wealth, and for other Purposes | therein mentioned. | [*Philadelphia: John Dunlap.* 1776.] Folio, pp. 3.   L. C. P.   3312

ADAMS. (S.) An | Oration | Delivered at the State-House, | in | Philadelphia, | to | A very numerous Audience ; | On Thursday the 1st of August, | 1776 ; | By Samuel Adams, | Member of the **** ********** the General | Congress | of | The ****** ****** of America. | . . . | . . . | . . . | . . . | . . . . | *Philadelphia*

Printed; | *London, Re-printed for J. Johnson, No. 4,* | *Ludgate-Hill.* | M.DCC.LXXVI. | 8vo. Half-title, 1 leaf; Title, 1 leaf; pp. 42.   3313

"An undelivered oration. See Wells' Life of Adams, vol. ii. p. 439; vol. iii. p. 403. There is no Philadelphia edition." Menzies' Catalogue.

ADVERTISEMENT. | [*Philadelphia:*]   *Printed by Melchior Steiner and Charles Cist.* [1776.] | Folio, 1 leaf.   L. C. P.   3314

Dated "Feb. 28, 1776," and signed "William Dewees, Sheriff." Notice, in English and German in parallel columns, of an election to fill a vacancy in the Assembly, caused by the resignation of Benjamin Franklin.

ADVERTISEMENT. *Philadelphia: Robert Aitken.* 1776.   3315

Aitken, in his Ledger, on Oct. 3d, charges Matthew Clarkson for printing 1004 advertisements of the Prize Schooner Peter, and on Nov. 2d, for printing 100 advertisements of Real Estate.

AN AFFECTIONATE | Address | to the | Inhabitants | of the | British Colonies | in | America. | By a Lover and Friend of Mankind. | . . . | . . . | . . . | . . . | . . . | . . . | . . . . | [*Philadelphia:*] *Printed* [*by W. and T. Bradford*] *in the Year* M.DCC.LXXVI. | 8vo. pp. vi, 55.   H. S. P.   3316

𝕯𝕰𝕹 𝖆𝕷𝖆𝕽𝕸 : | Ober | Eine Erweckungs = Zuschrift an das Volk von Pennsylvanien, | über den neuerlichen Schluß des Congreß, um alle von der Krone Großbrittannien | hergeleitete Macht und Gewalt gänzlich abzuschaffen. | [*Philadelphia: Henrich Miller.* 1776.] 4to. pp. (4).   H. S. P.   3317

THE ALARM : | Or, | An Address to the People of Pennsylvania, | On the late Resolve of Congress, for totally suppressing all | Power and Authority derived from the Crown of Great-Britain. | [*Philadelphia: Henry Miller.* 1776.] 4to. pp. 4.   3318

Du Simitiere says, "Distributed on Sunday, May 19th, 1776, in Philadelphia."

𝕯𝕬𝕾 | 𝖆𝕷𝕿𝕰 Zeugniß | und die | Grund= | Sätze | des Volkes | so man Quäfer nennet, | erneuert, | In Ansehung des | Königs und der Regierung ; | und | Wegen den nunmehr herrchenden Unru= | hen in diesem und andern Theilen von America. | An das Volk überhaupt gerichtet. |

Germantown, gedruckt bey Christoph Saur, dem | Juengern, auf Kosten der Verfasser. 1776. | 8vo. pp. 8.   H. S. P.   3319

THE AMERICAN Calendar for 1777. *Philadelphia: W. and T. Bradford.* 1776.   3320

𝕬𝕸𝕰𝕽𝕵𝕮𝕬𝕽𝕵𝕾𝕮𝕳𝕰 Reichs= Staats= Kriegs= Siegs= und Ge= schichts=Calender, auf das Jahr 1777. Zum Erstenmal herausgegeben. *Lancaster: Matthias Bartgis.* 1776.   3321

𝕬𝕹 die Unter=Officiers und Gemeinen der verschiedenen Companien Associators, | die zur Stadt und den Freyheiten von Philadelphia gehören. | [*Philadelphia: Henrich Miller.* 1776.] Folio, pp. (2).   3322

THE | ANCIENT Testimony | and | Principles of the People called Quakers, | renewed, | with respect to the | King and Government; | and | Touching the Commotions now prevailing in these and other Parts of | America. | Addressed to the | People in General. | [*Philadelphia:* 1776.] Folio, pp. 4.   H. S. P.   3323

ANNO Regni | Georgii III. | Regis, | Magnæ Britanniæ, Franciæ & Hiberniæ, | Decimo Sexto. | At a General Assembly of the Pro- | vince of Pennsylvania, begun and holden at Philadelphia, | the Fourteenth Day of October, Anno Domini 1775, in | the Sixteenth Year of the Reign of our Sovereign | Lord George III. by the Grace of God, of Great | Britain, France and Ireland, King, Defender of the | Faith, &c. | And from thence continued by Adjournments to the Sixth of April, 1776. | [*Penn Arms.*] | *Philadelphia: | Printed by Hall and Sellers, at the | New Printing-Office near the Market.* | MDCCLXXVI. | Folio, Title, 1 leaf; pp.   3324

𝕶𝕬𝕽𝕷𝕰 𝕬𝕹𝕷𝕰𝕵𝕲𝕰𝕽 | von dem | Verfahren | der | Convention | des | Staats von Pennsylvanien, | Gehalten zu Philadelphia, den Fünf= zehnten Tag July, 1776. | *Philadelphia, | Gedruckt und zu haben bey Henrich Miller, in der Rees-strasse,* 1776. | Folio, pp. 67. H. S. P.   3325

AN | APOLOGY | For the People called Quakers, | Containing some Reasons, for their not complying with human Injuncti- | ons and Instructions in Matters relative to the Worship of God. | Published by the Meeting for Sufferings of the said People at

Philadelphia, in pursuance of the | Directions of their Yearly Meeting, held at Burlington, for Pennsylvania and New-Jersey, the | 24th Day of the Ninth Month, 1756. | [At the end :] Re-published by the Direction of the Meeting for Sufferings, held at Philadelphia the | 27th of the Fourth Month, 1776. | *Philadelphia: Printed by Joseph Crukshank, in Market-street.* [1776.] | 4to. pp. 4.

THE | ART | of making | Common Salt. | Particularly adapted to the Use of the | American Colonies. | With | An Extract from Dr. Brownrigg's Treatise on the Art | of making Bay-Salt. | Detached from the Pennsylvania Magazine for March 1776. | *Philadelphia: | Printed by R. Aitken, Printer and Bookseller, opposite | the London Coffee-House, Front-Street.* | M.DCC.LXXVI. | 8vo. pp. 7, 1 plate.   L. C. P.   3327

Aitken sold 1000 copies to William Hooper, 500 to George Walton, and 300 to Thomas Stone.

ASTLEY. (P.)   The Modern | Riding-Master : | Or, a | Key to the Knowledge of the Horse, | And | Horsemanship ; | with several | Necessary Rules for Young Horsemen. | By Philip Astley, | Riding-Master, | Late of His Majesty's Royal Light Dragoons. | Adorned with various Engravings. | *Philadelphia : | Printed and sold by Robert Aitken, Printer | and Bookseller in Front-Street.* | MDCCLXXVI. | *(Price Eighteen Pence).* | 12mo. pp. 40.   3328

AT | A Meeting, | Held at the Philosophical Society-Hall, on Thursday Evening, | October 17th, 1776. | Colonel Bayard unanimously chosen Chairman. | [*Philadelphia :* 1776.]   Folio, pp. (2).

Resolutions against the new Constitution.

AT a Meeting of a Number of the Citizens | of Philadelphia, at the Philosophical Society's Hall, November the 2d, | Samuel Howell, Chairman, | Jonathan B. Smith, Secretary, | It was unanimously Resolved, to publish the following Address to the | Inhabitants of the City and Liberties of Philadelphia. | [*Philadelphia :* 1776.]   4to. 1 leaf.   H. S. P.   3330

A protest against the creation of the Council of Censors.

AT | A Meeting | Of a Number of the Citizens of Philadel-
phia, | In the Philosophical Society-Hall, the 8th | of November,
1776. | [*Philadelphia:* 1776.]   4to. 1 leaf.   H. S. P.   3331

Instructions to the Representatives of the City of Philadelphia, in Assembly, to
procure certain modifications of the Constitution of 1776, published for the consideration of the Citizens.

AUX | Habitants | De la Province du Canada. | [*A Philadel-
phie:*]   *Chez Fleury Mesplet & Charles Berger.*   [1776.] | Folio, 1
leaf.   L. C. P.   3332

Letter from Congress, dated " A Philadelphie, le 24 Janvier, 1776," and signed
" John Hancock, President."   The imprint is omitted on some copies.

ROBERT   BARCLAYS | Apologie | Oder | Vertheidigungs=
Schrift | der wahren Christlichen | Gottesgelahrtheit, | Wie solche | unter
dem Volk, so man aus Spott | Quaker, | das ist, Zitterer nennet, |
vorgetragen und gelehret wird. | Oder | Völlige Erklärung und Rettung
ihrer | Grundsätze und Lehren, durch viele aus der | Heil. Schrift, der
gesunden Vernunft, und den Zeug= | nissen so wohl alter als neuer be=
rühmten Scribenten | gezogene Beweißthümer. Nebst einer gründli= |
chen Beantwortung der stärksten Einwürffe, | so gemeiniglich wider sie
gebraucht | werden. | Anjetzo nach der zweyten Lateinischen und neunten
Englischen Herausgebung gantz von neuem ins Deutsche übersetzt. |
Germantown: | *Gedruckt bey Christoph Saur, dem Juengern,* 1776. |
16mo. pp. 797, (25).   H. S. P.   3333

BAXTER. (R.)   The Saint's Everlasting Rest.   By Richard
Baxter.   *Philadelphia: Robert Bell.*   1776.   3334

[BENEZET. (Anthony)]   Thoughts | on the | Nature of War,
&c. | [*Philadelphia:* 1776.]   8vo. pp. 24.   3335

Du Simitiere ascribes it to Benezet, with the date 1776.   (See the copy in the Library Co. of Philadelphia, 791, D.)   Appended to several copies I have met with is
the letter from the Rev. John Sayre, described as No. 3280, *supra.*

BIBLIA, | Das ist: | Die ganze Göttliche | Heilige Schrift | Alten
und Neuen | Testaments, | nach der Deutschen Uebersetzung | D. Martin
Luthers; | Mit jedes Capitels kurzen Summarien, auch | beygefügten
vielen und richtigen Parallelen: | Nebst einem Anhang | Des dritten und

vierten Buchs Esra, und des | dritten Buchs der Maccabäer. | Dritte Auflage. | *Germantown:* | *Gedruckt und zu finden bey Christoph Saur,* 1776. | 4to.   H. S. P.   3336

Collation: Title, 1 leaf; Vorrede, 1 page; Verzeichnisz aller Bücher des Alten und Neuen Testaments, 1 page; Old Testament, &c., pp. 1–992; New Testament, pp. 1–277; Register, pp. (3). The title to the New Testament is as follows: Das Neue | Testament | unsers | Herrn und Heylandes | Jesu Christi, | nach der Deutschen Uebersetzung | Dr. Martin Luthers, | mit kurzem | Inhalt eines jeden Capitels, | und vollständiger | Anweisung gleicher Schrift-Stellen. | Wie auch | aller Sonns- und Fest-tägigen | Evangelien und Episteln. | *Germantown: Gedruckt und zu finden bey Christoph Saur,* 1776. |

LES BIGARRURES d'un citoyen de Genève et ses conseils dedies aux Américains. 2 tomes. *A Philadelphie:* [*Winterthur.*] 1776.   3337

BLACKWELL. (T.) Schema Sacrum: | Or, a | Sacred Scheme | of | Natural and Revealed | Religion. | By Thomas Blackwell. | *Lancaster:* | *Printed by Francis Bailey, at the* | *Printing and Post-Offices, near the Market.* | MDCCLXXVI. | Sm. 8vo.   H. S. P.   3338

Collation: Title, 1 leaf; Second Title, 1 leaf; Contents, pp. (2); Preface, pp. i.–iv.; text, pp. 1–331; Subscribers, pp. i.–xxix. The second title reads: Schema Sacrum: | Or, a | Sacred Scheme | of | Natural and Revealed Religion: | Making | A Scriptural Rational Account | of | These Three Heads: | As First, of Creation, and that both in its Eternal Causes and | Springs in the Deity; and in the Wonderful Divine Procedure, | in the Six Days Work. | And Secondly, Of the Whole Complex Eternal Scheme of Divine | Predestination; as comprehending the whole great Events re- | lative to Angels and Men, with respect to Time and Eternity. | And Thirdly, Of the Wise Divine Procedure, in Accomplishing | the whole Parts of the foresaid Scheme. | In Discoursing of all which Heads, the several Principal Difficul- | ties made by the great Pretenders to Reason in our Day; against the Doctrine of the World's Creation by God; the eter- | nal Decrees of Divine Predestination; the constitution of Adam | as the Moral Head and Representative of all his Posterity; the | Divine Permission of the Fall of Man. The real and proper | Satisfaction of Justice by the Substitution and Obedience of | our Lord Jesus Christ, in the Name and Room of the Elect: | Together with the alledged Unaccountableness of the Superna- | tural Operations of the Holy Ghost in the Regeneration and | Sanctification of the Elect of God: | Are all particularly Considered, Cleared and Removed by Answers | and Arguments, founded upon Infallible Scripture and Solid | Reason. | By Thomas Blackwell. | . . . | . . . | . . . . | *Lancaster:* | *Printed by Francis Bailey, at the* | *Printing and Post-Offices, near the Market.* | MDCCLXXVI. |

[BRACKENRIDGE. (Hugh Montgomery)] The | Battle | of

| Bunker's-Hill. | A Dramatic Piece, | Of Five Acts, | In Heroic Measure. | By a Gentleman of Maryland. | . . . | . . . | . . . . | *Philadelphia:* | *Printed and Sold by Robert Bell, in Third-Street.* | MDCCLXXVI. | 8vo. 1 plate, pp. (8), 5–49, (1). H. S. P. 3339

[BRAXTON. (Carter)] An | Address | to the | Convention | of the | Colony and Ancient Dominion of | Virginia; | on the | Subject of Government in general, and recommending | a particular Form to their Consideration. | By a Native of that Colony. | *Philadelphia:* | *Printed by John Dunlap, in Market-Street.* | M,DCC,LXXVI. | Sm. 8vo. pp. 25. L. C. P. 3340

BROWN. (J.) A Pocket English Dictionary; containing Explanations of the most difficult Words, which are commonly made use of in the English Language. By John Brown, M.D. *Philadelphia: Robert Bell.* 1776. 3341

Advertised in the Pa. Gazette, Sept. 25, 1776. Perhaps referring to an edition printed elsewhere.

BY an Express arrived yesterday from South Carolina, we have | the following intelligence. | [*Philadelphia: B. Towne.* 1776.] Folio, 1 leaf. N. Y. H. S. 3342

An account of the attack on Fort Sullivan, dated " Philadelphia, July 20, 1776."

BY an Express, just arrived from New- | York, we have | His Majesty's | Most Gracious Speech, | To Both Houses of | Parliament, | On Friday, October 27, 1775. | [*Philadelphia:*] *Printed by John Dunlap.* [1776.] | Folio, 1 leaf. H. S. P. 3343

Dated " Philadelphia, January 8, 1776, 10 O'Clock, A.M."

[CARTWRIGHT. (John)] American Independence | the | Interest and Glory | of | Great Britain; Containing | Arguments which prove, that not only in Taxation, | but in Trade, Manufactures, and Government, | the Colonies are entitled to an entire Independency on | the British Legislature; and that it can only be | by a formal Declaration of these Rights, and forming | thereupon a friendly League with them, that the true | and lasting Welfare of both Countries can be promoted. | In a Series of Let-

ters to the Legislature. | . . . | . . . | . . . | . . . | . . . | . . . | . . . |
. . . | . . . | . . . | . . . | . . . . | *Philadelphia,* | *Printed and Sold*
by Robert Bell, in Third-Street. | MDCCLXXVI. | 8vo. pp. 125.

[CHALMERS. (George)] Plain Truth ; | addressed to the |
Inhabitants | of | America, | Containing, Remarks | On a Late
Pamphlet, | entitled | Common Sense. | Wherein are shewn, that
the Scheme of Independence | is Ruinous, Delusive, and Impracti-
cable : That were | the Author's Asseverations, Respecting the
Power of | America, as Real as Nugatory ; Reconciliation on |
liberal Principles with Great Britain, would be | exalted Policy :
And that circumstanced as we are, | Permanent Liberty, and True
Happiness, can only be | obtained by Reconciliation with that
Kingdom. | Written by Candidus. | . . . | . . . | . . . | . . . . |
Philadelphia : | *Printed and Sold by R. Bell, in Third-Street.* |
MDCCLXXVI. | 8vo. + The Second Edition.   H. S. P.   3345

Collation : The Printer to the Public, pp. (2) ; Title, 1 leaf ; Dedication, pp. (2) ;
Introduction, 1 page ; Memorandum, 1 page ; text, pp. 1–66 ; Rationalis, pp. 67–78 ;
Cato's [2d] Letter, pp. 79–84 ; Advertisement, pp. (2). Re-printed : Title as above
with the addition of a one-line Latin quotation. Collation : The Printer, &c., pp.
(2) ; Title, 1 leaf ; Dedication, pp. (2) ; Introduction, 1 leaf ; text, pp. 9–74 ; Rationalis, pp. 75–86 ; Cato, pp. 87–96. Congress on the Rights of Englishmen (Letter to
the Inhabitants of Quebec), pp. (6) ; Title to Additions to Plain Truth, 1 leaf ; Additions, pp. 97–136. The collation of the second edition is the same, except that the
reverse of the Introduction is occupied by a " Memorandum " concerning a Third
Edition. The title-page differs, in the substitution of " Honorable Connections," for
" Reconciliation," in the seventeenth line ; the addition of the words " The Second
Edition," and the omission of the Latin quotation. The title to the Additions is
as follows : Additions | to | Plain Truth ; | addressed to the | Inhabitants | of |
America, | Containing, further Remarks | On a Late Pamphlet, | entitled | Common
Sense : | Wherein, | Are clearly and fully shewn, that American Independence, | is
as illusory, ruinous, and impracticable, as a liberal | reconciliation with Great Britain,
is safe, honorable, | and expedient. | Written by the Author of Plain Truth. | . . . |
. . . | . . . | . . . | . . . | . . . . | [Imprint as in first title.]
  The authorship of this tract has been attributed to Alexander Hamilton (but not till
about 1792, and then only by his political enemies) ; to the Rev. Charles Inglis, on
a supposition which is effectually disposed of by Mr. Franklin Burdge (Magazine of
American History, ii., 59–60) ; to Joseph Galloway on no evidence at all ; contem-
poraneously to Richard Wells, of Philadelphia, who immediately denied the charge ;
and to George Chalmers. It is scarcely necessary to say that the tenor and style of
the tract are too much at variance with Hamilton's opinions and writings to allow
him to be suspected of being the author by any unprejudiced person. In regard
to Joseph Galloway, if the dedication to his old enemy, Dickinson, is not suffi-

cient, the laudatory references to the Proprietary Government of Pennsylvania are enough to preclude the slightest credence to the claim put forth for him. The writer's style, allusions to the eastern shore of Maryland (where Chalmers resided), admiration of a proprietary (the Maryland as well as Pennsylvania) form of government, and ardent Presbyterianism, all point to him as the author. His immediate appointment by the Government, on his arrival in England, to a lucrative office, and employment as a political writer, are more credibly explained by such a service as the production of "Plain Truth" than by any individual losses which he might have sustained through his loyalty. The second edition is announced as just published in the Pa. Gazette, May 8, 1776. Some copies of the Additions are partly printed on a coarse blue paper. In these there is generally pasted on the back of the title a slip of blue paper containing the following: " To Every Purchaser. The impossibility of obtaining White, constituted the law of necessity for part of these Additions to appear in Blue. The Philosopher reacheth beyond outward appearances.—The Patriot surmounteth every difficulty. And the Bookseller industriously attempteth business, agreeable to the prescriptions and decrees of the British and American Laws of Freedom concerning the Liberty of the Press. Third Street, April 24th, 1776."

CIVIL Prudence, recommended to the Thirteen United Colonies of North-America. *Philadelphia: Samuel Dellap.* 1776. 3346

Advertised in the Pa. Evening Post, Aug. 14, 1776, perhaps referring to the edition printed at Norwich, Conn.

CLAIRAC. ([Louis André de la Mamie de]) L' Ingenieur de Campagne: | Or, | Field Engineer. | Written in French | By the Chevalier de Clairac, | And Translated | By Major Lewis Nicola. | To which is added, | By Way of Appendix, | A Short Treatise on Sea Batteries, shew- | ing their Defects, and an Attempt | to remedy them. | Likewise, | An Explanation of all the Technical Terms used in | the Work, | By the Translator. | Illustrated with a variety of copper-plates. | *Philadelphia:* | *Printed and Sold by R. Aitken, Printer and | Bookseller, Front-Street.* | M.DCC.LXXVI. | 8vo. L. C. P. 3347

Collation: Title, 1 leaf; Dedication, 1 leaf; Advertisement and Directions, pp. (2); text, pp. 1–256; Errata, &c., pp. (2); 39 folded plates.

COMMITTEE Chamber, Philadelphia, May 18, 1776. | [*Philadelphia:* 1776.] 4to. 1 leaf. L. C. P. 3348

" On application of a number of the Inhabitants requesting the call of a meeting of the City and Liberties to be held at the State House, on Monday morning. The Committee give Notice that a meeting will be held at the aforesaid Time and Place."

A COMPLETE Tutor for the Fife. *Philadelphia:* 1776. 3349

THE | CONSTITUTION | of the | Common-Wealth | of | Pennsylvania, | as established by | The General Convention | Elected for that Purpose, | And held at Philadelphia, | July 15th, 1776, | And continued by Adjournments | to September 28, 1776. | *Philadelphia:* | *Printed by John Dunlap, in Market-Street.* | M,DCC,LXXVI. | Sm. 8vo. pp. 32.   H. S. P.   3350

DALRYMPLE. (C.)   Extracts | from a | Military Essay, | containing | Reflections | on the | Raising, Arming, Cloathing and Discipline | of the | British Infantry and Cavalry. | By Campbell Dalrymple, Esq; | Lieut. Colonel to the King's own Regiment of Dragoons. | *Philadelphia:* | *Printed by Humphreys, Bell, and Aitken.* | M,DCC,LXXVI. | 8vo. pp. 31, 8 plates.   L. C. P.   3351

[DALRYMPLE. (Sir James)] The | Rights | of | Great Britain Asserted | against the | Claims of America: | Being an | Answer | to 'the | Declaration | of the | General Congress. | Said to be Written by Lord George Germaine. | *London Printed: Philadelphia* | *Re-Printed, and Sold by R. Bell, in Third-Street.* | MDCCLXXVI. | 8vo. pp. 92, 1 folded leaf, (4).   H. S. P.   3352

DE FOE. (D.) Robinson Crusoe. By Daniel De Foe. *Philadelphia: Robert Bell.* 1776.   3353

DIRECTIONS to sail into and up Delaware Bay. | [*Philadelphia:* 1776?] Folio, 1 leaf.   L. C. P.   3354

AN | EPISTLE | from our | Yearly-Meeting, | Held in Philadelphia, for Pennsylvania, New-Jersey, | and the Western Parts of Maryland and Virginia, by | Adjournments, from the 21st Day of the Ninth Month, to | the 28th of the same, inclusive, 1776. | To our Friends and Brethren of the several Quarterly and Monthly | Meetings, in these and the adjacent Provinces. | [*Philadelphia:* 1776.] Folio, pp. 4.   L. C. P.   3355

THE | EPISTLE | from the | Yearly-Meeting | in | London, | Held by Adjournments, from the 27th of the Fifth Month to the 1st | of the Sixth Month 1776, inclusive. | To the Quarterly and

Monthly Meetings of Friends and Brethren in | Great-Britain, Ireland, and elsewhere. | [*Philadelphia:* 1776.] Folio, pp. 4.   3356

The last two pages contain An Epistle from the London Yearly Meeting " To Friends at their Yearly-Meeting at Philadelphia, for Pennsylvania and New-Jersey."

AN ESSAY of a Declaration of Rights, | Brought in by the Committee appointed for that Purpose, and now under | the Consideration of the Convention of the State of Pennsylvania. | [*Philadelphia: John Dunlap.* 1776.] Folio, 1 leaf.   H. S. P.   3357

AN | ESSAY | of a | Frame of Government | for | Pennsylvania. | *Philadelphia.* | *Printed by James Humphreys, junior.* | M,DCC,LXXVI. | 8vo. pp. 16.   3358

AN EXERCISE, containing a Dialogue and two Odes set to Music. *Philadelphia:* 1776. Sm. 8vo.   3359

Title from H. A. Brady's Catalogue, lot 410.

EXTRACT of a Letter from an Officer of Distinction in the | American Army. | [*Philadelphia:*] *Printed by John Dunlap.* [1776.] | Folio, 1 leaf.   H. S. P.   3360

This report of atrocities committed in New Jersey by British soldiers was published by order of the Council of Safety. It was also printed in the Pa. Packet, Dec. 27, 1776.

EXTRACT of a Letter from New-Town, (Bucks County,) December 27. | [*Philadelphia: W. and T. Bradford.* 1776.] 4to. 1 leaf.   L. C. P.   3361

An account of the Battle of Trenton.

EXTRACTS | from the | Journals of Congress, | relative to the | Capture and Condemnation of Prizes, | and the | Fitting out Privateers; | together with the | Rules and Regulations of the Navy, | And Instructions to the | Commanders of Private Ships of War. | *Philadelphia:* | *Printed by John Dnnlap,* | M,DCC,LXXVI. | 8vo. Title, 1 leaf; pp. 1–45.   H. S. P.   3362

EXTRACTS from the Proceedings of the | Provincial Conference of Committees for the | Province of Pennsylvania, | Held at Carpenter's Hall, Philadelphia, June 18, 1776. | [Colophon.] *Philadelphia: Printed by Styner and Cist, in Second-street.* [1776.]. | 4to. pp. 6. H. S. P. 3363

EXTRACTS | from the | Votes | of the | House of Assembly, | Of the Province of | Pennsylvania; | Containing | Rules and Regulations | for the better Government of the | Military Association in | Pennsylvania, the Articles | of said Association, and, the Re- | solutions directing the Mode of le- | vying Taxes on Non-Associators | in Pennsylvania. | Published by Order of the Committee of Safety. | *Philadelphia :* | *Printed by W. and T. Bradford.* [1776.] | 8vo. pp. 20. A. P. S. 3364

THE FALL | of | British Tyranny: | Or, | American Liberty | Triumphant. | The First Campaign. | A Tragi-Comedy of Five Acts, | as lately planned | At the Royal Theatrum Pandemonium, | at St. James's. | The Principal Place of Action in America. | Publish'd according to Act of Parliament. | . . . | . . . | . . . | . . . . | *Philadelphia :* | *Printed by Styner and Cist, in Second-street,* | *near Arch-street.* MDCCLXXVI. | 8vo. pp. viii, 66. H. S. P. 3365

Said to have been written by "Mr. Laycock, of Philadelphia."

FATHER Abraham's | Pocket Almanack | For the Year 1777; | . . . | . . . . | *Philadelphia :* | *Printed and Sold by John Dunlap.* [1776.] | 24mo. pp. 24. 3366

FOUR | Letters | on | Interesting Subjects. | *Philadelphia :* | *Printed by Styner and Cist, in Second-street.* | MDCCLXXVI. | 8vo. pp. (2), 24. H. S. P. 3367

Be Liberty thine. [Cut.] | THE FREEHOLDERS and Inhabitants | Of the respective Townships, in Lancaster County, qualified | by the Laws of the Province to vote for Members | of Assembly, | Are required to meet . . . . | *Lancaster, Printed by Francis Bailey, in King's Street.* [1776.] | Folio, 1 leaf. 3368

Notice of an Election, signed "John Ferree, Sheriff," and dated "Lancaster, April 4th, 1776."

FREYLINGHAUSEN. (J. A.) Ordnung des Heyls, nebst einem Verzeichniß der wichtigsten Kern = Sprüche der Heil. Schrift, darin die vornehmsten Glaubens=Artikel gegründet sind, wie auch einem sogenannten Güldenen A, B, C, und Gebetlein. Denen Einfältigen und Unerfahrnen zum Besten herausgegeben von Johann Anastasius Freylinghausen. *Philadelphia: Henrich Miller.* 1776. 3369

GENERAL Orders, | [*Philadelphia:* 1776.] 4to. 1 leaf. 3370

Dated "Head-Quarters, Philadelphia, Dec. 14, 1776," and signed "Israel Putnam, Major General." Appointing Col. Griffin, Adjutant-General, &c. Issued on Putnam's taking command in Philadelphia.

GENTLEMEN and Fellow Soldiers. | [*Philadelphia:* 1776.] 4to. 1 leaf. L. C. P. 3371

An address to the Pennsylvania Associators in favor of signing the regulations directed by the Assembly.

THE | GENUINE Principles | of the Ancient | Saxon, or English | Constitution. | Carefully collected from the best Authorities; | With some Observations, on their peculiar | fitness, for the United Colonies in general | and Pennsylvania in particular. | By Demophilus. | . . . | . . . | . . . | . . . | . . . . | *Philadelphia:* | *Printed, and Sold, by Robert Bell, in Third-Street.* | MDCCLXXVI. | 8vo. pp. 46. H. S. P. 3372

GESSNER. (S.) Der Tod Abels in fünf Gesängen. Von Salomon Geßner. *Germantown. Gedruckt bey Christoph Saur, dem Juengern.* 1776. Sm. 8vo. pp. 157. H. S. P. 3373

HABERMANN. (J.) Christliche | Morgen= und | Abend=Gebäter, | auf alle Tage in der Wochen, | durch | D. Johann Habermann. | Sammt andern schönen | Gebätern; | wie auch | D. Neumanns | Kern aller Gebäter | und schönen | Morgen= Abend= und an= | dern Liedern. | *Germantown,* | *Gedruckt und zu finden bey Christoph Saur,* 1776. | 24mo. pp. 1–62, 1–55. H. S. P. 3374

HEAD-QUARTERS, Philadelphia, Dec. 13th, 1776. | [*Philadelphia:* 1776.] 4to. 1 leaf. H. S. P. 3375

Signed "Israel Putnam, Major General." "The General will consider every attempt to burn the City of Philadelphia as a Crime of the blackest Dye."

HIS Majesty's | Most Gracious Speech | To Both Houses of Parliament, | On Friday, October 27, 1775. | *Philadelphia: Printed by Hall & Sellers.* [1776.] | 4to. 1 leaf.   H. S. P.   3376

HIS | Majesty's | most gracious | Speech, | To both Houses of Parliament, on Friday October 27, 1775. | [*Philadelphia:*] *Printed by William and Thomas Bradford,* [1776.] | 4to. 1 leaf.   3377

THE HISTORY of Little Goody Two-Shoes. *Philadelphia: Robert Bell.* 1776.   3378

𝖉𝖊𝖗 | 𝕳𝕺𝕮𝕳 = Deutſch= | Americaniſche | Calender, | Auf das Jahr | . . . | . . . | 1777. | (Welches ein gemein Jahr von 365 Tagen iſt.) | . . . | . . . | . . . | . . . | . . . | . . . | . . . | . . . | . . . | . . . | . . . . | Zum neun und dreyßigſten mal heraus gegeben. | *German-town: Gedruckt und zu finden bey Christoph Saur.* | . . . | . . . [1776.] | Sq. 8vo. pp. (48).   H. S. P.   3379

HOME, (Henry — Lord Kames.) Six Sketches | on the | History of Man. | Containing, | The Progress of Men as Indi-viduals. | I. The Diversity of Men, and of Languages. | II. Of Food, and Population. | III. Of Property. | IV. The Origin and Progress of Commerce. | V. The Origin and Progress of Arts. | VI. The Progress of the Female Sex. | With an Appendix, | Concerning, the Propagation of Animals, and the Care of | their Offspring. | By Henry Home, Lord Kaims, [*sic.*] | Author of the Elements of Criticism. | *Philadelphia:* | *Sold by R. Bell, in Third-Street, and R. Aitken, in Front-Street.* | M,DCC,LXXVI. | 8vo. Half-title, 1 leaf; Title, 1 leaf; Preface, pp. v–vi; Contents, 1 leaf; text, pp. 1–262; (2).   H. S. P.   3380

IN Assembly, | Thursday, December 5, 1776. P.M. | [*Philadel-phia:*] *Printed by John Dunlap.* [1776.] | 4to. 1 leaf.   L. C. P.   3381

" Resolved unanimously, That a Committee be appointed to bring in a Bill or Draught of a Militia Law."

IN Assembly, December 12, 1776.] | [*Philadelphia: John Dunlap.* 1776.] 4to. 1 leaf.   L. C. P.   3382

Resolution offering Bounties to Volunteers.

IN Assembly, December 24, 1776. | [*Philadelphia: John Dunlap. 1776.*] Folio, 1 leaf.   H. S. P.   3383

An "Address to the Inhabitants of Pennsylvania" on the approach of the British Army.

IN Committee Chamber, May 16, 1776. | [*Philadelphia: 1776.*] 4to. 1 leaf.   L. C. P.   3384

Recommendation " to all the Inhabitants of this City to forbear any kind of Insult to Quakers who will not observe the Fast recommended by Congress. This Committee hold Liberty of Conscience to be sacred."

IN Committee, | Of Inspection and Observation. | February 5th, 1776. | [*Philadelphia: 1776.*] 4to. 1 leaf.   L. C. P.   3385

" This Committee do hold up to the World, . . . John Drinker, Thomas and Samuel Fisher as Enemies to their Country" for refusing to receive the Bills of Credit emitted by Congress. Signed " Peter Z. Lloyd, Secretary."

IN Congress, | Saturday, March 16, 1776. | *Philadelphia: Printed by John Dunlap.* [1776.] | Folio, 1 leaf.   L. C. P.   3386

Recommending Friday, May 17th, as a day of " Humiliation, Fasting, and Prayer."

IN Congress, | March 23, 1776. | *Philadelphia: Printed by John Dunlap.* [1776.] | Folio, 1 leaf.   H. S. P.   3387

Preamble and five Resolutions concerning the fitting out of Privateers.

IN Congress, April 3, 1776. [*Philadelphia: 1776.*] Folio, 1 leaf.   N. Y. H. S.   3388

Resolution concerning Privateers.

IN Congress, May 6, 1776. [*Philadelphia: 1776.*] Folio, 1 leaf.

Instructions to commanders of American vessels.

IN Congress, | May 15, 1776. | *Philadelphia: Printed by John Dunlap.* [1776.] | Folio, 1 leaf.   L. C. P.   3390

Preamble and resolution recommending the " Assemblies and Conventions of the United Colonies, where no Government sufficient to the exigencies of their Affairs has been hitherto established, to adopt such Government as shall . . . best conduce to the happiness and safety of their constituents."

IN Congress, July 4, 1776. | A Declaration by the Representatives of the United States | of America, in General Congress Assembled. | [*Philadelphia: John Dunlap.* 1776.] Folio, 1 leaf. 3391

A broadside edition of the Declaration of Independence.

IN Congress, July 19, 1776. | [*Philadelphia:* 1776.] 4to. pp. (3). H. S. P. 3392

A resolution recommending the Convention of Pennsylvania to hasten the March of the Associators into New Jersey, with order of the same date from the Convention to the Colonel or Commanding Officer of the Battalion of the County of —.

IN Congress, | October 3d, 1776. | [*Philadelphia:*] *Printed by John Dunlap.* [1776.] | Folio, 1 leaf. L. C. P. 3393

" Resolved that 5,000,000 Dollars be immediately borrowed," &c.

IN Convention for the State of Pennsylvania. | Friday, August 9, 1776. | [*Philadelphia:* 1776.] 4to. 1 leaf. L. C. P. 3394

Rations allowed for the men in the " Flying Camp."

IN Convention | for the State of Pennsylvania. | Saturday, August 10, 1776. | [*Philadelphia: Henry Miller.* 1776.] Folio, 1 leaf. L. C. P. 3395

Seven Resolutions. The first orders the whole of the State Militia to march into New Jersey. The second exempts the Associators of several western counties from the effect of the first. The others relate to the " Flying Camp."

IN Convention | for the State of Pennsylvania. | Friday, August 16, 1776. | [*Philadelphia: Henry Miller.* 1776.] Folio, 1 leaf.

Three Resolutions concerning deserters from the Associators.

IN Convention | for the State of Pennsylvania. | Thursday, September 26, 1776. | *Philadelphia: Printed by Styner and Cist, in Second-street, near Arch-street.* [1776.] | Folio, 1 leaf. L. C. P. 3397

A resolution of the Convention altering the time for holding the election for members of Assembly.

IN Council of Safety. | Philadelphia, October 14, 1776. | [*Philadelphia: John Dunlap.* 1776.] | Folio, 1 leaf. A. P. S. 3398

"The Hessians have embarked from Staten-Island. Have your Battalion in perfect Readiness to march at the shortest Warning."

IN Council of Safety, | Philadelphia, November 14th, 1776, | 12 o'Clock, Thursday. | [*Philadelphia :*] *Printed by John Dunlap, in Market-Street.* [1776.] Folio, 1 leaf.   H. S. P.   3399

Circular letters to the commanding officers of the several battalions of militia. "We have certain Intelligence that the Enemy has actually sailed from New York Five Hundred Ships for this city, . . . you will march all your Battalion to this City without the least Delay." Some copies were issued without an imprint.

IN Council of Safety, November 27, 1776. | To the Freemen of the City and Liberties of Philadelphia. | [*Philadelphia : W. and T. Bradford.* 1776.] 4to. 1 leaf.   L. C. P.   3400

Call for a public meeting at the State-House, signed "David Rittenhouse, Vice-President."

IN Council of Safety, | December 3, 1776. | *Philadelphia: Printed by John Dunlap, in Market-street.* [1776.] | 4to. 1 leaf.

Appointing a committee to collect "all the old great coats, coats, surtouts, jackets and breeches from the inhabitants which they can spare."

IN Council of Safety, | Philadelphia, December 8, 1776. | [*Philadelphia: John Dunlap.* 1776.] Folio, 1 leaf.   L. C. P.   3402

Calling out the Militia. "The Enemy are at Trenton, and all the City Militia are marched to meet them."

IN Council of Safety, | Philadelphia, December 13, 1776. | [*Philadelphia :*] *Printed by John Dunlap.* [1776.] | 4to. 1 leaf.   3403

Notice of General Putnam's having taken command in Philadelphia.

IN Council of Safety, | Philadelphia, December 23, 1776. | [*Philadelphia :*] *Printed by John Dunlap.* [1776.] | Folio, 1 leaf.

An address on the approach of the British Army.

IN the Committee for Lancaster County, Feb. 29, 1776. | [*Lancaster: Printed by Francis Bailey,* 1776.] Folio, 1 leaf.   3405

Two resolves adopted Feb. 29 and March 1, relative to Military Associators, signed "J. Yeates, Chairman."

[INGLIS. (Charles)]   The True | Interest of America | Impartially Stated, | in certain | Strictures | On a Pamphlet intitled | Common Sense. | By an American. | . . . | . . . | . . . | . . . | . . . | . . . | . . . | . . . | . . . | . . . | . . . . | *Philadelphia.* | *Printed and Sold by James Humphreys, jun.* | *The Corner of Black-horse Alley Front-street.* | M,DCC,LXXVI. | 8vo. pp. 71. + The Second Edition. | [*Ibid.*] 8vo. pp. 71.   H. S. P.   3406

JONES. (J.)   Plain Concise | Practical Remarks, | on the treatment of | Wounds and Fractures ; | To which is Added, An Appendix, | on | Camp and Military Hospitals ; | principally | Designed, for the Use of young Military and Naval Surgeons, | in North-America. | By John Jones, M.D. | Professor of Surgery, in King's College, New York. | *Philadelphia :* | *Printed, and Sold, by Robert Bell, in Third-Street,* | MDCCLXXVI. | 8vo. pp. 114, 1 leaf.

JOURNAL | of the | Congress, | of the | United States | of | America ; | continued. | *Philadelphia :* | *Printed and Sold, by William and Thomas* | *Bradford, at the Coffee-House.* | M.DCC.LXXVI. | 8vo. Half-title, 1 leaf ; Title, 1 leaf ; pp. 1–218.   H. S. P.   3408

THE | JOURNALS | of the | Proceedings | of | Congress. | Held at Philadelphia, | From January to May, 1776. | *Philadelphia :* | *Printed by R Aitken, Bookseller, opposite the* | *London Coffee-house, Front-Street.* | M.DCC.LXXVI. | 8vo.   H. S. P.   3409

Collation : Title, 1 leaf ; Journal for January, pp. 1–93 ; Title, 1 leaf ; Journal for February, pp. 1–70 ; Title, 1 leaf ; Journal for March, pp. 73–146 ; Journal for April, pp. 147–237. The second title is : The | Journals | of | Congress. | For February, 1776. | *Philadelphia :* | *Printed and Sold by R. Aitken, Front-Street.* | M.DCC.LXXVI. | This edition appears to have been issued in monthly parts. Aitken says of it, "I was ordered [in April, 1776] to print no more in this large type, and to begin a new edition beginning with the session of Congress, which rendered the sale of the above abortive, meantime, I sold 80 copies. I also sold 14 reams of this edition to Benjamin Flower, for the use of the army for cartridges at 30s. per ream."

JOURNAL | of the | Proceedings | of the | Congress, | held at | Philadelphia, | May 10, 1775. | *Wilmington,* | *Printed and Sold by James Adams, in High-street,* 1776. | 8vo. pp. 110.   H.   3410

LAMBART, (Richard — 6th Earl of Cavan.) A | New System | of | Military | Discipline, | Founded upon Principle. | By a

General Officer. | *Philadelphia:* | *Printed and sold by R. Aitken,* *Printer and Bookseller,* | *opposite the London Coffee-House, Front-Street.* | M.DCC.LXXVI. | *Price, in Boards, One Dollar,—Bound, Ten Shillings.* | 8vo. pp. 267, (1).   H. S. P.   3411

LAMONT, (— de) and (—) DE LA VALLIERE. The | Art of War, | containing, | I. The Duties of all Military Officers in actual Service; includ- | ing necessary Instructions, in many capital Matters, by the | Knowledge of which, a Man may soon become an Ornament | to the Profession of Arms. By Monsieur De Lamont, Town- | Major of Toulon. | II. The Duties of Soldiers in General; including necessary | Instructions, in many capital Matters, by remaining Ignorant | of which, a Man who pretends to be a Soldier, will be every | Day in danger, of bringing Disgrace upon himself, and ma- | terial Injury, to the Cause of his Country. | III. The Rules and Practice of the greatest Generals, in the | Manœuvres of encamping, marching, order of Battle, | fighting, attacking, and defending strong Places, with the | Manner of surprising Towns, Quarters, and Armies; ex- | hibiting what is most requisite to be known, by all who | enter into the | Military Service. | By the Chevalier de La Valiere. | *Philadelphia:* | *Printed and Sold by Robert Bell, in Third-Street.* | MDCCLXXVI. | 8vo.

Collation : Title, 1 leaf; Contents, pp. (5); Advertisement, 1 page ; Title to Lamont's work, 1 leaf; Preface, pp. iii.–v. ; Introduction, pp. vii.–xi. ; text, pp. 13–61 ; Title to the Duties of Soldiers, 1 leaf; Preface, 1 leaf; text, pp. 67–143 ; Title to La Valliere's work, 1 leaf; Preface, 1 leaf; text, pp. 149–264. The several title-pages are as follows :

LAMONT. The | Art of War, | containing, | The Duties | of all | Military Officers, | In Actual Service ; | Including necessary Instructions in many capital Matters, | by the Knowledge of which a Man may soon become an | Ornament to the Profession of Arms. | Written by Monsieur De Lamont, Town Major of Toulon. | [Imprint as in general title.]

THE | ART of War, | containing, | The Duties | of | Soldiers in General, | In Actual Service ; | Including necessary Instructions in many capital Matters, | by remaining Ignorant of which, a Man will be every | day in danger, of bringing Disgrace upon Himself and | material Injury, to the Cause of his Country. | Written by a French Officer. | [Imprint as in general title.]

LA VALLIERE. The | Art of War, | containing, | The Rules and Practice | of the | Greatest Generals, | in the | Manoeuvres, | Of encamping, marching, order of Battle, fighting, attacking, | and defending strong Places, with the Manner of surprising | Towns, Quarters, and Armies; exhibiting what is most | requisite to be known, by all who enter into the | Military Service. | By the Chevalier De La Valiere. | [Imprint as in general title.]

Brunet mentions an edition of these three works published at the Elzevir press in 1671. I have followed his spelling of La Valliere's name.

LINN. (W.) A | Military | Discourse, | delivered in | Carlisle, | March the 17th, 1776, | to | Colonel Irvine's Battalion of Regulars, | and a very respectable number of the | Inhabitants. | Published at the request of the Officers. | By William Linn, A.M. Chaplain. | . . . | . . . . | *Philadelphia:* | *Printed in the Year* MDCCLXXVI. | 12mo. pp. 23.   L. C. P.   3413

LIST of the Sub-Committees, appointed by the | Committee for the city and liberties of Philadelphia, to | superintend the several districts of said city, &c. | [*Philadelphia: W. and T. Bradford.* 1776.] Folio, 1 leaf.   L. C. P.   3414

Signed by "Jonathan B. Smith, Secretary," and dated "February 26, 1776."

THE | MANUAL | Exercise, | as ordered by | His Majesty, | In the Year 1764. | Together with, | Plans and Explanations of the | Method generally Practised at Re- | views and Field-Days. | With Copper Plates. | *Philadelphia:* | *Sold by J. Humphreys, R. Bell, and R. Aitken.* | MDCCLXXVI. | 8vo. pp. 35, (1), 2 plates.

MINUTES | of the | Baptist Association, | Held at the Scots Plains, in the State of New Jersey, | October 15th and 16th, 1776. | [Colophon.] *Philadelphia:* | *Printed by Henry Miller, in Race-street.* [1776.] | Sq. 8vo. pp. 7.   3416

MINUTES | of the | Proceedings | of the | Convention | of the | State of Pennsylvania, | Held at Philadelphia, the Fifteenth Day of July, 1776. | *Philadelphia:* | *Printed and Sold by Henry Miller, in Race-Street.* | MDCCLXXVI. | Folio, pp. 67.   H. S. P.   3417

The Convention, besides framing a Constitution, exercised both legislative and executive powers; assuming, in fact, the government. The Proceedings as printed in the collection of Pennsylvania Conventions, issued in 1836, containing only the matter relating to the Constitution. This edition was issued in weekly parts.

MORTON. (P.) An | Oration, | Delivered at the King's Chapel in Boston, | April 8, 1776, | On the Re-Interment of the

Remains of the late | Most-Worshipful Grand-Master | Joseph Warren, Esquire, | President of the late Congress of this Colony, | and | Major-General of the Massachusetts Forces; | Who was Slain in the Battle of Bunker's Hill, | June 17, 1775. | By Perez Morton, M.M. | *Boston, Printed:* | *Philadelphia: Re-printed* | *by John Dunlap, in Market-Street.* | M,DCC,LXXVI. | 4to. pp. 16. 3418

NECESSARIES; | best | Product | of | Land; | best | Staple | of | Commerce. | *Philadelphia:* | *Printed by James Humphreys, junr.* | M,DCC,LXXVI. | 8vo. pp. 17, 1 leaf.   L. C. P.   3419

This was in opposition to the proposed introduction of Silk-culture and Wine-making in Pennsylvania, for which there had been a popular outcry started five or six years before. Du Simitiere says only 12 copies were printed.

DER NEUE, Verbessert= und Zuverläßige | Americanische | Calender | Auf das 1777ste Jahr Christi, | Welches ein Gemein Jahr von 365 Tagen ist. | [12 lines.] | Zum Fünfzehntenmal herausgegeben. | *Philadelphia, Gedruckt und zu finden bey Henrich Miller, . . .* | *. . .* | *. . .* | *. . .* | *. . . .* [1776.] | 4to. pp. (48).   H. S. P.   3420

NEW-YEAR Verses of the Carriers of the Pennsylvania Evening Post. *Philadelphia: B. Towne.* 1776.   3421

NEW-YEAR Verses of the Carriers of the Pennsylvania Gazette. *Philadelphia: Hall and Sellers.* 1776.   3422

NEW-YEAR Verses of the Carriers of the Pennsylvania Journal. *Philadelphia: W. and T. Bradford.* 1776.   3423

NEW-YEAR Verses of the Carriers of the Pennsylvania Ledger. *Philadelphia: James Humphreys, jun.* 1776.   3424

NEW-YEAR Verses of the Carriers of the Pennsylvania Packet. *Philadelphia: John Dunlap.* 1776.   3425

[NICHOLA. (Lewis)] A | Treatise | of | Military | Exercise, | calculated | for the Use of the Americans. | In which every Thing that is supposed can be of Use | to them, is retained, and such Manœuvres, as are | only for Shew and Parade, omitted. | To which is added | Some Directions on the other Points | of

Discipline. | *Philadelphia:* | *Printed by Styner and Cist, in Second-street,* | *near Arch-street.* MDCCLXXVI. | Sm. 8vo. pp. viii, 91, (1), 9 plates.   L. C. P.   3426

OBSERVATIONS : | On the | Reconciliation | of | Great-Britain, | and the | Colonies; | In which are exhibited, Arguments | for, and against, that Measure. | By a Friend of American Liberty. | . . . | . . . | . . . . | *Philadelphia:* | *Printed by Robert Bell, in Third-Street.* | MDCCLXXVI. | 8vo. pp. 40.   H. S. P.   3427

The " Plan of an American Compact with Great Britain, first published in New York," occupies pp. 33–40.

AN ORDINANCE | For the Appointment of | Justices of the Peace | For the State of Pennsylvania. | *Philadelphia: Printed by John Dunlap.* [1776.] | Folio, 1 leaf.   L. C. P.   3428

AN ORDINANCE | of the State of Pennsylvania, | Declaring what shall be Treason, and for Punishing the same, | and other Crimes and Practices against the State. | *Philadelphia: Printed by Styner and Cist, in Second-street, near Arch-street.* [1776.] | Folio, 1 leaf.   L. C. P.   3429

AN ORDINANCE | for rendering the Burthen of Associators and Non- | Associators in the Defence of this State as nearly | equal as may be. | [*Philadelphia: John Dunlap.* 1776.] Folio, pp. (3).   H. S. P.   3430

A PROPOSED ORDINANCE | of the State of Pennsylvania, | Declaring what shall be Treason, and for Punishing the same, | and other Crimes and Practices against the State. | *Philadelphia: Printed by Styner and Cist, in Second-street.* [1776.] | Folio, 1 leaf.

[PAINE. (Thomas)] The American Crisis. | Number I. | By the Author of Common Sense. | [*Philadelphia: Styner and Cist.* 1776.] 8vo. pp. 8.   H. S. P.   3432

[PAINE.] Common Sense; | addressed to the | Inhabitants | of | America, | On the following interesting | Subjects. | I. Of the Origin and Design of Government in general, | with concise Remarks on the English Constitution. | II. Of Monarchy and Hereditary Succession. | III. Thoughts on the present State of American Affairs. | IV. Of the present Ability of America, with some mis- | cellaneous Reflections. | . . . | . . . | . . . . | *Philadelphia :* | *Printed, and Sold, by R. Bell, in Third-Street.* | MDCCLXXVI. | 8vo. Title, 1 leaf; Introduction, pp. (2); text, pp. 1–79; Adver- tisement, 1 page.   H. S. P.   3433

Bell advertised a second edition in Pa. Evening Post, Jan. 27, 1776. (See Sa- bin's Dictionary for a number of editions printed elsewhere.)

[PAINE.] Common Sense; | addressed to the | Inhabitants | of | America, | On the following interesting | Subjects. | I. Of the Origin and Design of Government in general, | with concise Re- marks on the English Constitution. | II. Of Monarchy and Heredi- tary Succession. | III. Thoughts on the present State of American Affairs. | IV. Of ·the present Ability of America, with some mis- cel- | laneous Reflections. | A New Edition, with several Additions in the Body of | the Work. To which is added an Appendix ; to- gether | with an Address to the People called Quakers. | N. B. The New Addition here given increases the Work | upwards of one Third. | . . . | . . . | . . . . | *Philadelphia printed.* | *And sold by* *W. and T. Bradford.* [1776.] | 8vo.   H. S. P.   3434

Collation : Half-title, 1 leaf; Title, 1 leaf; Introduction, pp. (2); text, pp. 1–50. The Appendix begins in the middle of page 37. A Postscript, which is added to the introduction of the first edition, is dated " Philadelphia, February 14, 1776."

[PAINE.] Common Sense ; | with the whole | Appendix : | The | Address | to the | Quakers : | Also, the | Large Additions, And | A Dialogue between the Ghost of General Montgomery, | just arrived from the Elysian Fields; and an American | Dele- gate in a Wood, near Philadelphia : | On the Grand Subject of | American Independancy. | *Philadelphia :* | *Printed, and Sold, by* *R. Bell, in Third-Street.* | MDCCLXXVI. | 8vo.   H. S. P.   3435

Collation : Half-title and Advertisement, pp. (2); General title, 1 leaf; Title to Common Sense, 1 leaf; Introduction, pp. (2) ; text, pp. 1–79 ; Advertisement, 1 page; Large Additions to Common Sense, Title and Verses, pp. (2) ; text, pp. 81–147, (1) ; Bell to the Public, pp. (2); Dialogue, Title, 1 leaf; text, pp. 5–16. The title-page to Common Sense differs from that of the first edition, No. 3433, *supra*, only in the spacing of the 12th and 13th lines, and by the addition of " The Third Edition." The title of the Additions is given in No. 3439, *infra*, and the title of the Dialogue is No. 3437, *infra.*

[PAINE.] Common Sense : | Addressed to the | Inhabitants | of | America. | On the following interesting | Subjects. | I. Of the origin and Design of Government in general, | with concise Remarks on the English Constitution. | II. Of Monarchy and Hereditary Succession. | III. Thoughts on the present State of American Affairs. | IV. Of the present Ability of America, with some | miscellaneous Reflections. | A New Edition, with several Additions in the Body of | the Work : To which is added an Appendix ; toge- | ther with an Address to the People called Quakers. | The Fourth Edition. | . . . | . . . | . . . . | *Lancaster :* | *Printed by Francis Bailey, in King's-Street.* [1776.] | 8vo. pp. 63.   3436

[PAINE.] A | Dialogue | between | The Ghost | of | General Montgomery | Just arrived from the Elysian Fields ; | and an | American Delegate | In a Wood | near | Philadelphia. | [*Philadelphia :*] *Printed, and Sold by R. Bell, in Third-Street.* | MDCCLXXVI. | 8vo. Advertisement, 1 leaf ; Title, 1 leaf ; pp. 5–16.   3437

[PAINE.] Gefunde Bernunft | an die | Einwohner von Amerika, | über folgende wichtige Gegenstände : | I. Bon dem Ursprung und der Absicht der Re= | gierung überhaupt, mit kurzen Anmerkun= | gen über die Englische Landsverfassung. | II. Bon Monarchie und Erbfolge. | III. Gedanken über den gegenwärtigen Zustand | Americanischer Angelegenheiten. | IV. Bon der jetzigen Stärke von America, mit | einigen vermischten Betrachtungen. | Nebst | Einem Anhang, und einer Zuschrift an die | Repräsentanten des Bolfs, das den Namen | Quäfer führet. | . . . | . . . | . . . . | Aus dem Englischen übersetzt. | *Philadelphia,* | *Gedruckt bey Melchior Steiner und Carl Cist, in* | *der Zweyten-strasse.* 1776. | 8vo. pp. viii, 70.   H. S. P.   3438

[PAINE.] Large | Additions | to | Common Sense ; | Addressed to the inhabitants of America, | On the following interesting subjects. | I. The American Patriot's Prayer. | II. American Independancy defended, by Candidus. | III. The Propriety of Independancy, by Demophilus. | . . . | . . . | . . . . | IV. A Review of the American Contest, with some | Strictures on the King's Speech. Addressed to all | Parents in the Thirteen United Colonies, by a | Friend to Posterity and Mankind. | V. Letter to Lord Dartmouth, by an English American. | VI. Observations on Lord North's Conciliatory Plan, | by Sincerus. | To which are added and given | An Appendix to Common Sense; Together with an Ad- | dress to the People called Quakers, on their Testimony | concerning Kings and Governments, and the present | Commotions in America. | *Philadelphia :* | *Printed, and Sold, by R. Bell, in Third-Street.* | MDCCLXXVI. | pp. 79–147, (1). H. S. P. 3439

Little, if any part, of this collection was the work of Paine. The essays were mostly gathered up by Bell, who issued the pamphlet about the 20th of February, 1776.

[PENN. (William)] To the | Children of Light | in this | Generation, | Called of God to be Partakers of Eternal Life in Jesus Christ, | the Lamb of God, and Light of the World. | [*Philadelphia :* 1776.] 4to. pp. 4. F. 3440

Put forth by the Meeting for Sufferings to discourage assistance to the Revolutionary cause.

THE | PENNSYLVANIA | Evening Post. | MDCCLXXVI. | *Philadelphia :* | *Printed by Benjamin Towne, in Front-Street.* [1776.] | 4to. pp. (2), 618. 3441

THE PENNSYLVANIA Gazette. 3442

Numbers 2454 (Jan. 3, 1776) to 2501 (Nov. 27, 1776), four pages each, with "Supplements" of two pages to Numbers 2455, 2458, 2460, 2462, 2464, 2466 to 2469, 2471, 2472, 2476, 2480, 2485, 2496, and 2498. Publication was suspended from Nov. 27, 1776, to Feb. 5, 1777. Title and imprint as in No. 2913, *supra.*

THE PENNSYLVANIA Journal. 3443

Numbers 1726 (Jan. 3, 1776) to 1773 (Nov. 27, 1776), four pages each, with a "Supplement" of two pages to No. 1476; a "Postscript" of one leaf to No. 1744 and one of two pages to No. 1727, and a quarto leaf to No. 1745. Title and imprint as in No. 2317, *supra.* The publication of the paper was suspended from Nov. 30, 1776, until Jan. 29, 1777.

THE PENNSYLVANIA Ledger. 3444

Numbers L. (Jan. 6, 1776) to XCVII. (Nov. 30, 1776), four pages each, with a "Supplement" of one leaf to No. 54, and one of two pages to No. 62. Title and imprint as in No. 3255, *supra,* until No. 74, when the royal arms were withdrawn from the former. The publication of the Ledger was suspended with No. 97, until October 10, 1777.

THE PENNSYLVANIA Magazine. *Philadelphia: Robert Ait-ken.* 1776. 8vo. pp. 5–344, 5 plates. H. S. P. 3445

The magazine ended with the number for July. No title-page or index appear to have been issued. On page 74 is given for the first time in America the Manual Alphabet for the Deaf and Dumb, with an article upon its use.

THE PENNSYLVANIA PACKET. 3446

Numbers 219 (Jan. 1, 1776) to 268 (Dec. 27, 1776), four pages each, except the last two, which are only two pages, with "Postscripts" of one leaf to No. 237; of two pages to Numbers 220, 224, 229, 231, 233 to 236, 238 to 240, 243, 245, 254, 258, 262, 264, and 265; "Supplements" of one leaf to No. 245, and of two pages to No. 240, and an "Extra" of one leaf to No. 221. Title as in No. 3076, *supra*, until No. 234, when the old cut of the ship was restored. This was changed in No. 236 to a new and smaller cut of the same kind. From No. 234 the size of the sheet was reduced, and the paper printed in three columns. Imprint as in No. 3076, *supra*. The publication of the paper was suspended between Nov. 26 and Dec. 18.

THE PENNSYLVANIA Pocket Almanac for 1777. *Philadelphia: W. and T. Bradford.* 1776. 3447

POOR Will's Almanac for 1777. *Philadelphia: Joseph Cruk-shank.* 1776. 3448

POOR Will's | Pocket Almanack, | For the Year 1777; | . . . | . . . | . . . | . . . | . . . . | *Philadelphia:* | *Printed and Sold by J. Crukshank,* | *in Market-street, opposite the Presby-* | *terian Meeting house.* [1776.] | 24mo. pp. (24). H. S. P. 3449

PRICE. (R.) Observations | on the | Nature | of | Civil Liberty, | the | Principles | of | Government, | and the | Justice and Policy | of the | War with America. | To which is added, | An | Appendix, | containing | A State of the National Debt, an Estimate of the Money | drawn from the Public by the Taxes, and an Account of the | National Income and Expenditure since the last War. | . . . | . . . . | By Richard Price, D.D. F.R.S. | *London Printed, 1776.* | *Philadelphia:* | *Re-printed and Sold by John Dunlap, at the Newest* | *Printing-Office, in Market-Street.* [1776.] | 8vo. pp. 71. H. S. P. 3450

PRIMA | Morum & Pietatis | Præcepta. | Viz. | I. Dicta septem sapientum e Græcis. | II. Gulielmi Lilii Monita, pædagogica.

| III. Dion. Catonis Disticha moralia. | IV. Joan. Sulpitii Veru-
lani de moribus & civili- | tate Puerorum Carmen. | V. Rudi-
menta Pietatis, sire, Oratio Dominica, | Symbolum Apostolicum &
Decalogus; item | duorum Sacramentorum, Baptismi & Sacræ |
Cœnæ Domini Institutiones. | Quibus accessit. | Summula Cata-
chismi ad piam Juniorum Edu- | cationem apprime utilis; | Item,
| Præcipua Capita Christianæ Religionis, desumpta è sacra |
Scriptura Veteris ac Novi Testamenti. | . . . | . . . | . . . . | *Phila-
delphia:* | *Apud R. Aitken, Anno Domini* | M.DCCLXXVI. | 12mo.
pp. 34.   H. S. P.   3451

PROCEEDINGS | of the | Provincial Conference | of | Com-
mittees, | of the | Province of Pennsylvania; | Held at the Car-
penter's Hall, | at | Philadelphia. | Began June 18th, and con-
tinued by adjournments to | June 25, 1776. | *Philadelphia:* | *Printed
by W. and T. Bradford.* [1776.] | 8vo. pp. 31.   L. C. P.   3452

THE | PROCESS | for | Extracting | and | Refining | Salt-
Petre, | According to the Method practised at the | Provincial
Works in Philadelphia. | Published by Order of the Committee |
Of Safety. | *Philadelphia:* | *Printed by William and Thomas Bradford,
at the* | *London Coffee House.* | M,DCC,LXXVI. | 8vo. pp. 8.   3453

THE PROGRESS of the British and Hessian Troops through
New Jersey, | has been attended with such scenes of Desolation
and Outrage, as would | disgrace the most barbarous Nations. . . . .
| [*Philadelphia:* 1776.]   4to. 1 leaf.   H. S. P.   3454

An account of outrages committed on women in New Jersey. Published to excite
opposition to the British. Dated " Bucks County, December 14, 1776."

THE PROPOSED Plan or Frame of | Government for the
Common- | Wealth or State of Pennsyl- | vania. | (Printed for
Consideration.) | [*Philadelphia: Henry Miller.* 1776.]   Folio, pp.
12.   H. S. P.   3455

THE PROTEST | Of divers of the Inhabitants of this Prov-
ince, in behalf of themselves and others. | To the Honorable
the Representatives of the Province of Pennsylvania. | [*Phila-
delphia:* 1776.]   Folio, 1 leaf.   L. C. P.   3456

Dated by Du Simitiere, " Philadelphia, May 20, 1776." Against the Provincial Assembly continuing to act as a Legislative body.

RATIONALIS. A Reply to Common Sense. *Philadelphia:* 1776. 3457

Title from the Catalogue of Library Company of Philadelphia. This is not a separate publication, but is the first of Bell's addenda to Chalmers's Plain Truth, forming pp. 75–86 of that pamphlet.

REFLECTIONS | of a few | Friends of the Country, | upon several | Circumstantial Points; | In a Conference between Sandy, Pady, | Simon and Jonathan, and the Parson : | Or | A Looking-Glass | for the | Americans. | . . . | . . . | . . . | . . . . | *Philadelphia,* | *Printed by* [*Henry Miller*] *for the Author,* 1776. | Sm. 8vo. pp. 48. L. C. P. 3458

𝕽𝖊𝖌𝖎𝖒𝖊𝖓𝖙𝖘 = Verfaſſung von Pennſylvanien. | [*Philadelphia:* *Henrich Miller.* 1776.] 8vo. pp. 16. H. S. P. 3459

RÉGLEMENT | Militaire, | Concernant | La Police | et | La Discipline, | Que doivent observer les Troupes qui sont ou seront | dans la suite levées & payées par les Treize | Colonies Unies de l'Amerique Septentrionale. | Traduit de l'Anglais, Par F. Daymon. | *A Philadelphie;* | *Chez Fleury Mesplet & Ch. Berger,* | *Imprimeurs & Libraires.* | M.DCC.LXXVI. | 8vo. pp. 39. 3460

REMARKS | on | A Late Pamphlet | entitled | Plain Truth. | By | Rusticus. *Philadelphia:* | *Printed by John Dunlap, in Market-Street.* | M,DCC,LXXVI. | 8vo. pp. 31. H. S. P. 3461

𝕯𝖎𝖊 𝕽𝖊𝖕𝖗𝖆𝖘𝖊𝖓𝖙𝖆𝖓𝖙𝖊𝖓 der Vereinigten Staaten | von America, im Congreß verſammlet, | An das Volk überhaupt und an die Einwohner Pennſylvaniens | und der angrenzenden Staaten insbeſondere. | [*Philadelphia: Henrich Miller.* 1776.] Folio, 1 leaf. 3462

THE REPRESENTATIVES of the United States of | America, in Congress assembled, | To the People in General, and particularly to the Inhabitants | of Pennsylvania, and the adjacent States. | [*Philadelphia:* 1776.] Folio, 1 leaf. L. C. P. 3463

" We think it our Duty to address a few Words of Exhortation to you in this important Crisis," &c. " Philadelphia, December 10, 1776."

RESOLUTIONS directing the Mode of levying Taxes on Non-Associators. *Philadelphia: Henry Miller.* 1776.   3464

RUDDIMAN. (T.) The | Rudiments | of the | Latin Tongue: | Or, a | Plain and easy Introduction | to | Latin Grammar. | Wherein | The Principles of the Language are | Methodically digested both in English and | Latin. | With | Useful Notes and Observations, explaining the Terms | of Grammar, and farther improving its Rules. | To which is added, by the Publisher, | Several useful Extracts from Ross's Latin Grammar, which | renders this Edition more complete, than any hitherto | published. | By Tho. Ruddiman, M.A. | The First American Edition with Additions. | *Philadelphia:* | *Printed and sold by R. Aitken,* *opposite the London* | *Coffee-House, Front-Street.* 1776. | 12mo. pp. 126.   H. S. P.   3465

RULES | and | Articles | for the better | Government | of the | Troops | Raised, or to be raised and kept in pay by | and at the expence of the United | States of | America. | *Philadelphia:* | *Printed by John Dunlap, in Market-Street.* | M,DCC,LXXVI. | 8vo. pp. 36.   H. S. P.   3466

RULES and Articles for the Government of the Pennsylvania Forces. *Philadelphia: Henry Miller.* 1776.   3467

Adopted by the Assembly April 5, 1776, together with the " Rules" next mentioned. They were also printed in German.

RULES and Regulations for the better Government of the Military Association in Pennsylvania. *Philadelphia: Henry Miller.* 1776.   3468

SAUNDERS. (R.) A Pocket Almanac for 1777. By Richard Saunders, Phil. *Philadelphia: Hall and Sellers.* 1776.   3469

SAUNDERS. Poor Richard improved: | Being an | Almanack | . . . | . . . | . . . | . . . | . . . | . . . | . . . | . . . | . . . | . . . | For the | Year of our Lord 1777: | Being the First after Leap-Year. | . . . | . . . | . . . | . . . | . . . | . . . | . . . | . . . | . . . . | By Richard Saunders, Philom. | *Philadelphia:* | *Printed and* *Sold by Hall and Sellers.* [1776.] | Sm. 8vo. pp. (36 ?).   c.   3470

SCHNEEBERGER. (A. and B.) Das Raben = Geschrey, durch Br. Andreas Schneeberger | auf Antetum, 1776. | 8vo. 2 pp. Die Stimme der Turteltaube, durch Sch. Barbara | Schneeberger auf Antetum. [n. p.] 1776. | 8vo. 2 pp. 3471

SHARP. (A.) Der Gantz Neue Verbefferte Nord = Americanische Calender, auf das 1777ste Jahr Christi. Zum Zweytenmal heraus= gegeben und verfertiget von Anthony Sharp, Philom. *Lancaster : Francis Bailey.* 1776. 3472

SHARP. The Lancaster Almanac for 1777. By Anthony Sharp, Philom. *Lancaster : Francis Bailey.* 1776. 3473

SIMES. (T.) The | Military Guide | for | Young Officers, | By | Thomas Simes, Esq. | Author of the Military Medley. | In Two Volumes. | Vol. I. | *London, Printed.* | *Philadelphia,* | *Re-printed by J. Humphreys, R. Bell, and | R. Aitken, Printers and Booksellers.* | M.DCC.LXXVI. | 8vo. + Volume the Second. | [*Ibid.*] 8vo.

Collation: Volume I. Title, 1 leaf; Advertisement, pp. (2) ; Contents, pp. (4) ; text, pp. 1–384 (misprinted 284) ; 2 folded leaves ; Index, pp. (5). Volume II. Title, 1 leaf; 2d Title, 1 leaf; text, pp. (188) ; 1 plate. The second title is as follows : A New | Military, Historical, | and | Explanatory | Dictionary : | Including the | Warriors Gazetteer of Places remarkable | for Sieges or Battles. | By Thomas Simes. | *Philadelphia :* | *Sold by Humphreys, Bell, and Aitken.* | M,DCC,LXXVI. |

SMITH. (W.) An | Oration | In Memory of | General Montgomery, | and of the | Officers and Soldiers, | Who Fell with Him, December 31, 1775, | before | Quebec ; | Drawn up (and Delivered February 19th, 1776.) | At the Desire of the | Honorable Continental Congress, | By William Smith, D.D. | Provost of the College and Academy | of Philadelphia. | . . . | . . . | . . . | . . . . | *Philadelphia :* | *Printed by John Dunlap, in Market-Street.* | M,DCC,LXXVI. | 8vo. Half-title, 1 leaf; Title, 1 leaf; Preface, pp. (2); text, pp. 1–44. L. C. P. 3475

STILLMAN. (S.) Death, the last Enemy, destroyed by Christ. | A | Sermon, | Preached, March 27, 1776, | before | The Honorable | Continental Congress ; | on the Death of | The Honorable | Samuel Ward, Esq. | one of the | Delegates from the Colony | of

Rhode-Island, | who died of the Small-Pox, in this city, | (Phila-
delphia) March 26, Æt. 52. | Published at the desire of many who
heard it. | By Samuel Stillman, M.A. | *Philadelphia:* | *Printed by*
Joseph Crukshank, in Market-street. | MDCCLXXVI. | 8vo. pp. 28.

SWIETEN. ([Geraard] van) The | Diseases | incident to |
Armies. | With the | Method of Cure. | Translated from the
Original of | Baron Van Swieten, | Physician to their Imperial
Majesties. | To which are Added; | The Nature and Treatment,
| of | Gun-Shot Wounds. | By John Ranby, Esquire, Surgeon
general | to the British Army. | Likewise, | Some brief directions,
to be | observed by Sea Surgeons | in engagements. | Also, | Pre-
ventatives of the Scurvy at Sea. | By William Northcote, Sur-
geon, | many years in the sea-service. | Published, for the Use of
Military, and Naval Surgeons | In America. | *Philadelphia:* |
Printed, and Sold, by R. Bell, in Third-Street. | MDCCLXXVI. |
8vo. pp. 164.   L. C. P.   3477

Baron van Swieten's work ends on page 112, and is followed by a work with the
following title-page:
NORTHCOTE, (W.) and J. RANBY. Extracts | from the | Marine Practice | of |
Physic and Surgery. | With some brief directions to be | observed by sea-surgeons |
in engagements, &c. | By William Northcote, Surgeon, | many years in the sea-
service. | Including, | The Nature and Treatment, | of | Gun-Shot Wounds. | By
John Ranby, Esquire; surgeon general | to the British Army. | *Philadelphia:* |
Printed, and Sold, by R. Bell, in Third-Street. | MDCCLXXVI. |

THOUGHTS | on | Government: | Applicable to | The Present
State | of the | American Colonies. | In a Letter from a Gentleman
| To his Friend. | *Philadelphia:* | *Printed by John Dunlap.* |
M,DCC,LXXVI. | Sm. 8vo. pp. 28.   L. C. P.   3478

TO our Friends and Brethren in religious Profession, in | these
and the adjacent Provinces. | [*Philadelphia:* 1776.] 4to. pp. (2).

"Signed in . . . behalf of the Meeting for Sufferings, . . . 20th day of the
Twelfth Month, 1776, John Pemberton, Clerk." "That we may with Christian firm-
ness and fortitude withstand and refuse to submit to the arbitrary injunctions and
ordinances of men, who assume to themselves the power of compelling others, either
in person or by other assistance, to join in carrying on war." One of the inoppor-
tune epistles put forth by some members of the Society of Friends, the persistent
repetition of which largely influenced their being sent to Virginia.

TO the Associators of | Pennsylvania. | [*Philadelphia :*] *Printed by John Dunlap.* [1776.] | Folio, 1 leaf. H. S. P. 3480

Dated " War Office, Nov. 14, 1776." " Congress have received Intelligence that a Fleet of the Enemy, consisting of several hundred sail, were yesterday discovered near Sandy-Hook, steering to the Southward. . . . immediately put yourselves in array and march by Companies and Parts of Companies . . . with the utmost Expedition to this City."

TO the | Electors | and | Freeholders | of the | City of Philadelphia. | [*Philadelphia :* 1776.] Folio, 1 leaf. L. C. P. 3481

Dated by Du Simitiere, " Philadelphia, April 30, 1776." Issued on the election of four additional Assemblymen from Philadelphia, in favor of the selection of men of moderate views.

TO the Free and Independent Electors | of the City of Philadelphia. | [*Philadelphia :* 1776.] Folio, 1 leaf. L. C. P. 3482

Signed " Philirenæus." Du Simitiere dated his copy " Philadelphia, November 5, 1776." An election circular in support of the " Constitution of 1776."

TO the Privates of the several Battalions of Military | Associators in the Province of Pennsylvania. | [*Philadelphia :* 1776.] 4to. pp. 3. L. C. P. 3483

" Signed by Order of the Committee of Privates, Samuel Simpson, President." The second and third pages contain " The Protest of the Committee of the Privates of the Military Association belonging to the City and Liberties of Philadelphia," against the appointment by the Assembly of two Brigadier-Generals to command the Associators, as recommended by Congress.

TO the Public. | [*Philadelphia : W. and T. Bradford.* 1776.] Sm. folio, 1 leaf. L. C. P. 3484

The officers of the Pennsylvania Navy, concerning the " many misrepresentations . . . circulated respecting the quantity of ammunition, and other circumstances relating to the condition of the Gallies at the time of the late engagement" with the " Roebuck."

TO the several Battalions of Military Associators | in the Province of Pennsylvania. | [*Philadelphia :* 1776.] Folio, pp. (2). 3485

Signed by Thos. Nevil, John Chaloner, James Canmon, Andrew Epley, and William Thorne, Committee of Correspondence, dated " June 26, 1776," in regard to the choice of officers.

TO the Tories. | [*Philadelphia:* 1776.] 4to. 1 leaf. H. S. P. 3486

An election circular signed " Old Trusty," and dated " Tuesday, April 30, in the Year of our Lord 1776, and in the third Year of the Union."

TOUSTAIN DE RICHEBOURG. Pro aris et focis. Par Toustain de Richebourg. *A Philadelphie d'Amorique et non d'Ame- rique.* [*France.*] 1776.   W. 3487

TUCKER. (Josiah) The True | Interest of Britain, | Set Forth in Regard | to the | Colonies; | And the only Means of | Living in Peace and Harmony with Them, | Including Five dif- ferent Plans for effecting this desirable | Event. | By Jos. Tucker, D.D., Dean of Gloucester. | Author of the Essay on the Advan- tages and Disadvantages | which respectively attend France and Great-Britain, with | regard to Trade. | To which is added by the Printer, A few more Words, | on the Freedom of the Press in America. | *Philadelphia:* | *Printed, and Sold, by Robert Bell, in Third-Street.* | MDCCLXXVI. | 8vo. pp. 66; A few more Words, pp. (4); Advertisement, pp. (2). + The Second Edition.   3488

THE UNIVERSAL Almanac for 1777. *Philadelphia: James Humphreys, jun.* 1776.   3489

VIEW | of the | Title | to | Indiana, | A Tract of Country | on the | River Ohio. | Containing | Indian Conferences at John- son-Hall, in May, 1765 — the | Deed of the Six Nations to the Proprietors of Indiana — the | Minutes of the Congress at Fort Stanwix, in October and | November, 1768 — the Deed of the Indians, settling the | Boundary Line between the English and Indians Lands — | and the Opinion of Counsel on the Title of the Pro- | prietors of Indiana. | *Philadelphia:* | *Printed by Styner and Cist, in Second-* | *street, near Arch-street.* MDCCLXXVI. | 8vo. pp. 46.   L. C. P. 3490

VOTES | of the | House of Representatives, | From Monday, February 12, to Saturday, February 17, 1776. | [Colophon.] *Philadelphia: Printed and Sold by Henry Miller, in Race-Street.* [1776.] | Folio, pp. 173–175.   H. S. P. 3491

Continued weekly to April 6, and from May 20 to June 15, 1776, pp. 173–265.

The Assembly adjourned to meet on August 26, and on August 28 they adjourned until Sept. 23. They sat until the 26th of Sept., when the Provincial Assembly "rose" for the last time.

VOTES | and | Proceedings | of the | House of Representatives | of the | Province of Pennsylvania. | Beginning the Fourteenth Day of October, 1767. | Volume The Sixth. | [*Penn Arms.*] | *Philadelphia: | Printed and Sold by Henry Miller, in Race-Street.* | MDCCLXXVI. | Folio, Title, 1 leaf; pp. 766, 1 leaf.   H. S. P.   3492

WATTS. (I.) Horæ Lyricæ. Poems chiefly of the Lyric Kind. In Three Books. By Isaac Watts, D.D.   *Philadelphia: Robert Bell.* 1776?   3493

WEATHERWISE. (A.)   Father Abraham's | Almanack | For the Year of our Lord | 1777; | Being the First after Leap-Year. | . . . | . . . | . . . | . . . | . . . | . . . | . . . | . . . | . . . | . . . | . . . | . . . | . . . . | By Abraham Weatherwise, Gent. | . . . | . . . | . . . | . . . | . . . | . . . . | *Philadelphia: | Printed and Sold by John Dunlap, at the | Newest-Printing-Office, in Market-Street.* [1776.] | Sm. 8vo. pp. 32 +.   L. C. P.   3494

WETTENHALL. (E.)   Græcæ | Grammaticæ | Institutio Compendiaria. | In usum Scholarum. | Auctore | Edv. Wettenhall, D.D. | Nuper Episcopo Kilmor. & Ardag. | *Philadelphia.* | *Printed and Sold | By James Humphreys, junr.* | M,DCC,LXXVI. | 12mo. pp. (4), 93.   3495

WITHERSPOON. (J.)   The Dominion of Providence over the Pas- | sions of Men. | A | Sermon | preached | At Princeton, | On the 17th of May, 1776. | Being | The General Fast appointed by the Congress | through the United Colonies. | To which is added, | An Address to the Natives of Scotland residing in | America. | By John Witherspoon, D.D. | President of the College of New-Jersey. | *Philadelphia: | Printed and sold by R. Aitken, Printer and | Bookseller, opposite the London Coffee- | House, Front-Street.* | M.DCC.LXXVI. | 8vo. Title, 1 leaf; Dedication, 1 leaf; pp, 1–78; Errata, 1 leaf.   H. S. P.   3496

[YOUNG. (Arthur)] Rural Oeconomy: | Or Essays on the | Practical Parts of Husbandry. | Designed to explain several of the most important Me- | thods of conducting Farms of various kinds; includ- | ing many Useful Hints to Gentlemen Farmers, rela- | tive to the œconomical Management of their Business. | Containing, among other enquiries, | Of that Proportioned Farm, | which is of all others the | most profitable. | The best Method of conduct- | ing Farms that consist all of | Grass, or all of Arable Land. | The Means of keeping the most | Cattle the Year round on a | given quantity of Land. | The cheapest way of manuring | Land. | Considerations on the œcono- | mical conduct of Gentlemen | Farmers. | The comparative Profit of farm- | ing different Soils. | Of Experimental Agriculture. | Of the New Husbandry. | Of the Management of Borders | of Arable Fields. | Of periodical Publications con- | cerning Rural Oeconomics. | To which is added, | The Rural Socrates, | Being Memoirs of a Country Philosopher, | By the Author of the Farmer's Letters. | . . . | . . . . | The Second Edition. | *London, Printed:* | *Philadelphia: Re-printed and Sold* | *By James Humphreys, junr.* | M,DCC,LXXVI. | 8vo. pp. 245, (1). H. S. P. 3497

The Rural Socrates was written by Hans Caspar Hirzel, a Swiss physician.

THE YOUNG Clerk's Vade Mecum: Or, Complete Law Tutor. *Philadelphia: Robert Bell.* 1776. 3498

ZEISBERGER. (D.) Essay | of a | Delaware - Indian and English | Spelling-Book, | for the | Use of the Schools | of the | Christian Indians | on Muskingum River. | By David Zeisberger, | Missionary among the Western Indians. | *Philadelphia,* | *Printed by Henry Miller.* 1776. | Sm. 8vo. pp. (2), 113. H. S. P. 3499

1777.

THE | ACCOMPLISH'D Maid. | A new | Comic Opera. | As it is performed at the | Theatre-Royal in Covent-Garden. | The Music by | Signior Niccolo Piccini. | . . . | . . . | . . . . | *Philadelphia:* | *Printed and Sold by Robert Bell, in Third-Street.* | MDCCLXXVII. | 8vo. pp. 61, (1). H. S. P. 3500

AN ACCOUNT of the Births and Burials in Christ Church and St. Peter's. *Philadelphia:* 1777. 3501

AN ACT | To discourage Desertion, and to punish all such Persons as shall harbour or | conceal Deserters. | [*Philadelphia: John Dunlap.* 1777.] Folio, 1 leaf.   L. C. P. 3502

AN | ACT | to regulate the | Militia | of the | Common-Wealth | of | Pennsylvania. | *Philadelphia:* | *Printed by John Dunlap, in Market-Street.* | M,DCC,LXXVII. | 8vo. pp. 32.   L. C. P. 3503

ACT. A Supplement to the Act | intitled "An Act to regulate the | "Militia of the Common-Wealth of | "Pennsylvania." | [*Philadelphia: John Dunlap.* 1777.] 8vo. pp. 4.   L. C. P. 3504

ACT. A Supplement to the Act, intitled, "An Act to | "regulate the Militia of the Common-Wealth of Pennsylvania." | [*Philadelphia:*] *Printed by John Dunlap.* [1777.] | Folio, 1 leaf. 3505

ACT. Supplement to an Act for amending the several acts for electing Members of Assembly. *Philadelphia: Steiner and Cist.* 1777. 8vo. pp. 8. 3506

Title from Sabin's Dictionary, No. 60,651. Probably the same as No. 3569, *infra.*

EINE ACTE | zur | Anordnung | der | Miliz | der | Republik Penn=sylvanien. | Aus dem Englischen übersetzt. | *Philadelphia:* | *Gedruckt bey Steiner und Cist, in der Zweyten-strasse,* | *nahe bey der Arch-strasse.* 1777. | 8vo. pp. 28.   L. C. P. 3507

ADDENDA to the Rural Socrates. *Philadelphia: James Humphreys, junr.* 1777. 3508

Announced as in the Press at the end of Young's Rural Economy, and in the Pa. Journal, July 16, 1777. "Essays on Field Husbandry," by Jared Elliot, were also announced as in the press, in both advertisements.

AN | ADDRESS | of the | Convention | of the | Representatives | of the | State | of | New-York | to their | Constituents. | *Philadelphia:* | *Printed by John Dunlap.* | M,DCC,LXXVII. | 12mo. pp. 12.   L. C. P. 3509

AN ADDRESS to General St. Clair's Brigade at Ticonderoga. *Philadelphia: Styner and Cist.* 1777. 3510

AN | ADDRESS | to the | Inhabitants of Pennsylvania, | By | Those Freemen, of the City of Philadelphia, | who are now confined in the | Mason's Lodge, | By virtue of | A General Warrant, | Signed in Council | by the | Vice President | of the | Council of Pennsylvania. | *Philadelphia : | Printed by Robert Bell, in Third-Street.* | MDCCLXXVII. | 8vo. Title, 1 leaf; Quotation, 1 leaf; | pp. 1–52.   H. S. P.   3511

ADVERTISEMENT. *Philadelphia: Robert Aitken.* 1777. 3512

Aitken's Ledger contains during 1777 charges for printing the following advertisements, &c.:

Feb. 10. 200 copies Gen. Weedon's Advertisement from Head Quarters.
Feb. 11. 200 copies Maj. Nichola's Advertisement for Returns, &c.
Feb. 23. 500 copies Notices for Matthew Clarkson.
June 2. 200 copies Gen. Mifflin's Advertisement, 4to.
Sept. 24. Vanuxem's Circular Letter (in French). Folio.

ADVERTISEMENT. | A Return of Waggons and Horses | in Philadelphia, Germantown, and the | Country about is to be given . . . to | the Quarter Master General, . . . | . . . | . . . | . . . | . . . | . . . | . . . | . . . | . . . . . | *Philadelphia, Printed by James Humphreys, Junr.* [1777.] | Folio, 1 leaf.   3513

Dated "Philadelphia, October 10, 1777."

ADVERTISEMENT. | The Inhabitants of Philadelphia, German- | town and the Country about, are required to give | . . . | . . . | . . . a Return of | the Number of Horses, Waggons, Teams, and | Carts in their Possession. | . . . | . . . | . . . | . . . | . . . | . . . | . . . . . | *Philadelphia: Printed by B. Towne, in Front-street.* [1777.] | 4to. 1 leaf.   L. C. P.   3514

ALL Gentlemen | Sailors | Desirous of rendering themselves useful to their Country, let them | repair on Board His Majesty's armed Ship the | Vigilant, | Captain Christian, | Commander ; | . . . | . ·. · . | . . . | . . . | . . . . | *Philadelphia : Printed by James Humphreys, Junr.* | . . . [1777.] | 4to. 1 leaf.   L. C. P.   3515

ALL Gentlemen | Volunteers, | Who have a Desire to serve on Board the Stanley armed Brig, | belonging to His Majesty's

Ship the | Roebuck, | . . . | Will meet with the warmest en-
couragement . . . . | [*Philadelphia*: 1777.] 4to. 1 leaf. L. C. P. 3516

Dated " December 30, 1777."

ALL Persons having in their Possession any | Kind of Stores
and Provisions, belonging to | the Rebel Army, are . . . required
to report . . . | to the Quarter-Master or Commissary-General, |
. . . | . . . | . . . | . . . | . . . | Philadelphia, September 29,
1777. [*Printed by James Humphreys, junr.*] 4to. 1 leaf. L. C. P. 3517

ALL Persons having in their Possession Rum, | or any kind
of Spirituous Liquors, are here- | by ordered to report the same
to the Commissary- | General, before Twelve o'Clock To-morrow.
| . . . | . . . | . . . . | *Philadelphia : Printed by James Humphreys,
Junr.* [1777.] | Folio, 1 leaf. L. C. P. 3518

Dated " Commissary-General's Office, Philadelphia, October 6, 1777."

ALL the Male white Inhabitants residing | &c. [*Philadelphia*:
1777.] 4to. 1 leaf. L. C. P. 3519

A printed form of a call for a public meeting " to chuse by Ballot, one Captain, two
Lieutenants, one Ensign, and two Persons to be stiled Court-Martial Men,"
Signed " George Henry, Lieutenant of the City of Philadelphia," and dated " April
23, 1777."

AMERICANISCHE Calender. Der Hinckend- und Stolpernd- |
doch eilfertig-fliegend- und laufende Americanische Reichs-Volk, | Das ist
der Allerneueste- Verbesserte und Zuverläßigste. | Amerikanische Reichs-
Staats- Kriegs- Siegs- und | Geschichts- | Calender, | Auf das Jahr,
nach der Gnadenreichen Geburt unsers | Herrn und Heylandes Jesu
Christi, | 1778. | Welches ein Gemein-Jahr von 365 Tagen, das zweyte
nach dem Schalt Jahr ist, | darinen enthalten | Die Wochen- Monats-
und Merkwürdigt Tage; des Monds Auf- und Un- | tergang; seine
Zeichen, Grade, und Viertel; die Aspecten der Planeten, samt der | Wit-
terung; des Siebengestirns Aufgang Südplatz und Untergang; Auf- und
Untergang der Sonnen; nebst der Fluth oder dem hohen Wasser zu |
Philadelphia, Neu-York und andern Platze in America | Und andere
gewöhnliche Calender-Arbeit. | wie auch | Unterschiedliche kurzgefaßte
wunderliche kurzweilige Historien; nebst vielen | verschiedenen sehr merk-

würdigen Stücken, ꝛc. ꝛc. | Vornemlich nach dem Pennſylvaniſchen Horizon berechnet ; | Jedoch in den angrenzenden Landſchafften ohne merklichen Unterſchied zu gebrauchen. | Zum Zweytenmal herausgegeben. | *Lancaster, Gedruckt und zu finden bey Matthias Bartgis, in der Koenigin-* | *Strasse nahe bey dem Court-Hausz.* | . . . | . . . | . . . . [1777.] | Sm. 4to. pp. (38).   3520

The title is on the fifth page. In place of the cut on the first page is an abridged title, as follows : Der | Allerneueste Nord- | Americanische | Calender, | Auf das Jahr | . . . | . . . | 1778. | . . . | . . . | . . . | . . . | . . . . | *Lancaster, Gedruckt und zu finden bey Matthias Bartgis.* |

AN die hochgeehrten Glieder der | Aſſembly, | Des Pennſylvaniſchen Staats. | Das Memorial verſchiedener Einwohner der Graffſchaft Lan= caſter | giebt mit aller gebührenden Hochachtung zu erkennen. | [*Lancaster : Francis Bailey.* 1777.] Folio, 1 leaf.   H. S. P. 3521

APOCALYPSE de Chiokoyhikoy, Chef des Iroquois, Sauvages du Nord de l'Amérique. Ecrite par lui-même vers l'an de l'ère Crétienne 1305. Traduite en François sur l'original Iroquois. Avec un commentaire pour l'intelligence des endroits les plus difficiles du Texte, soigneusement revu et corrigé sous les yeux du Congrès général des Colonies Unies. Publié par ordre du Congrès général. *A Philadelphie, [Paris,] Chez W. Roberdson, Imprimeur Ordinaire des Colonies Confédérées.* 1777. 8vo. pp. iv, 111.

ARTICLES | of | Confederation | and | Perpetual Union | between the | States | of | New-Hampshire, Massachusetts-Bay, Rhode- | Island and Providence Plantation, Con- | necticut, New-York, New-Jersey, Pennsyl- | vania, Delaware, Maryland, Virginia, | North-Carolina, South-Carolina and Geor- | gia. | *Lancaster : | Printed by Francis Bailey.* | M,DCC,LXXVII. | Folio, pp. 26.   A. P. S. 3523

[BENEZET. (Anthony)] Serious Reflections affectionately recommended | to the Well-disposed of every Religious De- | nomination, particularly those who Mourn | and Lament on account of the Calamities | which attend us ; and the insensibility that | so generally prevails. | [*Philadelphia :* 1777 ?] Sm. 8vo. pp. 4.   F. 3524

BEY feiner Excellenz | G. Waſchington, Eſq. | General und oberſter
Befehlshaber über die Böl= | ker der vereinigten Staaten von America.
| *Lancaster: Gedruckt bey Frantz Bailey, in der Koenigs-Strasse.*
[1777.] | Folio, 1 leaf.   H. S. P.   3525

Dated "Dec. 20, 1777." For the same in English, see No. 3610, *infra*.

[BRACKENRIDGE. (Hugh Montgomery)] The | Death | of
| General Montgomery, | at the | Siege of Quebec. | A Tragedy.
| With an Ode, in honour of the Pennsylvania Militia, and | the
small band of regular Continental Troops, who sustained the |
Campaign, in the depth of winter, January, 1777, and repulsed
the | British Forces from the Banks of the Delaware. | By the
Author of a Dramatic Piece | on the Battle of Bunker's-Hill. |
To which are added, | Elegiac Pieces, | Commemorative of distin-
guished Characters. | . . . | . . . | . . . . | *Philadelphia:* | *Printed
and Sold by Robert Bell, in Third-Street,* | *Next Door to St. Paul's
Church.* | M,DCC,LXXVII. | 8vo. pp. 79, (5), 1 plate.   3526

[BRACKENRIDGE.] The | Death | of | General Montgom-
ery, | In Storming the | City of Quebec. | . . . | . . . | . . . | . . .
| . . . | . . . | . . . . | To which are added, | Elegiac Pieces, |
Commemorative of Distinguished Characters. | By different Gen-
tlemen. | . . . | . . . | . . . . | *Philadelphia:* | *Printed and Sold by
Robert Bell, in Third-Street,* | . . . . | M,DCC,LXXVII. | 8vo.   3527

Collation: Half-title, 1 page; explanation of plate, 1 page; 1 plate; Title, 1 leaf;
Dedication, pp. (2); The Author to the Public, pp. (2); Prologue, pp. (2); Dramatis
Personæ, 1 leaf; text, pp. 9–53; An Ode, pp. 55–64; Elegiac Pieces, Half-title, 1
leaf; pp. 67–79, (2).

[BURGOYNE. (John)] The | Maid | of the | Oaks: | A new
| Dramatic Entertainment. | As it is performed at the | Theatre-
Royal, in Drury-Lane. | . . . | . . . | . . . | . . . | . . . | . . . . |
Philadelphia: | *Printed and Sold by Robert Bell, in Third-Street.* |
MDCCLXXVII. | 8vo. pp. 67, 1 blank page, (4).   H. S. P.   3528

BURTON. (R.) The Fables of Æsop, with his Life, to which
are added Morals and Remarks, accommodated to the youngest
capacities. By Robert Burton. *Philadelphia: Robert Bell.* 1777.

CATALOGUE of Books to be Sold at Auction by Robert Bell December 18th, 19th and 20th. *Philadelphia: Robert Bell.* 1777.

𝕮𝕬𝕿𝕰𝕮𝕳𝕵𝕾𝕸𝖀𝕾, ober Kurzer Unterricht Chriſtlicher Lehre, wie berſelbe in benen Reformirten Kirchen unb Schulen ber Churfürſtlichen Pfalz, auch anberwärts getrieben wirb, mit Zeugniſſen ber Heiligen Schrift erflärt unb beſtätigt. *Philadelphia: Steiner und Cist.* 1777. 3531

𝕮𝕬𝕿𝕰𝕮𝕳𝕵𝕾𝕸𝖀𝕾. Der Kleine | Catechismus | bes ſel. | Dr. Martin Luthers, | nebſt | ben gewöhnlichen Morgen= Tiſch= unb | Abenb= Gebätern. | Wobey | Die Orbnung bes Heils in einem | Liebe, in furzen Säßen, in Frag | unb Antwort, unb in | einer Tabelle, | wie auch | ber Inhalt ber Heiligen Schrift | in Verſen, | hinzugefüget. | Zum Gebrauch ber Jugenb. | Nebſt einem | Anhang ber ſieben Buß= | Pſalmen, einem geiſtlichen Lieb, | unb bas Einmals=Eins. | *Germantown,* | *Gedruckt und zu finden bey Christoph Saur, jun.* | *und Peter Saur,* 1777. | 24mo. pp. (4), 140 +. H. S. P. 3532

CHAD'S Ford, September 11, 1777. 5 O'Clock, P.M. | *Phila-delphia, Printed by John Dunlap.* [1777.] | Folio, 1 leaf. 3533

Letters from Robert H. Harrison and General Washington to John Hancock, announcing the loss of the battle of Brandywine.

COLMAN, (G.) and D. GARRICK. The Clandestine Marriage. By George Colman and David Garrick. *Philadelphia: Robert Bell.* 1777. 3534

THE | CONSTITUTION | of the | Common-Wealth | of | Pennsylvania, | as established by the | General Convention | Elected for that Purpose, | And held at Philadelphia, | July 15th, 1776, | And continued by Adjournments | to September 28, 1776. | *Philadelphia:* | *Printed by John Dunlap, in Market-Street.* | M,DCC,LXXVII. | 12mo. pp. (6), 3–18. H. S. P. 3535

CONTINENTAL NAVY BOARD. 3536

Robert Aitken's Ledger contains the following charges against the Board:
Feb. 17. 300 Copies of an Advertisement for Seamen.
Feb. 26. 250 Copies of Letters and Orders for Continental Vessels.
April 1. 150 Copies of a Resolve of the Marine Committee.

April 12. 150 Copies of the Rules and Regulations.

Aug. 11. 100 copies of a Quarto Advertisement for the encouragement of the Navy in the River.

CROXALL. (S.) The Fables of Æsop and others, translated into English; with instructive applications. By Samuel Croxall, D.D. *Philadelphia: Robert Aitken.* **1777.**   3537

" This is the first edition of Croxall's Æsop's Fables printed in America. It contains 196 fables, and a neat engraving before every fable." Pa. Packet, May 13, 1777.

DAY and Night | Signals; | for the | Fleet | Belonging to the State of | Pennsylvania: | Under the Command of | — Esquire. | Published by Order of the Navy Board. | *Philadelphia:* | *Printed by William and Thomas Bradford, at the* | *London Coffee-House.* | M.DCC.LXXVII. | Sq. 8vo. 17 leaves.   H. S. P.   3538

The day signals, painted by hand, are given in the margins of leaves 2–14.

A DESCRIPTION of the Attack on Fort Sullivan, in a Letter from Sir Peter Parker to Mr. Stephens, Secretary of the Admiralty, and an extract of a Letter from Lieut. Gen. Clinton to Lord George Germaine, containing an account of the proceedings of the British fleet and army, before and after their Defeat at Sullivan's Island. *Philadelphia: Daniel Humphreys.* 1777.   3539

This was annexed " to A Plan of the Attack. Engraved from the original printed in London."

DOBBS. (F.) The | Irish Chief; | or, | Patriot King. | A new | Tragedy. | Performed at the Theatre in Smock-Alley, | Dublin. | Written by Francis Dobbs. | *Philadelphia:* | *Printed and Sold by Robert Bell, in Third-Street.* | MDCCLXXVII. | 8vo. pp. 58, (2).

DODSLEY. (R.) The | Blind Beggar | of | Bethnal Green. | [Cut.] | A Dramatic Performance : | With several Instructive and Entertaining Pieces. | By Robert Dodsley, Author of the Original Fables. | *Philadelphia:* | *Printed and Sold by Robert Bell, in Third-Street.* | MDCCLXXVII. | 8vo. pp. 108.   H. S. P.   3541

Collation : Half-title, 1 leaf; Title, 1 leaf; Dedication, 1 page; Persons, 1 page; The Blind Beggar, pp. 7–26; The King and the Priest, pp. 27–35; Poems and

Essays, pp. 37–76; Pleasure the Best Religion, pp. 77–86; Epistle to Mr. Pope, pp. 87–90; A Matrimonial History, pp. 91–108.

DODSLEY. Select Fables | of | Æsop | And other Fabulists. | In Three Books. | Containing, | I. Fables from the Antients. | II. Fables from the Moderns. | III. Original Fables newly Invented. | By Robert Dodsley. | . . . | . . . | . . . | . . . | . . . | . . . | . . . . | *Philadelphia:* | *Printed and Sold by Robert Bell, in Third-Street.* | MDCCLXXVII. | 8vo. Half-title, 1 leaf; pp. 371, (1).   L. C. P.   3542

THE | EPISTLE | from the | Yearly-Meeting | in | London, | Held by Adjournments, from the 19th of the Fifth Month 1777, | to the 24th of the same, inclusive. | To the Quarterly and Monthly Meetings of Friends in Great- | Britain, Ireland, and elsewhere. | [*Philadelphia:* 1777.] Folio, pp. 4.   F.   3543

Contains also the Epistle "To Friends at their Yearly Meeting at Philadelphia, for Pennsylvania and New-Jersey."

THE FARMERS and others | Are desired and required to bring in and deliver at His | Majesty's Magazines in this City, what Cattle, Sheep, | and Forage they can spare, for which they will be paid at the | following Rates— | *Philadelphia, Printed by James Humphreys, Junr.* [1777.] | 4to. 1 leaf.   L. C. P.   3544

Dated "Commissary General's Office, Philadelphia, Oct. 10."

FATHER Abraham's | Pocket Almanack, | For the Year 1778; | Being the Third Year of the Indepen | dence of America. | Fitted to the Use of Pennsylvania and the | Neighbouring States. | Containing | (Besides a Number of useful Lists, &c.) | The Articles of Confederation | and Perpetual Union | Between the States of America, | As proposed by Congress to the Legisla- | tures of the different States. | *Lancaster:* | *Printed by John Dunlap,* | *In Queen-Street.* [1777.] | Sm. 16mo. pp. (32).   H. S. P.   3545

FIVE or Six Hundred | Blankets | Are Wanted for the Troops. | . . . | . . . | . . . . | [*Philadelphia:* 1777.] 4to. 1 leaf.   3546

Dated "Philadelphia, October 31, 1777."

FRANKLIN. (B.) La Science du bonhomme Richard, ou moyen facile de payer les impôts. Par Benjamin Franklin, traduit de l'anglais par Quétant et Lecuy. *A Philadelphie: [Paris.]* 1777.

FRESH Important Intelligence, | Just arrived from the Northern Army. | *Lancaster, Printed by Francis Bailey.* [1777.] | Folio, pp. (2). A. P. S. 3548

<small>Dated "Sept. 23, 1777."</small>

GENERAL Orders. | Head-Quarters, Morris Town, January 22, 1777. | *Philadelphia: Printed by William and Thomas Bradford.* [1777.] | Folio, 1 leaf. L. C. P. 3549

GENERAL Orders. | Philadelphia, April 11. 1777. | [*Philadelphia: Robert Aitken.* 1777.] Folio, 1 leaf. L. C. P. 3550

<small>Aitken, in his Ledger, on April 11, 1777, charges Major Lewis Nichola for printing 150 General Orders in Folio, and on April 14 for printing 100 General Orders, signed by Schuyler, in quarto, and on April 16 for printing 100 General Orders, signed by Nichola, in quarto.</small>

GENERAL Return of Philadelphia Troops. *Philadelphia: Robert Aitken.* 1777. 3551

<small>Aitken, in his Ledger, on June 2, 1777, charges Major Lewis Nichola for printing 600 copies in folio.</small>

GESANG-BUCH. Vollständiges | Marburger | Gesangbuch, | zur Uebung der Gottseligkeit, | in 680 christlichen und trostreichen | Psalmen und Gesängen | Hrn. D. Martin Luthers, | und andrer Gottseliger Lehrer. | Ordentlich in XII. Theile verfasset. | Auch mit nöthigen Registern und einer Verzeichniß | versehen, unter welche Tittel die im Anhang befind= | lichen Lieder gehörig: | Auch zur Beförderung | des so Kirchen= als Privat = Gottesdienstes, | Mit erbaulichen | Morgen= Abend= Buß= Beicht= und | Communion = Gebätlein vermehret. | Fünfte und vermehrte Auflage. | *Germantown: | Gedruckt und zu finden bey Christoph Saur,* 1777. | 16mo. pp. (14), 522, (16), 14, 56. H. S. P. 3552

GRANDMAISON. (— de) A Treatise | on the | Military Service, | of | Light Horse, | and | Light Infantry, | In the Field, and in fortified Places. | By Major General De Grandmaison, | Formerly a Captain, with the Rank of Lieutenant | Colonel of Cavalry, in the·Voluntiers of Flanders. | Translated from the French, by Major Lewis Nichola. | *Philadelphia:* | *Printed and Sold by Robert Bell, in Third Street.* | MDCCLXXVII. | 8vo.   H. S. P.   3553

Collation : Half-title and Advertisement, pp. (2) ; Title, 1 leaf; Dedication, &c., pp. (2); Contents and Advertisement, pp. (2); text, pp. 5–228.

GLORIOUS | Authentic Intelligence. | October 21, 1777. | *Lancaster, Printed by Francis Bailey.* [1777.] | Folio, pp. (2).   3554

Announcement of Burgoyne's surrender.

HASELDEN. (T.) The Seaman's Daily Assistant. *Philadelphia : Joseph Crukshank.* 1777.   3555

HINTS and Instructions concerning the Collecting and Levying of the | Money paid to Substitutes in the Militia of Pennsylvania. | [*Philadelphia:* 1777 ?] 4to. 1 leaf.   L. C. P.   3556

HIS Excellency the | Commander in Chief | Having been pleased to appoint Mr. Francis | Gilbert, and Mr. John Henderson, | Wardens for the Port of Philadelphia. | All Masters of Vessells and Others concerned | are hereby ordered to obey them as such. | [*Philadelphia:* 1777.] 4to. 1 leaf.   L. C. P.   3557

Dated " 4th December, 1777."

DER | HOCH = Deutsch= | Americanische | Calender, | Auf das Jahr | . . . | . . . | 1778. | . . . | . . . | . . . | . . . | . . . | . . . | . . . | . . . | . . . | . . . | . . . | . . . | . . . . | Zum vierzigsten mal heraus gegeben. | *Germantown: Gedruckt und zu finden bey Christoph Saur, jun. und Peter Saur.* | . . . | . . . [1777.] | Sq. 8vo. pp. (48).

HOME. ([John]) Alonzo | and | Ormisinda. | A new | Tragedy | In Five Acts. | As it is performed at the | Theatre-Royal, in Drury-Lane. | Written by Mr. Home, | Author of the Tragedy of Douglas. | . . . | . . . . | *Philadelphia:* | *Printed, and Sold, by Robert Bell, in Third-Street.* | MDCCLXXVII. | 8vo. pp. 67, (2).   3559

HURT. (J.) The Love of our Country. | A Sermon, | preached before | The Virginia Troops | in New-Jersey. | By John Hurt,

Chaplain. | *Philadelphia: | Printed and Sold by Styner and Cist, in Second-street, | six Doors above Arch-street.* | MDCCLXXVII. | 8vo. pp. 23.   L. C. P.   3560

IN Congress, | April 11, 1777. | [*Philadelphia :*] *Printed by John Dunlap.* [1777.] | Folio, 1 leaf.   L. C. P.   3561

Appointing a " Committee . . . to make diligent enquiry respecting the truth of information just given to Congress, of a quantity of provisions being laid up in . . . Philadelphia." With the resolutions of the State Board of War on the same subject.

IN Congress, | April 14, 1777. | [*Philadelphia :*] *Printed by John Dunlap.* [1777.] | Folio, 1 leaf.   H. S. P.   3562

Appointing a Committee of three to confer with the authorities of Pennsylvania on the threatened invasion of that State, followed by the Report of the Committee, on the following day.

IN Council. | Philadelphia, April 9, 1777. | To the People of Pennsylvania. | [*Philadelphia :*] *Printed by Styner and Cist, in Second-street, near Arch-street.* [1777.] | Folio, 1 leaf.   H. S. P.   3563

An address on a rumored movement of the Royal troops towards Philadelphia.

IN Council. | Philadelphia, July 9, 1777. | [*Philadelphia : John Dunlap.* 1777.] Folio, 1 leaf.   L. C. P.   3564

Circular letter to the County Magistrates requesting a return of names of persons qualified " to take care of the Billeting and providing for the poor People who shall be sent out of Philadelphia, and to take an account of all the Flour, Wheat, Grain or other Stores, that they may find lodged in any Mills or Store-houses, within twenty miles westward of the Delaware."

IN Council. | Philadelphia, 28th July, 1777. | [*Philadelphia : John Dunlap.* 1777.] Folio, 1 leaf.   L. C. P.   3565

Circular letter to the Lieutenants of the Counties. Ordering the Militia to be called out on the expected arrival of the British in Delaware Bay.

IN Council. | Philadelphia, September 4, 1777. | [*Philadelphia :*] *Printed by Styner and Cist, in Second-street, near Arch-street.* [1777.] | 4to. 1 leaf.   L. C. P.   3566

A resolution that arms or blankets, taken into the field, by the Militia, and captured or unavoidably lost, shall be paid for by the State.

IN Council of Safety. | Philadelphia, January 22, 1777. | [*Philadelphia: Henry Miller.* 1777.] Folio, 1 leaf.   L. C. P.   3567

" Resolved that Colonel Melcher, Barrack-Master General, be directed to quarter the Militia upon the Non-Associators in this City." In English and German.

IN Council of Safety. March 11, 1777. *Philadelphia: Robert Aitken.* 1777. Folio.   3568

Aitken, on March 13, 1777, charges the Council for printing 150 copies of their orders respecting the cleaning of Houses in which troops were quartered. See Colonial Records, xi. 144.

IN General Assembly. | Thursday, June 5th, 1777. | [*Philadelphia:*] *Printed by Styner and Cist, in Second-street.* [1777.] | 8vo. pp. 8.   H. S. P.   3569

A Bill entitled " A Supplement to the Act, entituled, An Act for amending the several Acts for electing Members of Assembly," " printed for the Consideration of the Public."

IN General Assembly, | Friday, June 6, 1777. | [*Philadelphia:*] *Printed by John Dunlap.* [1777.] | Folio, pp. 2.   H. S. P.   3570

A Bill entitled " A Supplement to the Act, entitled An Act directing the mode of Collecting the Fines imposed on persons who do not meet and exercise, in order to learn the Art Military, according to the Resolves of the late Assembly of Pennsylvania," " printed for public consideration."

IN General Assembly, | For the State of Pennsylvania. | Thursday, June 12, 1777. P.M. | [*Philadelphia:*] *Printed by John Dunlap.* [1777.] | 4to. 1 leaf.   L. C. P.   3571

" Resolved, That this House will recommend it to the Inhabitants of this Common-Wealth, to give their Sense of the present Dispute respecting the calling of a Convention," to amend the Constitution.

IN General Assembly | For the Commonwealth of Pennsylvania. | Tuesday, June 17, 1777. P.M. | *Philadelphia: Printed by John Dunlap.* [1777.] | Folio, 1 leaf.   L. C. P.   3572

A. Bill entitled " An Act to empower the Trustees of the General Loan-Office of the State of Pennsylvania to pay out of the monies which remain in their hands, and cannot be again lent out for want of borrowers, unto the Treasurer of this State, any Sum not exceeding Thirty Thousand Pounds, with Directions to replace the same," " printed for public consideration."

IN General Assembly. | Monday, September 15, 1777. A.M. | *Philadelphia: Printed by Styner and Cist, in Second-street, near Arch-street.* [1777.] | Folio, 1 leaf.   L. C. P.   3573

A Bill entitled " An Act to impower the Supreme Executive Council of this Commonwealth, to provide for the Security thereof in special Cases where no Provision is already made by Law," " printed for public consideration."

IN Pursuance of a Writ to me | directed, ... | [*Philadelphia: Henry Miller.* 1777.] Folio, 1 leaf.   L. C. P.   3574

Notice of a special election to elect representatives for Philadelphia County, in place of John Dickinson, George Gray, Thomas Potts, and Isaac Hughes, who had not taken their seats. Printed in English and German in parallel columns.

JOURNALS | and | Proceedings | of the | General Assembly | Of the Common-Wealth of | Pennsylvania. | *Philadelphia:* | *Printed by John Dunlap, in Market-Street.* | M,DCC,LXXVII. | Folio, pp. 100.   L. C. P.   3575

Issued in eight parts, of which the last, pp. 83–100, were printed at Lancaster by Francis Bailey. Some of these parts are headed " Minutes | of the | General Assembly," | &c.

JOURNALS | of | Congress. | Containing the | Proceedings | From Sept. 5. 1774. to Jan. 1. 1776. | Published by order of Congress. | Volume I. | *Philadelphia:* | *Printed and sold by R. Aitken, Bookseller, Front-street,* | M.DCC.LXXVII. | 8vo. Title and Authorization, pp. (2); text, pp. 1–310; Index, pp. (12).   3576

JOURNALS | of | Congress. | Containing the | Proceedings | | In the Year, 1776. | Published by order of Congress. | Volume II. | *Philadelphia:* | *Printed and sold by R. Aitken, Bookseller, Front-street.* | M.DCC.LXXVII. | 8vo. Title and Authorization, pp. (2); text, pp. 1–513; Index, pp. (22).   H. S. P.   3577

Aitken was ordered to print this edition in April, 1776. (See No. 3409, *supra.*) There were to have been 700 sets, but Aitken says, " I printed 800 copies of the second volumes, 50 were carried to Lancaster, and committed to the care of Mr. Dunlap. I find of the 750 other copies only 532 were delivered. I allow 218 copies as they have been lost or embessled."

KELLY. (H.) The | Romance | of | An Hour: | A new | Comedy, | Of Two Acts. | As it is performed, with universal Applause, at the | Theatre-Royal, Covent-Garden. | Written by | Hugh Kelly, Esq; of the Middle Temple | Author of False Delicacy, a Word to the Wise, | Clementina, The School for Wives, &c. &c. | . . . | . . . | . . . | . . . . | *Philadelphia:* | *Printed and Sold by Robert Bell, in Third-Street.* | MDCCLXXVII. | 8vo.   3578

Collation : Half-title, 1 leaf; Title, 1 leaf; Advertisement, pp. (2); Prologue, 1 leaf; Dramatis Personæ, 1 leaf; text, pp. 11–49; Epilogue, pp. (2); List of Books, pp. (5).

LAWS | enacted in a | General Assembly | of the | Representatives | of the | Freemen | of the | Common-Wealth | of | Pennsylvania. | Begun and held at Philadelphia the Twenty-eighth day of November, | A.D. One Thousand Seven Hundred and Seventy-six, and continued by adjournments | to the Twenty-first day of March, A.D. One Thousand Seven Hundred and | Seventy-seven. | *Philadelphia:* | *Printed by John Dunlap, in Market-Street.* | M,DCC,LXXVII. | Folio, pp. 48, 1 leaf.   H. S. P.   3579

LAWS | enacted in a | General Assembly | of the | Representatives | of the | Freemen | of the | Common-Wealth | of | Pennsylvania. | Begun and held at Philadelphia the Tenth day of May, | A.D. One Thousand, Seven Hundred and Seventy Seven, and | continued by adjournment to Lancaster, until the Fourteenth | day of October, A.D. One Thousand, Seven Hundred and | Seventy Seven. | *Lancaster:* | *Printed by Francis Bailey, in Kings-Street.* | M,DCC,LXXVII. | Folio, Title, 1 leaf; pp. 51–65, 1 leaf.

MARSHALL. (—) Comedy in Embryo. By Miss Marshall. *Philadelphia: Robert Bell.* 1777.   3581

MILTON. (J.) Paradise Lost. | A | Poem, | in | Twelve Books. | The Author | John Milton. | With the Life of Milton. | By Thomas Newton, D.D. | . . . | . . . | . . . | . . . | . . . | . . . | . . . | . . . | . . . . | *Philadelphia:* | *Printed by Robert Bell, in Third-Street.* | MDCCLXXVII. | 8vo.   3582

Collation : Half-title and List of Books, pp. (2) ; 1 plate ; Title, 1 leaf ; Tonson to Lord Sommers, 1 page ; Marvel's Poem, pp. (2) ; The Verse, 1 page ; Arguments of the 12 books, pp. 9–15; text of Books I. to XI., pp. 1–328. Vol. II. Half-title, 1 leaf; Title, 1 leaf; The Stationer to the Reader, from the first edition, 1 page; "Contents of the second Volume," 1 page; Half-title to Poems, 1 leaf; Book XII., Paradise Lost, pp. 329–350; Index, pp. (32); Life of Milton, pp. 383–444; L'Allegro, Il Penseroso, Lycidas, Sonnets and Poems, pp. 445–474; Paradise Regained, pp. 475–545; Samson Agonistes, pp. 547–603; Comus, pp. 605–640. The title to the second volume is as follows: Paradise Regain'd. | A | Poem, | in | Four Books. | To which are added, | Samson Agonistes: | And | Poems on Several Occasions. | The Author | John Milton. | With the Life of the Author. | By Thomas Newton. D.D. | *Philadelphia:* | *Printed and Sold by Robert Bell, in Third-Street.* | MDCCLXXVII. | The collation given of the second corresponds with the printed "Contents of the second Volume." The portrait of Milton is a very good specimen of John Norman's work. This is the first American edition of Milton's Poems.

DER NEUSTE, Verbeſſert= und Zuverlaßige Americaniſche Cal=
ender auf das 1778ſte Jahr Chriſti. *Philadelphia: Henrich Miller.*
1777. 3583

THE NEW England Primer. *Philadelphia: Robert Aitken.*
1777. 3584

THE NEW | Testament | Of our Lord and Saviour | Jesus Christ: | Newly Translated out of the | Original Greek; | And with the former | Translations | Diligently compared and revised. | Appointed to be read in Churches. | *Philadelphia:* | *Printed and Sold by* | *R. Aitken,* | *Printer & Bookseller,* | *Front-Street.* | 1777. | 12mo. pp. 353, (1). H. S. P. 3585

The first edition of the New Testament printed in English in America. The imprint is in a rude type-metal cut.

NEW-YEAR Verses of the Carriers of the Pennsylvania Evening Post. *Philadelphia: B. Towne.* 1777. 3586

All the newspapers suspended publication on the approach of the British in November, 1776; the Evening Post was, however, not only the last to stop, but was the first to resume. It is possible that some of the other papers issued "New-Year Verses."

NEW-YEAR Verses of the Carriers of the Pennsylvania Packet. *Philadelphia: John Dunlap.* 1777. 3587

NEW YORK. The | Constitution | of the | State | of | New-York. | *Philadelphia:* | *Printed and Sold by Styner and Cist, in*

Second-street, | *six Doors above Arch-street.* | MDCCLXXVII. | 8vo. pp. 32.   L. C. P.   3588

NEWS. | *Lancaster, Printed by Francis Bailey.* [1777.] | Folio, pp. (2).   A. P. S.   3589

Probably issued in lieu of a regular newspaper. Dated "Nov. 1, 1777."

NO Person whatever is to presume to remove | any Merchandise or Goods of any Kind out | of the City, without first obtaining Leave . . . | . . . | . . . | . . . . | [*Philadelphia: James Humphreys, junr.* 1777.] 4to. 1 leaf.   L. C. P.   3590

Dated "Philadelphia, October 1, 1777."

NOTICE is hereby Given, | To all Seamen and Others, | Belonging to any of His Majesty's Ships | . . . now in or about this Town, | to give themselves up to the Commanding Officer | of the Delaware Frigate; . . . | . . . | . . . | . . . . | *Philadelphia, Printed by James Humphreys, Junr.* [1777.] | 4to. 1 leaf.   L. C. P.   3591

Dated "Philadelphia, October 8, 1777," and signed "J. Watt."

NOTICE is hereby Given, | To all Seamen and able-bodied | Landsmen, | Desirous to serve the King . . . | . . . to repair to the . . . | . . . Delaware Frigate, . . . | . . . | . . . | . . . | . . . | . . . | . . . . | *Philadelphia, Printed by James Humphreys, Junr.* [1777.] | 4to. 1 leaf.   L. C. P.   3592

Dated "Philadelphia, October 10, 1777," and signed "J. Watt, Commanding Officer."

NOTICE | Is Hereby Given, | To the Merchants, Adventurers, and Masters of | Vessels, that a Report of their Cargoes is to be | made to the Quarter-Master-General, or his Deputies, | before they land any Part of it: . . . | . . . | . . . | . . . . | *Philadelphia: Printed by James Humphreys, Junr.* | *In Market-street, between Front and Second-streets.* [1777.] | 4to. 1 leaf.   L. C. P.   3593

Dated "Philadelphia, November 24, 1777."

OBSERVATIONS on the Slaves and the Indented Servants, inlisted | in the Army, and in the Navy of the United States. | [*Philadelphia:*] *Printed by Styner and Cist, in Second-Street, near Arch-Street.* [1777.] | Folio, pp. (2).   H. S. P.   3594

[PAINE. (Thomas)] The | American Crisis. | Number II. | By the Author of | Common Sense. | *Philadelphia :* | *Printed and Sold by Styner and Cist, in* | *Sceond-strèet, six doors above Arch-street.* | . . . | . . . . | [1777.] | 8vo. pp. 9–24. + Number III. | [*Ibid.*] 8vo. pp. (2), 27–56. + Number IV. [*Ibid.*] *Where it may be had Gratis. Also at the Coffee-House.* | 8vo. pp. 57–60.   H. S. P.   3595

THE | PENNSYLVANIA | Evening Post. | MDCCLXXVII. | Volume III. | *Philadelphia :* | *Printed by Benjamin Towne, in Front-Street.* [1777.] | 4to. pp. (2), 606.   3596

THE PENNSYLVANIA Gazette.   H. S. P.   3597

Numbers 2502 (Feb. 5, 1777) to 2533 (Sept. 10, 1777), four pages each. Title and imprint as in No. 2913, *supra.* The publication of the paper was suspended on the approach of the British, and the press and materials removed to York, where the paper was printed from Jan. to June, 1778. These papers were not numbered. Publication was again suspended from June, 1778, to Jan., 1779, when the regular issue of the paper was resumed, and numbered in continuation from Sept. 10, 1777.

THE PENNSYLVANIA Journal.   3598

Numbers 1774 (Jan. 29, 1777) to 1807 (Sept. 17, 1777), four pages each. Title and imprint as in No. 2317, *supra.* The publication of the paper was suspended from Sept. 17, 1777, until about Dec. 23, 1778.

October 10, 1777. Number XCVIII. | THE | PENNSYL-VANIA : Ledger : | Or : the | Weekly : Advertiser. | Friday : October 10, 1777.   L. C. P.   3599

Numbers XCVIII. (Oct. 10, 1777) to CXIV. (Dec. 31, 1777), four pages each, except Numbers 98, 107, 109, 111, and 113, which contain only two pages. Imprint as in No. 3255, *supra*, until No. 104, when it was changed to the form given in No. 3769, *infra.* In No. 106 the title was also changed to the form there given, and with this issue the paper began to appear twice a week.

THE PENNSYLVANIA Packet.   3600

Numbers 269 (Jan. 4, 1777) to 304 (Sept. 9, 1777), four pages each, except Nos. 269 to 272, which are only two pages. The publication of the paper was resumed at Lancaster on Nov. 29, and continued weekly. These issues were not numbered. Title and imprint of the papers printed in Philadelphia as in No. 3446, *supra;* of those printed at Lancaster as in No. 3770, *infra.*

PENNSYLVANIA War-Office, April 13th, 1777. | [*Philadelphia:*] *Printed by John Dunlap.* [1777.] | Folio, 1 leaf. H. S. P. 3601

A letter from Henry Fisher, of Lewes, giving an account of the movement of British men-of-war in Delaware Bay, published by the Board of War.

PENNSYLVANIA War-Office, | Philadelphia, April 17th, 1777. | [*Philadelphia:*] *Printed by John Dunlap.* [1777.] | Folio, 1 leaf.   L. C. P. 3602

Appointing a committee of fifty to remove " all the Provisions and other Stores now in this City," &c.

PENNSYLVANIA War-Office, | Philadelphia, May 2d, 1777. | *Philadelphia: Printed by John Dunlap.* [1777.] | Folio, 1 leaf. 3603

Resolutions ordering 4000 blankets to be collected; fixing the quota to be supplied by the city of Philadelphia and the several counties, and appointing commissioners to carry out the resolutions.

THE | PHILADELPHIA | Almanack | For the Year 1778 | Calculated | For Pennsylvania and the | neighbouring Parts | To which is Added some useful Tables. | [Engraved on Copper by J. Norman. 1777 ?] 24mo. pp. 20. Plan of the City, 1 leaf folded.   H. S. P. 3604

THE | PLEA | of the | Colonies | On the Charges brought against them by | Lord Mansfield, and Others, | in a letter to | His Lordship. | By a Native of Pennsylvania. | *London, Printed in the Year* MDCCLXXVI. | *Philadelphia:* | *Re-printed and Sold by Robert Bell, in Third-Street.* | MDCCLXXVII. | 8vo. H. S. P. 3605

Collation : Half-title, 1 leaf; 1 plate ; Explanation, 1 leaf; Title, 1 leaf; Preface, pp. (2) ; text, pp. 1–38 ; List of Books, pp. (2). Reprinted from the second London edition. The first appeared in 1775.

POOR Will's Almanac for 1778. *Philadelphia: Joseph Crukshank.* 1777. 3606

POOR Will's | Pocket Almanack, | For the Year 1778 ; | . . . | . . . | . . . | . . . | . . . . | *Philadelphia:* | *Printed and Sold by J. Crukshank,* | *in Market-street, opposite the* | *Butcher's Shambles.* [1777.] | 24mo. pp. (24).   H. S. P. 3607

PRÉSERVATIF contre les mensonges politiques, addressé à l'auteur des observations sur les dangers de la patrie. *A Philadelphie:* [*Genève.*] 1777.   w. 3608

PROCLAMATION. By His Excellency | George Washington, Esq; | General, and Commander in Chief, of all the Forces of the . | United States of America. | Proclamation. | *Philadelphia: Printed by William and Thomas Bradford.* [1777.] | Folio, 1 leaf.   3609

Dated " Head Quarters, Morris Town, January 25th, 1777." Commanding all persons who have taken British protections, certificates, or passports, to surrender the same.

PROCLAMATION. By His Excellency | George Washington, Esquire, | General and Commander in Chief of the Forces | of the United States of America. | . . . | . . . I hereby enjoin and require all Persons | residing within seventy Miles of my Head Quarters to | thresh one Half of their Grain by the 1st Day of February, | and the other Half by the 1st Day of March next ensuing, | . . . | . . . | . . . | . . . | Given under my Hand, at Head Quarters, near | the Valley Forge, in Philadelphia County, this 20th | Day of December, 1777. | G. Washington. | . . . | . . . . | *Lancaster; Printed by John Dunlap.* [1777.] | Folio, 1 leaf. 3610

PROCLAMATION. [*Royal Arms.*] By His Excellency | Sir William Howe, K.B. | General and Commander in Chief, &c. &c. &c. | Proclamation. | *Philadelphia; Printed by James Humphreys, junr.* [1777.] | Folio, 1 leaf.   L. C. P. 3611

Dated " 28th of September, 1777," warning persons who have taken advantage of the proclamation of Aug. 27, offering Security and Protection, not to forfeit their Pretensions by their future conduct.

PROCLAMATION. [*Royal Arms.*] By His Excellency | Sir William Howe, K.B. | General and Commander in Chief, &c. &c. &c. | Proclamation. | [*Philadelphia: James Humphreys, junr.* 1777.] Folio, 1 leaf.   L. C. P. 3612

Dated " 1st of Oct., 1777," requiring all persons to take the Oath of Allegiance to His Majesty before Oct. 25th.

PROCLAMATION. [*Royal Arms.*] By His Excellency | Sir

William Howe, K.B. | General and Commander in Chief, &c. &c. &c. | Proclamation. | [*Philadelphia : James Humphreys, junr.* 1777.] Folio, 1 leaf.   L. C. P.   3613

Dated " the 8th of October, 1777," offering a land bounty to recruits for the Provincial Corps then raising.

PROCLAMATION.   Eine durch Seine Excellenz, Sir William Howe, Ritter | vom Bad, General und Oberbefehlshaber, 2c. 2c. 2c., herausgegebene | Proclamation. | *Philadelphia, gedruckt bey Christoph Saur, junr. und Peter Saur.* [1777.] | Folio, 1 leaf.   L. C. P.   3614

Dated " 8th October, 1777," offering a land bounty to recruits for the Provincial corps then raising.

PROCLAMATION.   By His Excellency | Sir William Howe, K.B. | General and Commander in Chief, &c. &c. &c. | Proclamation. | [*Philadelphia :* 1777.]   Folio, 1 leaf.   L. C. P.   3615

Dated "the 8th of October, 1777," offering free pardon to deserters who surrender themselves before December the 1st.

PROCLAMATION.   [*Royal Arms.*]   By His Excellency | Sir William Howe, K.B. | General and Commander in Chief, &c. &c. &c. | Proclamation. | [*Philadelphia : James Humphreys, junr.* 1777.] Folio, 1 leaf.   L. C. P.   3616

Dated " 7th of November, 1777," exemplary Punishment shall be inflicted on all Persons, who shall be found guilty of taking the Property of others unwarrantably.

PROCLAMATION.   [*Royal Arms.*]   By His Excellency | Sir William Howe, K.B. | General and Commander in Chief, &c. &c. &c. | Proclamation. | [*Philadelphia : James Humphreys, junr.* 1777.] Folio, 1 leaf.   L. C. P.   3617

Dated "the 24th of November, 1777," requiring shipmasters to make oath as to the Quantity and Quality of Liquors imported by them.

PROCLAMATION.   [*Royal Arms.*]   By His Excellency | Sir William Howe, K.B. | General and Commander in Chief, &c. &c. &c. | Proclamation. | [*Philadelphia : Printed by James Humphreys, Junr. | in Market-street, between Front and Second-streets.* [1777.] | Folio, 1 leaf.   L. C. P.   3618

Dated "4th of December, 1777," appointing Joseph Galloway, Superintendent-General.

PROCLAMATION. [*Royal Arms.*] By His Excellency | Sir William Howe, K.B. | General and Commander in Chief, &c. &c. &c. | Proclamation. | [*Philadelphia: James Humphreys, junr.* 1777.] Folio, 1 leaf. L. C. P. 3619

Dated "4th of December, 1777," appointing Joseph Galloway, Superintendent of Imports and Exports in Philadelphia, regulating the manner and restricting the kind of goods to be imported, &c.

PROCLAMATION, [*Royal Arms.*] By His Excellency | Sir William Howe, K.B. | General and Commander in Chief, &c. &c. &c. | Proclamation. | [*Philadelphia: James Humphreys, junr.* 1777.] Folio, 1 leaf. L. C. P. 3620

"For the Suppression of Vice and Immorality," issued December 14, 1777.

PROCLAMATION. [*Royal Arms.*] By His Excellency | Sir William Howe, K.B. | General and Commander in Chief, &c. &c. &c. | Proclamation. | [*Philadelphia: James Humphreys, junr.* 1777.] Folio, 1 leaf. L. C. P. 3621

Dated the "18th of December, 1777." Relating to importation of goods by vessels in His Majesty's service.

PROCLAMATION. By the Supreme Executive Council | of the Common-Wealth of Pennsylvania. | A Proclamation. | [*Philadelphia: Hall and Sellers.* 1777.] Folio, 1 leaf. L. C. P. 3622

Dated "March 7, 1777," recommending the observance of the 3d of April as a Fast Day, &c.

PROCLAMATION. By the Supreme Executive Council | of the Commonwealth of Pennsylvania, | A Proclamation. | *Philadelphia: Printed by Styner and Cist, in Second-street, near Arch-street.* [1777.] | Folio, 1 leaf. L. C. P. 3623

Issued Sept. 10, 1777, on the approach of the British.

PSALTERSPIEL. Das Kleine | Davidiſche | Pſalterſpiel | Der | Kinder Zions, | von Alten und Neuen auserleſenen | Geiſtes=Geſängen,

| Allen wahren Heils=begieri= | gen Säuglingen der Weisheit, | Infon= derheit aber | Denen Gemeinden des Herrn, | zum Dienst und Gebrauch mit Fleiß zu= | sammen getragen | in gegenwärtig=beliebiger Form und Ordnung, | Nebst einem dreyfächen, darzu nützlichen und der | Materien halben nöthigen | Register. | Zum vierten mal ans Licht gegeben. | *Germantown, gedruckt bey Christoph Saur,* 1777. | 16mo. pp. (6), 572, (22 +).   H. S. P.   3624

REGULATIONS, | Under which the Inhabitants may pur- chase the enume- | rated Articles, [viz : Rum, Molasses, Salt, and Medicines.] mentioned in the Proclamation of His | Excellency Sir William Howe, ... | [*Philadelphia:* 1777.] Folio, 1 leaf. 3625

Dated " Philadelphia, December 8, 1777," and signed " Joseph Galloway, Super- intendent General."

THE FOLLOWING REMONSTRANCE, was this Day pre- sented | to the President and Council, by the Hands of their Secretary. | To the President and Council of Pennsylvania. | The Remonstrance of | Israel Pemberton, John Hunt, and Samuel Pleasants, | [*Philadelphia:*] *Printed by Robert Bell, in Third-Street.* | Folio, 1 leaf.   H. S. P.   3626

Dated " 4th. 9th mo. 1777."

THE | RISE | and | Continuance | of the | Substitutes, | in the | Continental Army. | Containing, Extracts | I. From the Journals of Congress. | II. From the Committee of Congress. Appointed to confer | with the President, and Members of the Supreme Executive | Council, of the Common-Wealth of Penn- sylvania, the Board | of War of said State, and the Delegates representing the same | in Congress, concerning the Authority which should be | deemed eligible to be exercised during the recess of the | Council and Assembly. | III. From the Pennsyl- vania War-Office. | IV. From a Declaration of the Rights of Pennsylvania. | V. From the Plan or Frame of Government. | VI. From the Militia Act of Pennsylvania. &c. &c. | With the Opinion of several Eminent Lawyers. | . . . | . . . | . . . | . . . | . . . | . . . . | Published for the Use of all, Who are yet capable of noticing, the | proper discriminations, which will eternally exist between | Right and Wrong. | *Philadelphia :* | *Printed and Sold by Robert Bell, in Third-Street.* | MDCCLXXVII. | 8vo. Title, 1 leaf; Preface, 1 leaf; text, pp. 1–18.   L. C. P.   3627

[RUSH. (Benjamin)] Observations | upon the present | Government | of | Pennsylvania. | In | Four Letters | to the | People of Pennsylvania. | . . . | . . . | . . . | . . . | . . . | . . . | . . . | . . . . | *Philadelphia :* | *Printed and Sold by Styner and Cist, in Second-street,* | *six doors above Arch-street.* MDCCLXXVII. | 8vo. pp. 24.   L. C. P.   3628

> On the last page of some copies are four lines of errata.

SAUNDERS. (R.) A Pocket Almanac for 1778. By Richard Saunders, Phil. *York-Town : Hall and Sellers.* 1777.   3629

SAUNDERS. Poor Richard improved : Being an Almanac for 1778. By Richard Saunders, Philom. *York-Town : Hall and Sellers.* 1778.   3630

SELECT Essays : | Containing : | The Manner of raising and | dressing Flax, and Hemp. | Also, The whole Method of | Bleaching or Whitening | Linen-Cloth. | Likewise, Observations on | the Management of Cows | and Sheep. | The Manner of raising Rad- | ishes, Turnips, Cabbage | and other such Plants. | And an Enquiry, concerning | the materials that may be | used in making Paper. | With, Valuable Dissertati- | ons on other useful Subjects. | Collected from the Dictionary of Arts and | Sciences, and from various modern Authors. | . . . | . . . | . . . . | *Philadelphia :* | *Printed, by Robert Bell, next Door to* | *St. Paul's Church, in Third-Street, Philadelphia.* | M,DCC,LXXVII. | 8vo.   H. S. P.   3631

> Collation : Half-title, 1 leaf; Title, 1 leaf; Preface and Contents, pp. (2) ; List of Books, pp. (2) ; text, pp. 1–159 ; List of Books, 1 page ; 1 folded plate.

SEVEN | Rational | Sermons, | on the following subjects, | viz. | I. Against Covetousness. | II. On the Vanity of this Life. | III. Against Revenge. | IV. Of Mirth and Grief. | V. The Cruelty of Slandering in- | nocent and defenceless Women. | VI. The Duty of Children. | VII. Advantages of Education. | Written in England, by a Lady, the Translatress of Four | Select Tales from Marmontel. | . . . | . . . | . . . . | *Philadelphia :* | *Printed by Robert Bell,* *in Third-Street.* | MDCCLXXVII. | 8vo. pp. 77, (1).   H. S. P.   3632

SHARP. (A.)   Der Ganz Neue Verbesserte Nord = Americanische Calender, auf das 1778ste Jahr Christi.   Zum Drittenmal herausgegeben und verfertiget von Anthony Sharp, Philom.   *Lancaster: Francis Bailey.* 1777.   3633

A second edition was advertised in *Das Pennsylvanische Zeitungs-Blatt,* Feb. 11, 1778.

SHARP. (A.)   The Lancaster Almanac for 1778.   By Anthony Sharp, Philom.   *Lancaster : Francis Bailey.*   1777.   3634

SHARP. (A.)   The | Lancaster | Pocket Almanack, | For the Year 1778. | Being the Third Year of American | Independency. | Fitted to the use of Pennsylvania, and the neighbouring States. | Containing | A | variety of useful Lists and | Tables. | By Anthony Sharp, Philom. | *Lancaster :* | *Printed by Francis Bailey,* | *who is removed from the North to* | *the South-Side of King-Street,* | *a few doors below the Market.*   [1777.] | 24mo. pp. (24).   H. S. P.   3635

STANDING Orders for the Garrison | of Philadelphia. | [*Philadelphia : Robert Aitken.*   1777.]   Folio, 1 leaf.   3636

Signed by Lewis Nichola, Town Major, and dated by Du Simitiere May 31, 1777. Aitken, on June 2, charges Nichola £6 for printing 600 copies. According to his Ledger for this and other work done for Nichola, amounting to £52.13.11, he was never paid for.

STEVENS. (G. A.)   Songs, Comic, Satyrical, and Sentimental. By George Alexander Stevens.   *Philadelphia : Robert Bell.*   1777.

Advertised in the Pa. Ledger, Nov. 26, 1777.   Fine paper copies were sold for two dollars.   Common paper ones at fifty cents less.

A TESTIMONY given forth from our Yearly-Meeting, | held at Philadelphia, for Pennsylvania and New-Jersey, by Ad- | journments, from the 29th Day of the Ninth Month to the 4th | of the Tenth Month, inclusive, 1777. | [*Philadelphia :* 1777.] | 4to. 1 leaf.   L. C. P.   3638

A disavowal of the " Spank-Town Yearly-Meeting" address.

TEUCRO duce nil desperandum. | First Battalion of Pennsyl-vania Loyalists. | . . . | . . . | All Intrepid Able-bodied | Heroes, | Who are willing to serve His Majesty . . . | . . . | . . . | . . . have now . . . | . . . an Opportunity of manifesting their Spirit, . . . | . . . | . . . | . . . | . . . | . . . | . . . | . . . | . . . . | Each Volunteer will receive, . . . a Bounty . . . | . . . | . . . | . . . | . . . | . . . | . . . . | [*Philadelphia:* 1777.]   Folio, 1 leaf.   3639

THOMSON. (J.) The | Seasons: | Containing, | Spring. Au-tumn. | Summer. Winter. | With | Poems on Several Occasions. | By | James Thomson. | To which are added, | An Account of the Life and Writings of the Author. | . . . | . . . | . . . | . . . | . . . | . . . | . . . . | *Philadelphia:* | *Printed and Sold by Robert Bell, in Third-Street,* | *Next Door to St. Paul's Church.* | MDCCLXXVII. | 8vo. Half-title, 1 leaf; Title, 1 leaf; Dedication, 1 leaf; Contents, 1 leaf; text, pp. 1–251, (3).   3640

TO the Congress. | The Remonstrance of the Subscribers, | Citizens of Philadelphia. | [*Philadelphia :*] *Printed by Robert Bell, in Third Street.* [1777.] | Folio, 1 leaf.   H. S. P.   3641

Dated "5th, 9 mo. 1777."

TO the Freemen of the Common Wealth of | Pennsylvania. | [*Philadelphia:* 1777.]   4to. 1 leaf.   L. C. P.   3642

Call for a meeting of persons who have procured substitutes to serve in the Army, dated " Philadelphia, June 18th, 1777."

TO the | Inhabitants of Pennsylvania. | [*Philadelphia: Robert Bell.* 1777.]   Folio, pp. 2.   L. C. P.   3643

Dated "Mason's Lodge, Sept. 9, 1777." A copy of the Resolution of the Council ordering the Quakers and other persons confined in the Free-Mason's Lodge, to be sent to Virginia, followed by " The Remonstrance and Protest of the Subscribers."

TO the President and Council of Pennsylvania. | The Remon-strance of the Subscribers, Freemen, | and Inhabitants of the City of Philadelphia, now confined in | the Free-Mason's Lodge. | [*Philadelphia :*] *Printed by Robert Bell, in Third-Street.* | Folio, pp. (2).   H. S. P.   3644

Dated " September 5th, 1777."

TO the Public. | *Philadelphia : Printed by John Dunlap.* [1777.] | Folio, 1 leaf.   L. C. P. 3645

Dated "Pennsylvania War-Office, May 2d, 1777." Names of persons appointed throughout the State to make an assessment of Blankets for the use of the Troops.

A TORY Medley. | [*Philadelphia :* 1777.] Folio, 1 leaf. 3646

By Francis Hopkinson ? The characters are "The Broker," William Smith ; "The Printer," James Rivington ; and "The Quaker," Samuel Rhodes Fisher. It consists of four songs and a "Medley."

A | TREATY | and | Convention, | for the | Sick, Wounded, and Prisoners of War, | of the | Land Forces of His Majesty | The King of Great-Britain, | and of | His Most Christian Majesty. | *Philadelphia :* | *Printed by John Dunlap.* [1777.] | Sm. 8vo. pp. 16.

WANTED, | A Number of Hands to | Cut Wood | During the Winter Season, for the Use of the | Army. | . . . | . . . | . . . | . . . . | [*Philadelphia :* 1777.] 4to. 1 leaf.   L. C. P. 3648

Dated "Philadelphia, November 1, 1777."

WASHINGTON. (G.) An intercepted original Letter | from General Washington to | his Lady, in the Year 1776. | [*Philadelphia :* 1777.] Folio, 1 leaf.   L. C. P. 3649

Du Simitiere says, "Spurious : wrote in London by a Mr. Randolph of Virginia."

WATTS. (I.) Horæ Lyricæ: Poems chiefly of the Lyric Kind. In Three Books. By Isaac Watts, D.D. *Philadelphia : Robert Bell.* 1777.   3650

WEATHERWISE. (A.) Father Abraham's | Almanack, | For the Year of our Lord | 1778; | Being the Second after Leap-Year. | . . . | . . . | . . . | . . . | . . . | . . . | . . . | . . . | . . . | . . . | . . . . . . | . . . | . . . | By Abraham Weatherwise, Gent. | . . . | . . . | . . . | . . . | . . . . | *Lancaster :* | *Printed and Sold by John Dunlap, at his* | *Printing-Office, in Queen Street.* [1777.] | Sm. 8vo. pp. 24.   H. S. P. 3651

YOUNG. (E.) The | Complaint; | Or | Night-Thoughts | on

| Life, Death, and Immortality. | By the Reverend | Edward Young, LL.D. | To which are added, | A Poetical Paraphrase | on part of the Book of Job; | and his | Poem on the Last Day. | . . . | . . . | . . . | . . . | . . . | . . . | . . . . | *Philadelphia:* | *Printed and Sold by Robert Bell, in Third-Street.* | MDCCLXXVII. | 8vo.

Collation: Half-title, 1 leaf; Title, 1 leaf; Preface, 1 leaf; A Panegyric, &c., pp. (2); Night-Thoughts, pp. 1–295; Paraphrase, pp. 297–309; Notes, pp. 311–316; Poem on the Last Day, Title, 1 leaf; Verses, &c., pp. (4); text, pp. 323–357; List of Books, pp. (3). The Poem on the Last Day has the following title-page: A | Poem | on the | Last Day. | In Three Books. | By the Reverend | Edward Young, LL.D. | . . . | . . . . | *Philadelphia:* | *Printed, and Sold by Robert Bell, in Third-Street.* | M,DCC,LXXVII. |

ZUSCHRIFT | aus der | Versammlung | der Repräsentanten | des | Staates von Newyork | an die, | welche sie dazu bestellt haben. | Aus dem Englischen übersetzt. | *Philadelphia:* | *Gedruckt bey Steiner und Cist, in der Zweyten-* | *strasse, nahe bey der Arch-strasse,* 1777. | 8vo. pp. 21.

1778.

A Son Excellence, | Son Excellence Le Ministre | Plenipotentiaire de France | Auprés des Etats Unis de l'Amerique. | [*Philadelphie:* 1778?] Folio, pp. (4). L. C. P. 3654

"Epitre. A mon Jardin," in verse. The first page is occupied with the dedication in prose.

AN ACCOUNT of the Births and Burials in the United Churches of Christ Church and St. Peter's. *Philadelphia:* 1778.

AN ACT for the regulation of Waggons, Carriages and | Pack-Horses for the Public Service. | [*Lancaster: John Dunlap.* 1778.] Folio, pp. (2). L. C. P. 3656

AN ACT for the regulation of Waggons, Carriages and | Pack-Horses for the Public Service. | [*Philadelphia: John Dunlap.* 1778.] Folio, 1 leaf. L. C. P. 3657

AN ACT to prevent Forestalling and Regrating, and to | encourage Fair Dealing. | [*Lancaster: John Dunlap.* 1778.] Folio, pp. (2). A. P. S. 3658

ACT. A | Farther | Supplement | to the | Act | Entitled | "An Act to regulate the Militia | " of the Common-Wealth of Penn- | " sylvania." | *Lancaster: | Printed by John Dunlap, in Queen-street.* | M,DCC,LXXVIII. | 8vo. pp. 8.　　　L. C. P.　3659

ACT. A further Supplement to the Act intitled, " An Act directing the mode | and time of electing Justices of the Peace for the city of Philadelphia | and the several Counties in this Commonwealth, and for other pur- | poses therein mentioned. | *Philadelphia: Printed by John Dunlap.* [1778.] | Folio, 1 leaf.　3660

ACT. A Supplement to the Act intitled, " An Act for the further secu- | rity of the Government." | *Philadelphia: Printed by John Dunlap, in Market-Street.* [1778.] | Folio, 1 leaf.　L. C. P.　3661

AN | ADDRESS of the Congress | to the | Inhabitants of the United States of America. | *York-Town: Printed by Hall and Sellers.* [1778.] | Folio, 1 leaf.　　　H. S. P.　3662

ADDRESS of the Congress | to the | Inhabitants of the United States of America. | *Lancaster, printed by John Dunlap.* [1778.] | Folio, 1 leaf.　　　L. C. P.　3663

Dated " May 9, 1778," published May 14.

ALL Gentlemen | Sailors, | That are able and willing to serve His Majesty, | . . . | Let them Repair on Board | . . . | The Pearl, | John Linzee, Esq; Commander; | . . . | . . . | . . . . | [*Philadelphia:*] *Printed by James Humphreys, junr.* . . . | [1778.] | Folio, 1 leaf.　　　L. C. P.　3664

Issued Feb. 4, 1778.

ALL | Loyal Seamen | or | Able-Bodied Landmen, | Desirous of Serving his Majesty | . . . | . . . on Board the Galley | Phila-delphia, | . . . | . . . | . . . | Will meet with every Encouragement . . . | . . . | . . . | . . . . | [*Philadelphia:*] *Printed by James Humphreys, junr.* . . . [1778.] | Folio, 1 leaf.　　L. C. P.　3665

THE AMERICAN Calendar for 1779. *Philadelphia: Thomas Bradford.* 1778 ?　　　3666

THE AMICABLE Fire Company are re- | quested to meet at
the Cross Keys . . . | . . . | . . . at Six o'Clock this Even- | ing
. . . | . . . . | [*Philadelphia:* 1778.]   4to. 1 leaf.   L. C. P.   3667

Dated "Philadelphia, Jan. 26, 1778."

[ANSTEY. (Christopher)]   The Election Ball.   In Poetical
Letters, from Mr. Inkle at Bath, to his Wife at Gloucester, with a
Poetical Address to John Miller, Esq.   *Philadelphia: James Rob-
ertson.*   1778.   3668

THE | ARTICLES, | Published by Congress, | of a | Treaty of
Amity and Commerce, | and of a | Treaty of Alliance | Between
the Crown of France | And these United States, | Duly entered
into and executed at Paris, on | the 6th day of February last, by
a Minister | properly authorized by his Most Christian | Majesty
on the one part, and the Commissi- | oners of Congress on the
other part. | Also the | Articles | of | Confederation and Perpetual
| Union | Between the United States of America, as pro- | posed
by Congress to the Legislatures of the | different States. | *Lancas-
ter: Printed by John Dunlap.*   [1778.] | Sm. 12mo.   L. C. P.   3669

Collation: Title, 1 page; Treaty, pp. 2–12; Articles of Confederation, pp. (13);
Lists of Members of Congress, Pennsylvania Assembly, &c., pp. (4). The Articles
of Confederation and lists are from Father Abraham's Pocket Almanack for 1778.

AUCH noch Etwas fur Ordens= und Nichtordensleute der Mad.
Cagliostro.   *Philadelphia:* [*Wittekind in Eisenach.*]   1778.   W.   3670

AVIS au Public.   To the Public.   Öffentliche Bekanntmachung. |
Imprimè a Philadelphie par Henri Miller, | 1778. | Folio, 1 leaf.   3671

Printed in French, English, and German, in three parallel columns, with imprints
under each column. "Colonel De la Balme, a French Officer, . . . has begun to
erect about 28 miles from Philadelphia, a Row of Workshops, where such . . . as
are destitute . . . may . . . by means of their own Labour, overcome the Difficulties
of their Misfortunes. . . . The Diet is to be: Before going to work a Crust of good
Bread, or a Biscuit, and a Glass of the best Rum; Breakfast, Fruit, Potatoes and broil'd
Meat; For Dinner, Soup and boil'd Meat; Supper, Soup and roasted Meat. Fresh
Meat shall be served as much as can be, and from time to time some Beer or Cyder."

BECCARIA. ([Cesare Bonesana,] Marquis di)   An | Essay |
on | Crimes | and | Punishments. | Written by the | Marquis Bec-

caria, | of Milan. | With a | Commentary, | Attributed to Mon-
sieur De Voltaire. | . . . | . . . | . . . | . . . | . . . . | *Philadelphia :*
| *Printed and Sold by R. Bell, next Door to St. Paul's* | *Church, in*
Third-Street. | M.DCC.LXXVIII. | 8vo.   L. C. P.   3672

Collation : Half-title, 1 leaf ; Title, 1 leaf ; Contents, pp. (4) ; Preface, pp. 5–10 ;
Introduction, pp. 11–14 ; text, pp. 15–269 ; Sharp's Remarks, Half-title, and quotation, pp. (2) ; Title, 1 leaf ; Preface, pp. 275–288 ; text, 289–348 ; Rousseau on Duel-
ling, pp. 349–352 ; Index, pp. (3) ; Advertisement, 1 page. The title to Sharp's
tract is as follows : Remarks | on the | Opinions | of | Some of the most celebrated
Writers | on | Crown Law, | respecting the due distinction between Manslaughter
and Murder : | Being an Attempt to shew, | That the plea of sudden Anger | cannot
remove the imputation | and guilt of Murder, when a | Mortal Wound is wilfully
given | with a Weapon : | That the indulgence allowed by | the Courts to voluntary
Man- | slaughter in Rencounters, and | in sudden Affrays and Duels, | is indiscrimi-
nate, and without | foundation in Law : | And that impunity in such cases | of volun-
tary Manslaughter is | one of the principal causes of | the continuance and present
in- | crease of the base and disgrace- | ful practice of Duelling. | To which are added,
some thoughts | on the particular case of the | Gentlemen of the Army, when | in-
volved in such disagreeable | private differences. | With a Prefatory Address to the
Reader, concerning the | Depravity and Folly of modern Men of Honour, falsely so
called ; | including a short account of the Principles and Design of the | Work. | By
Grenville Sharp. | *Philadelphia :* | *Printed and Sold by Robert Bell, in Third-Street.*
| M.DCC.LXXVIII. |

BENEZET. (A.) A first Book for Children. A. B. C. D. E.
F. G. H. I. J. K. L. M. O. P. Q. R. S. T. U. V. W. X. Y. Z.
Note, When the above alphabets are defaced, this leaf may be
pasted upon the cover, and that on the other side used. By Anthony Benezet. *Philadelphia : Printed and sold by J. Crukshank, in*
Market-Street, between Second and Third Streets. 1778. 16mo. pp.
16 ?   3673

Title from Smith's Catalogue of Friends' Books.

[BENEZET.] Serious | Considerations | On several Important
| Subjects ; | viz. | On War and its Inconsistancy with the | Gos-
pel. | Observations on Slavery. | And | Remarks on the Nature
and bad Effects of | Spirituous Liquors. | [12 lines.] | *Philadelphia :*
| *Printed by Joseph Crukshank,* . . . .| . . . 1778. | 12mo. pp. 48.

[BENEZET.] Serious Reflections affectionately recommended
| to the Well-disposed of every Religious De- | nomination, par-
ticularly those who Mourn | and Lament on account of the Calam-

ities | which attend us; and the insensibility that | so generally prevails. | [*Philadelphia:* 1778 ?] Sm. 8vo. pp. 4.   H. S. P.   3675

[BENEZET.] Some | Necessary | Remarks | on the | Education | of the | Youth | in the Country-parts of this, and | the neighbouring | Governments. | [*Philadelphia:* 1778 ?] Sm. 8vo. pp. 8.   H. S. P.   3676

[BERTIE, (Willoughby —] Earl of Abingdon.) Thoughts] on the | Letter | of | Edmund Burke, Esq; | to the | Sheriffs of Bristol, | on the | Affairs of America. | By the Earl of Abingdon. | *Oxford, Printed:* | *Lancaster, Re-printed,* | *And Sold by John Dunlap,* | *In Queen-Street.* | M,DCC,LXXVIII. | 8vo. pp. 30; Advertisement, pp. (2).   H. S. P.   3677

A second edition was advertised in the Pa. Packet, June 3, 1778.

BRACKENRIDGE. (H. M.) Six | Political | Discourses | founded on | the | Scripture. | By Hugh Montgomery Brackenridge. | . . . | . . . | . . . | . . . . | *Lancaster:* | *Printed by Francis Bailey.* [1778.] | Sm. 8vo. pp. 88.   L. C. P.   3678

BROOKE. (H.) Gustavus Vasa, | The | Deliverer of his Country. | Inscrib'd | To his Excellency | General Washington, | Commander in Chief of the Forces of the Thirteen | United States of America. | . . . | . . . | . . . | . . . | . . . . | Written by | Henry Brooke, Esq, | Author of the Fool of Quality, of the History of Juliet | Grenville, &c. &c. &c. | *Philadelphia:* | *Printed and Sold by Robert Bell, next Door to* | *St. Paul's Church in Third-Street.* | M.DCC.LXXVIII. | 8vo. pp. 88, (8).   H. S. P.   3679

[BROWN. (William)] Pharmacopoeia | Simpliciorum | et | Efficaciorum, | in usum | Nosocomii Militaris, | ad exercitum | Fœderatarum Americæ Civitatum | pertinentis; | Hodiernæ nostræ inopiæ rerumque | angustiis, | Foroci hostium sævitiæ, belloque crudeli ex inopinatò | patriæ nostræ illato debitis, | Maxime accommodata. | *Philadelphiæ:* | *Ex Officina Styner & Cist.* MDCCLXXVIII. | Sm. 8vo. pp. 32.   L. C. P.   3680

This was the first Pharmacopœia published in the United States. A second edition was issued in 1781.

BY Order of His Excellency | Sir William Howe, K.B. | General and Commander in Chief, &c. &c. &c. | *Philadelphia : Printed by James Humphreys, Junior.* | . . . [1778.] | 4to. 1 leaf.   3681

Issued Jan. 15, 1778, requiring " all Merchants and Others to make a true return to the Barrack Master of Blankets and Rugs in their possession."

BY Order of His Excellency | Sir William Howe, K.B. | *Philadelphia: Printed by James Humphreys, Junr.* [1778.] | 4to. 1 leaf.   3682

Signed " Daniel Wier, Commissary General," dated " 22d of Feb., 1777." " It being expedient that a sufficient Quantity of Forage and Pasturage should be provided for the Use of the Horses in His Majesty's Service," &c.

CALENDRIER de Philadelphie, ou constitutions de Sancho Pansa et du bonhomme Richard de Pensylvanie. *Philadelphie: [Paris.]* 1778.   3683

Title from Weller's *Die falschen Druckorte.* Which also notes an edition printed " En Pensylvanie, 1778," and another " A Philadelphie, 1779," and says " Par Barbeu du Bourg."

CAMILLA. | His Majesty's Ship | The Camilla | Wants Men. | . . . | . . . . | *Philadelphia :] Printed by James Humphreys, junr.* . . . [1778.] | Folio, 1 leaf.   L. C. P.   3684

A CARD. | To the Electors of Philadelphia. | [*Philadelphia:* 1778.] 4to. 1 leaf.   L. C. P.   3685

Issued, says Du Simitiere, " October 13, 1778, in answer to a paragraph, signed an Elector, in the Pa. Packet, Oct. 16, 1778."

CATALOGUE of a small collection of Sentimental Food to be exhibited at Auction by Robert Bell, on the 15th, 16th and 17th of January. *Philadelphia: Robert Bell.* 1778.   3686

CATALOGUE of Books to be sold at Auction at Samuel Dellap's Auction Room, on Jan. 15th, and six or seven following evenings. *Philadelphia:* 1778.   3687

CATALOGUE of Books to be sold at Auction, May 21, 22, and 23. *Philadelphia : Robert Bell.* 1778.   3688

CATALOGUE of Books to be sold at Auction, by Robert Bell, April 23, 24, and 25. *Philadelphia: Robert Bell.* 1778.   3689

CATALOGUE of the Books in Bell's Circulating Library, Containing above 2000 volumes. *Philadelphia: Robert Bell.* 1778.   3690

DAVYS. (P.) Adminiculum Puerile, or an Help for School Boys. By P. Davys. *Philadelphia: James Humphreys, junr. ?* 1778.

Advertised in the Pa. Packet, Sept. 24, 1778, to be sold by John Dunlap. This was just after the sale of the confiscated effects of Humphreys, and it was probably from his press.

DE FOE. (D.) The | True Born | Englishman. | A Satyr. | By Daniel D'Foe. | *Philadelphia:* | *Re-printed in the Year* MDCCLXXVIII. | Sm. 8vo. pp. 38.   L. C. P.   3692

DESCRIPTION | of | Counterfeit Bills, | Which were done in Imitation of the True Ones ordered by the Honorable | the Continental Congress, | Bearing Date 20th May, 1777, and 11th April, 1778. | [*Philadelphia: John Dunlap.* 1778.] Folio, 1 leaf.   3693

DILWORTH. (T.) A New Guide to the English Tongue. By Thomas Dilworth. *Philadelphia: Robert Aitken.* 1778.   3694

DILWORTH. (T.) A New Guide to the English Tongue. By Thomas Dilworth. *Lancaster: Francis Bailey.* 1778.   3695

DIRECTIONS to sail into and up Delaware Bay. | [*Philadelphia:* 1778.] Folio, 1 leaf.   3696

Dated by Du Simitiere Feb. 9, 1778.

[*Royal Arms.*] | DRAUGHT of a Bill | For declaring the Intentions of the Parliament of Great Britain, | concerning the Exercise of the Right of imposing Taxes within | His Majesty's Colonies, Provinces, and Plantations in North- | America. | [*Philadelphia:*] *Printed by Macdonald and Cameron, in Chestnut-Street, a few Doors above the Barrack-Office.* [1778.] | Folio, 1 leaf.   3697

THE | ELDERS and Messengers | of the several | Baptist Churches, | . . . | . . . | . . . | . . . | . . . | . . . . | Being met in Association at Hopewell, in | New Jersey, October 13th and 14th, 1778; | [Colophon.] *Philadelphia: | Printed by Hall and Sellers.* [1778.] | Sm. 4to. pp. 7.   3698

THE | EPISTLE from the Yearly-Meeting | in London, | Held by Adjournments, from the 8th of the Sixth | Month 1778, to the 13th of the same, inclusive. | To the Quarterly and Monthly Meetings of Friends in Great- | Britain, Ireland, and elsewhere. | [*Philadelphia:* 1778.]   4to. pp. 4.   F. 3699

Contains also the Epistle to the Yearly Meeting in Philadelphia.

EVANS. (I.)   A | Discourse, | delivered, | on the 18th Day of December, 1777, the Day of | public thanksgiving, | Appointed by the | honourable | continental congress, | By the Reverend Israel Evans, A.M. | Chaplain to General Poor's Brigade. | And now published at the request of the General and Officers of the said Brigade, | To be distributed among the Soldiers | gratis. | *Lancaster: | Printed by Francis Bailey.* | M,DCC,LXXVIII. | 12mo. pp. 24.   3700

FATHER Abraham's | Pocket Almanack, | For the Year 1779; | *Philadelphia: | Printed and Sold by J. Dunlap.* [1778.] | 24mo. pp. (24).   3701

FIVE Hundred Pounds | Reward. | *Philadelphia: Printed by John Dunlap, in Market-street.* [1778.] | Folio, 1 leaf. L. C. P. 3702

A handbill in French and English, offering the above reward for the recapture of the " Virginia built pilot boat St. Louis," which had been seized and carried off by the crew. Signed " Anthony Marmajou," and dated " July 16, 1778."

FOR the Benefit of the Widows and Orphans | of the Army. | On Monday | [Jan. 19.] . . . | Will be Represented, at the Theatre in Southwark, | A Comedy, Called | No One's Enemy | But his Own, | and | The Deuce is in Him. | . . . . | *Philadelphia, Printed by James Humphreys, Junr.* [1778.] | Folio, 1 leaf.   L. C. P. 3703

[FOTHERGILL. (Samuel)]   Repent and be converted: | A | Sermon | Preached at a Meeting of the People called | Quakers,

1768. | Also The | Heads of a Sermon, | Preached at Horsley-down Meeting, upon the close of | a visit to Friends Families in that Quarter, the 19th | of the Eleventh Month, 1769. | *Philadelphia :* | *Printed, and Sold by Joseph Crukshank, in Market-* | *street, between Second and Third-street.* | M,DCC,LXXVIII. | 8vo. pp. 31.

[FRANKLIN. (Benjamin)]   La Science | Du Bonhomme Richard, | ou | Moyen Facile | De Payer les Impôts. | Traduit de l'Anglois. | Seconde Édition, | exactement semblable à la premiere. | [Cut.] | *A Philadelphie.* | *Et se trouve* | *A Paris, chez Ruault, Libraire,* | *rue de la Harpe,* 1778. | 24mo. pp. 151; List of Books, &c., pp. (5). + Troisieme Édition, | . . . . | *A Philadelphie :* | *Se vend à Paris,* | *chez Ruault,* . . . . | MDCCLXXVIII. | 24mo. pp. 151, (5).   H. S. P.   3705

Translated by Quétant and Lecuy, and printed at Lausanne, according to Weller's *Die falschen und finguten Druckorte.*

FROM our General Spring Meeting of | Ministers and Elders, held in Philadelphia, for Pennsylvania and New-Jersey, by Adjournments, | from the 21st of the Third-month to the 24th of | the same, inclusive, 1778. | To our Friends and Brethren in Religious Profession. | [*Philadelphia:* 1778.]   Folio, pp. 2.   F.   3706

GARRICK. (D.)   The | Lying Valet. | A | Comedy in two Acts. | Written | By David Garrick, Esq. | Printed at the Desire of some of the Officers in the American Army, who | intend to exhibit at the Play-house, for the Benefit of Families | who have suffered in the War for American Liberty. | *Philadelphia :* | *Printed by R. Bell, next Door to St. Paul's Church, Third-street.* | MDCCLXXVIII. | 8vo. pp. 23, (1).   H. S. P.   3707

THE GENTLEMAN and Lady's Pocket Memorandum Book for 1778.   *Philadelphia : James Humphreys, jun.*   1778.   3708

THE GENTLEMEN | Merchants and Citizens | Are requested to meet on Business of Import- | ance, This Evening. [*Philadelphia:* 1778.]   4to. 1 leaf.   L. C. P.   3709

Dated "Monday Morning, May 25, 1778."

𝕲𝕰𝕾𝕻𝕽𝕬𝕰𝕮𝕳 zwischen Doctor Beale, und dem Jehemmo. *Lancaster: Theophilus Cossart.* 1778.　　3710

GREGORY. (John) A Father's Legacy to his Daughters. By Dr. John Gregory. *Philadelphia: Robert Bell.* 1778.　　3711

[GREY. (Isaac)] A Serious | Address | to | Such of the People called | Quakers, | On the Continent of North-America, | As profess Scruples relative to the present Government: | Exhibiting | The ancient real Testimony of that People, concerning | Obedience to Civil Authority. | Written before the Departure of the British Army | from Philadelphia, 1778. | By a Native of Pennsylvania. | To which are added, for the Information of all rational | Enquirers, | An Appendix, | consisting of | Extracts from an Essay concerning Obedience | to the Supreme Powers, and the Duty of Subjects in all | Revolutions, published in England soon after the Revolu- | tion of 1688. | *Philadelphia: | Printed by R. Bell, next Door to St. Paul's Church, Third-street.* | M.DCC.LXXVIII. | 8vo.　　　　　　　　　　　　　　H. S. P.　3712

Collation: Advertisement, 1 page; Introduction, pp. (3); Title, 1 leaf; text, pp. 1–24. Appendix, pp. 25–41; Advertisement, 1 page; Note, 1 leaf.

[GREY.] A Serious | Address | to | Such of the People called | Quakers, | on the | Continent of North-America, | as profess | Scruples relative to the present Government: | Exhibiting | The ancient real Testimony of that People, concerning | Obedience to Civil Authority. | Written | Before the Departure of the British Army from Philadelphia, 1778, | By | A Native of Pennsylvania. | To which are added, | For the Information of all rational Enquirers, | An Appendix, | consisting of | Extracts from an Essay concerning Obedience | to the Supreme Powers, and the Duty of Subjects in all | Revolutions, published in England soon after the Revo- | lution of 1688. | The Second Edition. | *Philadelphia: | Printed by Styner and Cist, at the North-east Corner of | Race- and Second-streets,* MDCCLXXVIII. | 8vo. pp. 48.　　H. S. P.　3713

HIS Majesty's Ship | Liverpool, | Being Hauled off from the Wharf, | . . . | . . . every Man absent from her [is to] immediately repair | on Board. | . . . | . . . | . . . | . . . | . . . . | *Phila-*

delphia: Printed by James Humphreys, Junior, | . . . [1778.] | 4to.
1 leaf.   L. C. P.   3714

𝔇𝔈ℜ | ℌ𝔒ℭℌ = 𝔇𝔈𝔘𝔗𝔖ℭℌ= | Americanifche | Calender, | Auf das
Jahr | Nach der Gnadenreichen Geburt unfers | Herrn und Heylandes
Jefu Chrifti | 1779. | . . . | . . . | . . . | . . . | . . . | . . . | . . . |
. . . | . . . | . . . | . . . | . . . | . . . | . . . . | Zum ein und vierzigften
mal heraus gegeben. | *Philadelphia: Gedruckt und zu finden bey Johann
Dunlap, in der Markt-strasse.* | . . . | . . . | . . . | . . . | . . . .
1778.] | Sq. 8vo. pp. (32).   H. S. P.   3715

At the sale of Saur's confiscated effects, Dunlap bought the cuts and type of Saur's
Almanac, and called his first issue the 41st edition. The lines omitted are nearly the
same as in Saur's Almanac for 1777.

HUME. (D.) The | Life | of | David Hume, Esq; | The Philos-
opher and Historian, | Written by Himself. | To which are added,
The | Travels of a Philosopher, | Containing | Observations on
the Manners and Arts of various Nations, in | Africa and Asia. |
From the French of M. le Poivre, | Late Envoy to the King of
Cochin-China, and now Intendant of | the Isles of Bourbon and
Mauritius. | *Philadelphia:* | *Printed and Sold by Robert Bell, next
Door to* | *St. Paul's Church, in Third-Street.* | M,DCC,LXXVIII. |
8vo.   H. S. P.   3716

Collation: Title, 1 leaf; Life of Hume, pp. 3–8; Letter from Adam Smith, pp.
9–13; Title to Travels of a Philosopher, 1 leaf; text, pp. 17–62; Contents and List
of Books, pp. (2). The Travels of a Philosopher has the following title-page:
Travels | of a | Philosopher: | Containing | Observations | on the | Manners and
Arts | of | Various Nations, | in | Africa and Asia. | From the French of M. le
Poivre, | Late Envoy to the King of Cochin-China, and now Intendant of | the
Isles of Bourbon and Mauritius. | *Philadelphia:* | *Printed and Sold by Robert Bell,
next Door to* | *St. Paul's Church, in Third-Street.* | M,DCC,LXXVIII. |

IN Congress. April 23, 1778. | *York-Town. Printed by Hall
and Sellers.* [1778.] | Sm. Folio, 1 leaf.   N. Y. H. S.   3717

" Resolved, That it be recommended to the . . . States, to pass Laws pardoning
such of their Inhabitants as levied war against . . . these States, or aided the Enemy,
. . . as shall surrender themselves."

IN Congress, May 2, 1778. | [*Philadelphia: John Dunlap.* 1778.]
8vo. 1 leaf.   L. C. P.   3718

Resolutions authorizing the Managers of the United States lottery to employ agents in each State, and ordering the list of winning numbers to be printed.

IN Congress, | 27th May, 1778. | Establishment of the | American Army. | *York-Town: Printed by John Dunlap.* [1778.] | Folio, pp. (2).   A. P. S.   3719

JN der General Aſſembly | von Pennſylvanien, | Samstags, den 28ten November, 1778. | *Philadelphia, Gedruckt bey Steiner und Cist, am Eckt von der Rees- und Zweyten-strasse.* [1778.] | Folio, 1 leaf.

IN General Assembly of Pennsylvania, | Tuesday, September 1, 1778. | [*Philadelphia: John Dunlap.* 1778.]   Folio, 1 leaf. 3721

A Bill entitled "An Act for the recovery of the duties on negroes and mulatto slaves, which on the fourth day of July, one thousand seven hundred and seventy-six, were due to this state, and have since accrued and for appointing a Collector of the said duties," "printed for public consideration."

In General Assembly | Friday, September 4, 1778. | *Philadelphia: Printed by John Dunlap, in Market-Street.* [1778.] | Folio, 1 leaf.   L. C. P.   3722

A Bill entitled "A further Supplement to the Act entitled, 'An Act for the regulation of Waggons, Carriages and Pack-Horses for the public service,'" "printed for public consideration."

IN General Assembly | Monday, September 7, 1778. | [*Philadelphia: John Dunlap.* 1778.] Folio, 1 leaf.   L. C. P.   3723

A Bill entitled "A Supplement to the Act intitled, 'An Act for the further security of the Government,'" "printed for public consideration."

IN General Assembly | Of Pennsylvania, | Saturday, November 28, 1778. | *Philadelphia: Printed by John Dunlap.* [1778.] | Folio, 1 leaf.   H. S. P.   3724

Resolution directing the manner of voting by the people "for a Convention" and "against a Convention," and defining the points to be determined by the Convention. Printed also in German. 5000 copies in each language were ordered to be struck off.

IN General Assembly, | Thursday, December 3, 1778. P.M. | [*Philadelphia: John Dunlap.* 1778.] Folio, 1 leaf. L. C. P. 3725

A Bill entitled " An Act to establish and regulate Vendues in the City of Phila-delphia, the Northern Liberties thereof, and the District of Southwark," " printed for public consideration."

JEWELS and Diamonds for Sentimentalists, Now on sale at Bell's Book-Store, next door to St. Paul's Church, Philadelphia. *Philadelphia: Robert Bell.* 1778.   3726

JOURNALS | of | Congress. | Containing | the | Proceedings | From January 1, 1776, to January 1, 1777. | Published by order of Congress. | Volume II. | *York-Town: (Pennsylvania)* | *Printed by John Dunlap.* | M,DCC,LXXVIII. | 8vo. pp. (2), 1–520, i–xxvii.

JOURNALS | of | Congress, | containing | the | Proceedings | From January 1st, 1777, to January 1st, 1778. | Published by order of Congress. | Volume III. | *Philadelphia:* | *Printed by John Dunlap.* [1778.] | 8vo. pp. 603; Index to Vol. III., xxii; Index to Vol. I. pp. (12).   H. S. P.   3728

KUNZE. (J. C.) Einige | Gedichte und Lieder | von | Johann Christoph Kunze, | Ev. Luth. Pred. zu Philadelphia, in Nordame= | rika. | *Philadelphia :* | *Gedruckt und zu finden bei Christoph und Peter Saur,* | 1778. | Sm. 8vo. pp. (42), 132, (1).   H. S. P.   3729

LAWS | enacted in | The Second | General Assembly | of the | Representatives | of the | Freemen | of the | Common-Wealth | of | Pennsylvania. | At the Sitting which began at Lancaster on the Twenty- | seventh day of October, A.D. One Thousand Seven Hundred | and Seventy-seven, and continued by adjournment to the second | day of January, A.D. One Thousand Seven Hundred and | Seventy-eight. | *Lancaster:* | *Printed by John Dunlap, in Queen-Street.* | M,DCC,LXXVIII. | Folio, Title, 1 leaf; pp. 71–100. + Laws | Enacted in the Second Sitting | . . . | . . . | . . . | . . . | . . . | . . . | . . . . | [*Lancaster: John Dunlap.* 1788.] pp. 101–132. + Laws | Enacted in the Third Sitting . . . | . . . | . . . | . . . . | [*Lancaster: John Dunlap.* 1778.] pp. 133–136. + Laws | Enacted in the Fourth Sitting | . . . | . . . | . . . | . . . | . . . | . . . | . . . . | [*Philadelphia: John Dunlap.* 1778.] pp. 137–164.   H. S. P.   3730

LAWS | Enacted in the Third | General Assembly | of the | Commonwealth | of | Pennsylvania, | Which met at Philadelphia, | On Monday the twenty-sixth Day of October, in the | Year of our Lord One Thousand Seven Hundred | and Seventy-Eight, | And in the Third Year of the Independence of the United | States of North America. | *Philadelphia:* | *Printed by John Dunlap.* | MDCCLXXVIII. | Folio, Title, 1 leaf; pp. 167–177, (1).   3731

LETTERS | from | General Washington, | To several of his Friends in the | Year 1776. | In which are set forth, | A fairer and fuller View | of | American Politics, | Than ever yet transpired, | Or the Public could be made acquainted with | through any other Channel, | Together with | The Reverend Jacob Duché's (late | Chaplain to the Congress) Letter to Mr. | Washington, and an Answer to it, by | Mr. John Parke, a Lieutenant-Colonel in | Mr. Washington's Army. | [*Philadelphia:*] *Printed in the Year* 1778. | Sm. 8vo. Title, 1 leaf; pp. 52.   L. C. P.   3732

(By Permission.) | A | LIST | of the | General and Staff Officers, | and of the | Officers in the several Regiments | serving in North-America, | Under the Command of His Excellency General | Sir William Howe, K.B. | With the Dates of their Commissions as they Rank | in each Corps and in the Army. | *Philadelphia:* | *Printed by Macdonald & Cameron, a few* | *doors above the Barrack-Office,* | MDCCLXXVIII. | 8vo. pp. 56.   3733

A LIST | of the | Fortunate Numbers | in the | First Class | of the | United States Lottery. | [Colophon.] *Printed by Hall and Sellers.* [1778.] | 8vo. pp. 55.   L. C. P.   3734

LOUIS, | By the Grace of God, King of France and Navarre, | To All who shall see these Presents, | Greeting. | [*Lancaster:* *Francis Bailey.* 1778?] 4to. pp. (2).   L. C. P.   3735

Announcement of the appointment of C. A. Gerard to be Minister to the United States.

𝕷𝖀𝕿𝕳𝕰𝕽𝕵𝕾𝕮𝕳𝕰 und Reformirte A B C und Namen = Bücher, für Kinder, welche anfangen zu lernen. *Lancaster: Frantz Bailey.* 1778.

MACKAY. (F.) American Liberty | Asserted : | Or | British Tyranny | Reprobated : | In | A Discourse, delivered on Wednesday, the 22d Day | of April, 1778, to the Officers and Soldiers of Ge- | neral Woodford's Brigade. | By Fitzhugh Mackay, Chaplain. | . . . | . . . . | *Lancaster :* | *Printed by Francis Bailey, near the Court-House.* | MDCCLXXVIII. | Sm. 8vo. pp. 16.   c. 3737

McKEAN. (T.) A | Charge | delivered to the | Grand-Jury, | By the Honourable | Thomas McKean, Esquire, | Chief Justice of Pennsylvania, | At a Court of Oyer and Terminer, | and General Gaol Delivery, held at | York, for the County of York, on the 21st | Day of April, 1778; and published | at the special Request of the said Grand- | Jury. | *Lancaster :* | *Printed by Francis Bailey, in King's-Street.* | M,DCC,LXXVIII. | Sm. 8vo. pp. 18.   c. 3738

A MANUAL of Catholic Prayers, and other Christian Devotions for the use of those Roman Catholics who ardently aspire after salvation. *Philadelphia : Robert Bell.* 1778.   3739

The Advertised in the Pa. Evening Post, Dec. 28, 1778, with the following : " N. B. At said Bell's may be had Holy Bibles, for the pocket or the family, *with the Psalms of the Presbyterians.*"

HENRICH MILLERS, des Buchdruckers in Philadelphia, | nöthige Vorstellung | an die Deutschen in Pennsylvanien, ꝛc. | [*Philadelphia : Henrich Miller.* 1778.] Folio, 1 leaf.   H. S. P. 3740

MINUTES | Of the Second | General Assembly | of the | Common-Wealth | of | Pennsylvania, | Which met at Lancaster, on Monday, October | Twenty-Seventh, A.D. One Thousand Seven Hundred | and Seventy-seven. | *Lancaster :* | *Printed by John Dunlap, in Queen-Street.* | M,DCC,LXXVIII. | Folio, pp. 116.   3741

The Minutes of the 1st sitting occupy 41 pages ; of the 2d, pp. 43–76 ; of the 3d, pp. 77–86 ; of the 4th, pp. 87–116. The last two were probably printed by Dunlap in Philadelphia.

MINUTES | of the Third | General Assembly | of the | Commonwealth | of | Pennsylvania, | which met at Philadelphia, | On Monday the Twenty-sixth Day of October, A.D. One | Thousand Seven Hundred and Seventy-eight; | And in the Third Year | of the | Independence of America. | *Philadelphia :* | *Printed by John Dunlap, in Market-street.* | MDCCLXXVIII. | Folio, pp. 154. 3742

The first sitting, issued in four parts, occupies pp. 3–34 ; the second sitting, issued in twelve parts, pp. 35–118 ; and the third sitting, issued in eight parts, pp. 118–154. The first page of the last sitting was numbered 118, instead of 119, and the error was corrected by leaving a blank page after 140. Some of the sheets have Dunlap's imprint, and he, no doubt, printed the whole volume. The second and third sittings extend to Oct. 10, 1779.

MISCELLANIES | for | Sentimentalists : | Containing, | I. Life of David Hume, written by himself. | II. Travels of a Philosopher, by Le Poivre. | III. Principles of Politeness, and of Knowing | the World, by Lord Chesterfield. | IV. Maxims and Moral Reflections, by the | Duke De La Rochefoucault. | V. Travels of the Imagination ; a true Journey | from Newcastle to London, by J. Murray. | VI. American Independence, an Ever- | lasting Deliverance from British Tyranny, by Phi- | lip F—u. | VII. The humble Confession, Declaration, Recan- | tation, and Apology of Benjamin | Towne, Printer in Philadelphia. | *Philadelphia :* | *Printed and Sold by Robert Bell, in Third-Street.* | M.DCC.LXXVIII. | 8vo. 1 leaf.   H. S. P.   3743

A general title-page to volume of pamphlets, all of which will be found elsewhere under the authors' names, except Numbers II. and VI., which were issued with Numbers I. and V. respectively.

[MURRAY. (James)] The | Travels | of the | Imagination ; | A true Journey from | Newcastle to London. | To which are added, | American Independence, | an | Everlasting Deliverance | from | British Tyranny : | A Poem. | *Philadelphia :* | *Printed, by Robert Bell, in Third-Street.* | MDCCLXXVIII. | 8vo. pp. 126 ; List of Books, pp. (2).   H. S. P.   3744

The poem by Philip Freneau occupies pp. 114–126, and has the following title-page : American | Independence, | an everlasting | Deliverance | from | British Tyranny. | A Poem. | By Philip F—, Author of the American Village, | Voyage to Boston, &c. | . . . | . . . | . . . | . . . | . . . | . . . | . . . . | *Philadelphia :* | *Printed, by Robert Bell, in Third-Street.* | MDCCLXXVIII. |

DER NEUGESTELLTE, Verbeſſert= und Zuverläßige | Americaniſche | Staats=Calender | Auf das 1779ſte Jahr Chriſti, | Welches das britte nach bem Schalt=Jahr unb ein Gemein | Jahr von 365 Tagen ift. | [12 lines.] Zum Achtzehntenmal herausgegeben. | *Philadelphia, Gedruckt und zu finden bey Henrich Miller, . . .* | *. . .* | *. . .* | *. . .* | *. . . .* [1778.] | Sq. 8vo. pp. (40 ?).   H. S. P.   3745

THE NEW ENGLAND Primer. *Philadelphia : Robert Aitken.*
1778.   3746

THE NEW Testament, for the Use of Schools. *Philadelphia :*
Robert Aitken. 1778.   3747

Advertised in the Pa. Packet, Nov. 3, 1778.

NEW Year's Verses, | Addressed to the Kind Customers | of the | Pennsylvania Evening Post, | By the Printer's Lads who carry about the same. | Thursday, January 1, 1778. | [*Philadelphia : B. Towne.* 1778.] Folio, 1 leaf.   L. C. P.   3748

NEW-YEAR'S Verses | of those who deliver the | Pennsylvania Ledger | To the Subscribers. | Philadelphia, [*Printed by James Humphreys, junr.*] January 1, 1778. | Narrow folio, 1 leaf.   3749

NEW-YEAR Verses of the Carriers of the Pennsylvania Packet. *Lancaster : John Dunlap.* 1778.   3750

It is probable that no Carrier's Verses were printed by Hall and Sellers, and almost certain that none were issued by the Bradfords on New-Year's Day, 1778.

ON Friday Next, | The Tenth Day of April, | At the Theatre in Southwark, | For the Benefit of a Public Charity | will be represented, | The Wonder, | A Woman keeps a Secret : | To which will be added | A Trip to Scotland. | The Characters by the Officers of the Army | and Navy. | *Philadelphia : Printed by James Humphreys, Jun.* [1778.] | Folio, 1 leaf.   L. C. P.   3751

ON Friday next, | [April 24.] . . . | . . . | . . . | Will be Represented, A Comedy called | The Wonder, | A Woman keeps a Secret ! | To which will be added, by particular Desire, a Farce called the | Mock Doctor. | *Philadelphia : Printed by James Humphreys, Junr.* [1778.] | Folio, 1 leaf.   L. C. P.   3752

ON Friday next, | [May 1.] . . . | . . . | . . . | Will be Represented, A Comedy called | The Liar, | To which will be added, a Farce called | A Trip to Scotland. | *Philadelphia : Printed by James Humphreys, Junr.* [1778.] | Folio, 1 leaf. L. C. P. 3753

ON Monday, | [Jan. 26.] . . . | . . . | . . . | Will be represented a Comedy | called the | Minor, | To which will be added, The | Deuce is in him. | . . . . | *Philadelphia: Printed by James Humphreys, Junr.* | [1778.] Folio, 1 leaf. L. C. P. 3754

ON Monday, | [Feb. 16.] . . . | . . . | . . . | Will be represented a Comedy | called the | Constant Couple. | To which will be added, | Duke and no Duke. | . . . . | *Philadelphia, Printed by James Humphreys, Junr.* [1778.] | Folio, 1 leaf. L. C. P. 3755

ON Monday, | [March 2.] . . . | . . . | . . . | Will be represented a Comedy | called the | Constant Couple. | To which will be added, The | Mock Doctor. | *Philadelphia : Printed by James Humphreys, Junr.* [1778.] | Folio, 1 leaf. L. C. P. 3756

ON Monday, | [March 9.] . . . | . . . | . . . | Will be represented a Comedy | called | The Inconstant. | To which will be added, The | Mock Doctor. | *Philadelphia: Printed by James Humphreys, Junr.* [1778.] Folio, 1 leaf. L. C. P. 3757

ON Monday, | [March 16.] . . . | . . . | . . . | Will be represented a Comedy | called | The Inconstant. | To which will be added, A Farce called | Lethe. | *Philadelphia: Printed by James Humphreys, Jun.* [1778.] | Folio, 1 leaf. L. C. P. 3758

ON Monday, | [March 16.] . . . | . . . | . . . | Will be represented a Comedy | called | The Inconstant. | To which will be added, The | Mock Doctor. | *Philadelphia: Printed by James Humphreys, Jun.* [1778.] | Folio, 1 leaf. L. C. P. 3759

ON Monday Next, | [March 30.] . . . | . . . | . . . | Will be represented | The First Part of | King Henry IV. | To which will be added, A Farce called | Lethe. | *Philadelphia: Printed by James Humphreys, Jun.* [1778.] | Folio, 1 leaf. L. C. P. 3760

ON Monday next, | [April 13.] . . . | . . . | . . . | Will be represented, A Comedy called | The Wonder, | A Woman keeps a Secret! | To which will be added, | A Trip to Scotland. | *Philadelphia: Printed by James Humphreys, Jun.* [1778.] | Folio, 1 leaf. L. C. P. 3761

ON Wednesday, | [March 25,] . . . | . . . | . . . | Will be represented | The First Part of | King Henry IV. | To which will be added, the | Mock Doctor. | *Philadelphia: Printed by James Humphreys, Jun.* [1778.] | Folio, 1 leaf. L. C. P. 3762

ON Wednesday next, | [May 6.] . . . | . . . | . . . | Will be represented, A Comedy called | The Liar, | To which will be added, a Farce called | Duke and No Duke. | *Philadelphia: Printed by James Humphreys, Junr.* [1778.] | Folio, 1 leaf. L. C. P. 3763

[PAINE. (Thomas)] The | American Crisis. | Number V. | Addressed to | General Sir William Howe. | By the | Author of Common Sense. | *Lancaster: | Printed by John Dunlap,* | M,DCC,LXXVIII. | (Price 2s. 6d. single—2s. by the quantity.) | 8vo. Title, 1 leaf; pp. 63–88. H. S. P. 3764

" The Crisis, No. 6, which is ready for the press, will be published as soon as possible." Pa. Gazette, June 13, 1778.

PAINE. To the Public. | [*Philadelphia: B. Towne?* 1778.] Folio, 1 leaf. H. S. P. 3765

In regard to a publication signed " Plain Truth."

THE | PENNSYLVANIA | Evening Post. | MDCCLXXVIII. | Volume IV. | *Philadelphia: | Printed by Benjamin Towne, in Front-Street.* [1778.] | 4to. pp. (2), 458. 3766

After the entry of the British into Philadelphia, the Post was suspended for two weeks.

THE | PENNSYLVANIA Gazette. | Saturday, January 17, 1778. | [Colophon.] *York-Town: Printed by Hall and Sellers.* | Sm. Folio. H. 3767

The publication of the Gazette was, I believe, resumed at York, Pennsylvania, about December, 1777. It was probably published weekly, on Saturday, until June

20th, 1778. Until May it was a small folio of four pages in double columns. From May 2d it resumed its former size, and the title is as in No. 1693, *supra*. The papers issued on May 23, June 6 and 10, were only two pages each. There were "Postscripts" of one leaf quarto to the papers for May 2 and 9, and there was a regular issue on Wednesday, June 10th. None of these papers were numbered. The Gazette of Sept. 10, 1777, is No. 2533, and that of Jan. 5, 1779, No. 2534.

THE PENNSYLVANIA Journal.   3768

The publication of this paper, which was suspended Sept. 17, 1777, was resumed about December 23, 1778. Numbers 1808 and 1809 were published before 1779.

January 3, 1778. Numb. CXV. | THE | PENNSYLVANIA ⁝ Ledger : | Or the ⁝ Philadelphia | Market-Day ⁝ Advertiser. | Saturday, ⁝ January 3, 1778. | *Philadelphia : Printed by James Humphreys, Jun. in Market-street, between Front and Second-* | *streets, and nearly opposite the Guard-house :—By whom Essays, Articles of News, Advertisements, &c. are gratefully received,* | *and impartially inserted : And where Subscriptions are taken in for this Paper.* | Folio.   3769

Numbers CXV. (Jan. 3, 1778) to CLV. (May 23, 1778), four pages each, except Numbers 117 and 125, which contain two pages, and No. 120, six pages, with "Supplements" of two pages to Numbers 131, 132, and 135; "Extra Supplements" of four pages to Numbers 131 and 139, and of two pages to No. 132, and a "Postscript" of two pages to No. 134. Published on Wednesdays and Saturdays. The paper was discontinued just before the evacuation of the city by the British. Humphreys was declared a traitor, and his property confiscated by the State authorities.

THE | PENNSYLVANIA ⁝ Packet, | Or ⁝ the | General ⁝ Advertiser. | Wednesday, January 7, 1778. | *Lancaster : Printed by John Dunlap, in Queen-Street.* | Folio.   3770

The old cut of the ship was retained, as indicated by the dotted lines. Published without numbers, weekly, on Wednesdays, to June 17, with additional numbers on Monday, March 9, Saturday, May 23, and Saturday, June 6; with a "Supplement" of two pages, dated Jan. 29; a "Postscript" of four pages, dated April 25; and a "Packet Extraordinary" of four pages, dated May 14. The publication was suspended from June 17 to July 4, when it was resumed at Philadelphia, and the paper was issued "every Tuesday, Thursday, and Saturday" during the rest of the year. There was an "Extra" of four pages issued on Dec. 21. The paper for July 6 consists of one leaf only. From July 4 the imprint is as given in No. 3927, *infra*, and from July 16 the title is as there given.

THE PENNSYLVANIA Pocket Almanac for 1779. *Philadelphia : Thomas Bradford.* 1778.   3771

1778. | 1 Stück. | DAS | PENNSYLVANISCHE : Zeitungs=
Blat. | Oder: : Sammlung | Sowohl Answärtig= als Ein= : heimischer
Neuigkeiten. | Mittwochs, den 4 Februar. | [Colophon.] *Diese Zeitung*
wird alle Mittwochen ausgegeben von Frantz Bailey, in der Koenigs-
Strasse, nahe beym | Markt, allwo allerhand Buchdrucker-Arbeit in Eng-
lisch- und Deutscher Sprache verfertiget wird. [1778.] | Folio, pp. (4).

Continued to No. 21 (June 24, 1778), or perhaps later. Four pages each, with a
" Beylage" of two pages to No. 6, and one of 1 leaf quarto to No. 12.

PENNSYLVANISCHER Staatscourier. *Philadelphia : Christoph*
und Peter Saur. 1778.   3773

See Seidensticker's Bibliography under 1778, and Schlözer's Briefwechsel, III.
pp. 260–267.

THE PHILADELPHIA Pocket - Almanac for 1779. *Phila-*
delphia : John Norman. 1778.   3774

A PLAN for Liquidating Certain Debts of the State of
Pennsylvania, collecting Arrearages with greater Expedition,
restoring Confidence in the Government, and providing the Quota
of Federal Supplies. [n. p. 1778.] Folio, pp. 6.   3775

This title is No. 60,392 in Sabin's Dictionary, and is probably dated ten or more
years too early.

THE | POLITICAL Duenna: | A | Comic Opera, | In Three
Acts, | As it is performed by the Servants of his | Britannic
Majesty, | With Lord North's Recantation. | To which are added,
| A Letter to Mr. John Wesley on his calm Address to the
Ame- | ricans. Supposed to be written by the celebrated Junius.
| A Letter from an Irish Gentleman in London to his Friend
and | Countryman, in his Britannic Majesty's Service, in Amer-
ica. | *Philadelphia : | Printed and Sold by Robert Bell, next Door to |*
St. Paul's Church, in Third-street. | M.DCC.LXXVIII. | 8vo. pp.
56.   H. S. P.   3776

POOR Will's Almanac for 1779. *Philadelphia : Joseph Cruk-*
shank. 1778.   3777

POOR Will's Pocket Almanac for 1779. *Philadelphia : Joseph*
Crukshank. 1778.   3778

POPE. (A.)　An | Essay | on | Man. | In Four Epistles. | By Alexander Pope, Esq; | *Philadelphia:* | *Printed by Joseph* *Crukshank, in Market-* | *street, between Second and Third-street.* | MDCCLXXVIII. | 12mo. pp. (8), 38, (5.)　　　L. C. P.　3779

[PRATT. (Samuel Jackson)]　The | Pupil | of | Pleasure; | exhibiting, | The Adventures of a Man of Birth, Figure, Fortune, | and Character, ardent in the Pursuit of Pleasure, much | delighted with, attracted by, and formed upon the | Chesterfieldean System. | Two Volumes complete in One. | By Courtney Melmoth. | *Philadelphia:* | *Printed by Robert Bell, in Third-Street.* | M.DCC.LXXVIII. | 8vo. Title, 1 leaf; pp. 154; 157, (1).　　3780

This general title is followed by a second title : " The | Pupil | of | Pleasure. | In a Series of Letters. | By | Courtney Melmoth. | In Two Volumes. | Volume the First. | *Philadelphia:* | *Printed by Robert Bell, in Third-Street* | M.DCC.LXXVIII. | pp. 154. + Volume the Second. | [*Ibid.*] pp. 157, (1).

[PRATT.]　Travels for the Heart, written in France.　By Courtney Melmoth. In Two Volumes.　*Philadelphia : Robert Bell.* 1778.　　　　3781

PRICE. (R.)　Additional Observations | On the Nature and Value of | Civil Liberty, | and the | War with America : | Also | Observations on Schemes for raising Mo- | ney by Public Loans : | An Historical Deduction and Analysis of the | National Debt : | And a brief Account of the Debts and | Resources of France. | . . . | . . . | . . . | . . . | . . . | . . . . | By Richard Price, D.D. F.R.S. | *London, Printed :* | *Philadelphia : Re-printed by* *Hall and Sellers.* | M.DCC.LXXVIII. | 8vo. pp. i–x, 1–122, 1 folded leaf.　　　H. S. P.　3782

PRICE.　The | General Introduction | to the | Two Tracts | on | Civil Liberty, | the | War with America, | and the | Finances of the Kingdom. | By Richard Price, D.D. F.R.S. | *London, Printed :* | *Philadelphia : Re-printed by Hall and Sellers.* | M,DCC,LXXVIII. | 8vo. Title, 1 leaf; pp. xiv, 1 leaf.　　　H. S. P.　3783

PROCEEDINGS | of a | General Court Martial, | Held at Brunswick, | In the State of New-Jersey, | by order of | His

Excellency | General Washington, | Commander in Chief | Of the Army of | The United States of America, | For the Trial of | Major General Lee. | July 4th, 1778. | Major General Lord Stirling, President. | *Philadelphia :* | *Printed by John Dunlap, in Market-Street.* | MDCCLXXVIII. | Folio, pp. 62. H. S. P. 3784

Four sheets of this trial were printed by Aitken for Dunlap.

PROCEEDINGS | of a | General Court Martial, | Held at Major General Lincoln's Quarters, | Near Quaker-Hill, | In the State of | New-York, | By Order of his Excellency | General Washington, | Commander in Chief | Of the Army of | The United States of America, | For the Trial of | Major General Schuyler, | October 1, 1778. | Major General Lincoln, President. | *Philadelphia :* | *Printed by Hall and Sellers, in Market-Street.* | MDCCLXXVIII. | Folio, pp. 62. L. C. P. 3785

PROCEEDINGS | of a | General Court Martial, | Held at White Plains, | In the State of | New-York, | By Order of his Excellency | General Washington, | Commander in Chief | Of the Army of | The United States of America, | For the Trial of | Major General St. Clair, | August 25, 1778. | Major General Lincoln, President. | *Philadelphia :* | *Printed by Hall and Sellers, in Market-Street.* | MDCCLXXVIII. | Folio, pp. 52; 1 Folded map.

PROCLAMATION. [*Royal Arms.*] | By His Excellency Sir William Howe, K.B. | General and Commander in Chief, &c. &c. &c. | Proclamation. | [*Philadelphia :*] *Printed by James Humphreys, junr.* | *in Market-street, between Front and Second-streets.* [1778.] | Folio, 1 leaf. 3787

Dated "12th of Jan., 1778," "Naval Stores are known to be in this city, which may be needed for his Majesty's Service, all persons are to report such articles in their possession to the Quartermaster General before Jan. 19th."

PROCLAMATION. [*Royal Arms.*] | By Order of His Excellency | Sir William Howe, K.B. | General and Commander in Chief, &c. &c. &c. | Proclamation. | *Philadelphia : James Humphreys, junr.* 1778.] Folio, 1 leaf. 3788

Dated "9th of January, in the 18th year of his Majesty's Reign," signed by "Jos. Galloway," directing that "No Person shall appear in the street after the Evening Tattoo till the Revellie in the Morning without a Lantern."

PROCLAMATION. [*Royal Arms.*] | By Order of His Excellency | Sir William Howe, K.B. | General and Commander in Chief, &c. &c. | Proclamation. | [*Philadelphia :*] *Printed by James Humphreys, junr.* . . . [1778.] | Folio, 1 leaf. 3789

Dated "11th of January, 18th year of his Majesty's Reign," signed "Jos. Galloway," "That as all the Wood in the Neck of Land south of Philadelphia will be needed by H. M.'s Troops, all person are forbidden cut any wood in the Neck aforesaid."

PROCLAMATION. [*Royal Arms.*] | By Order of His Excellency | Sir William Howe, K.B. | General and Commander in Chief, &c. &c. | Proclamation. | [*Philadelphia : James Humphreys, junr.* 1778.] Folio, 1 leaf. 3790

Dated "4th of Feb. in 18th year of his Majesty's Reign," signed "Will. Erskine, Q. M. G.," directing "all Persons having Waggons, Carts or Horses to a return of them within five days."

PROCLAMATION. [*Royal Arms.*] | By Order of His Excellency | Sir William Howe, K.B. | . . . | Proclamation. | [*Philadelphia :*] *Printed by Macdonald & Cameron, in Chesnut-Street, a few Doors above* | *the Barrack-Office.* [1778.] | Folio, 1 leaf. L. C. P. 3791

Signed by "Jos. Galloway," dated "23d of March," "ill-disposed Persons under Pretence of bringing in Provisions have gone up and down the Delaware taking by force the property of His Majesty's loyal Subjects," &c.

PROCLAMATION. [*Royal Arms.*] | By Order of His Excellency | Sir William Howe, K.B. | . . . | Proclamation. | [*Philadelphia :*] *Printed by Macdonald & Cameron, in Chesnut-Street, a few Doors above* | *the Barrack-Office.* [1778.] | Folio, 1 leaf. 3792

Signed by "Jos. Galloway," dated "23d of March, 1778," "Whereas the Cart Ways of the Streets, Lanes, and Alleys of Philadelphia, are much incommoded with Mud, Dirt and other Filth," &c.

PROCLAMATION. By the Hon. Major General Arnold, Commander in Chief of the forces of the United | States of America, in the city of Philadelphia, &c. | A Proclamation. | [n. p. 1778.] Folio, 1 leaf. N. Y. H. S. 3793

Dated "June 17, 1778." Concerning the protection of property.

PROCLAMATION. By the Hon. Major General Arnold, Commander in Chief of the forces of the United | States of America, in the city of Philadelphia, &c. | A Proclamation. | [n. p. 1778.] Folio, 1 leaf. 　　　　　　　L. C. P.　3794

Dated "July 19, 1778." Proclaiming Martial Law.

A PROCLAMATION. | *Lancaster, Printed by John Dunlap,* [1778.] | Folio, 1 leaf. 　　　　　　　L. C. P.　3795

Dated "May 9, 1778." Issued by Congress against American Privateers attacking neutral vessels.

PROCLAMATION. Pennsylvania, ss. | A Proclamation. | By the Supreme Executive Council of the Common-Wealth | of Pennsylvania. | *Lancaster, Printed by John Dunlap.* [1778.] | Folio, pp. (2). 　　　　　　　L. C. P.　3796

Dated "May 8, 1778." Summoning certain persons to surrender themselves before June 25th, or be attainted of treason. On the reverse is "A Proclamation," | of Congress against American privateers seizing neutral vessels, dated "York," May 9, 1778.

PROCLAMATION. Pennsylvania, ss. | A Proclamation. | By the Supreme Executive Council of the Common-Wealth | of Pennsylvania. | *Lancaster: Printed by John Dunlap.* [1778.] | Folio, 1 leaf. 　　　　　　　L. C. P.　3797

Dated "May 21, 1778." Warning certain persons therein named to surrender themselves before July 6, 1778, or be attainted of high treason.

PROCLAMATION. Pennsylvania, ss. | A Proclamation. | By the | Supreme Executive Council | of the Commonwealth of | Pennsylvania. | *Philadelphia: Printed by John Dunlap, in Market-Street.* [1778.] | Folio, 1 leaf. 　　　　　　　L. C. P.　3798

Dated "Oct. 30, 1778." Warning certain persons therein named to surrender themselves before Dec. 15, 1778, or be attainted of high treason.

PROCLAMATION. Pennsylvania, ss. | By the | Supreme Executive Council | of the | Commonwealth of | Pennsylvania, | a | Proclamation. | *Philadelphia: Printed by John Dunlap.* [1778.] | Folio, 1 leaf. 　　　　　　　H. S. P.　3799

Dated "Nov. 26, 1778," appointing Dec. 30 as a Fast-Day.

QUEEN'S | Rangers. | All young and able-bodied | Men, |
(Seafaring Men excepted) | Who are desirous of serving their
King . . . | . . . | . . . | . . . will receive | their full Bounty . . . .
| *Philadelphia: Printed by James Humphreys, Jun.* | . . . [1778.]
| 4to. 1 leaf.   L. C. P.   3800

RECUEIL | des | Loix Constitutives | des | Colonies Angloises,
| confédérées | sous la dénomination | D'États-Unis | de l'Amé-
rique-Septentrionale. | Auquel on a joint les Actes d'Indépendance,
| de Confédération & autres Actes du Congrès | général, traduit
de l'Anglois. | Dédié à M. le Docteur Franklin. | *A Philadelphie,*
| *Et se vend à Paris, rue Dauphine,* | *Chez Cellot & Jombert, fils*
jeune; | *Libraires, la seconde porte cochere à* | *droite, au fond de la*
Cour. | M.DCC.LXXVIII. | 24mo.   H. S. P.   3801

Collation: Half-title, 1 leaf; Title, 1 leaf; Dedication, pp. (2); Advertisement,
pp. (2); Contents, pp. (3); Population of U. S. 1775, 1 page; text, pp. 1–370. This
translation, by Claude Ambrose Regnier?, was printed at Paris. It contains the
constitutions of six States.

DER REPUBLIKANISCHE Calender auf das 1779ste Jahr
Christi. Zum Ersten mal herausgegeben. *Lancaster, gedruckt und zu*
finden bey Theophilus Cossart, und Companie. 1778.   3802

ROCHEFOUCAULD. ([François,] Duc de la) Maxims | and
| Moral | Reflections | By the Duke | De La Rochefoucault. |
Printed according to the New Edition, revised and | improved at
London in 1775. | *Philadelphia:* | *Printed and Sold by Robert Bell,*
next Door | *to St. Paul's Church, in Third-Street.* | M.DCC.LXXVIII.
| 8vo. pp. 142; List of Books, pp. (2).   H. S. P.   3803

THE ROYAL Pennsylvania Gazette. | *Published by James*
Robertson in Front-Street, between Chesnut and Walnut-Streets. | *Phil-*
adelphia, Tuesday, March 3, 1778. (Number I.) | Folio, pp. 4.

Numbers 1 to 25 (May 26, 1778), four pages each, except Numbers 2, 4, and 6,
with a "Gazette Extraordinary" of four pages to No. 9. In No. 7 the title was
changed to (Number VII.) | The : Royal | Pennsylvania : Gazette. | Thursday :
March 24, 1778. | A cut of the Royal Arms was introduced, as indicated by the
dotted lines. Robertson was a follower of the Royal Army, and left Philadelphia
with it.

SAUNDERS. (R.) A Pocket Almanac for 1779. By Richard Saunders, Phil. *Philadelphia : Hall and Sellers.* 1778. 3805

SAUNDERS. Poor Richard improved: | Being an | Almanack | [10 lines] | For the | Year of our Lord 1779 : | Being the Third after Leap-Year. | [9 lines.] | By Richard Saunders, Philom. | *Philadelphia : | Printed and Sold by Hall and Sellers.* [1778.] | 8vo. pp. (36). H. S. P. 3806

[SHARP. (Anthony)] Der Ganz Neue Verbefferte | Nord=Americanifche | Calender, | auf das 1779fte Jahr Chrifti, | Welches ein gemein Jahr von 365 Tagen ift. | Und enthält | Die Wochen= Monaths= Namen = Feyer und andere dem Land= | man zu wiffen nützliche und merkwürdige Tage. | Wie auch : | Der Sonnen und des Mondes Auf= und Untergang; die Afpecten der Planeten, An= | zeige der Witterung, der Fluth, oder hohen Waffer zu Philadelphia, | des Siebengeftirno Aufgang, Sudplatz und Untergang : | Berechnet vornemlich nach der Pennfylvanifchen Himmels=Gegend, dabey aber | in angrenzenden Land= fchaften ohne merflichen Unterfchied zu gebrauchen : | Diefem find noch beygefüget, einige angenehme, nützliche und lehrreiche Erzehlungen, famt anderen | Calender=Arbeiten. | Zum Vierten mal herausgegeben | und verfertiget von David Rittenhouse, A.M. | *Lancaster : Gedruckt und zu finden bey Francis Bailey, in der Koenigs-strasse.* | . . . | . . . | . . . | . . . . [1778.] | Sm. 4to. pp. (40). 3807

Not having had an opportunity to personally examine a copy of one of this series of almanacs until the work was in press, the compiler was led to suppose by the advertisements in the newspapers that the pseudonym of Anthony Sharp appeared on the title- page, and the whole series has been entered under that name.

SHARP. The Lancaster Almanac for 1779. By Anthony Sharp. *Lancaster : Francis Bailey.* 1778. 3808

SHARP. The Lancaster Pocket Almanac for 1779. By Anthony Sharp. *Lancaster : Francis Bailey.* 1778. 3809

A SOLEMN | Warning | by the | Associated Presbytery, | in | Pennsylvania : | Addressed to | All Persons into whose Hands it may come | in these United States ; particularly to the | People under their Inspection. | Wherein | The great Sin, Danger and

Duty of | the Inhabitants of the Land, are pointed | out and declared. | ... | ... | .... | *Lancaster:* | *Printed by Francis Bailey.* [1778.] | Sm. 8vo. pp. 27.   L. C. P.   **3810**

SOME Observations relating to the Establishment of Schools, agreed to by the Committee, to be laid for consideration before the Yearly Meeting. [*Philadelphia:* 1778.] Folio, pp. 2?   **3811**

> Signed, on behalf of the Committee, by Anthony Benezet and Isaac Zane 9 mo. 29, 1778, with a Recommendation by the Yearly Meeting, dated 10 mo. 2, 1778. Title from Smith's Catalogue of Friends' Books.

STANHOPE, (Philip Dormer — Earl of Chesterfield.) Principles | of | Politeness, | and of | Knowing the World; | By the late | Lord Chesterfield. | Methodised and digested under distinct Heads, with Additions, | by the Reverend Dr. John Trusler: | Containing | Every Instruction necessary to complete the Gentleman and Man of | Fashion, to teach him a Knowledge of Life, and make him well | received in all Companies. | *Philadelphia:* | *Printed and sold by Robert Bell, next Door to* | *St. Paul's Church, in Third-Street.* | M,DCC,LXXVIII. | 8vo. pp. 88.   H. S. P.   **3812**

STANHOPE. Select Letters, written by the late Right Honourable Philip Domer Stanhope, Earl of Chesterfield, to his Son, Philip Stanhope, Esq; Late Envoy Extraordinary at the Court of Dresden. *Philadelphia: Robert Bell.* 1778.   **3813**

STERNE. (L.) The Koran, containing the Life, Character, and Sentiments of Tria Juncta in Uno, M.N.A. or Master of No Arts. By Laurence Sterne. In Two Volumes. *Philadelphia: Robert Bell.* 1778.   **3814**

STERNE. Letters to his most intimate Friends. By Laurence Sterne. Published by his Daughter. In Three Volumes. *Philadelphia: Robert Bell.* 1778.   **3815**

[TERMS of Enlistment of the Officers and Seamen of the several Row-Galleys established on the Delaware by Admiral Howe. n. p. 1778.] Folio, 1 leaf.   L. C. P.   **3816**

THEATRE. | For very particular Reasons, | The Play, | Advertised for | Monday next, must be | Postponed. | *Philadelphia :* *James Humphreys, Junr.* [1778.] | 4to. 1 leaf.   L. C. P.   3817

Dated " Saturday, February 28, 1778."

THEATRE. | On Account of the Indisposition | of one of the Actresses, | The Play, | Which was to have been | Performed | On Friday, | . . . | Is obliged to be | Postponed. | [*Philadelphia :*] *Printed by James Humphreys, junr.* . . . [1778.] Folio, 1 leaf.

Dated " April 8, 1778."

THEATRE. | This Week being Passion Week, | It is thought Proper to | Postpone | The Play | Advertised | For Monday the Thirteenth Instant, | Till Monday the 20th . . . | . . . . [*Philadelphia :* 1778.] 4to. 1 leaf.   L. C. P.   3819

Dated " Philadelphia, April 12, 1778."

TO Be Sold | By Public Auction, | *Philadelphia : Printed by John Dunlap, in Market-Street.* [1778.] | 4to. 1 leaf.   L. C. P.   3820

The household furniture of Samuel Shoemaker, now seized and confiscated to the State.

TO the | Inhabitants | Of the States of | Pennsylvania, New-Jersey and Delaware. | *Lancaster : Printed by John Dunlap, in Queen-Street,* | *near the Court-House.* [1778.] | Folio, 1 leaf.   3821

Rates to be paid for provisions, &c., for the Army. Dated " Jan. 30, 1778," and signed " Geo. Washington."

TO the | Militia of Pennsylvania. | [*Philadelphia : Macdonald and Cameron.* 1778.] Folio, 1 leaf.   L. C. P.   3822

A Tory address, signed " Nestor."

TREATIES | of | Amity and Commerce, | and of | Alliance | Eventual and Defensive, | between | His Most Christian Majesty | and the | Thirteen United States | of America. | *Philadelphia :* | *Printed by John Dunlap.* | MDCCLXXVIII. | 4to.   H. S. P.   3823

Collation : Title, 1 leaf ; Title to Treaty of Alliance, 1 leaf ; text, pp. 3–10 ; Title to Treaty of Commerce, 1 leaf ; text, pp. 11–34.

UNITED States Lottery; | The Scheme is, | That this Lottery consist of four Classes, of One Hundred Thousand Tickets each. | *Philadelphia : Printed by John Dunlap, in Market-street.* [1778.] | Folio, 1 leaf.   L. C. P.   3824

VICTOR. (H. B.) New and Complete Instructions for the Violin. By H. B. Victor. *Philadelphia :* 1778.   3825

Victor projected other volumes for the Flute, Guitar, and Harpsichord. Also a Dictionary explaining such Foreign words as occur in Music. Pa. Ledger, Jan. 31, 1778. The music was engraved by John Norman.

VOLTAIRE. ([François Marie Arouet] de) The | Man | worth | Forty Crowns | of | M. De Voltaire. | Translated from the French. | With | Notes, Historical and Critical. | By T[obias] Smollett, M.D. and T[homas] Francklin. | *Philadelphia :* | *Printed by Robert Bell, in Third-street.* | M.DCC.LXXVIII. | 8vo. pp. 116, (4).   H. S. P.   3826

VOLTAIRE. The Princess of Babylon. By Voltaire. *Philadelphia : Robert Bell.* 1778.   3827

VOLTAIRE. The Pupil of Nature. By Voltaire. *Philadelphia : Robert Bell.* 1778.   3828

VOLTAIRE. Zadic. By Voltaire. *Philadelphia : Robert Bell.* 1778.   3829

WANTED | by the | Barrack-Master, | A Number of | Wood-Cutters. | . . . | . . . | . . . . | *Philadelphia : Printed by James Humphreys, Junr.* | . . . . [1778.] | 4to. 1 leaf.   L. C. P.   3830

Dated by Du Simitiere Jan. 15, 1778.

WATTS. (I.) Hymns and Spiritual Songs. By Isaac Watts. *Philadelphia : Hall and Sellers.* 1778.   3831

WATTS. The Psalms of David. Imitated &c. By Isaac Watts. *Philadelphia : Hall and Sellers.* 1778.   3832

WEATHERWISE. (A.) Father Abraham's Almanac for 1779. By Abraham Weatherwise. *Philadelphia : John Dunlap.* 1778. 3833

WHEN the | Chimneys | of the | Barracks | Of the different Regiments want Sweeping, | They are to apply to | Christian Apple. | *Philadelphia: Printed by James Humphreys, Junior.* | . . . [1778.] | 4to. 1 leaf. L. C. P. 3834

Dated "January 7, 1778."

[WITHERSPOON. (John)] . . . | . . . | . . . | . . . | . . . | . . . | The humble confession, declaration, recantation, | and apology of Benjamin Towne, | Printer in Philadelphia. | [*Philadelphia: Robert Bell.* 1778.] 8vo. pp. 5, (1). H. S. P. 3835

ZIMMERMANN. ([Johann Georg von]) Strictures | on | National Pride. | Translated from the German of | Mr. Zimmermann. | Physician in Ordinary | To His Britannic Majesty at Hanover. | . . . | . . . . | *Philadelphia:* | *Printed and Sold by R. Bell, at the Circulating* | *Library, next door to St. Paul's Church,* | *in Third-street.* | M.DCC.LXXVIII. | 8vo. Half-title, 1 leaf; Title, 1 leaf; Preface, pp. iii–iv; Contents, pp. vii–viii; text, pp. 9–274; Index, pp. (5); Advertisement, 1 page. 3836

1779.

AN ACCOUNT of the Births and Burials in the United Churches of Christ Church and St. Peter's. *Philadelphia:* 1779.

AN ACT | To appoint a Representation for the City of Phila-delphia, and the several Counties in this Com- | mon-Wealth, in proportion to the number of taxable inhabitants in each. | *Philadelphia: Printed by John Dunlap.* [1779.] | Folio, 1 leaf. 3838

THE | ACTS | of the | General Assembly, | of the | Common-Wealth | of | Pennsylvania, | Enacted into Laws, since the Decla-ra- | tion of Independence on the Fourth Day | of July, A.D. 1776. | *Philadelphia:* | *Printed by John Dunlap.* MDCCLXXIX. | Folio, 1 leaf. 3839

A title-page for the "Session Laws" of the first two Assemblies.

THE ADDRESS of the Committee of the City and | Liberties of Philadelphia, to their Fellow-Citizens throughout the United

States. | *Philadelphia: Printed by Francis Bailey in Market-Street.* [1779.] | Folio, 1 leaf.   L. C. P. 3840

ADYE. (S. P.) A | Treatise | on | Courts-Martial. | Containing, | I. Remarks on Martial-Law, and | Courts-Martial, in general. | II. The Manner of Proceeding against | Offenders. | To which is added | An | Essay | on | Military | Punishments and Rewards. | By Stephen Payne Adye, | Captain in the Royal Regiment of Artillery, and | Judge-Advocate of the British Army in America. | *Philadelphia:* | *Printed and Sold by R. Aitken, opposite the* | *Coffee-House, Front-Street.* | MDCCLXXIX. | 12mo. pp. 136.

R. AITKEN, | Printer, | [12 lines.] The following | Books printed by R. Aitken, | Are to be Sold Single or by the Dozen. | [*Philadelphia: Robert Aitken.* 1779?] Folio, 1 leaf. L. C. P. 3842

ALLEN. (E.) A | Narrative | of | Colonel Ethen Allen's | Captivity, | From the Time of his being taken by the British, near Montreal, on | the 25th Day of September, in the Year 1775, to the Time of his | Exchange, on the 6th day of May, 1778 : | Containing, | His Voyages and Travels, | with the most remarkable Occurrences respecting himself, and many | other Continental Prisoners of different ranks and Characters, | which fell under his Observation, in the Course of the same; | particularly the Destruction of the Prisoners at New York, by | General Sir William Howe, in the Years 1776 and 1777. | Interspersed with some Political Observations. | Written by himself, and now published for the Information of the·| Curious of all Nations. Price Ten Paper Dollars. | . . . | . . . | . . . . | *Philadelphia:* | *Printed and Sold by Robert Bell, in Third-Street.* | M.DCC.LXXIX. | 8vo. pp. 46. 3843

ALLEN. A Narrative | of | Colonel Ethan Allen's | Captivity, | From the time of his being taken by the Bri- | tish, near Montreal, on the 25th day of | September, 1775, to the time of his ex- | change on the sixth day of May, 1778, con- | taining his | Voyages and Travels, | With the most remarkable occurrences respect- | ing himself, and many other Continental pri- | soners of different ranks and characters, | which fell under his observation in the | course of the same; particularly the destruc- | tion of the prisoners at New York, by gene- | ral sir William Howe; in the years 1776 and | 1777, interspersed with some political ob- | serva- tions. | Written by himself, and now published for the | information of the curious of all nations. | . . . | . . . | . . . . | *Philadelphia:* | *Printed for and sold by William Mentz,* | *in Cherry Alley.* 1779. | Sm. 8vo. pp. 64. 　　　　　　　　　　　　　A. P. S. 3844

THE AMERICAN Calendar for 1780. *Philadelphia: Thomas Bradford.* 1779. 3845

𝕬𝕸𝕰𝕽𝕴𝕮𝕬𝕽𝕴𝕾𝕮𝕳𝕰𝕹 | Hauß= und Wirthschafts= | Calender | Auf das 1780ste Jahr Christi, | Welches ein Schalt=Jahr von 366 Tagen ist. | Nach dem Pennsylvanischen Horizont berechnet; | Jedoch in den angrenzenden Staaten ohne merklichen Unter= | scheid zu gebrauchen. | Zum Erstenmal heraus gegeben. | *Philadelphia: Gedruckt und zu haben bey Steiner und Cist, in* | *der Zweyten-strasse, vier Haeuser oberhalb der Rees-strasse.* [1779.] | Sm. 4to. pp. (36). 　　　H. S. P. 3846

An das Volk in Pennsylvanien. | Erster Brief. | [*Philadelphia: Henrich Miller.* 1779.] Folio, pp. (2). 　　　H. S. P. 3847

ANSWER to Gre-Ma-Chre. *Philadelphia: B. Towne.* 1779.

ANSWER to the Banks of the Dee. A Song. *Philadelphia: B. Towne.* 1779. 3849

BANDOT. (S.) Discours prononcé le 4 Juillet, jour de l'Anni- | versaire de l'Indépendence, dans l'Eglise Catholique, | par le Reverend Pere Seraphin Bandot, Recollet, | Aumônier de Son Excellence Mr. Gerard, Ministre | Plénipotentiare de France auprès des Etats Unis de | l'Amérique Septentrionale. | *A Phila- delphie, de l'Imprimerie de Steiner & Cist.* [1779.] | Folio, 1 leaf.

THE BANKS of the Dee. A Song. *Philadelphia: B. Towne.* 1779. 3851

THE BATTLE of Monmouth. A Song. *Philadelphia: B. Towne.* 1779. 3852

BEAUMARCHAIS. (P. A. C. de) Observations sur le Mémoire

justificatif de la cour de Londres. Par Pierre Auguste Caron de
Beaumarchais. *A Londres et Philadelphie:* [*Paris.*] 1779. 3853

Title from Weller's *Die falschen Druckorte.* For a translation, see No. 4079, *infra.*

[BENEZET. (Anthony)] An Essay towards the most easy
introduction to the Knowledge of the English Grammar, compiled for the Pennsylvania Spelling Book. [*Philadelphia:* 1779 ?]
12mo. pp. 6 ?   3854

Title from Smith's Catalogue of Friends' Books. I have placed it in 1779, but the date is very uncertain.

BENEZET.   The | Pennsylvania | Spelling-Book, | or |
Youth's friendly Instructor and | Monitor: | Or an easy Plan,
for exciting the Attention, | and facilitating the Instruction
of Children | and others, in Spelling and Reading; and | ac-
quainting them with the essential Parts of | Orthography, Point-
ing, &c. | As also, training their Minds to early Sentiments | of
Piety and Virtue. | More particularly calculated for the use of
Pa- | rents, Guardians and others, remote from | Schools; in
the private Tuition of their | Children, and illiterate Domesticks,
&c. | The Second Edition, Improved and enlarged. | Compiled by
Anthony Benezet. | *Philadelphia:* | *Printed by Joseph Crukshank in
Market-* | *Street, between Second and Third-Streets.* | MDCCLXXIX.
| 12mo. pp. 168.   H. S. P. 3855

BRACKENRIDGE. (H. M[ontgomery]) An | Eulogium | of
the | Brave Men | who have | Fallen in the Contest | with |
Great-Britain: | Delivered on Monday, July 5. 1779. | Before |
A Numerous and Respectable Assembly of Citizens and Foreign-
ers, | in the German Calvinist Church, Philadelphia. | By Hugh
M. Brackenridge, A.M. | . . . | . . . | . . . . | *Philadelphia:* | *Printed
by F. Bailey, in Market-Street.* [1779.] | 4to. pp. 25. L. C. P. 3856

GENERAL BURGOYNE'S Defeat. · A Song. *Philadelphia:
B. Towne.* 1779.   3857

THE | CASE | of the | Sloop Active, &c. | [*Philadelphia: Hall
and Sellers.* 1779.] 4to. pp. 27.   H. S. P. 3858

Probably printed in connection with the Proceedings of the Supreme Executive Council of Pennsylvania against Benedict Arnold (see No. 3935, *infra*), who was accused of champerty in this case. For a meagre account of the almost romantic story of the capture of this vessel, the lengthy legal proceedings which grew out of it, and the important political questions to which it gave rise, see Westcott's *Historic Mansions of Philadelphia*, p. 260.

CATALOGUE of a Collection of Books, about 900 volumes, to be sold at Sheriff's Sale, March 4. *Philadelphia:* 1779.   3859

CHURCHMAN. (J.) An | Account | of the | Gospel Labours, | and | Christian Experiences | of a | Faithful Minister | Of Christ, | John Churchman, | Late of Nottingham in Pennsylvania, deceased. | To which is added a short Memorial of the Life and | Death of a fellow Labourer in the Church, our valuable | Friend Joseph White, late of Bucks County. | . . . | . . . | . . . . | *Philadelphia:* | *Printed by Joseph Crukshank, on* | *the North side of Market-Street, between* | *Second and Third-Streets.* | MDCCLXXIX. | 8vo. pp. i–vii, 1 blank page, 1–256. H. S. P.   3860

The "Testimony" concerning Joseph White occupies pp. 250–256, the remainder of the volume is mostly filled with Churchman's autobiography.

CIRCULAR Letter. *Philadelphia: Robert Aitken.* 1779.   3861

In March, 1779, Aitken printed *two* Circular Letters for Bache and Shee.

A | CIRCULAR Letter | from the | Congress | of the | United States of America | to their | Constituents. | *Philadelphia:* | *Printed by David C. Claypoole,* | *Printer to the Honorable the Congress.* [1779.] | 8vo. pp. 12.   H. S. P.   3862

COMMITTEE for the City and Liberties of Philadelphia. | [*Philadelphia:* 1779?] 4to. 1 leaf.   L. C. P.   3863

An election ticket. The Committee consisted of 120 members.

COMMITTEE-Room. | May 28. 1779. | *Philadelphia: Printed by Francis Bailey, in Market-Street.* [1779.] | Folio, 1 leaf.   3864

Regulating the price of provisions. The following order was for the same purpose.

COMMITTEE-Room. | May 31st, 1779. | *Philadelphia: Printed by Francis Bailey, in Market-Street.* [1779.] | Folio, 1 leaf.   3865

COMMITTEE Room, | June 10, 1779. | [*Philadelphia: John Dunlap.* 1779.] Folio, 1 leaf.   L. C. P.   3866

A circular letter to the Counties on the formation of local Committees similar to that of Philadelphia.

COMMITTEE Room, | June 18, 1779. | *Philadelphia: Printed by John Dunlap, in Market-Street.* [1779.] | Folio, 1 leaf.   3867

Signed " John Swift, Secretary." Regulating the prices of provisions and labor.

COMMITTEE-Room, | June 26, 1779. | *Philadelphia, Printed by Francis Bailey, in Market-Street.* [1779.] | Folio, 1 leaf.   3868

Prices of various articles for the month of July, as fixed by the Committee.

CONSIDERATIONS | on the | Mode and Terms | of a | Treaty of Peace | with | America. | . . . . | *London, Printed* 1778: | *Philadelphia: Re-printed, and Sold by Hall | and Sellers.* MDCCLXXIX. | 8vo. pp. 16.   H. S. P.   3869

DILWORTH. (T.) A New Guide to the English Tongue. By Thomas Dilworth. *Philadelphia: Robert Bell.* 1779.   3870

In the Pa. Gazette, March 31, 1779, Bell offers Dilworth's spelling-book by the dozen, hundred, or thousand copies. Hall and Sellers published an edition in July, and Crukshank another in December of this year.

DODGE. (J.)   A | Narrative | of the | Capture and Treatment | of | John Dodge, | By the English at Detroit. | Written by Himself. | *Philadelphia: | Printed by T. Bradford, at the Coffee-House.* | MDCCLXXIX. | 12mo. pp. 22.   L. C. P.   3871

ECHO from the Temple of | Wisdom, | announced by | Messieurs Common Truth, S.S.T.P. | Common Honesty, C.P.S. | Common Law, L.L.D. | And " Common Sense, Secretary to Foreign | Affairs, and Author of all the Writings | Under the Signature of Common Sense;" | or a | Constitutional Answer and Refutation | of an | Address to Mr. Silas Deane, | Approved of and agreed unto by a Majority of | Delegates in General Congress, | Of Senators, Orators, Grammarians, Rhetoricians, | Logicians, Lawyers, |Critics, Politicians, | Patriots, Public Spirited Whigs, Connoisseurs, | Casuists, Divines, and Republicans; | Mr. Common Sense himself Chief Speaker | in and among them. | In a Series of Letters, | By Socrates, Father of the House of | Congress. | . . . | . . . | . . . | . . . | . . . | . . . . | *Philadelphia :* *Printed in the Year* | 1779. | 8vo. pp. 51, (1).   L. C. P.   3872

THE | ELDERS and Messengers | of the several Baptist Churches, | . . . | . . . | . . . | . . . | . . . | . . . | . . . | . . . | Being met in Association at Philadelphia October 12th and 13th, 1779. | [Colophon.] *Philadelphia : Printed by David C. Claypoole.* [1779.] | Sq. 8vo. pp. 7.   3873

THE | EPISTLE | from the | Yearly-Meeting | in | London, | Held by Adjournments, from the Twenty-fourth of the Fifth Month | 1779, to the Twenty-ninth of the same, inclusive. | To the Quarterly and Monthly Meetings of Friends in Great-Britain, | Ireland, and elsewhere. | [*Philadelphia :* 1779.]   4to. pp. 4.   3874

[ESTAING. (Charles Hector Theodat, Comte d')] Déclaration | Addressée | Au nom du Roi | a tous les anciens François | De l'Amérique Septentrionale. | [Colophon.] *A Philadelphie, De l'Imprimere de Francois Bailey, Rue du Marche.* [1779.] | Folio, pp. 3, (1).   L. C. P.   3875

EVANS. (I.) A | Discourse, | delivered | At Easton, | On The 17th of October, 1779, | to the | Officers | and | Soldiers | Of the Western Army, | After their Return from an Expedition against | the Five Nations of hostile Indians. | By the Reverend Israel Evans, A.M. and | Chaplain to General Poor's Brigade. | Now Published at the particular Request of the Generals | and Field Officers of that Army. | And to be distributed among the Soldiers. —Gratis. | *Philadelphia :* | *Printed by Thomas Bradford, at the Coffee-House.* | M.DCC.LXXIX. | 8vo. pp. 40.   L. C. P.   3876

FAME let thy Trumpet Sound. A Song. *Philadelphia : B. Towne.* 1779.   3877

FATHER Abraham's | Pocket Almanack, | For the Year 1780 ; | *Philadelphia :* | *Printed and Sold by John Dunlap.* [1779.] | 24mo. pp. (24).   H. S. P.   3878

FELLOW Citizens, | Remember the proceedings on Mon- | day Morning at the Coffee-House, and on Tuesday | at the Town-Meeting. | The Liberty of the Press and | Freedom of Speech were then both | violently attacked. | Change both Men and Measures, or Ruin inevi- | tably awaits us.   The late public Insult offered to | the French Nation, through their Officer in this | City, sufficiently warrants this Caution. | Monday, | August 2d, 1779. | [*Philadelphia:* 1779.] | 4to. 1 leaf.   L. C. P.   3879

THE FEMALE Whig. A Song. *Philadelphia: B. Towne.* 1779.   3880

THE GAMESTER. A Song. *Philadelphia: B. Towne.* 1779.

GENERAL Militia Orders. | Philadelphia, October 27, 1779. | *Philadelphia: Printed by F. Bailey, in Market-Street.* [1779.] | Folio, pp. 2.   H. S. P.   3882

GERMAN Newspaper. *Philadelphia: Gedruckt und zu haben von Johann Dunlap, in der Englischen und Deutschen Buchdruckerei.* | Folio.   3883

I have met with only the second leaf of a number of this paper, issued in February.

GRE-Ma-Chre. A Song. *Philadelphia: B. Towne.* 1779.

HASELDEN. (T.)   The Seaman's Daily Assistant. By Thomas Haselden. *Philadelphia: Joseph Crukshank.* 1779.   3885

DER | HOCH = DEUTSH= | Americanische | Calender, | Auf das Jahr | . . . | . . . | 1780. | [12 lines.] | Zum zwey und vierzig= sten mal heraus gegeben. | *Philadelphia: Gedruckt und zu finden bey Johann Dunlap, in der Markt-strasse.* | . . . | . . . | . . . | . . . | . . . . [1779.] | Sq. 8vo. pp. (32).   H. S. P.   3886

HOPKINSON. (F.)   The Battle of the Kegs. By Francis Hopkinson. *Philadelphia: B. Towne.* 1779.   3887

IN Committee, July 14, 1779. | . . . | . . . | . . . | . . . . | To our Fellow-Citizens. | *Philadelphia: Printed by Thomas Bradford, at the Coffee-House.* [1779.] | Folio, 1 leaf.   3888

Signed "William Henry, Chairman." A plan for stopping the emission of paper money.

IN Council. | Philadelphia, February 3d, 1779. | *Philadelphia: Printed by Francis Bailey, in Front-street.* [1779.] | Folio, 1 leaf.

Resolutions exhibiting the charges of illegal and oppressive conduct against General Benedict Arnold, upon which the Attorney-General was directed to prosecute him.

IN Council. | Philadelphia, May 28th, 1779. | *Philadelphia: Printed by John Dunlap, in Market-street.* [1779.] | Folio, 1 leaf.

" Whereas it has been represented to this Board, that divers persons of suspicious characters, and to whom inimical practices are imputed, and also divers who are charged with forestalling and engrossing, have lately been restrained in their liberty, . . . Resolved, That the Magistrates of the City be requested and directed to order the Sheriff . . . to transmit . . . without delay, a list of all such persons."

IN Council. | Philadelphia, July 8, 1779. | *Philadelphia : Printed by Francis Bailey, in Market-Street.* [1779.] | Folio, 1 leaf.   3891

Irregularities and Abuses having lately happened in the Public Markets, " Resolved, That the Justices, High Sheriff, and Constables, be directed to attend at the Market, for the Preservation of the public Peace."

IN Council, | Philadelphia, October 13, 1779. | [*Philadelphia: John Dunlap.* 1779.] Folio, 1 leaf.   H. S. P.   3892

A circular letter to the Lieutenants of the counties, ordering the Militia to rendezvous at Trenton.

IN Council. | Philadelphia, October 26, 1779. | To the Merchants and Traders of | Philadelphia, and particularly the | Importers and Holders of Salt. | *Philadelphia : | Printed by F. Bailey, in Market-Street.* | M.DCC.LXXIX. | Sm. 8vo. pp. 6, 1 leaf.   3893

IN General Assembly, | Saturday, February 13, 1779. | *Philadelphia : Printed by John Dunlap.* [1779.] | Folio, pp. (3).   3894

A bill entitled " An Act to raise the Supplies for the Year One Thousand Seven Hundred and Seventy-Nine, published for consideration."

IN General Assembly, | Of Pennsylvania. | Thursday, April 1, 1779. | [*Philadelphia: John Dunlap.* 1779.] Folio, 1 leaf.   3895

A bill entitled " An Act for the regulation of the Markets in the City of Philadelphia, and for other purposes therein mentioned," "printed for public consideration."

THE | INDEPENDENT & Constitutional | Ticket, | for a General Committee, | Of the City of Philadelphia . . . . | [*Philadelphia: Francis Bailey.* 1779.] Folio, 1 leaf.   L. C. P. 3896

INSTRUCTIONS to the Agents | for Forfeited Estates. | *Philadelphia: Printed by Francis Bailey, in Market-Street.* [1779.] | Folio, 1 leaf.   H. S. P. 3897

JOURNALS | of | Congress, | from | Friday January 1st, | to | Monday February 1st, 1779. | *Philadelphia:* | *Printed by David C. Claypoole, Printer to* | *the Congress of the United States of America.* | MDCCLXXIX. | Folio, pp. 12.   H. S. P. 3898

JOURNALS | of | Congress, | from | Monday, February 1st, | to | Monday, March 1st, 1779. | *Philadelphia:* | *Printed by David C. Claypoole,* | *Printer to the Honorable the Congress of* | *the United States of America.* [1779.] | 8vo. pp. 50.   H. S. P. 3899

JOURNALS | of | Congress | from | Monday, March 1st, | to | Tuesday, March 30th, 1779, inclusive. | [*Ibid.*] 8vo. pp. 56. + JOURNALS | of | Congress, | from | Wednesday, March thirty-first, | to | Saturday, April tenth, 1779, | inclusive. | [*Ibid.*] pp. 24. Continued Weekly to Dec. 31, 1779, 38 parts in all.

JOURNALS | of | Congress, | containing | the | Proceedings | From January 1st, 1778, to January 1st, 1779. | Published by order of Congress. | Volume IV. | *Philadelphia:* | *Printed by David C. Claypoole,* | *Printer to the Honorable the Congress.* [1779.] | 8vo. Title, 1 leaf; text, pp. 1–748; Index, pp. i–lxxxix; Appendix, pp. (4).

LAWS | Enacted in the Second Sitting | of the Third | General Assembly, | Of the Commonwealth | of | Pennsylvania, | Which commenced at Philadelphia, on Monday the first day of | February, A. D. One thousand seven hundred and seventy-nine, | and continued till Monday the fifth day of April of the same year. | [*Philadelphia: John Dunlap.* 1779.] Folio, pp. 177–228. + Laws | Enacted in the Third Sitting | . . . | . . . | . . . | . . . | . . . | . . . | . . . . | [*Ibid.*] pp. 229–260.   H. S. P. 3901

LAWS | Enacted in the First Sitting | Of the Fourth | General Assembly, | Of the Commonwealth | of | Pennsylvania, | Which met at Philadelphia, on Monday the twenty-fifth day of October, in | the year of our Lord One thousand seven hundred and seventy-nine. | [*Philadelphia: John Dunlap*. 1779.] Folio, pp. 261–280, 1 leaf. 3902

THE LIBERTY Tree. A Song. *Philadelphia: B. Towne.* 1779.

MAGAW. (S.) A | Sermon | preached in | Christ-Church, | Dover, | On Monday, December 27th, 1779, | Being the Anniversary of | St. John the Evangelist; | At the Request of and Before | The General Communication of | Free and Accepted | Masons | of the | Delaware State: | By Samuel Magaw, A.M. | *Philadelphia:* | *Printed by John Dunlap, in Market-Street.* [1779.] | 8vo. pp. 16. L. C. P. 3904

MANSON. (D.) A New Primer. By David Manson. *Philadelphia: Joseph Crukshank.* 1779. 3905

MINUTES. | of the | First Session, | of the Fourth | General Assembly | Of the Commonwealth | of | Pennsylvania. | [*Philadelphia: John Dunlap.* 1779.] Folio, pp. 154–176, 1 leaf. 3906

No title-page. The minutes of the second sitting are paged 180–235; of the third sitting, 236–251; and of the fourth sitting, 252–298. The first page should have been numbered 155, and the error was corrected by dropping 300 from the paging.

[MORRIS. (Gouverneur.)] Observations | on the | American Revolution. | Published | According to a Resolution | of Congress, | By their Committee. | For the | Consideration of those who are desirous | of comparing | The Conduct of the opposed Parties, | and | The several Consequences which have | flowed from it. | *Philadelphia:* | *Printed by Styner and Cist, in Second-Street.* | MDCCLXXIX. | 8vo. Half-title, 1 leaf; Title, 1 leaf; pp. 122.

MORRIS. (Robert) To the Citizens of Pennsylvania. | *Philadelphia: Printed by Hall & Sellers.* [1779.] | Folio, pp. (2). 3908

In defence of his management of the public accounts.

THE MOTE Point of Finance, | or the | Crown Land equally divided. | [*Philadelphia:* 1779.]　4to. 1 leaf.　　　L. C. P.　3909

Signed " Lucius Quintius Cincinnatus," and dated " Phila., Sept. 21, 1779."

MULLER. (J.)　A | Treatise | of | Artillery: | Containing | I. General Constructions of | Brass and Iron Guns used | by Sea and Land, and their | Carriages. | II. General Constructions of | Mortars and Howitzers, | their Beds and Carriages. | III. Dimensions of all Car- | riages used in Artil- | lery. | IV. Exercise of the Regi- | ment at Home, and Ser- | vice Abroad in a Siege or | Battle. | V. Its March and Encamp- | ment, Ammunition, | Stores, and Horses. | VI. Lastly, The necessary | Laboratory Work for | Fire-Ships, &c. | To which is prefixed, | An Introduction, | with | A Theory of Powder applied to | Fire-Arms. | With large Additions, Alterations, and | Corrections, | According to the Second London Edition. | By John Muller, | Professor of Artillery and Fortification, | And Preceptor of Engineering, &c. to his Royal Highness the | late Duke of Gloucester. | *Philadelphia:* | *Printed by Styner and Cist, in Second-street,* | *For John Norman, Engraver.* 1779. | 8vo.　　　L. C. P.　3910

Collation : Title, 1 leaf; Dedication, 1 leaf; Contents, pp. (4) ; Introduction, pp. i.–xl. ; text, pp. 1–215 ; 32 plates (Frontispiece, 3 tables of piles of shot and plates i. to xxviii.).

𝕯𝕰𝕽 𝕽𝕰𝖀𝕲𝕰𝕾𝕿𝕰𝕷𝕷𝕿𝕰 und Verbefferte | Americanifche | Staats= Calender | Auf das 1780fte Jahr Chrifti, | Welches ein Schalt=Jahr von 366 Tagen ift. | [12 lines.] | Zum Zwanzigftenmal herausgegeben. | *Philadelphia: Gedruckt und zu haben bey Henrich Miller, in der Reesstrasse, zwischen* | *der Zweyten- und Dritten-strasse, und gerade gegenueber Moraeviaen-Ally.* [1779.] | Sq. 8vo. pp. (40 ?).　H. S. P.　3911

THE NEW RECRUIT, or the Gallant Volunteer.　A Song. *Philadelphia: B. Towne.* 1779.　　　3912

THE NEW ENGLAND Primer enlarged.　*Philadelphia: Styner and Cist.* 1779.　　　3913

Hall and Sellers published an edition in January, and Crukshank another in December.

THE NEWEST American Primer. *Philadelphia: Styner and Cist.* 1779. **3914**

NEW-YEAR Verses of the Carriers of the Pennsylvania Evening Post. *Philadelphia: B. Towne.* 1779. **3915**

NEW-YEAR Verses of the Carriers of the Pennsylvania Gazette. *Philadelphia: Hall and Sellers.* 1779. **3916**

NEW-YEAR Verses of the Carriers of the Pennsylvania Journal. *Philadelphia: Thomas Bradford.* 1779. **3917**

NEW-YEAR Verses of the Carriers of the Pennsylvania Packet. *Philadelphia: John Dunlap.* 1779. **3918**

NORTH CAROLINA. The | Constitution, | or | Form of Government, | Agreed to, and Resolved upon, | by the | Representatives of the Freemen | of the | State | of | North-Carolina, | Elected and chosen for that particular Purpose, | In Congress assembled, at Halifax, | The Eighteenth Day of December, in the Year of our Lord | One Thousand Seven Hundred and Seventy-Six. | *Philadelphia:* | *Printed by F. Bailey, in Market-Street.* | M,DCC,LXXIX. | Sm. 8vo. pp. 16. H. S. P. **3919**

NOUGARET. (P. J. B.) Eloge de Voltaire. Par Pierre Jean Baptiste Nougaret. *A Philadelphie:* [*Paris.*] 1779. w. **3920**

NOUGARET. Le bon Frère, parodie de Castor et Pollux. Par P. J. B. Nougaret. *A Philadelphie:* [*Paris.*] 1779. w. **3921**

NOUVELLES nouvelles en vers. *A Philadelphie.* 1779. **3922**

ON General Wayne's taking Stony Point. A Song. *Philadelphia: B. Towne.* 1779. **3923**

THE | PENNSYLVANIA | Evening Post. | MDCCLXXVIX. | Volume V. | *Philadelphia:* | *Printed by Benjamin Towne, in Front-Street.* [1779.] | 4to. pp. (2), 258. **3924**

January, 1779. Numb. 2534. | THE | PENNSYLVANIA | Gazette, | and | Weekly Advertiser. | Tuesday, January 5, 1779. |

*Philadelphia : Printed by Hall and Sellers, at the New-Printing- |
Office, near the Market.* | Folio.   3925

Numbers 2534 to 2585 (Dec. 29, 1779), four pages each.

January 6, 1779.   Number 1810. | THE | PENNSYLVANIA
Journal | and | Weekly Advertiser. | Wednesday, January 6,
1779. | [Colophon.]   *Philadelphia : Printed and Sold by Thomas
Bradford, at the Corner of Front and Market Streets, where | Persons
may be supplied with this Paper at Fifty Shillings a Year, and where
Advertisements are taken in.* | 3926

Numbers 1810 (Jan. 6, 1779) to 1320 (Dec. 29, 1779), four pages each.   Number
1822 is misnumbered 1282, and this error was carried on for several years.   The papers
for April 28 and May 5 are both numbered 1286, and this error was not corrected.

Saturday, January 2, 1779. | THE | PENNSYLVANIA :
Packet. | Or : the | General Advertiser | (Price Fifteen single,
One Shilling by the quantity.   Published every Tuesday, Thurs-
day and Saturday.) | *Philadelphia : Printed and Sold by John Dunlap,
in Market-street.*   [1779.] | Folio.   3927

Jan. 2 to Dec. 30, 1779, 157 numbers of four pages, including a " Packet Extraordinary," of Sept. 10th.   There is a " Supplement" of one leaf to the paper of Sept.
2d, and also a " Packet Extraordinary" of one leaf to the same issue ; of this there
were two editions.   There is also a " Packet Extraordinary" of two pages to the
paper of Feb. 23d ; an additional half-sheet of one leaf to the paper of July 6th ;
and a " Postscript" of one leaf to that of Dec. 16th.   The price of the paper was
omitted from the title of the issue of March 23d, and on and after Oct. 5th.   From
March 25th to Oct. 3d it was " Price 2s. 6d. single, 2s. by the quantity."

THE PENNSYLVANIA Pocket Almanac for 1780.   *Phila-
delphia : Thomas Bradford.*   1779.   3928

PERRIN. (J.)   A | Grammar | of the | French Tongue, |
grounded upon the | Decisions of the French Academy, | wherein
all the | Necessary Rules, Observations, and Examples | are | Ex-
hibited in a Manner intirely New. | By John Perrin. | . . . . |
According to the Second Edition, | printed at London. | *Philadel-
phia : | Printed by Styner and Cist, in Second-street,* | . . . . |
M.DCC.LXXIX. | 8vo. pp. xii, 1 leaf, 320.   H. S. P.   3929

1779.   Numb. I. | 𝔓𝔥𝔦𝔩𝔞𝔡𝔢𝔩𝔭𝔥𝔦𝔰𝔠𝔥𝔢𝔰 𝔖taatsregi𝔣ter. |

Enthaltend | Die neueſten Nachrichten von den merkwürdigſten In= und Ausländiſchen | Kriegs= und Friedens=Begebenheiten; | nebſt verſchiedenen andern gemeinnützigen Anzeigen. | Mittwochs, den 21 July. | *Diese Zeitung wird alle Mittwochen heraus gegeben von Steiner und Cist, Buchdruckern, in der Zweyten-strasse, vier Haeuser | oberhalb der Rees-Strasse; für Zwey Schillinge und Sechs Pens beym einzelnen Stück, und Zwey Schillinge beym Dutzend.* [1779.] | Folio, pp. (4).   A. P. S.   3930

This was the successor of Miller's paper. It was continued until about 1781, and was succeeded by Steiner's *Philadelphische Correspondenz.*

POOR Will's | Almanack, | for the | Year of our Lord, 1780; | [15 lines.] | *Philadelphia:* | *Printed and Sold by Joseph Crukshank,* | *in Market Street, between Second and Third-Streets.* [1779.] | Sm. 8vo. pp. (36).   H. S. P.   3931

POOR Will's Pocket Almanac for 1780. *Philadelphia: Joseph Crukshank.* 1779.   3932

A PRIMER. *Philadelphia: Walters and Norman.* 1779.   3933

" Adorned with a beautiful head of general Washington and other copper plate cuts." Pa. Evening Post, June 23, 1779. This was the first portrait of Washington engraved in America.

PROCEEDINGS | of the | General | Town-Meeting, | held | In the State-House Yard, | in the | City of Philadelphia. | On Monday the Twenty-Sixth, | And by Adjournments to | Tuesday the Twenty-Seventh of July last. | *Philadelphia:* | *Printed by F. Bailey, in Market-Street.* | M.DCC.LXXIX. | Sm. 8vo. pp. 26.   3934

PROCEEDINGS | of the | Supreme Executive Council | of the | State of Pennsylvania | In the Case of | Major General Arnold. | [*Philadelphia :*] *Printed by Hall and Sellers.* 1779. | 4to. pp. 11.

PROCLAMATION. [*Arms of Pennsylvania.*] | By His Excellency the President, and Council of | the Commonwealth of Pennsylvania, | A Proclamation. | [*Philadelphia :*] *Printed by Hall and Sellers.* 1779. | Folio, 1 leaf.   H. S. P.   3936

Dated " April 2, 1779." " Whereas there is just Cause to believe that our cruel and inveterate Enemies, despairing of the Conquest of America by open and manly

Force, are about to adopt the mean and savage Policy of Distress and Depredation,"
&c., &c.

PROCLAMATION. | *Philadelphia: Printed by Hall and Sellers.*
[1779.] | Folio, 1 leaf.   H. S. P.   3937

By Congress, appointing the first Thursday of May to be a " Day of Fasting,
Humiliation, and Prayer." Signed " John Jay, President," and dated " March 20,
1779."

PROCLAMATION. [*Arms of Pennsylvania.*] | By His Excel-
lency the President, and Council of | the Commonwealth of Penn-
sylvania, | A Proclamation. | [*Philadelphia:*] *Printed by Hall and
Sellers.* 1779. | Folio, 1 leaf.   H. S. P.   3938

Dated " April 16, 1779." Appointing the first Thursday in May to be a Fast Day.

PROCLAMATION. By the Honorable George Bryan, Esquire,
Vice-President, and the Supreme Executive Council of the Com-
monwealth of Pennsylvania. *Philadelphia: Printed by Hall and
Sellers.* 1778. Folio, 1 leaf.   3939

Dated " Oct. 11, 1779." Laying an embargo for thirty days.

[*Arms of Pennsylvania.*] | A PROCLAMATION | By His Ex-
cellency Joseph Reed, Esquire, President, and the | Supreme Ex-
ecutive Council of the Commonwealth of Pennsylvania. | [*Phila-
delphia:*] *Printed by Hall and Sellers.* 1779. | Folio, 1 leaf.   3940

Dated " June 22, 1779." Warning certain persons therein named to surrender
themselves before August 5th, or be attainted of high treason.

PROCLAMATION. [*Arms of Pennsylvania.*] By His Excel-
lency Joseph Reed, Esq; President, and the Su- | preme Execu-
tive Council of the Commonwealth of Pennsylvania, | A Proclama-
tion. | [*Philadelphia:*] *Printed by Hall and Sellers.* 1779. | Folio, 1
leaf.   L. C. P.   3941

Against the " Fort Wilson" rioters, dated " Oct. 6, 1779."

PROCLAMATION. [*Arms of Pennsylvania.*] By His Excel-
lency Joseph Reed, Esq; President, and the Supreme Executive |

Council of the Commonwealth of Pennsylvania, | A Proclamation. | [*Philadelphia :*] *Printed by Hall and Sellers.* 1779. | Folio, 1 leaf.

Concerning the Virginia Boundary Line, dated " Dec. 28, 1779."

[*Arms of Pennsylvania.*] | A PROCLAMATION | By His Excellency Joseph Reed, Esquire, President, and the | Supreme Executive Council of the Commonwealth of Pennsylvania. | [*Philadelphia :*] *Printed by Hall and Sellers.* 1779. | Folio, 1 leaf.   3943

Dated " April 30, 1779." Laying an embargo on outward-bound vessels for 15 days, in order that the State Ship of War should obtain its complement of men.

[REED. (Joseph)] Remarks | on | Governor Johnstone's Speech | In Parliament ; | with | A Collection | of all the | Letters and Authentic Papers, | relative to | His Proposition to engage the Interest of one of | the Delegates of the State of Pennsylva- | nia, | in the Congress of the States of Ame- | rica, to promote the Views of the British | Commissioners. | *Philadelphia :* | *Printed by Francis Bailey.* | M.DCC.LXXIX. | 4to. p̄p. 61.   H. S. P.   3944

REGULATIONS | for the | Order and Discipline | of the | Troops | of the | United States. | Part. I. | *Philadelphia :* | *Printed by Styner and Cist, in Second-street.* | MDCCLXXIX. | 12mo. pp. 154, (9), 8 plates.   L. C. P.   3945

REPORT | of | Commissioners | for | Settling a Cartel | for the | Exchange of Prisoners. | *Philadelphia :* | *Printed by David C. Claypoole* | *Printer to the Honorable the Congress of* | *the United States of America.* | MDCCLXXIX. | 8vo. pp. 20. ·   A. P. S.   3946

REPORT | of the | Committee of the Assembly, | On the State of the | Public Accounts, 1777 and 1778. | [Colophon.] *Philadelphia : Printed by John Dunlap, in* | *Market-street.* [1779.] | Folio, pp. 67.   L. S. P.   3947

REPORT | of the | Committee of the Assembly, | On the State of the | Public Accounts, 1779. | [Colophon.] *Philadelphia : Printed by John Dunlap.* [1779.] | Folio, pp. 39.   H. S. P.   3948

REPORTS | of the | Board of Treasury | Relative to Finance.

| [Of the United States.] [*Philadelphia : John Dunlap.* 1779?] Folio, 7 leaves.   L. C. P.   3949

𝕯𝕰𝕽 𝕽𝕰𝕻𝖀𝕭𝕷𝕴𝕶𝕬𝕹𝕴𝕾𝕮𝕳𝕰 Calender auf das 1780ste Jahr Christi. Zum Zweyten mal herausgegeben. *Lancaster, gedruckt und zu finden bey Theophilus Cossart und Companie.* 1779.   3950

ROBERDEAU. ([Daniel]) At a General Meeting of the Citizens | of Philadelphia, and Parts adjacent, at the State-House Yard in this City, on | Tuesday the 25th of May 1779, General Roberdeau was unanimously requested | to take the Chair; who introduced the Business with the following Address : | *Philadelphia : Printed by Francis Bailey, in Market-Street.* [1779.] | Folio, 1 leaf.

Meeting in regard to appointing a Committee to regulate the retail prices of rum, sugar, flour, coffee, and tea.

ROSLIN Castle. A Song. *Philadelphia : B. Towne.* 1779. 3952

[SAINTE-CROIX. (Guillaume Emanuel Joseph de)] De l'etat, et du sort des colonies des anciens peuples. *A Philadelphie :* [*Paris.*] 1779.   3953

SAUNDERS. (R.) A Pocket Almanac for 1780. By Richard Saunders, Phil. *Philadelphia : Hall and Sellers.* 1779.   3954

SAUNDERS. Poor Richard improved : | Being an | Almanack | . . . | . . | . . . | . . . | . . | . . | . . . | . . . | . . . | . . . | For the | Year of our Lord 1780 : | Being Bissextile or Leap-Year. | . . . | . . . | . . | . . . | . . | . . . | . . . | . . . | . . . | By Richard Saunders, Philom. | *Philadelphia :* | *Printed and Sold by Hall and Sellers.* [1779.] | Sm. 8vo. pp. (36).   H. S. P.   3955

THE | SCHOOL | for | Scandal. | A | Comedy. | . . . | . . . | . . . | . . . | . . . | . . . . | The Third Edition. | *London : Printed.* | *Philadelphia ;* | *Re-printed and Sold by Thomas Bradford, at the* | *Coffee-House.* | M.DCC.LXXIX. | 8vo. Title, 1 leaf; Dedication, pp. iii–iv; Dramatis Personæ, 1 leaf; text, pp. 1–46.   3956

A political adaptation of Sheridan's play.

SHARP. (A.) Der Ganz Neue Verbefferte Nord = Americanifche Calender, auf das 1780fte Jahr Chrifti. Zum Fünftenmal herausgegeben und verfertiget von Anthony Sharp, Philom. *Lancaster: Francis Bailey.* 1779.   3957

SHARP. The Lancaster Almanac for 1780. By Anthony Sharp. *Lancaster: Francis Bailey.* 1779.   3958

SHARP. The Lancaster Pocket Almanac for 1780. By Anthony Sharp. *Lancaster: Francis Bailey.* 1779.   3959

SIR, | You are returned one of the Overseers of the Poor. . . . . | [*Philadelphia :* 1779.] 4to. 1 leaf.   L. C. P.   3960

Notice of election and a list of the Overseers, dated "Philadelphia, March 13, 1779."

A SOLDIER and his Lady, or Tom and Kate. A Song. *Philadelphia: B. Towne.* 1779.   3961

SOME | Account | of | Isaac Shoemaker, | of the | Township of Cheltenham, in the County of Philadel- | phia, (Son of John Shoemaker of the same place) | who departed this Life on the 31st. day of the se- | venth month 1779, in the twenty-fifth year of his | Age. | [*Philadelphia:* 1779 ?] 8vo. pp. 8.   3962

STEUBEN. ([Frederick William Augustus,] Baron) For the | Use of the Militia | Of Pennsylvania. | An | Abstract | Of a System of | Military Discipline : | Framed by | The Hon. the Baron Steuben, | Major General and Inspector General of the | Armies of these United States. | Approved by | His Excellency General Washington. | Confirmed by | The Hon. the Congress. | *Philadelphia :* | *Printed by Francis Bailey, in Market-Street.* | M.DCC.LXXIX. | Sm. 8vo. pp. 38.   L. C. P.   3963

Die | TÄGLICHEN | Loofungen | der | Brüdergemeine | für das Jahr | 1780. | *Philadelphia,* | *Gedruckt bey Steiner und Cist, in der Zweyten-Strasse.* [1779.] | 8vo. pp. (58).   H. S. P.   3964

TAXATION Royal Tyranny, | Or the errors of the American

Congress demonstrated by | a geometrical axiom. | [*Philadelphia :* 1779.]   4to. 1 leaf.   L. C. P.   3965

Signed "Vox Populi," and dated "Phila., Sept. 22, 1779."

[TICKELL. (Richard)]   Anticipation. | Containing the Substance of   His Majesty's | Most Gracious Speech | to both | Houses of Parliament. | On the | Opening of the approaching Session ; | Together | With a full and authentic Account of the Debates which will | take Place in the House of Commons, on the Motion for the | Address, and the Amendment. | With Notes. | (First published three Days before the Opening of the Session.) | . . . | . . . . | The Sixth Edition. | *London, Printed ; | Philadelphia : | Re-printed and Sold, by T. Bradford, at the Corner of Front | and Market Streets.* 1779. | 8vo. Half-title, 1 leaf; Title, 1 leaf; Advertisement, 1 leaf; text, pp. 1–33.   L. C. P.   3966

TO the inhabitants of Pennsylvania in general, and particularly | those of the city and neighbourhood of Philadelphia. | [*Philadelphia : Thomas Bradford.* 1779.] Folio, pp. 2.   L. C. P.   3967

"Signed by order of a meeting of tanners, curriers, and cordwainers, held at the Committee room, 11th day of July, 1779.   James Roney, Chairman."

TO the | Inhabitants | of the | United States of America. | *Philadelphia : Printed by David C. Claypoole, Printer to the | Honorable the Congress of the United States of America.* [1779.] | Folio, pp. (2).   L. C. P.   3968

An address on the situation of the country, dated "May 26, 1779."

THE | UNITED States | Magazine : | A | Repository | of | History, Politics | and | Literature. | Volume I. | For the Year, 1779. | *Philadelphia : | Printed and sold by Francis Bailey, in Front-street.* [1779.] | 8vo. pp. 506.   H. S. P.   3969

Edited by Hugh Montgomery Brackenridge, better known as Hugh Henry B.
"It abounds in curious and interesting original matter relative to the American Revolution."

VINCENT. (—) Lettres d'un membre du congrès Américain

à divers membres du Parlement d'Angleterre. *A Philadelphie,* [*Paris.*] 1779.   w.   3970

VOUS êtes prié de la part | du Ministre Plenipotentiare de | France, d'assister au Te Deum, | qu'il sera chanter Dimanche 4 de | ce Mois, à midi dans la Chapelle | Catholique neuve pour celebrer | l'Anniversaire de l'Independance | . ... | . . . . | *A Philadelphie, De l'Imprimere de Francois Bailey, Rue du Marché.* [1779.] | Sm. 4to. 1 leaf.   L. C. P.   3971

WAR and Washington. A Song. *Philadelphia: B. Towne.* 1779.   3972

WEATHERWISE. (A.) Father Abraham's | Almanack, | For the Year of our Lord | 1780 ; | Being Bissextile or Leap-Year, | And the Fifth Year of American | Independence. | . . . | . . . | . . . | . . . | . . . | . . . | . . . | . . . | . . . | . . . | . . . | . . . | . . . . | By Abraham Weatherwise, Gent. | *Philadelphia :* | *Printed and Sold by John Dunlap,* | *In Market-Street.* [1779.] | Sm. 8vo. pp. (32).   H. S. P.   3973

[WEBSTER. (Pelatiah)] An | Essay | on | Free Trade | and | Finance, | humbly offered to the | Consideration | of the | Public. | By a Citizen of Philadelphia. | *Philadelphia :* | *Printed and Sold by Thomas Bradford, at the Coffee-House.* | M.DCC.LXXIX. | 8vo. pp. 20.   H. S. P.   3974

[WEBSTER.] A Second | Essay | on | Free Trade | and | Finance, | humbly offered to the | Consideration | of the | Public. | By a Citizen of Philadelphia. | *Philadelphia :* | *Printed and Sold by Thomas Bradford, at the Coffee-House.* | M.DCC.LXXIX. | 8vo. pp. 20.   H. S. P.   3975

WHEN America first at Heaven's Command. A Song. *Philadelphia : B. Towne.* 1779.   3976

WHEN the Cares of Day. A Song. *Philadelphia : B. Towne.* 1779.   3977

WHEREAS the rapid and alarming depreciation of the currency

. . . . *Philadelphia: Printed by F. Bailey, in Market-Street.* [1779.] | Sm. folio, 1 leaf.   L. C. P.   3978

Signed " Blair McClenaghan, Chairman of the Committee for enquiring into the State of Trade," and dated by Du Simitiere, Phila., Aug. 10, 1779. A resolution calling upon retail tradesmen to send in " an attested Account of the Prices they severally sold for or charged at in the Year 1774."

GENERAL WOLFE. A Song. *Philadelphia: B. Towne.* 1779.   3979

THE WORLD Turned Upside Down. Moral Essays in Verse. Decorated with 34 copper plate cuts. *Philadelphia: Walters and Norman.* 1779.   3980

YE Fair Married Dames. A Song. *Philadelphia: B. Towne.* 1779.   3981

1780.

AN ACCOUNT of the Births and Burials in the United Churches of Christ Church and St. Peter's. *Philadelphia:* 1780.

AN | ACT | for the | Regulation | of the | Militia | of the | Commonwealth | of | Pennsylvania. | Published by Order of the | General Assembly. | [*Philadelphia: Thomas Bradford?* 1780.] 8vo. pp. 20.   L. C. P.   3983

𝔄𝔐𝔈ℜℑ𝔒𝔄ℜℑ𝔖𝔒𝔈ℌ𝔈ℜ | Haus= und Wirthschafts= | Calender | Auf das 1781ste Jahr Christi, | Welches ein Gemeines Jahr ist von 365 Tagen. | . . . | . . . | . . . . | Zum Zweytenmal heraus gegeben. | *Philadelphia: Gedruckt und zu haben bey Steiner und Cist, in | der Zweyten-strasse, vier Haeuser oberhalb der Rees-strasse.* [1780.] | Sm. 4to. pp. (40).   H. S. P.   3984

BARCLAY. (R.) An Apology for the True Christian Divinity ; being an Explanation and Vindication of the Principles and Doctrines of the People called Quakers. By Robert Barclay. The Tenth Edition. *Philadelphia: Joseph Crukshank.* 1780.   3985

[BENEZET. (Anthony)] Christian Piety : | By Philalethes. | With Extracts from different Authors. | *Philadelphia:* 1780 ?] 12mo. pp. 36.   F.   3986

[BENEZET.] An | Extract | from a | Treatise | on the | Spirit of Prayer, | or | The Soul rising out of the Vanity of Time into the Riches | of Eternity. | With some | Thoughts on War : | Remarks on the Nature and bad effects of the use | of Spirituous Liquors. | And | Considerations on Slavery. | . . . | | . . . | . . . | . . . | . . . | . . . | . . . | . . . | . . . | . . . | . . . | . . . . . | Philadelphia : | Printed by Joseph Crukshank, in Market-street, | between Second and Third-streets. | MDCCLXXX. | 12mo. pp. 84.   F.   3987

[BENEZET.] Notes on the Slave Trade, &c. | [Philadelphia : Joseph Crukshank. 1780 ?] Sm. 8vo. pp. 8.   L. C. P.   3988

BENEZET. Observations | sur | L'Origine, | Les Principes, | et | L'Establisement en Amerique, | De la Societé | Connue sous la Denomination | de | Quakers ou Trembleurs : | Extrait de divers Auteurs. | Redigés, principalement, en faveur des Etrangers. | Par Antoine Benezet, | A Philadelphie. | Chez Joseph Crukshank, dans la Rue du Marché, entre | la Seconde et la Troisieme Rue. | MDCCLXXX. | Sm. 8vo. pp. 36.   H. S. P.   3989

[BENEZET.] Serious Reflections affectionately recommended | to the Well-disposed of every Religious De- | nomination, particularly those who Mourn | and Lament on account of the Calamities | which attend us ; and the insensibility that | so generally prevails. | [Philadelphia : 1780 ?] Sm. 8vo. pp. 4.   F.   3990

The first three pages are the last three of Christian Piety, renumbered but not re-set.

BENEZET. A Short | Account | of the People called | Quakers ; | Their Rise, Religious Principles and Settlement | in America, | Mostly collected from different Authors, for the | Information of all serious Inquirers, particularly | Foreigners. | By Anthony Benezet. | Philadelphia : | Printed by Joseph Crukshank, in Market-street, between | Second and Third-streets. | M,DCC,LXXX. | 8vo. pp. 27.   H. S. P.   3991

BENEZET. A Short | Account | of the People called | Quakers ; | Their Rise, Religious Principles and Settle- | ment in

America, | Mostly collected from different Authors, for | the In-
formation of all serious Inquirers, | particularly Foreigners. | The
Second Edition. | By Anthony Benezet. | *Philadelphia: | Printed by
Joseph Crukshank, in Market-street, be-* | *tween Second and Third-
streets.*   [1780?] | 12mo. pp. 36.   3992

[BENEZET.] Short Observations on | Slavery, | Introductory to
some Extracts from | the writing of the Abbe Raynal, | on that im-
portant Subject. | [*Philadelphia:* 1780?] 12mo. pp. 12. M. S. 3993

[BENEZET.] Some | Necessary | Remarks | on the | Educa-
tion | of the | Youth | in the Country-parts of this, and | the
neighbouring | Governments. | [*Philadelphia:* 1780?] Sm. 8vo.
pp. 8.   F. 3994

THE BLESSED Effects of a Holy Life and | Daily Conversa-
tion with God, | exemplified in a short Extract of the Life | of
Amelle Nicolas, a poor | ignorant Country Maid. | [*Philadelphia:
Joseph Crukshank.* 1780?] 12mo. pp. 12.   F. 3995

One of Benezet's tracts, without date or imprint.

[BRISSOT de Warville. (Jean Pierre)] Testament | Politique
| de | L'Angleterre. | *A Philadelphie: [Paris?]* | M.DCC.LXXX.
| Sm. 8vo. pp. 88.   H. S. P. 3996

B[ROOK.] (M[ary]) Reasons | for the | Necessity | of | Silent
Waiting, | in order to the | Solemn Worship of God. | To which
are added, | Several Quotations from | Robert Barclay's Apology.
| By M. B. | *London: Printed.* | *Philadelphia:* | *Re-printed, by Joseph
Crukshank, in Market-* | *street, between Second and Third-streets.* |
MDCCLXXX. | 8vo. pp. 32.   F. 3997

BUCHANAN. (J.) A | Regular | English Syntax. | Wherein
is exhibited | The Whole Variety | of | English Construction, |
properly exemplified. | To which is added | The elegant Manner of
arranging Words, and | Members of Sentences. | The Whole re-
duced to Practice, | For the Use of private young Gentlemen and
Ladies, | as well as of our most eminent Schools. | By James

Buchanan. | From the London Edition. | *Philadelphia :* | *Printed by Styner and Cist, in Second-Street.* | M.DCC.LXXX. | 8vo. pp. xxiii, 165, (1).   H. S. P.   3998

BUMBO. (J.) The American Almanac for 1781. By Jacob Bumbo. *Philadelphia : Thomas Bradford.* 1780.   3999

[BURGH. (James)] The | Art | of | Speaking. | Containing, | I. An Essay; in which are given Rules for expres- | sing properly the principal Passions and Humours, | which occur in Reading, or public Speaking; and | II. Lessons taken from the Ancients and Moderns, | (with Additions and Alterations, where thought use- | ful) exhibiting a Variety of Matter for Practice; the | emphatical Words printed in Italics; with Notes of | Direction referring to the Essay. | To which are added, | A Table of the Lessons; | and | An Index of the various Passions and Humours | in the Essay and Lessons. | ... | ... | ... | .... | The Fifth Edition. | *Philadelphia :* | *Printed and sold by R. Aitken, in Market-* | *street, three doors above the Coffee-house.* | M.DCC.LXXX. | 12mo. pp. 277, (11).   4000

CARRÉ. (—) A Table of French Verbs. Together with re- marks on particular irregularities. By Mr. Carré. *Philadelphia : Francis Bailey.* 1780.   4001

CATALOGUE of a Collection of valuable Books to be sold by Auction at the House of David Franks, Nov. 1, 1780. *Philadel- phia : Robert Bell.* 1780.   4002

A CATALOGUE of the Library of the Late Reverend Francis Alison, D.D. To be sold at Auction August 31, 1780. *Philadel- phia : John Dunlap ?* 1780.   4003

CRISP. (S.) An | Epistle | to | Friends | Concerning the Present and Succeeding | Times. | Being a Faithful Exhortation and Warning to all | Friends, who Profess the Truth, to beware of the | manifold Wiles of the Enemy, and to stand Armed | in the Light of the Lord God of Heaven and Earth, | (against his As- saults) that so they may be ready | to Answer the Call and Re- quirings of the Lord. | Also something signified of the Misery of the Suc- | ceeding Times, that all may be Prepared, and | that the Evil Day may not overtake any unawares, | but such as turn away their Ear from Counsel. | By one who is a Traveller in the way of Peace, and hath | Good will towards all Men, and more especially to the | Household of Faith, Stephen Crisp. | . . . | . . . . | *London : Printed in the Year,* 1666. *And now* | *Re-printed (being the Sixth Edition) and Sold by* | *J. Crukshank, in Market-Street, Philadelphia.* 1780. | Sm. 8vo. pp. 36.   N. Y. H. S.   4004

DILWORTH. (T.)   A New Guide to the English Tongue. By Thomas Dilworth. *Philadelphia: Steiner and Cyst.* 1780. + *Philadelphia: John Dunlap.* 1780.   4005

EXTRACT from an | Address | in the | Virginia Gazette, | Of March 19, 1767. | By a respectable Member of the Community. | [*Philadelphia: Joseph Crukshank.* 1780.] Sm. 8vo. pp. 4.   4006

FATHER Abraham's Pocket Almanac for 1781. *Philadelphia: John Dunlap.* 1780.   4007

[FOTHERGILL. (Samuel)]   The | Necessity | and | Divine Excellency | of a | Life | of | Purity and Holiness, | Set forth with pathetic Energy, by an eminent Minister of the | Gospel amongst the People called Quakers. | In | Seven Discourses | and | Three Prayers, and an Epistle | to his | Brethren in Religious profession in the Island of Tortola. | Now collected and re-published, that the instructive and important | Truths therein contained, may be spread and become more | generally useful. | . . . . | *Philadelphia : | Re-printed by Joseph Crukshank, in Market-Street between | Second and Third-Streets.* 1780. | 8vo. pp. 148.   H. S. P.   4008

Several of the tracts in this volume have separate title-pages, as follows : Two | Discourses | and a | Prayer, | publickly delivered | On Sunday the Seventeenth and Tuesday the | Nineteenth Days of May, 1767, | At the Quakers Yearly Meeting, | At the Fryers, in Bristol. | The Whole taken down in Characters, | By a Member of the Church of England. | To which is added, a Preface. | The Fifth Edition. | [Imprint as in general title.] Pp. 17–51. The | Prayer of Agur, | illustrated in a | Funeral Discourse: | And the | Advantages Resulting | from an | Early and Stead-fast Piety. | Preached extempore, | By the Author of Two Discourses and a Prayer. | Publickly delivered | At the Quaker's Yearly-Meeting, in | Bristol. | . . . | . . . . | The Third Edition. | [Imprint as in general title.] Pp. 53–90. The Grace of our Lord Jesus Christ, the Love of God, | and a Divine Communion, recommended and inforced, in | A | Sermon | publicly delivered | At a Meeting of the People called Quakers, | held | In Leeds, the 26th of the Sixth Month, commonly | called June, 1769. | Carefully taken down in characters at the | same time, by James Blakes, Jun. | [Imprint as in general title.] Pp. 91–116. Repent and be converted: | A | Sermon | preached at a | Meeting of the People called Quakers, 1768. | Also the | Heads of a Sermon, | preached | At Horsleydown Meeting, upon the close of a visit | to Friends Families in that Quarter, the 19th of the | Eleventh Month, 1769. | [Imprint as in general title.] Pp. 117–148.

THE GENTLEMAN and Lady's Pocket Memorandum Book and Almanac for 1781. *Philadelphia: William Mentz.* 1780. 4009

GRIFFITH. (J.) A | Journal | of the | Life, Travels, and Labours | in the | Work of the Ministry, | of | John Griffith, | Late of Chelmsford in Essex, in Great Britain, | formerly of Darby, in Pennsylvania. | *London Printed: | Philadelphia: Re-printed | By Joseph Crukshank in Market-street, | between Second and Third-streets.* | MDCCLXXX. | 8vo. Title, 1 leaf; Testimony, pp. i–iv; Journal, pp. 1–426.   H. S. P.   4010

DER | HOCH=DEUTSCH= | Americaniſche | Calender, | Auf das Jahr | . . . | . . . | 1781. | [12 lines.] | Zum drey und vierzigſten mal heraus gegeben. | *Philadelphia: Gedruckt und zu finden bey Johann Dunlap, in der Markt-strasse* | . . . | . . . | . . . | . . . | . . . [1780.] | Sq. 8vo. pp. (32).   H. S. P.   4011

State of Pennsylvania. | IN General Assembly, | Thursday, September 21, 1780. [*Philadelphia:*] *Printed by John Dunlap.* [1780.] | Folio, pp. 3.   4012

A Bill entitled " An Act for establishing a Land-Office, and for the other purposes therein mentioned," " printed for public consideration."

JENYNS. (S.) A | View | of the | Internal Evidence | of the | Christian Religion. | . . . | . . . . | By Soame Jenyns, Esq. | The Eighth Edition, corrected. | *Philadelphia: | Printed by Joseph Crukshank, in Market-street, | between Second and Third-streets.* | MDCCLXXX. | 8vo. pp. 76.   H. S. P.   4013

JOURNALS | of | Congress, | from | January 1st, 1780, | to | January 1st, 1781. | Published by Order of Congress. | *Phila-*

delphia : | *Printed by David C. Claypoole,* | *Printer to the Honorable* *the Congress.* [1780.] | 8vo. pp. 403.   H. S. P.   4014

Issued in monthly parts.

KOPPELBERGER (J.) Ein neues Lied, | welches auf eine fon= berbare Art gemacht ist, wenn man den ersten Buchstaben von jedem Verse | nimmt ; vom ersten bis zum letzen Verse an buchstabirts den Namen | „ Leonard Detweiler,‟ | welches auf sein Verlangen gemacht worden ist, von einem Dichter mit Namen | Johannes Koppelberger. | [n. p. 1780 ?] Folio, 1 leaf.   H. S. P.   4015.

LAWS | enacted in the | Second Sitting | of the fourth | Gen- eral Assembly, | Of the Commonwealth | of | Pennsylvania. | Which Commenced at Philadelphia, on Wednesday the 19th day | of January, in the Year of our Lord One thousand seven hun- dred | and eighty. | [*Philadelphia : John Dunlap.* 1780.] Folio, pp. 283–365, (1). + Laws | enacted in the | Third Sitting | . . . | . . . | . . . | . . . | . . . | . . . . | [*Ibid.*] Folio, pp. 367–384. + Laws | enacted in the | Fourth Sitting | . . . | . . . | . . . | . . . | . . . | . . . . | [*Ibid.*] pp. 385–394, 1 leaf.   H. S. P.   4016

LAWS | Of the First Sitting of the Fifth | General Assembly | Of the Commonwealth of | Pennsylvania, | Which met at Phila- delphia, on Tuesday, the twenty-third | Day of October, in the Year One thousand se- | ven hundred and eighty. | [*Philadelphia :*] *Printed by John Dunlap.* [1780.] | Folio, pp. 397–417, (1).   4017

LEE. (A.) Extracts | from a | Letter | written to the | Presi- dent of Congress, | by the Honorable | Arthur Lee, Esquire, | In Answer to a Libel published in the Pennsylvania Gazette | of the Fifth of December, 1778, | by | Silas Deane, Esquire. | In which every Charge or Insinuation against him in that | Libel, is fully and clearly refuted. | *Philadelphia :* | *Printed by Francis Bailey.* | M.DCC.LXXX. | Sm. 4to. pp. 74.   H. S. P.   4018

LEE. Observations | on certain | Commercial Transactions | in | France, | Laid before Congress. | By | Arthur Lee, Esquire. | *Philadelphia :* | *Printed by F. Bailey, in Market-street.* | M,DCC,LXXX. | Sm. 4to. pp. 51.   H. S. P.   4019

[McNUTT. (A —)] Considerations | on the | Sovereignty, In- dependence, | Trade and Fisheries | of | New Ireland, | (Formerly known by the Name of Nova Scotia) | and the | Adjacent Islands: | Submitted to the | European Powers, | That may be engaged in settling the Terms of Peace, | among the Nations at War. | Pub- lished by Order of the Sovereign, Free | and Independent Com- monwealth of | New Ireland. | [*Philadelphia: Robert Aitken.* 1780.] 12mo. pp. 24.   H. S. P. 4020

[McNUTT.] The | Constitution | and | Frame of Government Of the Free and Independent | State and Commonwealth | of | New Ireland, | As prepared by the special Direction | of the Peo- ple, for the Consider- | ation of their Convention, when | met. | Composed by those who are invested with | proper Authority for that Purpose. | [*Philadelphia:*] *Printed by R. Aitken,* | *for the Free and Independent State of* | *New Ireland.* | [1780.] 12mo. pp. 39, 1 blank page, Advertisement, pp. (5).   H. S. P. 4021

[McNUTT.] To the Inhabitants of the State of New Ireland, and all others on both Sides of the Atlantic, who | are interested in the great and important Contest betwixt the rising Empire of North America | and the Island of Great Britain. [*Philadelphia: Robert Aitken.* 1780.] Folio, 1 leaf.   H. S. P. 4022

MATLACK. (T.) An | Oration, | Delivered March 16, 1780, | before the | Patron, Vice-Presidents and Members | of the | American | Philosophical Society, | held | At Philadelphia, | for promoting | Useful Knowledge. | By Timothy Matlack, Esquire, | A Member of the said Society and Secretary of the Supreme Executive Council | of the State of Pennsylvania. | *Philadelphia:* | *Printed by Styner and Cist, in Second-Street.* M.DCC.LXXX. | 4to. pp. 27.   H. S. P. 4023

[MAUDUIT. (Israel)] Strictures | on the | Philadelphia | Mischianza or Triumph | upon leaving | America Unconquered. | With | Extracts, containing the Principal Part of a | Letter pub- lished in the American Crisis. | In order to shew, | How far the King's Enemies think his General | deserving the Public Honours. | N. B. A flattering Account of this Mischianza was pub- | lished in the Philadelphia Gazette, and copied into the | Morning Post of the 13th of July last; and a larger one | by a still more flattering Panegyrist, may be found in the | Gentleman's Magazine for August last. | *London Printed:* | *Philadelphia,* | *Re-Printed by F. Bailey, in Market-Street.* | M.DCC.LXXX. | Sm. 8vo. pp. 22. 4024

MINUTES | of the | Baptist Association, | Held at Philadelphia, October 17 and 18, 1780. | [*Philadelphia:*] *Printed by R. Aitken, Bookseller, three Doors above the Coffee-House, Market-Street,* [1780.] | Sm. 4to. pp. 4.   4025

MINUTES | Of the First Sitting of the Fifth | General Assembly | Of the Commonwealth | of | Pennsylvania, | Which met at Philadelphia, on Monday the Twenty-third day of | October, in the Year of our Lord One Thousand | Seven Hundred and Eighty. | [Colophon.] *Philadelphia: Printed by John Dunlap.* [1780.] | Folio, pp. 301–357.   L. C. P. 4026

The minutes of the second sitting, issued in 1781, are paged 359–434; of the third sitting, 435–473; and of the fourth sitting, 475–496.

MORNING | Prayer. | [Colophon.] [*Philadelphia:*] *Printed by John Dunlap.* [1780.] | Sm. 4to. 10 leaves.   4027

For use at the University of Pennsylvania.   Printed in script-type on one side only.

THE NEW | Testament | Of our Lord and Saviour | Jesus Christ. | Newly translated out of the | Original Greek; | And with the former | Translations | Diligently Compared and Revised. | Appointed to be Read in Churches. | *Philadelphia:* | *Printed and Sold by Hall and Sellers, in Market-* | *Street.* M,DCC,LXXX. | 12mo. pp. (347).   4028

THE NEW Testament. *Philadelphia: Francis Bailey.* 1780.

Advertised in the Pa. Gazette, March 8, 1780.

NEW-YEAR'S | Verses, | For the Lad who carries | The Evening Post. | [*Philadelphia: B. Towne.* 1780.] Narrow folio, 1 leaf.   A. A. S. 4030

NEW-YEAR Verses of the Carriers of the Pennsylvania Gazette. *Philadelphia: Hall and Sellers.* 1780.   4031

NEW-YEAR Verses of the Carriers of the Pennsylvania Journal. *Philadelphia: Thomas Bradford.* 1780.   4032

NEW-YEAR Verses of the Carriers of the Pennsylvania Packet. *Philadelphia: John Dunlap.* 1780.   4033

[PAINE. (Thomas)]   The | Crisis | Extraordinary. | [Colophon.]   *Philadelphia: | Sold by William Harris at his store in Second- | street, five doors below Market-street. | (Price Four Dollars single, or Thirty Six | Dollars the Dozen.)* | 8vo. pp. 16.   L. C. P. + The Second Edition.   4034

"On the subject of taxation," dated "Philadelphia, October 6, 1780." It is number X of the collected edition. Pages 15 and 16 contain a postscript on Arnold's treason, which is omitted in the collected edition. A second edition was announced in the Pa. Packet, Oct. 31, 1780. In some copies the words "at his store" are omitted from the imprint.

[PAINE.]   Public Good, | being | An Examination | Into the Claim of Virginia to the | Vacant Western Territory, | and | Of the Right of | The United States to the Same. | To which is added, | Proposals for laying off a new State, | to be applied as a Fund for carrying on | the War, or redeeming the | National Debt. | By the Author of Common Sense. | *Philadelphia: | Printed by John Dunlap, in Market-Street.* | M,DCC,LXXX. | 8vo. pp. 38.

THE PENNSYLVANIA Gazette.   4036

Numbers 2580 (Jan. 5, 1780) to 2637 (Dec. 27, 1780), four pages each. Title and imprint as in No. 3925, *supra.*

THE PENNSYLVANIA Journal.   4037

Numbers 1321 (Jan. 5, 1780) to 1372 (Dec. 27, 1780), four pages each. Title and imprint as in No. 3926, *supra,* until No. 1340, when the former was changed back to the old form of No. 2914, *supra,* and until 1747, when the imprint was changed to the form given in No. 4136, *infra.*

THE PENNSYLVANIA Packet.   4038

Jan. 1 to Dec. 30, 1780, 120 or 121 numbers, of four pages each, of which the paper of April 6th is called a "Packet Extraordinary," as is one (No. 691) of the two

papers dated Dec. 19th (the other of the same date is No. 690).   After the first of
April the paper was issued only twice a week, but in none of the six copies which I
have examined is there any paper between Sept. 12th and 19th, while the regular
semi-weekly issue calls for a paper on Sept. 16th, it is for this reason that I say
about 120 or 121 papers. With the paper for Dec. 2d (which has the day of the week
Tuesday, instead of Saturday, as it ought to have been) the numbering of the paper
was resumed, and the papers for December are Numbers 684 to 694, two of which,
Numbers 690 and 691, were issued on Dec. 19th.   Title and imprint as in No. 3928,
supra, until April 8th, when the last line of the former was changed to " Published
every Tuesday and Saturday." The imprint was changed, Oct. 17th, to " Philadelphia : Printed and Sold by John Dunlap and David C. Claypoole."

THE | PENNSYLVANIA | Pocket Almanac, | For the Year
1781, | Being the First after Bissextile or | Leap-Year. | Calcu-
lated for the Use of the State of | Pennsylvania, and the neigh-
bour- | ing States. | *Philadelphia :* | *Printed and Sold by Thomas
Brad-* | *ford, at his Book-Store, adjoining* | *the Coffee-House.* [1780.]
| 24mo. pp. (24).   H. S. P.   4039

PERRIN. (J.) The | Practice | of the | French Pronunciation
| alphabetically exhibited : | Wherein | The several Sounds of
the Letters are distinguished, and the | Words which have the
same Sound are placed in one Class : | With two | Spelling Vocab-
ularies, | French and English. | By John Perrin. | *Philadelphia :*
| *Printed by Styner and Cist, in Second-Street,* | *four Doors above
Race-Street.* | MD,CC,LXXX. | 8vo. pp. iv, 108.   H. S. P.   4040

PLAN | for | Conducting | the | Hospital Department of the
| United States. | *Philadelphia :* | *Printed by David C. Claypoole,* |
Printer to the Honourable the Congress. [1780.] | 8vo. pp. 8.   4041

PLAN | for | Conducting | the | Inspector's Department of the
| United States. | *Philadelphia :* | *Printed by David C. Claypoole,*
| *Printer to the Honourable the Congress.* [1780.] | 8vo. pp. 8. 4042

PLAN | For Conducting | The Quartermaster General's | De-
partment, | Agreed to In Congress, | July 15th, 1780. | *Philadel-
phia :* | *Printed by David C. Claypoole,* | *Printer to the Honourable the
Congress.* | M,DCC,LXXX. | 8vo. pp. 15.   L. C. P.   4043

THE | PLAIN Path | to | Christian Perfection, | shewing |
That we are to seek for Reconciliation and | Union with God,

solely by renouncing ourselves, | denying the World, and follow-
ing our Blessed | Saviour, in the Regeneration. | Translated from
the French. | . . . | . . . | . . . | . . . | . . . | . . . | . . . | . . . |
. . . . | *Philadelphia:* | *Printed by Joseph Crukshank, in Market-*
| *Street, between Second and Third Streets.* | MDCCLXXX. | 12mo.
pp. xi, 91. F. 4044

POOR Will's | Almanack, | for the | Year of our Lord, 1781 ;
| Being the First after Leap-Year. | . . . | . . . | . . . | . . . | . . . |
. . . | . . . | . . . | . . . | . . . | . . . | . . . | . . . | . . . . | *Phila-*
delphia: | *Printed and Sold by Joseph Crukshank,* | *in Market Street,*
between Second and Third-Streets. [1780.] | Sm. 8vo. pp. (36). 4045

POOR Will's | Pocket Almanack, | For the Year 1781 ; | *Phil-*
adelphia: | *Printed and Sold by Joseph Crukshank.* [1780.] | 24mo.
pp. (24). H. S. P. 4046

PRINCIPLES and Articles | Agreed on by the Members of the
| Constitutional Society, | In Philadelphia ; | And Proposed for the
Consideration of the Lovers and Supporters of Civil Go- | vern-
ment in other Parts of the State. | *Philadelphia: Printed by Fran-*
cis Bailey, in Market-Street. [1780.] | Folio, 1 leaf. L. C. P. 4047

PROCEEDINGS | of a | Board | of | General Officers, | Held
by Order of | His Excellency Gen. Washington, | Commander in
Chief of the Army of the United States | of America. | Respect-
ing | Major John André, | Adjutant General of the British Army.
| September 29, 1780. | *Philadelphia:* | *Printed by Francis Bailey,*
in Market-Street. | M.DCC.LXXX. | 8vo. Half-title, 1 leaf ; pp.
21. L. C. P. 4048

The half-title reads : Proceedings | of a | Board of General Officers, | Held by
Order of His Excellency General | Washington, Commander in Chief of | the Army
of the United States of America : | Respecting Major André, Adjutant Gene- | ral to
the British Army, Sept. 29, 1780. | To which are Appended, The Several | Letters
which passed to and from New- | York on the Occasion, &c. | Published by Order of
Congress. |

PROCEEDINGS | of a | General Court Martial | of the Line,
| Held at Raritan, | in the State of | New-Jersey, | By Order of
his Excellency | George Washington, Esq. | General and Com-

mander in Chief | Of the Army of | The United States of America, | For the Trial of | Major General Arnold, | June 1, 1779. | Major General Howe, President. | Published by Order of Congress. | *Philadelphia:* | *Printed by Francis Bailey, in Market-Street.* | M.DCC.LXXX. | Folio, pp. 55. H. S. P. 4049

PROCLAMATION. [*Arms of Pennsylvania.*] | By His Excellency Joseph Reed, Esq; President, and the Su- | preme Executive Council of the Commonwealth of Pennsylvania, | A Proclamation. | [*Philadelphia:*] *Printed by Hall and Sellers.* 1780. | Folio, 1 leaf.

Dated "April 16, 1780." Offering £1000 reward for "the Author, Printer or Publisher of a seditious Paper, dated 'Philadelphia, April 14, 1780,' and signed 'Slow and Sure.'"

PROCLAMATION. [*Arms of Pennsylvania.*] By His Excellency | Joseph Reed, Esq. President, | And the Supreme Executive Council, of the Commonwealth of Pennsylvania. | A Proclamation. | [*Philadelphia: Francis Bailey.* 1780.] Folio, 1 leaf. L. C. P. 4051

Dated "April 22, 1780." Offering a reward of $3000 for every Indian or Tory Prisoner, and $2500 for every Indian Scalp.

PROPOSALS by the Philadelphia Baptist Association for printing by subscription an Abridgment of Dr. Gill's Exposition. *Philadelphia:* 1780. Folio. B. M. 4052

DER REPUBLIKANISCHE Calender auf das 1781ste Jahr Christi. Zum Dritten mal herausgegeben. *Lancaster, gedruckt und zu finden bey Theophilus Cossart und Companie.* 1780. 4053

SAUNDERS. (R.) A Pocket Almanac for 1781. By Richard Saunders, Phil. *Philadelphia: Hall and Sellers.* 1780. 4054

SAUNDERS. Poor Richard improved: | Being an | Almanack [10 lines] | For the | Year of our Lord 1781: | Being the First after Leap-Year. | [9 lines.] | By Richard Saunders, Philom. | *Philadelphia:* | *Printed and Sold by Hall and Sellers.* [1780.] | 8vo. pp. (36). 4055

THE SENTIMENTS of an | American Woman. | [*Philadelphia: John Dunlap.* 1780?] Folio, pp. (2). H. S. P. 4056

SHARP. (A.) Der Ganz Neue Verbeſſerte Nord = Americaniſche Calender, auf das 1781ſte Jahr Chriſti. Zum Sechſtenmal herausgegeben und verfertiget von Anthony Sharp, Philom. *Lancaster: Francis Bailey.* 1780.   4057

SHARP. The Continental Almanac for 1781. By Anthony Sharp. *Philadelphia: Francis Bailey.* 1780.   4058

SHARP. The Continental Pocket Almanac for 1781. By Anthony Sharp. *Philadelphia: Francis Bailey.* 1780.   4059

A SHORT | VINDICATION | of the | Religious Society called Quakers, | Against the Aspersions of a nameless Writer in the Pennsylvania Packet of the | 12th Instant. | [*Philadelphia:* 1780.] 4to. pp. 4.   H. S. P.   4060

SLOW and Sure. *Philadelphia:* 1780. Folio? 1 leaf.   4061

Copies of a seditious paper, dated "Philadelphia, April 14, 1780," and signed "Slow and Sure," were pasted up at several street corners. President Reed offered £1000 reward for the arrest of the author. See Colonial Records, xii. 319.

TABLE | for | The Payment | of | Principal and Interest of | Loans, | agreeable to | The Resolutions | of | Congress, | of | The twenty-eighth day of June, | 1780. | *Philadelphia:* | *Printed by David C. Claypoole,* | *Printer to the Honourable the Congress.* | M,DCC,LXXX. | 8vo. pp. 23.   H. S. P.   4062

DIE | TÄGLICHEN | Looſungen | der | Brüdergemeine | für das Jahr | 1781. | *Philadelphia,* | *Gedruckt bey Steiner und Cist, in der Zweyten-Strasse.* [1780.] | 8vo. Title, 1 leaf; pp. (62). H. S. P.   4063

TO the | Citizens | of | Pennsylvania. | [*Philadelphia:* 1780.] Folio, 1 leaf.   L. C. P.   4064

An Anti-Constitution address, signed "By Order of the [Constitutional] Society, Richard Bache, Chairman."

TO the Public. | [*Philadelphia:*] *Printed by John Dunlap.* [1780.] | 4to. 1 leaf.   L. C. P.   4065

Dated "Phila., July 29, 1780," and signed by "David Schaffer, Isaac Melcher, and Adam Melcher," whose estates had been seized as the property of Andrew Allen.

WEATHERWISE. (A.) Father Abraham's Almanac for 1781. By Abraham Weatherwise. *Philadelphia: John Dunlap.* 1780.

[WEBSTER. (Pelatiah)] A Fourth | Essay | on | Free Trade | and | Finance, | humbly offered to the | Consideration | of the | Public. | By a Citizen of Philadelphia. | *Philadelphia:* | *Printed and Sold by Hall and Sellers, opposite the Jersey* | *Market.* MDCCLXXX. | 8vo. pp. 16.   L. C. P.   4067

The Third Essay was published in the Penna. Packet, Jan. 6th and 8th, 1780.

[WEBSTER.] A Fifth | Essay | on | Free Trade | and | Finance, | humbly offered to the | Consideration of the Public. | By a Citizen of Philadelphia. | *Philadelphia:* | *Printed and Sold by Francis Bailey, in Market-Street.* | M.DCC.LXXX. | 8vo. pp. 23.

1781.

AN ACCOUNT of the Births and Burials in the United Churches of Christ Church and St. Peter's. *Philadelphia:* 1781.

State of Pennsylvania. | AN ACT | Directing the Mode of adjusting and settling the Payment of Debts | and Contracts entered into and made between the first Day of January, One thousand seven hundred and seventy-seven, and the | first Day of March, One thousand seven hundred and eighty-one, and for other Purposes therein mentioned. | [*Philadelphia: T. Bradford.* 1781.] Folio, 1 leaf.   4070

State of Pennsylvania. | AN ACT for the repeal of so much of the Laws of | this Commonwealth as make the Continental Bills of | Credit and the Bills emitted by the Resolves or Acts of | the Assemblies of the said Commonwealth a Legal | Tender, and for other purposes therein mentioned. | [*Philadelphia: T. Bradford.* 1781.] Folio, pp. (2).   H. S. P.   4071

AN | ADDRESS | from the | Baptist Church, | in | Philadelphia, | to their | Sister Churches | of the same denomination, | throughout the | Confederated States | of | North America. | Drawn up by a Committee of the Church, | appointed for said

Purpose. | *Philadelphia :* | *Printed by Robert Aitken, at Pope's Head,* | . . . . | M,DCC,LXXXI. | 8vo. pp. 16.   L. C. P.   4072

AN ADDRESS | To those of the People called Quakers, who have been | disowned for Matters religious or civil. | *Philadelphia : Printed by Francis Bailey.* [1781.] | Folio, 1 leaf.   H. S. P.   4073

From the Meeting of "Free Quakers, Philadelphia, 4th mo. 24th, 1781."

ADVERTISEMENT.   *Philadelphia : Robert Aitken.*   1781.

Aitken, in his Ledger, on Feb. 2d, charges William Nicholls for printing 1920 Advertisements, and on May 18, John Kean, of York, Pa., for printing 500 Advertisements.

𝕬𝕸𝕰𝕽𝕵𝕮𝕬𝕽𝕵𝕾𝕮𝕳𝕰𝕽 | ℌau𝔰= unb 𝔚irt𝔥ſ𝔠𝔥aft𝔰= | 𝕮alenber | 𝔄uf ba𝔰 1782ſte 𝔍a𝔥r 𝕮𝔥riſti, | . . . | . . . | . . . | . . . . | 𝔍um 𝔇ritten= mal 𝔥erau𝔰 gegeben. | *Philadelphia : Gedruckt und zu haben bey Melchior Steiner, in* | *der Rees-strasse, zwischen der Zweyten- und Dritten-strasse.* [1781.] | Sm. 4to. pp. (40).   H. S. P.   4075

𝕬𝕸𝕰𝕽𝕵𝕮𝕬𝕽𝕵𝕾𝕮𝕳𝕰𝕽 | ℌau𝔰= unb 𝔚irt𝔥ſ𝔠𝔥aft𝔰= | 𝕮alenber | 𝔄uf ba𝔰 1782ſte 𝔍a𝔥r 𝕮𝔥riſti, | . . . | . . . | . . . | . . . . | 𝔍um 𝔇ritten= mal 𝔥erau𝔰 gegeben. | *Philadelphia : Gedruckt und zu finden bey Carl Cist, in der* | *Markt-strasse, zwischen der Vierten- und Fünften-strasse.* [1781.] | Sm. 4to. pp. (40).   H. S. P.   4076

This appears to be identical with the preceding in every respect, except the imprint.

ARRANGEMENT | of the | Pennsylvania | Line, | January 17, 1781. | [*Arms of Pennsylvania.*] *Philadelphia :* | *Printed and Sold by Francis Bailey.* [1781.] | 16mo. pp. 15.   L. C. P.   4077

[BARTON. (William)] Observations | on the | Nature and Use | of | Paper-Credit; | and the | Peculiar Advantages | to be derived from it, in | North-America : | From which are inferred the Means of | Establishing and Supporting it, | including | Proposals for Founding | a | National Bank. | *Philadelphia :* | *Printed and sold by R. Aitken, at Pope's Head,* | *Three Doors above the Coffee House, in Market Street.* | M.DCC.LXXXI. | 8vo. pp. 40.   H. S. P.   4078

The words "and sold" do not appear in the imprint of some copies.

[BEAUMARCHAIS. (Pierre Auguste Caron de)] Observations | on the | Justificative Memorial | of the | Court of London. | Paris, Printed by the Royal Authority. | *Philadelphia:* | *Printed by F. Bailey, in Market-Street.* | M.DCC.LXXXI. | Sm. 4to. pp. 129.

Translated by P. S. Du Ponceau. See No. 3853, *supra.*

[BENEZET. (Anthony)] Notes on the Slave Trade. | [*Philadelphia: Joseph Crukshank.* 1781.] Sm. 8vo. pp. 8.   F. 4080

[BENEZET.] Short Observations on | Slavery, | Introductory to some Extracts from | the writing of the Abbe Raynal, | on that important Subject. | [*Philadelphia: Joseph Crukshank.* 1781?] 12mo. pp. 12.   F. 4081

BIDDLE. (O.) An | Oration, | Delivered the Second of March, 1781, | at the request of the | American | Philosophical Society | for promoting | Useful Knowledeg, | Before the said Society | And a large and respectable Assembly of | Citizens and Foreigners. | By Owen Biddle, | One of the Secretaries to the said Society. | *Philadelphia:* | *Published by Order of the Society, and* | *Printed by Francis Bailey, in Market-Street.* | M.DCC.LXXXI. | 4to. pp. 36.

BROWN. (W.) Pharmacopoeia | Simpliciorum & Efficaciorum, | in usum | Nosocomii Militaris, | ad exercitum | Fœderatarum Americæ Civitatum | pertinentis; | Hodiernæ nostræ inopiæ | rerumque Augustiis, | Feroci hostium sævitiæ, belloque | crudeli ex inopinato patriæ nostræ | illato debitis, | Maxime accommodata. | Auctore Gulielmo Brown, M.D. | Editio Altera. | *Philadelphiæ:* | *Ex Officina Coroli Cist.* | M.DCC.LXXXI. | 12mo. pp. 32.   4083

𝔅𝔯ü𝔡𝔢𝔯𝔩𝔦𝔠𝔥𝔢 Vermahnungen an einige Brüder Freimaurer. Von dem Bruder Sebbag. *Philadelphia:* [*Logan in Petersburg.*] 1781.   w. 4084

BUMBO. (J.) The | American | Almanac, | For the Year of our Lord, | 1782. | (Being the Second after Bissextile or Leap-Year.) | Containing, | The Motions of the Sun and Moon; the true Places | and Aspects of the Planets; the Rising and Setting | of the Sun; the Rising, Setting, and Southing of | the Moon; the

Lunations, Conjunctions, Eclipses, | Rising, Setting, and Southing of the Planets; | Judgment of the Weather; Festivals, and other | Remarkable Days, Quakers Yearly Meetings, Courts, | Roads, &c. &c. | Also, | A Variety of useful and enter- | taining Matter. | Fitted to the Latitude of 40 Degrees North, and near | Five Hours West from London; but may, without | sensible Error, serve all the Northern States. | By Father Jacobus Bumbo. | *Phil-adelphia:* | *Printed by T. Bradford and P. Hall, and* | *Sold at the Book-store, adjoining the Coffee-House.* [1781.] | Sm. 8vo. pp. (36).

CATALOGUE of Books to be sold at Auction, Oct. 23. *Phil-adelphia: Robert Bell.* 1781. 4086

THE SHORTER CATECHISM, for the use of Baptist Congregations. *Philadelphia: Robert Aitken.* 1781. 4087

A CONFESSION of Faith, Put forth by the Elders and Brethren Of many Congregations of Christians (Baptized upon Profession of their Faith) In London and the Country. Adopted by the Baptist Association met at Philadelphia, Sept. 25, 1742. The Eighth Edition. To which are added, Two Articles viz. Of Imposition of Hands, and Singing of Psalms in Publick Worship, Also A Short Treatise of Church Discipline. *Philadelphia: Robert Aitken.* 1781. 4088

CONSIDERATIONS | on the Subject of | Finance. | In which the causes of the depreciation of the Bills | of Credit emitted by Congress are briefly stated | and examined, and a Plan proposed for restoring | Money to a certain, known value. | [*Philadelphia:* 1781.] 8vo. pp. 16. L. C. P. 4089

THE | CONSTITUTION | of the | Common-Wealth | of | Pennsylvania, | As established by the General Convention | elected for that Purpose, and held at Phi- | ladelphia, July 15th, 1776, and continued | by Adjournments to September 28th, 1776. | To which is Prefixed, | The Confederation | of the | United States of America. | [*Arms of Pennsylvania.*] | *Philadelphia:* | *Printed by F. Bailey, in Market-Street.* | M.DCC.LXXXI. | 8vo. pp. 67. 4090

THE | CONSTITUTIONS | of the | Several Independent

States | of | America; | the | Declaration of Independence; | the | Articles of Confederation | between the said States; | the | Treaties between His Most Christian Majesty | and the United States of America. | Published by order of Congress. | *Philadel-* *phia:* | *Printed by Francis Bailey, in Market-Street.* | M.DCC.LXXXI. | Sm. 8vo. Title, 1 leaf; Authorization, 1 leaf; pp. 3–226. 4091

> Two hundred copies were printed by order of Congress.

CULLEN. (W.) First Lines | of the | Practice of Physic, | For the Use of Students, | in the | University of Edinburgh. | By William Cullen, M.D. & P. | Vol. I. | According to the Second Edition, | Printed at Edinburgh. | *Philadelphia:* | *Printed* *by Steiner and Cist.* | M,DCC,LXXXI. | 8vo. Title, 1 leaf; Subscribers, pp. (2); From the Editor (Benjamin Rush), 1 leaf; Preface, pp. ix–x; Contents, pp. xi–xv; text, pp. 1–388. 4092

DILWORTH. (T.) The | Schoolmasters Assistant: | Being a | Compendium of Arithmetic, | both | Practical and Theoretical. | In Five Parts. | Containing | I. Arithmetic in Whole Numbers, | wherein all the common Rules, | having each of them a suffi- | cient | Number of Questions, with their | Answers, are methodi- | cally and | briefly handled. | II. Vulgar Fractions, wherein se- | veral Things, not commonly met | with, are there distinctly treated | of, and laid down in the most | plain and easy Manner. | III. Decimals, in which, among | other Things, are considered the | Extraction of Roots; Interest, | both Simple and Compound; | Annuities, Rebate, and Equa- | tion of Payments. | IV. A large Collection of Questi- | ons, with their Answers, serv- | ing to ex- ercise the foregoing | Rules; together with a few | others, both pleasant and di- | verting. | V. Duodecimals, commonly call- | ed Cross Multiplication; where- | in that Sort of Arithmetic is | thoroughly considered and ren- | dered very plain and easy; to- | gether with the Method of prov- | ing all the foregoing Operations | at once by Division of several | Denominations, without reduc- | ing them to the lowest Term | mentioned. | The Whole being delivered in the most familiar Way of Question and | Answer, is recommended by several eminent Mathematicians, Ac- | comptants, and Schoolmasters, as necessary to be used in Schools by all | Teachers, who would have their Scholars thoroughly understand, | and make a quick Progress in Arithmetic. | To which is prefixt, | An Essay on the Education of Youth ; humbly offered to the | Consideration of Parents. | By Thomas Dilworth, | Author of the New Guide to the English Tongue ; Young Book-Keeper's | Assistant, &c. &c. and Schoolmaster in Wapping. | *Philadelphia : | Printed and Sold by R. Aitken, Bookseller, in Market-Street, | Three Doors above the Coffee-House.* | M.DCC.LXXXI. | Sm. 8vo. Portrait, 1 leaf ; pp. 220, 1 leaf folded. H. S. P. 4093

THE | DISCIPLINE | of the | Society of Friends, | by some styled the | Free Quakers, | Unanimously agreed to in their Meeting for Business, | held in Philadelphia, on the Sixth Day of the | Eighth Month, 1781. | [*Philadelphia: Francis Bailey.* 1781.] Folio, pp. (4). H. S. P. 4094

[DODSLEY. (Robert)] The | Oeconomy | of | Human Life. | In Two Parts. | Part the First. | Translated from an Indian Manuscript, | written by an ancient Bramin. | To which is prefixed, | An Account of the Manner in which | the said Manuscript was discovered. | In a Letter from an English Gentleman, | now residing in China, to the Earl of ***. | *Philadelphia : | Printed and Sold by R. Aitken, | at Pope's Head, Three Doors above | the Coffee-House, Market Street.* | M,DCC,LXXXI. | Sm. 12mo. pp. 107, (1). + Part the Second. | Translated from an Indian Manuscript, | found soon after that which contained the | original of the first part, and written by | the same hand. | in | A second Letter from an English Gentle- | man, residing in China, to the Earl of ***. | [*Ibid.*] Sm. 12mo. pp. 131, (1). F. 4095

[DODSLEY.] The | Oeconomy | of | Human Life. | Translated from an Indian Manuscript, | written by an ancient Bramin. | To which is perfixed, | An account of the manner in which the | said Manuscript was discovered. | In | A Letter from an English Gentleman, | now residing in China, to the Earl of ***. | *Philadelphia : | Printed and sold by Joseph Crukshank, | in Market-street, between Second and | Third-streets.* 1781. | 18mo. pp. xii, (2), 54. + The | Oeconomy | of | Human Life. | Part the Second. | Translated from an Indian Manuscript, | found soon after that which contained | the original of the first part, and writ- | ten by the same hand. | In | A second Letter from an English | Gentleman, residing in China, to the | Earl of ******. | *Philadelphia :* | *Printed and sold by Joseph Crukshank,* | *in Market-street, between Second and* | *Third-streets.* 1781. | 18mo. pp. iv, (2), 70.   4096

AN EPISTLE from Titus to Timothy. | Quillsylvania; [*Philadelphia :*] *Printed for the Author.* [1781.] | Sm. Folio, 1 leaf. 4097

Doggerel lines on a rencounter between Whitehead Humphreys and Timothy Matlack, in Market-street, on Jan. 1, 1781.

AN | EULOGIUM | on | General Washington | being appointed | Commander in Chief | of the | Federal Army in America. | *Philadelphia :* | *Printed and sold by B. Towne in* | *Pewter Platter Alley.* 1781. | Sm. 8vo. pp. 15.   A. P. S.   4098

EXTRACT of a Letter from Trenton, dated Jan. 20. | 1781. | [*Philadelphia: David C. Claypoole.* 1781.] Folio, 1 leaf. H. S. P. 4099

An account of the British intrigue with the revolted Pennsylvania Line. Dated " Philadelphia, January 22, 1781."

FATHER Abraham's Pocket Almanac for 1782. *Philadelphia : John Dunlap.* 1781.   4100

[FORRESTER. (James)] The | Polite Philosopher : | Or, | An Essay on the Art which makes a Man | happy in himself, and agreeable to others. | . . . | . . . | . . . | . . . | . . . | . . . | . . . | . . . | . . . | . . . | . . . | . . . | . . . | . . . . | The Ninth Edition. | *Philadelphia :* | *Re-printed and sold by T. Bradford* | *and P. Hall.* | MDCCLXXXI. | 18mo. pp. 54.   L. C. P.   4101

Wednesday, April 25, 1781. Number I. | THE | FREEMAN'S : Journal : | Or, : the | North American : Intelligencer. | Open to All Parties, but Influenced by None. | *Philadelphia, Printed by Francis Bailey, in Market-Street, between Third and Fourth-Streets.* | Folio.   4102

Numbers I. (April 25, 1781) to XXXVI. (Dec. 26, 1781), four pages each, with " Postscripts" of one leaf to Numbers 22, 23, 24, 30, and 31, and one of two pages to No. 23. A cut of "Justice" divides the title, as indicated by the dotted lines.

[FRENEAU. (Philip)]   The British Prison-Ship: | A | Poem, | In Four Cantoes. |

Viz. Canto
{
1 The Capture,
2 The Prison-Ship,
3 The Prison-Ship, continued.
4 The Hospital-Prison-Ship. |
}

To which is added, | A Poem on the Death of Capt. N. Biddle, | who was blown up, in an Engagement with the | Yarmouth, near Barbadoes. | . . . | . . . | . . . | . . . | . . . | . . . | . . . | . . . | . . . | . . . | . . . | . . . | . . . | . . . | . . . | . . . . | *Philadelphia:* | *Printed by* | *F. Bailey, in Market-Street.* | M.DCC.LXXXI. | Sm. 8vo. pp. 23.

FROM the Monthly Meeting of Friends, | Called by Some | The Free Quakers, | Held by Adjournment at Philadelphia, on the 9th Day of the 7th Month, | 1781. | To those of our Brethren who have disowned us. | [*Philadelphia:* 1781.] Folio, 1 leaf.   4104

A GENTLEMAN just arrived from New-York, has favoured us with a | Paper, printed there, containing the following Intelligence. | [*Philadelphia:*] *Printed by David C. Claypoole.* [1781.] | Folio, 1 leaf.   H. S. P.   4105

Dated " Philadelphia, Wednesday Evening, February 7, 1781." The King's Speech at the opening of Parliament.

GREGORY. ([John])   A | Father's Legacy | to his | Daughters. | By the late | Dr. Gregory, | of | Edinburgh. | *Philadelphia:* | *Printed and Sold by R. Aitken,* | *at Pope's Head Three Doors* | *above* | *the Coffee House, Market Street.* | M.DCC.LXXXI. | Sm. 12mo. pp. 114, (2).   F. 4106.

GRIFFITH. (J).   Some | Brief Remarks | upon sundry | Important Subjects, | Necessary to be understood and attended to by all | professing the Christian Religion. | Principally addressed to | the People called Quakers. | By John Griffith. | *London, Printed:* | *Philadelphia,* | *Re-printed* | *By Joseph Crukshank in Market-street,* | *between Second and Third-streets.* | MDCCLXXXI. | 8vo. Title, 1 leaf; Preface, pp. (4); Contents, 1 leaf; text, pp. 1–112.   4107

[GROSVERNOR. (Benjamin)]   The Mourner, or the Afflicted relieved. *Philadelphia: Robert Aitken.* 1781.   4108

HALE. (Thomas)   To the | Friends of Liberty and | the Con-
stitution. | [*Philadelphia :* 1781.]   4to. 1 leaf.   L. C. P.   4109

HELMUTH. (J. H. C.) Empfindungen | des | Herzens | in |
einigen Liedern | von | Just Heinrich Christian Helmuth, | Evangelisch-
Lutherischen Prediger in Philadelphia. | *Philadelphia,* | *Gedruckt bey*
Melchior Steiner, in der Rees-strasse, | *nahe bey der Dritten-strasse.*
1781. | Sm. 8vo. pp. (8), 81, (3).   H. S. P.   4110

Der | Hoch = Deutsch= | Americanische | Calender, | Auf das
Jahr | . . . | . . . | 1782. | [12 lines.] | Zum vier und vierzigsten
mal heraus gegeben. | *Philadelphia : Gedruckt und zu finden bey Johann*
Dunlap, in der Markt-strasse. | . . . | . . . | . . . | . . . [1781.]
| Sq. 8vo. pp. (32).   H. S. P.   4111

[*Arms of Pennsylvania.*] | IN Council, | Philadelphia, March 10,
1781. | [*Philadelphia :*] *Printed by F. Bailey.* [1781.] | Sm. folio, 1
leaf.   H. S. P.   4112

A Resolve prescribing the form of receipt to be taken by the Recruiting Commissioners, for the Bounty of £9 granted to men enlisting for the war prior to 1780.
Signed " T. Matlack, Secretary."

IN Council, | May 4, 1781. | [*Philadelphia :*] *Printed by F. Bailey.*
[1781.] | Folio, 1 leaf.   L. C. P.   4113

An address, signed " Joseph Reed, President," in defence of the resolution of
Council regulating the rate of exchange between specie and Continental paper money.

INTELLIGENCE from the Southward. | [*Philadelphia :*] *Printed*
by David C. Claypoole. [1781.] (*Price Three Dollars.*) | Folio, 1
leaf.   H. S. P.   4114

Dated " Philadelphia, March 31, 1781."   Gen. Greene's account of the battle of
Guilford. The depreciation of Continental paper is shown by the price of this
broadside.

JANEWAY. (J.) A Token for Children. By James Janeway.
Philadelphia : Robert Aitken.   1781.   4115

JOURNALS | of | Congress, | from | January 1st, 1780, | to |
January 1st, 1781. | Published by Order of Congress. | *Philadel-*
phia : | *Printed by David C. Claypoole, Printer to the Honorable the*

Congress. [1781.] | 8vo. pp. 403; Index, pp. xxxviii; Appendix, pp. (3).   H. S. P.   4116

JOURNALS | of | Congress, | and of the | United States | In Congress Assembled. | For the Year 1781. | Published by Order of Congress. | Volume VII. | *Philadelphia:* | *Printed by David C. Claypoole.* | M,DCC,LXXXI. | 8vo. pp. 522, (4), lxxix.   4117

[KUNZE. (Johann Christoph)] Etwas | vom | rechten Lebenswege. | [Cut.] | *Philadelphia,* | *Gedruckt und zu finden bei Melchior Steiner.* 1781. | 8vo. pp. (12), 1–243.   4118

KUNZE. Ein Wort | für den | Verstand und das Herz | vom | rechten und gebanten | Lebenswege | von Johann Christoph Kunze, A.M. | Ev. Pred. zu Philadelphia, in Nordamerika. | *Philadelphia:* | *Gedruckt bey Melchior Steiner, in der Reesstrasse, zwischen | der zweiten und dritten Strasse.* 1781. | 8vo. pp. (8), 243, 1 leaf.   H. S. P.   4119

LAWS | Enacted in the Second Sitting | of the Fifth | General Assembly, | Of the Commonwealth of | Pennsylvania, | Which Commenced at Philadelphia, on Tuesday the sixth | day of February, in the year of our Lord One thousand | seven hundred eighty and one. | [*Philadelphia:*] *Printed by John Dunlap.* [1781.] | Folio, pp. 395–432, (2), for 419–456, (2). + Laws | enacted in the Third Sitting, | . . . | . . . | . . . | . . . | . . . | . . . | . . . | . . . . | [*Ibid.*] pp. 459–476. + Laws | enacted in the Fourth Sitting | . . . | . . . | . . . | . . . | . . . | . . . | . . . . [*Ibid.*] pp. 477–488.

MINUTES | of the | First Session, | of the | Sixth General Assembly, | of the | Commonwealth | of | Pennsylvania, | Which commenced at Philadelphia, on Monday, the twen- | ty-second Day of October, in the Year of our Lord One | thousand seven hundred eighty and one. | *Philadelphia:* | *Printed by John Dunlap, in Market-street.* | MDCCLXXXI. | Folio, Title, 1 leaf; pp. 499– 712.   H. S. P.   4121

The first sitting occupies pp. 499–562, the second sitting, pp. 563–650, and the third sitting, pp. 651–712. The second and third sittings were held in 1782.

MINUTES | of the | Philadelphian | Baptist Association, | In

M.DCC.LXXXI. | [Colophon.] [*Philadelphia :*] *Printed by R. Aitken, in Market-Street.* [1781.] | Sq. 8vo. pp. 8.   4122

THE MONTHLY Meeting of Friends, called by some | The Free Quakers, | (Distinguishing us from those of our Brethren who have disowned us) | Held at Philadelphia, the fourth Day of the 6th Month, 1781. | To our Friends and Brethren in Penn-sylvania, New- | Jersey, and elsewhere. | [*Philadelphia:* 1781.] Folio, 1 leaf.   L. C. P.   4123

MORGAN. ([John]) Conclusion of doctor Morgan's | Remarks on doctor Shippen's | feeble Attempts to Vindicate | himself. | [*Philadelphia: David C. Claypoole.* 1781.] Folio, 1 leaf.   4124

Probably issued as a Supplement to the Pa. Packet, Jan. 6, 1781. Part of a very bitter personal controversy, which began to appear in the Packet in July, 1780.

THE NEW ENGLAND Primer. *Philadelphia: T. Bradford and P. Hall.* 1781.   4125

THE NEW | Testament | Of our Lord and Saviour | Jesus Christ: | Newly Translated out of the | Original Greek; | And with the former | Translations | Diligently compared and revised. | [Cut.] | *Philadelphia:* | *Printed and Sold by R. Aitken, Bookseller,* | *opposite the Coffee-House, Front-Street.* | M.DCC.LXXXI. | 12mo. pp. (335).   H. S. P.   4126

Not paged. Signatures A to CC, 12 pp. each, and Dd, 11 pp. This is the New Testament of the Bible issued by Aitken in 1782, see No. 4184, *infra.* O'Callaghan notes a misprint (*thy* for the) in 1 Tim. iv. 16.

THE NEW Testament. *Philadelphia: Hall and Sellers.* 1781.

Advertised in the Pa. Gazette, Aug. 29, 1781.

NEW YEAR'S | Verses, | For the printer's lads who carry | The Evening Post | To the customers. | [*Philadelphia: B. Towne.* 1781.] | Narrow folio, 1 leaf.   A. A. S.   4128

NEW-YEAR Verses of the Carriers of the Pennsylvania Ga-zette. *Philadelphia: Hall and Sellers.* 1781.   4129

NEW-YEAR Verses of the Carriers of the Pennsylvania Journal. *Philadelphia: Thomas Bradford.* 1781.   4130

NEW-YEAR Verses of the Carriers of the Pennsylvania Packet. *Philadelphia: David C. Claypoole.* 1781.   4131

OBSERVATIONS | upon the | Effects | of certain late | Political | Suggestions, | By the Delegates of Georgia. | *Philadelphia:* | *Printed by R. Aitken, Bookseller, in Market-Street,* | . . . . | M.DCC.LXXXI. | Sm. 4to. pp. 10, 1 leaf folded.   L. C. P.   4132

> Relates to the commercial importance of Georgia, and the means of recovering it from the British.

[PAINE. (Thomas)]   Plain Facts: | Being | An Examination | into the | Rights of the Indian Nations of America, | to their respective Countries; | and | A Vindication of the Grant, | from | The Six United Nations of Indians, | to | The Proprietors of Indiana, | against | The Decision | of the | Legislature of Virginia; | Together with | Authentic Documents, | proving | That the Territory, Westward of the Allegany | Mountain, never belonged to Virginia, &c. | *Philadelphia:* | *Printed and Sold by R. Aitken, Bookseller, in Market-* | *Street, Three Doors above the Coffee-House.* | M.DCC.LXXXI. | 8vo. pp. 164, 1 leaf.   H. S. P.   4133

THE PENNSYLVANIA Evening Post. *Philadelphia: B. Towne.* 1781.   A. A. S.   4134

THE PENNSYLVANIA Gazette.   4135

> Numbers 2638 (Jan. 3, 1781) to 2689 (Dec. 26, 1781), four pages each. Title and imprint as in No. 3925, *supra*.

THE PENNSYLVANIA Journal. *Philadelphia: Printed and Sold by Thomas Bradford.*   4136

> Numbers 1373 (Jan. 3, 1781) to 1452 (Dec. 29, 1781), four pages each. Title as in No. 2914, *supra*. Imprint as above, until No. 1390, when it was changed to " *Philadelphia: Printed and Sold by T. Bradford and P. Hall.*" This was changed in No. 1399 to the form given in No. 4230, *infra*. In July they began to appear twice a week.

Tuesday, January 2, 1781. | THE | PENNSYLVANIA Packet,

| or, the | General Advertiser. | Vol. X.)   Published every Tuesday and Saturday.   (Numb. 690. | *Philadelphia: Printed and Sold by David C. Claypoole.* | Folio.   4137

Numbers 695 (Jan. 2, 1781) to 826 (Dec. 29, 1781), four pages each, with " Postscripts" of one leaf to No. 768, and to one of the two numbers 797 ; of three pages to June 9 (misnumbered 780 for 740), and of four pages to No. 741.   No. 740 is misnumbered 780 ; the papers for March 17 and 20 are both numbered 716 ; those of Oct. 16 and 18, 795 ; and those of Oct. 23 and 25, 797.   The paper for Nov. 17 is misdated 15, and it and the regular Nov. 15 are both numbered 807.   This error, as well as that of two numbers 716, were corrected in the succeeding pages, but the other cases of duplication do not seem to have been detected.   After No. 741 the paper was published three times a week, necessitating a slight change in the title. The imprint was slightly changed in No. 816.

THE PENNSYLVANIA Pocket Almanac for 1782.   *Philadelphia: Thomas Bradford.*   1781.   4138

PERRIN. (J.)   Instructive and Entertaining | Exercises | with the | Rules of the French Syntax. | By John Perrin. | . . . . | *Philadelphia:* | *Printed by Charles Cist, in Market-Street, near* | *Fifth-Street.* | M,DCC,LXXXI. | Sm. 8vo. pp. v, 216, 1 leaf folded. 4139

𝕻𝕳𝕴𝕷𝕬𝕯𝕰𝕷𝕻𝕳𝕴𝕾𝕮𝕳𝕰 Correſpondenʒ.   *Philadelphia: Melchior Steiner.*   1781.   Folio.   4140

This paper, begun about May 1, 1781, was continued until about 1796.   There is an imperfect file of it in the collection of the Historical Society of Pennsylvania.

𝕻𝕳𝕴𝕷𝕬𝕹𝕿𝕳𝕽𝕺𝕻𝕴𝕾𝕮𝕳𝕰 Gedanken von der Natur der Sprach-zeichen.   *Philadelphia: [Eichenberg in Frankfurt.]*   1781.   w.   4141

A PLAIN | Almanack, | for the | Year of our Lord, 1782; | Being the Second after Leap-Year. | Shewing, | The Days of the Month; the Days of the Week; | The | Time of the Rising and Setting of the Sun and Moon; | Full and Change of the Moon; Rising, Setting and | Southing of some of the Planets; Equation of Time; | Eclipses; Tide Table; Roads, &c. | Also, | A Variety of Essays, in | Prose and Verse. | *Philadelphia:* | *Printed and Sold by Joseph Crukshank,* | *in Market-Street, between Second* | *and Third-Street.* [1781.] | Sm. 8vo. pp. (36).   H. S. P.   4142

POOR Will's | Almanack, | for the | Year of our Lord, 1782;

| Being the Second after Leap-Year. | . . . | . . . | . . . | . . . |
. . . | . . . | . . . | . . . | . . . | . . . | . . . . | *Philadelphia:* |
Printed and Sold by Joseph Crukshank, | *in Market-Street, between
Second* | *and Third-Street.* [1781.] | Sm. 8vo. pp. (36).   H. S. P.   4143

POOR Will's Pocket Almanac for 1782.   *Philadelphia: Joseph
Crukshank.*   1781.   4144

PROCLAMATION.   [*Arms of Pennsylvania.*]   By His Excel-
lency Joseph Reed, Esq; President, and the Su- | preme Execu-
tive Council of the Commonwealth of Pennsylvania, | A Procla-
mation. | [*Philadelphia:*] *Printed by Hall and Sellers.* [1781.] |
Folio, 1 leaf.   L. C. P.   4145

Dated "May 11, 1781." Recommending the acceptance of the Paper Currency
for all kinds of debts.

PROCLAMATION.   [*Arms of Pennsylvania.*] | By His Excel-
lency Joseph Reed, Esquire, President, and the Supreme | Execu-
tive Council of the Commonwealth of Pennsylvania, | A Procla-
mation. | [*Philadelphia:*] *Printed by F. Bailey, in Market-Street.*
[1781.] | Folio, 1 leaf.   L. C. P.   4146

Dated "July 14, 1781." Prohibiting Receivers of Taxes from accepting counterfeit British Half-pence.

𝕻𝕾𝕬𝕷𝕿𝕰𝕽𝕾𝕻𝕵𝕰𝕷. Das Kleine | Davidische | Pfalterspiel | der |
Kinder Zions, | von Alten und Neuen auserlesenen | Geistes-Gesängen,
| Allen wahren Heils-begierigen | Säuglingen der Weisheit, | Infon-
derheit aber | Denen Gemeinden des Herrn, | zum Dienst und Gebrauch
mit Fleiß zu- | sammen getragen | in gegenwärtig-beliebiger Form und
Ordnung, | Nebst einem dreysachen, darzu nützlichen und | der Materien
halben nöthigen | Register. | *Philadelphia:* | *Gedruckt bey Steiner und
Cist.* 1781. | 16mo. pp. (6), 575, (23).   H. S. P.   4147

REED. (Joseph) My late Engagements of a public Nature have
prevented my taking earlier Notice of a Report . . . That I had
been or was concerned in trading in New York . . . . [*Philadelphia: Francis Bailey.* 1781.] 4to. 1 leaf.   H. S. P.   4148

REED.   The following Paper having been much misrepresented

. . . . | *Philadelphia: Printed by F. Bailey, in Market-Street.* [1781.] | Folio, 1 leaf. H. S. P. 4149

In defence of his address of Jan. 15, 1781, concerning raising by subscription the money to pay the Pennsylvania Troops.

REMARKS | Upon a Pamphlet intitled | " An Address | From the | Baptist Church in Philadelphia, | To their | Sister Churches of the same | Denomination, | Throughout the Confederated | States of North America." | In which some Mistakes are rectified, | And the | Matters of Fact set in a true Light. | *Philadelphia:* | *Printed by Ben. Towne.* 1781. | Sm. 4to. pp. 28. H. S. P. 4150

REPORT | Of the Committee of the Assembly, on the state of the | Public Accounts, | For the Year One thousand seven hundred and eighty. | [*Philadelphia:*] *Printed by John Dunlap.* [1781.] | Folio, pp. 46. H. S. P. 4151

DER | REPUBLIKANISCHE | Calender, | Auf das 1782ste Jahr Christi, | Welches ein gemein Jahr von 365 Tagen ist. | Und enthält | Die Wochen= Monats = Namen = und Feyer=Tage, | des Monden Auf= und Untergang; seine Zeichen, Grade und Viertel; | die Aspecten der Planeten, samt der Witterung; des Sieben= | gestirns Aufgang, Südplatz und Untergang; Auf= und | Untergang der Sonnen; nebst der Fluth oder dem | hohen Wasser zu Philadelphia: | Wie auch | Verschiedene angenehme und lehrreiche Stücke, | nebst nützlichen Tabellen, 2c. 2c. 2c. | Und andere gewöhnliche Calender = Arbeit. | Eingerichtet vor den 40sten Grad der Norder=Breite; sonderlich | vor Pennsylvanien; kann aber doch in den angrenzenden Land= | schaften ohne merklichen Unterscheid gebraucht werden. | Zum Vierten mal heraus gegeben. | *Lancaster, Gedruckt und zu finden bey Theophilus Cossart und Companie,* | *nahe bey der Prison, und gerade gegen ueber den drey gruenen Baeumen.* | Sq. 8vo. pp. (32).

RESOLUTIONS, | Acts and Orders | of | Congress, | For the Year 1780. | Volume VI. | Published by Order of Congress. | [*Philadelphia:*] *Printed by John Dunlap.* [1781.] | 8vo. pp. 257, xliii.

RUSH. (B.) The | New Method | of | Inoculating | for the | Small Pox; | delivered | in a Lecture in the Uni- | versity of Philadelphia, | Feb. 20th, 1781. | By Benjamin Rush, M.D. | *Phila-*

delphia, Printed by Charles Cist, | *in Market-Street.* | M.DCC.LXXXI.
| 12mo. pp. 28. 4154

SAUNDERS. (R.) A Pocket Almanac for 1782. By Richard
Saunders, Phil. *Philadelphia: Hall and Sellers.* 1781. 4155

SAUNDERS. Poor Richard improved: | Being an | Almanack
| [10 lines] | For the | Year of our Lord 1782: | Being the Second
after Leap-Year. | [9 lines.] | By Richard Saunders, Philom. |
Philadelphia: | *Printed and Sold by Hall and Sellers.* [1781.] | 8vo.
pp. (36). H. S. P. 4156

SAUR. (C.) Ein Einfältiges Reim=Gedichte, welches Chriſtoph |
Saur gemacht hat auf ſeinen Namen und Ge= | burts=Tag, als er ſechzig
Jahr alt war den 26ſten | September, 1781. | [n. p. 1781.] 8vo. pp. 4.

SHARP. (A.) Der Ganz Neue Verbeſſerte Nord = Americaniſche
Calender, auf das 1782ſte Jahr Chriſti. Zum Siebentenmal heraus=
gegeben und verfertiget von Anthony Sharp, Philom. *Lancaster:
Francis Bailey.* 1781. 4158

SHARP. The | Continental | Almanac, | [Cut] | for the |
Year of our Lord, 1782: | Being the Second after Leap-Year. | The
Seventh Year of American Independence. | By Anthony Sharp,
Philom. | *Philadelphia:* | *Printed and Sold by Francis Bailey, in* |
Market-street, between Third and Fourth-streets. [1781.] | Sm. 8vo.
pp. (36). H. S. P. 4159

SHARP. The Continental Pocket Almanac for 1782. By
Anthony Sharp. *Philadelphia: Francis Bailey.* 1781. 4160

A SHORT Introduction to Latin Grammar, for the use of the
University and Academy of Pennsylvania. *Philadelphia: Charles
Cist.* 1781. 4161

[STANHOPE, (Philip Dormer — Earl of Chesterfield.)] Lord
Chesterfield's | Advice to his Son, | on | Men and Manners: | Or,
a new | System of Education. | In which the | Principles of
Politeness, | the art of acquiring a | Knowledge of the World,
| with every | Instruction necessary to form a | Man of Honour,

Virtue, Taste, | and Fashion, | are laid down in a | Plain, Easy, Familiar Manner, | adapted to every | Station and Capacity. | The whole arranged on a | Plan entirely New. | *London, Printed:* | *Philadelphia: Re-printed and Sold* | *by T. Bradford and P. Hall.* | M.DCC.LXXXI. | 18mo. pp. i–viii, 1–126.   L. C. P.   4162

𝔇𝔍𝔈 | 𝔗Ä𝔊𝔏𝔍𝔆𝔥𝔈𝔑 | Loosungen | der | Brüdergemeine | für das Jahr | 1782. | *Philadelphia,* | *Gedruckt bey Melchior Steiner, in der Rees-Strasse.* [1781.] | 8vo.   H. S. P.   4163

Collation: Title and "Vorrede," pp. (2) ; Die Taglichen Loosungen, pp. (62) ; Die Taglichen Lehrtexte, pp. (69) ; Tageregister, pp. (3).

. . . | . . . | . . . | . . . | . . . | . . . | . . . | . . . | . . . . | TO the President and Executive Council, the General | Assembly of Pennsylvania, and others whom it may | concern; | The following Representation on Behalf of the | People called Quakers. | [*Phila-delphia:* 1781.]   Folio, pp. (3).   L. C. P.   4164

Dated "12mo. 6th, 1781," and at the end "11th mo. 22d."

TO the Representatives of the Freemen of the Commonwealth of Pennsylvania, in | General Assembly met.   Divers Freemen of the said Commonwealth beg Leave | to shew, | [*Philadelphia:* 1781.]   4to. 1 leaf.   L. C. P.   4165

A petition from the "Free Quakers," presented Dec. 2, 1781.

TO the Representatives of the Freemen | of the Commonwealth of Pennsylvania, | in General Assembly met. | The Memorial and Remonstrance of Isaac Howell and White Matlack, | in behalf of themselves, and others, who have been disowned by the People called | Quakers, &c. | [*Philadelphia:* 1781.]   Folio, pp. (4).   4166

WATTS. (I.) Divine Songs for Children. By Isaac Watts. *Philadelphia: Robert Aitken.* 1781.   4167

WATTS. The Psalms of David, Imitated, &c. By Isaac Watts. *Philadelphia: Robert Aitken.* 1781.   4168

WEATHERWISE. (A.) Father Abraham's Almanac for 1782. By Abraham Weatherwise. *Philadelphia: John Dunlap.* 1781.

WEBB. (E.) A | Letter | from | Elizabeth Webb | to | Anthony William Boehm, | with his | Answer. | *Philadelphia:* | *Printed and Sold by Joseph Crukshank, in* | *Market-Street,* M,DCC,LXXXI. | 12mo. pp. 44.   H. S. P.   4170

[WESLEY. (Charles)] Hymns | for | those that seek | and | those that have | Redemption | in the | Blood | of | Jesus Christ. | *Philadelphia:* | *Printed by Melchior Steiner.* | M,DCC,LXXXI. | 12mo. pp. 65, (4).   H. S. P.   4171

WESLEY. (J.) Hymns | and | Spiritual Songs, | intended for the use of | Real Christians, | of all denominations. | By John Wesley, M.A. | Late Fellow of Lincoln College, Oxford. | . . . | . . . | . . . | . . . | . . . | . . . | . . . | . . . . | *Philadelphia:* | *Printed by Melchior Steiner.* | M,DCC,LXXXI. | 12mo. pp. 136, (4).   H. S. P.   4172

WESLEY. (J. and C.) A | Collection | of | Psalms and Hymns. | Published by John Wesley, M.A. | Fellow of Lincoln-College, Oxford; | and | Charles Wesley, M.A. | Student of Christ-Church, Oxford. | *Philadelphia:* | *Printed by Melchior Steiner,* | M,DCC,LXXXI. | 12mo. pp. 144, (4).   H. S. P.   4173

[WHARTON. (Charles Henry)] A | Poetical Epistle | to his Excellency | George Washington Esq. | Commander in Chief of the | Armies of the United States | of America, | from | An Inhabitant of the State of Maryland. | *London Printed:* | *Philadelphia Re-printed and sold* | *By George Kline,* | *In Third-Street, near Arch-Street.* 1781. | 12mo. pp. 10.   4174

WINCHESTER. (E.) The | Seed | of the | Woman | Bruising the Serpent's Head. | A Discourse | delivered at the | Baptist Meeting House, | in | Philadelphia, Sunday April 22, 1781. | By Elhanan Winchester. | Published by Request. | *Philadelphia: Printed* [*by B. Towne*] *in the Year* | 1781. | 8vo. pp. 58.   H. S. P.   4175

Collation; Sermon, pp. 18; Attempt to collect the Scripture Passages in favour of Universal Redemption, pp. 19–35; The Objections brought from the Scriptures against that Doctrine, pp. 36–58. No. 4150, *supra*, may have been written by Winchester.

1782.

AN ACCOUNT of Births and Burials | in the | United Churches of Christ Church and St. | Peter's, in Philadelphia, | From December 25, 1781, to December 25, 1782. | By William Young, Clerk, and George Stokes, Sexton. | [*Philadelphia:* 1782.] Folio, 1 leaf.   L. C. P.   4176

ACT of the Associate Reformed Synod, | for a | Public Fast. | At Philadelphia, 1st November, 1782. | [*Philadelphia:*] *Printed by Robert Aitken, in Market Street, near the Coffee House.* [1782.] | Folio, 1 leaf.   L. C. P.   4177

EJNE ACTE zur Jncorporirung der zur Unterſtützung nothleidender Deutſchen beyſteurenden Deutſchen Geſellſchaft in Pennſylvanien. *Philadelphia: Gedruckt bey Melchior Steiner* . . . . 1782. 8vo. pp. 30.

THE | ACTS | of the | General Assembly | of the | Commonwealth of Pennsylvania, | Carefully compared with the Originals. | And an | Appendix, | Containing the Laws now in Force, passed between the 30th | Day of September, 1775, and the Revolution. | Together with | The Declaration of Independence; the Constitution of the State of | Pennsylvania; and the Articles of Confederation of the United | States of America. | Published by order of the General Assembly. | [*Arms of Pennsylvania.*] | *Philadelphia:* | *Printed and Sold by Francis Bailey,* | *in Market-Street.* | M,DCC,LXXXII. | Folio.   H. S. P.   4179

    Collation: Title, 1 leaf; Authorization, &c., 1 leaf; The Declaration, pp. i.–vi.; Constitution, pp. vii.–xxi.; Articles of Confederation, pp. xxii.–xxxi.; Directions to Binder, 1 page; text, pp. 1–527; Index, pp. i.–viii. Edited by Thomas McKean, and generally known as McKean's Laws.

AMERJCANJSCHER | Haus= und Wirthſchafts= | Calender | Auf das 1783ſte Jahr Chriſti, | . . . | . . . | . . . | . . . . | Zum Vierten= mal heraus'gegeben. | *Philadelphia: Gedruckt und zu haben bey Melchior Steiner,* | *in der Rees-strasse, zwischen der Zweyten- und Dritten-strasse.* [1782.] | Sm. 4to. pp. (40).   H. S. P.   4180

AMERJCANJSCHER | Haus= und Wirthſchafts= | Calender | Auf das 1783ſte Jahr Chriſti, | . . . | . . . | . . . | . . . . | Zum Vierten=

mal herau3 gegeben. | *Philadelphia: Gedruckt und zu haben bey Carl Cist,* | ... | .... [1782.] | Sm. 4to. pp. (40). ⌐ H. S. P.   4181

> The first fourteen pages are identical with the preceding. Throughout the rest of the pages the reading matter is generally different.

[BASSVILLE. (N. J. H. de)] Réflexions d'un instituteur sur un roman int. Adèle et Théodore [de Madame de Genlis]. *A Philadelphie: [Paris.]* 1782.   w.   4182

BENEZET. (A.)   The | Plainness and Innocent Simplicity | of the | Christian Religion. | With | Its salutary Effects, compared to the corrupting Nature | and dreadful Effects of War. | With | Some Account of the blessing which attends on a Spirit influenced by | divine Love, producing Peace and Good-Will to Men. | ... | ... | ... | ... | ... | ... | ... | ... | ... | .... | Collected by Anthony Benezet. | *Philadelphia:* | *Printed by Joseph Crukshank, in* | *Market-Street, between Second and* | *Third-streets.* | MDCCLXXXII. | 12mo. pp. 48.   H. S. P.   4183

THE | HOLY BIBLE, | Containing the Old and New | Testaments: | Newly translated out of the | Original Tongues; | And with the former | Translations | Diligently compared and revised. | [*Arms of Pennsylvania.*]   *Philadelphia:* | *Printed and Sold by R. Aitken, at Pope's* | *Head, Three Doors above the Coffee* | *House, in Market-Street.* | M.DCC.LXXXII. | 24mo. Title, 1 leaf; pp. (1114).

> Not paged. Signatures A to Zz (omitting J, V, and W), 24 pp. each, and Aaa, 10 pp. The Title is really the first leaf of A, but it is followed by an inset of two pages, containing the proceedings in Congress, and the names, &c., of all the Books of the Bible. 2 Kings vii. 12, contains a misprint, *not* for now. The sixth chapter of Hosea is numbered vii. This was the first Bible printed in English in America. For title and collation of the New Testament see No. 4126, *supra.*

BOND. (T.)   Anniversary Oration, | Delivered May 21st, | before the | American Philosophical Society, | held in Philadelphia, | For the Promotion of Useful Knowledge. | For the Year 1782. | By Doctor Thomas Bond, | Vice-President of that Society. | ... | .... | *Philadelphia:* | *Printed by John Dunlap.* [1782.] | 8vo. Title, 1 leaf; pp. 34.   L. C. P.   4185

BRJEFWECHSEL zwischen S. Maj. dem Kaiser Joseph dem

Zweiten und J. K. Hoheit dem Kurfürsten zu Trier, wegen der Kaiser=
lichen Religions=Edikte. Aus dem Französischen. *Philadelphia: Bei John
Hurter.* 1782.   w. 4186

BUMBO. (J.)   The | American | Almanac, | For the Year of
our Lord, | 1783. | (Being the Third after Bissextile or Leap-
Year.) | [14 lines.] | By Father Jacobus Bumbo. | *Philadelphia :* |
*Printed by T. Bradford, in Front-Street, four | Doors below the Coffee-
House.* [1782.] | Sm. 8vo. pp. (36).   H. S. P. 4187

THE | CASE | of the | Episcopal Churches | in the | United
States | Considered. | . . . | . . . | . . . | . . . . | *Philadelphia :* |
Printed by David C. Claypoole. | M,DCC,LXXXII. | 8vo. pp. 35 ;
Errata, 1 leaf.   H. S. P. 4188

CATALOGUE of a Collection of Books belonging to the Rev.
Robert Smith, of South Carolina, and Mr. James Cannon, de-
ceased, late of this city. To be sold at Auction, April 24th.
Philadelphia : Francis Bailey ?   1782.   4189

CATALOGUE of a Curious and Valuable Collection of Books,
to be sold on Oct. 11th.   *Philadelphia.*   1782.   4190

CATALOGUE of a Gentleman's very valuable library to be
Sold at Auction, Oct. 17th, 18th, 19th, 24th, 25th and 26th.   *Philadelphia : Robert Bell.*   1782.   4191

CATALOGUE of Books to be sold at Auction, Jan. 30th.
Philadelphia : Robert Bell.   1782.   4192

,Other book sales by Bell were advertised for May 1 and Nov. 2. On each occasion " Printed Catalogues [were] to be had at the Sale."

CLARKE. (J.)   Erasmi | Colloquia Selecta ; | or, the | Select
Colloquies | of | Erasmus. | With an | English Translation, | as
literal as possible. | Designed for the Use of Beginners in the
Latin Tongue. | The Eighteenth Edition. | By John Clarke, |
Author of the Essays upon Education and Study. | *Philadelphia :*
| *Printed and Sold by Joseph Crukshank, | in Market-Street, between
Second and | Third-Streets.*   MDCCLXXXII. | 12mo. pp. v, 222.

[DUPONT DE NEMOURS. (Pierre Samuel)] Memoirs | sur | La Vie et les Ouvrages | de | M. Turgot, | Ministre d'Etat. | Premiere Partie. | . . . | . . . . | . . . . | *Philadelphie.* [*Paris.*] | 1782. | 16mo. pp. i–viii, 1–148. + Seconde Partie, | Contenant son Ministere aux Finances & | sa Retraite. | [*Ibid.*] 16mo. pp. 268.

DU SIMITIERE. (Pierre Eugene) American Museum. | [*Philadelphia:*] *Printed by John Dunlap.* [1782.] | 4to. 1 leaf.   4195

A descriptive handbill, dated "June 1, 1782."

EPITAPH. | *Philadelphia:* | *Printed by F. Bailey, in Market-Sreet,* 1782. | Folio, 1 leaf.   L. C. P.   4196

Mock epitaph on George III.

EVANS. (I.) A | Discourse | delivered | Near York in Virginia, | on the | Memorable Occasion | of the | Surrender of the British Army | to the | Allied Forces of America and France, | before | The Brigade of New-York Troops and the Division of | American Light-Infantry, under the Command of the | Marquis de la Fayette. | By Israel Evans, A.M. | Chaplain to the Troops of New Hampshire. | (On the 13th day of December, the day of General Thanksgiving, this Dis- | course, nearly in its present form was delivered in the second Presbyterian | church in Philadelphia. The author is indebted for its publication to the | generosity of a number of gentlemen in this city; and it is principally in- | tended for the gratification of the brave soldiery fighting in the cause of | America and, mankind.) | *Philadelphia:* | *Printed by Francis Bailey, in Market-street.* | M.DCC.LXXXII. | 8vo. pp. 45, (1).   H. S. P.   4197

FATHER Abraham's Pocket Almanac for 1783. *Philadelphia:* *John Dunlap.* 1782.   4198

THE FREEMAN'S Journal.   4199

Numbers XXXVIII. (Jan. 2, 1782) to LXXXVIII. (Dec. 23, 1782), four pages each, with a "Postscript" of one leaf to No. 56. Title and imprint as in No. 4102, *supra.* In No. 53, the words "Vol. II. | Price, Six-Pence," are introduced in the title under the cut, and in No. 54, "Vol. II." was placed above it.

GOLDSMITH. (O.) The Deserted Village. By Oliver Goldsmith. *Philadelphia:* 1782.   4200

GRAVINES. (— de) The Ladies Friend. By Monsieur de
Gravines. *Philadelphia: Robert Aitken.* 1782.   4201

𝔇𝔈𝔑 𝔥𝔬𝔠𝔥 = 𝔇𝔈𝔘𝔗𝔖𝔥= Americaniſche Calender, Auf das Jahr
1783. *Philadelphia: Johann Dunlap.* 1782.   4202

THE | INDEPENDENT Gazetteer; | or, the | Chronicle of
Freedom. | . . . | . . . . | Numb. I) Saturday, April 13, 1782.
(Price Six-pence.) | *Philadelphia: Printed by E. Oswald, at his
Printing-Office, near the Bunch of | Grapes Tavern, in Third-Street,
where Subscriptions, at Three Dollars per Annum, Essays, Articles of
Intelligence, | &c. for this Paper, are gratefully received.—Advertisements
of no more Length than Breadth, are inserted | the first Three Weeks for
one Dollar, and for every Continuance after, one third of a Dollar; those
exceeding a Square, | are inserted in the same Proportion.* | Folio. 4203

Numbers 1 (April 13, 1782) to 52 (Dec. 28, 1782), four pages each, with " Supplements" of two pages to Numbers 5 and 52. From the 14th of September to the end
of the year the paper was issued twice a week.

INTELLIGENCE from the Moon; found on board one of the
Dutch East Indiamen, captured by Commodore Johnstone. *Philadelphia: Theophilus Cossart.* 1782.   4204

JOURNALS | of the | House of Representatives | of the |
Commonwealth of Pennsylvania. | Beginning the twenty-eighth
Day of November, 1776, and | Ending the second Day of October,
1781. | With the | Proceedings | of the several | Committees and
Conventions, | Before and at the Commencement of the | Amer-
ican Revolution. | Volume the First. | [*Arms of Pennsylvania.*] |
Philadelphia: | *Printed by John Dunlap.* | MDCCLXXXII. | Folio.
Title, 1 leaf; pp. 1–698, for 697, (1).   H. S. P.   4205

JOURNALS | of | Congress. | Containing | the | Proceedings
| From January 1, 1779, to January 1, 1780. | Published by
Order of Congress. | Volume V. | *Philadelphia:* | *Printed by David
C. Claypoole.* | M,DCC,LXXXII. | 8vo. pp. 464, (15), lxxiv.   4206

KUNZE. (J. C.) Eine Rede von den Absichten und dem bisherigen Fortgange der privilegirten deutschen Gesellschaft. Von Ehrw. Johann Christoph Kunze. *Philadelphia.* 1782. 4207

LAWS | enacted in | The Sixth | General Assembly | of the | Representatives | of the | Freemen | of the | Commonwealth | of | Pennsylvania, | At the Sitting which commenced at Philadelphia on Monday, | the Twenty-second Day of October, and continued by Adjourn- | ment to Friday, the Twenty-eighth Day of December, A.D. | One Thousand Seven Hundred and Eighty-one. | Vol. II. | *Philadelphia :* | *Printed by Hall and Sellers, in Market-street.* | M,DCC,LXXXII. | Folio, pp. 8. + Laws | Enacted in the Second Sitting | . . . | . . . | . . . | . . . | . . . | . . . | . . . . | [*Ibid.*] pp. 9–81, (2). + Laws | Enacted in the Third Sitting | . . . | . . . | . . . | . . | . . . | . . . | . . . . | [*Ibid.*] pp. 85–110, 1 leaf. H. S. P. 4208

LAWS | enacted in | The Seventh | General Assembly | of the | Representatives | of the | Freemen | of the | Commonwealth | of | Pennsylvania, | At the Sitting which commenced at Philadelphia, on Monday, | the Twenty-eighth Day of October, and continued by Adjourn- | ment to Wednesday, the Fourth Day of December, A.D. | One Thousand Seven Hundred and Eighty-two. | *Philadelphia :* | *Printed by Hall and Sellers, in Market-street.* | M,DCC,LXXXII. | Folio. Title, 1 leaf; pp. 115–126. 4209

LYTTELTON. (T.) Letters | of the late | Thomas Lord Lyttelton : | With | His Poems on several Occasions, | and | A Sketch of his Lordship's Character. | *Philadelphia :* | *Printed and Sold by Robert Bell, in Third-Street.* | M,DCC,LXXXII. | 8vo. pp. 80. 4210

[MACKENZIE. (Henry)] Julia de Roubigné, | A Sentimental Novel. | In a Series of Letters. | Published by | The Author of The Man of Feeling, | and The Man of the World. | In Two Volumes. | Vol. I. | The Third Edition. | *Philadelphia, Printed by Charles Cist,* | *in Market-Street.* | M.DCC.LXXXII. | 16mo. pp. viii, 111. + Vol. II. pp. iv, 119. L. C. P. 4211

MACKENZIE. The Man of Feeling. By Henry Mackenzie. *Philadelphia : Robert Bell.* 1782. 4212

[MACPHERSON. (John)]   An | Introduction | to the | Study of Natural Philosophy. | [*Philadelphia* : 1782.]   Folio, pp. (2).   4213

MARTIN. (H.)   A | Narrative | of a | Discovery | of a | sovereign specific, | for the cure of | Cancers. | With several other improvements lately | made in Medicine. | With a | Postscript, | on a singular case of a | Stone | taken out of the Tongue. | By Hugh Martin, | Physician and Surgeon in the American Army. | *Philadelphia :* | *Printed by Robert Aitken.* | M.DCC.LXXXII. | 8vo. pp. 15.   4214

MINUTES | of the | First Session, | of the | Seventh General Assembly, | of the | Commonwealth | of | Pennsylvania ; | Which commenced at Philadelphia, on Monday, the | twenty-eighth Day of October, in the Year of our Lord | One thousand seven hundred and eighty-two. | *Philadelphia :* | *Printed by John Dunlap.* [1782.] | Folio.   Title, 1 leaf; pp. 715–968.   H. S. P.   4215

The first session occupies pp. 715–780, the second, pp. 781–883, and the third, which sat until Sept. 26, 1783, pp. 883–968.   The first page of the last Session should have been 885.

MINUTES | of the | Baptist Association, | Held in Philadelphia, October, 1782. | [*Philadelphia : Robert Aitken.*   1782.]   Sq. 8vo. pp. 8.   4216

DER NEUE, Verbeſſert= und Zuverläßige | Americaniſche | Calender, | Auf das 1783ſte Jahr Chriſti, | Welches ein Gemein Jahr von 365 Tagen iſt. | Darin enthalten | Die Wochen= Monaths= und Merkwürdige Tage; des Monden | Auf= und Untergang; ſeine Zeichen, Grade, und Viertel; die Aſpecten der | Planeten, ſamt der Witterung; des Sieben= geſtirns Aufgang, Sudplaß | und Untergang; Auf= und Untergang der Sonne; nebſt der | Fluth oder dem hohen Waſſer zu Philadelphia; | Und andere gewöhnliche Calender=Arbeit. | Vornemlich nach dem Penn= ſylvaniſchen Horizont berechnet; | Jedoch in den angrenzenden Staaten ohne merklichen Unterſcheid zu gebrauchen. | Zum Erſtenmal heraus= gegeben. | *Philadelphia, Gedruckt und zu haben bey Joseph Crukshank, in der Markt-strasse.* [1782.] | Sq. 8vo. pp. (40).   H. S. P.   4217

NEUJAHRS=Verſe | des | Herumträgers der Philadelphiſchen Cor=

refponben$. | Den 1ften Januar, 1782. | [*Philadelphia: Melchior Steiner.* 1782.] 4to. 1 leaf.   H. S. P.   4218

THE | NEW Testament | of our | Lord and Saviour | Jesus Christ, | newly translated out of the | Original Greek : | And with the | Former Translations diligently | compared and revised. | Appointed to be read in Churches. | *Philadelphia:* | *Printed by Joseph Crukshank, in Market-Street,* | *between Second and Third-Streets.* | MDCCLXXXII. | 12mo. pp. (452).   4219

THE | NEW Testament | of our | Lord and Saviour | Jesus Christ, | newly translated out of the | Original Greek: | And with the | Former Translations diligently | compared and revised. | Appointed to be read in Churches. | *Philadelphia:* | *Printed by Joseph Crukshank, in Market-Street,* | *between Second and Third-Streets.* | MDCCLXXXII. | 12mo. pp. (440).   4220

NEW-Year Verses of the Carriers of the Freeman's Journal. *Philadelphia: Francis Bailey.* 1782.   4221

NEW-YEAR Verses of the Carriers of the Pennsylvania Evening Post. *Philadelphia: B. Towne.* 1782.   4222

NEW-YEAR Verses of the Carriers of the Pennsylvania Gazette. *Philadelphia: Hall and Sellers.* 1782.   4223

NEW-YEAR Verses of the Carriers of the Pennsylvania Journal. *Philadelphia: T. Bradford and P. Hall.* 1782.   4224

NEW-YEAR Verses of the Carriers of the Pennsylvania Packet. *Philadelphia: David C. Claypoole.* 1782.   4225

PAINE. (T.) Letter | addressed to the | Abbe Raynal | on the | Affairs of North-America. | In which | The Mistakes in the Abbe's Account | of the | Revolution of America | are corrected and cleared up. | By Thomas Paine, M.A. | of the University of Pennsylvania, and author of the Pamphlet | and other Publications, entitled, " Common Sense." | *Philadelphia:* | *Printed by Melchior Steiner, in Race-street,* | *near Third-street.* | *And Sold by Robert Aitken, Bookseller, in Market-* | *street, three Doors above the Coffee-*

House. | M,DCC,LXXXII. | 8vo.   Half-title, 1 leaf; Title, 1 leaf; Introduction, pp. i–iv; text, pp. 5–77.   H. S. P. + The Second Edition.   [*Ibid.*]   A. P. S.   4226

PAINE.   A Letter to the Earl of Shelburne, on his Speech, July 10, 1782, respecting the acknowledgment of American Independence.   By Thomas Paine.   *Philadelphia:* 1782.   8vo.   4227

The American Crisis, No. XIV.

THE PENNSYLVANIA Evening Post.   *Philadelphia: B. Towne.* 1782.   A. A. S.   4228

THE PENNSYLVANIA Gazette.   4229

Numbers 2690 (Jan. 2, 1782) to 2741 (Dec. 24, 1782), four pages each, with " Supplements" of two pages to Numbers 2694, 2698, 2699, 2702 to 2705, 2727, 2728, and 2735, of four pages to No. 2701 ; and " Postscripts" of two pages to Numbers 2696, 2719, and 2732.   Title and imprint as in No. 3925, *supra*, until No. 2735; when the former was changed to the form given in No. 4334, *infra*.

THE PENNSYLVANIA Journal.   *Philadelphia: Printed by T. Bradford and P. Hall.   Advertisements, &c. for this Paper, | are received at the Book-Store in Market-street, adjoining the Coffee-House, or the Printing-Office in Lætitia-Court. |*   4230

Numbers 1453 (Jan. 2, 1782) to 1554 (Dec. 28, 1782), four pages each, with a " Postscript" of two pages to No. 1488.   Published on Wednesdays and Saturdays. Title as in No. 2914, *supra*.   After No. 1498 Hall's name was omitted in the imprint, and the spacing somewhat changed.

THE PENNSYLVANIA Packet.   4231

Numbers 827 (Jan. 1, 1782) to 983 (Dec. 31, 1782), four pages each, with a " Supplement" of one leaf to No. 914 ; " Postscripts" of two pages to Numbers 933 and 935, and one of one leaf to No. 950.   Published three times a week.   Title and imprint nearly the same as in No. 4137, *supra*.

THE PENNSYLVANIA Pocket Almanac for 1783.   *Philadelphia: Thomas Bradford.* 1782.   4232

A PLAIN | Almanack, | for the | Year of our Lord, 1783; | Being the Third after Leap-Year. | Shewing, | The Days of the Month; the Days of the Week; | The | Time of the Rising and

Setting of the | Sun and Moon ; | Full and Change of the Moon; Rising, Setting and Southing | of some of the Planets; Equation of Time ; Eclipses; | Friends Yearly Meetings; Table shewing the Value | and Weight of Coins; Table of Interest; Table of Tide ; | Roads, &c. | Also, | A Variety of Essays, in | Prose and Verse. | *Philadelphia :* | *Printed and Sold by Joseph Crukshank,* | *in Market-Street, between Second* | *and Third-Street.* [1782.] | Sm. 8vo. pp. (36).

POOR Will's | Almanack, | for the | Year of our Lord, 1783; | Being the Third after Leap-Year. | . . . | . . . | . . . | . . . | . . . | . . . | . . . | . . . | . . . | . . . | . . . | . . . | . . . | . . . . | *Philadelphia :* | *Printed and Sold by Joseph Crukshank,* | . . . | . . . . [1782.] | Sm. 8vo. pp. (36).   H. S. P.   **4234**

POOR Will's | Pocket Almanack, | For the Year 1783. | *Philadelphia :* | *Printed and Sold by Joseph Crukshank.* [1782.] | 24mo. pp. (24).   H. S. P.   **4235**

[PRATT. (Samuel Jackson)] Emma Corbett: | Exhibiting | Henry and Emma, | the | Faithful Modern Lovers, | as | delineated by themselves, | In their Original Letters. | Published by Courtney Melmoth. | Author of the Pupil of Pleasure, &c. &c. | . . . | . . . | . . . | . . . | . . . . | Three Volumes Complete in One. | *Philadelphia ;* | *Printed and Sold by Robert Bell, in Third-Street.* | MDCCLXXXII. | 8vo. pp. 48. + The Second Volume. | [*Ibid.*] 8vo. pp. 48. + The Third and Last Volume. | [*Ibid.*] 8vo. pp. 48.   L. C. P.   **4236**

" Founded upon incidents which occurred at or near Philadelphia in the winter of 1777."

PROCEEDINGS | of a | General Court Martial, | Held at Philadelphia, | In the State of | Pennsylvania, | By Order of his Excellency | General Washington, | Commander in Chief | Of the Army of | The United States of America, | For the Trial of | Major General Howe, | December 7, 1781. | Major General Baron Steuben, President. | *Philadelphia :* | *Printed by Hall and Sellers, in Market-Street.* | M,DCC,LXXXII. | Folio, pp. 31.   H. S. P.   **4237**

PROCLAMATION. [*Arms of Pennsylvania.*] | Pennsylvania,

ss. | By the President and Supreme Executive Council of the Commonwealth | of Pennsylvania, | A Proclamation. | [*Philadelphia:*] *Printed by Francis Bailey.* [1782.] | Folio, 1 leaf.   4238

Dated " Nov. 20, 1782." On the observance of Sunday.

PROPOSALS | To Amend and Perfect the Po- | licy of the Government | of the United States of | America; | Or, | The fulfilling of the Prophe- | cies in the latter Days, com- | menced by the Indepen- | dence of America. | Containing, A new Mode of Elec- | tions, with a Method of Supporting | Government without taxing or | fining the People. | . . . | . . . | . . . | . . . | . . . | | . . . | . . . . | [*Philadelphia:*] *Printed* [*by B. Towne*] *for the Author,* 1782. | 12mo. pp. 36.   A. P. S.   4239

RAYNAL. ([William Thomas]).   The | Revolution | of | America. | By the Abbe Raynal, | Author of the philosophical and political history of the establish- | ments, and commerce of the Europeans in both the Indies. | Price Half a Dollar. | *Philadelphia:* | *Printed for Robert Bell, in Third-Street.* | M,DCC,LXXXII. | 8vo. pp. 72.   H. S. P. + The second edition, | Price One Dollar. | [*Ibid.*] 8vo. pp. 72.   L. C. P.   4240

𝔇𝔈𝔯 𝔯𝔈𝔓𝔘𝔅𝔏𝔍𝔠𝔄𝔯𝔍𝔰𝔠𝔥𝔈 Galender auf das 1783ste Jahr Christi. Zum Funfftenmal heraus gegeben. *Philadelphia: Theophilus Cossart.* 1782.   4241

REGULATIONS for the Order and Discipline of the Troops of the United States. Part I. *Philadelphia: Charles Cist?* 1782. 12mo. pp. 77, (1), iv, 8 plates.   4242

ROBIN ([Claude C.]) Nouveau | Voyage | dans | L'Amérique Septentrionale, | en l'année 1781; | et | Campagne | de l'armée | De M. le Comte de Rochambeau. | Par M. l'Abbe Robin. | *A Philadelphie,* | *Et se trouve à Paris,* | *Chez Moutard, Imprimeur-Libraire de la Reine,* | *de Madame, et de Madame Comtesse d'Artois,* | *rue des Mathurins, Hôtel de Cluni.* | M.DCC.LXXXII. | 16mo. pp. ix, 222.   L. C. P.   4243

RULES and Articles | for the | Better Government | of the | Troops raised, or to be raised, | And kept in Pay, | By and at the Expense of the | United States | of | America. | *Philadelphia : Printed in the Year* | 1782. | Sm. 8vo. pp. 39.   H. S. P.   4244

SAUNDERS. (R.)   A Pocket Almanac for 1783.   By Richard Saunders, Phil.   *Philadelphia : Hall and Sellers.*   1782.   4245

SAUNDERS.   Poor Richard improved : | Being an | Almanack | [10 lines] | For the | Year of our Lord 1783 : | Being the Third after Leap-Year. | [9 lines.] | By Richard Saunders, Philom. | *Philadelphia : | Printed and Sold by Hall and Sellers.* [1782.] | 8vo. pp. (36).   H. S. P.   4246

A | SERMON, | On the Present Situation of | the Affairs of | America | and | Great - Britain. | Written by a Black, | And printed at the Request of several Persons of | distinguished Characters. | *Philadelphia : | Printed by T. Bradford and P. Hall.* | M,DCC,LXXXII. | 8vo. pp. 11.   H. S. P.   4247

SEWARD. ([Anna])   Monody | on | Major Andre, | Who was executed at Tappan, | November — 1780. | By | Miss Seward. | To which are added, | Major Andre's | Letters, | Addressed to Miss Seward, when at his 18th Year. | *Philadelphia : | Printed and Sold by Enoch Story, in Third | Street, Third Door from Chestnut-street.* [1782.] | Sm. 8vo. pp. 56.   N. Y. H. S.   4248

SHARP. (A.)   Der Gantz Neue Verbefferte Nord = Americanifche Calender, auf das 1783fte. Jahr Chrifti.   Zum Achtenmal herausgegeben und verfertiget von Anthony Sharp, Philom.   *Lancaster : Francis Bailey.*   1782.   4249

SHARP.   The Continental Almanac for 1783.   *Philadelphia : Francis Bailey.*   1782.   4250

SHERIDAN. (R. B.)   The Real and Genuine School for Scandal.   By Richard Brinsley Sheridan.   *Philadelphia : Robert Bell.*   1782.   8vo. pp. 64.   L. C. P.   4251

A SHORT | Account | of the | Convincement | of | Edward Andrews. | [*Philadelphia : Joseph Crukshank.* 1782?] Sm. 8vo. pp. 4.   F.   4252

SIBYLLÆ Americanæ | genethliacum | Ludovico XVII. | Regni Gallici Delphino | Prognosticum. | *Philadelphiœ :* | *Apud Benjaminum Towne.* | M,DCC,LXXXII. | 4to. pp. 16. L. C. P. 4253

SMITH. (R.) The | Obligations | of the | Confederate States of North America | To Praise God. | Two Sermons. | Preached at Pequea, December 13th, 1781, the | day recommended by the honourable Congress to | the several States, to be observed as a Day of | Thanksgiving to God, for the various inter- | positions of his providence in their favour, during | their contest with Great Britain, particularly those | of the present year, crowned by the capture of | Lord Cornwallis with his whole army. | By Robert Smith, A.M. | Minister of the Gospel at Pequea. | Published by Request. | *Philadelphia :* | *Printed by Francis Bailey, in Market-Street.* | M.DCC.LXXXII. | Sm. 8vo. Title, 1 leaf; Preface, 1 leaf; pp. 1–36.   c.   4254

STANHOPE, (Philip Dormer — Earl of Chesterfield.) The Principles of Politeness. By Lord Chesterfield. *Philadelphia : Robert Aitken.* 1782 ?   4255

𝕯𝕴𝕰 | 𝕿𝕬𝕲𝕷𝕴𝕮𝕳𝕰𝕽 | Loofungen und Lehrterte | der | Brüder=gemeine | für das Jahr | 1783. | *Philadelphia :* | *Gedruckt bey Melchior Steiner, in der Rees-strasse, nahe | bey der Dritten-strasse.* 1782. | 8vo. pp. (51), (63).   H. S. P.   4256

" Die taglichen Lehrtexte," pp. (63), in the copy examined were printed in Germany.

THOMAS. (D.) The | Novelty of Novelties examined : | or, | The New System of Religion compared | with Ancient Scriptures, | and | Found to be contrary to them all. | Being | some friendly Remarks on Mr. Winchester's late | Sermon, | entitled | The Seed of the Woman bruising the Serpent's Head. | By David Thomas. A.M. | . . . | . . . | . . . | . . . . | *Philadelphia :* | *Printed for the Author. [by B. Towne.]* | M,DCC,LXXXII. | 8vo. Half title, 1 leaf; pp. 37.   4257

TO the Inhabitants of Pennsylvania. | [*Philadelphia :* 1782.] 4to. pp. 7.   L. C. P.   4258

Signed " A Freeholder." Du Simitiere writes on it, " For the Election of October, 1782."

THE UNIVERSE, a miscellany, or moral view of the Intellectual World, and the Analogy of Nature. *Philadelphia: Theophilus Cossart.* 1782. 4259

Advertised in the Freeman's Journal, Oct. 2, 1782, as " to be published by subscription, if a sufficient number of sentimentalists should offer to encourage the publication."

WEATHERWISE. (A.) Father Abraham's | Almanack, | For the Year of our Lord | 1783; | Being the Third after Leap-Year, | And the Eighth Year of American | Independence. | . . . | . . . | . . . | . . . | . . . | . . . | . . . | . . . | . . . | . . . | . . . | . . . | . . . . | By Abraham Weatherwise, Gent. | *Philadelphia :* | *Printed by John Dunlap.* [1782.] | Sm. 8vo. pp. (32). H. S. P. 4260

WINCHESTER. (E.) The Outcasts Comforted. | A Sermon | Delivered at the University in Philadelphia, | January 4, 1782, | To the Members of the | Baptist Church, | Who have been rejected by their Brethren, | For holding the Doctrine of | The final Restoration of all | Things. | By Elhanan Winchester. | Published at the earnest Desire of the Hearers. | . . . | . . . | . . . | . . . | . . . . | *Philadelphia :* | *Printed* [*by B. Towne,*] *in the Year* 1782. | 8vo. pp. 18. H. S. P. 4261

1783.

AN ACCOUNT of the barbarous Murder of Col. Crawford, and the miraculous escape of Dr. Knight and John Slover, from Captivity with the Indians in 1782. *Philadelphia: Francis Bailey.* 1783. 4262

AN ACCOUNT of the Births and Burials in the United Churches of Christ Church and St. Peter's. *Philadelphia :* 1783.

ADDRESS | and | Recommendations | to | The States, | by | The United States in Congress | assembled. | *Philadelphia :* | *Printed by David C. Claypoole.* | M,DCC,LXXXIII. | 8vo. H. S. P.

Collation: Title, 1 leaf; Address, pp. 3–14; Estimate of the National Debt, 1 page; Report, pp. 1–9; Estimate of the Produce of the Import on Imported Articles,

1 page; Extract of a Letter from Franklin, 1 page; Letter from the Minister of France, pp. 1–3; Contract with France, pp. 1–6; Contract with Holland, pp. 1–5; Address, &c., of the Army, pp. 1–4; Extract of a Letter from Washington, &c., pp. 1–20. In some copies the last part is expanded to 26 pages by the insertion of additional matter.

ADVENTURES of a Hackney Coach. *Philadelphia: Enoch Story.* 1783. 　　　　　　　　　　　　　　　　　　　　　　4265

ADVERTISEMENT. *Philadelphia: Robert Aitken.* 1783.

The following charges appear in Aitken's Ledger during 1783:

May 16. Lewis Grant. To printing 100 Advertisements			£.0.15.0
July 20. } John Kean, of Yorktown. { To printing and paper			5. 0.0
Nov. 2. 　　　　　　　　　　　{ To printing Advertisement			1. 0.0
Sept. 22. William Turnbull. To printing 100 Advertisements			10.0
Sept. 23. } Matthew Clarkson. { To printing 250 Circular Letters			1. 5.0
Oct. 22. 　　　　　　　　　{ To printing Advertisement			2.10.0
Nov. —. Peter January. To printing 100 Advertisements of his house in Spruce St.			

AHIMAN Rezon | abridged and digested: | As a | Help to all that are, or would be | Free and Accepted Masons. | To which is added, | A Sermon, | Preached in Christ-Church, Phila- delphia, | At a General Communication, | Celebrated, agreeable to the Constitutions, on | Monday, December 28, 1778, as the Anniver- | sary of St. John the Evangelist. | Published by Order of | The Grand Lodge of Pennsylvania, | By William Smith, D.D. | *Philadelphia:* | *Printed by Hall and Sellers.* | M,DCC,LXXXIII. | 8vo. 1 plate; pp. i–xvi, 1–166. 　　　　　　　H. S. P.　4267

THE ALTERNATIVE. | The | Constitution | and a | Roasted Turkey; | or | A new Constitution | with | Buttermilk and Pota- toes | for | Mechanics. | [*Philadelphia:* 1783.] 4to. 1 leaf. 　4268

An election poster, dated by Du Simitiere Oct. 14, 1783.

𝕬𝕸𝕰𝕽𝕵𝕮𝕬𝕽𝕵𝕾𝕮𝕳𝕰𝕽 | Haus= und Wirthschafts= | Calender | Auf das 1784ste Jahr Christi, | Welches ein Schalt=Jahr ist von 366 Tagen. | . . . | . . . | . . . . | Zum Fünftenmal heraus gegeben. | *Philadel- phia: Gedruckt und zu haben bey Melchior Steiner,* | . . . . [1783.] | Sm. 4to. pp. (40). 　　　　　　　　　　　　H. S. P.　4269

𝕬𝕸𝕰𝕽𝕵𝕮𝕬𝕽𝕵𝕾𝕮𝕳𝕰𝕽 | Stadt und Land | Calender | Auf das

1784ſte Jahr Chriſti, | Welches ein Schalt-Jahr iſt | von 366 Tagen. | *Philadelphia:* | *Gedruckt und zu haben, bey haben Carl Cist, in der* | *Markt-strasse,* | *zwischen der Vierten und Fuenften-strasse.* [1783.] | Sm. 4to. pp. (40).   H. S. P.   4270

[BENEZET. (Anthony)]   Notes on the Slave Trade, &c. | [*Philadelphia: Enoch Story.* 1783.]   Sm. 8vo. pp. 8.   F.   4271

BENEZET.   A Short | Account | of the People called | Quakers ; | Their Rise, Religious Principles and | Settlement in America. | Mostly collected from different Authors, for | the information of all serious Inquirers, | particularly Foreigners. | The Third Edition. | By Anthony Benezet. | *Philadelphia :* | *Printed by* | *Enoch Story, at his Printing-Office,* | *in Strawberry-Alley, opposite Trot-* | *ter's Alley.* | MDCCLXXXIII. | Sm. 8vo. pp. 40.   F.   4272

BENEZET.   Kurzer Bericht | von den Leuten, die man | Quäker | nennet ; | Ihrem Urſprung, ihren Religionsgründen, | und von ihrer Niederlaſſung in America. | Meiſtentheils aus verſchiedenen Autores zu- | ſammen ge- | zogen, zum Unterricht aller aufrichtigen Nachforſcher, | und inſonderheit für Ausländer. | Durch Anton Benezet. | Aus dem Engliſchen überſetzt. | *Philadelphia:* | *Gedruckt bey Melchior Steiner, in der Rees-* | *strasse.* 1783. | 12mo. pp. 45.   H. S. P.   4273

[BOISGELIN. (Jean de Dieu Raymond de Cucé de)]   Recueil de pièces direrses en vers.   *A Philadelphie:* [*Paris.*]   1783.   4274

BROWNELL. (A.)   Enthusiastical | Errors, | Transpired and detected, | By Abner Brownell, | In a Letter to a Father, | Benjamin Brownell. | . . . | . . . | . . . | . . . | . . . | . . . | . . . | . . . | . . . | . . . | . . . | . . . | . . . | . . . | . . . | . . . . | [*Philadelphia?*] *Printed* [*by B. Towne ?*] *for the Author, in the Year* 1783. | 8vo. pp. 44.   F.   4275

BUCHANAN. (J.)   A | Regular | English Syntax. | Wherein is exhibited | The Whole Variety | of | English Construction, | properly exemplified. | To which is added | The elegant Manner of arranging Words, | and Members of Sentences. | The Whole reduced to Practice, | For the Use of private young Gentlemen and | Ladies, as well as of our most eminent | Schools. | By James

Buchanan. | *Philadelphia: | Printed by Charles Cist, in Market |
Street.* M.DCC.LXXXIII. | 12mo. Title, 1 leaf; pp. xxxi, 197.

BUMBO. (J.) The American Almanac for 1784. By Jacobus
Bumbo. *Philadelphia: T. Bradford.* 1783.   4277

BURKE. (Æ.) An | Address | to the | Freemen | of the |
State of South-Carolina. | Containing Political Observations on
the following | Subjects, viz. | I. On the Citizens making a tempo-
rary Submission to the British | Arms, after the reduction of
Charlestown in 1780. | II. On Governor Rutledge's Proclamation
of the 27th of | September, 1781. | III. On the Mode of conduct-
ing the Election, for the Assembly | at Jacksonborough. | IV. On
the Exclusion Act, which cuts off the Citizens from | the Rights
of Election. | V. On the Confiscation Act. VI. On the Amerce-
ment Act. | VII. The Conclusion, with Remarks to prove the Ne-
cessity of | an Amnesty, or Act of Oblivion. | By Cassius. | Sup-
posed to be written by Ædanus Burke, Esquire, | one of the Chief
Justices of the State of South-Carolina. | . . . | . . . | . . . | . . . .
| *Philadelphia: | Printed and Sold by Robert Bell, in Third-Street. |
Price one-third of a Dollar.* MDCCLXXXIII. | 8vo. pp. 32.   4278

BURKE. Considerations | on the | Society or Order | of | Cin-
cinnati ; | Lately Instituted | By the Major-Generals, Brigadier-
Generals, and | other Officers of the American Army. | Proving
that it creates | A Race of Hereditary Patricians, | or | Nobility.
| Interspersed with remarks | On its Consequences to the Free-
dom | and Happiness of the Republic. | Addressed to the People of
South- | Carolina, and their Representatives. | By Cassius. | Sup-
posed to be written by Ædanus Burke, Esquire, | one of the Chief
Justices of the State of South-Carolina. | . . . . | *Philadelphia: |
Printed and Sold by Robert Bell, in Third-Street. | Price, one-sixth of a
Dollar.* M,DCC,LXXXIII. | 8vo. pp. 16.   H. S. P.   4279

[CADWALADER. (John)] A | Reply | to | General Joseph
Reed's | Remarks | on a | Late Publication | in the | Independent
Gazetteer, | With some Observations on his | Address | to the |
People of Pennsylvania. | *Philadelphia: | Printed and Sold by T.*

Bradford, in Front-Street, the Fourth | Door below the Coffee-House.
MDCCLXXXIII. | 8vo. pp. 54.   H. S. P.   4280

CATALOGUE. Just published and now selling at | Bell's
Book-Store, in Third-Street, | Price one quarter of a Dollar. | A |
Catalogue | of a large | Collection | of | New and Old | Books, |
in | Arts, Sciences, and Entertainment, | for | Persons of all De-
nominations, | With the selling Price Printed to each Book; |
Now on Sale, at said Bell's Book-Store, | near St. Paul's Church,
in Third-Street. | *Philadelphia: | Printed by Robert Bell, in Third-
Street.* | M,DCC,LXXXIII. | 8vo. pp. 88.   H. S. P.   4281

Containing, besides advertisements of a dozen of Bell's more recent publications,
the titles of 2421 works and 21 maps and atlases which he had for sale.

CATALOGUE of a Collection of scarce and valuable Books,
belonging to a gentleman just arrived from Europe, with the price
of each book affixed. *Philadelphia: Francis Bailey.* 1783.   4282

CATALOGUE of Books to be sold at Auction, Feb. 19. *Philadelphia: Robert Bell.* 1783.   4283

Other book sales by Bell were advertised for May 6, Oct. 30, Nov. 13, and Dec.
3. On each occasion " Printed Catalogues [were] to be had at the Sale."

CATALOGUE of the Circulating Library of William Pritchard.
Philadelphia: 1783.   4284

THE COMPOSITORS and Distributors of the Independent
Gazetteer, | humbly address the following Verses on the New-
Year, | 1783, to the Customers. | [*Philadelphia: Eleazer Oswald.*
1783.] 4to. 1 leaf.   L. C. P.   4285

[CRAWFORD. (Charles)] The | Christian: | A | Poem; | in
| Four Books. | To which is prefixed a | Preface in Prose | In
Defence of Christianity; | with an | Address | to the | People of
America. | . . . | . . . | . . . . | *Philadelphia: | Printed and Sold by
Joseph Crukshank, | in Market-Street, between Second and | Third-
Streets.* MDCCLXXXIII. | 12mo. pp. xl, 111.   L. C. P.   4286

[CRAWFORD.] Liberty: | A | Pindaric Ode. | . . . . | *Phila-*

delphia : | *Printed for the Author, by Robert Aitken, at Pope's Head* | *in Market-Street.* | M.DCC.LXXXIII. | Sq. 8vo. pp. 16.   4287

CRAWFORD. A Poem on the Death of Montgomery. By Charles Crawford. *Philadelphia: Robert Aitken ?* 1783.   4288

[CRAWFORD.] A | Poetical | Paraphrase | on our | Saviour's Sermon | on the | Mount. | . . . | . . . | . . . . | *Philadelphia :* | *Printed for the Author, by Robert Aitken, at Pope's Head,* | *in Market Street.* | M.DCC.LXXXIII. | 4to. pp. 24.   H. S. P.   4289

CROXALL. (S.) The Fables of Æsop and others. With instructive applications, and a print before each Fable. By Samuel Croxall, D.D. The Second American Edition. *Philadelphia: Robert Aitken.* 1783.   4290

CULLEN. (W.) First Lines of the Practice of Physic. Part II. Containing Nervous Diseases. By William Cullen, M.D. *Philadelphia: Charles Cist.* 1783.   4291

CUNNINGHAM. (L.) The | Case of the Whigs | who | Loaned their Money on the Public | Faith | Fairly Stated. | Including | A Memento for Congress to review their | Engagements, and to establish the Honour and | Honesty of the United States of America. | By Letitia Cunningham. | *Philadelphia :* | *Printed by Francis Bailey, in Market-Street.* | M,DCC,LXXXIII. | Sm. 8vo. pp. 51.   L. C. P.   4292

. . . | . . . | . . . | . . . .] THE | DEFINITE Treaty, | Between Great-Britain and the United States of America, sign- | ed at Paris the 3d day of September, 1783. | *Philadelphia: Printed by David C. Claypoole, in Market-street.* [1783.] | Folio, 1 leaf.   4293

Dated "New-York, November 26." "Last Sunday night arrived the Lord Hyde Packet, in 47 days from Falmouth."

[ELLIS. (William)] 'An Authentic | Narrative | of a | Voyage | to the | Pacific Ocean : | Performed by | Captain Cook, and Captain Clerke, | in His Britannic Majesty's Ships, | The Resolution, and Discovery, | In the Years, 1776, 1777, 1778, 1779, and 1780. | Including, A faithful account of all their Discoveries in this | Last Voyage, the Unfortunate Death of Captain Cook, at | the Island of O-why-ee, and the return of the Ships to | England under Captain Gore. | Also A Large Introduction, | Exhibiting, an Account of the several Voyages round the | Globe; with an abstract of the principal expeditions to | Hudson's Bay, for the Discovery of a North-West-Passage. | By an Officer on Board the Discovery. | Volume the First. | *Philadelphia:* | *Printed and Sold by Robert Bell, in Third-Street.* | *Price two thirds of a Dollar.* M,DCC,LXXXIII. | 8vo. pp. 229, (1); Advertisements, pp. (2).

The first volume, which ends on page 112, is followed by the title (1 leaf) and text (pp. 115–229) of the second volume.

FATHER Abraham's Pocket Almanac for 1784.   *Philadelphia: John Dunlap.*   1783.   4295

[FLETCHER. (John)] An | Appeal | to | Matter of Fact and Common Sense. | Or a | Rational| Demonstration | of | Man's corrupt and lost Estate. | [14 lines.] | *Bristol: Printed,* | *Philadelphia:* | *Re-printed by Melchior Steiner,* | *in Race-Street, near Third-Street.* | M.DCC.LXXXIII. | 12mo. pp. 271.   H. S. P.   4296

[FOTHERGILL. (Samuel)] The | Necessity | and | Divine Excellency | of a | Life | of | Purity and Holiness, | Set forth with pathetic Energy, by an eminent Minister of the | Gospel amongst the People called Quakers. | In | Seven Discourses | and Three Prayers, and an Epistle, | to his | Brethren in Religious Profession in the Island of Tortola. | Now collected and re-published, that the instructive and important | Truths therein contained, may be spread and become more | generally useful. | . . . . | The Second Edition. | *Philadelphia:* | *Re-printed by Joseph Crukshank, in Market-street,* | *between Second and Third-streets.* | MDCCLXXXIII. | 8vo. pp. 148.   H. S. P.   4297

For the first edition see No. 4008, *supra.* There are four separate titles, as in the first edition, which do not differ greatly from those described. The Prayer of Agur is called "The Fourth Edition," and the last two titles are dated "1784."

THE FREEMAN'S Journal.   4298

Numbers LXXXIX. (Jan. 1, 1783) to CXLI. (Dec. 31, 1783), four pages each, with a " Postscript" of two pages to No. 129. Title and imprint as in No. 4102, *supra*, until No. 138, when the latter was slightly changed.

FRY. (J.) Select Poems, containing Epistles, &c. occasionally written on various subjects. To which is now added, the history of Elijah and Elisha. By John Fry. *Philadelphia: Joseph Cruk-shank.* 1783.   4299

FULLER. (S.) Some | Principles and Precepts | of the | Christian Religion. | By Way of Question and Answer. | Recommended to Parents and Tutors | for the Use of Children. | By Samuel Fuller. | . . . | . . . | . . . | . . . | . . . | . . . | . . . | . . . | . . . . | *Philadelphia:* | *Printed by Joseph Crukshank,* | *in Market-street, between Second* | *and Third-streets.* MDCCLXXXIII. | Sm. 12mo. pp. ix, (6), 48.   H. S. P. 4300

[GURNEY. (John)] An | Affectionate | Address | to the | Youth | of | Norwich Monthly Meeting. | . . . | . . . | . . . | . . . | . . . . | The Third Edition. | *Philadelphia:* | *Printed and sold by Joseph Crukshank,* | . . . | . . . 1783. | 12mo. pp. 36. H. S. P. 4301

The Half-title reads, " Two | Epistles | to the | Youth | of | Norwich Monthly-Meeting, | in | Great-Britain." | Gurney's Address, which ends on page 27, is followed by Joseph Phipps' To the Youth of Norwich Meeting, the title of which will be found under No. 4338, *infra*.

DER HOCH = DEUTSCH = Americanifche Calender, auf das Jahr 1784. *Philadelphia: Johann Dunlap.* 1783.   4302

[HOLROYD, (John Baker — Earl of Sheffield.)] Observations | on the | Commerce | of the | American States | with | Europe and the West Indies; | Including the several Articles of | Import and Export. | Also, an | Essay | on | Canon and Feudal Law. | By John Adams, Esquire; | Ambassador Plenipotentiary, from the | United and Independent States of North America, | To their High Mightinesses the States General of the | United Provinces of Holland. | To which is Annexed, the Political Character of the said | John Adams, Esquire; | By An American. | Price Half a Dollar. | *Philadelphia:* | *Printed and Sold by Robert Bell, in Third-Street.* | M,DCC,LXXXIII. | 8vo.   4303

Collation : General title, 1 leaf; Title to Observations, 1 leaf; text, pp. 3–43;

Title to Adams' Essay, 1 page; text, pp. 45–58; Character of Adams, pp. 58–62; Additional Notes on American Commerce, by Lord Sheffield, pp. 63–73; Short Dissertation upon Commerce, pp. 73–77; List of Books, 1 page. The second title is as follows: Observations | on the | Commerce | of the | American States | with | Europe and the West Indies ; | Including the several Articles of | Import and Export. | Price Half a Dollar. | [Imprint as in general title.] The third title is : An | Essay | on | Canon and Feudal Law. | By John Adams, Esquire ; | Ambassador Plenipotentiary, from the | United and Independent States of North America, | To their High Mightinesses the States General of the | United Provinces of Holland. | To which is annexed, the Political Character of the said | John Adams, Esquire ; | By an American. | [Imprint as in general title.] Sheffield's Observations were issued separately.

HOPKINS. (S.) An Inquiry concerning the future State of those who die in their Sins. By Samuel Hopkins, D.D. *Philadelphia: Francis Bailey.* 1783. 4304

[HUMPHREYS. (David)] The | Glory | of | America; | or, | Peace triumphant over War: | A | Poem. | *Philadelphia:* | *Printed for the Author, by E. Oswald and D. Humphreys,* | *at the Coffee-House.* | M.DCC.LXXXIII. | Sq. 8vo. pp. 16. H. S. P. 4305

IN Assembly, | Tuesday, December 2d, 1783, A.M. | [n. p. 1783.] 4to. 1 leaf. H. S. P. 4306

Report of the Committee relative to the Preparations to be made for Public Demonstrations of Joy, on the Peace, with a "description of the Triumphal Arch and its Ornaments."

THE INDEPENDENT Gazetteer. 4307

Numbers 53 (Jan. 4, 1783) to 113 (Dec. 27, 1783), four pages each, with a "Supplement" of two pages to No. 75, and "Postscripts" of two pages to Numbers 101 and 102. During February and March the paper was published twice a week, but it appeared only once a week during the other ten months. Title and imprint as in No. 4203, *supra*, until No. 75, when the latter was changed to *Philadelphia : Printed by E. Oswald, and D. Humphreys, at the Coffee-House,* . . . | . . . | . . . | . . . . | The imprint was slightly changed in No. 106 and the paper was enlarged by the addition of a fourth column.

JOHNSON. (J[ohn]) The | Advantages | and | Disadvantages | of the | Marriage State ; | As entered into with religious or irreligious Persons. | Represented under the Similitude of a Dream. | By J. Johnson. | The Seventh Edition. | *Philadelphia :* | *Printed and Sold by Joseph Crukshank,* | . . . | . . . 1783. | *Sold also by Lot Tripp, near New-Milford,* | *Connecticut.* | 12mo. pp. 24. H. S. P. 4308

JONES. (S.)   The Doctrine of the Covenants. | A | Sermon | Preached | at | Pennepeck in Pennsylvania, | September 14, 1783. | Wherein is shewn | That there never was a Covenant of Works | made with Adam; nor any other Covenant | ever made with Man, respecting Things purely | of a Spiritual Nature. | By Samuel Jones A.M. | *Philadelphia: | Printed and Sold by F. Bailey, in Market-Street.* | M,DCC,LXXXIII. | Sm. 8vo. pp. 55.   H. S. P.   4309

JOURNAL | of the | Council | of | Censors, | Convened, at Philadelphia, on Monday, the | Tenth Day of November, One Thousand Seven | Hundred Eighty and Three. | *Philadelphia: Printed by Hall and Sellers.* | M.DCC.LXXXIII. | Folio, pp. 179.

The journal extends to September 25, 1784.

JOURNAL | of the | United States | In Congress Assembled, | containing | The Proceedings | from | The First Monday in November 1782, | to | The First Monday in November 1783, | Volume VIII. | Published by Order of Congress. | *Philadelphia: | Printed by David C. Claypoole.* | M,DCC,LXXXIII. | 8vo. pp. 489, xxxvi.   H. S. P.   4311

KEMPIS. (T. à)   Of the | Imitation | of | Christ: | In Three Books. | Translated from the Latin | of Thomas A Kempis. | By John Payne. | *London: Printed, | Philadelphia: Re-Printed | And Sold by Joseph Crukshank, in | Market-Street, between Second | and Third-Streets.* | MDCCLXXXIII. | 12mo. pp. 44, 211.   H. S. P.   4312

LAWS | Enacted in the Second Sitting | of the Seventh | General Assembly | Of the Commonwealth of | Pennsylvania, | Which commenced at Philadelphia, on Wednesday, the Fifteenth | Day of January, in the Year of our Lord One Thousand Seven | Hundred Eighty and Three. | [Colophon.] [*Philadelphia:*] *Printed by Hall and Sellers.* [1783.] | Folio, pp. 127–184, for 183. + Laws | Enacted in the Third Sitting | . . . | . . . | . . . | . . . | . . . | . . . | . . . . | [n. p. 1783.] pp. 185–254, (2).   H. S. P.   4313

LAWS | Enacted in the First Sitting | Of the Eighth | General Assembly, | Of the Commonwealth of | Pennsylvania, | Which commenced at Philadelphia on Monday the twenty- | seventh Day of October, in the Year of our Lord One | Thousand Seven Hundred Eighty and Three. | [Colophon.]   [*Philadelphia:*]   *Printed by Thomas Bradford.*   [1783.] | Folio, pp. 255–270, 1 leaf.   4314

LESLIE. (C.)   A | Short and Easy | Method | with the | Deists. | Wherein the certainty of the Christian | Religion is demonstrated. | In a Letter to a Friend. | By Mr. Charles Leslie. | *Philadelphia:* | *Re-printed for a Society of Gentlemen by Robert Aitken, in* | *Market-Street, the third door above the Coffee-House.* | M.DCC.LXXXIII. | 12mo. pp. 36.   H. S. P.   4315

MACKENZIE. ([Henry])   The | Man | of the | World. | A New Work of Entertainment, | By Mr. Mackenzie, | of Edinburg. | Author of Julia de Roubigne, | And of the Man of Feeling. | . . . | . . . | . . . | . . . . | The First Volume. | *Philadelphia:* | *Printed and Sold by Robert Bell, in Third-Street.* | MDCCLXXXIII. | 8vo. pp. 48. + The Second Volume. [*Ibid.*] 8vo. pp. 48. + The Third and Last Volume. [*Ibid.*] 8vo. pp. 64.   L. C. P.   4316

MANUEL de franc-maçons et des franc-maçonnes. | *Philadelphie: [Paris.]*   1783.   W.   4317

MINUTES | of the | First Session | of the | Eighth General Assembly | of the | Commonwealth | of | Pennsylvania, | Which commenced at Philadelphia, on Monday, the Twenty- | seventh Day of October, in the Year of our Lord One | Thousand Seven Hundred and Eighty-three. | *Philadelphia:* | *Printed by Hall and Sellers, in Market-street.* | M,DCC,LXXXIII. | Folio, pp. 361, 3.

The first sitting occupies pp. 3–82; the second, pp. 83–252; and the third, pp. 253–361. The second and third sittings were held in 1784.

MINUTES | of the | Baptist Association, | Held at Philadelphia, October, 1783. | [*Philadelphia: Robert Aitken.* 1783.]   Sq. 8vo. pp. 7.   4319

MOLLINEUX. (M.)   Fruits of Retirement, or, Miscellaneous Poems, Moral and Divine. By Mary Mollineux. *Philadelphia: Joseph Crukshank.* 1783.   4320

MOORE. (J.)   A | View | of | Society and Manners | in |

France, Switzerland, | Germany, and Italy : | With | Anecdotes relating to some Eminent Characters. | By John Moore, M.D. | During his Travels through those Countries, with his | Grace, the present Duke of Hamilton. | . . . | . . . | . . . . | The First Volume. | *Philadelphia :* | *Printed and Sold by Robert Bell, in Third-Street.* | MDCCLXXXIII. | 8vo. pp. 100. + Number Second. 8vo. pp. (6), 107–190. + Number Third. 8vo. pp. (5), 196–281, (1). A | View | of | Society and Manners | in | Italy : | With | Anecdotes relating to some Eminent Characters. | By John Moore, M.D. | During his Travels through those Countries, in the years | 1777 and 1778, with his Grace, The present | Duke of Hamilton. | . . . | . . . . | The First [should be Second] Volume. | *Philadelphia :* | *Printed and Sold by Robert Bell, in Third-Street.* | MDCCLXXXIII. | 8vo. pp. 117, 1 leaf. + Number Second. 8vo. pp. (8), 129–239. + Number Third. 8vo. pp. (4), 249–358, 1 leaf.   4321

THE MOTHER'S Catechism, on the plan of the Rev. Mr. Willison, containing the great foundation doctrines of the Christian Religion in short questions and answers. *Philadelphia : Francis Bailey.* 1783.   4322

[MURRAY. (James)] Sermons | to | Ministers of State. | By the Author of, | Sermons to Asses. | Dedicated to Lord North, Prime Minister of | England, for the use of the religious, political, | and philosophical Rationalists, in Europe, and | America. | . . . | . . . | . . . | . . . . | Price Half a Dollar. | *Philadelphia :* | *Printed and Sold by Robert Bell, in Third Street.* | MDCC,LXXXIII. | 8vo. pp. 79, (1).   H. S. P.   4323

𝕯𝖆𝖘 𝕹𝖊𝖚𝖊 | Teſtament | unſers | Herrn und Heylandes | Jeſu Chriſti, | nach der Deutſchen Ueberſetzung | D. Martin Luthers. | Mit | Kurzem Inhalt eines jeden Capitels, | und | Vollſtändiger Anweiſung gleicher Schriftſtellen. | Wie auch | aller Sonn= und Feſttägigen | Evangelien und Epiſteln. | *Philadelphia :* | *Gedruckt bey Melchior Steiner, in der Rees-* | *strasse, nahe bey der Dritten-strasse.* 1783. | 16mo. Title, 1 leaf; Verzeichniss der Bucher des Neuen Testaments, 1 leaf; pp. 1–533 ; Register, pp. (5).   H. S. P.   4324

𝕹𝕰𝖀𝕵𝕬𝕳𝕽𝕾 = Verſe | des | Herumträgers der Philadelphiſche Cor=

refponden3. | Den 1ften Januar, 1783. | [*Philadelphia: Melchior Steiner.* 1783.] 4to. 1 leaf.   H. S. P.   4325

NEW-YEAR Verses of the Carriers of the Freeman's Journal. *Philadelphia: Francis Bailey.* 1783.   4326

NEW-YEAR Verses of the Carriers of the Pennsylvania Gazette. *Philadelphia: Hall and Sellers.* 1783.   4327

NEW-YEAR Verses of the Carriers of the Pennsylvania Journal. *Philadelphia: Thomas Bradford.* 1783.   4328

NEW-YEAR Verses of the Carriers of the Pennsylvania Packet. *Philadelphia: David C. Claypoole.* 1783.   4329

OBSERVATIONS | on a | Late Pamphlet, | entituled, | " Considerations upon the Society | or Order of the Cincinnati ;" | clearly evincing the | Innocence and Propriety | Of that Honourable and Respectable | Institution. | In Answer to Vague Conjectures, False Insinuations, | and Ill-founded Objections. | By an Obscure Individual. | . . . | . . . | . . . | . . . | . . . | . . . | . . . | . . . . | *Philadelphia :* | *Printed and Sold by Robert Bell, in Third-Street.* | *Price, one-fourth of a Dollar.* M,DCC,LXXXIII. | 8vo. pp. 28 ; Advertisement, pp. (4).   H. S. P.   4330

PENINGTON. (I.) Select Pieces | on | Religious Subjects, | first published | About the Middle of the | Last Century. | By | Isaac Penington. | *London, Printed :* | *Philadelphia :* | *Re-printed and sold by Joseph Crukshank,* | *in Market-Street, between Second and* | *Third-Streets.* MDCCLXXXIII. | 8vo. pp. i–iv, 1 leaf, 3–98, (2).   H. S. P.   4331

PENN. (W.) Primitive Christianity | revived, | By William Penn. | Also, | Select Essays | on | Religious Subjects, | from the | Writings | of | Isaac Penington. | *Philadelphia :* | *Printed and Sold by Joseph Crukshank, in Market-* | *Street, between Second and Third-Streets.* | MDCCLXXXIII. | 8vo.   H. S. P.   4332

Collation : General title, 1 leaf ; Title to Primitive Christianity, 1 leaf ; text, pp. 3–66 ; Title to Select Pieces by Penington, 1 leaf ; Preface, pp. iii.–iv. ; Epistle, 1 leaf ; text, pp. 3–98 ; List of Books, pp. (2). For the title to Penington's tract see No. 4331, *supra.*

PENN. Tender | Counsel and Advice, | by way of | Epistle, | To all those who are sensible of | Their Day of Visitation, | And who have received | The Call of the Lord, | By the light and spirit of his Son in their | hearts, to partake of the great salva- | tion, where-ever scattered throughout | the world; Faith, Hope and Cha- | rity, which overcome the world, | be multiplied among you. | By William Penn. | The Fifth Edition. | *Phila- delphia:* | *Printed by Enoch Story, in* | *Strawberry Alley.* 1783. | 12mo. pp. 49.   4333

January. 1783. Numb. 2740. | THE | PENNSYLVANIA Gazette. | Wednesday, January 29, 1783. | [Colophon.] *Philadel- phia: Printed by Hall and Sellers, at the New-Printing-* | *Office, near the Market.* | 4334

Numbers 2742 (Jan. 1, 1783) to 2794 (Dec. 31, 1783), four pages each, with " Sup- plements" of two pages to Numbers 2744, 2751, 2759, 2777, and 2782, of four pages to Numbers 2753 and 2778; and " Postscripts" of two pages to Numbers 2761 and 2768, and of four pages to No. 2754.

THE PENNSYLVANIA Journal. *Philadelphia: Printed by Thomas Bradford. Advertisements, &c. for this Paper are re-* | *ceived at the Book-Store in Front-street, Four Doors below the Coffee-House, or at the Printing-Office in Lætitia-Court.* | 4335

Numbers 1554 (Jan. 1, 1783) to 1656 (Dec. 31, 1783), four pages each, with " Sup- plements" of two pages to Numbers 1624, 1628, 1635, 1636, 1638 to 1640, 1643, 1645 to 1647 (misnumbered 1646), 1650, and 1652. The papers for Feb. 1 and 5 are both numbered 1653, and for June 14 and 18 are both numbered 1600, and these errors are not corrected. No. 1616 is misnumbered 1619, but this mistake was corrected in the next number. Published twice a week. Title as in No. 4230, *supra.*

THE PENNSYLVANIA Packet.   4336

Numbers 984 (Jan. 2, 1783) to 1640 [1140] (Dec. 30, 1783), four pages each, with a " Postscript" of one leaf to No. 1099. No. 1100 is misnumbered 1600, and this error is carried to the end of the year. Title and imprint as in No. 4231, *supra,* until No. 1607, when they were changed to the form given in No. 4516, *infra,* and the paper was enlarged by the addition of a fourth column.

THE PENNSYLVANIA Pocket Almanac for 1784. *Philadel- phia: Thomas Bradford.* 1783.   4337

PHIPPS. (J.) The | Original and Present State | of | Man, | Briefly Considered; | wherein is shewn, | The Nature of his Fall, and the Necessity, Means, and | Manner of his Restoration, through the Sacri- | fice of Christ, and the sensible Operation of | the Divine Principle of Grace and Truth, | held forth to the World | by the | People called Quakers. | To which are added, | Some Remarks on the Arguments of Samuel | Newton, of Nor- wich. | By Joseph Phipps. | . . . | . . . | . . . . | *London, Printed:* | *Philadelphia: Re-Printed* | *And sold by Joseph Crukshank, in* | *Market- Street, between Second and* | *Third-Streets.* MDCCLXXXIII. | 8vo. pp. (4), 209.   H. S. P.   4338

A PLAIN Almanac for 1784.   *Philadelphia: Joseph Crukshank.* 1783.   4339

POOR Will's | Almanack, | for the | Year of our Lord, 1784; | Being Bissextile or Leap-Year. | . . . | . . . | . . . | . . . | . . . | . . | . . . | . . . | . . . | . . . | . . . | . . | . . . | . . . | . . . . | *Philadelphia:* | *Printed and Sold by Joseph Crukshank,* | . . . | . . . [1783.] | Sm. 8vo. pp. (36).   H. S. P.   4340

POOR Will's Pocket Almanac for 1784.   *Philadelphia: Joseph Crukshank.* 1783.   4341

POWNALL. (T.) A Memorial addressed to the Sovereigns of America. By Thomas Pownall.   *Philadelphia: Thomas Bradford.* 1783.   4342

PROCLAMATION. By the United States in Congress | Assembled, | A Proclamation. | *Philadelphia: Printed by David C. Claypoole.* [1783.] | Folio, 1 leaf.   L. C. P.   4343

Dated "Sept. 22, 1783." Forbidding the purchase of land from the Indians.

PROCLAMATION. By His Excellency | Elias Boudinot, Esquire, | President of the United States in Congress Assembled. | A Proclamation. | *Philadelphia, Printed by David C. Claypoole.* [1783.] | Folio, 1 leaf.   L. C. P.   4344

"Whereas a body of armed Soldiers in the service of the United States, and quartered in the Barracks of this City, having mutinously renounced their obedience to their Officers, did . . . proceed, . . . in a hostile and threatening manner, to the Place in which Congress were Assembled, and did surround the same with Guards : . . . and whereas the said Soldiers still continue in a state of open Mutiny and Revolt, so that the Dignity and Authority of the United States would be constantly exposed to the repetition of Insult, ... I do therefore, . . . hereby summon the honourable the Delegates . . . to meet in Congress . . . at Princeton, in the State of New-Jersey." Dated " Philadelphia, June 24, 1783."

PROCLAMATION. [*Arms of Pennsylvania.*] | By the President of the Supreme Executive Council of the Commonwealth | of Pennsylvania, | A Proclamation. | [*Philadelphia :*] *Printed by Francis Bailey.* [1783.] | Folio, 1 leaf.   L. C. P.   4345

Signed " John Dickinson," and dated " Jan. 6, 1783," announcing the Judgment of the Court of Commissioners, appointed to determine the controversy between Pennsylvania and Connecticut, in regard to the settlement of Wyoming. " We are unanimously of Opinion, that the State of Connecticut has no Right to the Lands in Controversy."

PROCLAMATION. [*Arms of Pennsylvania.*] | By the President and the Supreme Executive Council of the Commonwealth | of Pennsylvania, | A Proclamation. | [*Philadelphia :*] *Printed by Francis Bailey.* [1783.] | Folio, 1 leaf.   L. C. P.   4346

Dated " March 6, 1783." Concerning the " boundary between this State and Virginia."

PROCLAMATION. By the United States of America | In Congress Assembled. | A Proclamation, | Declaring the Cessation of Arms, as well by Sea as by Land, agreed upon between the United | States of America and His Britannic Majesty; and enjoining the Observance thereof. | *Philadelphia, Printed by David C. Claypoole.* [1783.] | Folio, 1 leaf.   L. C. P.   4347

Dated " April 11, 1783."

PROCLAMATION. [*Arms of Pennsylvania.*] | By the President and the Supreme Executive Council of the Commonwealth | of Pennsylvania, | A Proclamation, | Declaring the Cessation of Arms, as well by Sea as by Land, agreed upon between | the United States of America and His Britannic Majesty; and enjoining the | Observance thereof. | [*Philadelphia :*] *Printed by Francis Bailey.* [1783.] | Folio, 1 leaf.   L. C. P.   4348

Dated " April 16, 1783."

PROCLAMATION. [*Arms of Pennsylvania.*] | Pennsylvania, ss. | By the President and the Supreme Executive Council of the Commonwealth | of Pennsylvania, | A Proclamation. | [*Philadelphia :*] *Printed by Francis Bailey.* [1783.] | Folio, 1 leaf.   4349

Dated " July 24, 1783." Offering a reward for the apprehension of the murderer of James Molineaux.

PROCLAMATION. [*Arms of Pennsylvania.*] | Pennsylvania, ss. | By the President and the Supreme Executive Council of the Commonwealth | of Pennsylvania, | A Proclamation. | [*Philadelphia :*] *Printed by Francis Bailey.* [1783.] | Folio, 1 leaf.   4350

Dated " July 26, 1783." Offering a reward for the apprehension of Moses, Abraham, Levi, and Malin Doan.

PROCLAMATION. [*Arms of Pennsylvania.*] | By the President and the Supreme Executive Council of the Commonwealth | of Pennsylvania. | A Proclamation. | [*Philadelphia :*] *Printed by Francis Bailey.* [1783.] | Folio, 1 leaf.   L. C. P.   4351

Dated " July 31, 1783." Against settlers on vacant lands north of the west branch of the Susquehanna, and west of the Ohio.

PROCLAMATION. [*Arms of Pennsylvania.*] | By the President and The Supreme Executive Council of the Commonwealth | of Pennsylvania. | A Proclamation. | [*Philadelphia :*] *Printed by Francis Bailey.* [1783.] | Folio, 1 leaf.   L. C. P.   4352

Dated " Aug. 30, 1783." Concerning counterfeit " British Half-Pence."

PROCLAMATION. [*Arms of Pennsylvania.*] | Pennsylvania, ss. | By the President and the Supreme Executive Council of the Commonwealth | of Pennsylvania, | A Proclamation. | [*Philadelphia : Francis Bailey.* 1783.] | Folio, 1 leaf.   L. C. P.   4353

Dated " Oct. 30, 1783." Appointing the 2d Thursday in December as a day of Public Thanksgiving.

THE | PSALMS | of | David, | In Metre : | Allowed by the Authority of the General Assem- | bly of the Kirk of Scotland, and appointed to be | sung in Congregations and Families : | With an | Analysis, | Or brief View of the Contents of each Psalm, taken from the | Exposition of Mr. Matthew Henry, Author of | the Commentary on the Bible. | *Philadelphia :* | *Printed and Sold by R. Aitken, Market-Street.* | M.DCC.LXXXIII. | 16mo. pp. 398.

[REED. (Joseph)] Remarks | on a | Late Publication | in the | Independent Gazetteer; | with a | Short Address | to the | People of Pennsylvania | on the Many | Libels and Slanders | which have | Lately Appeared against the Author. | *Philadelphia :* | *Printed by Francis Bailey, in Market-Street.* | M,DCC,LXXXIII. | 8vo. pp. 72.   H. S. P.   4355

A second edition was advertised in the Pa. Gazette, Feb. 25, 1783.

RICHARDSON. (J.) An | Account | of the | Life | of that | Ancient Servant of Jesus Christ, | John Richardson, | Giving a Relation of many of | his Trials and Exercises in his Youth, and | his Services in the Work of the Ministry, | in England, Ireland, America, &c. | . . . | . . . | . . . . | *Philadelphia :* | *Printed and sold by Joseph Crukshank,* | *in Market-street, between Second | and Third-streets.* MDCCLXXXIII. | 8vo. pp. i–vi, 1–236; List of Books, pp. (2).   L. C. P.   4356

Richardson's autobiography is preceded by a brief sketch of his father, and the " Testimonies" of two Quaker Meetings.

ROBERTS. (D.) Memoirs of the Life of John Roberts, alias Hayward. By Daniel Roberts. *Philadelphia : Joseph Crukshank.* 1783.   4357

ROBIN. [(Claude C.)] New Travels | through | North-America: | In a Series of Letters; | Exhibiting, the History of the Victorious Campaign of the | Allied Armies, under his Excellency General Washington, | and the Count de Rochambeau, in the Year 1781. | Interspersed with political, and philosophical Observations, upon | the genius, temper, and customs of the Americans; Also | Narrations of the capture of General Burgoyne, | and Lord Cornwallis, with their Armies; | and a variety of interesting particulars, which occurred, | in the course, of the | War in America. | Translated from the original of the Abbé Robin; | one of the Chaplains to the French Army in America.

| . . . | . . . | . . . | . . . | . . . | . . . | . . . | . . . . | *Philadelphia:* |
Printed and Sold by Robert Bell, in Third-Street. | M,DCC,LXXXIII.
Price Two Thirds of a Dollar. | 8vo. pp. 112.   H. S. P.   4358

[ROBIN.] Voyage | dans | L'Amérique Septentrionale, | en
l'année 1781, | et | Campagne | De l'Armée | De M. le Cte. de
Rochambeau. | *A Philadelphie, [Paris.]* | 1783. | 16mo. pp. 192.

[RUSH. (Benjamin)] Observations upon the present Government of Pennsylvania. In Four Letters to the People of Pennsylvania. First printed in the year 1777. *Philadelphia: Charles
Cist.* 1783.   4360

RUSH. A | Syllabus | of a | Course | of | Lectures | on |
Chemistry, | for the | Use of the Students of Medicine | in the
College of Philadelphia. | By Benjamin Rush, M.D. | *Philadelphia:*
| *Printed by Charles Cist,* | *in Market-Street,* | M.DCC.LXXXIII.
| Sm. 12mo. pp. 39, 1 leaf folded.   A. P. S.   4361

[SAINT-VICTOR. (L. G. de)] Recueil précieux de la maçon-
nerie adonhiramite. Par un chevalier de tous les ordres maçon-
niques. *A Philadelphie: [Paris.]* 1783.   w.   4362

SAUNDERS. (R.) A Pocket Almanac for 1784. By Richard
Saunders, Phil. *Philadelphia: Hall and Sellers.* 1783.   4363

SAUNDERS. Poor Richard improved: | Being an | Almanack
| [10 lines.] | For the | Year of our Lord 1784: | Being Bissextile
or Leap-Year. | [9 lines.] | By Richard Saunders, Philom. |
Philadelphia: | *Printed and Sold by Hall and Sellers.* [1783.] | 8vo.
pp. (36).   H. S. P.   4364

SCHMETTOW. (W. F. von) Auch Fragmente. Von W. F. von
Schmettow. *Philadelphia: [Hammerich in Altona.]* 1783. w. 4365

[SCOTT. (Helenus)] The | Adventures | of an East-India |
Rupee. | Wherein are interspersed, | Various Anecdotes | Asiatic,
and European. | . . . | . . . | . . . | . . . | . . . . | Price Half a
Dollar. | *Philadelphia:* | *Printed and Sold by Robert Bell, in Third-
Street,* | M,DCC,LXXXIII. | 8vo. pp. 64.   L. C. P.   4366

A | SERMON | on the | Evacuation | of | Charlestown. | By an Æthiopian. | *Philadelphia :* | *Printed for the Author, and Sold by Will. Woodhouse,* | *in Front-street, next Door to the Old Coffee-House.* | M.DCC.LXXXIII. | 8vo. pp. 16.   N. Y. H. S. 4367

SHARP. (A.) Der Gantz Neue Verbeſſerte Nord = Americaniſche Calender, auf das 1784ſte Jahr Chriſti. Zum Neuntenmal heraus= gegeben und verfertiget von Anthony Sharp, Philom. *Lancaster : Francis Bailey.* 1783.   4368

SHARP. The Continental Almanac for 1784. *Philadelphia : Francis Bailey.* 1783.   4369

SHERIDAN. (T.) A | Rhetorical Grammar | of the | English Language, | Calculated solely for the Purposes of Teaching | Propriety of Pronunciation, | and | Justness of Delivery, | In That Tongue, | by the | Organs of Speech. | By Thomas Sheridan, A.M. | Author of the Lectures on Elocution. | The American Edition is published under the Inspection of | Archibald Gamble, A.M. Professor of English | and Oratory, in the University of Pennsylvania. | *Philadelphia :* | *Printed and Sold by Robert Bell, in Third* | *Street, and Francis Bailey, in Market Street.* | M,DCC,LXXXIII. | Sm. 8vo. pp. xvi, 218, (2).   H. S. P. 4370

SMITH. (Francis) To Captain Alexander Patterson, | acting as a Justice of the Peace for Northumber- | land County, in Wyoming. | [n. p. 1784.] Sm. folio, 1 leaf.   L. C. P. 4371

Dated " Northampton County, 15th Nov. 1783."

STATE | of the | Accounts | of | Andrew Kachline, Esq. | late | Sub-Lieutenant | of | Bucks County, | deceased, | From the time of his appointment, March 1780, until the time of his | death in the spring, 1781. | In which is exhibited the amount of the fines he received within that | period, and accounted for : | Together with lists, shewing the sums paid by the persons respective- | ly, of whom the same were received : | Likewise the amounts of fines outstanding, and the appropriation and | disposal of the monies collected. | *Philadelphia :* | *Printed by Robert*

Aitken, three Doors above the Coffee- | *House, in Market Street.* | M,DCC,LXXXIII. | 8vo. pp. 14.   H. S. P. 4372

A | STATE | of the | Accounts | of | Archibald Thompson, Esquire, | late a | Sub-Lieutenant | of | Philadelphia County. | *Philadelphia :* | *Printed by Hall and Sellers.* | MDCCLXXXIII. | 8vo. Title, 1 leaf; pp. 1–41.   H. S. P. 4373

STATE of the Accounts of Benjamin Brannon, Esq. | late a Sub-Lieutenant of Chester County, from the time of his Appoint- | ment in March 1777, until the time of his Resignation in De- | cember fol- | lowing. | [*Philadelphia :* 1783.] 8vo. pp. 3.   4374

STATE of the Accounts of Col. Adam Hubly, Lieutenant of Lancaster County, and the several Sub-Lieutenants, from March 1781, to January 1782. *Lancaster?* 1783. 8vo. pp. (101). 4375

STATE | of the | Accounts | of | Col. George Smith, | A Sub-Lieutenant of the County of Philadelphia. | In which is exhibited, for the information of the Pub- | lic, the Amount of the Fines received and accounted | for by him, between March 1777, and April 1780 ; | Together with Lists of the Fines composing the same, | and the Names of the Persons from whom received, | respectively arranged in Companies and Classes. | Likewise, the Disbursements out of those Monies, and | Payments thereof into the Treasury. | *Philadelphia :* | *Printed by Francis Bailey, in Market-Street.* | M.DCC.LXXXIII. | 8vo. pp. 72.   H. S. P. 4376

STATE | of the | Accounts | of | Jacob Engle, Esquire, | late a | Sub-Lieutenant | of | Philadelphia County. | *Philadelphia :* | *Printed by John Dunlap,* | MDCCLXXXIII. | 8vo. Title, 1 leaf; pp. 1–128.   H. S. P. 4377

STATE | of the | Accounts | of | Jacob Morgan, Senior, | late | Lieutenant | of | Berks County, | From March 1777 to March 1780. | In which is exhibited the amount of the monies received by him with- | in that time for militia fines, and accounted for : | Together with lists shewing by whom they were paid; and the a- | mount of fines incurred within that period, which were not received

| by him but are outstanding, (except the exercise fines of the first | four battalions for the year 1779, the returns of which as repre- | sented were not made to him, but delivered to his successor.) | Likewise the application of the monies, and payments thereof to the | Treasury. | *Philadelphia :* | *Printed by Robert Aitken, three Doors above the Coffee* | *House, in Market-street.* | M.DCC.LXXXIII. | 8vo. pp. 54.   H. S. P.   4378

A | STATE | of the | Accounts | of | John Gill, Esquire, | late | Sub-Lieutenant | of | Bucks County. | *Philadelphia :* | *Printed by John Dunlap.* | MDCCLXXXIII. | 8vo.   Title, 1 leaf; pp. 17.

STATE | of the | Accounts | of | John Hay, Esquire, | late | Sub-Lieutenant | of | York County, | From the time of his appointment under the militia law in March | 1777, to the first of March 1780. | In which is set forth the amount of the fines received within that pe- | riod from delinquents of the 2d and 3d battalions, for non- | performance of militia duty and exercise : | Together with Lists shewing the names of the persons by whom | payments have been made, and the sums received from | them respectively. | Likewise the disbursements made by him, and the payments to | the Treasury. | *Philadelphia :* | *Printed by Robert Aitken, three Doors above the Coffee-* | *House, in Market Street.* | M,DCC,LXXXIII. | 8vo. pp. 12.   H. S. P.   4380

STATE | of the | Accounts | of | John Lacey, Junior, | and | George Wall, Esquire, | late | Sub-Lieutenants | of the | County of Bucks, | As they have been liquidated and settled. | In which is exhibited, for the information and satisfaction of the pub- | lic, the amount of the fines received by them, and accounted for | from March 1777 to March 1780, from the fourth battalion ; | With lists of the names of the persons, and the sums paid by them | respectively, arranged in the order of their companies and classes : | Likewise the disbursement and appropriation of the monies thus | collected. | *Philadelphia :* | *Printed by Robert Aitken, three Doors above the Coffee-* | *House, in Market Street.* | M,DCC,LXXXIII. | 8vo. pp. 20.   H. S. P.   4381

STATE | of the | Accounts | of | Joseph Hart, | Esquire, |

Lieutenant | of | Bucks County, | From the time of his appointment in March 1780, to the 1st of | March, 1783 ; | In which is set forth the amount of the fines incurred within that pe- | riod by delinquents of the 1st battalion, for non-performance of | militia duty and exercise, and the outstanding fines due thereby, | before his appointment, agreeable to lists delivered by the late | Lieutenant of the said county. | Together with lists shewing the names of the persons by whom pay- | ments have been made, and the sums received from them respectively. | Likewise the disbursements made by him, and the payments to the | Treasury. | *Philadelphia :* | *Printed by Robert Aitken, in Market Street,* | *near the Coffee House.* | MDCCLXXXIII. | 8vo. pp. 24.   H. S. P.   4382

STATE | of the | Accounts | of | Lewis Gronow, Esquire, | late a | Sub-Lieutenant | of | Chester County, | From March 1777, to March 1780, as they have been adjusted and | settled; in which is set forth the amount of the monies received | by him for fines incurred within the period aforesaid, and | accounted for. | Together with Lists shewing the names of the persons from whom the | same were received, and the sums paid by them respectively, ar- | ranged in the order of the companies : | Likewise the disbursements and payments made to the Treasury. | *Philadelphia :* | *Printed by Robert Aitken, three Doors above the Coffee* | *House, in Market-street.* | M.DCC.LXXXIII. | 8vo. pp. 22.   H. S. P.   4383

STATE of the Accounts of Peter Richards, Esq; late a Sub-Lieutenant of Philadelphia County. *Philadelphia :* 1783. 8vo. pp. 8.   H. S. P.   4384

STATE | of the | Accounts | of | Robert Smith, Esquire, | Lieutenant | of | Chester County, | From March 1777, to March 1780, as they have been adjusted and | settled; in which is exhibited the amount of the monies received | by him for fines incurred within that time, and accounted for | from the 4th and 7th battalions of Chester county militia. | Likewise lists shewing by whom the same were paid ; also the dis- | bursements of the money, and the payments thereof to the treasury. | *Philadelphia :* | *Printed by Robert Aitken, three Doors above the Coffee* | *House, in Market-street.* | M.DCC.LXXXIII. | 8vo. pp. 12.   H. S. P.   4385

A | STATE | of the | Accounts | of | Samuel Dewees, Esq; | late | Sub-Lieutenant | of | Philadelphia County. | *Philadelphia:* | *Printed by John Dunlap.* | MDCCLXXXIII. | 8vo. Title, 1 leaf; pp. 1–23.   H. S. P.   4386

STATE | of the | Accounts | of | Thomas Levis, | a | Sub-Lieutenant | of | Chester County, | From March 1777 to March 1780. | As they have been adjusted and settled; in which is exhibited the | amount of the monies received by him for fines incurred within | that time in Col. Davis's battalion of militia; and accounted for. | Together with Lists shewing by whom the same were paid. | Likewise his disbursements and payments thereof into the Treasury. | *Philadelphia:* | *Printed by Robert Aitken, three Doors above the Coffee* | *House, in Market-street.* | M.DCC.LXXXIII. | 8vo. pp. 11.   H. S. P.   4387

STATE of the Accounts | of Wm. Antes, Esq. Sub Lieutenant | of Philadelphia County, as they have been | settled and adjusted. | [*Philadelphia:* 1783.] 8vo. pp. 17.   H. S. P.   4388

A | STATE | of the | Accounts | of | William Coats, Esquire, | Lieutenant | of | Philadelphia County. | *Philadelphia:* | *Printed by Robert Aitken, in Market Street,* | *near the Coffee House.* | MDCCLXXXIII. | 8vo. Title, 1 leaf; pp. 28.   H. S. P.   4389

STATE | of the | Accounts | of the | Collectors of Excise, | for | Berks County, | From the 4th of August 1774, (to which time they were settled by | the Committees of Accounts of Assembly) until the 24th of No- | vember 1781. | In which is exhibited, | The Amount of the Monies received by them respectively, and ac- | counted for; | Also, Lists shewing the names of Persons from whom Excise became | due, and was received. | Likewise the Payments made thereof to the Treasurer. | *Philadelphia:* | *Printed by Robert Aitken, three Doors above the Coffee-* | *House, in Market-Street.* | M,DCC,LXXXIII. | 8vo. pp. 7.   H. S. P.   4390

STATE | of the | Accounts | of the | Collectors of Excise, | for | Chester County, | From August 1, 1776, to August 10, 1782. | In which is exhibited, | The Amount of Excise received and accounted for, | and a List of the Persons by whom the same was paid, | and the Sums received from them respectively. | Likewise, | The Payments to the Treasury. | *Philadelphia :* | *Printed by Francis Bailey, in Market-Street.* | M,DCC,LXXXIII. | 8vo. pp. 4.   4391

STATE | of the | Accounts | of the | Collectors of Excise, | for | Cumberland County, | From the 10th of August 1774, (to which time they | were settled by the Committees of Accounts of Assem- | bly and the Ballances paid) until the 20th of Janu- | ary 1783. | In which is exhibited, | The Amount of the Monies received by them re- | spectively, and accounted for; | Also, Lists shewing the names of Persons from whom | Excise became due, and was received. | Likewise, the Payments made thereof to the Treasurer. | *Philadelphia,* | *Printed by F. Bailey, in Market-Street.* | M,DCC,LXXXIII. | 8vo. pp. 7.   H. S. P.   4392

STATE | of the | Accounts | of the | Collectors of Excise, | for | Lancaster County, | From the Twenty-eighth of February, One Thousand Seven Hundred | and Seventy-six (to which Time they have been settled by the | Committees of Assembly, and the Ballances paid) until the Tenth | Day of August, One Thousand Seven Hundred and Eighty-two : | In which is exhibited, | The Amount of the Monies received and accounted for : | Also, | Lists, shewing the Names of the Persons from whom Excise | became due, and was received : | Likewise, the Payments made to the State Treasurer. | *Philadelphia :* | *Printed by Hall and Sellers, in Market-street.* | M,DCC,LXXXIII. | 8vo. pp. 11.   H. S. P.   4393

STATE | of the | Accounts | of the | Collectors of Excise | for | Northampton County. | *Philadelphia :* | *Printed by John Dunlap.* | M,DCC,LXXXIII. | 8vo.   Title, 1 leaf, pp. 12.   H. S. P.   4394

STATE | of the | Accounts | of the | Collectors | Of Excise | for | The Counties | of | Bedford, Northumberland, Westmoreland and | Washington. | *Philadelphia :* | *Printed by Francis Bailey, at Yorick's Head, in Market Street.* | M.DCC.LXXXIII. | 8vo. pp. 4.

STATE | of the | Accounts | of the | Collectors of Excise | for | York County, | From the 1st of August, 1774, (to which time they have been settled | by the late Committees of Accounts of Assembly) to the 31st | of May, 1781. | In which is set forth the amount of the monies received by them re- | spectively on account of the Excise of the said county, with lists | shewing by whom the same were paid; likewise the payments | made to the Treasury. | *Philadelphia:* | *Printed by Robert Aitken, in Market Street,* | *near the Coffee House.* | MDCCLXXXIII. | 8vo. pp. 8.   4396

STATE | of the | Accounts | of | The Hon. George Wall, Esquire, | Sub-Lieutenant | of | Bucks County, | From 20th March 1780, to the 1st April 1783. | In which is exhibited the Amount of the Monies received by him for | Militia Fines, and accounted for: | Together with Lists, shewing by whom they were paid; likewise the | Application and Payment of the Monies. | *Philadelphia:* | *Printed by Robert Aitken, three Doors above the* | *Coffee-House, in Market-Street.* | M,DCC,LXXXIII. | 8vo. pp. 34.   H. S. P.   4397

STATE | of the | Accounts | of the late | Lieutenant and Sub-Lieutenants | of | Lancaster County, | From March 1777, to the 15th Feb. 1780. | Shewing the amount of fines received by them respectively, | and accounted for; the persons from whom ┤ received; and the application and pay- | ment of the money. | *Philadelphia:* | *Printed by John Dunlap.* | M,DCC,LXXXIII. | 8vo Title, 1 leaf; pp. 77, (1).   H. S. P.   4398

STATE of the Accounts of the late Lieutenant and Sub-Lieutenants of Northampton County, . . . from March 1777 to September 4, 1779. [Colophon.] [*Philadelphia.*] *Printed by Hall and Sellers.* [1783.] 8vo. pp. 40.   H. S. P.   4399

TABLES | for | The Payment | of | Principle and Interest | of Loans, | agreeable to | The Resolutions | of | Congress | of | The twenty-eighth day of June, | 1780. | *Philadelphia:* | *Printed and Sold by T. Bradford* | *in Front Street, the fourth door from* | *the Coffee-House.* 1783. | 18mo. pp. 36.   4400

ＤＪＥ | ＴＡＧＬＪＣＨＥＮ | Loosungen nnd Lehrtexte | der | Brüdergemeine | für das Jahr | 1784. | *Philadelphia:* | *Gedruckt bey Melchior Steiner, in der Rees-strasse, nahe* | *bey der Dritten-strasse.* 1783. | 8vo. pp. (128).   H. S. P.   4401

THREE | Letters | addressed to the | Public, | on | The follow- ing Subjects : | I. The Nature of a Fœderal Union.—The Powers vested in | Congress, and therein of Sovereignty. | II. The civil and military Powers.—The Dispute between | General Greene and Governor Gerard, respecting Flags of | Truce. | III. The public Debt.—The Act of Confederation defective—a remedy suggested. —The Five per Cent. Import Act con- | sidered and recommended. | . . . . | *Philadelphia :* | *Printed by T. Bradford, the fourth Door* | *below the Coffee-House,* 1783. | 8vo. pp. 28.   H. S. P.   4402

Signed " Tullius," and dated " Charles-Town, May 5th, 1783."

𝕰𝕴𝕹 𝕹𝕰𝖀 𝕿𝕽𝕬𝖀𝕰𝕽 = 𝕷𝕴𝕰𝕯, | Wie man vernomen von einem Menschen, der von dem Tod ist wieder komen. | Die Melodie thut so anfangen : Ihr Suender kommt gegangen. | [n. p. 1783 ?]   Folio, 1 leaf.   H. S. P.   4403

Said to have been written " by old Dr. Fahnestock, certainly he was the Doctor that relieved the spirit mentioned in the Hymn. A. H. Cassell."

TURFORD. (H.)   Grounds of a Holy Life.   By Hugh Turford. *Philadelphia : Joseph Crukshank.*   1783.   4404

𝖂𝕬𝕳𝕽𝕳𝕰𝕴𝕿 | und | Guter Rath | an die | Einwohner Deutschlands, | besonders in | Hessen. | . . . | . . . | . . . | . . . | . . . . | *Phila- delphia, Gedruckt bey Carl Cist, in der* | *Markt-strasse,* 1783. | Sm. 8vo. pp. 35.   H. S. P.   4405

WASHINGTON. (G.)   A | Circular Letter, | from | His Ex- cellency | George Washington, | Commander in Chief | of the | Armies of the | United States | of | America ; | Addressed to the Governors of | the several States, on his | resigning the Command of the | Army, and retiring from pub- | lic Business. | *Philadel- phia :* | *Printed by Robert Smith, jun.* | *back of the Fountain Inn, be-* | *tween Second and Third streets.*   [1783 ?] | 16mo. pp. 51, (1).   4406

I have followed the date given in the Menzies Catalogue, which is, however, in my opinion, several years too early.

WEATHERWISE. (A.)   Father Abraham's Almanac for 1784. By Abraham Weatherwise.   *Philadelphia : John Dunlap.*   1783.

WEBB. (E.) Einige | Glaubens= | Bekentniſſe | und göttliche | Erfahrungs=Proben, | in einem Send=ſchreiben | von | Elizabetha Webb | an | Anton Wilhelm Böhm, | Capellan zum Prinzen Georg von Däne= mark, | Im Jahr 1712. | Aus der Engliſchen Sprache überſetzt von J. M. | Jorck, Im Jahr 1783. | *Philadelphia, Gedruckt bey Carl Cist, in der* | *Markt-Strasse,* 1783. | Sm. 8vo. pp. 55.   H. S. P.   4408

WEBB. A | Letter | from | Elizabeth Webb | to | Anthony William Boehm, | with his | Answer. | *Philadelphia:* | *Printed and Sold by Joseph Crukshank,* | *in Market-Street.* | MDCCLXXXIII. | 12mo. pp. 44.   H. S. P.   4409

[WEBSTER. (Pelatiah)] A | Sixth Essay | on | Free Trade | and | Finance; | Particularly shewing what | Supplies of Public | Revenue may be drawn from | Merchandize, | Without injur- ing our Trade, or burdening our | People. | Humbly offered to the Public. | By a Citizen of Philadelphia. | *Philadelphia:* | *Printed and Sold by T. Bradford, in Front-street, three Doors be-* | *low the Coffee-House.* MDCCLXXXIII. | 8vo. pp. 32.   H. S. P.   4410

[WEBSTER.] A | Dissertation | on the | Political Union | and | Constitution | of the | Thirteen United States, | of | North- America: | Which is necessary to their Preservation and Happi- ness, | humbly offered to the Public, | By a Citizen of Philadelphia. | *Philadelphia:* | *Printed and Sold by T. Bradford, in Front-street, three Doors below* | *the Coffee-House,* MDCCLXXXIII. | 8vo. pp. 47.   H. S. P.   4411

WIE geht es denn eigentlich in den Klöſtern der Bettelmönche zu? *Philadelphia:* [*Stettin in Ulm.*] 1783.   w.   4412

WINCHESTER. (E.) The | Gospel | of | Christ | No Cause of Shame: | Demonstrated in two Discourses on | the Subject. | By Elhanan Winchester. | . . . | . . . . | *Philadelphia:* | *Printed by B. Towne.* 1783. | 8vo. pp. 140.   H. S. P.   4413

1784.

AN ACCOUNT of the Births and Burials in the United Churches of Christ Church and St. Peter's. *Philadelphia:* 1784.

ACCOUNTS | of | Pennsylvania. | Volume I. | [*Philadelphia: Hall and Sellers.* 1784.] 8vo.   H. S. P.   4415

Collation: Half-title, 1 leaf; Advertisement and Contents, pp. (2); Index, pp. 1–17. General title and index to 17 pamphlets printed in 1783 and 1784, which are separately described.

AN ADDRESS | of the | Council of Censors | to the | Freemen of Pennsylvania. | [*Philadelphia:*] *Printed by Hall and Sellers.* [1784.] | Folio, 1 leaf.   H. S. P.   4416

ADVERTISEMENT. *Philadelphia: Robert Aitken,* 1784.   4417

The following charges appear in Aitken's Ledger during 1784:

March 6. Ebenezer Hazard. Printing 3 quires sheet Advertisement.
March 7. John Kean, Yorktown. Printing advertisement.
May 23. Matthew Clarkson. Printing 100 Advertisements, Ship Rudolph.
July 15. William Turnbull. Printing 100 Advertisements.
Sept. —. The same. Printing 100 Advertisements.
Sept. 9. Turnbull and Marsenié. Printing 60 Hand-Bills, of a Sloop for Halifax.
Sept. 9. Thomas Leiper. Printing 1000 folio Advertisements.
Oct. 2. Matthew Clarkson. Printing Advertisements of the Brig General Washington, for Virginia.
Oct. 21. John Shields. Printing 480 Large folio crammed Advertisements.
Oct. 22. John Purdon. Printing 500 folio Advertisements.
Dec. 7. Clement Biddle. Printing 50 Advertisements.

AN ALARM. | To the Freemen and Electors of | Pennsylvania. | [*Philadelphia:* 1784.] Folio, 1 leaf.   H. S. P.   4418

AMERICANISCHER | Haus- und Wirthschafts- | Calender | Auf das 1785ste Jahr Christi, | Welches ein gemein Jahr ist von 365 Tagen. | . . . | . . . | . . . . | Zum Sechstenmal heraus gegeben. | *Philadelphia: Gedruckt und zu haben bey Melchior Steiner,* | . . . . [1784.] | Sm. 4to. pp. (40).   H. S. P.   4419

AMERICANISCHER | Stadt und Land | Calender | Auf das 1785ste Jahr Christi, | Welches ein Gemeines- Jahr ist | von 365 Tagen. | *Philadelphia:* | *Gedruckt und zu haben bey Carl Cist, in der* | *Zweyten-strasse, nah bey der Rees-strasse.* [1784.] | Sm. 4to. pp. (40).

ANDERSON. (J.) Letters. By the Rev. John Anderson.
Philadelphia: Robert Aitken. 1784.   4421

AN ARITHMETICAL Card. *Philadelphia: Sold by William Poyntell.* 1784.   4422

AT a Meeting at the Council Chamber, | 15th September, 1784. | [*Philadelphia:* 1784.] Sm. Folio, 1 leaf.   4423

A Resolve directing surveys to be made in the counties of Westmoreland, Washington, and Fayette, to persons claiming title under the laws of Virginia.

AT a Meeting of Clergymen and Lay-Delegates from sundry Congregations of the Episcopal Church in the State of Pennsylvania, held . . . in Philadelphia on . . . 25th . . . May, 1784. [*Philadelphia:* 1784.] Folio, 1 leaf.   H. S. P. 4424

BAILEY'S | Pocket Almanac, | being an | American | Annual Register, | For the Year of our Lord 1785 ; | And of the Empire the Tenth. | The First after Bissextile. | . . . | . . . . | [Cut.] | *Philadelphia:* | *Printed and Sold by Francis Bailey,* | *at Yorick's Head, in Market-Street.* [1784.] | Sm. 16mo. pp. (80), 1 map, 1 plate. 4425

BEATTIE. (J.) The | Minstrel : | Or, | The Itinerant | Poet, and Musician. | A Descriptive Poem, | On the | Progress of Genius ; | In Two Books. | By James Beattie, L.L.D. | . . . | . . . | . . . | . . . | . . . | . . . | . . . | . . . | . . . . | *Philadelphia:* | *Printed and Sold by Robert Bell, in Third-Street.* | M,DCC,LXXXIV. | 8vo. pp. 38.   H. S. P. 4426

BEATTIE. Poems on several Occasions. By James Beattie.
Philadelphia: Robert Bell. 1784.   4427

BELKNAP. (J.) The | History | of | New-Hampshire. | Volume I. | Comprehending the events of one complete | Century, from the discovery of the | River Pascataqua. | By Jeremy Belknap, A.M. | Member of the American Philosophical Society, held at Philadelphia | for promoting useful Knowledge. | . . . | . . . | . . . | . . . . | *Philadelphia:* | *Printed for the Author by Robert*

Aitken, in | *Market Street, near the Coffee-House.* | M.DCC.LXXXIV. | 8vo. pp. viii, 361, lxxxiv.   H. S. P.   4428

The second volume was printed at Boston in 1791, and the third in 1792, when the first volume was reprinted.

BELL'S | Address | to every | Free-Man; | but especially to the | Free Citizens | of | Pennsylvania, | Concerning, A | Tyrannical Embargo, | now laid upon the | Free-Sale of Books by Auction. | [15 lines.] | *Philadelphia:* | *Printed and Sold by Robert Bell, in Third-Street.* | M,DCC,LXXXIV. *Price four Pence.* | 8vo. pp. 7, (1). | [*Ibid.*] 8vo. pp. 15, (1).   L. C. P.   4429

BELL'S | Memorial | on the | Free Sale of Books: | To which are added | Sentiments | on what is | Freedom, | and what is | Slavery. | By a Farmer. | . . . | . . . | . . . . | *Philadelphia:* | *Printed and Sold by Robert Bell, in Third-Street.* | M,DCC,LXXXIV. | 8vo. pp. 52.   4430

[BENEZET. (Anthony)]   A | Collection | of | Religious | Tracts, | Plainly setting forth the great | Truths of the Gospel, | For the Instruction of the Youth and others | particularly those of the | Black People. | [16 lines.] | *Philadelphia:* | *Printed by Enoch Story, in* | *Strawberry-Alley.* M,DCC,LXXXIV. | 12mo. pp. 72.   F.   4431

[BENEZET.]   In the life of the lady Elizabeth | Hastings, . . . | [*Philadelphia: Enoch Story.* 1784.] Sm. 8vo. pp. 8.   F.   4432

[BENEZET.]   Some | Observations | on the | Situation, Disposition, | and | Character | of the | Indian Natives | of this | Continent. | . . . | . . . | . . . | . . . | . . . | . . . | . . . . | *Philadelphia:* | *Printed and sold by Joseph Crukshank, in* | *Market-Street.* | MDCCLXXXIV. | 12mo. pp. 59.   L. C. P.   4433

BINGHAM. (W.)   A | Letter | from an | American, | Now resident in London, | to a | Member of Parliament, | On the Subject of the | Restraining Proclamation; | and containing | Strictures | on | Lord Sheffield's Pamphlet, | on the | Commerce | of the | American States. | Said to be written by William Bingham,

Esquire; | late Agent for the Congress of the United States | of America, at Martinico. | To which are added, | Mentor's Reply to Phocion's Letter; | with some Observations on Trade, | addressed to the Citizens of New-York. | *Philadelphia:* | *Printed and Sold by Robert Bell, in Third-Street.* | M,DCC,LXXXIV. | 8vo. pp. 48.

Collation: Title, 1 leaf; Bingham's Strictures, pp. 2–16; Mentor's Reply to Phocion's Letter, pp. 17–24; Phocion's Second Letter, Title, 1 leaf; pp. 29–48. The title to the last is as follows: Colonel Hamilton's | Second Letter, | from | Phocion | to the | Considerate Citizens | of | New York, | On the Politics of the Times, | In Consequence of the Peace: | Containing Remarks on | Mentor's Reply. | [Imprint as in general title.] Sabin says Bingham's tract was issued in 1783.

BLAIR. (H.) Lectures | on | Rhetoric | and | Belles Lettres. | By Hugh Blair, D.D. | One of the Ministers of the High Church, and Professor of | Rhetoric and Belles Lettres in the University | of Edinburgh. | *Philadelphia:* | *Printed and Sold by Robert Aitken, at Pope's Head in* | *Market-Street.* | MDCCLXXXIV. | 4to. pp. viii, 1–454, (12).   L. C. P.   4435

BLAESER. (P.) Ein Brief, Weiland von Peter Bläfer an feinen Freund Michael Billmeyer, Buchdrucker in Germantown, worin er ihm einen Bericht ertheilt wie es ihm in feiner Gegend ergangen ift, daß man ihm wie auch andern, feines tugendfamen Betragens halben den Un Namen Strabler beygelegt habe 2c. [n. p. about 1784.]   4436

[BORDLEY. (John Beale)] A | Summary View | of the | Courses of Crops, | in the Husbandry | of | England & Maryland; | with | A Comparison | of their Products; | and | a System of | Improved Courses, | proposed | for Farms in America. | *Printed by Charles Cist, at Philadelphia:* | MDCCLXXXIV. | Sq. 8vo. pp. 22.   H. S. P.   4437

A | BRIEF View | of the | Accounts | of the | Treasury of Pennsylvania, | From the time of the commencement of the Revolution to the | First of October, 1781: | Extracted from the books of the Comptroller-General, and | by him laid before the General Assembly, agreeable to the | directions contained in the 17th section of the Act for me- | thodizing the department of accounts, passed the 13th day | of April, 1782. | In which is exhibited, | The

monies in the Treasury at the commencement, the seve- | ral re-
ceipts and payments during that time, and the balance | on hand at
the end thereof: | Also, | The Accounts of the State Treasurer, con-
tinued from the said | First of October, 1781, to the First of Oc-
tober, 1782: | Likewise, | The accounts of the several counties for
their taxes to October | 1782, continued from the report of the Com-
mittee of Ac- | counts of Assembly for the year 1781: | Together
with, | The state of the outstanding debts, due by the counties for
| their deficiencies in payment of taxes. | *Philadelphia: | Printed
by Hall and Sellers.* | M,DCC,LXXXIV. | 8vo. pp. 237.   4438

BUCHAN. (W.) Domestic Medicine: | Or, a | Treatise | on
the | Prevention and Cure | of | Diseases | by | Regimen and Sim-
ple Medicines. | With | An Appendix, containing a Dispensatory |
for the Use of Private Practitioners. | By William Buchan, M.D. |
Fellow of the Royal College of Physicians, Edinburgh. | Carefully
Corrected from the latest London Edition, | To which is now
added, a Complete Index. | *Philadelphia: | Printed for Joseph
Crukshank, Robert Bell, and James Muir, | of Philadelphia: And for
Robert Hodge, of New-York.* | M.DCC.LXXXIV. | 8vo. pp. 540.

BUMBO. (J.) The | American | Almanac, | For the Year of
our Lord, | 1785. | (Being the first after Leap-Year.) | [14 lines.]
| By Father Jacobus Bumbo. | *Philadelphia: | Printed by T. Brad-
ford, in Front-Street, the | fourth Door below Market-street.* [1784.] |
Sm. 8vo. pp. (40).   H. S. P.   4440

BURKE. ([Edmund]) Mr. Burke's Speech on the 1st December 1783, upon the question for the Speaker's leaving the
chair, in order for the House to resolve itself into a Committee on
Mr. Fox's East-India Bill. *Philadelphia: Thomas Bradford.* 1784.

BY the United States | in Congress Assembled. | April 30,
1784. | [*Philadelphia:* 1784.] Folio, 1 leaf.   H. S. P.   4442

Recommending the States to empower Congress to prohibit the importation of
merchandise in vessels of subjects of foreign powers who shall not enter into treaties
of Commerce.

A | CANDID Examination | of the | Address | of the | Minority | of the | Council of Censors | to the | People of Pennsylvania: | Together with | Remarks upon the Danger and Inconveniences | of the principal Defects of the Con- | stitution of Pennsylvania. | By One of the Majority. | *Philadelphia:* | *Printed in the Year* 1784. | Sm. 8vo. pp. 40.   H. S. P.   4443

CARVER. (J.) Three Years | Travels, | through the | Interior Parts of North America, | for more than | Five Thousand Miles, | containing, | An Account of the great Lakes, and all the Lakes, | Islands, Rivers, Cataracts, Mountains, Minerals, | Soil, and Vegetable Productions of the North-West | Regions of that vast Continent; | with a | Description of the Birds, Beasts, Reptiles, | Insects, and Fishes, peculiar to the Country. | Together with a concise | History of the Genius, Manners, and | Customs of the Indians | Inhabiting the Lands that lie adjacent to the Heads and to the | Westward of the great River Mississippi; | and an | Appendix, | Describing the uncultivated Parts of America that are the | most proper for forming Settlements. | By Captain Jonathan Carver, | of the Provincial Troops in America. | *Philadelphia:* | *Printed and sold by Joseph Crukshank, in Market-street,* | *and Robert Bell, in Third-street.* | MDCCLXXXIV. | 8vo. pp. xxi, 217.   4444

THE | CASE | of our | Fellow-Creatures, | the | Oppressed Africans, | respectfully recommended to | The Serious Consideration | of the | Legislature | of | Great-Britain, | By the People called Quakers. | *London, Printed:* | *Philadelphia:* | *Re-printed by Joseph Crukshank, . . .* | . . . . | MDCCLXXXIV. | 8vo. pp. 13, (3).

CATALOGUE of Books for sale by Jackson and Dunn. *Philadelphia: Robert Aitken.*   8vo? pp. 10?   4446

CATALOGUE of Books for sale by William Prichard. *Philadelphia:* 1784.   4447

CATALOGUE of Books to be sold at Auction April 8. *Philadelphia: Robert Bell.*   1784.   4448

Other book sales by Bell were advertised for April 15th and 22d.

CATALOGUE of Books to be sold at Auction, on March 11, 12

and 13, by Alexander Boyd and John Bayard, Auctioneers. *Philadelphia:* 1784.   4449

CATALOGUE of a Collection of Modern Erudition, to be sold at Auction by Alexander Boyd. *Philadelphia:* 1784.   4450

A CATALOGUE of French, Latin, English, German, and Dutch Books for sale by Boinod and Gaillard. *Philadelphia:* 1784.

A CATALOGUE of several Hundred New and Old Medical Works, for sale by Robert Bell. *Philadelphia: Robert Bell.* 1784.

𝔇𝔢𝔯 𝔎𝔩𝔢𝔦𝔫𝔢 | 𝔠𝔞𝔱𝔢𝔠𝔥𝔦𝔰𝔪𝔲𝔰 | des sel. | Dr. Martin Luthers, | nebst | den gewöhnlichen Morgen= Tisch= und | Abend= Gebätern. | Wobey | Die Ordnung des Heils in einem | Liede, in kurzen Sätzen, in Frag und Antwort, | und in einer Tabelle, | wie auch der | Inhalt der Heiligen Schrift | in Versen, | hinzugefüget. | Zum Gebrauch der Jugend. | Nebst einem | Anhang der sieben Buß=Psalmen, | einem geistlichen Lied, und das | Einmal Eins. | *Philadelphia:* | *Gedruckt und zu haben bey Klein und Reynolds,* | *in Carter's-Alley, in der Zweyten-strasse,* | *zwischen der Chesnuss und Walnuss-strasse.* | 1784. | 24mo. Title, 1 leaf; Inhalt und Ordnung, pp. (2); Text, pp. 1–139, (1).

𝔇𝔢𝔯 𝔎𝔩𝔢𝔦𝔫𝔢 𝔠𝔞𝔱𝔢𝔠𝔥𝔦𝔰𝔪𝔲𝔰. *Germantown: Leibert und Billmeyer.* 1784.   4454

CHAMBAUD. (L.) Fables Choisies, | A l'usage des Enfants, | et | Des autres personnes qui commencent à | apprendre | La Langue Françoise, | Avec un Index alphabétique de tous les mots | traduits en Anglois. | Par L. Chambaud. | *A Philadelphie:* | *Chez Charles Cist,* M.DCC.LXXXIV. | 12mo. pp. v, (3), 93, 66.   4455

A | CHOICE | Collection | of | Hymns, | from | Various Authors, | adapted to | Publick Worship: | Designed for the edification of the | pious of all Denominations; but more | particularly for the use of the Bap- | tist Church in Philadelphia. | *Philadelphia:* | *Printed by Enoch Story, Jun. living in* | *Strawberry-Alley.* 1784. | 12mo. pp. 180.   4456

A | CIRCULAR Letter, | addressed | To the State Societies | of the | Cincinnati, | by | The General Meeting, | Convened at

Philadelphia, May 3, 1784. | Together with | The Institution, | As altered and amended. | *Philadelphia:* | *Printed by E. Oswald and D. Humphreys, at the* | *Coffee-House.* M,DCC,LXXXIV. | 8vo. pp. 8.   L. C. P.   4457

THE | CONSTITUTION | of the | Commonwealth of Pennsylvania, | as established by the | General Convention. | Carefully compared with the original. | To which is added, | A | Report of the Committee | appointed to enquire, | " Whether the Constitution has been preserved inviolate in every Part, and | " whether the legislative and executive Branches of Government, have per- | " formed their Duty as Guardians of the People, or assumed to themselves | " or exercised other or greater Powers, than they are intitled to by the | " Constitution." | As adopted by the | Council of Censors. | Published by their Order. | *Philadelphia:* | *Printed by Francis Bailey, at Yorick's Head,* | *in Market-street.* | M.DCC.LXXXIV. | 8vo. pp. 64.   H. S. P.   4458

CO[O]MBE. (T[homas]) The | Peasant | Of Auburn, | Or, the Emigrant, | A Poem. | By T. Combe, D.D. | . . . | . . . . | [Cut.] | *Philadelphia:* | *Printed and Sold by Enoch Story, Jun.* [1784 ?] | 8vo. pp. 48.   L. C. P.   4459

COPIES | of | Sundry Petitions, &c. | presented by | Isaac Austin, | setting forth | His Claim to the New Ferry, | in the | City of Philadelphia. | As also, | Copies of Sundry Petitions, &c. | from | George A. Baker, | drawn forth | In Consequence of the Claim of said | Isaac Austin. | *Philadelphia,* | *Printed by Francis Bailey, at Yorick's Head, Market Street.* | MDCCLXXXIV. | 8vo. pp. 35.

CRANZ. (A. F.) Charafteriſtif oder Gemälde aus dem jeṭt lebenden Berlin. Von A. F. Cranz. *Philadelphia:* [*Hesse in Berlin.*] 1784.

LE COURRIER de l'Amerique. *A Philadelphie: Boinod et Gaillard.* 1784.   4462

" Boinod and Gaillard, Booksellers, at the solicitation of their friends to publish a newspaper in the French language, inform the public that they have digested a plan of publication, which they are distributing gratis." Pa. Gazette, June 30, 1784. Scharf and Westcott's History of Philadelphia gives the title of this paper as above, and says it was commenced but had only a short existence.

CRAWFORD. (C.) Observations | upon | Negro-Slavery. | . . . | . . . | . . . | . . . | . . . | . . . | . . . . | The Author | Charles Crawford. | *Philadelphia:* | *Printed and sold by Joseph Crukshank, in Market-* | *Street, between Second and Third-* | *Streets.* MDCCLXXXIV. | 12mo. pp. 24.　　　4463

CRAWFORD. Poems on various Subjects. By Charles Crawford. *Philadelphia: Joseph Crukshank.* 1784.　　　4464

DAVIDSON. (R.) Geography Epitomized; or a Description of the Terraqueous Globe, attempted in Verse. By Robert Davidson. *Philadelphia:* 1784.　　　4465

DAY (T.) Fragment of an Original Letter on the Slavery of the | Negroes; Written in the Year 1776, by Thomas Day, Esq. | *Philadelphia:* | *Printed by Francis Bailey, at Yorick's Head.* | M,DCC,LXXXIV. | Folio, 1 leaf.　　　H. S. P.　4466

DECLARATION and Testimony of the Doctrine and Order of the Church of Christ, adopted by the Associate Presbytery of Pennsylvania. *Philadelphia: Robert Aitken.* 1784.　　　4467

DESLON. (C—.) Observations sur les deux rapports des Commissaires nommés par S. M., pour l'examen du magnetisme animal. Par C. Deslon. *A Philadelphie:* [*Paris.*] 1784.　4468

DILWORTH. (T.) The | Schoolmasters Assistant: | Being a | Compendium of Arithmetic, | both | Practical and Theoretical. | In Five Parts. | Containing. | I. Arithmetic in Whole Numbers, | wherein all the common Rules, | having each of them a sufficient | Number of Questions, with their | Answers, are methodically and | briefly handled. | II. Vulgar Fractions, wherein se- | veral Things, not commonly met | with, are there distinctly treated | of, and laid down in the most | plain and easy Manner. | III. Decimals, in which, among other | Things, are considered the Extrac- | tion of Roots; Interest, both Sim- | ple and Compound; Annuities, Re- | bate, and Equation of Payments. | IV. A large Collection of Questions, | with their Answers, serving to | exercise the foregoing Rules; | together with a few others, both | pleasant and diverting. | V. Duodecimals, commonly called |

Cross Multiplication; wherein that | Sort of Arithmetic is thoroughly | considered, and rendered very | plain and easy; together with | the Method of proving all the | foregoing Operations at once by | Division of several Denominati- | ons, without reducing them to the | lowest Term mentioned. | The Whole being delivered in the most familiar Way of Question and | Answer, is recommended by several eminent Mathematicians, Accomptants, | and Schoolmasters, as necessary to be used in Schools by all Teachers, who | would have their Scholars thoroughly understand, and make a quick | Progress in Arithmetic. | To which is prefixt, An Essay on the Education of Youth; humbly | offered to the Consideration of Parents. | By Thomas Dilworth, | Author of the New Guide to the English Tongue; Young Book-keeper's | Assistant; &c. &c. and Schoolmaster in Wapping. | . . . | . . . | . . . | . . . | . . . | . . . . | *Philadelphia :* | *Printed and sold by Joseph Crukshank, in Market-Street,* | *between Second and Third-Streets.* MDCCLXXXIV. | 12mo.   Portrait? 1 leaf; pp. xiv, (10), 192, 1 folded leaf.   H. S. P.   4469

DISCOURS sur l'origine, les progrès et les révolutions de la franche-maçonnerie philosophique. *A Philadelphie : [Paris.]* 1784.

DUFFIELD. (G.) A | Sermon, | Preached in the | Third Presbyterian Church, | in the | City of Philadelphia, | On Thursday, December 11, 1783. | The day appointed by the United States in Congress | assembled, to be observed as a day of thanksgiving, for | the restoration of peace; and the establishment of our In- | dependence, in the enjoyment of our rights and pri- | vileges. | By George Duffield, A.M. | Pastor of the said Church. | Published at the request of the Committee of the said | Congregation. | . . . | . . . | . . . | . . . | . . . . | *Philadelphia :* | *Printed by F. Bailey, at Yorick's Head, in Market-Street.* | M.DCC.LXXXIV. | 8vo. pp. 28, (2).   N. Y. H. S.   4471

ELLIOT. (J.) The | Medical | Pocket-Book; | For Those Who Are, | And For All Who Wish, To Be, | Physicians. | Containing a short but plain Account of the | Symptoms, Causes, and Methods of Cure, | of the Diseases incident to the Human |

Body: | Including such as require | Surgical Treatment: | To-gether with the | Virtues and Doses of Medicinal | Compositions and Simples. | Extracted from the best Authors, | And digested into Alphabetical Order. | By John Elliot, M.D. | *Philadelphia:* | *Printed and Sold by Robert Bell, in Third-Street.* | M,DCC,LXXXIV. | 8vo. pp. 74.   4472

AN | ENQUIRY | into | Public Abuses, | arising for Want of a | Due Execution of Laws, | provided for the | Suppression of Vice, | in the | State of New-Jersey: | Calculated to draw the Attention of | the Executive Authority, and | People at large, to the Necessity of an | united Exertion, that may produce a | Reformation. | . . . | . . . . | *Philadelphia:* | *Printed and sold by Hall and Sellers; also sold by* | *Isaac Collins, Printer in Trenton;* *Thomas Red-* | *man, Haddonfield; and John Redman, in Salem.* | M,DCC,LXXXIV. | Sm. 8vo. pp. 22.   4473

AN | ESSAY | on | Matter. | In Five Chapters. | . . . | . . . | . . . | . . . | . . | . . . | . . . | . . . | . . . . | *Philadelphia: Printed for the Author.* | M,DCC,LXXXIV. | 8vo. Half title, 1 leaf; Title, 1 leaf; Apology, pp. (2); Contents, 1 leaf; text, pp. 1–26. 4474

AN ESSAY on the Causes of the Decline of the Foreign Trade. *Philadelphia: Thomas Bradford.* 1784.   4475

EVANGELIUM Nicodemi, | Oder: | Historischer Bericht | Von dem | Leben | Jesu Christi, | Welches | Nicodemus, | Ein Rabbi und Oberster der Jüden, | beschrieben, | Wie er solches selbst gesehen und erfahren, | Weil er ein Nachfolger und heimlicher Jünger Jesu | Christi gewesen; | auch sind | Viel schöne Stücke und Geschichte | dabey zu finden, | Welche die Evangelisten nicht beschrieben haben. | Nebst einer Historie | Von einem Rabbi und Obersten der Jüden, | Welcher öffentlich bekannt: | Daß Christus Gottes Sohn sey. | Aus des Hn. Philippi Kegelii. Anhang zum Geistlicher | Weg-Weiser nach dem himmlischen Vatterlande ꝛc. | genommen. | Wie dann auch | Die erschrecklichen Straf-fen und Plagen | der XII. Judischen Stämme. | *Lancaster, Gedruckt bey Jacob Bailey.* 1784. | Sm. 8vo. pp. 247.   H. S. P.   4476

THE EVERY Thing, or an History of the Late War in America, in Miniature, in Two Odes, or Poems, to be said or sung. By Crispianus. *Philadelphia:* 1784. 4477

FATHER Abraham's Pocket Almanac for 1785. *Philadelphia: John Dunlap.* 1784. 4478

FEMALE Fortitude, or the Power of Love. *Philadelphia: Kline and Reynolds.* 1784. 4479

FENELON. Les | Aventures | de | Télémaque, | Fils d'Ulysse, | Par Messire | Francois de Salignac | de la Mothe Fenelon, | Précepteur de Messeigneurs les Enfans de France, & depuis, Archevêque de Cambray, &c. | Nouvelle Edition | Avec des Notes & des Remarques pour l'intelligence | de la Mythologie & de ce Poëme. | *A Philadelphie* | *Chez Boinod et Gaillard.* | MDCCLXXXIV. | 24mo. pp. i–xl, 1–448, 11 plates. 4480

FOR Sale at Public Vendue, | On Thursday the 10th Day of March, at the late Dwelling House of | Pierre Eugene du Simitiere, Esq. | . . . . | The American Museum. | *Philadelphia, Printed by Charles Cist, at the Corner of Front and Arch-streets.* [1784.] | Folio, 1 leaf. L. C. P. 4481

The Catalogue comprises 36 lots. Under No. 17 is grouped the Americana, most, if not all, of which was bought for the Library Company of Philadelphia, which thereby obtained some of the most valuable books and pamphlets now in its possession.

FOX. (G.) A | Looking-Glass | for the | Jews: | Wherein | They may clearly see that the Messiah is come, | by the Prophets in the Old Testament (above | Sixteen Hundred Years since) and the manifest | Testimonies since. | And also, | They may see their own Blindness and Ignorance | of their own Prophets, and of the Messiah | unto this Day. | By which my desire is, | They may turn to Him, that their Eyes may be opened, | that they may see Him whom they have pierced. | Written by George Fox, | in the year of our Lord, 1674. | *London, Printed:* | *Philadelphia:* | *Re-printed by Joseph Crukshank, in Market-* | *Street, between Second and* | *Third-Streets.* 1784. | 12mo, pp. 44; List of Books, &c., pp. (4). 4482

THE FREEMAN'S Journal. *Philadelphia: Printed by Francis Bailey, at Yorick's Head in Market-Street.* |　　　　　4483

Numbers CXLII. (Jan. 7, 1784) to CXCII. (Dec. 29, 1784), four pages each, with a "Supplement" of two pages to No. 144. Title as in No. 4102, *supra*.

FREYMUETHIGE Gedanken über die sogenannte "Anrede von der | Minorität im Rath der Censoren," denen freyen und unabhängigen Deutschen Bür= | gern des Staats von Pennsylvanien, übergeben von | Einem freyen Deutschen Bürger des Staats. | [*Philadelphia: Melchior Steiner.* 1784.] Folio, pp. (2).　　　H. S. P.　4484

GOETHE. ([Johann Wolfgang von]) The Sorrows and Sympathetic Attachments of Werther : a German Story, in a Series of Letters. By Mr. Goethe, Doctor of the Civil Law. In Two Volumes. *Philadelphia: Robert Bell.* 1784.　　　4485

HAMILTON. ([Alexander]) A | Letter | from | Phocion, | to the | Considerate Citizens | of | New York, | on the Politics of the Times, | in Consequence of the Peace. | Said to be written by Colonel Hamilton, | late Aid to his Excellency General Washington, | and a Member of the American Congress. | . . . | . . . | . . . | . . . | . . . . | *Philadelphia:* | *Printed and Sold by Robert Bell, in Third-Street.* | M,DCC,LXXXIV. | 8vo. pp. 13. H. S. P. + [*Ibid.*] 8vo. pp. 15, (1).　　　L. C. P.　4486

" Letters on the Stage," pp. 13–15, and List of Books, 1 page, added by the printer, probably mark a second edition. Hamilton's second Letter from Phocion was advertised as separately published in the Pa. Gazette, April 14, 1784. I have only met with it as an addendum to Bingham's Strictures on Lord Sheffield, No. 4419, *supra*.

THE HAPPY Man. *Philadelphia: Robert Aitken.* 1784　4487

In June, 1784, Aitken printed 100 copies for James Slatter, Pedler.

HELTON. (J.) Reasons | for quitting the | Methodist Society; | Being a | Defence | of | Barclay's Apology. | In answer to | A Printed Letter | to a | Person | joined with the | People Called Quakers. | In a Letter to a Friend. | By John Helton. | The Third Edition, corrected. | . . . . | *Dublin: Printed* | *Philadelphia:* | *Reprinted by Joseph Crukshank, in Market-street,* | *between Second and Third-streets.* | MDCCLXXXIV. | 8vo. pp. 56.　　　F.　4488

HILLIARD-D'AUBERTEUIL. (—) Mis Mac Rea, | Roman | Historique, | Par M. Hilliard D'Auberteuil. | [Cut.] | *A Phila-delphie.* [*Paris.*] | M.DCC.LXXXIV. | Sm. 12mo. pp. i–xii, 1–146.

THE | HISTORY | of the | Old and New | Testament, | inter-spersed with | Moral and Instructive | Reflections, | chiefly taken from | The Holy Fathers. | From the French. | By J. Reeve. | The Third Edition. | *Philadelphia:* | *Printed by M. Steiner, in Race-street,* | *For C. Talbot, late of Dublin, Printer and Bookseller.* 1784. | 8vo. pp. vi, (2), 536 for 436.   H. S. P.   4490

"Reeve's History of the Bible was a translation, more or less abridged, of what is known as *La Bible de Royaumont.* It is attributed generally to Louis Isaac le Mais-tre, better known as de Sacy, who died at Pompone, 1684; but is ascribed by others to Nicolas Fontaine, who was imprisoned with Sacy. They were both Jansenists. The Rev. Joseph Reeve was an English Jesuit. He died at Ugbrook Park, England, in 1820." J. G. Shea, LL.D. The volume contains a long list of subscribers.

DER | HOCH=DEUTSCHE | Americanische | Calender, | Auf das Jahr | 1785. | [11 lines.] | Zum Ersten mal heraus gegeben. | *German-town: Gedruckt und zu finden bey Leibert und Billmeyer.* | . . . | . . . | . . . . [1784.] | Sq. 8vo. pp. (40).   H. S. P.   4491

A continuation of the series begun by the first Christopher Sower in 1738. Dun-lap, who purchased the confiscated effects of the younger Sower in 1778, disposed of his interest in the Almanac to Leibert and Billmeyer in 1784, and it was continued by them for many years.

[HOLME. (Benjamin)] A Serious | Call | in | Christian Love | to all | People, | To turn to the | Spirit of Christ | in themselves; | That they may come to have a right Understanding of the | Things of God, and be enabled thereby to serve him | acceptably: With some Observations on the following | Heads; | 1. The Uni-versality | of God's Love in | sending His Son to | die for all Men. | 2. The Holy Scrip- | tures. | 3. Worship. | 4. Baptism. | 5. The Supper. | 6. Perfection. | 7. The Resurrection. | 8. Swearing. | . . . | . . . | . . . . | *Philadelphia:* | *Printed by Joseph Crukshank,* *in* | *Market-street between Second* | *and Third-streets.* [1784?] | 8vo. pp. 58.   H. S. P.   4492

HUTCHINS. (T.) An | Historical Narrative | and | Topo-graphical Description | of | Louisiana, | and | West-Florida, |

comprehending the | River Mississippi with its Principal Branches | and Settlements, and the Rivers Pearl, | Pascagoula, Mobile, Perdido, | Escambia, Chacta-Hatcha, &c. | The | Climate, Soil and Produce | whether | Animal, Vegetable, or Mineral; | with | Directions for Sailing into all the Bays, Lakes, Harbours and Rivers on | the North Side of the Gulf of Mexico, and for Navigating between the | Islands situated along that Coast, and ascending the Mississippi River. | By Thomas Hutchins, | Geographer to the United States. | *Philadelphia:* | *Printed for the Author, and sold by Robert* | *Aitken, near the Coffee-House, in* | *Market-street.* | M.DCC.LXXXIV. | 8vo. pp. 94, 1 leaf.   H. S. P.   4493

ILLUMINATIONS | for | legislators, | and for | sentimentalists; Containing, | I. Sentiments on what is Freedom, and | what is Slavery, By a Farmer. | II. Sentiments on Liberty, exhibited in | Observations on the Revolution of America, | By Abbe Raynal. | III. Sentiments on Government, Law, Arbitrary Power, Liberty, | and Social Institutions, | By John James Rousseau, originally of Geneva. | IV. Sentiments on Government, and | on the English Constitution. | By J. L. De Lolme, Advocate, and Citizen of Geneva. | . . . . | Re-published by Robert Bell, Printer, Book-seller, | Book-Auctionier, and Provedore to the Sentimentalists in | America. | [*Philadelphia:*] *Printed and Sold by Robert Bell, in Third-Street.* | M,DCC,LXXXIV. | 8vo. pp. (4), 52.

State of Pennsylvania. | IN the Council of Censors, | Friday, September 24th, 1784, P.M. | The draught of an Address from this Council to the Freemen of the Common- | wealth of Pennsylvania, read Yesterday, and laid on the Table for considera- | tion, was taken up for a second reading, and the same being considered was | adopted as follows; viz. | [Colophon.] *Philadelphia: Printed by Francis Bailey, at Yorick's Head.* [1784.] | Folio, pp. (2).   H. S. P.   4495

THE INDEPENDENT Gazetteer.   4496

Numbers 114 (Jan. 3, 1784) to 165 (Dec. 24, 1784), four pages each, with a "Supplement" of one leaf to No. 117. Title as in No. 4203, *supra,* and imprint as in note to No. 4307, *supra,* until No. 138, when it was changed to *Philadelphia: Printed by Eleazer Oswald, at the Coffee-House,* . . . | . . . | . . . | . . . . |

𝕵𝕰𝕾𝖀𝕴𝕿𝕰𝕹𝕲𝕴𝕱𝕿, wie es unter Clemens XIII entdeckt, unter Clemens XIV unterdrückt und unter Pius VI noch fortschleicht. *Philadelphia:* [*Hartmann in Wien.*] 1784. w. 4497

JOHNSON. (S.) Abridgment of the Lives of the British Poets. Parts I. II. and III. Cowley, Denham, and Milton. By Samuel Johnson. *Philadelphia.* 1784. 4498

JOURNAL | of the | Committee of the States: | Containing | The Proceedings | from | The First Friday in June, 1784, | to | The Second Friday in August, 1784. | Published by Order of Congress. | [*Philadelphia:*] *Printed by John Dunlap.* | *Printer to the United States in* | *Congress Assembled.* | M,DCC,LXXXIV. | 8vo. pp. 47. h. s. p. 4499

JOURNAL | of the | United States | In Congress Assembled: | Containing | The Proceedings | from | The Third Day of November, 1783, | to | The Third Day of June, 1784. | Volume IX. | Published by Order of Congress. | *Philadelphia:* | *Printed by John Dunlap,* | *Printer to the United States in* | *Congress Assembled.* [1784.] | 8vo. pp. 317, xviii. h. s. p. 4500

KENRICK. (W.) A Rhetorical Grammar of the English Language. By William Kenrick. *Philadelphia: Robert Bell.* 1784.

KUNZE. (J. C.) Eine | Aufforderung | an das | Volk Gottes in Amerika | zum | frohen Jauchzen und Danken. | An dem von einem Erlauchten Congres wegen erhaltenen Friedens und | erlangter Unabhängigkeit auf den 11ten December, 1783, aus= | geschriebenen Dankfeste in der Zions=kirche zu Philadelphia | vorgestellt, und auf Verlangen verschiedener | Zuhörer dem Druck übergeben, | nebst dem, | Anhange einer andern Predigt | änlichen Inhalts, und an dem Dank= und Bettage | des Jares 1779 gehalten, von | Johann Christoph Kunze, | der heil. Schrift Doctor, Professor der orient. und der deutschen | Sprache auf der Univers. zu Philadelphia und | Ev. Luther. Pred. daselbst. | *Philadelphia:* | *Gedruckt bei Melchior Steiner, in der Rees-strasse, zwischen* | *der Zweiten- und Dritten-strasse.* 1784. | 8vo. pp. 101. h. s. p. 4502

𝕶𝖀𝕽𝖅𝕰 | Fragen | Ueber die | Christliche | Glaubens=Lehre. | Nach | Heil. Schrift=Zeugniß | beantwortet und bewähret. | Den Christlichen

Glaubens-Schülern | zu einem anfänglichen Unterricht | nützlich zu ge=
brauchen. | *Philadelphia,* | *Gedruckt bey Carl Cist, in der* | *Zweyten-
strasse,* 1784. | Sm. 8vo. pp. (10), 140.   H. S. P.   4503

LANGHORNE, ([John]) and [Edmund] CARTWRIGHT.
The | Fables | of | Flora. | By Mr. Langhorne. | with | Armine |
and | Elvira. | A Legendary Tale, by Mr. Cartwright. | . . . | . . .
| . . . . | *Philadelphia :* | *Printed and Sold by Robert Bell, in Third-
Street.* | M,DCC,LXXXIV. | 8vo.   H. S. P.   4504

Collation : Title, 1 leaf; Dedication, &c., pp. (2); Fables, pp. 1–26; Armine, &c.,
pp. 27–43 ; Advertisement, 1 page.

LAWS | Enacted in the Second Sitting | Of the Eighth |
General Assembly, | of the | Commonwealth | of | Pennsylvania,
| Which commenced at Philadelphia, on Tuesday, the | thirteenth
Day of January, in the Year of our Lord, One | Thousand Seven
Hundred Eighty and Four. | [Colophon.] *Philadelphia : Printed
by Thomas Bradford.* [1784.] | Folio, pp. 271–368, i–iii. + Laws |
Enacted in the Third Sitting | . . . | . . . | . . . | . . . | . . . | . . .
| . . . | . . . | . . . . | [*Ibid.*] pp. 371–399, i–ii.   H. S. P.   4505

LAWS | Enacted in the First Sitting | Of the Ninth | General
Assembly, | of the | Commonwealth | of | Pennsylvania, | Which
commenced at Philadelphia, on the twenty-fifth | Day of October,
in the Year of our Lord, One Thousand | Seven Hundred and
Eighty-Four. | [Colophon.] [*Philadelphia :*] *Printed by Thomas
Bradford.* [1784.] | Folio, pp. 401–415, (1).   H. S. P.   4506

Pages 402 and 403 are misnumbered 442 and 443. The publication of the " Session Laws" was continued in folio until 1801, and since then in octavo.

LESSONS for Lovers. By Ovid Americanus. To which is
added The Thunder Storm, a Poem. *Philadelphia : Robert Bell,*
1784. 8vo. pp. 35.   4507

THE | LIFE | and | Adventures | of | Ambrose Gwinett, | Ap-
prentice to an Attorney at Law, | Who for a Murder which he
never committed, was tried, | condemned, executed, and hung in
chains, in Old England; yet | lived many Years afterwards, and
in his Travels found the | Man in the West-Indies actually alive;

for the supposed | Murder of whom he had been really executed. | Demonstratively proving that | Condemnations upon circumstantial Evidence are injurious | to Innocence, incompatible with Justice, | and therefore ought always to be discountenanced especially | in Cases of Life and Death. | To which is Added, | An Account of John Matthieson, an ingenious | Scotsman, lately executed in London, for | forging the Notes of the Bank of England. | *Philadelphia:* | *Printed and Sold by Robert Bell, in Third-Street.* M,DCC,LXXXIV. | 8vo. pp. 32.   L. C. P.   4508

Collation: Title, 1 leaf; Life of Gwinett, pp. 3–16; Life of Matthieson, pp. 17–22; A Narrative of the Extraordinary Adventures of four Russian Sailors, who were cast away, and lived six Years on the Desert Island of East-Spitzenbergen, pp. 23–32.

THE | LIFE | Travels | and | Adventures, | of | Edward Wortley Montague Esq; | Son to the most famous Traveller, | Lady Mary Wortley Montague, | Exhibiting | His very extraordinary Transactions in England, France, | Italy, Turkey, Arabia, Egypt, and the | Holy Land: | With Remarks on the Manners and Customs of the | Oriental World. | Volume the First. | *Philadelphia:* | *Printed and Sold by Robert Bell, in Third-Street.* | M,DCC,LXXXIV. | 8vo. pp. 40. + Volume the Second. [*Ibid.*] 8vo. Title, 1 leaf; pp. 43–90.   L. C. P.   4509

𝕯𝕬𝕾 𝕷𝖀𝕿𝕳𝕰𝕽𝕵𝕾𝕮𝕳𝕰 und Reformirte A. B. C. und Namen=büchlein. *Germantown: Leibert und Billmeyer.* 1784.   4510

MACKLIN. (C.) The | True-Born Irishman; | or the | Irish Fine Lady. | A | Comedy | in | Two Acts. | By Mr. Charles Macklin, | Author of Love a-la-mode, the True-Born | Scotchman, &c. | *Philadelphia:* | *Printed by William Spotswood.* | 1784. | 12mo. pp. 36.   4511

MAGAW. (S.) A | Sermon | delivered in | St. Paul's Church, | On Saturday, December 27, 1783, | The Anniversary of | St. John the Evangelist; | (For the Benefit of the Poor) | by direction, and in the presence of | the Ancient and Honorable Fraternity | of | Free and Accepted Masons | Of the several Lodges | in | Philadelphia. | By Samuel Magaw, D.D. | Vice-Provost of the University of | Pennsylvania. | *Philadelphia: Printed by Hall and Sellers.* | M,DCC,LXXXIV. | 8vo. pp. 32.   H. S. P.   4512

MANSON. (D.) A New Primer. By David Manson. *Philadelphia: Robert Aitken.* 1784.   4513

[MARKOE. (Peter)] The | Patriot Chief. | A | Tragedy. | . . . | . . . | . . . | . . . | . . . | . . . | . . . . | *Philadelphia:* | *Printed for the Author, and sold by Wm. Prichard,* | *at his Circulating Library, and Book-Store, in Market-Street,* | MDCCLXXXIV. | 8vo. pp. (4), 70.

MARSHALL. (W.) Religious Instruction to the Rising Generation. | A | Catechism | for | Youth, | containing the | Principles | of | Practical Religion : | Agreeable to the Doctrine of the Holy Scriptures exhibited in | the Westminster Confession of Faith, and the Larger and | Shorter Catechisms. | To which is added | a | Catechetical Explanation | of | Sundry Terms belonging to Religion, | Alphabetically digested : | In which are specified the distinguishing Tenets of the various De- | nominations of Christians and religious Sects that now appear. | By William Marshall, A.M. | Minister of the Gospel to the Scots Presbyterian Church in Philadelphia. | . . . | . . . | . . . | . . . | . . . . | *Philadelphia:* | *Printed for the Author, and sold by Robert Aitken, in Market-Street.* | MDCCLXXXIV. | 12mo. pp. iv, 172.   4515

The Catechism has a separate title-page, with the date 1783.

MENDENHALL. (T.) Tables of Difference of Latitude and Departure, constructed to every quarter of a Degree of the Quadrant, and to answer for all Distances from one-tenth of a Perch or Mile to twelve hundred; particularly suited to the purposes of Land Surveying. By Thomas Mendenhall. *Philadelphia: Joseph Crukshank.* 1784.   4516

MINUTES | of the | Baptist Association, | Held at New-York, October, 1784. | [Colophon.] *Philadelphia: Printed by R. Aitken, at Pope's Head, Market Street.* [1784.] | Sq. 8vo. pp. 8.   4517

MINUTES | of the | First Session | of the Ninth | General Assembly | of the | Commonwealth | of | Pennsylvania, | Which commenced at Philadelphia on Monday, the | Twenty Fifth Day of October, in the Year of our Lord, | One Thousand Seven Hundred and Eighty Four. | [*Arms of Pennsylvania.*] | *Philadelphia:* |

Printed by Francis Bailey, at Yorick's Head | in Market-Street. |
MDCCLXXXIV. | Folio, pp. 402.   H. S. P.   4518

The first session ends on page 103, the second on page 328, and the third on page
402. The Assembly sat until Sept. 23, 1785, and the Minutes of the second and
third sessions were not printed till 1785.

A | MONODY | In Honor of the | Chiefs | Who have fallen in
the Cause of | American Liberty, | Spoken at the Theatre, | in |
Philadelphia, December 7, 1784. | With the Vocal Accompany-
ments : | And | A Rondelay, | Celebrating | American Indepen-
dency. | . . . . | [*Philadelphia :*] *Printed by Thomas Bradford.*
[1784.] | Sm. 4to. pp. 8.   4519

Not delivered till Dec. 14. The vocal parts were sung by a " Lady." A very rare
tract, but few having been printed.

NARRATIVE concerning the maintenance of the Reformation
Testimony, Approved by the Associate Presbytery of Pennsylvania. *Philadelphia : Robert Aitken.*   1784.   4520

A | NARRATIVE | of the | Captivity | and | Sufferings | of |
Benjamin Gilbert | and his | Family ; | Who were surprised by
the Indians, and taken from | their Farms, on the Frontiers of
Pennsylvania, | In the Spring, 1780. | *Philadelphia :* | *Printed and
sold by Joseph Crukshank, in Market-Street,* | *between Second and
Third-Street.* | MDCCLXXXIV. | 8vo. pp. 96.   H. S. P.   4521

The authorship of this Narrative has been attributed to Thomas Austin and to
William Walton. See Comly's Hist. of Byberry, Memoirs of the H. S. P., Vol. II.,
Part II., p. 195. Benjamin Gilbert was probably the author of Numbers 1109 and
2523, *supra,* and the tract ascribed to him in the additional titles under 1769.

𝔑𝔈𝔘𝔍𝔄𝔥𝔯𝔰=𝔙𝔢𝔯𝔰𝔢 𝔡𝔢𝔰 𝔥𝔢𝔯𝔲𝔪𝔱𝔯ä𝔤𝔢𝔯𝔰 𝔡𝔢𝔯 𝔓𝔥𝔦𝔩𝔞𝔡𝔢𝔩𝔭𝔥𝔦𝔰𝔠𝔥𝔢 𝔈𝔬𝔯𝔯𝔢𝔰𝔭𝔬𝔫=
𝔡𝔢𝔫𝔷. 𝔇𝔢𝔫 1𝔰𝔱𝔢𝔫 𝔍𝔞𝔫𝔲𝔞𝔯 1784. *Philadelphia : Melchior Steiner.*   1784.

NEW-YEAR | Verses, | For those who carry the | Pennsylva-
nia Gazette | To the | Customers. | January, 1, 1784. | [*Philadel-
phia : Hall and Sellers.* 1784.] | Folio, 1 leaf.   H. S. P.   4523

NEW-Year Verses of the Carriers of the Freeman's Journal.
Philadelphia : Francis Bailey.   1784.   4524

NEW-YEAR Verses of the Carriers of the Independent Gazetteer. *Philadelphia: E. Oswald and D. Humphreys.* 1784. 4525

NEW-YEAR Verses of the Carriers of the Pennsylvania Journal. *Philadelphia: Thomas Bradford.* 1784. 4526

NEW-YEAR Verses of the Carriers of the Pennsylvania Packet. *Philadelphia: David C. Claypoole.* 1784. 4527

DJE ÖSTERREJCHJSCH = ungarifche Provinz der gefchuhten Auguftiner Mönche. *Philadelphia:* 1784. w. 4528

OVID. Les Héroïdes d'Ovide. [Traduit par J. R. de Boisgelin.] *A Philadelphie: [Paris.]* 1784. + Les Héroïdes du galant Ovide. *A Philadelphie: [Paris.]* 1784. w. 4529

THE PENNSYLVANIA Gazette. 4530

Numbers 2795 (Jan. 7, 1784) to 2847 (Dec. 29, 1784), four pages each, with "Supplements" of two pages to Numbers 2800, 2805, 2811, 2817, 2819, 2825, 2827, 2835, and 2844. Title and imprint as in No. 4334, *supra.*

THE PENNSYLVANIA Journal. 4531

Numbers 1657 (Jan. 3, 1784) to 1761 (Dec. 29, 1784), four pages each, with "Supplements" of two pages each to Numbers 1708, 1712, 1715, 1719 to 1722, 1727, 1728, 1739, 1740, 1744, and 1750. Number 1754 is misnumbered 1755, and the error is not corrected. Published twice a week. Title and imprint as in No. 4335, *supra.*

THE | PENNSYLVANIA Mercury | and | Universal Advertiser. | Price Six-pence. Friday, August 20, 1784. Numb. I. | *Philadelphia: Printed by Daniel Humphreys, at the New Printing-Office in Dock-street, near the Drawbridge; where Advertisements, | Articles and Letters of Intelligence, &c. are gratefully received, and every kind of Printing-Work performed with Diligence and Dispatch.* | Folio.

Numbers 1 to 20 (Dec. 31, 1784), four pages each.

THE PENNSYLVANIA Packet, | And General Advertiser. | Thursday, January 1, 1784. | Vol. XIII.) Published every Tuesday, Thursday and Saturday. Price Six-Pence. (Num. 1641. | [Colophon.] *Philadelphia: Printed and sold by David C. Claypoole, in Market-street.* | Folio.

The Pennsylvania Packet, and Daily Advertiser. | Price Four Pence.) Tuesday, September 21, 1784. (No. 1755. | [Colophon.] *Philadelphia: Printed and sold by John Dunlap and David C. Claypoole, on the South side of Market-street, the third | House East of Second-street, where Subscriptions, Advertisements, &c. for this Paper are thankfully received.* | Folio.   4533

> Numbers 1641 (Jan. 1, 1783) to 1842 (Dec. 31, 1784), four pages each. The paper for Aug. 24 is misnumbered 1745 for 1743, and that for Nov. 12 is misnumbered 1790 for 1800. The first of these errors was immediately corrected, but the other was carried on through the year. The imprint was slightly changed in Numbers 1697 and 1703. On Sept. 21 (No. 1755) the Packet became the first daily paper issued in America, with title and imprint as above. It is now represented by the North American.

THE PENNSYLVANIA Pocket Almanac for 1785. *Philadelphia: Thomas Bradford.* 1784.   4534

THE PHILADELPHIA Price Current, | Published by Subscription every fourteen Days, in which are contained the Prices | of Merchandise, Duties on Importation and Exportation, regulated by John Mac- | pherson, Broker, with the assistance of Twenty eminent Merchants, Fac- | tors, and Others; likewise, the Course of Exchange, the Premiums of Insurance | to and from the most considerable Places of Trade. And as Pennsylvania Currency | is not understood in all parts of Europe, &c. Mr. Macpherson has set down the | Value of all Commodities in Spanish milled Dollars, and the Ninetieth Parts of a | Spanish milled Dollar. | [*Philadelphia:* 1784.] Folio, pp. (2).   H. S. P.   4535

> I have met with only three numbers, viz.: Nos. 1, 15, and 29.

THE | PHILADELPHIAD; | or, | New Pictures of the City: | Interspersed with a candid review and display of some first-rate | Modern | Characters | Of Both Sexes: | Delineated in a friendly and satirical manner, and containing | sketches of the materials that distinguish the following | places, viz. | Court-House, Hospital for Lunatics, | New-Jail, Bell's-Book-Store, | Theatre, State-House, and | Bagnio, Coffee-House. | With other entertaining Anecdotes, humorous, | moral and sentimental. | Vol. I. | . . . | . . . | . . . . | *Philadelphia:* | *Printed for the Editor by Kline & Reynolds, and sold* | *at their Printing-Office, in Carter's-alley, and by all the* | *Booksellers in Town and Country.* 1784. | Sm. 8vo. pp. 83. + Vol. II. [*Ibid.*] Sm. 8vo. pp. 59, (1).   H. S. P.   4536

A PLAIN Almanac for 1785.   *Philadelphia: Joseph Crukshank.* 1784.   4537

PLATTES. (G.) A Discovery of | Subterranean Treasure: | Containing | Useful Explorations. | Concerning all Manner of Mines and Minerals, from the Gold to the | Coal; with plain Directions and Rules for the finding of them in | all Kingdoms and Countries. | In which | The Art of Melting, Refining and Assaying of them is plainly | Declared, so that every ordinary man, that is moderately ingeni- | ous, may with small charge presently try the value of such Ores, | as shall be found either by Rule or by Accident. | Whereunto is added | A Real Experiment whereby every ignorant man may presently try | whether any piece of Gold that shall come to his hands be True | or Counterfeit, without defacing or altering the form thereof, | and more certainly than any Goldsmith or Refiner could formerly | Discern. | Also a | Perfect way to try what colour any Berry, Leaf, Flower, Stalk, | Root, Fruit, Seed, Bark, or Wood will give: With a Perfect | way to make Colours that they shall not stain nor fade like | ordinary Colours. | Very necessary for every one to know, whether he be a Traveller by | Land or by Sea, in what Country, Dominion, or Plantation soever | he shall either sojourn or Inhabit. | By Mr. Gabriel Plattes. | *Philadelphia:* | *Printed and Sold by Robert Bell, in Third-Street.* | M,DCC,LXXXIV. | 8vo. pp. 37, (3). N. Y. H. S.   4538

A POCKET Memorandum Book; Or Daily Journal for 1785, with various useful tables. *Philadelphia: Joseph Crukshank.* 1784.

THE | POLITICAL Establishments | of the | United States | of | America, | in | A Candid Review of their Deficiencies. | Together | With a Proposal of Reformation, | Humbly Addressed | To the Citizens of America. | By a Fellow Citizen. | *Philadelphia:* | *Printed and Sold by Robert Bell, in Third-Street.* | M,DCC,LXXXIV. | 8vo. pp. 28.   H. S. P.   4540

POOR Will's | Almanack, | for the | Year of our Lord, 1785; | Being the First after Leap-Year. | . . . | . . . | . . . | . . . | . . . | . . . | . . . | . . . | . . . | . . . | . . . | . . . | . . . | *Philadelphia:* | *Printed and Sold by Joseph Crukshank,* | . . . | . . . [1784.] | Sm. 8vo. pp. (36).   H. S. P.   4541

POOR Will's Pocket Almanac for 1785.   *Philadelphia: Joseph Crukshank.*   1784.   4542

PRIESTLEY. (J.)   An | Appeal | to the | Serious and Candid Professors | of | Christianity. | On the following Subjects. | I. The Use of Reason in Matters of Religion. | II. The Power of Man to do the Will of God. | III. Original Sin. | IV. Election and Repro- bation. | V. The Divinity of Christ, and | VI. Atonément for Sin by the Death of Christ. | By Joseph Priestly, L.L.D. F.R.S. | and a Lover of the Gospel. | To which are added, | A concise History of the Rise of those Doctrines : | And the | Triumph of Truth; | Being An Account of the | Trial of Mr. E. Elwall, | For Heresy and Blasphemy, at Stafford Assizes. | . . . | . . . . | *Phila- delphia:* | *Printed and Sold by Robert Bell, in Third-Street.* | M,DCC,LXXXIV. | 8vo. pp. 57, (1).   H. S. P.   4543

> The Appeal ends on page 33, and is followed by Elwall's Trial, which ends on page 41. On page 42 there is a new title : A | General View | of the | Arguments | for the | Unity of God ; | from Reason, from the Scripture, | and from History. | Containing, | I. Arguments from Reason against the Trinitarian Hypothesis. | II. Arguments from Reason against the Arian Hypothesis. | III. Arguments against the Trinitarian and the Arian Hypothesis | from the scriptures. | IV. Arguments from History against the Deity, and pre- | existence of Christ; or a summary View of the Evidence | for the primitive Christians having held the doctrine of | the simple Hu- manity of Christ. | V. Maxims of Historical Criticism, by which the preceeding | Articles may be tried. | By Joseph Priestley, L.L.D., F.R.S. | [Imprint as above.]

PROCLAMATION.   [*Arms of Pennsylvania.*] | Pennsylvania, ss. | By the President and the Supreme Executive Council of the Commonwealth | of Pennsylvania, | A Proclamation. | [*Phila- delphia: Francis Bailey.*   1784.]   Folio, 1 leaf.   L. C. P.   4544

> Dated "March 24, 1784."   Offering a reward for the murderer of Richard Marple.

PROCLAMATION.   By the President and the Supreme Ex-

ecutive Council of the Commonwealth of Pennsylvania, | A Proc-
lamation. | [*Philadelphia :* 1784.]   Folio, 1 leaf.   H. S. P.   4545

Dated " Jan. 22, 1784," announcing the conclusion of the Peace of Paris.

PROCLAMATION.   Pennsylvania, ss. | By the President and
the Supreme Executive Council of the Commonwealth | of Penn-
sylvania, | A Proclamation. | [*Philadelphia :* 1784.]   Folio, 1 leaf.

Thomas Leaming, Jr., and Elizabeth Houston, having been robbed in Penn Street,
Southwark, £300 reward was offered for the apprehension of the robbers. Dated
" May 15, 1784."

𝕯𝕰𝕽 | 𝖕𝕾𝕬𝕷𝕿𝕰𝕽 | des | 𝕶önigs | unb | 𝖕ropheten Dabibs, | ver=
beutfchet von | D. Martin 𝕷uther | mit kurzen Sumarien ober Jn= |
halt jebes 𝖕falmen. | Unb mit vielen | 𝖕arallelen ober gleichen Schrifft=
ftellen. | Erfte Auflage. | *Germanton* | *gedruckt bey Leibert und Bill-*
meyer. | 1784. | 24mo. pp. 252.   H. S. P.   4547

𝕯𝕴𝕰 | 𝕽𝕰𝕲𝕴𝕰𝕽𝖀𝕹𝕲𝕾𝖁𝕰𝕽𝕱𝕬𝕾𝕾𝖀𝕹𝕲 | ber | 𝕽epublik 𝖕enn=
fylvanien | wie folche von ber zu dem Zweck erwählten | unb | vom 15ten
July, bis zum 28ften September, 1776, | von Tag zu Tag in 𝖕hilabelphia
gehaltenen | General Convention | veftgefetzt worden. | Aus dem Eng=
lifchen überfetzt. | *Philadelphia,* | *Gedruckt bey Francis Bailey, in der*
Marckt-strass= | *se, zwischen der Dritten- und Vierten-strasse.*   1784. |
Sm. 8vo. pp. 47.   4548

𝕯𝕴𝕰 | 𝕽𝕰𝕲𝕴𝕰𝕽𝖀𝕹𝕲𝕾𝖁𝕰𝕽𝕱𝕬𝕾𝕾𝖀𝕹𝕲 | . ber | 𝕽epublik 𝖕enn=
fylvanien, | wie folche von ber | General Convention, | bie zu dem Zweck
erwählet | unb | vom 15ten Julii, 1776, bis zum 28ften September, 1776,
| in 𝖕hilabelphia gehalten wurde, | veftgefetzt worden. | Aus dem Eng=
lifchen überfetzt. | *Philadelphia :* | *Gedruckt bey Melchior Steiner, in der*
Rees-strasse, nahe | *bey der Dritten-strasse.*   1784. | 8vo. pp. 49.   4549

Contains also (pp. 19–49) : " Der Bericht der Committee des Raths der Censoren."
See No. 4458, *supra.*

REPORT | of the | Committee | of the | Council of Censors, |
appointed to enquire, | " Whether the Constitution has been pre-
served inviolate in every Part, and | " whether the legislative and
executive Branches of Government, have per- | " formed their Duty

as Guardians of the People, or assumed to themselves | " or exercised other or greater Powers, than they are intitled to by the | " Constitution ;" | On the | Executive Branch of Government. | As Adopted by the said Council. | Published by their Order. | *Philadelphia :* | *Printed by Francis Bailey, at Yorick's Head,* | *in Market-Street.* | M.DCC.LXXXIV. | 8vo. pp. 15.   H. S. P.   4550

A | REPORT | of the | Committee | of the | Council of Censors, | appointed to enquire, | " Whether the Constitution has been preserved inviolate in every | " part, and whether legislative and executive branches of | " government have performed their duty as guardians of the | " people, or assumed to themselves or exercised other or | " greater powers, than they are entituled to by the Constitu- | " tion." | *Philadelphia :* | *Printed by Francis Bailey, at Yorick's Head,* | *in Market-Street.* | MDCCLXXXIV. | 8vo. pp. 27.   L. C. P.   4551

RULES | for the | Regulation | of the | Society for the Relief | of Free Negroes, and | others, unlawfully held in Bon- | dage. | Instituted in Philadelphia in the Year 1784. | To which are prefixed, | The Acts of the General Assembly | of Pennsylvania, respecting the gradual | Abolition of Slavery. | *Philadelphia :* | *Printed by Joseph Crukshank,* . . . | . . . | . . . MDCCLXXXIV. | 8vo. Title, 1 leaf; pp. 16.   L. C. P.   4552

[RUSH. (Benjamin)]   Considerations | upon the present | Test-Law | of | Pennsylvania : | Addressed to the Legislature | and Freemen of the State. | *Philadelphia : Printed by Hall and Sellers.* | MDCCLXXXIV. | Sm. 8vo. pp. 23.   H. S. P.   4553

SAUNDERS. (R.) A Pocket Almanac for 1785. By Richard Saunders, Phil.   *Philadelphia : Hall and Sellers.* 1784.   4554

SAUNDERS. Poor Richard improved : | Being an | Almanack | [10 lines] | For the | Year of our Lord 1785 : | Being the First after Leap-Year. | [9 lines.] By Richard Saunders, Philom. | *Philadelphia :* | *Printed and Sold by Hall and Sellers.* [1784.] | 8vo. pp. (36).   H. S. P.   4555

𝕾𝕰𝕹𝕯𝕾𝕮𝕳𝕽𝕰𝕵𝕭𝕰𝕹 an meinen 𝔅ruber ʒu 𝕳anober, 𝔍. 𝔉. 𝕾. . . .

über meinen britten Aufenthalt zu Augsburg. *Philadelphia: [Nuernberg.]* 1784. w. 4556

[SERVAN. (J. M. A.)] Apologie de la Bastille. Par un homme en pleine campagne. *A Philadelphie: [Lusanne.]* 1784.

SHARP. (A.) Der Ganz Neue Verbefferte | Nord=Americanifche | Calender | Auf das 1785fte Jahr Chrifti, | Welches ein gemein Jahr von 365 Tagen ift. | Und enthält, | Die Wochen= Monaths= Namen= Feyer und andere dem Land= | man zu wiffen nützliche und merkwürdige Tage; des Monden Auf= und | Untergang; feine Zeichen, Grade und Viertel; die Afpecten der Pla= | neten, famt der Witterung; des Sieben= geftirns Aufgang, Sub= | platz und Untergang; Auf= und Untergang der Sonnen; nebft | der Fluth oder dem Hohen Waffer zu Philabelphia; | Und andere gewöhnliche Calender = Arbeit. | Wie auch: | Verfchiedene angenehme Poetifche Stücke; Gefchichten, 2c. 2c. | Berechnet vornemlich. nach der Pennfylvanifchen Himmels = Gegend; | Jedoch in den angren= zenden Landfchaften ohne merklichen Unterfcheib zu gebrauchen. | Zum Zehndenmal herausgegeben | und verfertiget von Anthony Sharp, Philom. | *Lancaster, Gedruckt und zu finden bey Francis Bailey, in der Koenigs-strasse.* | . . . | . . . | . . . | . . . | . . . . [1784.] | Sm. 4to. pp. (36). 4558

SHARP. The Continental Almanac for 1785. By Anthony Sharp. *Philadelphia: Kline and Reynolds.* 1784. 4559

SMITH. (Devereaux) To the People of Pennsylvania. | [*Phila-delphia:* 1784.] Folio, 1 leaf. 4560

[SMITH. (William)] An | Account | of | Washington College, | in the | State of Maryland. | Published by Order of the Visitors and Governors of the | said College, for the Information of its Friends and | Benefactors. | *Philadelphia: | Printed by Joseph Crukshank, in | Market-street, between Second and | Third streets.* MDCCLXXXIV. | 8vo. pp. 50, 1 plate. A. P. S. 4561

STANCLIFF. (J.) An | Account | of the | Trial | of | Doctor Joseph Priestley, | For the horrid Crime of High-Treason | against the | King of Heaven and Earth, | and Supreme Governor of | the United States of | North-America. | (Delivered under the

II.—57

Similitude of a Dream) | By John Stancliff, Minister of the Gospel. | . . . | . . . . | *Philadelphia:* | *Printed by Charles Cist, in Arch-Street,* | *the North-east Corner of Fourth-Street.* | M.DCC.LXXXIV. 8vo. pp. 24.   H. S. P.   4562

STANCLIFF. The | Riddle | of | Riddles unriddled. | A | Sermon | preached in | Philadelphia, July the 15th, 1784. | By John Stancliff, | Minister of the gospel. | *Philadelphia: Printed for the author.* | 1784. | 8vo. pp. 27.   4563

STATE | of the | Accounts | of | Adam Orth, Esq. | late | Sub-Lieutenant | of | Lancaster County. | From the time of his last Settlement, Aug. | 1778, to March 1780, and for the out- | standing fines, incurred before the time | last mentioned in the several Battalions | throughout the County to the 1st of | April 1783. | *Philadelphia:* | *Printed by F. Bailey, at Yorick's Head, in Market-Street.* | M,DCC,LXXXIV. | 8vo. pp. 23.   H. S. P.   4564

STATE | of the | Accounts | of | Andrew Boyd, Esq. | a | Sub-Lieutenant | of | Chester County. | From March 1777, to March 1780. | In which is exhibited. | The amount of the Monies received by him for Fines incurred | within that Time in the 8th Battalion of militia, and accounted | for. Together with Lists shewing by whom the same were paid, | so far as these Lists were obtained. | Likewise, | His Disbursements and Payments thereof into the Treasury. | *Philadelphia:* | *Printed by F. Bailey, at Yorick's Head, in Market-Street.* | MDCCLXXIV. [1784.] | 8vo. pp. 12.

STATE | of the | Accounts | of | Conrad Foos, | Collector of Excise, | Berks County, | From November 24th 1781, to the 22d of August | 1783. | In which is exhibited, | The Excise accruing within said time the monies received | by the said Collector on account thereof. And | the sums yet due. | Together, | With the Payments made to the Treasurer of the State. | *Philadelphia:* | *Printed by Robert Aitken, three Doors above the Coffee | House, in Market street.* | MDCCLXXXIV. | 8vo. pp. 6.   H. S. P.   4566

STATE | of the | Accounts | of | Edward Bartholomew, | Collector of Excise | for the | City and County of Philadelphia, |

From the Time of his Appointment, Nov. 21, | 1782, to the 22d
of Nov. 1783. | In which is exhibited, | The Amount of the
Monies received by him, on account of Excise ac- | crued before
his Appointment; and the Amount of Monies received | on ac-
count of Excise accruing within the period aforesaid; together |
with a list of the Persons by whom the same were paid. | Also
the Payments thereof to the Treasurer. | Likewise the Excise
accruing since the Time of his Appointment, which | is repre-
sented to be yet outstanding. | And the amount of the Quantity
exported. | *Philadelphia :* | *Printed by F. Bailey, at Yorick's Head, in
Market-Street.* | M,DCC,LXXIV.　[1784.] | 8vo. pp. 25.　　　4567

STATE | of the | Accounts | of | Jacob Barnitz Esquire, | Col-
lector of Excise, | York County, | From November 20th 1782, to
the 1st of May | 1784. | In which is exhibited, | The Excise ac-
cruing within said time the monies received | by the said Collector
on account thereof.　And | the sums yet due. | Together, | With
the Payments made to the Treasurer of the State. | *Philadelphia :*
| *Printed by Robert Aitken, three Doors above the Coffee-* | *House, in
Market street.* | M,DCC,LXXXIV. | 8vo. pp. 8.　　H. S. P.　4568

STATE | of the | Accounts | of | Jesse Jones, Esq. | Late
Collector of Excise | for | Northampton County. | *Philadel-
phia:* | *Printed by F. Bailey, at Yorick's Head, in Market-Street.* |
M,DCC,LXXXIV. | 8vo. pp. 4.　　H. S. P.　4569

STATE | of the | Accounts | of | John Buchanan Esquire, |
Collector of Excise, | Cumberland County | From the 20th of
January to the 25th of April | 1783. | In which is exhibited, |
The Excise accruing within said time the monies received | by
the said Collector on account thereof.　And | the sums yet due. |
Together, | With the Payments made to the Treasurer of the
State. | *Philadelphia :* | *Printed by Robert Aitken, three Doors above the
Coffee* | *House, in Market street.* | M,DCC,LXXXIV. | 8vo. pp. 7.

STATE | of the | Accounts | of | Joshua Anderson, Esq. | late
| Sub-Lieutenant | of | Bucks County. | From March 1780, to
April 1783. | In which is set forth the Amount of the Fines re-
ceived within that | Period from Delinquents of the Fourth Bat-

talion, for non-per- | formance of Militia Duty and Exercise. To-
gether with Lists | shewing the Names of the Persons by whom
Payments have been | made, and the Sums received from them
respectively. Likewise | the Disburseme⸗ ts made by him, and
the Payments to the Trea- | sury. | *Philadelphia : | Printed by F.
Bailey, at Yorick's Head, in Market Street.* | M,DCCLXXIV. [1784.]
| 8vo. pp. 38.　　　　　　　　　　　　　　H. S. P.　4571

STATE | of the | Accounts | of | Samuel Cunningham, Esq. |
late | Collector of Excise | for | Chester County. | From August
10, 1782, to Nov. 7, 1783, and | until he ceased to act as Collector.
| In which are exhibited. | The amount of the Monies received
and accounted for : also, Lists | shewing the names of the Persons
from whom Excise became | due, and was received. | Likewise, |
The Payments made to the State Treasurer. | *Philadelphia : | Printed
by F. Bailey, at Yorick's Head, in Market-Street.* | MDCCLXXXIV.
| 8vo. pp. 6.　　　　　　　　　　　　　　H. S. P.　4572

STATE | of the | Accounts | of | Thomas Strawbridge, Esq. |
late | Sub-Lieutenant | of | Chester County. | From the time of
his appointment under the Militia Law in | March 1777, to the 8th
of April 1778. | In which is set forth the Amount of the Fines
received within that | Period from Delinquents of Col. Evans's
Battalion, for | non-performance of Militia Duty and Exercise : |
Together with Lists shewing the Names of the Persons by whom
Pay- | ments have been made, and the Sums received from | them
respectively. | Likewise, the Disbursements made by him, and the
Payments to the | Treasury. | *Philadelphia: | Printed by F. Bailey,
at Yorick's Head, in Market-Street.* | M,DCC,LXXXIV. | 8vo. pp. 7.

STATE | of the | Accounts | of | William Crispin, Esq. | late
| Collector of Excise | for the | City & County of Philadelphia.
| Revised and Settled. | *Philadelphia : | Printed by F. Bailey, at
Yorick's Head, in Market Street.* | MDCCLXXIV. [1784.] | 8vo.
pp. 16.　　　　　　　　　　　　　　　　H. S. P.　4574

STATE | of the | Accounts | of | William Hay, Esq. | Collector
of Excise | for | Lancaster County. | From August 10, 1782, to
August 10, 1783. | In which is exhibited. | The amount of the

Monies received and accounted for: also Lists | shewing the names of the Persons from whom Excise became | due, and was received. | Likewise, | The Payments made to the State Treasurer. | *Phila-delphia:* | *Printed by F. Bailey, at Yorick's Head, in Market Street.* | MDCCLXXIV. [1784.] | 8vo. pp. 11.   H. S. P.   4575

STATE | of the | Accounts | of the | Collectors of Excise, | for | Bucks County, | From the 1st of July, 1776 (to which time the Accounts of the Excise of the said County, | have been settled and paid) to the 21st of | November, 1783. | In which is exhibited, | The Excise accruing with said time the monies re- | ceived by the respective Collectors on account there- | of. And the sums yet due. | Together, | With the Payments made to the Treasurer of the State. | *Philadelphia:* | *Printed by F. Bailey, at Yorick's Head, in Market-Street.* | M,DCC,LXXXIV. | 8vo. pp. 18.   H. S. P.   4576

STATE | of the | Accounts | of the | Lieutenant and Sub-Lieutenants | of | Chester County. | From March 1780, to April 1783. | In which is exhibited. | The amount of the Monies received for fines, by them respective- | ly, and accounted for; with lists of the persons by whom the | same were paid, arranged in the order of their companies and | classes. | Likewise, | Their disburse-ments and payments to the treasury. | *Philadelphia:* | *Printed by F. Bailey, at Yorick's Head, in Market Street.* | MDCCLXXIV. [1784.] | 8vo. pp. 88.   H. S. P.   4577

STATE | of the | Accounts | of the | Lieutenant & Sub Lieuten-ants | of the | City of Philadelphia, | and | Liberties. | From March 1777, to April 1783. | Wherein is exhibited, the amount of the fines paid by the six bat- | talions of infantry, and the artillery battalion, which were in- | curred within that time, for non-per-formance of militia duty, | and exercise. Together with lists, shewing from whom the same | were received, arranged in the order of battalions, companies, | and classes. Likewise, the ac-counts of disbursement and | appropriation thereof. | *Philadelphia:* | *Printed by Francis Bailey, at Yorick's Head,* | *in Market-Street.* | M,DCC,LXXXIV. | 8vo. pp. 165.   H. S. P.   4578

STATE | of the | Accounts | of the | Lieutenant & Sub-Lieutenants | of | Westmoreland County. | From March 1777, to April 1783. | For Fines incurred by sundry persons for non-performance of | their tour of duty, when thereunto called, agreeable to | the several militia laws; for monies received on account of | those fines; for payments ordered by council placed in their | hands for the defence of the frontiers; and for the appro- | priation and disbursement thereof. | *Philadelphia :* | *Printed by F. Bailey, at Yorick's Head, in Market-Street.* | M,DCC,LXXIV. [1784.] | 8vo. pp. 18.

STATE | of the | Accounts | of the | Sub-Lieutenants | of | Washington County, | From the 28th March 1781, when the | County was erected, to the 1st April | 1783. | And of the | Lieutenant of the said County, | From the Time aforesaid, to the 27th of | October 1783. | For Fines incurred by sundry Persons for non-performance of | their Tour of Duty agreeable to the Militia Law; for Mo- | nies received on account of those fines; for Payments ordered | by Council; and for the appropriation and Disbursement of | the Monies received. | *Philadelphia :* | *Printed by F. Bailey, at Yorick's Head, in Market-Street.* | M,DCC,LXXXIV. | 8vo. pp. 8.   H. S. P.   4580

𝕿𝕬𝕲𝕰𝕭𝖀𝕮𝕳 | des | Raths | der | Censoren, | Versammlet zu Phila= delphia, | Am Montage, den Zehnten November, Ein Tausend Sieben Hundert | und Drey und Achtzig. | Aus dem Englischen übersetzt. | *Philadelphia :* | *Gedruckt bey Melchior Steiner, in der Rees-strasse, nahe bey der Dritten-strasse.* 1784. | Folio, pp. 147.   4581

THOUGHTS on Taxation, in a Letter to a Friend. With Observations on the consequences resulting from the proposed plan, humbly addressed to the good people of the State of New York. *Philadelphia :* 1784.   4582

TO the | Citizens of Pennsylvania. | [*Philadelphia :*] *Printed by Hall and Sellers.* [1784.] | Folio, 1 leaf.   H. S. P.   4583

> In regard to the withdrawal from the Assembly of nineteen members on the third reading of a supplement to the Test-law, "Signed, in behalf and by order of the Majority, George Gray, Speaker." And dated "Assembly Chamber, September 29, 1784."

TO the Freemen of Pennsylvania. | [*Philadelphia: Hall and Sellers.* 1784.] Folio, pp. 12. H. S. P. 4584

Reasons for dissent of a minority of the Council of Censors on a resolution to print the report of a committee appointed to investigate the conduct of the Legislature.

. . . | . . . | . . . . | TO the | General Assembly of Pennsylvania. | The | Representation | of | A Number of the Citizens of Philadelphia, Members of the | Religious Society of the People called Quakers. | [*Philadelphia:* 1784.] Folio, pp. 2. L. C. P. 4585

Against the repeal of the Law against theatrical performances, dated " 1st mo. 31st, 1784."

TO the real Patriots and Supporters of American | Independence. | [*Philadelphia:* 1784.] Sm. 4to. 1 leaf. L. C. P. 4586

Dated " Philadelphia, June 28, 1784.' " " An Independent Patriot," on the surrender of Chevalier Longchamp to the Court of France.

THE UNITED States Journal or the Continental Advertiser. *Philadelphia:?* 1784. 4587

Announced in July, 1784, as to be published on Mondays, after a sufficient number of subscribers' names had been received by the projector, Andrew Brown, with whom were associated Boinod and Gaillard and Charles Cist.

THE UNIVERSAL FRIENDS' Advice. *Philadelphia: Francis Bailey.* 1784. 4588

WEATHERWISE. (A.) Father Abraham's Almanack for 1785. By Abraham Weatherwise. *Philadelphia: John Dunlap.* 1784. 4589

[WEDDERBURN. (—)] Inkle & Yarico, | an | Opera, | as performed with great applause, | At the Theatre Royal,—London. | *Philadelphia:* | *Printed and Sold at E. Story's office, in Fourth-* | *Street, nearly opposite the Indian Queen Tavern.* [1784.] | Sm. 8vo. pp. 66. 4590

[WHARTON. (Charles Henry)] A | Letter | to the | Roman Catholics | of the | City of Worcester, | from the | Late Chaplain of that Society. | Stating the Motives which induced him to re- | linquish their Commu- | nion, and become a Member of the Prot- | estant Church. | . . . | . . . | . . . | . . . | . . . | . . . | . . . | . . . | . . . | . . . | . . . | . . . | . . . | . . . | . . . | . . . | . . . | . . . | . . . | . . . . | *Philadelphia:* | *Printed by Robert Aitken, at the Sign of Pope's Head in* | *Market Street, near the Coffee-House.* | M.DCC.LXXXIV. | 8vo. pp. 40.　　　　H. S. P.　4591

At the end, "Entered according to Act of Assembly." This is the earliest example of copyright in America I have met with.

WINCHESTER. (E.)　The | Divinity of Christ, | Proved from the | Scriptures | of the | Old and New Testament. | In several | Letters to a Friend. | By Elhanan Winchester. | . . . . | [*Philadelphia: B. Towne.　1784.*] | 8vo. pp. 39.　　　　H. S. P.　4592

𝖣𝖨𝖤 𝖂𝖀𝖭𝖣𝖤𝖱𝖡𝖠𝖱𝖤 Geſchichte von Ambroſe Gwinnett. Aus dem Engliſchen. *Philadelphia: Charles Cist.　1784.*　　　　4593

THE | YOUNG Man's | Magazine, | containing | the substance of | Moral Philosophy, | and | Divinity : | Selected from the works of the most | eminent for Wisdom, Learning, | and Virtue, among the | Ancients and Moderns. | . . . | . . . | . . . | . . . | . . . | . . . | . . . . | *Philadelphia:* | *Printed by Enoch Story, in Strawberry-* | *Alley, about mid-way.*　M,DCC,LXXXIV. | 12mo. pp. 35.　4594

ADDENDA.

1696.

DER APOSTOLISCHE Kirchen = Engel. *Philadelphia:* [*Germany.*] 1696. 4595

This and the four following titles, as well as several others marked w., are from Weller's *Falschen Druckorte.*

1700.

[DIPPEL. (J. C.)] Wein und Oel in die Wunden des gestäupten Pabstthums der Protestirenden. *Philadelphia, durch Nicodemum Pamphilum.* [*Bielcke in Jena.*] 1700. w. 4596

1703.

DER durch die gottlose Verführer und Babels=Pfaffen 2c. in göttlichen Eifer entbrannte Christliche. *Philadelphia:* [*Germany.*] 1703. 4597

KURTZE Erörterung, worinnen der Verfall des sogenannten heutigen Christenthums meistentheils bestehe. *Philadelphia:* [*Germany.*] 1703. w. 4598

1707.

GEDANKEN eines christlich=gesinnten Layen von der Vereinigung der protestantischen und reformirten Kirchen. *Philadelphia:* [*Germany.*] 1707. w. 4599

1718.

AN ACT | Passed in a | General Assembly | of the | Province of Pennsilvania, | Begun at Philadelphia the Fourteenth Day of Octber | and continued by Adjournments till the twenty-second | of February, in the Fourth Year of His Majesties Reign | Annoq; Domini 1717. | [*Royal Arms.*] | *Philadelphia;* | *Printed and Sold by Andrew Bradford at the Sign of the* | *Bible, in the Second Street.* | MDCCXVIII. | Folio, pp. 6. H. S. P. 4600

GUELDIN. (S.) Kurze Apologie der unschuldig verdächtig gemachten Pietisten zu Bern. Von Samuel Güldin. *Philadelphia:* 1718. w. 4601

1721.

NEW JERSEY. Speeches and Addresses during the sitting of the Assembly, begun at Burlington, the 28th day of February 1721, with the Acts and Laws of that Session. [*Philadelphia:*] *Printed by Andrew Bradford.* 1721. Folio, pp. 32. 4602

1725.

EDWARD HORNE'S Letter to Jo- | seph England, concerning James | Steel and Thomas Shute. | [*Philadelphia: Andrew Bradford.* 1725.] Folio, pp. 4. H. S. P. 4603

1729.

GESPRÄCH im Reiche der Geistlich-Todten und Geistlich-Lebendigen. *Philadelphia:* [*Germany?*] 1729. w. 4604

A | JOURNAL | of the | Votes and Proceedings | of the | House of Representatives | of the | Province of Pennsylvania. | Anno Domini, 1728. | [*Philadelphia: Andrew Bradford.* 1729.] Folio, pp. 60. H. S. P. 4605

Issued at four different times; the first three parts have the imprint at the end of each.

WEISS. (G. M.) Der In Der Americanischen Wildnusz, &c. Von Georg M. Weiss, Prediger. *Philadelphia: Gedruckt bey Andrew Bradfordt.* 1729. 12mo. pp. 29. 4606

Title from the Catalogue of Dr. W. Kent Gilbert's sale of Feb., 1873, lot 1494.

1730.

[DIPPEL. (J. C.)] Geistliche | Fama, | mitbringend | verschiedene | Nachrichten | und | Geschichte | von | göttlichen Erweckungen und Füh= | rungen, Wercken, Wegen | und Gerichten, | allgemeinen und besonderen Begebenheiten, | die zum Reich Gottes gehören. | Erstes Stück | . . . . | *Gesammlet und gedruckt* | *in Philadelphia* [*Buedingen*] | 1730. | 16mo. pp. 80. H. S. P. 4607

1731.

[DIPPEL. (J. C.)] Geistliche | Fama, | . . . | . . . | . . . | . . . | . . . | . . . | . . . | . . . . | Zweytes Stück. | . . . . | *Gesammlet und gedruckt* | *in Philadelphia* [*Buedingen.*] 1731. | 16mo. pp. 112. + Drittes Stück. [*Ibid.*] pp. 112. + Viertes Stück. [*Ibid.*] pp. 96. + Fünfftes Stück. [*Ibid.*] 1731. pp. 120. H. S. P. + Sechtes Stück. [*Ibid.*] 1732. 4608

THE VOTES, &c. of the House of Representatives of Pennsylvania. Oct. 14, 1730, to Sept. — 1731. *Philadelphia: B. Franklin and H. Meredith.* 1731. Folio, pp. 80. H. S. P. 4609

VOTES | and | Proceedings | of the | House of Representatives | of the | Province of Pennsylvania, | Met at Philadelphia, on Thursday the Fourteenth of | October, Anno Dom. 1731, and continued by adjournments. | [*Penn Arms.*] | *Philadelphia:* | *Printed and Sold by B. Franklin, at the New Printing-* | *Office near the Market.* M,DCC,XXXI. | Folio, pp. 36. H. S. P. 4610

1732.

VOTES | and | Proceedings | of the | House of Representatives | of the | Province of Pennsylvania, | Met at Philadelphia, on Saturday the Fourteenth of | October, Anno Dom. 1732, and continued by Adjournments. | [*Penn Arms.*] | *Philadelphia:* | *Printed and Sold by B. Franklin, at the New Printing-* | *Office near the Market.* M,DCC,XXXII. | Folio, pp. 14 +. H. S. P. 4611

1734.

VOTES | and | Proceedings | of the | House of Representatives | of the | Province of Pennsylvania, | Met at Philadelphia, on the Fourteenth of October | Anno Dom. 1734, and continued by Adjournments. | [*Penn Arms.*] | *Philadelphia:* | *Printed and Sold by B. Franklin, at the New Printing-* | *Office near the Market.* M,DCCXXXIIII. | Folio, pp. 30 +. H. S. P. 4612

1738.

PADLIN. (Benjamin.) Eine | Ernstliche Ermahnung, | An Junge und Alte: | Zu einer | Angeheuchelten Prüfung | Ihres Hertzens und

Zuſtandes. | Kurtzlich aus Engeland nach Amerika geſandt, und wegen seiner Wichtigkeit | Aus dem Engliſchen ins Deutſche treulich überſetzt; Von einem Liebhaber der Wahrheit. | *Germanton Gedruckt und zu finden bey Christoph Sauer.* 1738. | Folio, 1 leaf.   H. S. P.   4613

1740.

GEWJSSENHAFFTE Vorſtellung | Vom Mangel rechter | Kinder= Zucht, | Und zugleich | Wie ſolche zuverbeßern wäre, | Freunden und Feinden zum Nachdencken. | Aus gedrungenem Gemüthe dargeleget, | Und als eine Beylage zu der Sermon, von | der Haus=Religion dienlich. | . . . | . . . | . . . | . . . | . . . . | [*Germantown:*] *Gedruckt* [*bey Christoph Saur,*] *im Jahr* 1740. | 16mo. pp. 32.   H. S. P.   4614

MY dear | Fellow-Traveller, | Here hast Thou | A Letter, | Which | I have wrote to Thee out of the Fulness | of my Heart | And | With many Tears | For Thy Salvation's sake ; | And | The Lamb of God | Hath sprinkled it with His Blood, | That it will be profitable for Thee, | If Thou abidest by thy Heart. | Or now findest thy Heart. | [*Philadelphia: B. Franklin.* 1740 ?] Sm. 12mo. pp. 23.   H. S. P.   4615

1741.

LAW. (W.) Die | Gründe und Urſachen | Der Chriſtlichen | Wieder= geburth, | Oder | Die Neue=Geburth | Durch Chriſtum, | Dargelegt zu einer Betrachtung vor | alle Bekenner Chriſti und Gottes. | Von | William Law. | Aus dem Engliſchen ins Deutſche überſetzt. | *Germanton:* | *Gedruckt bey Christoph Saur,* 1741. | 16mo. Title, 1 leaf; Einleitung, pp. (2) ; text, pp. 95.   4616

1742.

BECHTEL. (J.) Kurtzer | Catechismus | Vor etliche | Gemeinen Jeſu | Aus der Reformirten Religion | Jn | Pennsylvania, | Die ſich zum alten Berner Synodo | halten : | Herausgegeben | von | Johannes Bechteln, | Dienern des Worts Gottes. | *Philadelphia,* | *Gedruckt bey Benjamin Franklin,* | 1742. | 24mo. pp. 44.   H. S. P.   4617

     This edition of Bechtel's Catechism was printed in Germany.

BECHTEL. A Short | Catechism | for some | Congregations of Jesus | Of the | Reformed Religion | In Pennsylvania, | Who keep to the ancient Synod of Bern; | Agreeable to | The Doctrine | Of the | Moravian Church. | First published | In German, | By John Bechtel, | Minister of the Word of God. | *Philadelphia:* | *Printed by Isaiah Warner, almost opposite* | *to Charles Brockden's in Chesnut-* | *Street.* MDCCXLII. | Sm. 12mo. pp. 36.   4618

CREAGHEAD. (A.) A | Discourse | concerning the | Covenants: | Containing | The Substance of Two Sermons, | preached at Middle-Octarara, | January 10 and 17. 1741, 2. | Upon Joshua IX. 15. | By Alexander Creaghead. | [4 lines.] *Philadelphia:* | *Printed by B. Franklin for the Author.* 1742. | 8vo. pp. 48.   4619

[ZINZENDORFF. (Nikolaus Ludwig von)] Oratio. [*Philadelphia: B. Franklin.* 1742.] Sm. Folio, pp. 4.   H. S. P. 4620

An address presented to Gov. Thomas by Zinzendorff on his arrival in Pennsylvania.

1745.

[ECKELIN. (Israel)] DJE RJCHTSCHNUR und Regel | eines Streiters Jesu Christi, | welcher in die ewige Schätze | der Weißheit verliebet ist. | *Ephrata. Anno.* MDCCXLV. | Folio, 1 leaf.   4621

This is the same as No. 926, *supra.*

1746.

ADVERTISEMENT. | [*Philadelphia: B. Franklin.* 1746.] 4to. 1 leaf.   H. S. P. 4622

Geo. Harrison's " Marble Shop, at the Sign of the Mason's Arms." Dated "July 14."

1748.

[BURGH. (James)] Britain's | Remembrancer. | Being | Some Thoughts on the proper | Improvement of the present | Juncture. | The Character of this Age and | Nation. | A brief Viow from History, of | the Effects of the Vices which | now prevail in Britain, upon | the greatest Empires and States | of former Times. | Remarkable Deliverances this | Nation has had in the most | imminent Dangers; with sui- | table Reflections. | Some Hints, shewing, what is | in the Power of the several | Ranks of People, and of every | Individual in Britain, to do | to-ward securing the State | from all its Enemies. | The Seventh Edition. | *London: Printed.* | *Philadelphia: Re-printed by Godhard* | *Armbrister for B[enjamin]. L[ay]. and are to be sold by him,* | *and the Printer hereof,* 1748. | Sm. 8vo. pp. 47.   L. C. P.   4623

𝕷𝕰𝕿𝕵𝕿𝕰 Zugabe zum flüchtigen Pater.   *Philadelphia:* [*Blochberg in Leipzig.*] 1748.   w.   4624

𝖁𝕰𝕽𝕳𝕬𝕹𝕯𝕷𝖀𝕹𝕲𝕰𝕹 des Coetus von Pennsylvanien.   *Philadelphia:* 1748.   4625

Title furnished by the Rev. Jos. Henry Dubbs, D.D., of Lancaster.

1749.

LUTHER. (M.) The Small Catechism of Dr. Martin Luther. *Philadelphia: B. Franklin and J. Boehm.* 1749.   4626

I am indebted to the Rev. B. M. Schmucker, of Pottstown, for this and several other similar titles.

1751.

TO the | Quarterly and Monthly Meetings of | Friends in Great Britain, Ireland, | and America. | [*Philadelphia:* 1751.] Sm. 8vo. pp. 8.   F.   4627

The report of a committee of the Yearly Meeting, on the Act of Parliament for regulating the Calendar, with a four-page testimony from the London Meeting for Sufferings against the "Heathenish" names of the days and months.

1754.

DAVENPORT. (J.) The Faithful Minister Encouraged. A Sermon. By the Rev. James Davenport. *Philadelphia: James Chattin.* 1754.   4628

Webster's History of the Presbyterian Church, p. 542.

𝕻𝕬𝕽𝕬𝕯𝕵𝕾𝕵𝕾𝕮𝕳𝕰𝕾 | Wunder-Spiel, | Welches sich | In diesen letzten Zeiten und Tagen | In denen Abend-Ländischen Welt-Theilen als ein Vor- | spiel der neuen Welt hervor gethan. Bestehende | In einer gantz neuen und ungemeinen Sing- | Art auf Weise der Englischen und himm- | lischen Chören eingerichtet. | Da dann das Lied Mosis und des Lamms, wie auch das hohe Lied Salomo- | nis samt noch mehrern Zeugnüssen aus der Bibel und andern Heiligen | in liebliche Melodyen gebracht.

Wobey nicht weniger der Zuruf der | Braut des Lamms, sammt der Zu=
bereitung auf den herrlichen | Hochzeit=Tag trefflich Præfigurirt wird. |
Alles nach Englischen Chören Gesangs=Weise mit viel Mühe und grosem
Fleiß ausgefertiget von einem | Friedsamen, | Der sonst in dieser Welt
weder Namen noch Titul suchet. | [Cut.] | *Ephratæ Sumptibus Societatis :*
| 1754. | Folio, Title, 1 page; Chor-Gesaenge, pp. 1–212; Regis-
ter, 1 page. 4629

> The only copy I have met with of this volume, once the property of Sister Barbara,
> of the Ephrata community, is one of the most remarkable specimens of Pennsylvania
> bookmaking. The text begins on the reverse of the title. The page, not quite 14
> inches in length, contains usually six lines of type, besides the heading, every two
> lines being divided by spaces of three inches, which are filled with manuscript music
> for four voices. The end of each musical phrase is marked by more or less elaborate
> penwork in two or three colors, amounting occasionally to an illumination, generally
> in the shape of a floral design.

1756.

OATH to be administered to all such Persons as enter into the
King's Service, in the Pay of the Government of Pennsylvania.
[n. p. about 1756.] 4to. 1 leaf. 4630

1757.

DILWORTH. (T.) A New Guide to the English Tongue. By
Thomas Dilworth. *Philadelphia :* 1757. 4631

TO the Freeholders of the County of | Philadelphia. | [*Philadel-
phia : B. Franklin, and D. Hall.* 1757.] Folio, pp. (2). 4632

> An election address.

1758.

[DAVYS. (P.)] Adminiculum Puerile : | Or, an Help for |
School-Boys. | Containing | I. Fundamental Exercises for Young
Beginners. | II. English Examples fitted to the Syntax-Rules of
the | Lord Bishop of Cork's Grammar, with some | Annotations.
| III. Some necessary Cautions to prevent Mistakes which | Boys
are generally guilty of in making Latin. | IV. English for Latin
Verses. | V. Some Examples of Themes in English, with larger
| Discourses on Subjects. | VI. Three Indexes : The first con-
taining all the Words | in the Fundamental Exercises : The second,

those | under the Syntax-Rules and Cautions : And the third | those in the Verses with Latin for them. | To which is subjoined | 1st, The Syntax Rules. 2d, A Prosody. And 3d, All | the short Examples of Clark's Introduction. | . . . | . . . . | *Dublin printed : | Philadelphia Re-printed by W. Dunlap, | for the Use of the College and Academy there.* | 1758. | 16mo. pp. (10), 119, (47), 17. 4633

FRANCKEL. (D. H.) Eine | Danck=Predigt | wegen des wichtigen und wundervollen | Siegs, | welchen | Sr. Königl. Maj. in Preussen | am 5ten December, 1757. | über die, der Anzahl nach ihm weit überlege= | ne, gesamte | Oesterreichische Armee in | Schlesien, | preißwürdig erfoch= ten. | gehalten | am Sabbath den 10ten desselben Monats | in der Juden Schule zu Berlin | von | David Hirschel Fränckel, | Ober Rabbi. | *Philadelphia, Gedruckt und zu haben das Stueck fuer 6 Pentz | bey Anton Armbruester.* [1758.] | 8vo. pp. 16. H. S. P. 4634

1759.

DES | KINDER = Büch= | leins | Tom vii. | d. i. | Ein Versuch zu einem | Losungs=Büchel aus | der Bibel für Sie | Aufs Jahr 1758. | *Barby | Gedruckt im Jahr* 1758. | *Zum andern mahl gedruckt zu Philadelphia.* [1759 ?] | Sm. 16mo. Title, 1 leaf; Preface, pp. (4); Losungs, pp. (117). H. S. P. 4635

TRAITÉ et Convention | pour les | Malades, Blessés et Pri- sonniers de Guerre des Troupes de Terre, | de Sa Majesté très Chrétienne, et de Sa Majesté | Britannique. | A | Treaty and Con- vention | for the | Sick, Wounded, and Prisoners of War, of the Land Forces, | of His Majesty the King of | Great Britain | and of | His Most Christian Majesty. | *Philadelphia : | Printed by W. Dunlap, at the Newest-Printing-Office | on the South Side of the Jersey Market.* 1759. | 8vo. pp. 24 ? 4636

UNTERSUCHUNG ob etwa die heutigen europäischen Völker Lust haben möchten dereinst Menschenfresser oder wenigstens Hottentotten zu werden. *Philadelphia : [Schwerin.]* 1759. w. 4637

1760.

ABHANDLUNG von der Unverletzlichkeit der Waffen= und Kriegs= verträge. *Philadelphia : [Schwerin.]* 1760. w. 4638

ERSKINE. (R.) Gospel Sonnets; | or, | Spiritual Songs. | In Six Parts. | I. The Believer's Espousals. | II. The Believer's Joint-ure. | III. The Believer's Riddle. | IV. The Believer's Lodging. | V. The Believer's Soliloquy. | VI. The Believer's Principles. | Concerning | Creation and Redemption, | Law and Gospel, | Justi-fication and Sanctification, | Faith and Sense, | Heaven and Earth. | The Ninth Edition. | In which the Holy Scriptures are extended. Not to be | found in any former Edition. | By the late Reverend Mr. Ralph Erskine, | Minister of the Gospel at Dumfermline. | *Edinburgh: Printed.* | *Philadelphia: Re-printed by W. Dunlap, at the* | *Newest-Printing-Office in Market-Street, for G. Noel,* | *Book-seller in New-York,* M,DCC,LX. | 12mo, pp. 1–22, 1–363. H. S. P. 4639

LEYDT. (J.) *ΑΔΠΟΕΛΕΥΘΕΡΙΑ ΕΙΣ ΕΙΡΠΝΠΝ* | i.e. | Ware Vryheyt tot Vrede | ofte | Berigt, | Hoe | Onderhandeling, Vrede | en Vereniging Zoekende | gepasseerd is: | en Wat den Ge-lukkigen Urtslag | gestremd heeft | mitsgaders. | Een Verde-diging | van het | Examineren en Promoveren | door de Cœtus verrigt: | De Gronden aanwyzende waarap het gedaan is. | Door Johannes Leydt, | Predicant te Nieuw Brunswyck, &c. | . . . | . . . | . . . | . . . | . . . | . . . | . . . | . . . | . . . | . . . . | *Te Philadelphia.* | *By Hendrik Miller; in de Tweede-straat;* | *in 't tweede Huys van de Rees-straat;* 1760. | 4640

1761.

ADVERTISEMENT. | [*Philadelphia:* 1761.] 4to. 1 leaf. 4641

Dated "Phila., Jan. 29, 1761," and signed "Richard Peters and Richard Hock-ley." "All persons settled in the Proprietaries' Manor of Springton are to take notice that their plantations will be exposed at public vendue unless they come and agree with us, the Proprietaries' Agents, before May next."

LUTHER. (M.) The Small Catechism of Dr. Martin Luther. *Philadelphia: Henry Miller.* 1761. 4642

WEATHERWISE. (A.) Mr. Weatherwise's | Pocket-Alma-nac, | (On an entire New Plan.) | For 1762. | Being the Second after Bissextile, | or Leap-Year. | Containing, | The Sun's Rising and Setting; the Ri- | sing, Setting and Southing of the | Planets; the Lunations, Conjuncti- | ons, Eclipses, Judgment of the | Weather; remarkable Days; High | Water at Philadelphia;

Quakers | Yearly Meetings, Fairs, Courts, | Roads, a Table of the Value and | Weight of Coins, &c. | By A. Weatherwise, Gent. | *Printed and sold by W. Dunlap,* | *at the Newest Printing-Office, on* | *the South Side of the Jersey-Mar-* | *ket, Philadelphia.* [1761.] | 24mo. pp. (24). H. S. P. 4643

1762.

EINE | NÜTZLICHE | Anweisung | Oder Beyhülffe | Vor die Teutschen | Um | Englisch zu lernen: | Wie es vor neu-Ankommende und andere | im Land gebohrne Land- und Handwercks-Leute, | welche in der Englischen Sprache erfahrene und | geübte Schulmeister und Pre- ceptores erman- | gelen, vor das bequemfte erachtet worden; | mit ihrer gewöhnlichen Arbeit und | Werckzeug erläutert. | Nebst einer | Grammatic, | Vor diejenigen, | Welche in andern Sprachen und deren | Fundamenten erfahren sind. | *Germanton.* | *Gedruckt und zu finden bey* *Christoph Saur,* 1762. | Sm. 8vo. pp. (4), 287, (4). H. S. P. 4644

CATECHISMUS, | Oder | Kurtzer Unterricht | Christlicher Lehre, | Wie derselbe in denen | Reformirten Kirchen und Schulen | Der | Chur- Fürstlicher Pfaltz, | Auch anderwerts, getrieben wird. | Mit Zeugnissen der heiliger Schrift | erklärt und bestätigt. | Nach vorhergegangener Col- lation mit den alten | Exemplarien. | *Philadelphia.* | *Gedruckt bey Peter* *Miller und Comp.* | M,D,CC,LXII. | 16mo. Title, 1 leaf; Prelim- inary Matter, pp. 1–14; text, pp. 1–344. 4645

LEYDT. (J.) Ware | Vryheyt | tot | Vrede, | Verdedigd | Tegen de zo genoemde | Kortbondige Wederlegginge | der voor- gevende | Liefhebbers van Waarheyt en Vrede; aanwyzende | Dat zy de Tsamen voeginze van Waarheyt en Vrede | niet gelukkig ge- troffen, nog de Coetus Verga- | deringe, nog derzelver Authoriteyt om te Exa- | mineren en Promoveren gelijt hebben. | Door | Jo- hannes Leydt, | Predicant te Nieuw Brunswyk, &c. | . . . | . . . | . . . | . . . | . . . . | *Te Philadelphia.* | *Gedrukt by Hendrik Miller,* *in de Twede Straat.* | MDCCLXII. | 4646

1763.

THE | CHRISTIAN'S Duty, | To | Render to Cæsar the Things that are Cæsar's, | Considered; | With Regard to the Pay- ment of the present | Tax of Sixty Thousand Pounds granted to

| the King's Use. | In which all the Arguments for the Non-pay- | ment thereof are examined and refuted : | Addressed to the Scrupulous among the People | called Quakers. | By a Lover of his King and Country. | *Philadelphia, Printed ; Parthenopolis :* [*Ephrata :*] | *Re-printed by J. George. Zeisiger,* | MDCCLXIII. | 16mo. pp. 28. H. 4647

DER | EHRLICHE Kurtzweilige Deutsche ; | Americanische | Ge= schichts und Haus | Calender, | Auf das Jahr | Nach der Gnadenreichen Geburt unsers | Herrn und Heylandes Jesu Christi | 1764. | (welches ein Schalt=Jahr von 366 Tagen ist) | Darinnen | Ordentlich angezeiget werden die Wochen Tage, | der Tag des | Monats, der Sontags Buch= staben, samt den Evangelien, die Neue und Alte Zeit des | Monds Viertel, der Planeten Lauf, und muthmasliche Witterung, der Sonnen Auf= und Unter= | gang, der Venus (des Morgen= und Abend=Sterns) Auf= und Untergang des Monds | Zeichen und Grad, dessen Auf= und Untergang, des 7* Gestirns Aufgang, Süd Platz und | Untergang, Erklärung der Zeichen, Anzeigung der Finsternüssen, Aber=lass Taffel, Cour= | ten. Jahrmärckte oder Fären, Auflaufung der Fluth (oder Teide in Phi= | ladelphia ꝛc.) Nebst einige Historie von Listigen Welt=händel. | Einge= richtet auf den 40ten Grad Norder= | Breite, sonderlich | Vor Pennsyl= vanien, doch auch in den angränzenden Landen ohne sonderlichen | Un= terscheid zu gebrauchen. | Zum Ehrstenmal heraus gegeben. | *T-Schesnuet-Huell : Gedruckt und zu haben bey N. Hasselbach.* | *Auch sind solche zu heben bey G. Christoph Reinhold, Buchbinder, in Philadelphia in* | *der Second-strasse, und bey A. Armbruester und bey den auswaertigen Kraemern.* | Sm. 4to. pp. (40). 4648

A | HYMN-BOOK | for the | Children | Belonging to the Brethren's | Congregations. | Taken chiefly out of the German | Little Book. | In three Books. | . . . . | *Philadelphia,* | *Printed* [*by Henry Miller*] *in the Year* MDCCLXIII. | 12mo. Title, 1 leaf; Preface, pp. i–xxx ; text (of the first book), 1–64. H. S. P. 4649

DER | LEHR = TEXTE | der | Brüder=Gemeine | und insonderheit | der | Kinder | Aus den Briefen Pauli | an die Gemeinen | aus den Heiden | Zweyte Auflage, | zum Gebrauch | des Jahrs | 1764. | . . . | . . . . | *Gedruckt zu Philadelphia* [*bey Henrich Miller*], 1763. | 8vo. pp. (48). H. S. P. 4650

𝕯𝕴𝕰 | 𝕿𝕬𝕲𝕷𝕴𝕮𝕳𝕰𝕹 | Looſungen | der | Brüder=Gemeine | für das Jahr | 1764. | *Gedruckt zu Philadelphia [bey Henrich Miller]*, 1763. | 8vo. pp. (46); Register, pp. (9).   H. S. P.   4651

A | WORD in season | To all protestants of all denominations throughout Great Britain, | Ireland, and America; | Or | Genuine christianity and popish bigotry always the | same. | As exemplified in the late martyrdom and conduct of the Reverend | Mr. Rochette, and three Noblemen, who were executed with | him at Thoulouse in France, Feb. 19. 1762, on account of | their attachment to the protestant religion. | In | A letter, written the day after, by a Person who was an eye-witness | of the bloody transaction. | . . . | . . . | . . . | . . . | . . . . | *London printed, Philadelphia Reprinted* | *by Anthony Armbruster, in Race-street.*   [1763.] | Sm. 8vo.   Title, 1 leaf; pp. 2–7.   H. S. P.   4652

1764.

Eine luſtige | 𝕬𝕽𝕴𝕬, | über die letztgeſchehene Unruhen in Philadelphia. | [*Philadelphia: Henrich Miller.*   1764.]   4to. 1 leaf.   4653

BARKLY. (Gilbert) A Representation to the Public, of Affaires between Gilbert Barkly of Philadelphia, and John Hay of Quebec. *Philadelphia:* 1764.   4654

HAY. (John) Answers | to a | Printed Libel, | entitled | " A Representation to the Public, of Affaires | " between Gilbert Barkly of Philadelphia, and John | " Hay of Quebec." | [*Philadelphia: ?* 1764.]   Folio, pp. (4).   H. S. P.   4655

Dated "Quebec, 22d October, 1764." Probably printed and circulated in Philadelphia.

Ein ſchön weltlich | 𝕷𝕴𝕰𝕯. | [*Philadelphia: Anton Armbruester.* 1764.]   Folio, 1 leaf.   H. S. P.   4656

1765.

HILLIARD | Magna. | Being the Life and Adventures | of | Moll Placket-Hole. | With a prefatory Dialogue, and some moral | Reflections, on the Whole. | . . . | . . . | . . . | . . . . | [*Philadelphia:*] *Printed [by Anthony Armbruster] in the Year* 1765. | 8vo. pp. 7.   H. S. P.   4657

DES | HERUMTRÄGERS des Staatsboten | Neujahrs = Verse, | seinen resp. | Geehrten Kundleuten | überreicht | der 1ten Jenner, 1765. | [*Philadelphia: Henrich Miller.* 1765.] Folio, 1 leaf. H. S. P. 4658

[Cut.] A | NEW Song. | About Miss Ketty, leaving the Country to the Tune | Derry down, down, down, Derry down. | [*Philadelphia: Anthony Armbruster.* 1765.] Narrow folio, 1 leaf. 4659

THIS | POEM, | Humbly dedicated to Sir Q— C—o. at his Study over a | Pot of Charcole. | [*Philadelphia: Anthony Armbruster.* 1765.] Folio, 1 leaf. H. S. P. 4660

A lampoon on Isaac Hunt.

A | PROPHECY, | or a | Warning to all Sinners. | [*Philadelphia: Anthony Armbruster.* 1765.] Sm. Folio, 1 leaf. H. S. P. 4661

A | WO and A Warning, | or | The three cruel Mothers. | Chap. II. | [*Philadelphia: Anthony Armbruster.* 1765.] Narrow folio, 1 leaf. H. S. P. 4662

1766.

GOOD News for America. | To the Sons of Liberty. | [*Philadelphia: Anthony Armbruster.* 1766.] Folio, 1 leaf. H. S. P. 4663

On the repeal of the Stamp Act.

JOYFUL News for America, | And the downfall of the Stamp-Act; | [*Philadelphia:* 1766.] Narrow folio, 1 leaf. H. S. P. 4664

The Historical Society of Pennsylvania has two copies of this song, at the end of one of which is: "Composed by Thomas Plant, Poet from London."

1767.

Die | ins Wasser gefallene | HOLTZ=FÄLLENDE AXT, | als | der Geist der Gnaden oder Selbst | Verlangnung und des Gebäts, | welche der | Prophetische=Geist Elisa | wieder schwimmend machet | mit | einem abgeschnittenen Stecken der neueren | und beweglischen | Aufrührungen | zur Aufraffung | wieder aufs neue in Walde so mancher | schönen Zeugnissen das geistliche | Bauholz nach Northdurft | zu fällen | um eine | göttliche Wohnung in seliger | Abgeschiedenkeit auffertigen zu lassen. | *gedruckt* 1767. | 16mo. 4665

Collation: Die Holtz-fällende Axt, pp. 56; Vergleichlicher Beschluss zum Geistl. Liebes-Zwang, pp. 57–87; Chamberlain's Errinnerung an die Englische Nation, pp. 88–114; and Die alles selig neu und herrlich nachrende Stimme Gottes, pp 115–124. The Rev. Joseph Henry Dubbs, D.D., of Lancaster, to whom I am indebted for this title, says, "The place of publication is not mentioned, but it is evidently American."

MATHER. (C.) The Everlasting Gospel. The Gospel of Justification by the Righteousness of God, as it is held and preached in the Churches of New England. Expressed in a brief Discourse on that important Article; made at Boston in the Year 1699. By Cotton Mather. The Second Edition. *Philadelphia:* 1767. 18mo.

Title from Sabin's Dictionary, 46,310.

𝕯𝖎𝖊 | 𝕿𝖆𝖌𝖑𝖎𝖈𝖍𝖊𝖓 | Loosungen | der | Brüder = Gemeine | für das Jahr | 1768. | *Philadelphia, Gedruckt* [*bey Henrich Miller*] *im Jahr 1767.* | 16mo. Title, 1 leaf; pp. (42). H. S. P. 4667

1769.

[GILBERT. (Benjamin.)] A Discourse shewing that there can be no Salvation to the Soul who doth not know a Being made perfect in this Life. *Philadelphia: John Dunlap.* 1769. 4668

1770.

ADVERTISEMENT. *Philadelphia:* 1770. 4669

In doggerel verse, by Louis Fay, perruquier, etc., dated "Nov. 1770." Sabin, No. 23,941.

ARTICLES | Agreed upon by those Members of the Unitas | Fratrum whose Names are hereunto subscribed, | making Provision for the Support of their | Widows. | [*Philadelphia: Henry Miller.* 1770.] Folio, pp. 8. H. S. P. 4670

In English and German in parallel columns.

1771.

' AN | EPISTLE | from our | Yearly-Meeting, | Held in London, by Adjournments, | from the 20th of the Fifth Month, 1771, | to the 25th of the same, inclusive. | [*Philadelphia:* 1771.] Folio, pp. 3. L. C. P. 4671

RULES | of the | Brotherly Association | for the | Support of

Widows. | [*Philadelphia : Henry Miller.* 1771 ?] 8vo. Half title, 1 leaf; pp. 8, 2.   H. S. P.   4672

> A reprint of the rules of an English Moravian charitable society.

1773.

[RUSH. (Benjamin)] An | Address | to | The Inhabitants | of the | British Settlements | in | America, | upon | Slave-Keeping. | *Philadelphia :* | *Printed by John Dunlap in Market-* | *street.* M.DCC.LXXIII. | 8vo. pp. (2), 30.   4673

SHEWEN. (W[illiam]) Counsel | to the | Christian-Traveller : | Also, | Meditations and Experiences | made public, | As a Testimony to the right Way of | God, revealed and made known in this the Day | of his glorious Appearing in his People ; that | they may be encouraged to walk therein to the | End thereof. | The Fifth Edition, Revis'd and Corrected. | To which is Added, | A Treatise concerning Thoughts and Imaginations, Good and | Evil ; also, a few Words concerning the Life of a Christian, | and Christian Worship. | By W. Shewen. | . . . | . . . | . . . . | *Dublin, Printed ; And,* | *Lancaster, Re-printed by Francis Bailey* | *for Caleb Johnson.* | MDCCLXXIII. | 8vo. pp. xv, 95.   H. S. P.   4674

1774.

AT a Meeting at the Philosophical Society's Hall on Friday, June 10th, and then by Adjournment on Satur- | day, of the Committee and a Number of respectable Inhabitants called in from all Societies in Town, to | devise, consult, and deliberate upon Propositions, to be laid before the General Meeting of the Inhabitants. | The following Propositions were unanimously agreed on. | [*Philadelphia :* 1774.] Folio, 1 leaf.   L. C. P.   4675

CHAMBERLAIN. (T.) Nachdrückliche | Buſs = Stimme | und Warnungs-Poſaune | von Himmel | an alle boßhafte Sünder auf Erden ; | Oder Thomas Chamberlain's | Letzte Leichen Rede | welche er nur einen Augenblick vor ſeinen | Ende, zur allgemeinen Erbauung, vor | einer voller Gemeine abgelegt. | Sammt : | Einer beſonderen Nachricht verſchiedener mer= | würdiger Dinge, welche ſeine Ehrwürder Kurz | von ſeinen Abſchied aus dieſer Welt in einem | Geſicht geſehen, deſſen eigentliche Auflöſung

| ihm ebenfalls gezeigt wurbe. | Zweite Auflage. | Aus bem Englischen ins Deutsche übersetzt. | *Germantown, gedruckt von Christoph Saur, jun.* 1774. | Sm. 8vo. pp. 22.   4676

I am indebted to the Rev. Jos. Henry Dubbs, D.D., of Lancaster, for this title.

[DODSLEY. (Robert)] The | Chronicle | of the | Kings of England, | from the Reign of | William the Conqueror, | First King of England, | down to | His present Majesty George III. | Containing a true History of their | Lives, and the Character which | they severally sustained, whe- | ther in Church or State, in | the Field, or in private | Life. | *Philadelphia:* | *Printed and sold by Robert Bell | and Benjamin Towne.* | MDCCLXXIV. | 12mo. pp. 119.   H. S. P.   4677

[KELLY. (Hugh)] The | School for Wives : | A | Comedy. | As it is performed at the | Theatre-Royal | in | Drury-Lane. | The Sixth Edition. | *Philadelphia:* | *Re-printed and Sold by John Dunlap,* | *in Market-street.* | MDCCLXXIV. | 16mo. pp. 101.   H. S. P.   4678

LUTHER. (M.)   Der kleine Catechismus des sel. Dr. Martin Luthers.   *Philadelphia: Henrich Miller.*   1774.   4679

1775.

COMMITTEE, | For the City of Philadelphia and Northern Liberties, to be and continue until the 16th | day of February A.D. 1776, and no longer. | [*Philadelphia: W. and T. Bradford,* 1775.] Folio, 1 leaf.   L. C. P.   4680

An election ticket.   There are several others of the same period in the DuSmitiere Broadsides belonging to the Library Company of Philadelphia.

PHILADELPHIA, June 7, 1775. | [*Philadelphia:* 1775.]   4to. 1 leaf.   L. C. P.   4681

Proceedings of the Philadelphia Committee concerning Capt. Torrance and Blair McClenaghan, who were suspected of importing and selling Irish linen.

1776.

DISCOURS de son Excellence Monsieur Jean Hancock, Président du Congres de Philadelphie. *A Philadelphie:* MDCCLXXVI. 8vo. pp. 32.   4682

" A rare and curious satirical brochure."   Sabin, No. 30,176.

FOSTER. (W.) True Fortitude delineated. | A | Sermon, | Preached at Fags Manor, | to | Captain Taylor's Company | of | Recruits, | on the | Lord's Day, February 18th, 1776, | (And now published by Request) | By the | Rev. William Foster, A.M. | . . . | . . . . | *Philadelphia:* | *Printed by John Dunlap, in Market-Street.* | M,DCC,LXXVI. | 8vo. pp. 24.   L. C. P.   4683

𝕯𝕴𝕰 𝕶𝕴𝕹𝕯𝕰𝕽 Bibel. *Germantown: Christoph Saur.* 1776. 24mo. pp. (24), 463, (21 +).   H. S. P.   4684

PHILADELPHIA, May 20. | [*Philadelphia:* 1776.] Folio, 1 leaf.   L. C. P.   4685

Proceedings of a public meeting in favor of Independence.

1777.

EXTRACT uit de Dag-Registers van het Noord-Amerikaansche Congres, Betrekkelyk tot het neemen en verbeurdverklaaren van Scheeps-Pryzen en het uitrusten van Kaapers; benerens de Ordonnantiën en Schikkingen der Zee-Vwot, ende Instructiën voor de Bevelhebbers der Particuliere Oorlogschepen. *Philadelphia:* 1777. 8vo. pp. 48.   4686

This title is No. 23,510 of Sabin's Dictionary, in which it also again appears as No. 55,429, with 1775 instead of 1777 as the date of publication. It is a translation of No. 3362, *supra.*

1779.

APOLOGIE des Franc-Maçons, par le Frère **** Membre de la Loge ** Ecossaise de P *. *A Philadelphie, l'an* 5651. [1779.] 12mo. pp. (8), 119.   4687

BRACKENRIDGE. (H. M.) Eine | Lobrede | auf diejenigen | tapfern Männer, | welche | in dem Streit | mit | Grofs-Brittannien | gefallen: | Gehalten am Montag den 5ten July, 1779. | Vor | einer zahlreichen und ansehnlichen Versammlung von | Bürgern und Ausländern, in der Deutschen | Reformirten Kirche zu Philadelphia. | Von Hugh M. Brackenridge, A.M. | . . . | . . . | . . . . | *Philadelphia,* | *Gedruckt bey Steiner und Cist, in der Zweyten-strasse,* | *zwischen der Rees- und Wein-strasse.* [1779.] | 16mo. pp. 24.   4688

1780.

L'AMÉRIQUIADE. Poème. *A Philadelphie.* [*Amsterdam ?*]
1780. 8vo. pp. 22. 4689

LETTERS | on | Appreciation. | [*Philadelphia : Thomas Brad-*
ford. 1780.] 8vo. pp. 20. H. S. P. 4690

1781.

L'AMÉRIQUAIN | aux Anglois, | ou | Observations | d'un
membre | des États Unis de l'Amérique, | à divers ministres d'An-
gleterre, | Traduit par M. D. B ✳ ✳ ✳. | *A Philadelphie.* [*Paris ?*]
M.DCC.LXXXI. | 8vo. Title, 1 leaf; Errata, 1 leaf; pp. 108.

[MAGAW. (Samuel)] A | Sermon, | Preached in Christ-
Church, Dover ; | before | the | General Communication | of |
Free and Accepted | Masons | of the | Delaware State : | On Wed-
nesday, December 27th, 1780. | Being the | Anniversary | of | St.
John the Evangelist. | *Philadelphia :* | *Printed by David C. Claypoole.*
| M.DCC.LXXXI. | 8vo. pp. 16. H. S. P. 4692

1782.

THE | EPISTLE | from the | Yearly-Meeting, | in | London,
| Held by Adjournments, from the 20th of the Fifth Month 1782,
| to the 25th of the same, inclusive. | To the Quarterly and
Monthly Meetings of Friends in Great- | Britain, Ireland, and
elsewhere. | [*Philadelphia :* 1782.] Folio, pp. 4. L. C. P. 4693

LUTHER. (M.) Der kleine Catechismus des sel. Dr. Martin
Luthers. *Philadelphia : Melchior Steiner.* 1782. 4694

SOUTH CAROLINA. Acts Passed at a General Assembly
Begun and Holden at Jacksonsburg, in the State of South Carolina, on the 8th of January, 1782, continued to the 26th day of
February of the same Year. *Philadelphia : Printed by John Dunlap.*
1782. Folio. 4695

1783.

[BENEZET. (Anthony)] Branntewein | und | Verderben. | [*Phila-*
delphia : Carl Cist. 1783.] 12mo. pp. 22. H. S. P. 4696

ESQUISSE | Intéressant | du Tableau fidele des causes qui ont occasioné | les révolutions actuelles de l'Amérique sep- | tentrionale, ornée d'Anecdotes historiques & | politiques sur la naissance de la République | des treize Provinces- | Unies de l'Amérique, | contre le Roi d'Angleterre, avec da démons- | tration des objets intéressants qui regardent | chaque état des Provinces-Unies, telle qu'elle | se trouve fixée par la traité fait à Versailles | entre les Puissances belligérantes & ses Al- | liés, le 20 Janvier, 1783. | Revu & corrigé à Versailles. | *A Philadelphie.* MDCCLXXXIII. | 8vo. pp. 124. 4697

For this, as well as numerous other titles in this volume, I am indebted to Mr. William C. Lane, of Harvard College Library.

PHILADELPHIA, August — 1783. | [*Philadelphia :* 1783.] Sm. Folio, 1 leaf. H. S. P. 4698

Circular Letter from the Whig Committee, on the election.

RECKETT, (W.) and J. GOUGH. Some | Account | of the | Life and Gospel Labours, | of | William Reckett, | Late of Lincolnshire in Great-Britain. | Also, | Memoirs | of the | Life, Religious Experiences, | and | Gospel Labours, | of | James Gough, | Late of Dublin, deceased. | *Philadelphia :* | *Printed and sold by Joseph Crukshank,* | *in Market-street, between Second* | *and Third-streets.* 1783. | 12mo. H. S. P. 4699

Collation : Title, 1 leaf; Life of Reckett, pp. 1–164 ; Memoirs of Gough, pp. i.–xxiv., 1–182 (2). The special title-pages are as follows : Some | Account | of the | Life | and | Gospel Labours | of | William Reckett. | *London, Printed :* | *Philadelphia : Re-printed* | *By Joseph Crukshank, in Market-* | *street, between Second and Third streets.* 1783. | Memoirs | of the | Life, | Religious Experiences, | and | Labours in the Gospel, | of | James Gough, | Late of the City of Dublin, deceased. | Compiled from his original Manuscripts, by his | Brother John Gough. | *Dublin, printed in* 1782. | *Philadelphia : Re-printed* | *By Joseph Crukshank,* . . . | . . . | . . . . 1783. |

REMARKABLE Particulars in the Life of the Rev. John Newton. *Philadelphia :* 1783. 4700

Title from the Catalogue of the Loganian Library. The volume of pamphlets, of which this was one, cannot now be found.

CORRIGENDA.

ANNO Regni | Georgii | Regis. | Magnæ Britanniæ, Franciæ & Hiberniæ | Novo. | At a Sessions of the General Assembly for the Pro- | vince of New-Jersey begun the Five and twentieth Day of | May, 1725. and continued to the 23th of August follow- ing, | at which time the following Acts were passed and Pub- | lished. | [*Royal Arms.*] | *Printed and sold by William Bradford in New-York and by* | *Andrew Bradford in Philadelphia*, 1725. | Folio, pp. 24.   N. Y. H. S. 257

EVANS. (D.) The | Minister of Christ, | and the | Duties of his Flock; | As it was Delivered in a | Sermon | At Abington in Pensilvania, | December 30. 1731. | At the Ordination of | Mr. Richard Treat | To the Gospel Ministry there. | With an Ap- pendix of the Questions then pub- | lickly proposed, and the Charges given. | Published at the Request of some of the Au- ditory. | By David Evans, Minister at Tredyffren. | . . . | . . . | . . . | . . . | . . . . | *Philadelphia:* | *Printed by B. Franklin*, 1732. | Sm. 12mo. pp. 108.   438

VOTES &c. of the House of Representatives of Pennsylvania, Met at Philadelphia, October 14, '1733. *Philadelphia: B. Franklin*, 1734. Folio, pp. 61.   H. S. P. 495

[ROWE. (Eliza)] The | History | of | Joseph. | A | Poem. | In Ten Books. | By a Female Hand. | *Philadelphia :* | *Printed and Sold by B. Franklin*, 1739. | 16mo. pp. 63.   605

476

TENNENT. (G.) The | Danger | of | An Unconverted | Ministry. | Considered in a | Sermon | On Mark vi. 34. | Preached at Nottingham, in Pennsylvania, | March 8. Anno 1739–40. | By Gilbert Tennent, A.M. | And Minister of the Gospel in New-Brunswick, | New-Jersey. | . . . | . . . | . . . | . . . | . . . . | *Philadelphia: | Printed by Benjamin Franklin, | In Market-street,* 1740. | 16mo. pp. 31.   661

LAW. (W.) The | Grounds and Reasons | of | Christian Regeneration, | or, the | New-Birth. | Offer'd to the Consideration of | Christians and Deists. | By William Law, M.A. | *London, Printed.* | *Philadelphia Reprinted, by Andrew | Bradford, at the Sign of the Bible, in | Front-Street,* MDCCXLI. | 16mo. Title, 1 leaf; Introduction, pp. (3); text, pp. 1–95.   H. S. P.   710

ANTES. (Henrich) Befanntmachung. | [*Germantown: Christoph Saur.* 1742.] 4to. 1 leaf.   H. S. P.   744

EDWARDS. (J.) The | Distinguishing Marks | Of a Work of the | Spirit of God. | Applied to that Uncommon Operation that | has lately appeared on the Minds of many of | the People of this Land: | With a particular Consideration of the extraordinary | Circumstances with which this Work is attended. | A Discourse | Delivered at New-Haven, September 10th, 1741. | Being the Day after the Commencement; | And now published at the earnest Desire of many | Ministers and other Gentlemen that heard it; with | great Enlargements. | By Jonathan Edwards, A.M. | Pastor of the Church of Christ at Northampton. | With a Preface by the Rev. Mr. Cooper of Boston. | . . . | . . . | . . . . *Boston, Printed: | Philadelphia, Re-printed and Sold by Benjamin | Franklin, in Market-Street,* 1742. | Sm. 8vo. pp. i–xvi, 1–84.   760

HJRTEN | Lieder | Von | Bethlehem, | Zum Gebrauch | Vor alles was arm ift | Was flein und gering ift. | *Germantown, gedruckt bey Christoph Saur.* 1742. | 24mo. Title, 1 leaf; pp. 1–128; Register, pp. (10).   765

BECHTEL. (J.) En kort | Catechismus | För några | Jesu Foersamlingar | Utaf then | Reformerta Religionen | Uti Pennsylvania, | Som hålla sig til thet Berniska Synodo; | Hwilket är | Enligit med Lärone uti then | Maehriska Kyrkian. | Först utgifwen i thet Tyska Språket | Af Johanne Bechtel, | Guds Ords Tienare. | *Philadelphia :* | *Tryckt hos Benjamin Franklin,* | *Aohr* 1743. | Sm. 12mo. pp. 35. H. S. P. 803

GILLESPY. (G.) Remarks | upon | Mr. George Whitefield, | proving | Him a Man under Delusion. | . . . | . . . | . . . | | . . . | . . . . | By George Gillespy, | Minister of the Gospel, in the County of | New-Castle, in America. | *Philadelphia :* | *Printed by B. Franklin, for the Author.* 1744. | Sm. 8vo. pp. 24. H. S. P. 880

GÜLDENE | Aepffel | In | Silbern Schalen | Oder : | Schöne und nützliche | Worte und Wahrheiten | Zur Gottseligkeit. | Enthalten | In Sieben Haupt-Theilen, | die in diesem Buch zusamen gestellet sind ; | Nemlich, In : | (1) Michael Sattlers Send-Briefen u. Acten; (2) Tho- | mä von Imbroichs Bekantnüß und Briefen; (3) Susan- | na von Holtz Testament und Brief; (4) Matthia Cervas | und Conrad Rochs Send- Briefen ; (welche alle aus den | Gefängnüssen geschrieben.) (5) Neunzehen Glaubens- | Articulen; (6) Christlichen Gebethen, samt Fürstellung | des Gebeths eines Gottlosen und Frommen; (7) Ei- | nem Unterricht von Singen der Christen. | Nebst angehängten Vorreden, | und einem zwey- fachen Register. | *Ephrata, im Jahr des Heils,* 1745. | 16mo. pp. (8), 519, (14). H. S. P. 932

There were two title-pages printed for this volume. The copies most frequently met with contain but one of them ; occasionally a copy is found with both.

GRÜNDLICHER | Unterricht | Von der | Einsammlung des Willens der | Seelen durch die stille Gebäts- | Andacht in die Gegen- | wart Gottes, | ans Licht gegeben | aus Liebe zu allen Seelen, welche gezo- | gen werden von dem verborgenen | Magneten der Liebe | Gottes, | von einem Schüler | der geheimen in Gott verborgenen | Gebäts-Andacht | *Germanton gedruckt [bey Christoph Saur] im Jahr,* 1746. | 24mo. pp. 131. H. S. P. 995

VOTES | and | Proceedings | of the | House of Representa- tives | of the | Province of Pennsylvania. | Met at Philadelphia, on the Fourteenth of October, | Anno Dom. 1745, and continued by Adjournments. | [*Penn Arms.*] | *Philadelphia :* | *Printed and Sold by B. Franklin, at the New Printing-* | *Office near the Market,* M,DCC,XLVI. | Folio, pp. 59.   H. S. P. 996

VOTES | and | Proceedings | of the | House of Representatives | of the | Province of Pennsylvania, | Met at Philadelphia, on the Fourteenth of October, | Anno Dom. 1746, and continued by Adjournments. | [*Penn Arms.*] | *Philadelphia :* | *Printed and Sold by B. Franklin, at the New Printing-* | *Office near the Market,* M,DCC,XLVII. | Folio, pp. 36, 1 leaf.   H. S. P. 1043

BOEHM. (J. P.) Der Reformierten Kirchen | in Pennſylvanien | Kirchen-Ordnung, | Welche | im Jahr 1725. von D. Joann Philipp Böhm, da= | mahls von den verſammelten Gliedern der Reformierten Kirchen einhellig erwählten | Prediger aufgeſtellet, und vor der Menge der Glieder vorgeleſen, welche alle Glieder vor | nützlich und gut gehalten, und auch willig angenommen haben. Nach Erwählung | der nöthig ge- achten Aelteſten aber und mit geſammtlichen Rath derſelben | An die | Wohlehrwürdige und Hochgelehrte Herren | Herren, | Der Hoch=Ehr= würdigen Claſſe von Amsterdam | Correſpondirende Prebicanten, | Gualterus Du Bois, und Henricus Boel | zu Neu=York, | und | Vincentius Antonides von Langen Eyland | zur Cenſur übergeben. | Welche | Dieſelbe an gedachte Hoch=Ehrwürdige Claſſe von Am- | ſter= dam überſchickt, von dieſer Hochanſehnlichen Verſammlung vor gut und | ſtifftlich erkennet und erlaubt. Und darauf auch bey denen aufgerichteten Gemeinden feſt geſtel= | let worden. Und wurden bis hieher verſchiedene unter dieſe Ordnung ſich ſubmittirte Re= | formirte Gemeinden in gutem Frieden regieret. | Weilen aber | Das von denen Hoch=Ehrwürdigen und Chriſtlichen Synoden von Süd- und Nord= | Holland verwilligte Cœtus der Reform. Kirchen in Pennſylvanien, den letzt verwichenen 28 Sept. | ditz 1748ſten Jahrs in Philadelphia ſeinen ordentlich= und jährlichen Sitz gehalten, und dieſe | Ihme bekannt gemachte Kirchen=Ordnung vor nützlich und heylſam angemercket, ſo hat | dieſes E. Cœtus einſtimmig beſchloſſen, dieſelbe zu eines jeden Gliedes der Reformier= | ten Kirchen nützlichen Nachricht öffentlich im Druck zu befördern ; welches zu be= | werckſtelligen das gantze Ehrwürdige Cœtus überlaſſen, an | D. Johann

Philipp Böhm, Prediger zum Falckner=Schwam, Providenz | und Witpen, p. t. Cœtus Præses. | *Philadelphia, gedruckt bey Gotthard Armbriester, wohnhafft in der Arch-strasse, 1748.* | Sq. 8vo. pp. (8), 1–14.

H. S. P. 1049

EIN MYSTISCHER | das ist ein vor der alten Natur und Ver= | nunfft und Eigenheit verborgener | Seelen=Spiegel, | Worinnen ein von Gott | ergriffenes und erleuchtetes | Gemüth sehen kan, | was die Seele des Menschen im Abfall | von Gott vor eine Lebens=Gestalt | bekommen; | Und was die Seele im Anfang ihrer Neuen= | Geburt aus der göttlichen Natur in ihren | Buß=Uebung erlanget, nehmlich, einen | Eiffrigen Ernst | durch die ersten Anzündungen der Feuer=Gestal= | ten des inwendigen Feuer=Eifferigen Hun= | gers nach Gott; welches aber noch | nicht die sanffte göttliche Lichts= | Geburt ist. | Und wie nicht anderst, als im demüthigen | Ersincken des Willens in Gottes | Willen erst die Lichts=Geburt er= | erbohren wird, | Ohne welche Gestalt die Seele nicht kan zu | Gott in sein Licht=Reich zur Ruhe eingehen. | Ge= schrieben aus Erkantnus und Erfahrung. | *Germanton gedruckt bey Christoph Saur,* | 1748. | 16mo. pp. 62.

H. S. P. 1067

LISCHY. (J.) Jacob Lischys | Reformirten Predigers | Zweyte | Declaration | Seines Sinnes, | an seine | Reformirte Religions= Genossen | in | Pensylvanien. | Auf Begehren guter Freunde heraus gegeben. | *Germanton, gedruckt bey Christoph Saur, 1748.* | Sq. 8vo. pp. 20.

H. S. P. 1082

TREUHERTZIGE | und Einfältige | Anweisung | Wie sich solche Gut= | willige Seelen zu | verhalten haben, | welche | Theils von den groben Welt=Geistern | und Lock=Vögeln zum Mitmachen, | Theils | Von denen Unlautern Seelen=Werbern | und Neben=Buhlern unter guten Schein | zu ihrer Nachfolge gereitzet, gelocket, an= | gefochten und überlauffen wer= den. | Dargelegt | Zur Prüfung, Verwahrung, und | Warnung von Einem | Durch Schaden gewitzigten Gemüth. | · · · | · · · | · · · | · · · | · · · | · · · · | *Germanton gedruckt bey Christoph Sauer* | 1749. | 16mo. pp. 40.

H. S. P. 1162

VOTES | and | Proceedings | of the | House of Representatives | of the | Province of Pennsylvania. | Met at Philadelphia, on the

Fourteenth of October, | Ann Dom. 1748, and continued by Adjournments. | [*Penn Arms.*] | *Philadelphia :* | *Printed and Sold by B. Franklin, at the New* | *Printing-Office, near the Market.* MDCCXLIX. | Folio, pp. 57, (1).   H. S. P.   **1164**

CLARKE. (R.) The | Prophetic Numbers | of | Daniel and John | calculated; | In order to shew the Time, | when the | Day of Judgement | for | This First Age of the Gospel, is to be expected: And the Setting up the | Millennial Kingdom | of | Jehovah and his Christ. | By Richard Clarke, | Minister of the Gospel of Jesus Christ. | The Third Edition, with Additions. | . . . | . . . | . . . | . . . | . . . | . . . | . . . | . . . | . . . | . . . . | *Philadelphia :* | *Printed and Sold by Wm. Bradford, at the Corner of* | *Front and Market-Streets,* M,DCC,LIX. | 8vo. pp. 24.   **1623**

𝕯𝕴𝕰 | 𝕰𝕽𝖅𝕰𝕳𝕷𝖀𝕹𝕲𝕰𝕹 | von | Maria le Roy | und | Barbara Leininger, | Welche vierthalb Jahr unter den In- | dianern gefangen gewesen, und am 6ten May | in dieser Stadt glücklich angekommen. | Aus ihrem eignen Munde niedergeschrieben und | zum Druck befördert. | *Philadelphia gedruckt und zu haben in der teut-* | *schen Buchdruckerey das Stueck vor 6 Pentz.* | M,DCCLIX. | 8vo. pp. 14. H. S. P. **1626**

M. TOBIAS WAGNERS | Abschieds-Rede | an seine Lutherische | Gemeinden in Penn- | sylvanien | Welche er zu unterschiedlichen Zeiten | als Prediger alle 14. Tag oder 4. | Wochen bedienet; vornehmlich in | 1. Richmond von 1743. bis 1759. | 2. Ruscombaner von 1749. bis 1759. | 3. Windsor von 1758. bis 1759. | 4. Carltown von 1749. bis 1755. | 5. Lancaster von 1751. bis 1753. | 6. Bern von 1745. bis 1750. 7. Dulvehafin von 1743. bis 1746. | 8. Allemängel von 1749. bis 1754. | 9. Der Protestan. Kirche von 1744. bis 1746. | 10. Freunds Kirche von 1744. bis 1746. | 11. North-Kill von 1744. bis 1746. | 12. Elsass von 1748. bis 1752. | 13. Reading etliche mal angenommen, etliche | mal abgedanckt. | *Ephratæ Typis Societatis* | MDCCLIX. | Sm. 8vo. pp. 39.   H. S. P. **1651**

MARTIN. (Jacob) Copie | Eines Briefs oder eine Antwort auf die Frage : | Ob alle Menschen die zur Seeligkeit gelaugen, zuvor ins inwendige Leben müssen | dersezt werden? | [*Ephrata :* 1760 ?] Folio, 1 leaf.   L. C. P. **1685**

VOTES | and | Proceedings | of the | House of Representatives | of the | Province of Pennsylvania, | Met at Philadelphia, on the Fifteenth of October, Anno | Domini 1759, and continued by Adjournments. | [*Penn Arms.*] | *Philadelphia:* | *Printed and Sold by B. Franklin, at the New-Printing-Office,* | *near the Market.* MDCCLX. | Folio, pp. 58.　　　　　H. S. P.　1705

ABEL. (T.) Subtensial Plain | Trigonometry, | Wrought with a | Sliding-Rule, | With | Gunter's Lines: | And also | Arithmetically, | In a very concise Manner. | And this Method apply'd to Navigation, | and Surveying. | To which is added, | I. Mensuration of Masons Work. | II. A Solution of Rota, or Aristotle's Wheel. | III. A brief Discourse upon Gravity. | By Thomas Abel, | Of Bourn in Lincolnshire, Old England. | *Philadelphia: Printed and Sold for* | *the Author, by Andrew Steuart,* 1761. | Sm. 8vo. Title, 1 leaf; To the Reader, and Contents, pp. (2); text, pp. 1–86; 7 plates.　　　　　H. S. P.　1709

LAMPE. (F. A.) D. Fried. Adolph Lampens | Jn ſeinem Leben erſtgeweſenen Theologiä Profeſ= | ſoris zu Utrecht, nachher aber zu Bremen, | und ſehr geiſtreichen Dieners des göttlichen | Wortes in der Reformirten Kirchen, ꝛc. | Mit hohem Holländiſchen Staaten Privilegio. | Zu erſt an das Licht gekommene, und in der Hollan= | diſch= und Bremiſchen Schulen ein= geführte, | Erſte | Wahrheits=Milch, | Für Säuglinge am Altar und Ver= ſtand. | (Oder kurtzgefaßte Grund=Lehren des Re= | formirten Chriſten= thums.) | Aufs neue nachgeſehen, von einigen dunckelſchei= | nenden Redensarten geſäubert, auch in etwas | vermehrt und mit der Vorrede des Predigers bey | der Reformirt=Hochteutſchen Gemeine zu An= | weil in New=Jerſey, | Dr. Caspar Michael Staples, | unter Vorwiſſen des Ehrwürd. Pennſylvani= | ſchen Cötus, | Zum Druck befördert, und verlegt von Willhelm | Räß. | *Philadelphia, Gedruckt bey Anton Armbrue-* | *ster, in Moraevien-Ally.* 1762. | Sm. 8vo. Title, 1 leaf; Texts, 1 folded leaf; Vorrede und Notes, pp. (4); text, pp. 1–40.　　　1823

AGUECHEEK. (A.) The Universal American | Almanack, | or Yearly | Magazine. | . . . | . . . | . . . | For the Year of our

Lord 1764; | . . . | . . . | . . . | . . . | Being Bissextile, or Leap-Year. | [20 lines.] | By Andrew Aguecheek, Philom. | *Philadel-phia: Printed by Andrew Steuart, at the | Bible-in-Heart, in Second-street.* [1763.] | Sm. 8vo. pp. (40).   L. C. P. 1867

AN | AUTHENTICK Account | of the | Proceedings | against | John Wilkes, Esq; | Member of Parliament for Aylesbury, | And late | Colonel of the Buckinghamshire Militia. | Containing | All the Papers relative to this interesting Affair, from that Gen- | tleman's being taken into Custody by his Majesty's Messengers, | to his Discharge at the Court of Common Pleas. | With | An Abstract of that precious Jewel of an Englishman, | The Habeas Corpus Act. | Also | The North Briton, No. 45. | Being the Paper for which Mr. Wilkes was sent to the Tower. | Addressed to all Lovers of Liberty. | *London, Printed.* | *Philadelphia, Re-Printed: And to be Sold* | *by W. Dunlap, in Market-Street,* M,DCC,LXIII. | 8vo. pp. 48.   H. S. P. 1872

[GRUBÉ. (Bernard Adam)] Dellawærisches | Gesang-Büch-lein. | [*Near Bethlehem: J. Brandmueller.* 1763.] | Sm. 8vo.   1897

The Historical Society of Pennsylvania has recently acquired the first eight pages of a copy of this curious work.

HARKER. (S.) An | Appeal | from the | Synod | of | New-York and Philadelphia, | to the | Christian World, | relating to the Censure and Sentence of the | said Synod, in their last Ses-sion at Phila- | delphia, against the Rev. Mr. Samuel | Harker, Pastor of the Church at Black- | River, in East-Jersey. | Written by himself. | *Philadelphia:* | *Printed and Sold by William Dunlap.* | M,DCC,LXIII. | 8vo. pp. 40.   M. 1899

TUNES | in | Three Parts, | For the several Metres of Dr. Watts's | Version of the Psalms; Some of which | Tunes are new. | Price One Shilling and 6 d. stitch'd. | *Philadelphia:* | *Printed by Anthony Armbruster, in* | *Moravian Alley,* 1763. | 12mo. Title, 1 leaf; pp. 1–43, (1).   H. S. P. 1930

ETLICHE Merckwürdige | Punckten | betreffende die Verwechselung des | Governments. | Gerichtet an die deutsche | Einwohner | der Provinz

𝔓enſylvanien. | *Philadelphia, gedruckt bey Anton Armbruester in der Aert-* | *Strasse, 1764.* | Sm. 4to. pp. 4.   H. S. P.   1986

COLMAN. (G.)   The | Man of Business, | a | Comedy. | As it is acted at the | Theatre-Royal in Covent-Garden. | By George Colman. | . . . . | The Third Edition. | *Philadelphia :* | *Re-printed and sold by John Dunlap,* | *in Market-street.* | MDCCLXXIV. | 12mo. pp. 82.   H. S. P.   2993

𝔇𝔈𝔕 𝔊𝔄ℜ𝔗ℨ 𝔑eue 𝔙erbeſſerte | 𝔑ord 𝔄mericaniſche | 𝔈alender, | 𝔇es | 1778ſten 𝔍ahres 𝔈hriſti, | 𝔈s iſt | 𝔇aſſelbe ein gemein 𝔍ahr von 365 𝔗agen, | 𝔘nd enthaelt | 𝔇ie 𝔚ochen= 𝔐onaths= 𝔑amen= 𝔉eyer und andere dem 𝔏and= | man zu wiſſen nützliche und merkwürdige 𝔗age. | 𝔚ie auch | 𝔇er 𝔖onnen und des 𝔐onds 𝔄uf= und untergang ; die 𝔄ſpec= ten der 𝔓laneten 𝔄n= | zeige der 𝔚itterung, der 𝔉luth oder des hohen 𝔚aſſers zu 𝔓hiladelphia. | und 𝔖iebengeſtirns 𝔄ufgang 𝔖udplaß und 𝔘ntergang. | 𝔅erechnet vornemlich nach der 𝔓ennſylvaniſchen 𝔥immels= 𝔊egend, dabey aber | in angrenzenden 𝔏andſchaften ohne merklichen unter= ſchied zu gebrauchen : | 𝔇ieſem ſind noch beygefüget einige angenehme, nützliche und lehreiche 𝔈rzehlungen, ſamt anderen | 𝔈alender 𝔄rbeiten. | ℨum 𝔇ritten mal herausgegeben und verfertiget von 𝔊ottlieb 𝔥immels= 𝔅ewunderer. | *Lancaster, Gedruckt und zu finden bey Franz Bailey in der Koenigs-strasse.* | *Auch koennen die auswaertigen Kraemer damit bedient werden bey den Herrn George Reynold, in Phil-* | *adelphia ; A. Witman und A. Schlaegel, in Reading ; Caspar Schnebely, in Lebanon ; Georg* | *Steg und Johann Kean, in York-taun ; Nicholas Reidenaur, in Baltimore, und andern.* [1777.] | Sm. 4to. pp. (44).   H. S. P.   3633

Page xi., line 10, *for* 1714 *read* 1744.

Page xiii., line 24, *for* Coffart *read* Cossart.

No. 175, *for* 1725 *read* 1722.

No. 253, *for* Memoral *read* Memorial.

No. 375, *for* Parry *read* Perry.

No. 714, note, *for* Ansonius *read* Ausonius.

No. 723 should be omitted, as, upon examination of the copy in the Philadelphia

Library (in whose printed catalogue it is said to have been printed in Philadelphia), it proves to be a fragment of a volume of sermons printed by J. P. Zenger in New York.

No. 763 was not written by Gruber.

No. 790, *after* Pennsylvania *add* Journal.

No. 824, *for* Gueldins *read* Gueldin.

No. 828, *for* Schrfftimaessiges *read* Schrifftmaessiges.

No. 838, *for* pp. 66 *read* pp. 61.

No. 916, *for* Biessel *read* Beissel.

No. 918 should be omitted, as it is only a variation of No. 600.

No. 957, *add* pp. 54.

No. 1013, Collation : With a slip between pp. 4 and 5, containing three additional verses to the 5th Hymn, and between pp. 44 and 45, one leaf containing " Der 80. Psalm."

No. 1100, *for* aufgeseszt *read* aufgesetzt.

No. 1111, *for* pp. (10). *read* Title, 1 leaf; To the Honourable, &c., 1 leaf; pp. 1–10.

No. 1165, *for* 1747 *read* 1749.

No. 1174, *for* Salignae *read* Salignac.

Nos. 1187, 1225, 1266, 1312, 1482, *for* Moore *read* More.

Nos. 1199 and 1221, *for* Thompson *read* Thomson.

No. 1219, the German paper referred to by Prof. Seidensticker in his bibliography is not that of 1751, and therefore no exception should have been taken to the title given by him.

Nos. 1222, 1471, 1901, 3886, 4202, *for* Deutch *read* Deutsch.

No. 1231, *before* Oder *insert* Anweisung.

No. 1243, *for* Zubley *read* Zubly.

No. 1251, *for* 233 *read* 223.

No. 1262, note, *for* Beardley *read* Beardsley.

No. 1287, *for* Allens *read* Allen.

No. 1372, *for* Mages *read* Magens.

No. 1416, *for* (62) *read* (61).

No. 1491, *for* Patterus *read* Paternus.

No. 1582, note, *for* Moon *read* Moore.

No. 1688, *for* Eingericteter *read* Eingerichteter.

No. 1726 was written by the Rev. Hugh Neill.

No. 1744, *for* Lyttleton *read* Lyttelton.

No. 1771, *for* pp. 17 *read* pp. 27.

No. 1804, *for* Frantz *read* Francke.

No. 1859, *for* [1765.] *read* [1762.].

No. 1873, *for* Balba *read* Barba.

No. 1890 was written by Francis Hopkinson.

No. 1897, *for* (J. A.) *read* (B. A.).

No. 1925 was written by S. How.

No. 1926, *for* School *read* Schools.

No. 1930, note, *for* 1764 *read* 2079.

No. 2010, *for* Lantzley *read* Cantzley.

No. 2016, *for* [Henrich Miller] *read* Anton Ambruester.

No. 2021, *for* Americanisher *read* Americanischer.

No. 2085, *for* ehmaligen *read* ehemaligen.

No. 2123, *for* Auterricht *read* Unterricht.

Nos. 2149, 2466, 2795, 3583, *for* zuverlaszige *read* zuverlaeszige.

No. 2278, *for* Bericht *read* Bericht.

No. 2788, *for* Litder *read* Lieder.

No. 2801, *for* Helbstmord *read* Selbstmord.

No. 2853, *for* David *read* Robert.

No. 3026 was written by Alexander Mack, and not by E. L. Gruber.

No. 3670, *for* fur *read* fuer.

No. 3911, *for* Reugestellte *read* Neugestellte.

No. 3924, *for* MDCCLXXVIX. *read* MDCCLXXIX.

No. 4110, *for* Empsindungen *read* Empfindungen.

No. 4218, *for* Neujahns *read* Neujahrs.

No. 4269, *for* Amenicanischer *read* Americanischer.

No. 4274, *for* direrses *read* diverses.

No. 4598, *for* Kuntze *read* Kurtze.

No. 4621, *for* Eckelin *read* Eckerlin.

INDEX.

The titles printed in these volumes are indexed under the names of the authors, when such names are given. Anonymous works are indexed under the first words of their titles. References are made to the numbers given to the titles in the regular order in which they appear, and not to the pages on which they are described. Almanacs, Lotteries, New-Year Verses, and Newspapers are grouped under those heads without cross-references. Numbers marked with an * will be found in the Corrigenda. In all cross-references the catchword referred to is printed in SMALL CAPS.

ALMANACS.

GENTLEMAN and Citizen's Pocket —, 1769-1771.

GENTLEMAN and Lady's Pocket Memorandum Book, 1778 & 1780.

HOCH-DEUTSCHE Americanische Calender, 1738-1784.

Kalendarium Pennsilvaniense, by S. ATKINS, 1685.

LADIES Memorandum Book, 1774.

LANCASTER —, 1771-1774.

Lancaster —, by A. SHARP, 1775-1779.

Lancaster Pocket — by A. SHARP, 1777-1779.

NEU-EINGERICHTETER Americanische Calender, 1746-1752, 1754-1767.

NEUE, Verbessert- u. Zuverläszige Americanische Calender, 1782.

NEUESTE, Verbessert- u. Zuverläszige Americanische Calender 1762-1779.

New Jersey —, by W. BALL, 1741-1758.

Pennsylvania —, by T. GODFREY, 1731-1735.

Pennsylvania—, by J. TAYLOR, 1702-1745.

Pennsylvania —, by T. THOMAS, 1759-1761.

PENNSYLVANIA Pocket —, 1759-1784.

Pennsylvania Town and Countryman's —, by J. TOBLER, 1754-1775.

PHILADELPHIA —, 1777.

PHILADELPHIA Newest —, 1774-1775.

PHILADELPHIA Pocket—, 1778.

PLAIN —, 1781-1784.

Pocket —, by R. SAUNDERS, 1740-1784.

POCKET memorandum Book, 1784.

Poor Richard's —, by R. SAUNDERS, 1732-1746.

Poor Richard improved —, by R. SAUNDERS, 1747-1784.

Poor Robin's —, 1741-1757 ; 1770-1771.

Poor Will's —, by W. BIRKETT, 1729-1751.

Poor Will's —, 1769-1784.

Poor Will's Pocket —, 1770-1784.

REPUBLICANISCHE Calender, 1778-1782.

Sheet ALMANACS, 1736 and 1741.

TEUTSCHE Pilgrim, 1730-1732.

UNIVERSAL —, 1772-1776.

Universal American —, by A. AGUECHEEK, 1759-1771.

WEATHERWISE, Pocket —, Number 4643.

Wilmington —, by T. Fox, 1763-1775.

ALONZO and Ormisindi, 3559.

ALPHABET. The, 2501.

ΑΛΗΟΕΛΕΥΘΕΡΙΑ ΕΙΣ ΕΙΡΠΝΠΝ, 4640.

ALSO sang ihrem Gotte, 742.

ALTE zeugnisz, 3319.

ALTERNATIVE. The, 4268.

AMERICA, 2457. — in tears, 1713.

AMERICAN crisis, 3432, 3595, 3764. — independence, 3344. — instructor, 399, 1062, 1298, 2528. — liberty, 3737. — magazine, 688, 1513, 2416. — museum, 4195. — traveller, 2513. — vine, 3196.

AMERICANUS examined, 2971.

AMÉRIQUAIN aux anglois, L', 4691.

AMÉRIQUIADE, L', 4689.

AMICABLE fire co., 3667.

AN das publicum, 2648. — das volk, 3847. — die deutschen, 2100. — die einwohner der stadt, 2972. — die einwohner von Irland, 3156. — die freyhalter, 1946. — die guten einwohner, 2850. — die hochgeehrten glieder der Assembly, 3521. — die unter-officers und gemeinen, 3322.

ANARCHY of the ranters, 1516, 2504.

ANCIENT testimony of the Quakers, 2851, 3323.

ANDERE anrede, 1947.

ANDERSON. John, 4421. Walter —, 2628.

ANECDOTE recommended, 3157.

ANGENEHME opfer, 1402.

ANGENEHMER geruch, 1450.

ANHANG zu dem charter, 860.

ANHANGEN an Gott. Das, 2071.

ANIMADVERSIONS on a pamphlet, 2196. — on the reasons, 752.

ANLEITUNG zur englischen sprache, 1169.

ANMERKUNGEN über ein wunder thier, 1948.

ANMUTHIGE erinnerung, 1684.

ANNERCH ir cymru, 173.

ANNIVERSARY oration, 4185.

ANNO regni, see Acts or Laws of DELAWARE. NEW JERSEY. PARLIAMENT. PENNSYLVANIA.

ANREDE an die deutschen freyhalter, 1951.

ANSTEY. Christopher, 3668.

ANSWER of Wm. Franklin, 2125. — to a printed libel, 4655. — to Gre-Ma-Chre, 3848. — to Lewis Evans' letter, 1452. — to Franklin's remarks, 1952. — to the banks of the Dee, 3849. — to the Bp. of London's pastoral, 611. — to the conduct of the Paxton men, 1953. — to the plot, 1954.

ANTES. Henrich, 744.

ANTI-Christ and sadducee, 31.

ANTI-pædo-rantism, 1022. — defended, 1186.

ANTICIPATION, 3966.

ANTIDOTE. The, 251.

ANTIENT testimony of the Quakers, 194.

ANTWORT auf Franklins anmerckungen, 2103.

APOCALYPSE de Chiokoyhikoy, 3522.

APOLOGIE de la Bastile, 4557. — des franc-maçons, 4687. — des ordens der freimaurer, 2420.

APOLOGY for the Quakers, 1453, 3326. — for the true christian divinity, 3162, 3985.

APOSTOLISCHE kirchen-engel, 4595.

APPEAL defended, 2429. — from the synod, 1899. — from the 28 judges, 39, 40, 41. — to matter of fact, 4296. — to the public, 2286. — to the public answered, 2349. — to the serious, 4543.

APPENDIX to the considerations, 3274.

APPROVED minister of God, 1128.

ARCADIA, 1826.

ARCHBISHOP of Cambray's dissertation on pure love, 576, 1174.

GREEN. Enoch, 2781. Jacob —, 2445.

GREGORY. John, 2888, 3167, 3216, 3294, 3711, 4106.

GRE-Ma-Chre, 3884.

GREW. Theophilus, 1302.

GREY. Isaac, 3712, 3713.

GRIFFITH. Benjamin, 1022, note. John —, 2363, 4010, 4107.

GROSSE gebet-buch. Das, 1303.

GROSVERNOR. Benjamin, 4108.

GROUND and nature of christian redemption, 2364.

GROUNDS and reasons of christian regeneration, 710. — of a holy life, 1329, 2832, 4404.

GROUP. The, 3307.

GRUBÉ. B. A., 1897, 1898.

GRUBER. Johann Adam, 707, 747, 762, 763.

GRUENDLICHER unterricht von den metallen, 1873.

GRUENDLICHES zeugnüsz. Ein, 1072.

GRÜNDE und ursachen der christlichen wieder-geburth, 4616.

GRÜNDLICHE anweisung, 1071.

GUALDO. J., 2446.

GUELDENE A. B. C. Das, 1177. — aepffel, 932.

GUELDIN. Samuel, 824, 4601.

GURNALL. William, 2654.

GURNEY. John, 4301.

GUSTAVUS Vasa, 3679.

GUTHREY. William, 825.

GUTHRIE. William, 2779.

GUYSE. John, 1733.

H.

H. E., 273. G. —, 2449.

HABERMANN. Johann, 1303, 1734, 1809, 2000, 3374.

HALBERT. Henry, 2130.

HALE. Matthew, 331, 635. Thomas —, 4109.

HALL. David, 1304, 1305, 1588, 1620, 2141, 2150, 2450, 2542. Joseph —, 1810. William —, 3027.

HAMILTON. Alexander, 4434, 4486. Dr. Alexander —, 1221. Andrew —, 282.

HAMMOND. William, 2543.

HANCOCK. John, 3217, 4682. Rev. John —, 826.

HANSON. Elizabeth, 327, 1342. Thomas —, 3218.

HAPPINESS, a characteristic poem, 3028. — of rewarding enemies, 1503.

HAPPY man. The, 4487.

HARKER. Samuel, 1899, 1900, 2069.

HARMER. Thomas, 2655.

HARMONIE der evangelien und episteln, 3200.

HARMONY between the old and new Testaments, 2998. — of the divine attributes, 2630. — of the Gospels, 1898.

HARRIS. Matthias, 1527.

HARRISON. Robert H., 3533.

HARTLEY. Thomas, 1628, 2303.

HASELDEN. Thomas, 3555, 3885.

HASENCLEVER. Francis, 2889.

HAUSAM. Anthony, 3219.

HAWLES. John, 2782.

HAY. John, 4655.

HAYES. Alice, 2222, 2223. Richard —, 2001.

HAYWARD. Samuel, *see* PIKE.

HEAD-QUARTERS, Philadelphia, Dec. 13th (1776), 3375.

HEAVEN upon earth, 2367.

HEIDELBERG catechism, 2304.

HEIDELBURG catechism, 2131.

HEILIGE und sichere glaubensweg. Der, 1804, 2532.

HEINOUS sin of drunkenness, 674.

HELMUTH. J. H. C., 4110.

HELP for parents, 437.

HELTON. John, 4488.

HENRY. Matthew, 636.

HERESIE and hatred, 62.

HERMIT. The, 1307. — of New Jersey, 4247.

HÉROÏDES d'Ovide. Les, 4529.

HERRLICHE erscheinung, 1923.

HERRN Pyrläi Ausruf-Zeddel, 744.

HERUMTRÄGERS des staatsboten, 2224. *See* NEW Year verses.

HERVEY. James, 1178, 1259, 1673.

HEYDELBERGISCHE catechismus, 2365.

HILDEBRAND. Johannes, 764, 827, 828, 1366.

HILL. Hannah, 127, 133, 141. John —, 3220.

HILLIARD D'Auberteuil, 4489.

HILLIARD Magna, 4657.

HINTS and instructions, 3556.

HIRTENLIEDER von Bethlehem, 765.

HIS Excellency, 3557. — Majesty's most gracious speech, 515, 3175, 3376, 3377. — Majesty's ship Liverpool, 3714.

HISTORICAL account of the expedition, 2169. — account of the late disturbance, 2002, 2003. — memorial, 1811. — narrative and topographical description, 4493.

HISTORISCHE beschreibung von den letzthin geschehenen unruhen, 2004. — nachricht von dem neulich in Lancaster caunty, 2005.

HISTORY and defence of Magna Charta, 2656. — of Belisarius, 2562. — of Diodorus Siculus, 239. — of France, 2628. — of Hypolitus, 2448. — of Ireland, 3044. — of Joseph, 605, 2320. — of little Goody Two-Shoes, 3378. — of New-Hampshire, 4428. — of Rasselas, 2368. — of the five Indian nations, 396. — of the kingdom of Basaruh, 199. — of the life of Thomas Ellwood, 3199. — of the old and new Testament, 4490. — of the Quakers, 350. — of the reign of Charles V., 2583. — of the war in America, 1768. — of the wars of Charles XII., 240. — of women, 3153.

END OF VOLUME II.

	DATE DUE		